Urban Transport VIII
Urban Transport and the Environment in the 21st Century

EIGHTH INTERNATIONAL CONFERENCE ON URBAN TRANSPORT AND THE ENVIRONMENT IN THE 21ST CENTURY

URBAN TRANSPORT VIII

CONFERENCE CHAIRMEN

L.J. Sucharov
Wessex Institute of Technology, UK.

C.A. Brebbia
Wessex Institute of Technology, UK.

F.G. Benitez
University of Seville, Spain.

INTERNATIONAL SCIENTIFIC ADVISORY COMMITTEE

E. Angelino
J.M. Baldasano
J.G. Bartzis
F. Benitez
R.D. Bornstein
C. Borrego
H-C. Chin
S. Clement
K.G. Goulias
Y.H. Hayashi
L.L.R. Int Panis
C.M. Jefferson
J.W.S Longhurst

L. Lundqvist
G. Mattrisch
J. Mertner
K. Miyamoto
P.S. Rana
M. Reneland
F. Robuste
G. Sciutto
E. Taniguchi
M.A.P. Taylor
R.Van der Heijden
J.H.R. Van Duin
A. Yeh

Organised by:
Wessex Institute of Technology, UK.
With the support of the Ministry of Science and Technology of Spain and the University of Seville.

International Series on Advances in Transport

Objectives

The objective of this Series is to provide state-of-the-art information on all aspects of transport research and applications. This covers land, water and air systems with emphasis on multi-mode operation. The books in the Series deal with planning operation and management as well as engineering aspects of transport. Environmental topics and sustainability are an important part of the Series. City, national and international transport are covered and encompassing interdisciplinary aspects.

Transport strategies
Planning and funding
Transport and economic issues
Operations and management
Private and public initiatives and police
Regulation and standardisation
Transport and land use planning
Sustainable transport
Environmental issues
Information technology and electronic aspects
Multi-media and advanced training techniques
Management information systems
Human interface and decision support
Traveller psychology and behaviour
Emerging technologies
Transport and energy
Air transportation

Railway systems
Water and sea transport
Road transport
Urban transport systems
Terminal and interchanges
People movers
Multi-mode systems
Traffic integration
Infrastructure
Scheduling and traffic control
Vehicle technology
Safety and accident prevention
Hazardous transport risk
Hazardous remediation
Transport in extreme conditions
Freight transport

Urban Transport VIII
Urban Transport and the Environment in the 21st Century

Edited by

L.J. Sucharov
Wessex Institute of TEchnology, UK.

C.A. Brebbia
Wessex Institute of Technology, UK.

F.G. Benitez
University of Seville, Spain.

WITPRESS Southampton, Boston

Published by

WIT Press
Ashurst Lodge, Ashurst, Southampton, SO40 7AA, UK
Tel: 44 (0) 238 029 3223; Fax: 44 (0) 238 029 2853
E-Mail: witpress@witpress.com
http://www.witpress.com

For USA, Canada and Mexico

Computational Mechanics Inc
25 Bridge Street, Billerica, MA 01821, USA
Tel: 978 667 5841; Fax: 978 667 7582
E-Mail: info@compmech.com
US site: http://www.compmech.com

British Library Cataloguing-in-Publication Data

A Catalogue record for this book is available
from the British Library

ISBN: 1-85312-905-4
ISSN: 1462-608X

The texts of the papers in this volume were set
individually by the authors or under their supervision.
Only minor corrections to the text may have been carried
out by the publisher.

No responsibility is assumed by the Publisher, the Editors and Authors for any injury and/or damage to persons or property as a matter of products liability, negligence or otherwise, or from any use or operation of any methods, products, instructions or ideas contained in the material herein.

Preface

Transportation in cities with its consequent environmental and social concerns continues to rise up the agenda of city authorities and central governments around the world. Sometimes the concern is not orderly but crisis ridden. The UK is a case in point where the railway system has suddenly been found to be in woeful condition after a series of major fatal accidents. A lesson that emerges is that even with the best planned urban transport systems, their safety, maintenance and operational use, require as much study and design of procedures and information systems as goes into the transport system itself.

On the broader front, the continuing need for better urban transport systems in general and the need of a healthier environment has led to a steadily increasing level of research around the world. This is reflected in these proceedings, which are larger than in any previous year and are a tribute to the delegates and the standing of the conference. This is especially so for delegates who would have been preparing their presentations at the time of the 11 September tragedy which curbed many people's wish to travel.

These proceedings show continuing research in urban transport systems although control, information and simulation systems grow steadily more prominent. There have been more papers on accessibility in cities while safety research remains an important area of work. The many papers on emissions underline the health concerns in cities while noise is becoming a significant area of study.

We would like to extend a warm welcome here in Seville to all delegates to the Conference and an appreciation to all authors in preparing their papers. Our special thanks goes to the International Scientific Advisory Committee who have given so generously of their time to review abstracts and then the papers, often under tight deadlines.

We are pleased to inform delegates and readers that the next Conference in the series Urban Transport and the Environment IX will take place in the attractive island of Crete on 10 to 12 March 2003.

The Editors
Seville 2002

Contents

Section 1: Urban accessibility and mobility

Section 2: Urban transport systems

Section 3: Traffic control

Section 4: Simulation

Section 5: Information systems

Section 6: Finance and planning

Section7: Emissions

Section 8: Environmental noise

Section 9: Economic and social impact

Section 10: Safety

Section 11: Vehicle technology

Section 1:
Urban accessibility and mobility

Future aspects of sustainable urban mobility

G. Mattrisch & C. Hoffmann
*DaimlerChrysler "Society and Technology " Research Group
Berlin/Palo Alto*

Abstract

The future of urban mobility is closely linked with sustainability issues. In this paper basic mobility strategies/policies are outlined, the main future conflict areas of mobility and sustainability are described. Specific sustainability potentials of mobility policy approaches are assessed, and the main findings related to future research issues are discussed.

1 Introduction

The future of urban mobility seems to be inevitably characterized by a threatening triangle of driving forces: Growing mobility demand, stagnant levels of infrastructure and transportation supply, and increasing societal pressure. In this paper the most relevant policy options are outlined, and their specific sustainability potential is discussed.

Due to the complex nature of mobility and transportation it is more than justified to consider mobility policies as assessment objects, rather than single measures or single pilot projects. The perception of one-dimensional measures or isolated projects as sources of follow-up problems in the sense of not-intended impacts is not really new, but it is getting more common. One consequence of this statement is that generally spoken complex and dynamic systems require integrated approaches and monitoring. In terms of applied mobility sciences an essential shift from confined measures to more complex and integrated mobility policy scenarios can be stated. Advanced mobility research programs like "Legal and Regulatory Measures for Sustainable Transport in Cities" (LEDA, 13), "Mobility Management Strategies for the next Decades" (MOST, 22), or "Mobility in Agglomerations" (23) might give proof for this paradigm shift.

The progressiveness of these approaches is constituted by new combinations of any mobility-relevant elements, thus exceeding conventional borders. From our point of view, the entity of those elements and combinations is best named mobility systems.

Additionally, while in the past much attention was given to issues such as reduction of unnecessary traffic and influencing modal split towards public transport in order to reduce undesired impacts of mobility, more and more awareness in the quality of mobility is evident. Like service offers in any other segment of everyday life, high-quality mobility systems have to be cheap, fast, reliable, and needs-oriented. This way the quality of mobility and transportation is directly linked with quality-of-life and economic productivity, but too much physical movement can essentially impair quality-of-life (e.g. well-being, possibility of comfortable and safe mobility, health, prosperity and an intact environment).

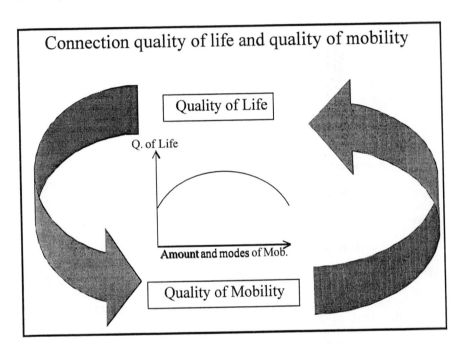

Fig. 1: Mobility and Quality-of-life

We assume that by means of integrated approaches in research and intervention programs mentioned above, some progress into this direction can be achieved. Adequate monitoring and evaluation procedures are applied and scientific and political support for comprehensive mobility policies are developed.

2 The future of urban mobility

Anticipating urban transportation contexts ten years ahead, the situation in developed countries probably will not be entirely different from today, though somewhat worse on average. The specific future states in different locations will obviously depend on the development of several factors such as demography, economic growth, environmental concerns, and - last but not least - transportation policy.

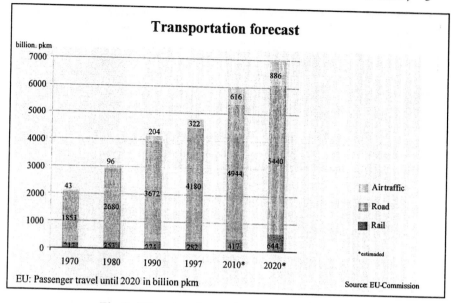

Fig. 2: Transportation forecast 2020 (see 21)

Given this framework of future urban mobility, what are the most crucial future issues to be dealt with on the agenda of mobility research? Altogether, we see four clusters :

- Framing conditions of urban mobility - legal, administrative, resources, society, environment,
- Technology - vehicles, systems, information/communication,
- Services - traffic management, scheduling, booking,
- Mobility behaviour - frequencies, distances, patterns, modes, and purposes of mobility and transportation.

Within any of these clusters changes and developments of different kinds can be expected, and at least some of these changes are outcomes of specific mobility policies. This paper will develop a structure of relevant mobility policy options, to assess the specific sustainability potential of these options, and point out research questions derived from previous findings.

Our starting hypothesis is, that sustainable future mobility policies will consist of integrated solutions, and that they will be basically needs-oriented. Bearing in mind that answers in this context require several social-science-based competencies, we now open up the chapter of conflict areas related to mobility and sustainability.

3 Urban mobility and sustainability

Given the three main driving forces sketched above - growing mobility demand, stagnant supply and societal awareness - the potential future states of urban mobility can be quite in line with sustainable development, but it is also a permanent source of latent conflict.

For the purpose of this paper, we use the definition of sustainability as it was elaborated at the "Sustainable Cities" conference in Rio de Janeiro in 2000:

"The concept of sustainability as applied to a city is the ability of the urban area and its region to continue to function at levels of quality of life desired by the community without restricting the options available to the present and future generations and causing adverse impacts inside and outside the urban boundary. (...) Urban transportation systems play a critical role due to their interaction with other urban systems such as environment, energy, land-use, safety and security, and in many cases may be viewed as the nucleus for sustainable cities. Sustainability in cities is extremely unlikely to be achieved without addressing the urban transportation problems."

The potential span between urban mobility either as active support of sustainable development in this sense or a source of possible conflict is constituted by future performance levels in six areas:

- More commuting time due to worsening traffic conditions, more travel time for recreation.
  Over the last decades, daily travel frequencies have been remarkably constant, as was the daily time used for being mobile (16). Furthermore, we see an equally stable trend towards longer distances, which in sum implies an increase in average systems speed, this way allowing travelers to overcome more distance in the same time. We assume that by increasing traffic volumes this compensation effect might not continue forever. More likely we expect decreasing average system speed and a higher susceptibility to interference of complex, highly optimized and high-occupancy transportation systems instead. While some people might argue that this effect is quite welcome, we would evaluate this possible development as negative: as a loss of quality-of-life and as an unnecessary risk in terms of sustainability.

- Environmental impacts.
  The literature on environmental consequences of urban transport and mobility is manifold, but in most cases related to past situations. Anyway, we would like to refer to some approaches with future perspectives via modeling, simulation, or scenarios. Due to complexity, dynamics, and stochasticness of the relevant cause-effect-relationships, precise knowledge as in natural sciences can not be achieved. This way future statements in this field have to be understood as assessments, based on the best knowledge available.
  Carbon-dioxide as an example: on the one hand easy to calculate, as emissions are directly linked to fuel consumption; on the other hand some open questions: What reduction potential using existing technologies are given; to what extent can new technologies like fuel cells contribute; will over-compensation by increasing traffic-volumes take place, in developing countries especially (as many experts are arguing) ? Taking into account risks and chances under complex and insecure conditions, any reduction of

traffic-related carbon-dioxide emissions is positive, the more reduction the better.

Ozone is a similar case, with a difference that local and regional impacts of ozone emissions have to be considered. ALLEGRINI et al. (2) developed a diffusion model, which can be used for local forecasting. To date it is not entirely clear how sensitive ozone emissions are to different mobility scenarios, but without any doubt low ozone emission levels are desirable.

Local emissions of NO_x and HC are crucial, as their negative impact on quality-of-life is obvious. By introducing and enforcing catalytic converters, the situation in countries with such policies has eased a bit at least, but there is still necessity and potential to lower emission levels even more. This is also due to the fact that for these groups of gaseous emissions mobility and transportation are pre-dominant sources. In Santiago de Chile for example, 70 % of NO_x-emissions are contributed by road transport, as FRESARD/OSSES (10) pointed out. As for HCs, the level is 46 %, or 49 % in the case of Finland (11). Although different assessments about the environmental and health impacts of emission levels have been published, for any mobility policy decreasing gaseous emissions should be beyond any dispute.

In this context we want to draw attention to a quite common misunderstanding: modal-split measures influencing modal split towards public transport do not automatically reduce emission levels. DE NOCKER et al. (7) and ROMILLY (15) calculated "break-even" occupancy levels, and due to differences in related elements, technologies etc. in Belgium and Scotland their results in terms of bus occupancy differ remarkably (25 % and 55 % respectively). Anyway, minimum occupancies have to be considered in terms of emission effects.

Another remark: environmental impacts of alternative transport measures or mobility policies have to be evaluated in an integrative way (8), as environmental gains and losses have to be calculated for every relevant factor, and too often specific additional ecological impacts are disconsidered.

Traffic-related noise is considered as a serious problem with regards to public health. For Germany, the Federal Environment Agency points out that about 40 % of the total population is exposed to noise levels representing potential health risks. On the other hand, traffic-caused noise patterns to an essential degree can be influenced by mobility and transportation policies, as was showed in scenarios on acoustic environments (18). In general, noise prediction models have been developed towards a quite remarkable level, so that results of simulation studies and sensitivity analyses might play some role in the evaluation of mobility policies and measures. The first pilot projects on noise-level related speed limits have been scheduled (5).

Another environmental concern is the conservation of qualities of landscapes and habitats. Our assessment of future developments is quite simple - we do not expect a notable portion of transportation infrastructure expansion within agglomerations - too strong financial and societal constraints have to be assumed. Some resources might be put into infrastructure maintenance and - to some degree - upgrading of existing infrastructure.

- Financial aspects
As already touched upon, aspects of financing will set serious constraints for the design of future transportation and mobility policies. In several countries difficulties in this context are already linked with the task of maintaining the existing infrastructure. There is an intensive search for models of funding and raising money from private investors, as private business models or approaches of public-private-partnerships. Besides methodological issues of calculating cost-benefit-ratios, life-cycle-costs, and other aspects of project financing (1), private investment may potentially play a significant role in any major projects related to transportation infrastructure and development of mobility services.
This brings some additional aspects to the agenda: How is funding for development, operation, maintenance, and repair going to be organized; how can some fair originators' principle be developed, assigning costs of damages and wear outs to the real causes; what fee levels are justified for which infrastructure use?
  Answers to these questions will not at all be simple, and the issues will be heavily discussed over the course of time. The pattern of the debate might be similar, as it has been about social costs of transportation and mobility policies (14). Anyway, cost-effectiveness of mobility will definitely remain a major issue.

- Safety and security issues
Road transport has been becoming safer over the last decades, due to several factors such as vehicle technology, rescue systems, and driving behavior. However, considering that safety indicators (e.g. fatal accidents per million passenger km) are about double in figures in some south-west European countries compared to Scandinavia (not including traffic-caused fatalities and injuries in some developing countries) should lead to the conclusion that road traffic safety can be essentially influenced by mobility policies (see 13; 19). This statement is more or less valid for any mode of transportation. In vehicle technology including assistance or automated systems major efforts are currently underway. In this way, a continuing trend towards decreasing accident rates can be expected, but eminently behavioral aspects might be an additional focus.
  Real and perceived security of mobility systems and public transportation (e. g. of molestation, sexual violence, terrorism or robbery) seems to be an issue
    (a)   not being empirically surveyed very much and
    (b)   definitely of growing importance over the coming years.
Of course, some topics have been analyzed and described with regards to security impacts like light-rail passenger cabin concepts, design of stopping places, lighting parameters in multi-storey car-parks, but comprehensive

evaluation of different mobility systems with regard to their security qualities still seem to be a task yet to be done.

Solutions for these problems are to be developed combining technology (e. g. easy access-emergency phones, presence of personnel), traffic management (e. g. management of speed and risky areas), the modification of infrastructure into mistake-avoiding structures and the design of public transportation towards improved real and perceived security.

In mobility services, the perceived security of the whole service is only as high as the perceived security of the weakest link (e. g. the way to the busstop). In general, accidents and violence are regarded with greater weight than "business as usual" - without reference to any real statistical data. This means that trust in new mobility options has to be built by enabling long-term positive experiences (by addressing real safety and security problems) and by professional risk communication strategies.

- Conflicts in the use of space

  Physical mobility requires space. In some metropolitan areas the amount of space in use for mobility purposes is exceeding 20%. By the way, the degree of area reserved for rail and air transportation is surprisingly high. Furthermore, taking the ratio between space and mobility performance into account, pedestrian and bicycle mobility can be quite inefficient in certain areas (4).

  In future there could be an optimization by combining different modes of transport depending on the aim of mobility. By means of Intelligent Transport Systems (ITS) and dynamic spatial restrictions related to sustainability degrees of vehicles, conflicts in the use of traffic space could be essentially diminished.

- Social impacts

  It is often argued that mobility opportunities are not distributed socially equal using this argument as evidence for the necessity of more subsidies for conventional public transport. We don't see any substantial justification for this kind of conclusion, and would rather encourage intensive search and experiments as innovative solutions like needs oriented mobility services and fair pricing - thus opening up potentials for highly efficient mobility offers, consequently decreasing demand for public subsidies in the long term.

  Mobility business is labour-intensive - quite often public transport organizations are the biggest local employers. Due to automation and cost-cutting tendencies some job reduction seems to be predetermined, and therefore any mobility policy with a positive or at least neutral job balance would be important.

A systemic evaluation of various combinations of policy options with regard to their ability to solve or to mitigate the problems addressed, or in other words an assessment of their sustainability potential is carried out in the following chapter.

4 Main sustainability indicators

Before evaluating political measures, there has to be a definition of goals. For this we have summarised the most common sustainability indicators and estimated the probable effects of political measures on them. We assume, that a satisfaction of a wide range of sustainability needs indicators is best for a sustainable urban mobility. For a detailed list of sustainability indicators we refer e. g. to TERM 2000 (17).

In our analysis we identified technology, products and behaviour as interfering factors, which at least influence sustainability. These have to be managed in an intelligent combination by political measures and an adequate "design" of framing conditions.

Policy Instruments	Intermediate factors			Indicators of environmental impact		Habitat and Landscape	Safety	Security	Social Impacts
	Technology	Products/Services	Behaviour	Global Impact (CO2), Energy Resources	Local Emissions, Noise				
Air quality based traffic restrictions	+++	++	+++	++	+++	0	0	0	++
Air quality based pricing	+++	+++	++	+++	++	0	0	0	+/-
Infrastructure extension/ development.	0	0/+	+++	+	++	+/-	+	+	+/-
Infrastructure management	+	+	+++	+/0	+	0	++	++	0
Taxes, tariffs, prices	++	++	+++	+++	++	0	+	0	+/-
Vehicle/systems technology	++	++	0	+++	++	0	++	+	0
Intelligent transportation systems (incl. public transport), traffic management	+	++	+++	++	++	0	+	++	0
Mobility services...	0	+	++	++	+	0	+	++	+

Figure 3: Sustainability-impacts of different political measures

As seen in the structure of marked areas in Fig. 3, there is no group of political measures, which satisfies all the requirements of sustainability. The table rather suggests that intelligent combination of measures into urban mobility policies might provide vital sustainability effects.

5 Policy options

Among academics and practitioners several alternative policy options to cope with urban transport and mobility issues are being discussed. We suggest structuring them into the following policy areas:

- *Air quality based traffic restrictions* (e. g. reduced access to certain areas, reduction of speed, environmental zones), and *air quality based pricing*, (e. g. emission-based city-toll or emission-based-road-pricing), which are able to reduce in "real-time" and close-to-origin the environmental impacts of traffic and could – in the long term – promote technological change.
- *Infrastructure extension/development* (e. g. building of new railways or roads or infrastructure for public transport), *infrastructure management* (e. g. systems for influencing collective or individual traffic, like flexible traffic signals), Intelligent Transportation Systems (including public transport), and other traffic management schemes, which may have positive economic effects by optimizing existing traffic and promoting new possibilities of transportation.
- *Mobility services* (e. g. Car Sharing, Integrated Mobility Services), which allow an efficient combination of different kinds of vehicles and by this an environmentally based optimization of transportation.
- *Taxes, tariffs, prices*, which strengthen economic influence on decisions about certain modes of traffic and – in the long term – might influence the development of technology for vehicles and systems and the development of attractive mobility services.
- *Vehicle and systems technology* (e. g. fuel cells or other alternative drives), which enable more environmental friendly transportation without reducing capacities.

6 Enlarged option landscape

Further analysis of the evaluation results leads to some new, additional mobility policy options, which are sketched briefly:

To influence technology and products (like certain mobility services) we assume that combining air quality based pricing (e.g. eco-selective city tolls) with taxes, tariffs and prices, and the support of industries for developing new vehicle and systems technology might be most promising.

According to findings of social sciences like environmental psychology, in order to influence behaviour, it is important to have a pull-effect by means of comfortable and attractive possibilities of "moving sustainable" like intelligent transportation systems (e. g. information technology) and mobility services and a push-effect through air quality based pricing and restrictions.

Overall, there has to be a well coordinated infrastructure management and an advanced, sustainability-supporting infrastructure (which is more than roads and railways, e. g. design of park-and ride-areas, location planning, safe and comfortable intermodal mobility management, etc.).

One open question in this context is how to identify and how to deal with target conflicts. Mobility is the materialization of different interests (and the resulting behaviour) of many different sub-groups and organizations. Conflicts might arise e. g. in costs (and the responsibility of funding), speed (e. g. between old and young people), growth (e. g. industry vs. living in quiet areas close to cities), time, resources, interest groups (different life situations, etc).

These conflicts can never be entirely solved, therefore there has to be local conflict management. Mobility systems generally should provide much flexibility by design, so that quick changes due to unexpected conditions and conflicts are possible.

7 Conclusions

- Comprehensive influence on all relevant sustainability indicators can be achieved only by broad combinations of measures, since most instruments listed above work only within limited sustainability ranges.

- Optimal effects on sustainability can be expected with a co-ordinated combination of technical developments, infrastructure organization, restrictions, and pricing/taxes. For this a close co-operation between politics, economy, and other actors must take place. This is to be found for example in pilot projects like "Mobilität in Ballungsräumen" or World Business Council for Sustainable Development (WBSCD, 20), establishing forms of public-private partnerships.

- For most measures traffic impacts on associated environmental media cannot be predicted exactly. Therefore accurate and on-line monitoring, and if necessary readjustment of measures are recommended.

- There is a risk of negative reciprocal effects, if e.g. changes in infrastructure like road construction and other measures (e. g. air quality based restrictions) on sustainability.

- Information systems alone do not promote environmental friendly transport systems or vehicles. Solutions have to be developed in the integration of systems, in the combination of different kinds of vehicles and in an efficient, innovation-supporting combination of measures.

- A focal factor of environmentally fair mobility systems is - apart from technology - human behaviour. The psychology of the choice of modes of transport, use of certain technologies and organization of personal mobility are usually not explicitly mentioned and are not sufficiently considered. Social Sciences like environmental psychology or sociology offer knowlegde about human factors in mobility which should be considerend (see (3), (5), (9), (12)).

- Innovations in the mobility sector could cause essential sustainability effects, especially mobility services are relevant (e. g. tax reduction for companies offering new mobility services, support for networking of companies in the sector of sustainable mobility, support in cross-linking different modes of transportation).

What are possible future developments of sustainable urban mobilities ? We did not intend to elaborate final answers, but rather wanted to sketch the road-map to alternative scenarios. Beyond specific findings an idea or a concept of what we would label as "Systemic Mobility" is rising. And it seems as if it requires some amount of research and evaluation to identify the most suitable solutions.

References

(1) ABDUL-MALAK, M.-A. U.: Parameters for an Integrated Life-cycle Anasis of Transportation Projects, In: Urban Transport IV, Wessex Institute of Technology, Southampton 1998, p. 159 - 168

(2) ALLEGRINI, I. et al.: Statistical Analysis of Ozone Concentration - A Forecasting and Control Model in Urban Areas, In: Urban Transport V, Wessex Institute of Technology, Southampton 1999, p. 93 - 104

(3) BAMBERG, S., GUMBL, H., SCHMIDT, P. (2000). *Rational Choice und theoriegeleitete Evaluationsforschung am Beipiel der Verhaltenswirksamkeit verkehrspolitischer Maßnahmen.* Opladen.

(4) BOUWMAN, M.: A comparison of short distance transport modes, In: : Urban Transport V, Wessex Institute of Technology, Southampton 1999, p. 415 - 424

(5) BRÜDERL, J., PREISENDÖRFER, P. (1995). Der Weg zum Arbeitsplatz. Eine empirische Untersuchung der Verkehsmittelwahl. In Diekmann, A. & Franzen, A. (Hrsg.), *Kooperatives Umwelthandeln* (S. 69-88). Chur, Zürich: Rüegger.

(6) BRUNNER, P.; TIEFENTHALER, H.: Verkehrslautstärke beeinflußt erlaubte Höchstgeschwindigkeit, In: Internationales Verkehrswesen, 10/2001, p. 474 - 477

(7) DE NOCKER, L.; INT PANTIS, L..; TORFS, R.: External Costs of Passenger Transport in Belgian Cities, In: Urban Transport V, Wessex Institute of Technology, Southampton 1999, p. 501 - 510

(8) DE VLIEGER, I. et al.: Multidisciplinary Study on Reducing Air Pollution from Transport - Methodology and Emission Results, In: Urban Transport VII, Wessex Institute of Technology, Southampton 2001, 429 - 440

(9) DICK, M. (2001). *Die Situation des Fahrens. Phänomenologische und ökologische Perspektiven der Psychologie. Diss., Bremen.*

(10) FRESARD; F.; OSSES, M.: Topographical Effects on Global Emissions from Mobile Sources in Urban Networks, In: Urban Transport VII, Wessex Institute of Technology, Southampton 2001, p. 521 - 532

(11) GRANBERG, M.; NIITTIMÄKI, J.: Traffic performance-based Air Quality Management, In: Urban Transport VII, Wessex Institute of Technology, Southampton 2001, 399 - 408

(12) KAROPKA, H.-J., MILLER, B., OPPEL, T. & BIHN, F. (2000). Wie erlebt der Kunde den öffentlichen Nahverkehr? *Der Nahverkehr, 11/2000,* 18-22.

(13) LEDA Endbericht 2000, www.leda.org

(14) ROBUSTE, F. et al.: Social Costs of Metropolitan Passenger Transport in Barcelona, In: Urban Transport VII, Wessex Institute of Technology, Southampton 2001, p. 751 - 763

(15) ROMILLY, P.: Transport and the Environment - A Multi- and Interdisciplinary Approach, In: Urban Transport VII, Wessex Institute of Technology, Southampton 2001, p. 409 - 418

(16) SHELL, 2001, Shell PKW-Szenarien: Mehr Autos – weniger Verkehr?, Deutsche Shell AG

(17) TERM 2000. Indicators on transport and environment in the EU, European Environment Agency, Copenhagen, February 2000

(18) VAN WALSUM, E. et al.: Scenarios for the Acoustic Environment in Flanders in 2010, In: Urban Transport VII, Wessex Institute of Technology, Southampton 2001, 555 - 564

(19) These topics are described in a future perspective by: WASCHKE, T.; METZNER, A.; CARSTEN, S. & F. WEBER (1999): Perspectives of Mobility in Future Societies. Symposium on "Engine & Environment", Graz.

(20) WBSCD (World Business Council for Sustainable Development): Mobilität 2001 - Ein Überblick, Genf 2001

(21) VDA - Verband Deutscher Automobilhersteller, Jahresbericht 2000

(22) www.mo.st

(23) www.mobiball.de

Inter-organisational co-operation in improving access to activity centres by public transport

R.E.C.M. van der Heijden[1,2] , A. van der Elst[2] & W.W. Veeneman[3]
[1] *Nijmegen School of Management, Nijmegen University, the Netherlands*
[2] *Department of Transport & Logistics, Delft University, the Netherlands*
[3] *Department of Organisation and Management, Delft University, the Netherlands*

Abstract

The accessibility to city centres and large attraction parks increasingly becomes an issue of concern for location owners. They seek possibilities to offer transport services as an alternative to car use. In doing so, co-operation with public transport companies is important. These companies do not yet have the culture and opportunities to develop tailor-made services. Institutional changes yielding more market incentives and good information sharing should help to bridge the gaps between these parties. In particular a shared view on the service level to be offered, based on investigation of visitors' preferences, should be the starting point for inter-organisational co-operation.

1 Introduction

In the Netherlands, for some considerable time, the well-known problems related to growing mobility (traffic congestion, use of scarce space, environmental deterioration, decreasing access to economic centres) have been regarded as a responsibility of public authorities. Both entrepreneurs and drivers tended to consider themselves victims of increased car use, yielding an attitude of looking at local, regional and national authorities to solve these problems. Strategies for solution have long been dominated by building car-focused infrastructures (roads, parking facilities). Non-infrastructure strategies (such as e.g. selective pricing, causing behavioural changes, significantly improve public transport services, large scale business related transport management, or modal shift towards rail and water) have long received less attention.

Fortunately, the Second (1990) and the Third (2001) Dutch National Transport Structure Plan, accepted as the basis for public transport policy development, stress the relevancy of broad strategies based on the simultaneous application of various instruments. The Plan, compared to public policy plans in other Western countries, offers a new perspective on to the increasing problems of the transport system and the ways to cope with them (Banister, 1994). Analyses of the Plan however, reveal that the ambitions are (too) high and not always coherent and systematically formulated and co-ordinated. Moreover, the practical realisation of strategies appears to be extremely difficult. Nevertheless, since the second half of the nineties one can experience throughout society a growing awareness of the problem complexity, resulting in the acceptance of the need for applying a variety of steering instruments and an active involvement of many other actors outside public authorities. Incentives to this mental shift have been given by several institutional changes, reducing the traditionally important role of public authorities and strengthening private initiatives. This is in particular clear for the sector of public transport, but also in the field of infrastructure design, construction, maintenance and exploitation significantly changes are introduced.

The new mind-set in transport policy also effects the attitude of entrepreneurs with shopping, recreational or conferencing facilities regarding issues such as location decision making, accessibility for visitors and use of alternative transport modes. Many of these facilities are located at spots difficult to be reached by car, for instance in inner cities. The problem with inner cities and large entertainment parks is the enormous amount of cars to be parked at top-days. Due to that congestion at local roads is induced, time is lost for parking entrance and exit and unattractive walking distances to the gates of the park or the shopping malls occur. Hence, customers experience growing difficulty in reaching these locations. Increasingly, entrepreneurs are aware of the fact that they themselves have to take initiatives in order to offer visitors attractive transport alternatives to reach the destination. Access to the location becomes a part of the marketing mix for the activities employed at that location (Van der Elst, 1999).

This development yields many questions, such as: what do visitors prefer with respect to accessibility? What are strategies by the entrepreneur to react to these preferences? Can an ex ante assessment be made of the cost-effectiveness of these strategies? With who should be co-operated to implement certain strategies? Does this co-operation also imply new financial risks? Are there institutional barriers for these strategies? And so on. Since offering transport services generally is no part of the services offered by the entrepreneurs, these questions can only be answered adequately in co-operation with transport companies and (local) public authorities. This makes the issue of improving accessibility increasingly subject of an inter-organisational co-ordination challenge between parties with diverging interests. In this context, the public authorities' position of key actor is released in favour of private stakeholders' initiatives. Accordingly, decision-making processes adapt to these new roles.

This paper further explores these changing roles, focusing on the interaction between real estate managers, shopkeepers, public transport companies and municipal authorities. The aim is to explore the complexity and to identify some pitfalls of new initiatives. The structure of the paper is as follows. In section 2 the problem of co-operation is more in-depth addressed from a theoretical perspective. In section 3 the analysis in section 2 is illustrated by the development of the Utrecht City Project (UCP). Since public transport companies play a special and crucial role in the context described above, the question whether they pick up the new challenges satisfactory will be addressed in section 4. Finally, some conclusions will be drawn in section 5.

2 Problems of co-operation

In the introduction it was argued that increasingly 'location-owners' (shopkeeper organisations, recreational businesses, congress centres and real estate companies) consider accessibility as an essential aspect of the service offered to visitors. Their attitude towards accessibility is shifting from passive to active and they are willing to pay for quality improvements. For instance, a big recreational attraction facility in the Netherlands (Dolfinarium Hardewijk) faces the problem that 80% of the 1 million visitors annually arrive by car. Therefore, recently an accessibility plan was elaborated in co-operation with public transport companies: NS-Reizigers (railway) and MIDnet (bus). The implementation of the plan however suffers from severe procedural problems (local authorities) and diverging interests of the transport service providers. Another example is the Efteling fairytale-park, taking initiatives to increase accessibility by running dedicated shuttle busses to the Efteling from various places in the Netherlands. Co-operation with public transport companies appeared to be very difficult. Another example is the policy to construct several Park & Ride facilities at the edge of city centres / urban areas (Whitfield and Cooper, 1998; Fradd and Duff, 1998). In some cases, these facilities are 'dressed-up' with additional services like grocery stores, fast food restaurants, and the like, in order to increase the attractiveness of parking at these places and using public shuttle services to for instance the inner city area. So far, only few of such facilities, combined with high quality shuttle services, are realised. Moreover, in several cases these facilities are wrongly located and the additional services appear to be less viable.

These examples indicate that the establishment of an effective and viable co-operation structure is quite difficult. There are several reasons for this situation, basically all related to different perceptions, interests and positions. *Firstly*, as indicated above, the mutual relationship between public authorities and public transport companies is changing rapidly, due to institutional changes (see e.g. Veeneman, 2002). These companies are increasingly challenged to operate as companies with full responsibility for their business results. Deregulation has increased the degree of freedom for enterprising behaviour substantially. On the other hand tendering of concessions seems to favour a growing stronghold over public transport by the public authorities. Consequently, the success of public transport development for the release of congested locations has become more dependent upon creative service development by the public transport companies and the ability and willingness of public authorities to allow public transport companies to develop service in co-operation with the other parties mentioned.

Secondly, irrespective the growth in freedom for enterprising behaviour, public transport companies and public authorities are very supply-focused and are therefore less flexible in terms of transport services. This can simply be argued by the cost/benefit structure in public transport. Bundling and regularity, hence mass production with a low level of differentiation, leading to effective planning and efficient resource use, seem success factors for arriving at significantly improved business results. However, location-owners often face very different visiting patterns (different days in the week, different periods of the year, weather-dependency, special events) demanding for a large flexibility (tailor-made) in provided transport services. This does not fit well to the basic service focus of the transport companies and generates many discussions on what is good for the passenger/visitor.

Thirdly, local and regional authorities sometimes have to take initiatives to investment in conditions favouring public transport. There might be a need e.g. to create Park & Ride facilities, or to facilitate the intended quality improvement of public transport services by e.g. free bus lanes or priority in traffic regulation. Moreover, car-access to the area should be made less attractive (decreasing parking lots, increasing price of parking). Such measures are often subject of intensive public debate, e.g. because of the image of an unfavourable cost-effectiveness ratio of these investments.

Finally, there is a permanent discussion about who is the problem owner, who benefits from various measures and who should bear the costs. Is the visitor the one who has the problem and benefits from attractive alternative transport services, or is it the local authority facing less congestion with these facilities? Or is it the location-owner trying to be sufficiently competitive and market-attractive? It often happens, that due to this fuzziness, perceptions of the need for changing the state-of-the-art, differ substantially among parties: in general the claim for changing the situation by one party seems to be larger in situations where another party is assumed to bear the responsibility. Moreover, the question might arise whether a somewhat lower level of access is acceptable because of compensation by other features of the destination, such as exclusive shops or cultural facilities.

Bridging these differences in perception and position is important for being successful in creating attractive services for large amounts of visitors to spatially concentrated activity centres. Evidently, the question is how to bridge. Van der Elst (1999) stresses the importance of breakthroughs in the contingency of the problem and the processes to cope with it. In relation to the contingency, it is important (a) to make differences in perception transparent what kind of (new) services for whom and when? (b) to reach an agreement on an operational view on accessibility (performance indicators and standards) and (c) to shift attention from an infrastructure approach towards a service level approach. Moreover, with respect to planning and decision-making processes, several strategies aimed at creating commitment among the key players have been suggested in policy and management literature (e.g. Kickert et al, 1997). From the analysis above with regard to problems of co-ordination, we learn that it is essential to feed these processes with information (facts and figures) in order to eliminate mistakes, reduce fuzziness and, hence, enhance decision-making. Since we know that information imbalance between key players often appears to be an obstacle for progress, it seems in particular important to create in a specific case a platform of all key players for information exchange. This helps to improve shared problem recognition, to develop a sense of urgency for actions and to facilitate shared strategy development.

In the next section, some aspects of the co-operation problem are illustrated by the development of the Utrecht City Project (UCP), the Netherlands.

3 Illustration: Utrecht City Project

The Utrecht City Project (UCP) is a plan for the functional and physical reconfiguration of the area around Utrecht central railway station. The present number of shops, cafes, offices, conference facilities and apartments will substantially be increased. The Utrecht central railway station is the largest node in the Dutch railway network. The station and its facilities have to be adapted to new developments, such as changes in the present rail services and the introduction of high-speed trains. UCP intends to enlarge the regional and national economic importance of the area, resulting in about 75 million visitors to the Utrecht central railway station yearly. It is clear that tackling the transport and accessibility problems of this scale is a major challenge.

In order to cope with this challenge, a Platform UCP has been created. Key players, such as the owner of the shopping mall called 'Hoog Catharijne', the railway station manager, different parts of the railway company, the city authorities and the owner of a large conference centre (Jaarbeurs), participate in the Platform. The Platform is the bases for public-private partnership in project development. Agreement has been reached that the Ministry of Transport will finance a part of the plan. The rest is partly financed by the municipality and partly by the private investors. Within the Platform, much discussion focuses on the accessibility of the node, but the parties have different perceptions of the problem and the potential solutions. The private parties put more emphasis on the car-accessibility, whereas the public authorities want to stimulate the access by high quality public transport. So, the question is relevant what accessibility means for different market segments of visitors and how to react to diverging preferences.

The potential visitor takes a variety of factors into consideration when taking a decision on visiting a particular destination. The part-worth utilities attached to these factors are combined to an overall utility for the destination. This overall utility is an indicator for the attractiveness of the destination. In case more than one destination is a serious option for the potential visitor, differences in utility (attractiveness) strongly influence destination choice. As noted before, the weight of the factor 'accessibility' as compared to the weight for other factors grows. The factor refers to the effort by a visitor to arrive at the destination. This effort is linked to e.g. travel time, travel costs, quality of information, comfort and pleasure. Consequently, the quality of the travel service from the place of origin to the destination is important. For instance: frequently used rules of thumb assume that the ratio of travel time by public transport and travel time by car at short distances (agglomeration level) should not exceed 1.5. At longer distances, this ratio should drop to 1.1 to 1.2. In current practice, ratios for many OD-relations are often significantly higher.

In order to find out how much weight visitors attach to accessibility, or more precisely the underlying aspects, market segments have to be distinguished. In a preliminary analysis for UCP (Van der Elst, 1998), the following criteria for segmentation were distinguished:

- travel mode (car, public transport, multi-modal)
- trip motive (business, recreation)
- intended activities at the destination (work, conference, shopping)
- zone of origin.

In total 18 market segments were distinguished. Visitors were asked in a questionnaire to evaluate different aspects of accessibility. Moreover, interviews were held among location owners to ask their opinion about the standards (minimum or maximum level to be pursued) with respects to various accessibility aspects. The images resulting from the questionnaire appeared to differ in many respects from the images resulting from the interviews with the location owners in the UCP area.

For instance, it was found that the location owners accept a higher percentage of visitors by car or by public transport being unsatisfied with respect to information provision, than the visitors do. For the location owners a maximum of (on average) 27% unsatisfied car visitors and 40% public transport visitors appeared to be acceptable. However, the visitors themselves indicate maximum (average) percentages of respectively 8% and 36%.

Another difference in perception was revealed with respect to transfer times. Again maximum levels were investigated. The location owners in the UCP area indicate a maximum transfer time for travellers by public transport of 4 minutes (in case of shopping), 5 minutes (in case of going to work) and 3 minutes (in case of going to a conference in the UCP area). The visitors themselves, however, indicated maximum acceptable transfer times of respectively 11, 9 and 10 minutes (average figures). Moreover, it was found that the current transfer times on average were lower than the maximum acceptable level for the travellers.

Finally, a third example is the difference in perception of the quality of the service level with regard to facilities at the railway stations and parking facilities. On average about 20% of the visitors was not satisfied, which indicates more people to be unsatisfied than was indicated to be acceptable by the location owners.

Overall, various gaps between the preferences of travellers with regard to accessibility and the images held by location owners were revealed. This includes information to travellers, access for car users to parking houses or to public transport services, social safety, quality of facilities at transfer nodes, and travel time by car as well as travel time by public transport from the larger Utrecht agglomeration to the UCP area. A remarkable finding was that the key players in the UCP project assume more serious gaps between the actual accessibility quality and the preferences of the visitors, than the visitors indicate. Since these key players heavily influence decision-making, these cognitive biases put a claim on the negotiation and decision making process between location owners, public authorities and transport companies. One conclusion is that decision takers need to improve their knowledge with respect to the accessibility preferences of visitors to the UCP area.

Apart from the need for knowledge improvement with respect to preferences (and thus the nature of the problem), it appears to be very difficult in the UCP project to make a shift in the discussion from measures at the level of infrastructure and traffic management, towards service concepts. Consequently, much attention is for instance paid at the number of parking lots, road capacity extensions and traffic measures. Instead, it might be much more productive to discuss performance of transport services in terms of the combination of frequency, reliability, information level, cost and comfort. In this respect, the idea of 'multi-modal chains' or 'seamless multi-modal mobility' has become a focus point in the discussions in the past years. Research indicates that co-ordination of tariff systems, information provision and inter-organisation of services is crucial for realising this type of services to the visitors (e.g. Gobits, 1998; De Vries, 1999). Such a focus clearly implies the need for a more customer-focused attitude of the transport providers. However, it also requires an active role of location owners with regard to e.g. providing real-time information and/or organising tailor-made transport facilities (such as bus shuttles, bicycles for rent) as addition to the mass transport services. And finally, it also requires a development directed towards thinking and co-operating in a regional context (Van der Maas, 1998).

From the interviews with the location owners in the UCP area it was concluded, that gradually the awareness about the need for thinking in terms of service level agreements between the key players grows. The regional focus has to be strengthened yet, for instance by accepting some new players in the Platform UCP (regional bus companies, representatives of some larger municipalities in the region). Clearly, there exists a tension between broadening a discussion in favour of better regional commitments at the cost of a lower process speed, and limiting the number of participants in favour of quick progress. Limiting the number of participant might however generate serious resistance after decisions have been taken. To solve this tension, a good process design is necessary. With regard to UCP, the structuring of the problem from a regional systems view is essential. Consequently, the discussions and strategy development cannot be limited to only a few key players. A systems view based on seamless multi-modal transport service concepts, in combination with improved insights in customers' preferences, should be the basis for specifying performance levels for accessibility to the UCP area (see e.g. Van der Heijden & Marchau, 2001).

In the following section, some special attention will be paid to the position of the transport companies. Until now, they often appear to be rather inflexible players in the game. Although understandable, this does not match very well the need for a customer-focused flexible attitude. The question is whether they can play their role better within the present institutional context

4   The public transport companies

It is obvious that in the complex arena of parties who become increasingly dependent upon each other, the public transport companies play a crucial role. These companies have a long record of mass passenger transport and have important resources to negotiate with municipal authorities and location owners. In fact, the future reaction of public transport companies to the needs of the location owners for innovative access concepts is critical for the success or failure of marketing strategies for these special areas that, amongst others, compete on the bases of innovation in accessibility. A first question is whether the public transport companies are sufficiently aware of their role and their present position? A second question is whether public authorities will understand the need for flexibility to define concessions for public transport?

The present situation in the field of public transport is characterised by institutional transition and due to that business uncertainty (Veeneman, 2002). The national government is releasing its hold on public transport and regional authorities are taking over. This decentralisation leads to a wide variety of institutional changes. The public control over the sector is changing from general regulation and subsidisation to a formal commissioning of public transport services, often through formal tendering procedures. Local authorities are looking for a way to make their new role work. Moreover, public transport companies are exploring the boundaries of their new role. They seem keen within the new institutional order to develop services that fit the needs of location owners. On the other hand they need to reorganise their business to improve the cost-income ratio, leaving little room for creative development of services.

Nevertheless, the recent institutional changes seem to offer better opportunities for developing inter-modal transport services and to improve the total service quality, from the perspective of the passengers. The massive changes in the sector make it possible to introduce more flexibility into the development of services. In stead of 'trip providers', these companies might develop towards 'access providers'. Such a development would very much resemble developments in freight transport, where various transport companies have transformed themselves into logistic providers. There are several examples indicating that the old supply orientation gradually shifts towards a more customer-oriented approach. Barriers between different services have been lifted in the services of e.g. public transport companies 'NoordNet' and 'Synthus' in the Netherlands. New service providers (among which car lease-companies) have come to the market, which offer seamless use of different types of transport (public transport, taxis, and rental cars) with the introduction of the so-called 'Odessey'-travelcard. More and more location owners (convention centres like 'Jaarbeurs', attraction parks like 'Dolfinarium' and 'Efteling') have been able to provide some form of alternative transport for their visitors. These services are specifically tailored to the needs of their customers. And other than the traditional public transport operators have come in to the market to offer these services.

Such a shift from a mass transport perspective towards a service perspective is a welcome answer to the shift in the meaning of place from 'being there' to 'being easy to reach'. Traditional and new public transport companies are willing to offer the services, and visitors are serviced better as their wishes form the basis for their development. A major question is how local and regional public authorities will steer institutional changes to strengthen this development, or that their changed position with respect to public transport will generate the desire to have a firm grip over all public transport service development.

5 Conclusions

This paper addressed the complexity of inter-organisational co-operation in respect to improving accessibility to special activity areas, focusing on public transport services. Location owners are increasingly aware of the problems of local access by car and fear a lower attractiveness and a decreasing market share. Therefore, they are more and more willing to take responsibility and help to realise innovative concepts for accessibility. In terms of marketing, these innovative concepts can be considered as a part of the marketing strategy of the location owners.

This involvement requires co-operation with other organisations, in particular municipalities and public transport companies. This inter-organisational co-operation however suffers from diverging interests, lack of knowledge, information imbalance, fuzziness in problem boundaries and dynamic positions and responsibilities. Some of these aspects have been illustrated by the Utrecht City Project.

It was concluded that improving the knowledge about the market segmentation of visitors to the location and their variation in preferences is important to arrive at a more operational view on accessibility and the related standards/goals for the specific area on hand. Clearly, this operational view and the goals set by the key players should take into account the potential compensation by other functional features of the area. Important is not only to focus on the local infrastructure and traffic aspects. A focus on the regional position and pursued service level for access seems more productive. It offers the possibility to combine a great number of instruments to bring accessibility at a level requested by targeted customers. Involvement of other regional parties in these discussions and the according decision making imply a recognition of the systems dynamics at the regional level and improves the support for accessibility strategies shared by public and private stakeholders.

A crucial category of actors in this complex game is the category of public transport companies. Some special attention is paid to their position. The present situation is characterised by transition and institutional uncertainty. However, it is concluded that the recent institutional changes seem to offer good opportunities for developing inter-modal transport services and to improve the total service quality, from the perspective of the passengers. In stead of 'trip providers', these companies might develop towards 'access providers'. In particular this change would imply a major step forward.

REFERENCES

Banister, D. (1994): *Transport Planning in the UK, USA and Europe*, E&FN Spon, London

De Vries, M. (1999): *The Importance of Additional Information for Trip Planning Tools; Stated Preferences of Public Transport Users*, Ma Thesis School of Systems Engineering, Policy Analysis and Management, Delft University of Technology

Fradd, C. and A. Duff (1998): The potential for rail based park and ride to Heathrow, in: *PTRC-Conference 1998, seminar Public Transport Planning and Operations*, PTRC, London, pp.75-90

Gobits, D. (1998): *The Trip Planning Tool that Users Need*, Ma-thesis School of Systems Engineering, Policy Analysis and Management, Delft University of Technology

Kickert, W. E., Klijn and J. Koppenjan (1997): *Managing Complex Networks; Strategies for the Public Sector*, Sage, London

Van der Elst, A. (1998): *Het UCP-Gebied: Wel of Niet Bereikbaar*, Ma-thesis School of Systems Engineering, Policy Analysis and Management, Delft University of Technology (in Dutch)

Van der Elst, A. (1999): Normalisation of Accessibility: the Concept, Paper to be published in the *conference proceedings of the TRAIL PhD-Conference*, December 1999

Van der Heijden, R. & V. Marchau (2001): Innovating road traffic management by ITS: a future perspective, forthcoming in *International Journal of Technology, Policy and Management*

Van der Maas, C. (1998): Successful Public Transport in Urban Regions: a European Study on Policy and Practice, in: *PTRC-Conference 1998, seminar Public Transport Planning and Operations*, PTRC, London, pp.201-211

Veeneman, W. (2002): Bridging the gap; institutional changes in public transport, Dissertation, forthcoming Delft University of Technology

Whitfield, S. and B. Cooper (1998): The travel effects of park and ride, in: *PTRC-Conference 1998, seminar Public Transport Planning and Operations*, PTRC, London, pp.63-74

The structural dependency on car use for the Swedish urban population

M. Reneland
Department of City & Mobility,
School of Architecture
Chalmers University of Technology, Sweden

Abstract

Using GIS techniques, this project, financed by KFB The Swedish Transport and Communications Research Board, deals with the 45 Swedish towns with more than 20 000 inhabitants (those in the Stockholm region are excluded), and shows characteristic information about population, employees within different categories (retail shops, amusements, and care), car ownership etc. within a pedestrian zone (1 km from the centre point of each town), and a bicycle zone of 3 km.

The findings show that most of the Swedish towns have a similar structure. High population density, many employees, many retail shops, small proportion green areas and low car ownership characterize the central parts. With increased distance from the town centre the population density, number of employees and number of retail shops decrease while the proportion of green area and the car ownership increases.

However I consider that a great deal of the Swedish urban population have a convenient (maximum 15 minutes) distance by bicycle from their home to a large proportion of the town services and workplaces. In 1995, 65% of the population in the towns studied, i.e. 1 705 000 inhabitants, lived within a distance of 3 km from the town centre. Furthermore, a large proportion lived within convenient walking distance (maximum 15 minutes). In 1995, 18% of the population in the towns studied, i.e. 468 000 inhabitants, lived within a distance of 1 km from the town centre. Since the proportion of short car trips is very high in urban areas, (70-80% are shorter than 4 km), there is a great potential for reduction of car use in towns. This reduction could probably take place without any serious losses in the economy of individuals, companies and society, which gives considerable freedom of choice for the Swedish government and local authorities when it comes to the design of a traffic policy for a sustainable society.

Background

Empirical knowledge about the distances from the homes of the urban population and different types of destinations, such as the workplaces and services, is crucial to the question of urban sustainability. Short distances mean that the urban population is more likely to use sustainable means of transportation, walking and cycling, and the environmental impact from car driving will be less than for long distances.

As Swedish towns are small, there are reasons to believe that a great proportion of the urban population has comfortable walking and cycling distances to workplaces and services. This study is initialized by research questions as:

- What is the proportion of the Swedish urban population dependent on the car or public transportation use for everyday mobility, and on the other hand, what proportion, which are able to walk or cycle?
- Are there any differences between towns of different sizes, population density etc. when it comes to dependency upon car use?

Aims

The aim of this paper is to describe the proportion of the urban population living within walking and cycling distances to town centres.

Study design

This study [1] is part of the research project *Accessibility in Swedish towns 1980 and 1995*, and deals with the 45 Swedish towns with more than 20 000 inhabitants (those in the Stockholm region are excluded). The background of the project is a comprehensive database with the location of different types of services (libraries, schools, retail food stores, chemist's shops, post offices and public transportation networks), and information about population, employees within different categories (retail, amusements, and care), car ownership etc. registered on the coordinates of each respective real estate. These disaggregated population statistics are provided by Statistics Sweden and are available to researchers as well as to the planning activities of the local authorities. The digital population statistics based on real estate coordinates supplied by Statistics Sweden are less than the same organisation's table values. For both 1980 and 1995, the average deviation for all 45 towns was 1980, 4.18%, and 1995, 2.06%. When it comes to employees, the difference is larger according to Statistics Sweden. The reason for this being the differences between address information for workplaces and address information for real estate coordinates. This means that workplaces with difficult addresses are lost at random.

In the analyses, a centre point has been chosen for every town, located in the middle of the pedestrian precincts. From this centre point, three different circular distance zones have been used. The first one, with a radius of 1000 metres, is assumed to correspond to a theoretically factual walking distance 30% longer, which means 1300 metres. Even with a low average walking speed, 5 km/h, it is possible to walk this distance within 15 minutes. The second distance zone, 3000 metres as the crow flies, corresponds to a cycling distance of 3900 metres, which is also possible to manage within 15 minutes at an average speed of 15 km/h. The third zone of 5000 metres is used to identify the suburban areas in the large towns.

Each town's geographical boundaries have been adjusted to the digital urban area boundaries for 1980 and 1995 as stipulated by Statistics Sweden (SCB). A simplified description of the definition of an 'urban area' is as follows: "An urban area encompasses all agglomerations of buildings with at least 200 inhabitants, on condition that the distance between these buildings does not normally exceed 200 metres" [2]. The analyses have been performed in three stages:

- First the differences between the four zones of 0-1000 m, 1000-3000 m, 3000-5000 m and >5000 m have been measured.
- Secondly the characteristics of the distance zone 0-1000 m, the "pedestrian town", have been measured.
- Thirdly the characteristics of the distance zone 0-3000 m, the "bicycle town", have been measured.

The four distance zones compared

From table 1 can be seen that population density decreases according to the distance from the town centre point, that large towns have higher population density than small ones and that population density has increased in the town centres between 1980 and 1995, especially in large towns.

Table 1: Population density 1980 and 1995 (inhabitants/hectare) for the largest, the smallest, one middle-sized town and an average for the 45 largest towns.

	0 – 1000		1000 – 3000		3000 – 5000		>5000	
	-80	-95	-80	-95	-80	-95	-80	-95
Göteborg (478 791)	27	32	29	32	27	26	18	17
Gävle (66 110)	45	49	16	16	11	12	8	8
Katrineholm (19 757)	32	32	15	13	7	13	-	-
Average for 45 towns	29	34	20	19	17	17	15	15

Table 2 Employee densities 1997 (employees/hectare) for the largest, the smallest, one middle-sized town and an average for the 45 largest towns.

	0 – 1000	1000 – 3000	3000 – 5000	>5000
Göteborg (478 791)	49	15	8	2
Gävle (66 110)	41	8	1	1
Katrineholm (19 757)	19	5	-	-
Average for 45 towns	31	7	4	3

From table 2 can be seen that employee density decreases according to the distance from the town centre point, and that large towns have higher employee density than small ones in the distance zones 0-1000 m and 1000-3000 m.

From table 3 can be seen that the number of employees per 100 inhabitants decreases according to the distance from the town centre point, and that large towns have higher values than small ones.

Table 3 Employees 1997 per 100 inhabitants 1995 for the largest, the smallest, one middle-sized town and an average for the 45 largest towns.

	0 – 1000	1000 – 3000	3000 – 5000	>5000
Göteborg (478 791)	153	46	31	13
Gävle (66 110)	83	51	12	8
Katrineholm (19 757)	58	35	4	-
Average for 45 towns	89	34	25	18

From table 4 can be seen that the proportion of high-income households increases according to the distance from the town centre point, that large towns have higher proportion of high-income households in the town centre area than small ones, which in turn have a very high proportion of high-income households in the zones 3000-5000 m and >5000 m.

Table 4 Proportion of low-income households (L) 1993 (0-99 000 SEK/year), and high-income households (H) 1993 (>240 000 SEK/year) of all house holds within a zone, for the largest, the smallest, one middle-sized town and an average for the 45 largest Swedish towns.

	0 – 1000		1000 – 3000		3000 – 5000		>5000	
	L	H	L	H	L	H	L	H
Göteborg (478 791)	35	14	39	13	39	12	34	20
Gävle (66 110)	41	9	35	13	27	30	24	27
Katrineholm (19 757)	43	7	34	21	19	43	-	-
Average for 45 towns	40	10	38	13	34	20	33	23

Table 5 Proportion of green area 1995 for the largest, the smallest, one middle-sized town and an average for the 45 largest Swedish towns.

	0 – 1000	1000 – 3000	3000 – 5000	>5000
Göteborg (478 791)	25%	37%	44%	47%
Gävle (66 110)	15%	42%	48%	44%
Katrineholm (19 757)	15%	34%	50%	-
Average for 45 towns	23%	37%	41%	44%

From table 5 can be seen that the proportion of green areas increases according to the distance from the town centre point, but that there are great differences between towns due to land use patterns. The proportion of green areas has a significant relationship to the population density in the different distance zones of a town.

From table 6 can be seen that the number of cars per 1000 households depend on the distance from the town centre point, and that the number of cars is lower in the large towns compared to the small ones.

Table 6 Number of cars 1993 per 1000 households 1995 for the largest, the smallest, one middle-sized town and an average for the 45 largest towns.

	0 – 1000	1000 – 3000	3000 – 5000	>5000
Göteborg (478 791)	441	410	445	536
Gävle (66 110)	452	582	774	867
Katrineholm (19 757)	520	687	903	-
Average for 45 towns	495	560	629	648

The "pedestrian town"

In this paper, the "pedestrian town" is the same as the 0-1000 m distance zone from the centre point of each town. In the analyses, every town has only one centre point despite the number of inhabitants. Two towns, Göteborg and Malmö are split up in three and two local authority areas. These have been allotted one centre point for each local authority area. A large town such as Göteborg has of course several sub-centres with commercial and social services. In some analyses, seven main sub-centres are added to the original three. In some analyses values are calculated according to both these situations.

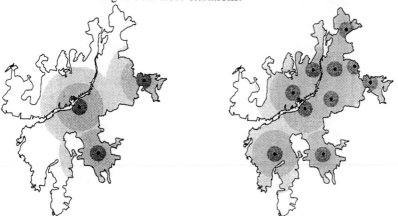

Figure 1 Göteborg, with distance zones 0-1000 m, 1000-3000 m, 3000-5000 m and >5000 m from three and ten centre points.

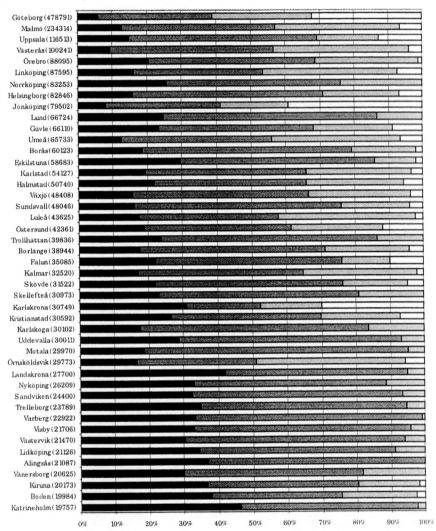

Figure 2 Proportion of population 1995 within 0-1000 m (black), 1000-3000 m (dark grey), 3000-5000 m (light grey) and >5000 m (white) from the town centre point. Names of towns and number of inhabitants 1995.

From figure 2 one can see that the larger town the less proportion of the inhabitants to be found in the pedestrian town and the bicycle town. On average for all 45 towns 18,0% of the inhabitants live within the pedestrian town, which means that ca 468 300 inhabitants can reach their town centres within 15 minutes walk. In 1980, the corresponding proportion was 16,0%, which means that a degree of compaction has taken place in the pedestrian town.

In Göteborg, the largest town in the sample, 5,9% of the inhabitants live within the pedestrian town when three centre points are considered. With ten centre points, the proportion is 22,2%, which is well above the average for all 45 towns.

Two towns differ from those of the same size. In Karlskrona (figure 3), an old naval town which has expanded into its hinterland, the town centre, surrounded by water, being in one end of the town. Almost the same proportion of the population live in the zone >5000 m in Karlskrona as in the large town Göteborg.

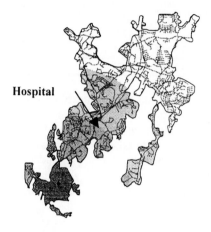

Figure 3 Karlskrona, with distance zones 0-1000 m, 1000-3000 m, 3000-5000 m and >5000 m from the town centre point.

In Örnsköldsvik (figure 4), the town centre is in the middle but the surrounding mountains, inlets from the sea and lakes have given the town a highly laciniated shape with long internal distances.

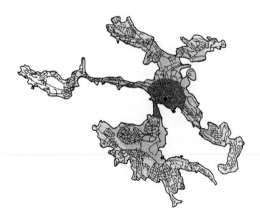

Figure 4 Örnsköldsvik, with distance zones 0-1000 m, 1000-3000 m, 3000-5000 m and >5000 m from the town centre point.

Table 7 Proportion of employees 1997, different categories, within the pedestrian town (distance zone 0 – 1000 m from the town centre point) for the largest, the smallest, one middle-sized town and an average for the 45 largest towns.

	Proportion of employees, different categories			
	Total	Retail	Amusements	Health Care
Göteborg (478 791)	24,1%	38,1%	57,4%	18,7%
Gävle (66 110)	42,2%	57,9%	82,4%	16,3%
Katrineholm (19 757)	59,6%	76,1%	95,1%	94,0%
Average for 45 towns	39,6%	52,4%	72,9%	43,1%

In a town with a large number of inhabitants (and a large number of employees) a smaller proportion of all employees is to be found within the pedestrian town than in a small town (table 7). The differences in population and employee density are not enough to compensate for the differences in scale. The difference between Göteborg with three (24,1%) and ten (34,1%) centre points when it comes to employees is not as big as when it comes to population. This means that sub-centres mainly offer services, and not work places.

Hospitals are very often the largest work place in a town. In small ones, the hospital often is situated within the pedestrian town, e.g. Katrineholm, Motala, Uddevalla and Falun. Then the proportion of employees in total and in the category Health Care is high.

In this paper has been assumed that the number of employees in the category Retail reflects the attractiveness of retail as a destination for retail-oriented trips. Again, the scale effect gives a lower proportion of retail within the pedestrian town in large towns than in small ones. One important reason is the existence of sub-centres in the large towns, which have been neglected in this study. Göteborg with its three (38%) and ten (52%) centre points throws light on these circumstances.

Small towns may have different structural characteristics, when it comes to retail localization. Both Uddevalla and Motala had about 30 000 inhabitants in 1995. In Uddevalla, about 86% of the employees in the retail sector is within the pedestrian town compared to 50% in Motala. While in Uddevalla the town centre dominates the retail structure, in Motala two competing centres have been developed, one in the town centre and one on the outskirts of the town.

In the same way as for retail an assumption has been made that the number of employees in the category Amusements reflects the attractiveness of these destinations for trips. To this category belongs those employed by restaurants, bars, theatres etc. A very high proportion of the employees of this category can be found in the pedestrian town of both large and small towns. The city life takes place in the town centre. This is where to amuse oneself.

Those employed in medical care, social care, chemist's shops etc belong to the category Health Care. The proportion of the employees in this category to be found within the pedestrian town varies a lot between different towns dependent on where the hospital is located.

The "bicycle town"

On average for all 45 towns, 64,7% of the inhabitants live within the "bicycle town", which means that ca 1 705 300 inhabitants are able to reach their town centres by bicycle within 15 minutes. To get a view over all towns in the study see figure 2.

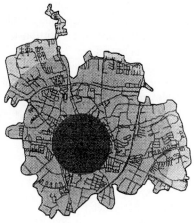

Figure 5 Lund, with distance zones 0-1000 m, 1000-3000 m and 3000-5000 m from the centre point.

Lund (figure 5) is special in many respects. It is a high-density town (in average 28,0 inhabitants/hectare 1995), almost circular and although it is a large town (66 724 inhabitants 1995) almost all of the town area is within the distance zone 0-3000 metres. Together this creates ideal prerequisites for cycling, and in Lund the population is to great extent cycle-oriented.

Table 8 Proportion of employees 1997, different categories, within the "bicycle town" (distance zone 0 – 3000 m from the town centre point) for the largest, the smallest, one middle-sized and an average for the 45 largest Swedish towns.

	Proportion of employees, different categories			
	Total	Retail	Amusements	Health Care
Göteborg (478 791)	64,7%	72,1%	86,4%	46,2%
Gävle (66 110)	92,2%	92,1%	95,4%	92,8%
Katrineholm (19 757)	99,8%	100,0%	100,0%	100,0%
Average for 45 towns	79,8%	82,7%	91,4%	81,8%

Once again, Karlskrona differs due to its shape and the location of the town centre. When it comes to the proportion of employees in total (53,2%) and the Health Care sector (11,8%) the explanation being that the hospital is situated just outside the bicycle town (see figure 3).

The large towns are those with only a small proportion of employees in retail within the bicycle town (table 8). The main reason for this being that the retail structure of large towns includes sub-centres. The large town Västerås (54,1%) differs from the towns of the same size, for example Uppsala (84,1%). Both towns have the same retail structure with two shopping centres almost located at the same distance from the town centre, but in Västerås situated just outside the distance zone 0-3000 m and in Uppsala situated just inside the same distance zone. Therefore, the difference in proportion of employees in retail is more profound in the analysis than in reality.

The proportion of employees in the Amusements category is very high in all towns as it also was in the pedestrian town. The differences between small and large towns found in the pedestrian town are levelled out in the bicycle town.

When it comes to the proportion of employees in Health Care the same tendency to levelling out can be found. However some towns differ from those of the same size. Karlskrona has been mentioned before.

Discussion

The findings from this study show that the 45 Swedish towns studied have a similar structure. The central part has high population density, many employees, high retail activity and small proportion of green areas. With increasing distance from the town centre the population density, number of employees and the proportion of retail employees decrease and the proportion of green areas increases.

The situation today reveals how the Swedish towns have grown over time. The central part consists mainly of the compact centre dating from the beginning of the industrial era at the end of the 19th Century with some older buildings. During the 1960s and 1970s most central areas were exposed to city renewal with department stores, office blocks and buildings for local administration. Modern town planning from 1930 onwards characterizes the outskirts of the town. This means a hierarchical road system, traffic differentiation, neighborhood units and a lot of more or less green areas, which together give these areas low population density and long distances between the residents' homes and destinations such as workplaces, services etc.

On average for all the 45 towns studied, 80% of all employees, and 83% of all retail employees are to be found within 3 km from the centre point of the town. This means that a great deal of possible destinations for the citizens' trips are to be found within the bicycle town. Although the population density is low in Swedish towns, a great proportion of the inhabitants can still walk or cycle from their homes to most of the urban destinations of importance. 65%, 1 705 000, inhabitants lived within 3 km from the centre point of their town, which means that they can reach their town centre in 15 minutes by bicycle. A great deal of them, 18% or 474 000, can choose to walk in 15 minutes. This does not mean that one knows whether a specific individual living within the bicycle town really has his/her workplace within this distance, or uses the facilities there. But the probability for this is high.

As the proportion of short car trips is very high in urban areas, 70-80% are shorter than 4 km, there is a great potential for modal change[3]. Changing from car use to walking or cycling should be possible without any greater losses in the economy for individuals, companies or society as a whole. Of course there are both economic and welfare costs and benefits distributed amongst individuals and companies, but there seems to be a freedom of action for politicians at the local or central level when designing the future transport policy for urban sustainability. In most Swedish towns there is also a potential to provide more citizens with convenient walking and cycling distances to workplaces and facilities with means of compaction. The proportion of green areas is high, and those of low ecological and recreational quality could be used for new buildings.

In other research reports, I have shown that the distances between where people live and destinations like schools, post offices, food stores and libraries have been extended between 1980 and 1995 [4] [5] [6] [7]. Development appears to lead away from urban sustainability if nothing is done. Many tendencies in the present liberal political era are encouraging "freedom of choice" instead of "sustainability". To develop urban sustainability is not mainly a question of preserving rare plants and animals, but merely a question of changed life-stiles. Car use is of greatest importance. Not all political issues of importance for sustainability are correctly labelled. In recent years it has been decided that parents can choose schools for their children for other reasons than vicinity, a question of "freedom of choice". This will bring about more short car trips when parents drive their children to school, thus creating a worsened school environment when it comes to traffic safety and pollution. This political issue has been wrongly labelled.

Another question of importance in order to make a modal change from car use to walking and cycling is to create high quality footpaths and cycleways. Especially when it comes to cycling, traffic safety is so low that it can be questioned if benefits are larger than costs. High quality footpaths and cycleways should be:

- safe
- continuous
- secure
- direct
- convenient
- well maintained
- adapted to the needs of different user groups, and should
- create good accessibility within the urban area.

The first step in this direction should be to analyse the existing footpath and cycleway networks. In order do this I have developed a GIS method which focuses on the standard setting user groups (children, the elderly and the disabled) in Swedish traffic policy, and on women and their demands concerning safety, security and attractiveness [8]. But this is another question.

References

[1]   Reneland M., *Tätortsbefolkningens strukturella bilberoende*, rapport

2000:5, Tema Stad & Trafik, Chalmers tekniska högskola, Göteborg.

[2]   SCB, *Tätorter 1995*, Statistiska meddelanden Be-16-SM-9601, Statistiska centralbyrån, Stockholm, 1996.

[3]   Vägverket, *Mer cykeltrafik på säkrare vägar – Nationell strategi för ökad och säker cykeltrafik*, publikation 2000:8, Vägverket, Borlänge, 2000.

[4]   Reneland M., *Befolkningens avstånd till service*, STACTH 1998:5, Stads- och trafikplanering, Chalmers tekniska högskola, Göteborg, 1998.

[5]   Reneland M., *Elevers avstånd till närmaste skola*, STACTH 1998:6, Stads- och trafikplanering, Chalmers tekniska högskola, Göteborg, 1998.

[6]   Reneland M., *Pensionärers avstånd till service*, STACTH 1998:7, Stads- och trafikplanering, Chalmers tekniska högskola, Göteborg, 1998.

[7]   Reneland M., *Kollektivtrafikens effektivitet*, STACTH 1998:8, Stads- och trafikplanering, Chalmers tekniska högskola, Göteborg, 1998.

[8]   Reneland M., *GIS-metod för kartering och analys av gång- och cykel-vägnät - tillgänglighetsanalyser för barn, kvinnor och äldre under antagna villkor beträffande säkerhet och trygghet*, rapport 2000:7, Tema Stad & Trafik, Chalmers tekniska högskola, Göteborg, 2000.

Accessibility indices and planning theory

M.-C. Brodde Makrí
Department of Technology and Society, Lund University, Sweden

Abstract

Accessibility is an important factor in land-use planning and several methods have been developed to calculate and to predict it. Nevertheless, it is seldom applied in planning situations, maybe because many land-use planners and elected officials lack the knowledge and resources needed to use traffic models. Consequently, accessibility is often used as a concept and a goal in daily planning, but is seldom translated into operational forms. One way to bridge this gap is the introduction of accessibility indices for planning situations as an alternative. In this paper, a theoretical analysis is conducted in order to place accessibility in the theoretical context of urban and land-use planning. Main theories of urban and regional planning are analysed with focus on their explicit and implicit relations to accessibility. The aspects of planning theory that are dealt with are urban design, planning procedures, planning legislation and societal goals (i.e. equity and sustainability). The indices discussed here are mainly integral place accessibility measures, containing a range of available opportunities with respect to their attractiveness and travel impedance. The applicability of the chosen indices has been evaluated quantitatively and qualitatively. The goal, by means of introducing accessibility indicators addressed to planners, architects, and elected officials, is to contribute to bridging the gap between the general discussions about accessibility in the planning context and the use of quantitative measures in accessibility models.

1. Introduction

This paper contains a general discussion of the issues touched on by accessibility indices (AI) as well as a theoretical discussion on the role of accessibility in the planning process. The aim is to investigate is included explicitly or implicitly in the town planning ideals that has affected the design of our towns, whether it has a place in the most common planning paradigms, and to discuss the use of AI as a tool in the planning process.

The indices used and discussed in this project are mainly integral place accessibility measures (PAI), containing a range of available opportunities with respect to how they measure attractiveness and travel impedance. The reason for this is that the aim of the overall project and, not just this paper, is to develop and evaluate tools suitable for qualified and continuing discussions in planning. This kind of discussion is by necessity more one of areas than of individuals living there. Though the research is carried out on a geographically aggregated level, the accessibility discussion in this paper is valid for all types of AI.

2. Why accessibility

One of the ongoing discussions among politicians, planners and researchers is how to find ways of limiting the negative effects of traffic without diminishing its positive effects. Ways are being sought to increase accessibility (i.e. the ease of reaching activities) keeping mobility (produced vehicle kilometres) invariable. In the EU Commission's report of 1999, "European Sustainable Cities", this is given particular emphasis through the concept of "sustainable accessibility". In Sweden, the 1998 transport political decision based on the government bill 1997/98:56, "Transport Policy for Sustainable Development", stipulates accessibility as one of five traffic policy goals.

The mobility achieved in an extended transport network is no longer a goal in itself. Today we know that building new and/or expanding existing roads lead to increased amounts of traffic (e.g. Goodwin 1997, Naess 2000). Moreover, high road standards attract businesses and enterprises, which move from central locations accessible to all, to remote areas accessible only by car which in turn leads to increased amounts of car traffic. Today the aim is rather to achieve good accessibility to satisfy our needs of interaction. The basic assumption is that people travel for a purpose in order to reach certain activities, not just for the fun of it. Even though this it may seem contradictory to the fact that roads generate traffic, it is assumed to be consistent in broad outline and is the starting point for several researchers who deal with peoples travelling patterns (e.g. Bertil Vilhelmson and Lars-Göran Kranz). This perception is called the "activity axiom".

On the other hand, high accessibility levels do not necessarily imply a reorientation towards sustainability. By means of choices, individuals optimise their own utility and not the society's. For the individual, higher accessibility signifies an increased quality of life in the form of greater freedom to choose activities and the amount of time to devote to them. In such a society attention is paid to a social sustainability, since all the social groups, regardless of age, income and state of health, can avail themselves of certain facilities.

Another motive for raising accessibility goals during the planning process is that it provides an opportunity to build in an environmental sustainability potential gradually in the urban environment. The accessible society acquires an environmental sustainability potential in that it does not have an in-built structural compulsion for motorised transport. Bertil Vilhelmson illustrates this in his report Tidsanvändning och resor (1997). He carries out a hypothetical experiment in which we wake up one day and have no access to cars. For many of us this means that normal daily activities are inaccessible within the available time budget. This naturally leads to new travelling patterns and to new routines (for example change of workplace). In the long run this has an inevitable impact on the location of housing and activities.

3. Why accessibility indices

Accessibility as a term has long been used by politicians and planners in descriptions of concepts and planning goals. Nevertheless, it has seldom been an integral part of performance measures used to evaluate policies, and has seldom been applied in planning situations. The introduction of AI for planning situations as an alternative is one way to bridge this gap. Even though simplification of PAI is a possible drawback, this is outweighed by the fact that they are relatively plain, easy to understand and simple to apply. In the last few years we have witnessed an increased interest in translating the concept of accessibility into this type of operational form. The field of application for PAI is wide. For the uninitiated, indices presented as digital maps are the easiest to understand. This provides a communication platform for the planner, from which he can spread information as well as facilitate a dialogue between all the parties concerned. Naturally, the indices are also useful in their numeric format. Socio-economic evaluations are an example of their applicability. Accessibility is not usually regarded as measurable and therefore excluded from calculations and only included in verbal descriptions.

One prerequisite for PAI to be accorded legitimacy, is that they should concern issues that are relevant to urban development and the planning process. The latter is discussed in the present paper. Another prerequisite is the existence of independent connections between PAI and travel patterns. This has been analysed in a field study where the effect of accessibility on people's travelling was estimated. Data on the traffic network was combined with available data on population and potential destinations into a series of AI and added as layers on a digital map. A study focusing on the land-use impact on travelling patterns was then carried out in order to obtain a quantitative evaluation (Brodde Makri forthcoming 2002). Home- and work- based PAI with different modes were compared to actual travel behaviour (i.e. number of trips, distances, travel time and trip-linking) obtained from travel diary data in RES, Statistic Sweden. The study was carried out on a regional level with the county of Scania, in the south of Sweden, as a case study.

4. Definition of accessibility

Accessibility can be regarded as an indicator of the built-up environment's potential for sustainability, as well as a dimension of people's quality of life and is therefore a notion of importance. A general definition for it is "the ease with which various activities, including the needs of citizens, trade and industry and public services, can be reached" (Swedish National Road Administration,1998) and can be considered to summarise the characteristics of the built-up environment and of the traffic system.

The concept of accessibility may be regarded as including many different aspects (Davidsson, forthcoming) such as 1) *physical accessibility*.- being able to reach a point in spite of any physical hindrances, 2) *mental accessibility* - understanding and being able to use a given area and its facilities, 3) *social accessibility* - having friends and a job; being able to get to and from work, meet friends and participate in social activities, 4) *organisational accessibility* - having access to travel opportunities, information and service regarding a journey and 5) *financial accessibility* - being able to afford available public or private means of transport. A different aspect connected to the modern lifestyle, mentioned by Gudmundsson (2000) in "Driving Forces of Mobility" is 6) *virtual accessibility* –being able to access information and people without moving from a certain place, by using electronic facilities.

In consequence, accessibility can be ascribed either to people or places. Today, the tendency is towards a concentration on individual aspects of accessibility, both in qualitative analyses, e.g. Ståhl (fothcomming 2002) and in traffic models, e.g. Miller (1999). This approach of relating individuals travel patterns with their physical, socio-economic, and accessibility prerequisites is suitable for a deeper understanding of the underlying mechanisms of movement.

Notwithstanding, this paper departs from the general practice in that it deals with measures suitable for geographically aggregated levels and there are several reasons for that. The first is that the project aims to develop tools for qualified and continuing planning discussions, which by necessity deal with areas and not with individuals living in it. The second is that we have chosen to develop measures, which are relatively plain and easy to work and communicate with. We believe that, in spite of the simplifications, the measures will provide a general understanding of the accessibility situation in the studied areas and provide planners with a usable tool.

4.1 Definition of place accessibility measures

Place accessibility (PA) is derived from patterns of land-use and from the transportation system. Measures of PA normally consist of two elements: a transportation (or resistance or impedance) element and an activity (or motivation or attraction or utility) element (Handy and Niemeier, 1997; Kwan, 1998). The transportation element comprises the travel distance, time, or cost for one or more modes of transport, while the activity element comprises the amount and location of various activities.

Ingram (1971) was first to subdivide the concept into relative and integral accessibility. Relative place accessibility was defined as the degree of interconnection between two points on the same surface, and integral place accessibility as the degree of interconnection between one point and all other points on the same surface.

PA are operationalised in several ways depending on the issue at hand, the area of the application, and means and limitations concerning resources and feasible data (Handy and Niemeier, 1997, Ingram, 1971). They range from the very simple, e.g. distance measures, to the more complex, e.g. utility measures. Depending on the complexity, various degrees of accuracy are obtained.

Distance measures are the simplest accessibility measures, counting the distance from one location to different opportunities. They can be measured as average distances, weighted area distances or distances to the closest opportunity. The estimation of these distances can be performed in several ways, from simple straight-line distances to more complicated impedance formulations.

Cumulative-opportunity measures are evaluations of accessibility with regard to the number or proportion of opportunities accessible within a certain travel distance or time from a given location. These measures provide an idea of the range of choices available to residents within an area and are attributable to the work of several researchers. All potential destinations within the cut-off area are usually weighted equally, but even cumulative indices, which take the spatial distribution of opportunities into consideration, may be used.

Gravity-based measures derive from the denominator of the gravity model for trip distribution (Geertman and van Eck, 1995; Sonesson, 1998). They are obtained by weighting opportunities in an area with a measure indicating their attraction and discounting them by an impedance measure (for example Geertman and van Eck, 1995; Kwan, 1998; Handy and Niemeier, 1997).

The definition of relative accessibility A_{ij} at location i is the attraction at destination j discounted by the distance decay function between these two points. The integral accessibility A_i for the residents of zone i is measured as: where

$$A_i = \frac{\sum_j a_j * f(d_{ij})}{A}$$

a_j is the attraction in zone j
d_{ij} is the travel time, distance or cost from zone i to zone j
$f_{(d_{ij})}$ is the impedance function
A is a standardising factor

Utility-based measures are based on random utility theory, and consist of the denominator of the multinomial logit model, also known as logsum (Handy and Niemeier, 1997; Sonesson, 1998). Utility theory is based on the assumption that individuals maximise their utility. This means that the individual gives each destination a utility value, and that the likelihood of an individual choosing a particular destination depends on the utility of that choice compared to the utility of all the other choices. (Sonesson, 1998). The utility function contains variables representing the attributes of each choice, reflecting the attractiveness of the destination, travel impedance, and socio-economic characteristics of the individual or household. Accessibility A_n for individual n can, for example, be measured as (Handy and Niemeyer 1997):

$$A_n = \ln\left(\sum_{\forall \in C_n} \exp(V_{n(c)})\right)$$

where
$V_{n(c)}$ is the observable temporal and spatial transportation components of indirect
   utility of choice c for person n
C_n is the choice set for person n

4.2   Some general issues

As mentioned above, different situations and purposes demand different approaches to accessibility. Regardless of the chosen approach, according to Handy and Niemeier (1997), some interrelated issues such as a) the degree and type of disaggregation (spatial, socio-economic etc), b) the definition of origins and destinations, c) the measurement of travel impedance and d) the measurement of attractiveness, have to be resolved.

Consequently, the planner is confronted with imperative choices that make him reflect over the information he wishes to convey. In this way he obtains flexibility through the broad spectrum of measures, variables and issues he is able to choose from. He has the opportunity to balance accuracy, the size of the investigated area, the size of the zones, etc. against the requisite costs for acquiring data and make an optimal choice. Instead of working traditionally with a model that is a "black box" to him, the planner works with a transparent tool, which lets him decide what the measures reflect.

5.   Accessibility and Planning Theory

Planning theory consists of two partly conflicting areas called scientific or descriptive and normative (Naess och Saglie 2000). Scientific planning theory attempts to describe what reality looks like. It operates on meta level and deals with scientific theory about the planning process, methods for the planning process and the need for planning tools and communication instruments. Normative planning theory assumes that planners are able to evaluate reality and work normatively on planning issues. Questions concerning the connection between localisation and transport often fall within the normative sphere. Indeed, almost all the available theory about traffic planning is normative. This paper attempts to remedy this by incorporating accessibility in the descriptive elements of planning theory.

5.1   Accessibility in Descriptive Planning Theory

Planning theory has mainly been developed in an attempt to understand and explain the mechanisms behind planning. Irrespective of whether it concerns the physical environment or any other area, there are common features characteristic of the planning process, i.e. distribution of power between actors, interaction between decision-making levels, extent of long-term perceptions etc.

Prevailing political ideologies during the second half of the century gave rise to various planning traditions which have been analysed by several scientists. Some of these theories and doctrines are presented below.

Rationalism deserves to be dealt with separately, especially since rationalistic methodology dominated planning for long periods in the 1900s. In Sweden, there was a widespread belief in the welfare state and in social engineering. Society's planners had visions and the belief that rational planning could achieve the Good Society. This was questioned by the planners themselves in the 70s (Nylund 1995) and later on in the 80s and 90s by public opinion. Despite this, it has maintained a dominant position within planning because it is the starting point that other theories relate to.

Rationality implies that the decision-making planner always chooses the alternative that optimises his material interests and utility. (Nyström 1999). According to Andreas Faludi (1984), the rationale of planning theory is "that of planning promoting human growth by the use of rational procedures of thought and action". Human growth is enhanced by planning in two ways; it shows the best way of achieving particular goals and adds to existing knowledge, and thereby to future growth. When localisation is discussed in a national economic context it is assumed that individuals and companies make rational choices. In the case of physical planning it is presupposed that land use can be evaluated in terms of utility or financial gains that are quantifiable before the choice of localisation.

Planners held much of the power in the era of rationalism. The urban ideals of functionalism and "small house neighbourhoods", which differed considerably, were tried but neither gave satisfactory results. This was due to the fact that planners and politicians were far too powerful and quantitative in their working methods. They chose to optimise a few utilities such as accessibility to workplaces or local shops, but largely neglected the qualitative aspects. This resulted in unpleasant and unpopular neighbourhoods. The remnants of rationalism in the urban environment clearly illustrate the effects of one-sided methods. The implication here is that decision makers should be careful about relying only on experts intent on optimising one particular aspect to the detriment of others. An holistic approach to the planning process including as many of the aspects and actors as possible is to be preferred.

John Friedmann (1987) divides rationality into market and social rationality. The former was described above, while social rationality is based on the assumption that people belong to a social group whose interests are more important than the individual's. Planning is mainly motivated by social rationality. Planning in a capitalistic society falls somewhere between these two forms (ibid).

Rationalism gave way to several other new theories dealing with different planning aspects. This can be likened to a paradigm shift as described by Kuhn (1962) in "The Structure of Scientific Revolutions ". Rationalism and the other theories were grouped together by Friedman (1987) as follows:

Social reform – the most dominant form within planning theory, has a social reforming perspective with both economic growth and welfare as the goals. The starting point for this type of planning is often social injustice. It is a centralised decision-making process (ibid). Since rationalism was the dominating doctrine, planners enjoyed high status. Thus accessibility to a limited number of activities was decisive for localisation of housing and activities.

Policy analysis – is a purely rational model. Planning is efficiency-oriented and only carried out by highly specialised practitioners. Analyses are based on economics, mathematics and statistical calculations with the use of advanced computer technology (ibid). Measures of accessibility can only be carried out by certain experts who are familiar with modelling techniques. Others involved in the planning process must therefore take this into account and follow their recommendations. At best, the models are used by others as "black boxes", i.e. the user has no control over the process but relies blindly on the measurement results.

Social learning – is dialectic. Planners, politicians and public opinion have an open dialogue and learn from one another's experiences. Social experiments and pilot projects can e.g. provide knowledge and a basis for future planning (ibid). Here, accessibility may well be expressed as a simple index easily understood by all the involved parties. AI become an instrument with which to spread information and knowledge, a tool for fruitful dialogue.

Social mobilisation – has its staring point in the belief that people should act collectively, and can be inspired by revolutionary ideas like anarchism and Marxism. Planning here is seen as system-changing rather than system-retaining. This is more an ideology than a method. The planner has no real power other than through the people for whom he is planning. An measure is produced by him at the request of the collective and constitutes a basis for their collective decision-making.

Planning is a continuous process involving a lot of decisions which may in turn lead to deadlocks, gradually decreasing the room for negotiation. If, for example, a decision is made at an early stage, there is a risk that the planning process will have to be started again. To avoid such deadlocks, a decision can be made subsequently as required. This planning procedure is called "incrementalism" (Nyström, 1999). Since AI are easy to produce, they can be useful tools in incremental planning.

At the end of the 80s the public sector's resources began diminishing at the same time as private actors became more dominant in land-use planning. This led to a new phenomenon of municipality representatives making agreements with private developers. Although this was undemocratic, it was done to keep the developers interested and to guarantee that the plan would not be changed. This is referred to as "negotiation planning" (ibid). This form of planning is often carried out above the head of the planner. There is a distinct lack of an holistic approach and participation by citizens. Accessibility is certainly very important to investors, but is often directed at mobile social groups with considerable purchasing power. This situation presents an opportunity to use AI to, for example, describe the effects of localisation and discuss aspects of equity.

From the 60s onwards it is possible to distinguish three epochs in Swedish traffic planning (Davidsson, forthcoming). The first was the "Criterion epoch" where norms or national values were used for securing the quality and standard that were sought in physical planning (e.g. Swedish Parking Regulations, SCAFT 1968). The second was the "Adjusting epoch" where plans were evaluated according to scales, for example, walking distances from a bus stop, vehicle speeds and safety at crossings, in order to accord it a level of quality (e.g. TRÅD 1982). Now, we are heading into the "Direction epoch" where planners and politicians at regional and local levels are given overriding goals that have to be put into operation. This is a difficult task but it also gives a certain freedom of choice of interpretation. Easily understood indicators, used to check whether a change is in the direction of the goal, are suitable tools for direction planning. Even if the various measures counteract one another, this does not necessarily impede their use and development. On a national level the counterparts for these indicators are "the green key figures" developed by the Delegation on the Environment for the Swedish government.

6. General Conclusions

The discussion conducted in this paper covers only a small section of the many dimensions of planning theory. Different types of planning, decision-making levels, methodology, tools of implementation, organisational issues etc. have not been taken up here. The overall conclusion is that accessibility can be expressed and used in many ways. Since different situations and purposes demand different approaches, there is no best approach to measuring accessibility. An awareness of the assumptions upon which each method is based is a prerequisite when choosing a method to determine accessibility.

The accessibility indices that is most suitable ought to be decided by the issue at hand , the practical constraints in any given situation and the planning tradition in his professional context. Since different planning situations demand different information, it is appropriate to make new choices every time new planning issues are dealt with.

What is vital is that the practitioner is aware of the whole spectrum of opportunities so that he can choose the most fitting measure. More importantly, the way in which the AI are applied will have consequences for the end product, the built-up environment. In the aim to achieve an "accessible" and "good" society, transparency, information dissemination, co-determination and communication are principles that should be given priority at all levels of physical planning.

References

(1) Breheny, M., Sustainable development and urban form, London, 1992.
(2) Brodde Makri, M-C., Accessibility indices as instruments of physical planning - an evaluation, Department of Technology and society, Lund University, forthcoming 2002.

(3)   Davidsson, T., Stadsmiljö och trafik, National Board of Housing, Building and Planning, Karlskrona, forthcoming 2002.

(4)   Faludi, A., Planning Theory, 4th edition, London, 1984.

(5)   Friedman, J., Planning in the public domain: From knowledge to action, Princeton, New Jersey, 1987.

(6)   Geertman, & Ritsema van Eck, GIS and models of accessibility potential: an application in planning, Int. J. Geographical Information Systems, vol. 9, no. 1, pp. 67-80, 1995.

(7)   Goodwin, P., Solving Congestion - inaugural lecture for the professorship of Transport Policy, University College, London, 1997.

(8)   Handy, S., & Niemeier, Measuring accessibility: an exploration of issues and alternatives, Environment and Planning A vol. 29, pp. 1175-1194, 1997.

(9)   Hägerstrand, T., Carlestam, G., Sollbe, B., What about People in Regional Science?, Ninth European Congress of the Regional Sience Association, Regional Science Association Papers, In "Om tidens vidd och tingens ordning". BFR, Stockholm, 1991.

(10)   Ingram, The Concept of Accessibility: A Search for an Operational Form, Regional Studies, vol.5, pp. 101-107, 1971.

(11)   Krantz, L-G., Rörlighetens mångfald och förändring: befolkningens dagliga resande i Sverige 1978 och 1996, Dissertation, School of Economics and Commercial Law, Göteborg University, 1999.

(12)   Khakee, A.,. Samhällsplanering, Lund University, 2000.

(13)   Kwan, M-P., Space-Time and Integral Measures of Individual Accessibility: A Comparative Analysis Using a Point-based Framework, Geographical Analysis, vol. 30, no.3, pp. 191-216, 1998.

(14)   Makrí, M-C., Folkesson, C., Accessibility Measures for Analyses of Land-Use and Travelling with Geographical Information Systems, Department of Technology and society, Lund University, 1999.

(15)   Miller, H., Measuring space-time accessibility benefits within transportation networks, Basic theory and computational procedures. Geographical Analysis, 31, 187-212, 1999.

(16)   Naess, P., Saglie, I-L., Surviving between the trenches: Planning research, methodology and theory of science, European Planning Studies, Vol. 8, No. 6, 2000, pp. 729-750, 2000.

(17)   Nylund, K., Det förändrade planeringstänkandet, NORDPLAN, Dissertation no 19, Stockholm, 1995.

(18)   Nyström, J., Planeringens grunder, Lund University, 1999.

(19)   Sonesson, Estimering av efterfrågan på långväga persontransporter: En ekonomisk-teoretisk belysning av gängse modeller samt en ny ansats till uppskattning av efterfrågesamband, Dissertation No. 36, Linköping University, 1998.

(20)   Song, Some tests of alternative accessibility measures: A population density approach, Land Economics, 72(4), pp. 474-482, 1996.

(21)   Vilhelmsson, B., Tidsanvändning och resor - att analysera befolkningens rörlighet med hjälp av en tidsanvändningsundersökning, School of Economics and Commercial Law, Göteborg University, KFB-report 1997:12, 1997.

Analysis of non-home-based trips in the Dallas-Fort Worth metropolitan area

J.J. Lour[1] & A. Anjomani[2]
[1]Denver Regional Council of Governments, USA
[2]School of Urban and Public Affairs
University of Texas at Arlington, USA

Abstract

In the Dallas-Fort Worth metropolitan area, these two cities have long been recognized as having very different public policies in addition to numerous other differences. The research presented here evaluates the possible benefits of evaluating these two areas separately in the travel mode choice analysis. Described are preliminary non-home-base individual mode choice models in the form of multinomial logit function for the Dallas segment and the Fort Worth part of the region area to assist in further exploration of the different travel mode choice characteristics of the two areas. In general, comparison results indicate that separate mode choice models for the Dallas area and the Fort Worth area will provide better accuracy to serve each area's transportation planning and forecasting purposes.

1 Introduction

In the United States increased attention is being directed to improving public transportation system. Over this new century, mass transit likely will once again become a potent force for shaping cities as well as serving them. The Dallas area has actively pursued this goal to serve its future.

The Dallas and Fort Worth share a metropolitan area that has experienced tremendous growth in the last three decades. In preparing to tackle the current and future gridlock of the transportation system the transit mode and car pool mode are more encouraged in the Dallas area while the drive-alone mode is more encouraged in the Fort Worth area. In brief, Dallas has gone one step further than Fort Worth. A rail transit system is under construction for the

Dallas area that will give the east part of the Dallas-Fort worth metropolitan region a whole new look.

Similar to the Dallas-Fort worth region, metropolitan areas all around the world have evolved into multi-center configurations with some segments having different characteristics. Yet the Urban Transportation Planning Process (UTPP), and the modal choice analysis step in this process treats a metropolitan area as a homogeneous entity suitable for application of different steps and techniques of the planning process. This paper discusses the need for calibration of more than one set of models in a metropolitan area for its different major segments, particularly with regard to mode choice analysis of non-home-base trips.   The Dallas-Fort Worth metropolitan area is used to test the appropriateness of this approach.

1.1 Research objective

This paper attempts to study the non-home-base trip mode choice behaviors within a metropolitan area. Using the Dallas-Fort Worth area as an example of a multicenter metropolitan area this study presents the need to have travel mode choice models treated separately for the areas inside a metropolitan region.

Dallas and Fort Worth have long been recognized as two very different cities in spite of their close physical proximity. It is necessary to test the hypothesis that separate calibrations are needed of the individual choice models for this metropolitan area in order to have a better understanding of behavior of travelers in these areas.

1.2 The study areas

For the purpose of this study two sub-areas within the metropolitan area were selected.   The area within the Dallas county limits plus the City of Plano is defined as the Dallas area, and the area within Tarrant County limits is defined as the Fort Worth area.   There are two purposes for defining the study areas in this say: The attempt was to separate the geographical and demographical balance of the two major centers. Similarly, in this way the major highway system, the primary transit services, and the policy-making bodies can be separated symmetrically.

2 Research approach

The most important and common starting point for individual choice models is the notion of utility maximization (DOT [1]; Horowitz [2]). It is assumed that the decision maker is able to assign at least an ordinal ranking to the alternatives available in terms of their relative desirability (i.e., the alternative's utility). Being a rational person, the decision maker will then choose the alternative with the maximum utility (i.e., the one that maximizes the benefits).

The utility maximization principle provides a valuable framework for the analysis of travel choice behavior.   However, deterministic utility principle sometimes is inadequate due to the inability to functionalize the exact utility of an individual and to measure accurately all of the variables relevant to travel choice (Horowitz [2]). A vast amount of research has been devoted to develop better tools to analyze this type of choice making behavior (Aldrich and Nelson [3], Ben-Akiva and Lerman [4], Brand [5], Cervero [6], Hensher and Johnson [7], Meyer and Miller [8], Kanafani [9], and Train [10]). Among them, individual choice analysis in the form of multinomial logit function, or logit model – a transformation from deterministic principle into probabilistic behavior – is taken to develop the mode choice models in this study.

Logit models are particularly and, in some respects, uniquely suitable for analyzing and forecasting mode split. This potential was noted relatively early in their development (Brand [5]).

With a good data set, individual mode choice analysis gives the transportation planner the opportunity to evaluate the impacts of polices over which he or she has some control. This is because most transportation policies are directed at changing the level-of-service characteristics of alternative travel modes. A typical practice can be an analysis of the car pool trips and the transit ridership change caused by using high occupancy vehicle (HOV) lanes or transit fare reduction in the service area. Such changes would tend to have the most direct impact on mode choice and, because of the sequential, non-feedback structure of the traditional travel demand forecasting process, would show little or no impact on trip generation or distribution.

The linear utility expressions found in individual mode choice models consist mainly of variables that describe the level of service provided by each alternative mode. By modifying the values of these variables, a planner can represent a variety of transportation policies. The impact of these changes can then be evaluated by examining the resultant changes in mode choice probabilities.

Another property of individual choice model is that almost any number of alternative choices may be included in the model provided that a capable multinomial logit regression package and a good data set are available.

In summary, because the logit models have these properties – including their sensitivity to changes in the deterministic components of utility, their dependence on utility differences, and a well established theoretical and empirical background – they are appropriate to be applied to the model choice analysis of the Dallas-Fort worth metropolitan area in this study.

2.1 The choice set and variables

Before the development of the mode choice models used in this project, it is necessary to define the universal choice set C (a group of defined alternative modes that individuals may take) for the problem under study. This step requires some decisions about which alternatives can be ignored. In principle, a traveler's choice set consists of every mode the traveler may choose. There are no rigorous analytic methods, however, for assigning a choice set to travelers. Thus, in the practical sense, the choice set can be defined to contain every mode for which probability of being chosen is large enough to be practically significant. In this project, for the Dallas-Fort worth metropolitan area, the universal choice set was defined to have three major travel modes of transit mode, carpool mode and drive-alone mode.

After the choice set has been defined, the particular variables entering into the utility functions for each alternative are identified. Like the identification of the choice set, however, there is no standard list of variables that always should be used in mode choice models or a standard procedure for selecting them. Six variables were selected for the models for their availability, suitability, a prior theoretical justification, and evidences shown in other empirical case studies. Some of these were deleted from the specific model because their regression parameters were shown to be insignificant to some models.

The selected variables to test these models were two basic types. The socioeconomic attributes included household annual income (INCM), traveler's occupation (OCCP), household auto ownership (AINH), and household size (PINH). The service attributes included travel time (TT) and out-of-pocket travel cost (OPCO). These variables then was used in mode choice models calibration for the Dallas area (model A), the Fort Worth area (model B), and the Dallas-Fort worth metropolitan area (model C).

Another important aspect of selecting variables for the mode choice model is deciding how these variables will be entered into the utility function. In this project, various functional forms of variables have been tested to develop the operational models that are used. For example, the variable "travel time (TT)," other than its linear form, was tested in the form of in (TT and $TT^{2)}$. After a careful comparison of the test results, all variables were entered in their linear form, a method also used in many other empirical studies.

2.2 Model calibration

The final operational models in multinomial logit function were defined and designed to provide the information with an operational capability. Selection criteria for the variables to remain in the models included consistency of the variables with behavioral theory and statistical significance of the calibrated coefficients (parameters). As was discussed earlier, the three major alternative travel modes was defined as:

1. Transit mode
2. Carpool mode
3. Drive-alone mode

The models were checked for specification errors that multinomial logit models in particular are prone to (Aldrich and Nelson [3], Ben-Akiva and Lerman [4], Kmenta [11], McFadden [12], Pindyck and Rubinfeld [13]). The final operational models and the statistical test results are presented in Table 1 and interpreted in the following discussion.

Table 1: coefficients and test statistics for Non-Home-Based models

	Model A	Model B	Model C
Intercept $_1$	-1.827 (0.968) [3.56]	-4.042 (1.963) [4.24]	-2.347 (0.862) [7.41]
Intercept$_2$	-0.053 (0.234) [NS]	-0.636 (0.300) [4.52]	-0.290 (0.183) [2.52]
AINH$_1$	-3.631 (0.733) [24.53]	-2.448 (1.233) [3.94]	-3.441 (0.600) [32.86]
AINH$_2$	-0.573 (0.105) [30.01]	-0.269 (0.117) [5.23]	-0.A426 (0.077) [30.32]
PINH$_1$	0.360 (0.309) [NS]	0.476 (0.734) [NS]	0.439 (0.274) [2.58]
PINH$_2$	0.151 (0.059) [6.59]	0.170 (0.065) [5.78]	0.152 (0.044) [12.24]
TT$_1$	0.048 (0.015) [9.92]	0.057 (0.015) [13.63]	0.050 (0.010) [22.72]
TT$_2$	-0.010 (0.006) [2.78]	0.0002 (0.006) [NS]	-0.006 (0.004) [NS]
POCO$_1$	0.782 (0.350) [4.99]		0.865 (0.339) [6.49]
POCO$_2$	-0.311 (0.375) [NS]		-0.569 (0.404) [NS]
SAMPLE SIZE	1045	809	1854
$L(0)$	-1148.1	-888.8	-2031.3
$L(\beta)$	-612.1	-513.5	-1330.4
L.R.	1072	750.6	1801.9
L.R. Index	0.47	0.42	0.44

Notes to Table 1

1. Model A, B, and C represent models calibrated for the Dallas area, the Fort Worth area, and a combined sample of the two study areas (the D-FW area), respectively.
2. Numbers in ( ) were standard errors for the estimated coefficient.
3. Numbers in [ ] were chi-square statistics for the estimated coefficient.
4. At the joint model estimation test (SAS [14]), when a variable showed a less than 0.05 level of significance (LOS), it was deleted from the model.
5. [NS] denotes that the estimated coefficient was not significantly different from zero at a 0.15 LOS.
6. $L(0)$: the value of the log likelihood function when all the coefficients are zero. It is the log likelihood of the most naïve possible condition; that is, the choice probabilities are 1/3 for each of the three alternatives.
7. $L(\beta)$: The value of the log likelihood function at its maximum.
8. *L.R.*: Likelihood Ratio, $-2 (L(0) - L(\beta))$, which is a statistic used to test the null hypothesis that all coefficients were zero.
9. *L.R. Index*: Likelihood Ratio Index, $\rho 2 = 1 - (L(\beta) / L(0))$, an informal goodness-of-fit index that measures the fraction of an initial log likelihood value explained by the model.

Each model has two utility functions, U_1 and U_2 to represent the relative choice utilities of transit vs. drive-alone and car-pool vs. drive-alone, respectively. In Table 1, variables are identified with subscript "1" and "2" to distinguish these two utilities. Other properties and significant characteristics of the models are presented here.

Four independent variables are included to explain the mode choice distribution in our non-home-based (NHB) models (see Table 1). In Model B, however, out-of-pocket cost (OPCO) is deleted since it was statistically insignificant in the model. Parameters for household auto ownership (AINH) are all negative indicating a shift from taking transit or using a car pool to driving depending on the number of cars owned by the traveler in all three samples. The magnitude of coefficients is higher for the Dallas case, especially for car pool, indicating less likelihood of using transit and carpool when number of cars owned is greater.

Household income and occupation type of traveler were found insignificant in all cases in models calibrated for this study although they were proved and used as significantly important socio-economic factors in a number of studies for other areas. The reason might be that in Sunbelt metropolitan areas owning a car is, practically speaking, a basic requirement for every adult regardless of one's income or occupation.

Parameters of household size (PINH) give an indication that travelers are more likely to take transit or car pool than drive alone if the household size is relatively large. Comparing the three models, the magnitude of coefficients are almost the same for the car pool case, indicating no difference in terms of this variable in the models. However, the household size for the Dallas and Fort Worth areas for the transit is not significant, indicating the difference of the two models in terms of this variable with model C.

When travel time (TT) becomes longer, travelers may choose more often to use transit or car-pool instead of drive-alone. The magnitude of the coefficients for the transit case are almost the same indicating no difference in terms of this variable in the models. The parameters of TT are not significantly different from zero for the choice between car pool mode and drive-alone mode (i.e., in U_2 utility function) in model B and C at 0.05 LOS, while it was barely significant in Model A at 0.05 LOS with negative sign. This simply indicates that, for a non-home-based trip, the travelers do not consider travel time in their choice between car pool or drive-alone.

On the other hand, when the relative out-of-pocket cost (OPCO) becomes higher, travelers may shift from driving to taking the bus. The insignificance of this variable for the Fort Worth area (model B) means that, in this area, out-of-pocket cost is not a determinant in the decision of modal choice. This is an interesting finding and may need some explanation. One reason might be that the Fort Worth area is relatively less congested. Another reason might be a sociological factor related to attachment to the car regardless of the economics of the situation.

2.3 Model validation

To verify the accuracy of the calibration, observation-prediction comparisons are calculated for each model. This is done by rewriting the calibrated logit models in a FORTRAN program that calculates the choice probabilities for all the observations in the data set. The prediction distribution over the modes are calculated for each model in two different ways: 1) in the test at the aggregate level, the individual probabilities of each mode are summed to give the expected value estimate of the mode share distribution; 2) in the test at the disaggregate level, the mode choice of each individual is predicted by the highest probability method and the percentage of individuals predicted to choose each mode is then calculated. The predicted modal distributions of the Dallas model and the Fort Worth model are compared with the actual modal distribution and the modal distribution predicted by the D-FW model in Tables 2 and 3. Overall, the first test shows a high level of accuracy. For detailed discussions on this topic, see Aldrich and Nelson [3], Koppelman and Chu [15], Parody [16].

Table 2: Results from the model validation test: models for the Dallas area

Observations and Predictions	Transit (%)	Carpool (%)	Drive alone (%)
Observation	0.8	26.7	72.5
Aggregate	0.8 [0.8]	26.7 [29.4]	72.5 [69.8]
Disaggregate	0.5 [0.4]	1.2 [1.0]	98.3 [98.6]

Note: Numbers in [ ] were predicted by the D-FW model.

Table 3: Results from the model validation test: models for the Fort Worth area

Observations and Predictions	Transit (%)	Carpool (%)	Drive alone (%)
Observation	0.4	32.4	67.2
Aggregate	0.4 [0.4]	32.4 [28.9]	67.2 [70.6]
Disaggregate	0.2 [0.2]	0.0 [0.2]	99.8 [99.6]

Note: Numbers in [ ] were predicted by the D-FW model.

3 Findings

As was discussed, the coefficients are stable and consistent across the three models, and the averaging effect is found. POCO was proved significant in the Dallas model, but it has no effect in the Fort Worth model. For their goodness-of-fit, the Dallas model (0.47) has a higher L.R. index with a much smaller sample size when compared with the D-FW.

Comparing the magnitude and signs of variable coefficients, the variable coefficients from the D-FW model is an average from the other two. Regarding test statistics, although the standard errors for all variable coefficients are improved if the D-FW sample is used, with a data set almost twice as large as other models, D-FW models have likelihood ratio indexes (L.R. Index) that show there is not only no improvement on the goodness-of-fit, but a reduction occurs when it is compared to the L.R. indexes from the Dallas model or the Fort Worth model. These findings indicate that the D-FW metropolitan area is not homogeneous; therefore, it is more appropriate to have two separate models for the Dallas area and Fort Worth area.

Overall, like the attempt to predict the current travel mode choice distributions at the disaggregate level in the model validation tests, the attempt to present strongly significant differences between the two study areas was somewhat disappointing because the differences were not as strong as expected. Nevertheless, evidence was found from the background studies shown in the introduction and from the model comparison that positively supports the findings that the two study areas are distinct from each other in terms of the existing travel mode choice behavior.

4 Conclusion

One purpose of the study was to test the methodology of individual mode choice analysis to determine the feasibility for treating the modeling process separately for the Dallas area and Fort Worth area. Overall, the results suggest that mode choice analysis of the type used in this project should be treated separately for the Dallas area and the Fort Worth area. We can conclude that the region (the Dallas-Fort Worth metropolitan area) is not homogeneous in terms of public policies, population distributions, and employment distributions. Therefore, it is improper to treat the area in one model. Implementation of the DART plan is creating a whole new look in terms of its travel patterns in the eastern part of the metropolitan area. A much higher sensitivity of the modeling task for the mode choice will be needed for the area. As such, separate consideration for the two study areas in terms of the modeling seems even more reasonable.

References

[1] Department of Transportation (DOT, *A study of Individual Choice Models-Applications of New Travel Demand Forecasting Techniques to Transportation Planning*, 1977.
[2] Horowitz, J., Random utility travel demand models, transportation and mobility in an era of transition, New York, NY: Elsevier Science Publishers B.V., Chapter 8, 1985.
[3] Aldrich, J.H. & Nelson, F.D., *Linear Probability, Logit, and Probit Models*, Beverly Hills, CA: SAGE Publication, 1983.
[4] Ben-Akiva, M. & Lerman, S.R., *Discrete Choice Analysis*, Cambridge, MA: MIT Press, 1985.
[5] Brand, D., Approaches to travel behavior research. *Transportation Research Record No. 569*, 1976, pp. 12-33.
[6] Cervero, R., Suburban employment centers: probing the influence of site features on the journey to work, *Journal of Planning Education and Research*, Vol. 8, No. 2, pp. 75-85, Winter 1989.
[7] Hensher, D.A. & Johnson, L.W., *Applied Discrete-Choice Modeling*, New York, NY: Halsted Press, pp. 163-192, 1981.
[8] Meyer, M.D. & Miller, E.J., *Urban Transportation Planning*, 2nd edition; New York, NY: McGraw-Hill, Chapter 5, 2001.
[9] Kanafani, A.K., *Transportation Demand Analysis*, New York, NY: McGraw-Hill, Chapter 4, 5, 1983.
[10] Train, K., *Qualitative Choice Analysis*, Cambridge, MA: MIT Press, Chapter 2, 1986.
[11] Kmenta, J., *Elements of Econometrics*, New York, NY: Macmillan Publishing, Chapter 11, 1986.
[12] McFadden, D., Train, K. & Tye, W.B., An application of diagnostic test for the independence from irrelevant alternatives property of the multinomial logit model. *Transportation Research Record, No. 637*, pp. 39-46, 1976.

[13] Pindyck, R.S. & Rubinfeld, D.L., *Econometric Models and Economic Forecasts*, 4th edition; New York, NY: McGraw-Hill, pp. 298-329, 1998.

[14] SAS Institute, Statistical analysis system user's guide, Vol. 5, 1985.

[15] Koppelman, F.S. & Chu, C., Effect of sample size on disaggregate choice model estimation and prediction. *Transportation Research Record, No. 944*, pp. 60-69, 1983.

[16] Parody, T.E., Technique for determining travel choice for a model of nonwork travel. *Transportation Research Record. No. 673*, pp. 47-53, 1978.

Contrasting structures of metropolitan mobility in Spain

J. Roca Cladera, M.C. Burns, M. Moix Bergadà and J. M. Silvestro
Centro de Política de Suelo y Valoración (CPSV)
Universidad Politécnica de Cataluña, Spain

Abstract

This paper draws upon results emanating from an INTERREG IIC European Union project, examining the territorial and functional characteristics of the Spanish metropolitan urban regions, in the context of the nature of the overall urban system of South-western Europe. Part of the study included research concerning the *structure of mobility and its territorial paradigm* in the Spanish metropolitan urban regions. The metropolitan urban regions under investigation were Barcelona, Madrid, Málaga, Seville, Valencia y Bilbao. Data of mobility for employment related purposes alone, between municipalities, was used, owing to the absence of homogenous mobility data sources for other purposes. The results indicate two clearly contrasting patterns of spatial organisation within the metropolitan urban regions. In the cases of Madrid, Valencia, Seville and Málaga, one can observe clearly *monocentric models* of development and mobility. Here the vast majority of the flows between place of residence and place of work gravitate to the centre of the metropolitan urban region and which are characterised by extensive radial distances. However in the metropolitan urban regions of Barcelona and to a lesser extent Bilbao, demonstrate more *decentralised models* of mobility, with the presence of sub-centres and a greater internal complexity, with shorter distances travelled and. as a consequence, areas which are potentially more sustainable.

1 Introduction

From a theoretical standpoint, a model of metropolitan decentralisation, seen as one organised through a grouping of primary areas, which contain a network of smaller sub-centres, or urban sub-systems, offers the possibility of achieving considerable savings of time and energy in questions of metropolitan mobility. What this research indicates is that of the Spanish metropolitan urban regions forming part of this study, in practice the case of Barcelona is the one with the closest fit to this model of metropolitan decentralisation.

2 Methodology and theoretical background

The main objective of this analysis is in the context of a study of the territorial and functional characterisation of the Spanish metropolitan areas, and its integration within the south-west European urban system. Seven Spanish metropolitan areas (Barcelona, Madrid, Malaga, Seville, Valencia, Bilbao and Zaragoza) are considered, in order to seek to explain the nature of the urban mobility of each case.

Three kinds of clearly differentiated territorial spaces can be identified: economic agglomerations, morphologic agglomerations and finally spaces responding to the delimitation of functional urban regions. See for example the works of Hall and Hay[2] and Cheshire et al.[1].

However in light of the absence of an agreed methodology for the delimitation of metropolitan regions, this study has adapted the methodology used by the United States Census Bureau for the identification of the Spanish metropolitan areas, based upon travel to work journeys. The results differ considerably from other methodologies based upon morphological (NUREC [3]) and functional (GEMACA [4]) criteria.

The analysis of flows of journeys between place of residence and place of work enables the achievement of a clear understanding of the nature of the mobility patterns in the respective metropolitan regions.

3 Metropolitan delimitation

The methodology used to delimit these metropolitan areas involved an adaptation of the method used by the United States Bureau of Census (Office of Management and Budget [5]), based upon flows between place of residence and place of work at the municipality level of analysis. The delimiting process began by determining those municipalities from which at least 15% of the resident population's journeys to work were to the central city. This group of municipalities was treated as one area, to which outlying municipalities were added in a similar way as a second iteration, where the same 15% journey to work flow applied, repeating the process up to a fourth iteration.

The delimitation system adopted is that used in the states of New England because of its similarity with the Spanish (and Continental European) morphological structure and administrative institutions. In the study the agglomerations considered are Barcelona, Madrid, Malaga, Seville, Valencia, and Bilbao. Zaragoza was not considered owing to the non-availability of statistical information concerning mobility beyond the central municipality.

Following the North American system of metropolitan delimitation, some differentiated ambits have been identified: the Primary Metropolitan Areas (PMA) and the Consolidated Metropolitan Areas (CMA) linked between them to generate the CMA in the case of Barcelona.

The procedure to delimit the PMA consists in finding the CMA with the criteria described above and then in finding the PMA that exist therein, where these ambits have a minimum population of 75,000 inhabitants.

In the delimitation of the North American metropolitan areas there are two main elements that must be considered. The existence of an urban continuity clearly defined by the urbanised areas, and the functional and physical dependencies among the cities and towns originated by the daily commuting for job proposes determined historically.

4 The Spanish metropolitan areas

The approach to delimit the Spanish metropolitan areas MAs (see Table 1), is similar to that used in New England, based principally upon 1990 Census data and the following criteria:

1) Centre identification: a municipality with at least 50,000 inhabitants. Where there are employees that live in other municipalities, but commute to this centre for work purposes (in a proportion greater than 15% of the active population of those bordering municipalities).
2) Ring delimitation (three rings as maximum): Delimited by municipalities that send the proportion of commuters described above to the precedent central municipality of ring.
3) The group of the municipalities that constitutes the metropolitan area, has to have as least 75,000 inhabitants. (In the study the MAs with more than 500.000 inhabitants.)

4.1 Primary and Consolidated Metropolitan Areas

The methodology used differentiates the ordinary metropolitan areas (formed around a main central nucleus) from the consolidated metropolitan areas (formed by the linkage among the primary metropolitan areas). The difference between the former and the latter is that the latter incorporates a group of Primary Metropolitan Areas.

Table 1: Principal characteristics of the Spanish metropolitan areas

Metropolitan Area	Number of municipalities	Population (1998)	Area (km²)	Workplaces
Barcelona	217	4,348,272	4,592	1,560,393
Madrid	163	5,010,747	7,392	1,598,427
Málaga	26	715,252	1,654	167,385
Seville	56	1,346,413	6,672	322,852
Valencia	86	1,467,941	2,831	451,623
Bilbao	77	1,034,521	1,780	326,501
Zaragoza	25	625,593	2,548	

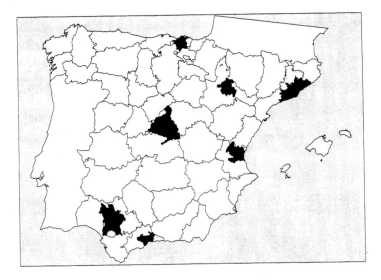

Figure 1: The Spanish metropolitan areas

A PMA is considered as an urban system that has an ordinary metropolitan area, but has an important link (>15%) with the remainder of the Consolidated Metropolitan Area (CMA). The condition to consider a PMA implies that its centre must be independent from the Consolidated Metropolitan Centre (>15%), and has to have a self-contention (>50%). An urban system is considered "consolidated" when there is an important complexity and de-centralisation, meaning reduced mobility dependent upon the main central municipality.

Of the 7 Spanish Metropolitan Areas, only Barcelona (see Figure 2) can be considered as a Consolidated Metropolitan Area (AMC) formed by six PMA (Sabadell, Terrassa, Granollers, Mataró, Vilanova, as well as Barcelona itself). The analysis shows Barcelona as the most de-centralised area.

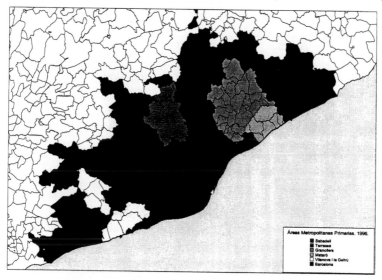

Figure 2: Consolidated Metropolitan Area of Barcelona

4.2 Outcommuting from the metropolitan municipalities

The dynamic of the inter municipal commuting shows a significant image of the labour market's outcommuting, in other words the employees that are *obliged* to commute to another municipality for job purposes.

The main results of the analysis of the labour market are described below (see Table 2):

a) Among all the metropolitan areas, Madrid shows the greatest degree of outcommuting (65%), followed by Barcelona (61%), Bilbao (58%), Seville (56%), Valencia and Malaga (50%).

b) Considering the number of employees that work in a municipality different to that of their residence, it is found that Barcelona (44%) and Bilbao (43%) have the highest values, followed by Madrid (39%), Valencia (32%), Seville (21%) and Malaga (9%).

c) With regard to the outcommuting from the metropolitan cores, Bilbao shows a figure of 25% and Barcelona 21% (the highest), followed by Valencia 18% and Madrid 15% (in the medium range), and Seville and Malaga 12% (with lowest outcommuting).

The maps of the Metropolitan Area (see Figure 3) shows, except for Barcelona, a clear concentration of the most open municipalities around the centres, as well as, a tendency of open reduction as the municipalities apart from the centres.

Table 2:

Metropolitan Area (MA)	Average outcommuting for the MA	Total outflow	Total outcommuting for the MA	Outcommuting from core municipality
Barcelona	0.61	674,757	0.44	0.21
Madrid	0.65	621,012	0.39	0.15
Málaga	0.5	13,852	0.09	0.12
Seville	0.56	66,125	0.21	0.12
Valencia	0.5	139,475	0.32	0.18
Bilbao	0.58	137,130	0.43	0.25

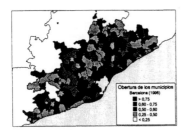

Figure 3a: Barcelona

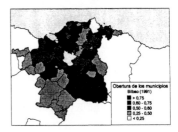

Figure 3b: Bilbao

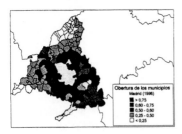

Figure 3c: Madrid

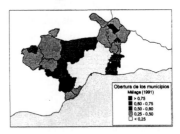

Figure 3d: Málaga

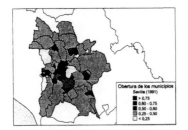

Figure 3e: Seville

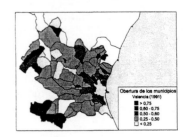

Figure 3f: Valencia

Figures 3a - 3f: Outcommuting within the Spanish metropolitan areas

The metropolitan areas like Barcelona and Bilbao with high outcommuting have a complex metropolitan structure, meanwhile the other metropolitan areas have a much less complex organisational structure, besides administrative facts such as the size of the core capital.

a) The metropolitan areas with high outcommuting are characterised by having cores with the smallest relative weight. For example the core municipality of Barcelona accounts for only 35% of the total population of its metropolitan area and Bilbao represents only 24%. On the other hand the core municipalities of Valencia, Seville, Madrid and Malaga have 50%, 52%, 58% and 74% of the respective metropolitan population.

b) The administrative size of the municipality also affects the degree of outcommuting. Barcelona with 98km^2 is smaller than Madrid with 605km^2, and Bilbao with 41 km^2 is smaller than Malaga with 394 km^2, Seville with 141 km^2 and Valencia with 134 km^2. So the spatial extent of the core municipality clearly affects the labour market's outcommuting.

4.3 The Sub Centres of the Metropolitan Areas

Beyond the distinctions between MA and CMA, and the degree of outcommuting, the structure of the metropolitan sub-centres shows the differences of the mobility for job purposes.

Here sub-centres are understood as those municipalities, other than the metropolitan core, with over 10.000 inhabitants that attract as least 15% of the workers from other municipalities.

Barcelona stands out from the other areas with 13 sub centres, followed by Madrid with 11, Bilbao with 4, Valencia and Malaga with 1, and Seville where the metropolitan core is at the same time the sub-centre.

The de-centralised structure of Barcelona compared with the rest of the metropolitan areas, stands out not only for the number of sub-centres, but by the level of autonomy of the sub-centres relative to the metropolitan core. Of the 13 sub-centres found in that metropolitan area only two (Mollet and Badalona) have flows >15% to the metropolitan core. On the other hand, in the case of Madrid the 11 sub-centres depend upon the core. In the rest of the metropolitan areas only Bilbao (with Mungia and Llodio) and Valencia (with Liria) show a degree of de-centralisation in their metropolitan area structure.

4.4 The radial distance from the core

The average radial distance of all the municipalities of the metropolitan areas measured from their core reveals the geometry of each area.

Despite the difference in the size and population between Madrid and Barcelona's MAs, the radial distance of the latter (34.1 km), due the existence of the coast and the coastal hill ranges, exceeds that of the Spanish capital (30.3 km).

Following these two principal metropolitan areas, one finds Seville with 25.5km, Valencia with 23.9km, Malaga with 20.7 and Bilbao with 14.9 km.

If the distance to the core is weighted by number of flows (excluding the internal journeys to each core municipality) the perception varies significantly: The functional space, considering the central distance, is quite different from the geometric space.

The longest average distance is that registered in the metropolitan area of Madrid (20.5) followed by Malaga (18.9 km) Seville (17.1 km), Barcelona (13.8 km) Valencia (12.6 km) and Bilbao (9.8 km).

This means a reduction of the distance to the centre in a proportion of 60% for Barcelona, 47% for Valencia, 34% for Bilbao, 33% for Seville, 32% for Madrid and only 9% for Malaga.

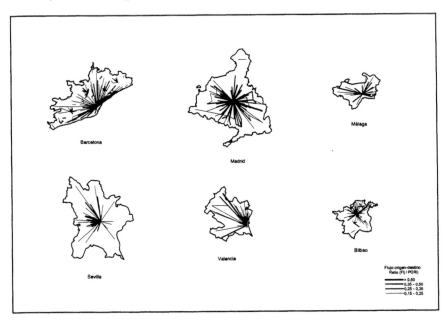

Figure 4: Metropolitan mobility

4.5 Distance to the main destination and total average distance

This reduction of the distance in Barcelona with regard to the rest of metropolitan areas is still shorter if one considers the average distance (considering the number of flows) to the main destination (not necessarily to the centre).

The average distance of Barcelona's Metropolitan Area (11.5 km) is the smallest after Bilbao (9.23 km). Valencia (12.7 km) represents the third metropolitan area with the shortest distance to the main destination.

In contrast, Madrid (19.8 km), Málaga (17.4 km), and Seville (17.0 km) show much higher journey distances to the principal destination.

If the total average distance is considered, i.e. the result of all the employment related journeys, including those within each municipality, the results are as follows:

Madrid is the MA with the greatest journeys (10.6 km) followed by Barcelona (6.7 km), Seville (5), Valencia (4.7), Bilbao (4.4), and Malaga (3.3).

Despite the clearly inferior territorial extension of the urban continuity of Barcelona, relative to Madrid, the Catalan capital shows a pattern of employment related mobility clearly more sustainable than that of Madrid. The same observation can be applied, with certain qualifications, to Bilbao relative to the comparable metropolitan areas of Seville and Valencia.

Table 3: principal indicators of the distance travelled in the work related journeys

Metropolitan areas	Average distance from the core (km)	Average distance weighted by flows (km)		
		to the core	To the principal destination	Total
Barcelona	34.1	13.8	11.5	6.7
Madrid	33	20.5	19.8	10.6
Málaga	20.7	18.9	17.4	3.3
Seville	25.5	17.1	17	5
Valencia	23.9	12.6	12.7	4.7
Bilbao	14.9	9.8	9.2	4.4

5 Conclusions

The Spanish Metropolitan Areas shows two clearly differentiated patterns of spatial organisation:

On the one hand one can identify the monocentric model, strongly hierarchical that is found in the metropolitan areas of Madrid, Valencia, Seville and Malaga. In these areas practically all the flows for job related purposes gravitate towards the centre, determining as general rule, long radial journeys.

On the other hand the more decentralised model: that can be found in Barcelona and to a lesser extent in Bilbao. In this model, the presence of sub-centres implies a strong complexity with shorter travel distances, meaning a potentially more sustainable system.

Barcelona is an exceptional example of metropolitan de-centralisation. Its metropolitan area is the only one of the Spanish cases organised by 'primary areas' PMA: i.e. Sabadell, Terrassa, Mataro, Granollers, Vilanova and Barcelona. Furthermore it is the only one that has a network of minor sub-centres (Sant Celoni, Malgrat, Martorell, Pineda, Vilafranca, and El Vendrel, as well as Badalona and Mollet) that act like cores of their own respective urban subsystems. This structure implies an important saving in metropolitan movement, despite its clearly complex geography.

References

[1] Cheshire, P. et al. (1988) *Urban Problems and Regional Policy in the European Community 12: analysis and recommendations for Community action*, Office of Publications of the European Commission, Luxembourg.

[2] Hall, P. and Hay, D. (1980) *Growth Centres in the European Urban System*, Heineman Educational Books, London.

[3] NUREC (1994) *Atlas of Agglomerations in the European Union*, NUREC, Duisburg.

[4] GEMACA (1996) Les Régions Métropoles de l'Europe du nord-ouest, limitres géographiques et structures économiques. IAURIF-GEMACA.

[5] Office of Management and Budget (1990) *Revised Standards for Defining Metropolitan Areas in the 1990s*. Federal Register, 30 March 1990.

Distinct measures of accessibility in traffic systems

J. Lyborg[1] & P. Envall[1]
[1]*Trivector Traffic, Sweden.*

Abstract

What gets measured matters – this is and always has been recognized as a fact in the business world. Many Swedish towns are today striving to improve accessibility to service areas, business centers and recreation. In spite of this, the actual conditions are seldom analyzed, since accessibility is recognized to be a complex aspect to measure. The main objective of this study is to measure accessibility between home and work (job opportunities) with GIS by comparing three transport modes in Växjö city, Sweden. Graphical outputs show that the bicycle is in many ways competitive to the car, when it comes to reaching job opportunities. This type of analysis can also be used to help decision-makers and politicians to increase the accessibility by other transport modes than car in their cities and regions. One can also pinpoint areas where there are gaps in bicycle networks or the public transport network, where improvements are needed, as well as locate potential areas for new exploitation.

1 Introduction

Over the last decades our global society has been highly influenced by automobility planning. Growing mobility has been seen as an indication of a well-functioning transport system and a society with increasing welfare. Excessive mobility can however lead to urban sprawl, longer travel distances and travel times as well as other problems that can be associated with lower welfare. A planning policy more focused on accessibility, i.e. siting new locations of activities that can be easily reached by other transport means than car, can reduce the size of some of the transport problems. The concept of accessibility should therefore gain more attention since it is believed that it cannot have a negative connotation.

The Swedish government has over the last few years also realised the importance of accessibility; hence the concept is one of five major transport political goals [1]. Nevertheless, it has been difficult to measure accessibility in the right way – some of the indicators used are so over-simplified that they can be misguiding, others are so complex that they are difficult to understand. These problems have made it difficult for politicians to grasp the importance of the concept [2]. Geographical Information Systems (GIS) provide a favourable working environment since transport data are spatial in nature. The main objective of this study is to measure accessibility between home and work (job opportunities) with GIS by comparing three transport modes in Växjö city, Sweden. The full version of the study can be found in Lyborg [3].

2 Methodological approach

An accessibility analysis can be performed in several different ways. In this case study GIS is used as the main tool to analyse and present the results. The accessibility is for instance measured as the number of job opportunities that can be reached within a certain time period from 147 statistical districts within Växjö city, comparing the transport modes car, public transport and bike.

Some limitations are required to keep the results on a comprehensible level. First, home-to-work trips are chosen since they are so-called forced trips [4]. They occur more or less daily and are often thought of as strenuous. They are not as wanted as recreational or vacational trips that often are associated with a pleasant and relaxing time. Work trips are also the group of activities that costs most in terms of transport time [4].

Second, the study only assesses the actual time aspect, without individual preferences or beliefs. It is also assumed that all trips are carried out straight from home to work without taking any stops, such as grocery shopping or leaving children at day care centre, into consideration. Third, socio-economic differences are not accounted for. For instance, a person may live very close to a large company, but if he does not have the skills or education to qualify for those jobs, then they are hardly accessible to employment. Nevertheless, adding too many factors can lead to results that are more complex and uncertain.

A digital copy of the Växjö road network enables realistic driving patterns. General car speeds [5] are determined by type of street (local or main street), number of lanes, type of area (residential, central or industrial) and speed limits (Table 1). 15 different street classes can be determined. The bike speed is set to 17 km/h, based i.e. on a study performed by [6]. Both car and bicycle network analyses are performed with a modified version of the GIS software ArcView Network Analyst. When creating the bus network, a public transport planning software is used. The resulting tables obtained from the three network analyses provide the basis for the actual accessibility analysis. AT50 (Accessibility Time at 50%), which shows the time it takes to reach 50% of the job opportunities, is proposed.

Table 1: The 15 street types with average speed results from the Västerås investigation [5] used in this study (res. = residential, ind. = industrial, CBD = Central Business District. The street types in *italic* letters are specific for Växjö.

No	Street type	No of lanes	Speed limit (km/h)	Average speed (km/h)	Standard error (km/h)
1	Local/*Main* res.	2	30	20.2*	4.2
2	Local res.	2	50	26.6	0.5
3	Main res.	2	50	46.6	0.5
4	Main/*Local* res.	2	70	52.9	1.1
5	Main res.	4	50	35.6	0.8
6	Main res.	4	70	35.7	1.5
7	Local ind.	2	50	27.1	1.2
8	Main ind.	2	50	46.7	1.6
9	Local CBD	2	50	14.3	0.8
10	Main CBD	2	50	26.6	1.0
11	Arterial	2	50	42.1	0.9
12	Arterial	2	70	53.6	1.4
13	Arterial	4	50	38.6	0.6
14	Arterial	4	70	52.1	0.5
15	Arterial	2/4	90	86.5	0.7

* Standard error of 4.2 km/h compared to an average of 0.9 km/h for the other 14 street types.

3 Results

Some statistics about the length of the trips for the three transport modes are presented in Table 2. It should be noted that the car can reach any of the 147 districts in less than 20 minutes, from wherever it starts within the city limits. The maximum time a bicycle trip takes is about twice as long as the car trip, while the maximum length for going by bus is more than six times as long.

However, Table 2 also shows that 90% of the trips can be performed in about 12 minutes with car, 22 minutes with bicycle and 43 minutes by bus. This implies that there are a number of bus trips that are very time consuming, but that most of the trips can be performed in about 40 minutes.

GIS also provides a suitable environment for production of maps. Figure 1 illustrates the accessibility by bicycle compared to car. High bicycle accessibility is achieved in dark-coloured areas. From these areas the bicycle can reach 90-100% of the job opportunities that can be reached by car in the same time period (20 minutes). Light-coloured areas are districts with very low accessibility, i.e. less than 50% of all job opportunities within the city borders can be reached by bicycle in 20 minutes. Bicycle accessibility is thus fairly high for most of the statistical districts. It is only the most peripheral areas where there are relatively few inhabitants that have a low level of accessibility.

Table 2: Trip lengths for car, bicycle and public transport in Växjö.

	Car (min)	Bicycle (min)	Bus (min)
Maximum	19.0	42.9	122.0
Average	7.7	12.0	24.3
Median	7.5	11.2	20.9
25:th percentile	5.1	5.6	14.2
75:th percentile	9.7	17.1	30.5
90:th percentile	11.6	22.3	43.3

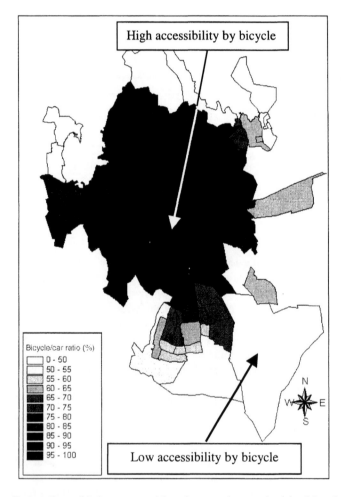

Figure 1:   Proportion of job opportunities that can be reached by bicycle in 20 minutes in Växjö city.

When looking at the same ratios for public transport and car, the general patterns are very different. Only the very central areas have an acceptable bus accessibility. Several of the densely populated areas do not cover enough job opportunities to reach acceptable levels of accessibility. Long waiting and transfer times are the main reasons why bus accessibility in Växjö city is so low.

Similar information can also be presented as graphs. From Residential Area North it takes 8 minutes to reach 50% of all job opportunities within the city limits, by bicycle it takes 14 minutes and by bus it takes 23 minutes (Figure 2). This graph illustrates a common travel behaviour in cities with small or no congestion. Travelling by car is the fastest transport mode, bicycle the second fastest and bus is the slowest transport mode.

The same type of graph for the Central Business District (Figure 3) illustrates that it takes only 6-7 minutes for both car and bicycle to reach 50% of all job opportunities. You can also reach a larger portion of the job opportunities by bicycle during the first five minutes than if you go by car from the CBD.

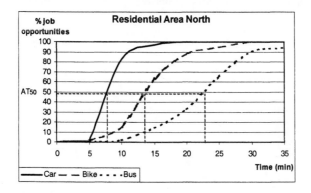

Figure 2: The proportion of job opportunities that can be reached at different time periods from Residential Area North.

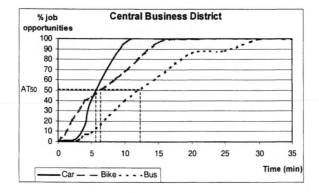

Figure 3: The proportion of job opportunities that can be reached at different time periods from the Central Business District.

Instead of comparing different transport modes one can also compare the accessibility by e.g. bicycle from different residential areas. In Figure 4 it is clear that the peripheral residential areas North, East and South have very similar curves. It takes roughly 15 minutes to reach 60% of all job opportunities from the three areas. If you travel from the CBD by bike, on the other hand, one can reach almost all job opportunities in the same time limit.

To the right in the graph is the curve for Residential Area West. This area has a very low bicycle accessibility during the first 10 minutes. The reason is probably that the area is secluded from the rest of the city by a lake.

The lake has on the other hand not affected the accessibility by bus and car to the same extent. In Table 3 it appears to take about 8 minutes to reach 50% of the job opportunities from the other residential areas and approximately 10 minutes from Residential Area West. It goes even faster to reach 50% of the job opportunities by bus from Residential Area West than it does from Residential Areas North and East. This can be a clear sign that the accessibility by bicycle from Residential Area West can be improved if new and/or more direct bicycle paths are built.

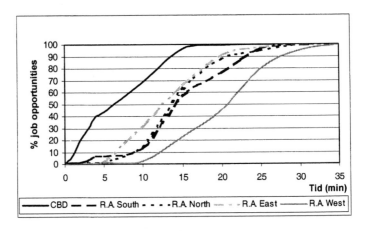

Figure 4:   The proportion of job opportunities that can be reached at different time periods from the four residential areas and the CBD by bicycle.

Table 3:   The time it takes to reach 50% of the job opportunities from the different residential areas.

	Car (min)	Bicycle (min)	Bus (min)
Res. Area North	7.9	13.6	23.0
Res. Area South	7.5	14.0	20.8
Res. Area East	7.9	12.6	25.4
Res. Area West	10.2	21.0	20.9
CBD	5.8	6.5	12.6

4 Conclusions

Vehicle usage cannot only be controlled by taxes and fees. Accessibility, environment and safety must instead control the development of the transport system. It requires a coordinated city- and traffic planning that manages new exploitation, job opportunities, service and recreation as well as the investments in and limitations of the traffic network.

There is however an infinite number of ways to measure accessibility. It can be carried out both quantitatively and qualitatively, for a single person or for an entire region. Despite difficulties in measuring accessibility, politicians around the world realize the importance of the concept, for the car driver, the biker, the child as well as for the elderly or disabled. One has to be able to reach work, service and recreation within a reasonable amount of time and with the transport mode most suitable for each and every one.

Public authorities can use this type of results to become aware of how new constructions affect the possibilities to use bicycle or public transport as the daily means of transportation. Low accessibility areas can then be "upgraded" by adding new or improved bike paths and/or a new or altered bus route in order to increase the accessibility. In addition, one can pinpoint areas that today might be unexploited, that are suitable for either residential or commercial development.

There seem to be difficulties transfering the results from the academic world to the actual planning process. New and more developed tools are probably required for this to happen. It is on the other hand important to find a balance between the too complex models and the more simple methods as soon as possible. The usage of GIS as a planning tool is becoming more and more common because of improvements in new analytical possibilities. The potential of using GIS in accessibility planning is thus large. However, the most important aspect is to move away from just having a high accessibility by car to high accessibility by bicycle and public transports as well in our struggle towards a sustainable society.

References

[1] Swedish Government, *Transport Development for a Sustainable Development*, Proposition 1997/98:56, Stockholm, 1998 (in Swedish).
[2] Cervero, R., Rodd, T. & Appleyard, B., Tracking accessibility: employment and housing opportunities in the San Fransisco Bay Area. *Environment and Planning A*, **31**, pp. 1259-1278, 1998.
[3] Lyborg, J. *Towards Accessibility Planning by Means of GIS – A Case Study on the Access to Potential Job Opportunities by Three Transport Modes.* LUMES, Lund University, 2000.
[4] Steen, P., Dreborg, K-H., Henriksson, G., Hunhammar, S., Höjer, M., Rignér, J. & Åkerman, J., *Journeys in the Future – Transports in a Sustainable Society*, Report 1997:7. KFB: Stockholm, 1997 (in Swedish).

[5] Ericsson, E., *Driving Pattern in Urban Areas – Descriptive Analysis and Initial Prediction Model*, Bulletin 185. Department of Technology and Society, Lund Institute of Technology, Lund University, 2000.

[6] Ljungberg, C., *Bicycle Traffic – A General Overview*, Report 78:1987, BFR: Stockholm, 1987 (in Swedish).

Innovative technologies for the public transportation in the Urban Mobility Plan of Padova

M. Andriollo[1], G. Del Torchio[2], G. Martinelli[3], A. Morini[3] & A. Tortella[3]
[1]*Department of Electrotechnics, Milan Polytechnic, Italy*
[2]*APS - Azienda Padova Servizi Spa, Padova, Italy*
[3]*Department of Electrical Engineering, Padova University, Italy*

Abstract

The reorganization of Padova public transportation system, established in the Urban Mobility Plan, aims at the development of three main lines along the north-south, east-west e north-south/east directions. The choice of advanced intermediate capacity rubber-tyred transport systems with guided running mode seems to be particularly suitable for Padova town planning, due to their favourable technical and economical characteristics. In fact their supply and traction systems ensure low air and noise emissions, while the inherent flexibility related to both the guidance and the supply modes allows efficient operation even in presence of other vehicles or obstacles along the critical route sections of the lines. Moreover the supply flexibility makes the lines easily compatible with historical-architectural structures. At present the first line is getting into construction and it is expected it will be put into operation by autumn 2003.

1 Introduction

Nowadays the need of urban mobility is satisfied by using various transportation systems with different characteristics and performances according to different utilization demands. In Tab.1 some data are reported, with reference to conventional transportation systems (bus, tram, light rail metro, conventional metro).
The wide ranges of the data reflect a partial overlapping and a substantial

Table 1: Performance characteristics of conventional transportation systems [1].

	Bus and trolley-bus	Tram[1]	Light rail metro[2]	Conventional metro
Vehicle capacity (passengers)[3]	60 ÷ 120	100 ÷ 200	100 ÷ 250	140 ÷ 280
Transport capacity (phd)[4]	1500 ÷ 3500	2000 ÷ 6000	6000 ÷ 15000	20000 ÷ 45000
Commercial speed (km/h)	5 ÷ 20	12 ÷ 20	18 ÷ 40	25 ÷ 60
Mean stop distance (m)	150 ÷ 300	150 ÷ 300	300 ÷ 600	400 ÷ 1000

[1] in shared lane   [2] or tram with predominant protected lane
[3] 4 standing passengers/m[2] included   [4] passengers per rush hour per direction

continuity in the performance values, due to the variety of operating conditions and specific technological features and infrastructures. In particular, when the transportation demand is within 2000 and 4000 phd (passengers per rush hour per direction), systems based on free drive operation (bus or trolley bus) or fixed guideway (tram) can be convenient.

Nowadays, tramways have got new interest especially if the transportation demand exceeds 4000-5000 phd and the town structure facilitates their application. Anyway tram systems have relatively high investment costs as well as low flexibility. On the contrary, conventional bus and trolley-bus lines sometimes do not meet the favour of passengers for low comfort or poor image, in addition to the reduced transport capacity and - for buses with diesel engine - to pollution problems. As a consequence many local governments of medium sized town (100,000-400,000 inhabitants) are involved in the modernization of the local transportation network by improving its image, ride comfort and efficiency in order to fit the passenger requirements and, at the same time, to reduce air and noise pollution as well as the traffic congestion caused by the increase of private cars.

The necessity of coping with these problems led to the development of new transport systems, different from tram and bus, to get the following targets:

- investment and operating costs lower than costs related to tramway;
- good service efficiency and modern image;
- reduced environmental impact as regards the historical-architectural structure of the town;
- reduced air and noise pollution.

These systems, commonly called "advanced intermediate rubber-tyred transport system with guided running mode", are of particular interest when transportation demand is between 2000 and 4000 phd.

2 Advanced intermediate transport systems

The intermediate systems support different technological solutions, but, in addition to the above-mentioned targets, they share the following features:

- good riding comfort and accessibility;

- intermediate capacity between tram and bus (2000-4000 phd);
- flexible operation with possibility to choose either guided or free-guided running mode; in case of guided mode, the guidance system can be either of mechanical type (central guiding rail or side kerbs) or of functional type (by means of optical, electronic or magnetic devices);
- electric propulsion with external supply (overhead wire or ground plant) and/or with on board supply (batteries or diesel-electric system);
- realization of an "integrated system" (set of constraints, infrastructures, fixed plants, devices for vehicle running control, devices for customer information and so on) according to the planning of a modern service.

As examples of such systems, the four technologies which nowadays have got a good level in experimentation and application are:

- TVR system (Transport sur Voie Réservée), by Bombardier Transport e Spie Enertrans consortium;
- TRANSLOHR system, by Lohr Industrie in collaboration with Parizzi (Alsthom group);
- CIVIS system, by Matra and Irisbus (IVECO group);
- STREAM system, by Ansaldo-Breda.

Their main features are described in the paper, with reference to the present development stage [2-10].

2.1   TVR

TVR (Fig.1) is a transport system based on [3]:

- Dual mode guidance
  - Guided running mode as a conventional tram using a central rail.
  - Un-guided running mode as a conventional articulated transit bus, excluding the rail and the external supply.
- Dual mode supply
  - External supply by overhead contact wire with pantograph-catenary system and the rail as return conductor. The vehicle is arranged to be supplied also by a twin wired overhead line like a trolley-bus.
  - On-board supply for 'off-wire' operation, provided by a 200 kVA diesel engine-electric generator system feeding an inverter at 750 V DC voltage.

The traction equipment consists of two 3-phase induction motors (150 kW each), located in the front and rear of the vehicle and fed by the inverter.
The vehicle is like a tram and consists of three articulated car-bodies, each one mounted on an aluminum frame to which all structural elements are bolted. The main technical characteristics are given in Tab.2.
The TVR technology has been chosen in Nancy to construct three lines (total length 25 km). The first line (11 km and 28 stations) was put into operation on December 2000. The power is supplied by a trolley using the pre-existing twin wired overhead line.

Figure 1: Bombardier TVR in Nancy [4].

2.2   TRANSLOHR

TRANSLOHR (Fig.2) is a transport system based on [5]:

- Dual mode guidance
  - Guided running mode using the coupling between a 'V' roller system and a central rail placed in a 20 cm deep concrete trench (Fig.3); the roller system drives the axle steering device.
  - Un-guided running mode as a conventional articulated transit bus, excluding the coupling with the rail and without the external supply.
- Dual mode supply
  - External supply by overhead contact wire with pantograph-catenary system and the rail as return conductor.
  - On-board supply for limited 'off-wire' operation, provided by batteries supported by a 5 kW diesel-electric system for their recharging.

Figure 2: TRANSLOHR system [6].

Table 2: Main technical characteristics of advanced intermediate rubber-tyred transport systems.

	CIVIS	STREAM	TRANSLOHR	TVR
Sizes (m)				
- width	2.55	2.50	2.20	2.50
- height	3.22	2.40	2.89	3.40
- length	12 18	12 18	25 32	24.5
Dual mode guidance	yes	yes	yes[1]	yes[2]
Traction	electric	electric	electric	electric
- external supply	twin wired overhead line	in the roadway	single wire or twin wired overhead line	single wire or twin wired overhead line
- on-board supply	diesel-electric/Euro 3	batteries (3-4 km)	batteries (1 km)[4]	diesel-electric/Euro 3
- bi-directional	no	no	yes	no
Vehicle capacity[3]	70 120	70 120	116 148	145
Per hour capacity (phd)[3]				
frequency 4 min	1050 1800	1050 1800	1740-2220	2175
3 min	1400 2400	1400 2400	2320-2960	2900
2 min	2100 3600	2100 3600	3480-4440	4350
Main performance data				
- commercial speed (km/h)	(20-25)[5]	(20-25)[5]	(20-25)[5]	(20-25)[5]
- maximum speed (km/h)	80	60-70	60-70	70
- maximum acceleration (m/s^2)	1.4	1.2	1.3	1.2
- minimum curve radius (m)	25[6]	12.5	10.5	12
- maximum slope (%)	13	-	13	13

[1] 'off-wire' operation only for short distances (for instance in depot)
[2] Italian road rules don't allow more than 18-m long vehicles
[3] 4 standing passengers/m^2 included
[4] possible integration with 5 kW diesel-electric system
[5] dependent on the length of the protected lane
[6] minimum compatible with optical guidance

Figure 3: TRANSLOHR guidance system [5].

The traction equipment consists of two 3-phase PM synchronous motors (peak power 220 kW), located in the front and rear of the vehicle, under the driving cabs; the motors are fed by an inverter (input voltage 750 V DC).

The TRANSLOHR vehicle is made up of three or four car-bodies; the main technical characteristics are reported in Tab.2.

Some prototypes have operated in test facilities with satisfactory results; till now no commercial line has been built.

2.3   CIVIS

Unlike the former systems, CIVIS (Fig.4) uses a functional guided running mode.

Figure 4: CIVIS vehicle [7].

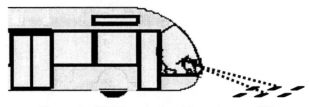

Figure 5: CIVIS optical guidance system [8].

Its main features are [7,8]:

- Dual mode guidance
  - Optical guidance: the vehicle follows the route thanks to a camera behind the windscreen reading a white dotted double-line on the roadway; the image is processed to detect any course deviation, which is immediately corrected by a motor controlling the steering column [7] (Fig.5). The driver always controls both acceleration and braking and may recover the manual driving at any moment, with a simple movement on the steering wheel. If needed, the functional guidance can be supported by a mechanical guidance based on side kerbs along the route: the contact between the kerb and small wheels (with vertical rotation axis) fixed on all the axles enables to recover the right direction, if vehicle goes outside the path because of adhesion loss or error in the optical guidance.
  - Un-guided running mode as a conventional bus, without optical guidance.
- Dual mode supply
  - External electric supply by twin wired overhead line (750 V DC voltage) like a conventional trolley-bus.
  - On-board supply for 'off-wire' operation, provided by a diesel engine-electric generator or - for limited movements - by batteries or low rate diesel-electric system.

The traction equipment consists of 3-phase induction hub-motors, each fed by a 75 kW converter. The main technical characteristics are given in Tab.2. The 12-m long vehicle (one car-body) uses rear motoring axles; the 18-m long vehicle, with two articulated car-bodies, operates both rear and intermediate driving wheels. The braking action is obtained by means of three independent systems (electric braking, front disk brake, oil bath brake acting on the rear driving wheels).

CIVIS vehicles with optical guidance have operated in test facility routes with satisfactory results; till now no commercial line has been built.

Figure 6: STREAM bus in Trieste [10].

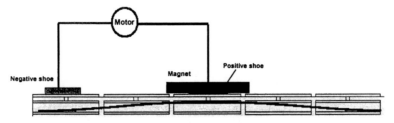

Figure 7: STREAM supply system [10].

2.4   STREAM

STREAM technology (Fig.6) utilizes an original electric supply system, innovative with respect to the other intermediate transport systems.
Its main features are [9,10]:

- Dual mode supply
  - External electric supply by a contact line installed in a trench (30-cm deep, 60-cm wide) along the roadway. The trench is formed by pre-fabricated box modules with the power conductor in the bottom and covered by insulated metal segments about 50-cm long. The contact line is normally connected to the ground: as a magnet, placed under the vehicle, passes over a metal segment, a force is performed which raises the power conductor from the trench bottom, so that it is put into contact with the metal plate (Fig.7). A collector, consisting of two sliding shoes with opposite polarities, supplies the traction energy: the current flows from the positive shoe to a passive metal segment through the negative shoe. The power is delivered by AC/DC converters placed along the line with output voltage of 500 V DC.
  - On board supply provided by batteries; for short distances (3-4 km), the vehicle can instantly and automatically disconnect the line and continue by using the on-board supplied energy.
- Dual mode guidance
  - Functional guidance system, based on the self-centring action of the current collector on the contact line; this enables to correct the vehicle path by steering the front wheels by means of an hydraulic cylinder.
  - Un-guided running mode when the vehicle is supplied by the on-board electric sources.

The 12-m long vehicle is propelled by two 80 kW induction motors in the rear wheels; the 18-m long vehicle by four motors placed in the rear wheels and in the middle axle. The main technical characteristics are reported in Tab.2.
A project based on STREAM technology is under experimentation in Trieste.

3   New public transportation system in Padova

In order to manage the mobility problems from a global point of view, Padova worked out an Urban Mobility Plan (PUM) [11], in which all the components involved in public mobility are analyzed and a new efficient integration among them is studied. In particular the following aspects are considered:

- different components of the public transportation network (regional railway system, urban and suburban lines, extra-urban lines and so on);
- interchange junctions between public transportation and road network;
- parking system;
- road network and its control model;
- sub-systems for non-motorized mobility: cycle tracks and pedestrian areas;
- public and private transport information system;
- public transport monitoring and regulation.

Such plan will be carried out step by step, taking into account both the present territorial scenery and the future developments within ten years, in terms of road infrastructures and town planning projects.

The PUM starting point is the re-design of the public transport system to get better service quality by means of innovation and re-qualification [1].

At present the public transportation network consists of 21 urban and suburban lines, with 7,5 millions vehicles km per year. In addition, extra-urban services develop a traffic of 1.05 millions vehicles km per year (1999). The main data of urban and suburban lines are reported in Tab.3.

Table 3: Main data related to the public transport in Padova.

Number of urban and suburban lines	21
Number of weekday trips	2336
Mean service frequency in primary lines (trips/hour)	10
Mean service frequency in auxiliary lines (trips/hour)	4
Rush hour commercial speed (km/h)	15.2
Daily commercial speed (km/h)	16.8
Number of operating vehicles	203
Mean transfer time from origin to destination (min)	17.2

The transport network has a radial configuration and most of the routes flows into two corridors which cross the downtown area, the first from north to south and the second from east to west. The 80 per cent of the urban lines converges towards the railway station: 13 routes reach directly the station square, 4 are located in close proximity. A third corridor, covered by a number of users lower than the other ones, links the station to the University scientific departments and to the hospitals.

The new public transportation system (just approved in the first stage of the PUM) is based on the following main features:

- Choice of innovative rubber-tyred systems with transport capacity intermediate between tram and bus and able to combine the features of both the conventional systems: guided running mode, low air and noise emissions, operating flexibility, easy insertion into the urban structure.
- Determination of three central corridors passing through the downtown area and in which a network of three main lines ("lines of force") is put

into operation. The routes, operated by intermediate transport systems with partially protected lane, are:
a)   north-south (Pontevigodarzere-Guizza), at present involving most of the users;
b)   east-west (Ponte di Brenta-Sarmeola di Rubano), connecting the areas in which the future development of Padova is expected;
c)   north-south/east, linking the railway station to the University scientific departments and to the hospitals.

The layout and the length of the lines, crossing each other at the railway station, are shown in Fig.8 and Tab.4, respectively.

- Integration of the main lines with secondary ones; these lines, with lower traffic intensity, can run, totally or partially, in the central corridors.
- Interchange parking (park & ride), located near the lines of force in strategic positions with respect to the main vehicular flows (Fig.8).
- Interchange nodes, located on the corridors, to allow the integration among the urban public network, the extra-urban public system and the regional railway transport service.

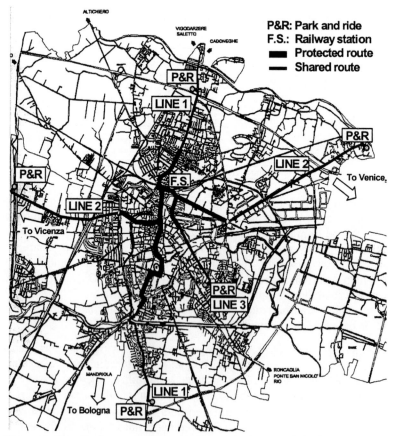

Figure 8: New Padova transportation network: layout of the lines of force.

Table 4: Length of the lines of force.

Route	Line #1	Line #2	Line #3	Total length
	Pontevigodarzere-Guizza (north-south)	Ponte di Brenta-Sarmeola di Rubano (east-west)	Railway station-S.Antonio Hospital (north-south/east)	
Length (km)	9.3	12.9	3.2	25.4
Protected length (km)	5.3 (57%)	4.2 (32%)	2.0 (62%)	11.5 (45%)

The problems related to the impact on both the historical-environmental peculiarity and the road systems as well as the technical, economical and organizing aspects of the network management introduce some constraints in the definition of the requirements of the lines of force:

- Need of dual mode supply to reduce - on the one hand - air and noise emissions (external electric supply) and, on the other hand, to attenuate the visual impact in downtown area or to run on routes outside the main corridors (on-board supply).
- Need of dual mode guidance for guided and free-guided operations. The guided mode is requested mainly to get accurate alignment at platforms for non-level passenger access and, where possible, to limit the lane width in some sections of the corridors. On the other hand, as normal operation in routes shared with other vehicles is required, the possibility to disconnect the guided mode allows maximum flexibility to overcome obstacles or to run outside the lane; furthermore the free-guided operation, together with on-board supply, is useful to move to and from the depot areas.
- Exigency to integrate, in the system design, both the trackway and the vehicle technology. The aim is to insert the new transportation system into the urban configuration, by re-planning the whole image of some urban areas and the system accessibility; this can be carried out by acting on the lane differentiation, on the fittings of the lane protection, on the architectural structure of stops and interchange junctions.
- Exigency that the vehicle layout reflects the innovation in the service and offers travel comfort in accordance with the updated technological progress (on-board, for both passengers and staff, as well as during the boarding or getting off operations).
- Need of central control of the system including the following capabilities:
  - radio link;
  - monitoring;
  - auto-location;
  - service management;
  - user information;
  - interface with the control system of traffic lights;
  - interface with the information system of the transport company.

In the PUM a technical-economical comparative analysis has been performed to evaluate the advantages deriving from the application of the described intermediate systems to the network of Fig.8 and Tab.4.

Table 5: Comparison of different solutions for the urban transport system of Padova [1].

Quantities	Unit	Present situation	Tram	Projects for the urban transport system	
				Intermediate system with functional guidance	Intermediate system with rail guidance
Length of the routes	km	-	6.5	25.4	25.4
Investment costs	billions ITL/km	-	18.1	8.3-11.1	17.7
Offered transport volume	thousand seats-km/day	1813	2277	2133	2240
Daily passengers	passengers/day	102,000	110,300	122,000	122,000
Travels with transfers	% of the total	11	56	22	22
Mean travelling time	minutes	17.2	18.4	16.2	16.2
Rush hour commercial speed	km/h	15.2	15.3	15.7	15.7
Daily commercial speed	km/h	16.7	16.9	17.3	17.3
Rate of protection of the routes	%	-	76	45	45
Per unit operating cost	ITL/passenger-km	377	329	282-296	311
Total operating costs (except amortization)	billions ITL/year	47.6	50.1	44.2-46.3	47.9
Total receipts	billions ITL/year	20.1	21.7	24.0	24.0

The analysis - reported in Tab.5 - compares the proposed scenery with the present arrangement in the public transport as well as with a tram-based network [1]. The tram option was foreseen in a previous project for the route Pontevigodarzere-Guizza (even if shorter in length) and later rejected for the following problems [1]:

- probably overestimated transport demand;
- lack of integration with a global project of the urban mobility (in particular it didn't take into account the planned developments of the east and west quarters of Padova);
- penalization on the private traffic and on the access to the trading and residential buildings, because of the barrier effect due to the rail;
- negative impact on historical-architectural areas of Padova;
- investment costs too high if compared with the expected benefits.

With reference to Tab.5, the criteria for the evaluation of the intermediate systems have considered range of values for some parameters (e.g. investment and operating costs) in order to take into account the different level of complexity of the examined technologies. On the contrary, the assumptions about the length of the protected routes and the mean operating speed are the same for all the technologies; the same transport capacity is obtained by assuming a different number of daily trips.

The advantages due to the introduction of rubber-tyred intermediate systems with guided running mode are:

- improvement in the daily service with an increase of about 20% in terms of offered seats;
- increase of the commercial speed;
- decrease of the mean travel time;
- decrease of the operating costs.

It's worth to notice that the mean travelling time related to the intermediate systems is lower than the one related to the tram, because the latter is applied only in north-south corridor and then a higher number of transfers is required.

As regard the realization of the three main lines, the beginning of the construction of line #1 is imminent, since a state co-financing of about 31 millions euros was assigned; for the other lines a state contribution has just been requested.

The announcement of a competition was published on the Official Journal of the European Community on May 11, 2001, by APS - Azienda Padova Servizi Spa, the company which manages the public urban transport of Padova. The contract includes the design and the realization of line #1, by means of a rubber-tyred intermediate system with mechanical or functional guided running mode; it requires the supply of both the rolling stock and the guidance system, the construction of the external supply system, the construction of the infrastructures and the system maintenance according to a "global service" principle.

The contract will be awarded to the most convenient tender with respect to the contract base-price (58,359,629.60 euros + VAT), on the basis of the projects which will be presented by January 31, 2002. The foreseen maximum period for the construction of the line is 540 days. In addition to the economical conditions, other aspects will be considered, such as the technical quality, the performances and the experimentation level of the proposed technology, the time required for the realization, the impact of works on town life, the features and the quality of the inside of the vehicle, the vehicle stylistic design and the architectural and environmental impact.

4   Conclusion

The reorganization of the public transport system of Padova, elaborated in the Urban Mobility Plan, recommends a solution based on a network of three main lines ("lines of force") as the most promising to meet the user demand and the most feasible from a technical and financial point of view.

The choice of rubber-tyred intermediate systems with mechanical or functional guided running mode and 18-m long vehicles seems to be very attractive for operating the three routes. The flexibility in the use of the guided mode - typical of these systems - enables the running even if other vehicles or obstacles are on the lane; a temporary disconnection from the guided mode enables also to run easily in presence of connections with other lines or if critical route sections are placed along the line. In addition, the flexibility due to the dual supply system ensures low impact on historical-architectural areas.

At present the first line is under its realization phase and it is expected it will be put into operation by autumn 2003.

References

[1] Transystem SpA, *Comune di Padova - Piano Urbano della Mobilità - First intermediate report*, May 18, 2000.

[2] Bjerkemo, S.A., Advanced Intermediate Public Transport Systems between the bus and the tram, *Cities of Tomorrow*, Gothenburg, August 23-24, 2001.

[3] http://www.bombardier.com

[4] http://www.grand-nancy.org/images/galerie/stan_tram1.jpg

[5] LOHR Industrie, *TRANSLOHR gamme de trams*, LOHR Report.

[6] http://www.teknoware.fi/English/lohr.htm

[7] http://www.matra-transport.fr

[8] http://www.transbus.org/civis.htm

[9] http://www.ansaldostream.com

[10] Ansaldo-Breda, *Magnetic pick-up electric transportation systems*, Ansaldo Report.

[11] Transystem SpA, *Comune di Padova - Piano Urbano della Mobilità - Final report*, Janauary 18, 2001.

Business structure and localization affects transport generation and traffic flow

M. Pettersson
City & Mobility, Chalmers University of Technology, Sweden

Abstract

Goods transports are increasing faster than the GNP and they are increasing most in the urban areas, which are great production and consumer areas. There are very little data referring to urban goods transports, and national statistics do not allow analyses on the intra- or interurban level. Studies indicate that the future capacity problems will occur not in the national main road system but in or around the urban areas. Today about 20% of the traffic (road vehicle kilometer) in the urban areas are goods transports generated by the commercial and industrial life. Despite this, town- and traffic planning focus personal transports by tradition.

To estimate the urban goods transports and to analyse how the business structure and localization affect the transport generation in urban areas, we need empirical data suitable for urban conditions. An empirical study has therefore been performed in 45 Swedish communities. The study has mapped all transports to and from a number of companies during one week.

The study will estimate the trip generation for businesses in different branches and of different sizes in terms of trip frequencies, vehicle kilometres and origin-destination analyses. The aim is to create a transport generation model that can be used in urban planning in terms of environmental decisions, business localization and land use. A second aim is to develop methods to analyse transports with GIS-tools. This paper will present the design of the empirical study, and it will focus a discussion on method and definitions in the field of transportation.

1 Introduction

Transportation is increasing faster than the GNP, and road transportation is increasing most. Trip frequencies are also increasing at the same time as the amount of goods carried each trip is decreasing. Since 1975 the total amount of goods carried in Sweden has decreased by 26 % and at the same time the performed transport work has increased by 62% [1]. Transports are getting longer and more frequent. Economic growth is the most important factor explaining the increase of transports. But geographical and organizational changes are also part of the explanation.

Goods transports are increasing mostly in the urban areas, which are production and consumer areas of great importance. According to SIKA there are not likely to be any severe capacity problems on the national road system, but in and around the urban areas capacity problems are expected. Yet neither national nor local authorities focus their attention on urban goods transports. By tradition local town and traffic planning focuses on personal transports while goods transports are neglected. The national level focuses on heavy transports and infrastructure planning in order to locate transport corridors and analyse the capacity of the national road network. One reason for this is that most goods transports are assumed to operate on a national and international arena. Yet 73% of the goods carried and 36 % of the traffic work have their origins and destinations within the same county [1].

The problem is two-fold, the local planning process, and the local and national process to achieve environmental goals. The local level decides about business localization and land, use but there is no data about how much transportation different businesses generate, or how the localization effects the transport generation to support their decisions. The local and national process to formulate and achieve environmental goals calls for action, both from technical development and from managing the increasing urban goods transports. But there is no data to support the formulation of goals, or the means to achieve them. To manage to reduce the negative effects of increasing urban transports and at the same time establish good accessibility for goods transports for commerce and industry is a great challenge and calls for knowledge about how transports are generated. This paper will present the data available, the design of an empirical study, some preliminair results and a transport generation model.

2 Aim

The project aims to create a transport generation model to be used in urban planning to support environmental decisions, business localization and land use. Further aims are to; provide a general description of the urban goods movements; produce key figures for transport generation; the number of transports generated by businesses of different branches and of different sizes; develop methods to analyse transports with Geographical Information Systems (GIS); create a GIS-database, which can be used for other analyses; calculate traffic work with GIS- tools.

3 Available transport data

National transport statistics are designed to create data for national infrastructure issues. These are shown by; how the amount of transportation is expressed, the one sided focus on links and how the studies are designed. This focus is reproduced on many levels in the society and influences the physical planning and the general transport discussions. It also affects the possibilities of using the data for other analyses.

3.1 How transport data is expressed

In the national statistics Swedish transports are expressed in four different measures; 1) goods carried, 2) transport frequencies, 3) traffic work and 4) transport work. These measures describe the same transports in quite different ways, and they give different results. Transport frequencies indicate that most transports are performed over short distances, 81% of the number of transports was shorter than 100 km, and 51% were shorter than 25 km. The goods carried also show dominance for short distances, 68% of the goods were carried less than 100 km, and 38% were transported less than 25 km. Transport work, on the other hand, indicates that long distances are more dominant, almost 80% of the transport work was performed over distances more than 100 km (figure 1). Traffic work also shows predominance for long distances, 66% of the traffic work was performed over distances more than 100 km. Most statistics, research investigations, data for political decisions etc. concerning transports, are presented as transport work (ton-km) and show a predominance for long heavy transports and under estimate short distance distribution and light goods, which are particularly frequent in urban areas.

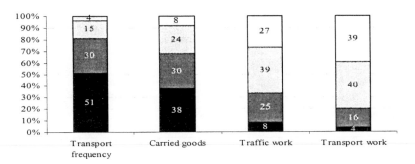

■ 0-24 km ■ 25-99 km ◻ 100 -299 km ◻ >300 km

Figure 1: Swedish transports 1999 in figures [1].

3.2 There are no transports without nodes

The national infrastructure emphasis is a focus on the links. In terms of nodes, and network, the local units are all nodes, and the roads are the links that constitute the network. The nodes are the dimensioning parts of the system. How crowded the network is on specific links is dependent on how the nodes are distributed. If a great deal of the local units are relocated the load on the network also will change. The amount of traffic on the links in the network is measured in several ways, but the generation at the nodes is seldom measured. When environmental issues and overcrowding are discussed, the most loaded links, and where infrastructure investments ought to be invested, come to focus. Studies of public and private personal transports always have an origin and a destination, and they always relate to where the living-, service- or work areas are located. But when analyzing goods transports the network seems to be the interesting part. If the impact from traffic is to be analysed, the nodes are more interesting parts of the system than the links. If the transport generation in the nodes is known (with O/D information), it is even possible to analyse the load on the links with GIS-tools.

To some extent, it is possible to affect the localization of the nodes. Some forms of business need authorization and permission from the local authority to set up. For these businesses it is possible to affect the localization. Another situation providing possibilities to affect localization is when a business needs land to set up or relocate an activity. Descriptions of the environmental consequences are also requested when starting or moving an activity. This also offers opportunities to control the nodes to optimal localizations, or at least possibilities of avoiding the most unfortunate localizations. Of course we are unable to rearrange the whole city to achive the optimal solution, but it is possible to influence localization if we know how the localization affects the transport generation and traffic flow.

3.2 Study design

In Sweden National statistics has produced comparable data since 1972. Since 1995, the statistics follows EU directives [2]. National Statistics and the official statistics of EU address the vehicle owner as the study unit. This does not allow analyses of transport generation based on localization or local unit size since one cannot calculate the total amount of transports from single units. The results are distributed in commodity groups, and are not possible to link to branch of business.

4 The empirical study

4.1 Method

Since transport generation is not possible to analyse with existing data, an empirical study has been performed in 45 Swedish communities. The study takes its point of departure in commerce and industry, in the companies that generate transports, in other words the nodes. Almost every business company orders goods and generates transports. This may be a shop ordering goods, an office ordering papers for its printer or an industry ordering or sending goods to or from its production. The study unit is the local unit of the businesses. A company may have one or more local units.

Since the aim is to analyse the transport generation for units of different sizes and with specific localizations, the local unit is more appropriate than the whole company, which may consist of several units with quite different activities, sometimes related to different branches. A sample was created from the Business Register of Statistics Sweden by selecting local units with 0-499 employees. The sample was stratified according to the branch and size of the community it was situated in. The questionnaire was delivered by post, but all units were also contacted by phone.

In the study all transports to and from the local units during a single week have been charted with origin and destination addresses, times of the day, types of goods and vehicles used (fig 2). The study sets out to estimate the trip generation for businesses in different branches and of different sizes in terms of trip frequencies, vehicle kilometres and origin-destination analyses. It is possible to show the transport generation for specific branches, for different community sizes and different local unit sizes. But the material does not provide statistically safe results for both branch and community size, or local unit size. If disaggregated to this level the uncertainties become too big.

4.2 Questions and analyses

The research question may be formulated, as "are there any relationships between transport generation, traffic work and business structure and localization?"

The question may be divided into three sub-questions; 1 How many transports do companies of different branches and of different sizes generate? 2 How large is the traffic work for companies of different branches and of different sizes? 3 How does localization affect the traffic work?

Enquiry questions   **Results**   **Models**
                         General description   Research questions

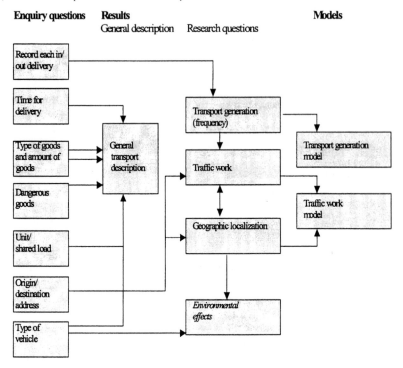

Figure 2:   How the questions in the questionnaire are related to analyses and models.

5 Results

Since this is an on going study, this section will bring you some results from the statistical part of the study. Primarily the presentation consists of results shown in the empirical study, with some remarks but no discussion.

5.1 The commercial and industrial structure

The analyse of the commercial and industrial structure in the 45 communities shows:

a homogeneous branch structure, commerce and industry has the same branch structure independent of community size (figure 3),

a homogeneous size structure, commerce and industry has the same size structure independent of community size (figure 4),

that the proportion of local units within each branch increases with community size. (Every branch has the greatest proportion of local units in the biggest community, and less in the smallest communities (figure 5).

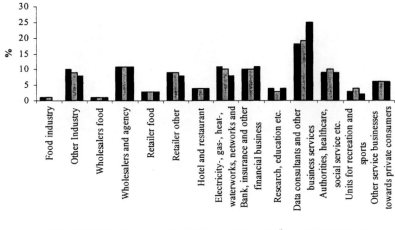

Figure 3: The branch structure is quite similar in communities of different sizes. The retailers, for example, constitute nearly 10 % of the local units independent of community size.

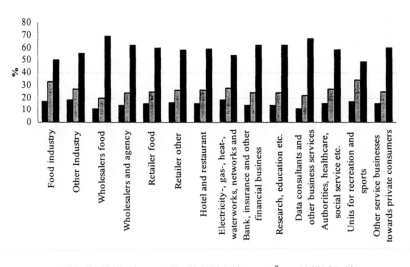

Figure 4: Commerce and industry has the same size structure independent of community size.

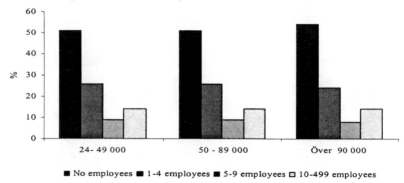

■ No employees ■ 1-4 employees ■ 5-9 employees □ 10-499 employees

Figure 5:   Every branch has the largest proportion of local units in the biggest
             community, and less in the smallest communities.

5.2 Local units without transports

A large proportion of the local units had no transports the week under review.

The largest proportion of local units with no transports was found among the
service branches (figure 6),

The largest proportion of local units with no transports was found among local
units with no employees (figure 7),

The proportion of local units with no transports decreased with increasing
local unit size (table 1),

The proportion of local units with no transports increased with the community
size.

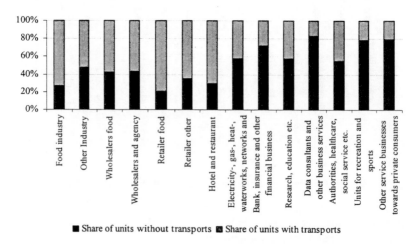

■ Share of units without transports ▨ Share of units with transports

Figure 6:   Share of local units with and without transports presented for various
             branches.

Table 1: Share of local units without transports presented for local unit size.

	Local units witout transports %
No employees	68
1-4 employees	23
5-9 employees	5
10-499 employees	4

5.3 Transport generation

Transport generation depends on branch (figure 7),
Transport generation increases with increasing size of local unit
(figure 8), transport generation does not depend on community size.The transport generation is highest for the industries, the wholesalers and the retailers. In all of these branches the generation is highest for food-related businesses. Transport generation is lowest in what we might call the service branches. (One exception not shown here is hospitals, which usually have a high transport generation, but this is not shown in the figures for health-care because they often have more than 500 employees).

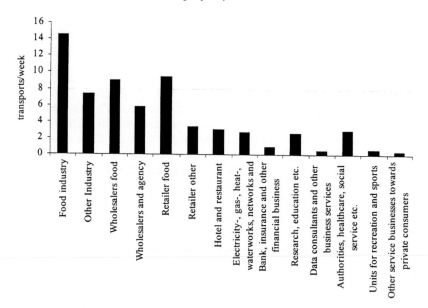

Figure 7. Transport generation in different branches.

Transport generation increases with increasing business size (figure 8, I). This is not surprising, but the small businesses without employees are also the greatest proportion of the businesses (figure 8, II). One consequence of this is that businesses without employees generate more than 20% of the total amount of transports in a community (figure 8, III). The largest companies generate nearly 40% of the transports. This shows that businesses without employees have low generation figures treated singularly, but together they are responsible for a great part of the transports. This is why I included them in the study. They are often excluded, because they have very few transports. But it is just this relationship that makes them interesting.

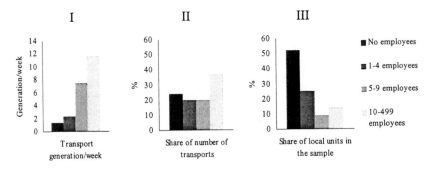

Figure 8. The importance of business without employees.

6 Transport generation model

The transport generation model is built on two sets of data in a GIS data bas: the actual Business Register from which you can outline the local units and the key figures for the transport generation from the empirical study. The model is a tool to analyse transport generation and to simulate how changes in business structure affect the amount and the flow of transports. This model can be used in urban planning with regard to business localization and land use in a specified geographical area, for example a community. By adding the key figures to the actual local units one is provided with a map over the transport generation nodes. If this model is combined with the model for traffic work one may also gain information about transport distances and emissions.

References

[1] Swedish institute for transport and communication analysis (SIKA). *Swedish domestic road goods transport and freight traffic by SJ and MTAB on the railway network in 1999. Final data. Statistical report TK 30 SM 0003.*
[2] Directive 78/546EEG and 89/462/EEG changes in the former.

Mobility Management in Lecco

L. Florio[1], C. De Micheli[2]
[1] *Politecnico di Milano, Italy.*
[2] *Agenzia per la Mobilità, Comune di Milano, Italy*

Abstract

The Province of Lecco has been testing the Public Transport Integrated System since 1998. The System consists in allowing the traveller to move from the public transport by road to that by rail, and vice-versa, bringing about important advantages in the reduction of acoustic and environmental pollution.
The memory reports the results of a survey with the judgements expressed on the quality and effectiveness of the service. As a whole, they are positive and confirm the validity of the technical solutions adopted.
A further important positive effect was reached thanks to the introduction of a Mobility Manager by the Commune and the Region for the commuting planning of the workers.

1 The Public Transport Integrated System in the Province of Lecco

The "municipal transport system in the Lecco area" (Servizio di trasporto metropolitano nell'area lecchese) is based on the fundamental requirements of transport system co-ordination and fare integration.
The passenger having the integrated ticket can travel choosing one mean of transport only, or both systems using both train and bus.
The trains of the F.S. spa were incremented by further trains paid by the Province in order to make the service similar to a subway. The experimental phase was concluded in September 1998. The organisation and planning of bus and train frequency has been improved and it will further be improved in the year 2001.
At first, the new mobility scenario of public transport was not welcomed by the users but, as it often happens, the project consolidation and the habit of using

combined means of transport produced an important rise in the sales of integrated ticket and passes.

The increase in the sales of "integrated ticket" ranged from 34 to 99%, and that of integrated passes from 17 to 40%, according to the lines.

The new system affected 3 railway stations and 13 bus lines.

2 Users survey

The users' judgement (on the base of different questionnaires on the means of transport and at the stop/station of the line interested) was analysed under four different aspects of the service:

1 *quality*   2 *costs*   3 *time to cover the distance*   4 *waiting times.*

The questionnaire is made by twelve pretty easy questions; the one used for busses is enclosed.

Each interviewed user expressed his judgement on the service by qualitative indicators.

The survey was dimensioned using the usual statistic techniques with the simple casual sampling technique (that is all elements of the universe have the same chance to be chosen) and resulted in 1006 interviews.

2.1 Statistical analysis on the judgement on "quality"

The overall complexity of commuting was classified in alternatives, meaning: excellent, good, sufficient, and insufficient. Then, a value was given to each answer (insufficient = 4, sufficient = 6, good = 8, excellent = 10), obtaining following results:

$n_{excellent} = 0$

$n_{good} = = 512$

$n_{sufficient} = 1722$

$n_{insufficient} == 732$

The average of the expressed judgements is equal to:

$\bar{n}_Q = (0+512+732+1722)/534 = 5.5543$

σ

Considering all quality judgements expressed by the sample, variance σ^2, is equal to:

$$\sigma^2 = \frac{\sum_{i=1...n}\left(n_Q^i - \bar{n}_Q\right)^2}{(n-1)} = 1.655$$

2.2 Statistical analysis on the judgement "time required to cover the distance"

The judgement on the time required by the mean of transport to reach the destination was classified as: Insufficient, Fair, Excessive, with following weights:
Insufficient = 8; Fair = 6; Excessive = 4.
The overall number of judgements obtained on the time to cover the distance were:

$n_{insufficient}$= 0
n_{fair} = 1293
$n_{excessive}$= 1276

The average of the expressed judgements is equal to:

$$\overline{n}_{tp} = (0+1293+1276)/534 = 4.807$$

number corresponding to a judgement placed between excessive and fair and, in any case, below "sufficient"
Variance σ^2, calculated among the judgements expressed by the sample on the time to cover the distance is equal to:

$$\sigma^2 = \frac{\sum_{i=1...n}\left(n_{tp}^i - \overline{n}_{tp}\right)^2}{(n-1)} = 0.988$$

2.3 Statistical analysis on the "waiting time for the means of transport"

The waiting time for the mean of transport was classified as follows:

Insufficient = 8, Fair = 6, Excessive = 4

The overall number of judgements was:
$n_{insufficient}$= 64
n_{fair} = 1866
$n_{eccessiv}$= 860

The average of the expressed judgements is equal to:

$$\overline{n}_{ta} = (64+1866+860)/534 = 5.22$$

Variance σ^2, calculated on the judgements expressed by the sample about the waiting time, is equal to:

$$\sigma^2 = \frac{\sum\limits_{i=1...n}\left(n^i_{ta} - \overline{n}_{ta}\right)^2}{(n-1)} = 1.071$$

3 Mobility management

A recent ministerial decree called "Sustainable mobility in urban areas" (1998), orders companies and public bodies with more than 300 workers in each productive unit as well as companies having more than 800 workers as a whole to introduce a "Mobility Manager" to optimise the systematic commuting of workers decreasing the use of private cars by mean of a "commuting plan".
The decree involves many subjects, among which:
Regions: they are required to have a plan for the improvement and the protection of the air quality;
Public Administrations: they are required to include a certain share of electric or not polluting vehicles in their car park (up to 50% in 2003).
Communes
Mobility management strategies can be summarised in persuasion, concession, and restriction strategies.

Persuasion Strategies
They identify information and communication programmes aimed at awaking public opinion to the problem and, as a consequence, at modifying people everyday habits.

Concession Strategies
They consist in new services for citizens, such as initiatives aimed at promoting and improving those systems presently available as well as the possibility to commute using two different means of transport.

Restriction Strategies
They represent already applied measures, such as park and road pricing or limited traffic areas. Those strategies can be implemented only by mean of a methodical involvement and a constant co-operation of all interested subjects (private citizens, companies, Public Administrations). Two professional figures were introduced in Italy: the area mobility manager and the company mobility manager.
The first is aimed at improving mobility within its reference area, reducing the use of private cars and individual mobility.
The latter is aimed at improving the access to the working place discouraging the personal use of private cars in favour of other collective, ecological and motor-free means of transport, and managing the commuting demand of workers (in terms of number of trips and time required/ distance covered).

Those aims can be met by the creation and adoption of a home-work commuting plan. It promotes alternative commuting ways that can be summarised as follows:

Car sharing

The use of a number of cars by private citizens (or companies) paying a fee according to the distance covered and the length of time they use the vehicle. Cars are booked at a call center, and the company managing the service is in charge of all ordinary and extraordinary maintenance of the cars.

Car pooling

Collective use of a vehicle by a group of people travelling along the same route. A call center manages the data bank and organises the group of cars using a specific software. This kind of transport is particularly suitable to the systematic demand that, due to its nature, does not undergo big changes.

Guaranteed ride home

The programme is made up by a set of tools allowing workers using collective means of transport to travel home any time a specific need arises: sudden illness, unforeseen delay, family problem or intermediate stops incompatible with the group needs.

The cars put at workers' disposal are insured by the company or by a taxi or by a public transport co-operation thanks to an agreement with the public transport

Measures for bicycles and scooters

In those areas allowing it, the encouragement to use bikes or scooters can be particularly effective.

In the first case, beyond the presence of bike ways, the company can create simple facilities to solve everyday problems linked to the use of that mean of transport.

Politics of available car parks

Companies are often obliged to provide their offices with car parks for workers only. But if the company has no space to do so, it should think of an optimal use of the areas available.

Incentives for workers

All initiatives part of the commuting plan should take into consideration some incentives in order to obtain a widespread support. Incentives can be of two different types: economic and not economic.

The company mobility manager has to try to change or to eliminate commuting by the decrease of the number of travelling vehicles or by the reduction of cars in the rush hours

Other ways are represented by teleworking (where possible) and the modification of working hours.

Benefits of the home-work commuting plan can be of two types: direct and indirect. In the first case, workers as well as the company have immediate and concrete facilitation. In the latter case, economic and not economic benefits come from the effects of the mobility plan.

4 Mobility management in the town of Lecco

The province of Lecco was highly industrialised in those suburbs strictly linked to the town up to the middle of last century. In the last ten years, this kind of production has led to an important dispersion in the territory both concerning the type of production and the size of all kinds of industries

A survey was carried out by us in different administrations. According to the results, there is only a limited number of private and public companies and industries in the metropolitan area of Lecco that could potentially take part to the project.

But there is a need of a mobility manager to ease the traffic flow still overcrowding Lecco metropolitan area.

This is the reason way it is suggested to acquire information in all public and/or private companies distributing questionnaires to the employees enquiring about:

Number of employees

Origin and destination of systematic commuting of each employee

The mean of transport used for the travel

The time required to cover the whole distance

The possibility of introducing a mobility manager dealing with all the home-work commuting of employees will be analysed in a second phase.

The proposed questionnaire should include information about:

a) Home address

b) Working place with complete address

c) Age and sex;

d) Time schedule: time of departure from home; time of arrival at the working place, time of departure from work and of arrival at home at the end of the working day; in case, specify time of the lunch break (for those who go home for lunch or similar);

e) Means of transport: write the mean of transport used to cover the distance (or the means, if more than one, in the right order). Specify if you drive the mean of transport used or if you are a passenger;

f) Parking: type of parking for those who travel with their own vehicle;

home-work distance;

g) Time required to cover the distance;

h) The reason for the choice of that mean of transport;

i) Judgement on the quality of the trip;

l) Worker's subjective perception of the monthly cost to commute to work.

References

1. Cascetta E. *"Teoria e metodi dell'ingegneria dei sistemi di trasporto"*, *UTET Torino1998*
2. De Luca M. *"Tecnica ed economia dei trasporti"*, *CUEN Napoli 1992*

- **ATTACH**

PROVINCIA DI LECCO	ORIGIN/DESTINATION SURVEY

INTERVIEWS FOR BUSSES

Reserved to the office

Station   : _____   1)_____

Name of Railway line .: _____   2)_____

Time of arrival/departure: _____,_____   3)_____

1   I) ORIGIN/DESTINATION AND REASON FOR THE TRIP

1. Where are you coming from?

Home	1	Tourism	6	
Usual working place	2	Hospital (treatments)	7	
Unusual working place	3	Public Officec	8	
School (student)	4	Station	9	
Shops	5	Personal reasons	10	

2.Place of origin   4) ____
(if possible, write the address)

_____

                                                5) ____

2. 3.Where are you going?

Home	1	Tourism	6	
Usual working place	2	Hospital (treatments)	7	
Unusual working place	3	Public Officec	8	
School (student)	4	Station	9	
Shops	5	Personal reasons	10	

6) ____

4. Destination
(if possible, write the address)

_____

7) ____

II) KNOWLEDGE OF THE INTEGRATED TRANSPORT SYSTEM

5. Do you know the integrated transport system
(bus/train) and do you use it?

He/She knows it: and use it___ doesn't know it___

and doesn't use it___

8) ____

6. Do you know the integrated ticked (one ticket only) and do you use it?

He/She knows it: and use it___ doesn't know it___   9)_____
                     and doesn't use it___

2   III) TRAVELLING MODALITY

**7. Which means of transport have you mainly used
to go to the station**

By foot	
Motorbike/ bike	
Car	
Bus	

10) _____

If the person interviewed uses his/her own vehicle:

7BIS. Where do you park your car/motorbike?
Free parking area __   Parking (not free) __

11) _____

8. How long does it take you to park?
Less than 5 min.__   between 5 and 10 min.__   more than 10 min.__

12) _____

**IV) HOW OFTEN DO YOU TRAVEL IN
A WEEK**

8. How often do you travel along this itinerary in a week? _____

13) _____

V) ECONOMIC EVALUATION

9. In your opinion, the cost of the trip is:
Excessive__   Fair__   Insufficient__

14) _____

VI) TIME REQUIRED TO COVER THE DISTANCE

10. In your opinion, the time required for your trip is :
Excessive___   Fair ___   Insufficient ___

15) _____

VII) WAITING TIME

11. The waiting time for the train is:
Excessive___ Fair ___   Insufficient ___

16) _____

VIII) SERVICE QUALITY

12. In your opinion, the quality of the service offered is:
Insufficient   __
Sufficient   __
Good   __
Excellent   __

17) _____

Section 2:
Urban transport systems

City distribution by railways?
A feasibility study of the city Graz

J.H.R. van Duin
Transport Policy and Logistics' Organisation,
Faculty of Technology, Policy and Management,
Delft University of Technology, The Netherlands

Abstract

The city of Graz in Austria is a semi large city (237.000 inhabitants) with an historical city centre with many small streets. The delivery of goods is not always without problems, and the predicted increase of freight transport within and around the city, gives reason to believe, that the delivery problems will increase in the near future. For this reason, the building of a freight transport centre in the south of Graz was initiated. The goal of this research is to find a rail transport option competitive with truck transport possible for a small amount of goods. In order to meet the punctuality constraints and the localisation of goods during transport possible, it is decided to use fifty boxes for the transport of the goods. These boxes are half as big as a standardised 20 ft container without making compromises in any service quality. Also the actual transport by train has to be as flexible as possible. Therefore the CargoSprinter is chosen for the transport between Werndorf and the Stations in Graz. This train is made for transport on short distances and can be coupled and uncoupled extremely quickly. The second step is the selection of train stations in Graz, suitable for transport and handling of fifty boxes. The third step consists of the calculation of competitiveness of the proposed transport type, using 32 different price scenarios. In the fourth step, the best price scenarios are tested on the actor preferences, because a transport system can only be successful when the actors support it. This feasibility study has shown that the intermodal transport option is not (yet) supported by the actors and is, therefore, not (yet!) a good transport alternative for unimodal transport.

1. Introduction

The city of Graz is a semi large city (237.000 inhabitants) in Austria with a historical city centre with many small streets. The delivery of goods is not always without problems, and the predicted increase of freight transport within and around city, give reason to believe that the delivery problems will increase in near future. These problem situations for freight delivery exist in many cities [1]. In Austria, not only road transport has increased during the last years, also rail transport increased substantially. For this reason, the building of a freight transport centre in the south of Graz (in Wendorf) was initiated. This freight transport centre is called GVZ-Wendorf (GueterVereinZentrum) and forms the basis of investigation in this paper.

Currently rail freight is transported into the city of Graz and is handled there. When the new freight terminal is put into use, the freight flows with destination Graz will not longer be unloaded in the city. This means that transport between the freight terminal and the city of Graz will be necessary. In order to prevent this transport to become all-truck-transport, the regional government of Styria is looking for alternative transport possibilities between the freight terminal and the city of Graz. The predicted increase of freight transport within the entire province of Styria makes the regional government is willing to find solutions that bring more freight on the rail in the entire region. A solution for the transport problem in Graz must fit in this plan and is therefore preferably a solution which includes rail transport. Although the regional government is not unwilling to provide subsidies for a good alternative, one of the most important demands is the competitiveness of the new transport alternative.

Therefore the aim of this study was to find a new transport option that makes competitiveness with truck transport possible for a small amount of goods that are transported between the terminal Werndorf and the city of Graz without making compromises in service quality.

2. Locations & Logistic concept

To choose for an intermodal final delivery it must be taken into account that the total transport distance is very short. If all stations in travel are supplied, the total transport distance does not even sum-up to a distance of 25 kilometres. Generally it is assumed that unimodal railtransport is only competitive for distances over 100 kilometres [2][3]. Another problem in the case of using railways is the need for switching and shunting activities. If goods up to station are transported by rail, at the stations transhipment of these goods is necessarily. This means that not only that transhipment vehicle/loading equipment has to be present, but also that sufficient loading area must be present.

2.1   Description of the stations

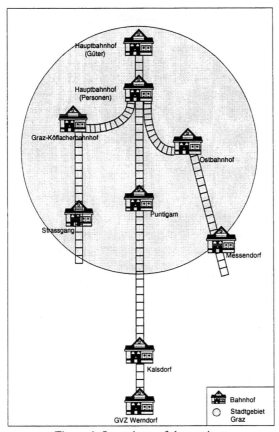

Figure 1: Locations of the stations

The station Kalsdorf is mainly a goods station, where containers and long trains load and unload. In addition is present storage space for containers. There is also a possibility to load crushed stones in railroad cars. Because no loading area for other transhipments is present, in principle this station is not very suitable for transhipment. However this station is closest located to Danzas. Danzas is a large transport company, that only transports by truck and considers in the future also intermodal transportation in direction Graz. If Danzas really brings its ideas for intermodal transport to execution, they must invest in addition in to change of the station Kalsdorf. Station Puntigam is a small station mainly created for transportation of passengers. Although also goods trains can hold here, no transhipment infrastructure as well as loading area is present. In the direct environment no possibilities such a stocks possibility are to be built. In further analysis this station is not regarded. Main station persons (HBFp) the main station is distributed into two section stations, whereby the HBFp is particularly equipped for passenger traffic. This station cannot be used thus for the transhipment of goods. In the study it is still important due to it's central position and all tracks are connected to this station. Main station of goods (HBFg) is the second station and is equipped for interconnection of tracks and the transhipment of goods. The station has several loading areas, which border usually directly at business or wholesale stocks. This station is very well suitable for the intermodal transport. The HBFg is included into further analyses. Graz Koeflacherbahnhof (GKB) is a mixed person and goods station. The station has no possibility for transhipment of goods, but the direct environment has a very useful loading area. However, more important to the usable loading area is the fact that the owner of this station, the Graz Koeflacher Railways (GKE) assured to be interested in the intermodal fine transport of the GVZ.

Additionally it would be necessary to use push-locomotives and to make brake tests for each attached railroad car. This process would cost much time and would make the fee too expensive. It was therefore decided to drive with a fixed course configuration. In this study on a relatively short course, consisting of one locomotive and ten railroad cars. This course is after fixed timetable six days per week to be driven and due to the business and shopping also on Saturday. Envelope of goods between course and truck will take place on existing stations in Graz. Altogether, it counts the city six stations about which four are in property of Austrian federal courses (OEBB) and two of the Graz Koeflacher Railways (GKE), a private company, who owns rails, stations and rail-mounted vehicles. The local conditions on the tracks determine the next fulfilment's in the logistic concept:

- Twice a day a turnaround trip by train;
- From GVZ Werndorf to Kalsdorf, to Graz-Koflacher station, to the main station, to Ostbahnhof;
- 15 minutes waiting times on every station, except the GVZ with a waiting time of 20 minutes;
- Arrival at Ostbanhof at latest at 2.00 am and 16:00 pm.;
- A trucking company drives with dedicated vehicles in three shifts;
- First and third shift will use cityboxes, second shift for own purposes;
- At the start minimal usage of 1 or 2 trucks;
- Combining routes between stations, shops and producers;
- Opportunity for pickup of citybox outside the normal delivery times.

2.2   Transport Vehicle: the Cargo Sprinter

Figure 2: Cargo Sprinter (source:Windhoff AG Online, 2001)

Due to the flexible requirements needed in this project there is chosen for the CargoSprinter. The CargoSprinter is a railcar featuring characteristics with regard to design and technology that are much related to a truck. For this reason, it is often called the truck on rail, combining the benefits of a fast, relatively cost effective and flexible means of transport. One transport unit can convey up to ten interchangeable containers respectively containers with a length of 7.8 m and 16 tons individual weight. The coupling is done within a few minutes by means of the automatic train coupling and non-contact data and energy transmission. In fact, each CargoSprinter unit is self-supporting, but within three minutes can be combined to a container train formation of up to seven units. At common target positions, the individual units are separated or combined to new formations.

In comparison with a truck the Cargo Sprinter features the same transporting capacity as five trucks, but requires one driver only. The speed of the train can be 120 km/h the CargoSprinter is considerably faster than the truck. In summary, Cargo Sprinters are high speed, high frequency distribution trains with a loading capacity of 26 TEU's.

2.3   Loading unit: The fifty box

The container must have good facilities to be transported on both transport systems. The transhipment must be easily both on train and truck and should be based on traditional transhipment equipment. The truck needs 4 extra twist-locks to load both containers. The box can be opened at two sites. This is very convenient when the boxes are stacked into the town in front of the shops.

The Fifty-box is as the name of the container almost describes the half of a 20-FT container.

Table 1: Characteristics of the Fiftybox S-LB380.

Length (inside)	3620 mm
Width (inside	2480 mm
Height (inside)	2800 mm
Weight	1.9 ton
Loading weight	6.1 ton
Total Weight	8.0 ton
Number of Euro-pallets	9
Max. Stack weight	5.5 ton

3.   Cost calculations

3.1   Assumptions

Starting point for the calculations are a demand of 40 Fifty-boxes to be transported. This implies two CargoSprinters. In the calculations the CargoSprinters are connected. The origin of the freight demand has been determined from Danzas and GVS Wendorf. Per trip about 10 containers come from Danzas and 30 containers come from GVS Wendorf. The frequency of the trains will be twice a day. The city of Graz has been divided into 15 regions. Each delivery is assumed to be delivered in the centre of the region. The 30 containers from GVZ Werndorf will be equally divided among the 15 regions. The 10 containers from Danzas will be divided among the regions closest to the centre. For the calculations some cost variants have been identified. One cost variant situation varies between trips with and without return loads. The return transport is the same only the difference is the opposite direction. For the cost calculations also the empty kilometres are counted in the total sum. Another cost alternative is the difference between a fixed price (based on a trip of 9 kilometres) and real costs. Also a distinction was made for calculations order-based and contract-based. For contract based transport a discount can be expected of 20%. Another alternative is the case that one truck transports two boxes and the situation that one truck caries four boxes. Also variants have been calculated for different values for the transhipment price. Calculations have been made with a price of 15€ and with a 20% discount price of 12€.

Table 2: Prices for unimodal Transport

Weight per load	15 Tons
Price for direct transport	0,65 €/Kilometre
Minimum price	6,36 €
Extra per Stop	31,77 €
Tariff per hour	31,77 €

Table 3: Calculation of intermodal Tariff without contract discount

Price groups	Week tariff	Evening tariff	Weekend tariff	**Intermodal tariff**
Price for direct transport (€/km.)	0,65	0,81	0,98	**0,81**
Minimum price (€)	6,36	07,95	09,54	**07,95**
Extra per stop (€)	31,77	39,71	47,66	**39,71**
Tariff per hour (€)	31,77	39,71	47,66	**29,71**

3.2 Costs comparison

Table 4: Cost results (one way in Euro's)

Alter native	Total costs	Truck costs	Truck costs/box	Tranship-ment costs	Train costs	Train costs/box	Difference
UNI	**2822,27**	**2822.27**	**70,56**	**0**	**0**	**0**	
1	3174,51	1883,84	47,10	600	690,67	17,27	-352,24
2	3054,51	1883,84	47,10	480	690,67	17,27	-232,24
3	4073,88	2783,21	68,58	600	690,67	17,27	-1251,60
4	3953,88	2783,21	68,58	480	690,67	17,27	-1131,60
5	**2797,74**	**1507,07**	**37,68**	**600**	**690,67**	**17,27**	**24,53**
6	**2677,74**	**1507,07**	**37,68**	**480**	**690,67**	**17,27**	**144,53**
7	3517,24	2226,57	55,66	600	690,67	17,27	-694,96
8	3397,24	2226,57	55,66	480	690,67	17,27	-574,96
9	3174,51	1883,84	47,10	600	690,67	17,27	-352,24
10	3054,51	1883,84	47,10	480	690,67	17,27	-232,24
11	4018,13	2727,46	68,19	600	690,67	17,27	-1195,86
12	3898,13	2727,46	68,19	480	690,67	17,27	-1075,86
13	**2797,74**	**1507,07**	**37,68**	**600**	**690,67**	**17,27**	**24,53**
14	**2677,74**	**1507,07**	**37,68**	**480**	**690,67**	**17,27**	**144,53**
15	3472,64	2181,97	54,55	600	690,67	17,27	-650,37
16	3352,64	2181,97	54,55	480	690,67	17,27	-530,37

Description:
1 = Fixed Price, transport order> 40 boxes, transhipment price 15
2 = Fixed Price, transport order> 40 boxes, transhipment price 12
3 = Fixed Price, transport order> 2 boxes, transhipment price 15
4 = Fixed Price, transport order> 2 boxes, transhipment price 12
5 = Fixed Price –20%, transport order> 40 boxes, transhipment price 15
6 = Fixed Price – 20%, transport order> 40 boxes, transhipment price 12
7 = Fixed Price –20%, transport order> 2 boxes, transhipment price 15
8 = Fixed Price –20%, transport order> 2 boxes, transhipment price 12
9 = Real Costs, transport order> 40 boxes, transhipment price 15
10 = Real Costs, transport order> 40 boxes, transhipment price 12
11 = Real costs, transport order> 2 boxes, transhipment price 15
12 = Real costs, transport order> 2 boxes, transhipment price 12
13 = Real costs –20%, transport order> 40 boxes, transhipment price 15
14 = Real costs – 20%, transport order> 40 boxes, transhipment price 12
15 = Real costs –20%, transport order> 2 boxes, transhipment price 15
16 = Real costs –20%, transport order> 2 boxes, transhipment price 12

From table 4 we can derive that only four from the 16 alternatives are competitive if no subsidies are given. Especially the alternatives 5,6 13 and 14 show these results. Interesting to observe is that even with a transhipment price of 15€ a competitive alternative can be find. It is also interesting to observe that a transport demand of 40 Fifty boxes make no difference between a fixed price fee and a price based on real costs. Other important fact is that without a price reduction for truck delivery no competitive alternative can be found.

The same calculations have been carried out for trips with return loads. The results are described in table 5.

Table 5 Cost results with return loads (in Euro's)

Alter native	Total costs	Truck costs	Truck costs/box	Tranship-ment costs	Train costs	Train costs/box	Difference
UNI	**3540,39**	**3540,39**	**44,25**	**0**	**0**	**0**	
1	4726,85	2836,18	35,45	1200	690,67	8,63	-1186,46
2	4486,85	2836,18	35,45	960	690,67	8,63	-946,46
3	5416,23	3525,56	44,07	1200	690,67	8,63	-1875,84
4	5176,23	3525,56	44,07	960	690,67	8,63	-1635,84
5	4159,61	2268,94	28,36	1200	690,67	8,63	-619,22
6	3919,61	2268,94	28,36	960	690,67	8,63	-379,22
7	4793,71	2903,04	36,29	1200	690,67	8,63	-1253,32
8	4553,71	2903,04	36,29	960	690,67	8,63	-1013,32
9	4726,85	2836,18	35,45	1200	690,67	8,63	-1186,46
10	4486,85	2836,18	35,45	960	690,67	8,63	-946,46
11	5388,62	3497,95	43,72	1200	690,67	8,63	-1848,23
12	5148,62	3497,95	43,72	960	690,67	8,63	-1608,23
13	4159,61	2268,94	28,36	1200	690,67	8,63	-619,22
14	3919,61	2268,94	28,36	960	690,67	8,63	-379,22
15	4771,63	2880,96	36,01	1200	690,67	8,63	-1231,24
16	4531,63	2880,96	36,01	960	690,67	8,63	-991,24

Contrary to our expectations that return loads should have a cost-efficient-effect, we can derive from this table that no competitive alternatives can be found unless artificial cost reductions will be applied. Reason for this irrationality is the relatively high trucking price as an element of the costs.

4.   Conclusions

In the study for the city of Graz we have been able to identify an intermodal transport service which can be competitive towards unimodal transportation. The conditions to the price setting of 2,9€ extra per Fiftybox must be financed with subsidies. It is exactly this reason that actors involved have doubts about the economic viability of this concept. All conditions must be met and all the transport demands in the 15 regions have to choose for this specific alternative. In practice this will be very hard to realise.

On the other hand we have learned in this study that we are able to provide more quantitative information about the economic viability with raising some simple assumptions about prices and related these prices to prices which are current practice in other fields. With sensitivity on the costs-parameters we have been able to identify the economical bandwidth of the concept.

Based on this insight the conclusion has been drawn that an intermodal transportation service is not yet a feasible solution for the future delivery of freight in the city of Graz.

Acknowledgement
I herewith thank Marit van der Zee for her master thesis work (e.g. Zee[4]) in which she made a detailed feasibility about the intemodal alternative for the city Graz.

References

[1]   E.Taniguchi, R.G.Thompson, T.Yamada, J.H.R van Duin, *'City Logistics: Network modelling and Intelligent Transport Systems'* , Elsevier Science, Pergamon, pag 260, ISBN 0-08-043903-9, January 2001

[2]   Deutsche Verkehrszeitung nr 122, *'Mehorn: LKW bis 150 km besser'*, 12. October 2000

[3]   Deutsche Verkehrszeitung nr 124, *'Alle Gueter auf die Bahn?'*, 17. October 2000

[4]   Zee, M.M. van der, 'Intemodaler Nachtransport in Graz – Chance oder Utopie', Faculty Technology, Policy and Management, Delft University of Technology, April 2001

A city and a transport system for a mutual enrichment

P. Vuaillat, D. Bouchet & J.-P. Berger
SEMALY, France

Abstract

Recent experiences in European cities and, increasingly, even on the other side of the Atlantic (Portland, Dallas, Sacramento, etc.) where, the joyfulness of the streets does not have the same meaning as in the Old World, have shown that the success of a transport project cannot be dissociated from the re-conquering of public space to the advantage of pedestrians. In middle sized cities, where travelling times are comparatively short, the amount of walking in an individual journey chain (arrival walk – transportation – final walk) is as important as the time spent on public transport itself. Travelling on public transport can thus be a time for pedestrians to sit back and relax, between two "arrival walks". Willing users of public transport become city-walking enthusiasts, people who love strolling around. This "quality of life", which increasing numbers of city-dwellers are seeking, does not arrive on a plate. It has to be conquered and the enjoyable journeys it offers you will be your reward. Even sceptics will be won over. They will acquire a taste for the enjoyment to be found. Now the two components which make this travel chain so attractive are both complementary and interactive. The new lay-out of public places (streets, squares and places for social interaction), as part of a modern public transport project, affects the speed and comfort of the form of transport itself (a key factor in its attractiveness) as well as the quality of station accessibility (another key factor). In other words, we would have little chance of attracting (and keeping) customers on urban public transport by creating a remarkable and rapid fixed link through areas which are "inhospitable" to pedestrians (car saturation, uncomfortable and inaccessible stations, poor connections etc.). Conversely, we would have no more success in restricting ourselves to designing high quality public spaces without an efficient transport system to accompany them. In urban public transport the attractiveness of the environment and operational efficiency are not mutually exclusive - each is a guarantee of the others quality.

1 A short history

The urbanisation of Europe during the 19th century was concomitant with the development of the means of communication, and especially tramways, which at that time often represented practically the only means of getting around. Commercial and social activities were essentially local and tramways acted as a link between districts shortening the increasingly long distances that had to be travelled. All the major thoroughfares were criss-crossed by trams and at the end of the century the largest towns were constructing underground railways.

After the Second World War, the development of road infrastructure systems favoured out-of-town areas. The population often preferred to abandon the town centre making the town mainly a place of interchange rather than a place to live. People only went there (and to a certain extend, continue to go there) for the day by car or inter-city trains which gradually turned in to commuter trains. Many European towns then abandoned their tramways to make room for cars and buses or the creation of an underground railway. This phenomenon took place to the detriment of urban life further strengthening the attraction of out-of-town areas.

Towns lost their souls, because what is a town? A human community that tends to live all its activities (social, family, professional, etc.) in space that is both unique and multiform.

From the early 80s, which marked the move from the industrial era to the services era, there was a resurgence of interest in the quality of urban life especially in France, and now increasingly abroad. This policy of upgrading town centres is based on deliberations about means of transport and in particular a relevant public transportation policy.

Today, the development of public transportation systems (notably tramways in many French towns) is an important revitalisation tool for many medium-sized towns just like it was in the 19th century for the development of the same towns during the industrialisation era.

2 Breaking the geographical and social barriers

2.1 The requirement for an urban transport plan which is coherent and non-exclusive

The car is, and will always be, the predominant means of transport in our western societies. For example, 90% of the French population in medium-sized towns have the use of a car and this percentage does not fall below 64% even in the Parisian urban area with the largest public transportation system in France.

However, the car is both the source of a nuisance for inhabitants living on main roads and the cause of traffic jams which penalise its users. Moreover, there is still a fringe of the population who do not have the use of a vehicle either permanently or occasionally and who are therefore dependant on other means of transport. Finally, it is generally agreed reducing the use of cars in towns and developing alternative means of transport contributes to an improvement in the life of citizens.

An opinion poll recently carried out in France shows that 72% of citizens think that the use of cars must be limited to improve traffic circulation in towns. In addition, policy managers are trying to combine and optimise the use of the various means of transport.

In France it is compulsory by law (Lepage Law) for towns with a population in excess of 100,000 to draw up an "Urban Transport Plan" from the standpoint reducing the car's nuisance value. The aim of the UPD is to enable everyone to travel around in the best conditions possible. It must describe the planning and operation concepts which must be implemented in order to:

- Promote travel within urban areas via a variety of less-polluting means of transport
- Reduce private automobile traffic and modify the management of parking by offering an alternative through the setting-up of park-and-ride facilities.
- Increase the capacity for transport by two-wheel vehicles on safe routes.
- Allow town-dwellers to re- conquest public space.

The assurance of having an Urban Transport Plan in harmony with city development incorporates concerns not to exclude any means of transport whether it is a question of pedestrians, cars or even bicycles, taxis, public transportation or the transport of goods. In addition, it must not exclude any geographic zones and must guarantee perfect traffic circulation throughout the entire town. No social stratum must be excluded by giving preference to one means of transport above another.

From this viewpoint, Public transportation network is naturally the main component thanks to the choice of the various systems and their routes.

2.2 Public transportation: a social bridge and a factor in social mixing

The charm of a town still lays in its diversity. Through the centuries new quarters have often been added to towns which have subsequently evolved with time and whose social characteristics have gradually been asserted. Social differentiation influences not only geographical zones but also the choice (sometimes imposed for economic reasons) of the means of transport used on a day-to-day basis.

To equip a town with an efficient and comfortable Public transportation network is to unite its social components. If the services offered by the public transportation network run at suitable times, workers will choose them to go to the factory at daybreak and the night watchmen for returning home late at night. Office workers and executives attracted by the offer of fast public transport during rush will leave their cars in the garage. Students readily choose more "sporty" means of transport such as the bicycle or at the moment roller-blades, but they remain reliant on public transportation network. For them, public transportation network is not only the only means of transport for getting to the campus but also for going out to have fun in the recreational districts of the town. If ease-of-access is guaranteed, pensioners, who have less agility to drive a private car, will choose to use public transportation for going to see their doctor or attend hospital.

This convergence of the interests of all social classes makes public transport not only a subject of interest and dialogue involving the whole population, but also the archetypal Public Place, the Agora of modern times, sometimes competing with the street itself.

It is interesting to note that during the coldest part of winter in Montreal, the underground railway replaces the street which has become inhospitable for pedestrians. An underground life besieges the shops that line the underground's corridors. Many towns combine inter-modal transport centres with the development of shopping centres or popular entertainment facilities.

2.3 Public transportation network as "Ariadne's thread" running through the town

The often chaotic growth of many towns and the rapid metamorphosis of some areas has tended to transform them into a veritable patchwork some of whose parts have become unconnected. The public transport system allows them to be efficiently reunited.

An underground railway line enables the main centres of activity to be rapidly linked and organises them by favouring interchange between them by overcoming the urban constraints and physical obstacles. It bolsters the economic activity around the stations.

A tramway line allows an intermediate service which is closer to the population and organises human activity into a "rosary" along the length of its route by stimulating synergies between the "beads".

Buses allow a local service which facilitates the connection of the most enclaved areas to busy transport routes or acts as a link between quarters with low interchange.

Obviously smaller towns will bring these three functions in to play thanks to different bus models and by building well-thought dedicated rights-of-way or even by constructing tramway lines for their busiest routes.

3 Strengthening the town's economic role

3.1 The town as an interchange for a web of intercity public transportation

The end of the last century experienced a spectacular increase in the number of intercity journeys involving all means of transport.
- Coaches travelling on a motorway network, and regional coaches.
- Regional and national trains or high-speed trains,
- Planes with ever larger airports, and which are themselves "aerial hubs".

For some of us, these intercity trips, which used to be sporadic, have sometimes become daily events.

The economic development of modern towns must be achieved via significant integration of this meshwork which exceeds the local or national level and which is often international, particularly in Europe with the development of European Regional capitals. This meshwork only has sense and is totally beneficial for the town if it is intimately interconnected with its public transport systems especially since intercity travellers are captive customers for public transportation.

By their design, interchange centres must incorporate functionality for the passengers and expandability for the operator. Similarly, their location on the system's busy lines is crucial.

3.2 Facilitating the transfer of out-of-town car drivers to public transport

The development of out-of-town areas has greatly favoured the development of the car, making commuters the main factor in the saturation of town centres. In order to restrict car use, it is important to make switching from one means of transport to another easy, and make connections. This means:
- Setting-up park-and-ride facilities on major roads, with well-indicated and easy access for motorists.
- It must be quick and simple to move between the car parking facilities and the boarding points for the different means of transport.
- Ensure a property or construction reserve that allows a rapid increase in the number of places so as to always be ahead of the increase in patronage.
- An attractive and reassuring architectural design that blends in with the surrounding environment.

More often than not, the construction of such centres is an opportunity to dynamise deserted out-of-town areas.

3.3 Facilitate travel between centres of economic activity

New service activities have a preference for the town centre. New industrial activities only set up in open out-of-town spaces. The development of railway interchanges or airport zones also generate centres of economic activities.

These centres, which are established in a variety of locations, need to be able to interchange, communicate with and transport the personnel necessary for their operation.

3.4 Create new zones attractive to property investors

As already demonstrated in the case of park-and –ride facilities or multi-modal interchanges, activity connected with transport systems generates economic activity. In addition, we have observed that the put in place of an extensive public transportation system in areas that need revitalising makes it easier to attract private investment in property. For instance, during the construction of line D of the underground railway in Lyon (France) 50% of the building permit applications lodged with the town hall concerned constructions to be built along the length of this line. The same phenomenon was observed a few years later during the construction of the tramway line.

4 Putting a human face on the town and its quarters

4.1 Enhancing life and interchange spaces

A town always has places or buildings whose architectural or historical value contribute to give a meaning to the built-up environment and urban life. Its inhabitants bring a culture that is their own and which must be recognised. Heritage and culture must therefore construct the social bonds.

The large-scale projects involved in the construction of transport infrastructures can have a catalytic action facilitating the implementation of urban improvement processes and consequently making a significant contribution to the self-fulfilment of the inhabitants and the pleasure of visitors.

Furthermore, this improvement in the architectural heritage must not be restricted to outstanding landmarks; it must also include the "ordinary" urban buildings. Outstanding heritage exists thanks to the link formed by the "public transportation line" with the day-to-day pieces of architecture. The variety of styles created as time goes by and dispersed in space will then be revealed.

4.2 Redistribute public space and give it back to pedestrians and residents

A recent opinion poll carried out on French residents about their perception of towns showed that the negative points are:

Traffic problems,
* Parking,
* The collapse of law and order
* Air and noise pollution.

On the other hand, the positive points are:
* Commercial dynamism,
* Cultural activities'
* Town architecture and the pleasure of taking a stroll.

The majority would also like the following improvements:
* Provision of protected ways for pedestrians and cyclists,
* Development of local green spaces,
* Easy parking,
* Efficient public transport.

Consequently, we can clearly understand that these improvements will be achieved by a more rational use of public space and a better repartition between its various uses.

The construction of dedicated rights-of-way does not mean a proportional reduction in the volume of car traffic flows. On the contrary, it presents an opportunity to deal with bottlenecks and optimise parking. In addition, the exercise makes it possible to identify and free up superfluous spaces unused for road and public transport systems for the benefit of pedestrians, green spaces or commercial or street activities.

Even if the construction of an underground railway does not have the same impact on public space, it nevertheless allows the layout of the town around the stations to be organised differently.

4.3 Make public transport more accessible, pleasant and secure

The synergy between the town and Transport operates through a balance mainly between the car and public transportation. But no coercive measures can be reasonably employed to impose this balance. It is better to ensure public transport itself is more attractive in the eyes of the public.

Whereas previously we have mainly spoken about what transport systems bring for towns, we are now going to talk about the need for progress that towns and their residents impose on decision makers and managers working for Public Transport systems, and we cannot help noticing that there is an increasing number of requirements that must be satisfied in a number of areas.

Accessible transport: all categories of the population expect to have easy access. Which supposes that the specific limitations of the various categories of users are integrated during the design phase of transport systems, including especially, people with reduced mobility, the visually impaired and children.

This is achieved:

- In the case of underground railways; by a systematisation of the installation of lifts and escalators and laying out platforms to guarantee their safety,
- In the case of carriages and buses; by designing interiors which make room for wheelchairs and pushchairs, and the consequent addition of suitably sized access doors.
- In the case of tram platforms and bus shelters; by clear accessibility, good protection from environmental conditions as well as suitable signing.

A quality of service which must be regular, frequent, fast, secure and safe
Urban transport must be ecological.
Finally, faced with the financial constraints that towns are confronted with, *it must demonstrate that it is ever more economical* with public money and prove that it is managed efficiently.

All these constraints imposed by the urban environment on players involved in transport (operators, designers, manufactures, organising authorities and legislators) are just so many challenges which contribute to making the economic sector a driving force for technological innovation and a vector for the development of local employment.

5 Assert the town's visual identity

Like London's red bus, San Francisco's cable car and Venice's Vaporetto, the means of public transport which dominates a town often becomes its symbol. Each mode of transport conveys a strong image within itself.

A strong and unique image for the whole public transportation network contributes significantly to the definition of the image for the entire town. In many cases the public transportation network is the first point of contact that a tourist or business traveller has with a town (other than the taxi driver). In fact, not only is he a captive passenger, on his return, and through a variety of ways (stories, photos, etc.), he will be the bearer of the town's image as seen while travelling around on the public transportation system.

This visual coherence is achieved for a network by:

- Identical colours and logos used on all the vehicles,
- Identical signing and symbol furniture (shelters, passenger-information media, benches and litter bins) throughout the network.

It also achieved through the quality of service and especially its cleanness, safety and reliability.

However, besides the network's general image, the technical choices made for the various means of transport do themselves contribute individually to strengthen the town's image.

The underground railway conveys an image of technology and economic power if it is modern, clean and spacious, especially if it is entirely automatic.

The tram is seen and allows the town to be seen. The tram has lost its old-fashioned image and now, thanks to the incorporation of the latest technologies into its design, brings modernity to the town.

As for its comfort and internal layout, the design of which encourages the occupants to look at the passing townscape, the passenger almost feels the pleasure of a walker rediscovering his town. The improvements brought to the trackside developments along the length of the line act as a boost to this pleasure. This means of transport has become synonymous with a clean and pleasant town.

The creation of a dedicated right-of-way (tram or bus) provides an excellent opportunity to give the town a new look by linking it to projects for the redevelopment of the public space.

6 Conclusion

I hope that my account will have shown how much public transportation influences towns and the extent to which towns impose challenges to innovate, manage and adapt on the players involved in transport systems. As an independent engineering company specialised in this sector, Semaly is proud to be an active player in many town's throughout the world and not only in Lyon where it is based. Everywhere, the challenges imposed on Semaly by towns are a source of passion and satisfaction for the company, whether it involves giving advice to its customers or carrying out projects for which it is responsible for the design and management of the construction. We deliver all the major public transportation infrastructure projects because first we learn to like the towns that that we are working with.

Some approaches on checkpoint dial-a-ride problems

A. Pratelli
Department of Civil Engineering "Vie e Trasporti"
University of Pisa, Italy

Abstract

The aim of this paper is to present some modelling approaches related to a special form of advanced public transport operations and called with different names such as route deviation line, point deviation bus line, corridor deviation line and checkpoint dial-a-ride. A checkpoint dial-a-ride transit system combines characteristics both of traditional fixed route transit and of advanced door-to-door dial-a-ride service. It resembles fixed route operations because some users have to walk to and from at a finite number of stops located on a corridor and always visited. The checkpoint dial-a-ride system also resembles a door-to-door service because some users are picked up and dropped on demand at another finite number of special stops, called deviated stops or checkpoints, located near their trip ends. Such checkpoints are the main elements of a route deviation bus operations, which accepts user demands and, by communicating with a central control unit, makes the bus deviate from its regular route to serve the off-fixed-line request and then return on the regular route. Route deviation bus systems has been proposed and applied in several countries in order to enhance effectiveness of urban transit during off-peak periods, as well-suited service for small cities or as part of a larger integrated transit system. Nevertheless, mathematical modelling of problems associated to route deviation bus systems has received few research contributions. In this paper we describe some of the most recent mathematical approaches to the deviation bus route design problem.

1 Introduction

In the family of paratransit a special range is covered by the so-called *checkpoint dial-a-ride* systems, also known as *route deviation* systems, or *corridor many-to-*

one systems. Such systems are based on information technology to improve transit operation and are intended to serve areas with demand densities too high for door-to-door services but not high enough for fixed route service.

A checkpoint dial-a-ride system is a mix of fixed route transit characteristics and door-to-door dial-a-ride transit characteristics. Such as in a door-to-door system the passengers may be picked up and dropped on demand at a finite number of special locations near their trip ends, called checkpoints or deviate stops, which are located outside the main, or regular, route and activated only on demand. When a deviate stop is activated, the bus leaves the main route at the closest "detour point", serves the deviate stop and finally takes the main line again. Such as in a fixed route system the users have to walk to and from the stops; and if demand is fairly low at all deviate stops, vehicles may operates almost as if on a line-haul operation mode. Each bus considers all the checkpoints in the same sequence and visits a deviate stop either if a passenger wishes to alight or a user is waiting for pickup there. If a deviate stop doesn't need a visit, it will be simply skipped and the bus route doesn't vary from the main path. Figure 1 displays a scheme of a part of a route deviation bus line.

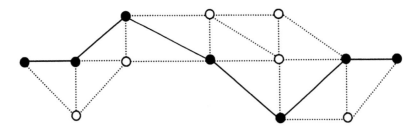

Figure 1: Scheme of a route deviation line: • scheduled operation of stops; o on demand stops; ____ main route; ...... alternative/variable route.

The *equipped* deviate stop is one of the main elements of a checkpoint dial-a-ride system which accepts user demands and, by communicating with an operation centre, makes the bus deviate from its regular route. The user interface at a deviate stop is a graphic screen, usually LCD display, plus few functional keys leading the user in his call choice and giving also to him information on the expected time of passage of next bus, other lines of the urban service and so on. After reading the time of passage on the screen, the passenger inserts coins or a smart card and confirm the subscription. The operation centre control system stores the booklet, actives the closest "detour point" and informs the driver of the on-coming bus of the need to proper deviation. When the bus reaches the deviated stop, data are reset in the control system.

Checkpoint dial-a-ride bus operation systems have been proposed and applied in order to enhance effectiveness and efficiency of urban transit during off-peak periods, as well-suited service for small cities or imbedded in larger integrated transit systems [1,2]. Nevertheless, the number of practical applications was not followed with a parallel modelling development, and only in the last decade few specific theoretical works have appeared in literature.

In the following sections, we intend to review three of the most recent contributions, each of them dealing with a different approach to the route deviation bus problem. Because of the large size and the high degree of heterogeneity that characterizes all reviewed models, we have opted for a brief textual description. Conclusions and insights for further research are presented in the closure.

2 The analytical approach

An analytical model was developed by Daganzo [3] in order to compare checkpoints dial-a-ride cost effectiveness to that of fixed route with no transfer and door-to-door dial-a-ride. The results are derived for a simple case, and involve some large simplifications, as is typical of the analytical approach. Urban areas with heterogeneous spatial characteristics are analyzed by supposing their internal characteristics (e.g., vehicle speeds, demand densities) as being approximately homogeneous. The main following assumptions are used in modelling the checkpoint dial-a-ride system:

(a) the service area is covered with a swath of width w and length L;
(b) buses travel at constant speed v;
(c) the tours are routed on the rectangular street network;
(d) the demand density λ, in passenger per unit time and unit area, is uniform and H is the buses dispatched headway, while the average wait equals $H/2$;
(e) buses operate on pre-set schedules with flexible routing designed to minimize the tour distance;
(f) the tours are routed on a rectangular grid network and departure headways are equal for all the service area and uniform within the study period.

Focusing our attention on the checkpoint dial-a-ride model, the main goal is to determine a near optimal checkpoint density, Δ, corresponding to an optimal distance, $d(w)$, between two consecutive stops. The extension of the service area, $A=Lw$, is also an variable to optimize. Let us assume that requests for service are independent Poisson variables, regarding any group of passengers travelling together as single requests. By consequence of the above assumption (d), the average number of requests for a stop will be $2\lambda H/\Delta$, while the probability π that a given checkpoint has at least one request is:

$$\pi = 1 - \exp\left(-\frac{2\lambda H}{\Delta}\right) \qquad (1)$$

To cover the region is used the travelling salesman building strategy described by Daganzo [4]. A swath of width w is cut through the region and the bus moves along the swath visiting sequentially the checkpoints that are activated without backtracking. Daganzo started his cost formulation from the equation for the approximate collection tour distance D in an optimized zone found by Stein [9] for a dial-a-ride analysis, based on the assumption that n points are randomly and independently dispersed over an area A and that an optimal travelling salesman tour has been designed to cover these n points:

$$D = k\sqrt{nA} \tag{2}$$

where k is a constant which is estimated to be 1.15 for Manhattan metric. Following his simple strategy for building a good travelling salesman tour in zones of irregular shapes, Daganzo [4] has evaluated how the collection tour distance of eqn (2) changes with zone shapes. He found that the expected total length of a bus path which visit sequentially all the n points moving along a unidirectional strip of width w without backtracking is given by:

$$D = nd(w) \tag{3}$$

where $d(w)$ is the expected distance between two consecutive points.
The total cost, C, is given by the weighted summation of waiting time plus walking time to a stop, or access time, plus travel time, plus cost of operation per passenger:

$$C = \beta \frac{H}{2} + \gamma \frac{0.8r}{v_0\sqrt{\Delta}} + \frac{L}{2v} + \alpha \frac{L}{\lambda A v H} \tag{4}$$

where: α is a conversion factor that turns the cost of one vehicle-hour of operation into one passenger-hour of riding; β and γ are constants to translate waiting and walking into riding time, respectively; and r is the network route factor between stops (the average spacing between stops is $r\Delta^{-1/2}$ and $r = 1.27$ for the Manhattan, or grid, metric); A is the size of the area which is to be served.
The first and the second terms of the right end of eqn (4) are access and waiting time per passenger, respectively. They depend only on Δ and H and thus are not influenced by the routing strategy. The third term is travel time (neglecting the time for a stop) at a given constant speed, v, which is proportional to tour length, L. The last term is cost of operation, which is proportional to L and inversely proportional to checkpoint density, Δ.
Finally, to minimize the total cost of eqn (4) for given values of H and Δ one should select a swath width w (the width of the corridor containing all the stops) which minimizes the expected tour length L; for then we obtain the smallest possible cost. Since, for a given H, eqn (1) gives π, then the number of stops per tour is fixed, and it suffices to minimize the distance between two consecutive stops, $d(w)$, of eqn (3):

$$d(w) \cong r\left[\frac{w}{3} + \frac{\psi(\pi\Delta w^2)}{\pi\Delta w}\right] \tag{5}$$

where $\pi\Delta$ represents the density of active checkpoints in the area immediately ahead of the bus at the time of visit, and $\psi(x) = (2/x^2)[(1+x)\log(1+x) - x]$ (see Daganzo [4]).

Equation (5) assumes that active checkpoints are randomly distributed along the swath. This is a reasonable assumption as long as π is small, but otherwise understates actual distances slightly, because intermediate distances between subsequent stops tend to be larger when stops are regularly spaced than when are randomly scattered.

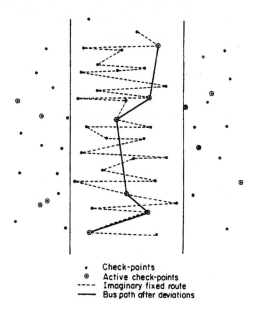

•	Check-points
◎	Active check-points
----	Imaginary fixed route
——	Bus path after deviations

Figure 2: Checkpoints, active checkpoints, swath, and the path of the bus [4].

3 The heuristic approach

Filippi and co-workers [5,6] proposed a two stage model for the route deviation line design problem which is based on a two recursive stage model. The first stage consists on demand estimation trough a regressive model. In the second stage, given a number N of possible deviated stops, the average length of the bus round trip is selected through a heuristic procedure. The whole procedure is iterated until convergence is reached both for number of passengers carried and for bus trip length. For demand estimation they used an updated version of a regression model developed by Burkhardt and Lago [10] to predict patronage for rural fixed route systems operating in small geographic areas:

$$Log \frac{PASSDAY}{PoP_o \times PoP_d} = a + bLogFREQ - cLogDS \qquad (6)$$

where $PASSDAY$ is the number of boarding or one-way passenger per day on the route (one-way passengers are approximately twice the number of round trip passenger); PoP_o is the population of the service area minus PoP_d which is the population of the largest borough traversed by the line, both expressed in hundreds of thousands; *FREQ* is the number of round trips on the route per day; *DS=(LF+LD)* is the round trip length given by the summation of the (fixed) length *LF* of main route and length *LD* which is the (variable) length of operated deviations per bus round trip; *a*, *b* and *c* are coefficients whose values derived from regression analysis on data of the specific case under examination.

The design variables are the number of passengers per day and the average length of the bus round trip. To determine the average length of one bus round trip one should know the demand at deviated stops which is derived from the number of calls. Given the average number of active deviations, one immediately obtains the average length of the bus round trip. The model assumes that calls for service are independent Poisson variables, and demand density is uniform on the service area. The probability π that a given deviate stop has at least one call during a time unit is $\pi = 1 - \exp(-m)$, where *m* is the average of calls per day and it is a function both of the headway – which is related to *FREQ* – and of the demand level.

Finally, the heuristic procedure determining the average number of passengers carried per day and the average length of the bus round trip is an iterative procedure which, recursively, applies a demand model, respect to a given value of average bus route length, then makes an estimation of service calls, drawn from a Poisson distribution based on the previous obtained demand level, which leads to the probability of activation for each deviated stops giving the average length of the bus route. The algorithm operates searching for demand/supply equilibrium and may be described in more general terms as the recursive solution of the following group of relationships:

$$PASSDAY^{(k)} = (PoP_o)(PoP_d)10\exp(-PASSDAY^{(k-1)})$$

$$PASSDEV^{(k)} = (Ad/A)PASSDAY^{(k)} \tag{7}$$

$$LD^{(k)} = 2DS^{(k-1)}[1 - \exp(-PASSDEV^{(k)}/(2FREQ \times N))]$$

$$DS^{(k)} = LF + LD^{(k)}$$

where: *k* is the counter; *A* is the whole service area and *Ad* is the area served through the *N* deviated stops; *PASSDEV* is the number of passenger at deviated stops per day.

In solving procedure (7) the initial solution ($k = 1$) is determined by solving eqn (6) with a bus route length $DS^{(1)}$ equal to *LF*. The convergence criterion is met when the relative change in the round trip length of the deviation bus becomes negligible, i.e., if the inequality $\left|(DS^{(k)} - DS^{(k-1)})/DS^{(k-1)}\right| \le \varepsilon$ holds respect to a pre-set approximation value.

4 The mathematical programming approach

Enhancement of system accessibility, increased served area and better service productivity are all the features related to a route deviation bus service whose are due to its route flexibility. Nevertheless, such flexibility may have a detrimental effect in terms of an increase of the variance of scheduled arrival times for main line stops, and of increased waiting and travelling times for passengers along the main line.

These aspects are explicitly taken into account in the systemic approach of Pratelli and Schoen [7,8] to design a deviation bus route line. Their attention is focused with the design problem which arise in planning the locations of deviated stops outside the main line. As said above, the objective function proposed with the model considers both the advantage of passengers served by the deviation devices and the disadvantages suffered by passengers on the bus, whose travel time increased during deviations, and by passengers downstream of the deviations whose waiting time also increases.

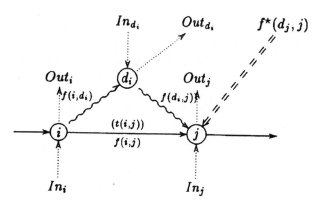

Figure 3: Fragment of a graph representing a route deviation bus line [8].

A graph is used to represent the relevant data structure, with nodes corresponding to bus stops and three kind of arcs: regular arcs, corresponding to the main bus line; deviated arcs, connecting possible locations of deviated stops to regular ones and vice versa; pedestrian arcs, for passengers walking from a potential deviate stop to the nearest regular stop. Figure 3 displays a fragment of a graph representing a route deviation bus line, where one can observe both some of the notations and symbols used in the following. The objective function is an aggregate measure of cost, which is built by a weighted summation extended to all customers and comprises three parts:

$$
\begin{aligned}
\min \Bigg\{ & K_b \left(\sum_{i=1}^{n-1} (t(i,i+1)f(i,i+1) + t(i,d_i)f(i,d_i) + t(d_i,i+1)f(d_i,i+1)) - T_0 \right) \\
& + K_f \sum_{i=1}^{n-1} t^*(d_i,i)f^*(d_i,i) \\
& + K_w \sum_{m=2}^{n} \sum_{i=1}^{m-1} (t(i,d_i) + t(i,d_i+1) - t(i,i+1)) ln(m) p_{di} \delta(d_i)
\end{aligned}
\tag{8}
$$

The first term is the cumulated time spent on the bus by all passengers, both on the regular line and along deviated arcs; of course, constraints have to be defined in order to impose that flow on arcs leading to a location which is not served by a deviated stop will be 0. The second term corresponds to the time perceived by passengers moving on foot to the nearest stop on the line. Finally, the third term includes the additional waiting time caused by an upstream deviation: at bus stop m there are, on average, $In(m)$ passengers waiting; if a deviation occurs right after an upstream stop i, with $i < m$, the travel time of the bus will change from its normal time $t(i,j)$ to the higher time required to serve the deviate stop, which is equal to $t(i,d_i)+t(d_i,i+1)$. Each term of eqn (8) is multiplied by a constant – namely K_b, K_f and K_w – in order to take into account the different time which is perceived while walking, or waiting, as opposed to time on board.

A deviation at regular bus stop i can only occur if the decision was taken of serving the deviate bus stop, $\delta(d_i)=1$, and either at least one passenger is waiting at deviated stop d_i, or a passenger on the bus just before stop i asks to be taken to the deviated stop. Because the expected traffic to a deviated stop is usually extremely low, it is assumed that both the process of passengers arriving at a deviated stop and the process of requests to be alighted at deviated stops form independent Poisson processes, with arrival rate λ_{di} and ρ_{di}, respectively. In this case, the probability that during a time unit a request for a deviation will occur is given by $p_{di}=1-\exp(-(\lambda_{di}+\rho_{di}))$. The following constraints represent the existing relationships between the different flows and the decision whether to activate or not deviated stops:

$$f(i,d_i) \leq M\delta(d_i) \tag{9}$$

$$f(d_i,i+1) \leq M\delta(d_i) \tag{10}$$

$$f^*(i,d_i) \leq M(1-\delta(d_i)) \tag{11}$$

$$f(i-1,i)+f(d_{i-1},i)+f^*(d_i,i)+In(i) = f(i,i+1)+f(i,d_i)+Out(i) \tag{12}$$

$$f(i,d_i)+In(d_i) = f(d_i,i+1)+f^*(d_i,i)+Out(d_i) \tag{13}$$

$$f(i,d_i) \geq p_{di}(f(i-1,i)+f(d_{i-1},i)+f^*(d_i,i)+In(i)+M(1-\delta(d_i))) \tag{14}$$

$$g \leq \sum_{i=1}^{n-1} \delta(d_i) \leq G \tag{15}$$

$$f(\cdot,\cdot), f^*(\cdot,\cdot) \geq 0 \tag{16}$$

$$\delta(d_i) \in \{0,1\} \tag{17}$$

Constraints (9), (10) and (11) just impose the logical conditions there can be a flow along a deviated arc only if the corresponding stop is activated; conversely, there can be a flow of user on foot only if the stop is not activated. Equations

(12) and (13) represent flow conservation at regular and deviated stops, respectively. Randomness in bus deviation is included assuming that, if the probability of at least one passenger waiting at deviated bus stop d_i is $p_{di} > 0$, and the decision was taken to enable that deviate stop, then passengers entering node i will split into two streams: one, proportional to p_{di}, on the deviated arc (i, d_i), the other, proportional to $(1 - p_{di})$, on the regular arc $(i, i+1)$. However, this modelling assumption does not imply that if probability p_{di} is positive, then every on coming bus will deviated: it simply means that, in such cases, every passenger who is on the bus just before the potential deviation, will actually deviate with probability p_{di}. This logical constraint is imposed through eqn (14) and leads to the following implications:

$$\delta(d_i) = 1 \implies f(i, d_i) \geq p_{di}(f(i-1, i) + f(d_{i-1}, i) + f^*(d_i, i) + In(i)) \qquad (18)$$

$$\delta(d_i) = 0 \implies f(i, d_i) \geq p_{di}(f(i-1, i) + f(d_{i-1}, i) + f^*(d_i, i) + In(i) - M) \quad (19)$$

Implication (18) forces an amount of flow which is at least p_{di} times the total flow into (or out of) node i to proceed along the deviated arc; because it is assumed that the triangular inequality holds, i.e. $t(i, d_i) + t(d_i, i+1) > t(i, i+1)$, at every optimal solution this constraint will be active. Implication (19) is redundant, as the right end side is always negative, and always dominated by the inequality (16) $f(i, d_i) \geq 0$. Again, as a consequence that it is more costly to proceed along the deviation than along the main line, if $\delta(d_i) = 0$, this last constraint will be active at optimal solutions. Through these logical implications it is thus possible to model the expected flows on all arcs by means of a mixed integer linear system of inequalities. Finally, constraint (15) is used to impose a minimum as well as a maximum total number of deviated stop to be activated.

5 Conclusions

This paper has presented three different models as many theoretical approaches proposed for the checkpoint dial-a-ride problem, which also called route deviation bus problem.

The analytic approach is useful to enhance the relations between decision variables and system parameters, and provides guidelines to determine at a strategically planning level when the checkpoint dial-a-ride service mode should be applied or not. Because the analytical model of Daganzo [3] is based on very crude approximations of reality, its results can provide only guidance to choose a checkpoint system macroscopic configurations worthy of more detailed simulations and refinements.

Heuristic models are a step forward. The work of Filippi and co-workers [5] makes possible an evaluation of a route deviation bus service in term of average values of the design variables. Even though this model has been tested on realistic data instances [6], its structure strongly relies on the specific form of an underlying aggregate demand model. This fact limits the model transferability from the calibration context to another study context.

High detailed problems which in the past were only approachable by simulation, can nowadays be solved, at least approximately, using mathematical optimization. The recent mathematical programming model developed by Pratelli and Schoen [7,8] may be quite useful for analysts in order to examine how some design parameters, such as time perceived by passengers, could influence the optimal location of concurrent deviated stops outside the main line. Moreover, despite the increasing realism and lot of details that can be reached with an optimization approach, considerable work remains to be accomplished in order to cope with large-scale bus route deviation networks.

Acknowledgements

This work was supported by "P.R.I.N. – anno 2000" of the Italian Ministry for University and Research. I herewith wish to thank Fabio Schoen of the University of Florence for his advice and useful comments.

References

[1] Flusberg, M., An innovative public transportation system for a small city: the Merril, Wisconsin, case study. *Transp. Res. Records* 606, TRB, 1976.

[2] Black, A., *Urban Mass Transportation Planning*. McGraw-Hill, 1995.

[3] Daganzo, C.F., Checkpoint dial-a-ride systems. *Transportation Research* **18B**, pp. 315-327, 1984.

[4] Daganzo, C.F., The length of tours in zones with different shapes. *Transportation Research* **18B**, pp. 135-145, 1984.

[5] Filippi, F., Pagliari, E. & Cecconi C., Un modello per la progettazione di trasporti pubblici a deviazione di percorso, *Proc. of 1st Int. Congr. Energia Ambiente Innovazione Tecnologica*, Caracas, pp. 859-864, 1989.

[6] Filippi, F. & Gori, S., Progettazione operativa di reti di trasporto pubblico in aree a domanda medio-debole. *Trasporti & Trazione* 5, pp. 215-225, 1994.

[7] Pratelli, A. & Schoen, F., A model for route deviation bus design, *Proc. of the 5th International Conference "Living and Walking in Cities"*, eds. R. Busi and M. Pezzagno, EUR191210 IT/EN: Brussels, pp. 71-84, 2000.

[8] Pratelli, A. & Schoen, F., A mathematical programming model for the bus deviation route problem. *Journal of the Operational Research Society* 52, pp. 494-502, 2001.

[9] Stein, D.M., Scheduling dial-a-ride transportation systems. *Transportation Science* 12, pp. 232-249, 1978.

[10] Burkhardt, J.E. & Lago, A.M., Predicting demand for rural transit systems. *Traffic Quarterly* 1, pp. 105-129, 1978.

Selecting an optimal traffic system for cities

D. Marušić[1], I. Lovrić[2]
[1] Faculty of Civil Engineering, University of Split, Croatia
[2] Faculty of Civil Engineering, University of Mostar,
Bosnia and Herzegovina

Abstract

Due to rapid development of cities, the existing transportation systems very often cannot satisfy the traffic demand. In these conditions it is necessary to reconstruct the existing and construct new transportation facilities. As investment in the transportation system is often greater than possibilities, it is very important to decide reach rational decisions.

Hence the investment policy must be rational and there is a simple rule: investment should be compensated as soon as possible by savings in the exploitation.

The main prerequisite for successful management of the transportation strategy is good knowledge of the interaction between national economy, intensity of perspective transportation work, capacity and investment.

This paper presents a methodology for determining the most convenient model of the whole transportation system or part of the system. The methodology is based on the assumptions that the program of investment in the planned period must be done so that the realized investment and resulting costs of exploitation give a minimal discount investment.

The methodology is based on the application of the method of discount investment i.e. there is a correlation between the rate of flow, capacity, stage investment and the exploitation of costs in the depending on time.

Accordingly, time-dependent investment interaction, in its application, manifests a real economic category.

Due to this methodology the transportation policy has a significant tool which can show: when, where and how much to invest and finally the expected benefits.

1 Introduction

The development of engineering sciences and new technologies has contributed to the more intensive development of society and an improvement in quality of living conditions. All these developments have directly influenced transportation so that its relevance to society has rapidly increased.

Further improvement is influenced by the adequate development of a transportation system. However, significant investment is a prerequisite for achieving an advanced technical level and the capacity required to satisfy increasing demands. Frequently, investment in the development of other economic activities and branches makes it difficult to meet the requirements of the transportation system; this is particularly true in cities.

The growth of modern cities changes in the structure of the city structure (migration of its inhabitants beyond the urban areas), changes the economic structure and changes the transportation demands.

These latter changes are manifested in the rapid increase in private vehicles which require larger transit areas than the city can provide. Due to the mentioned reasons, public transportation should be reintroduced since transportation requirements cannot be met exclusively by private vehicles.

Considering all these problems of urban and suburban transportation, it is necessary to take into account all changes which characterize the development of modern cities. These changes influence the following:

- *Change in the city structure* – is reflected in frequent migrations from the city center towards its periphery, suburban and satellite areas. This can be accounted by the availability of land and, therefore, less expensive housing and better living conditions in these suburban areas which have more favourable transportation conditions.

- *Change in the structure of the city's economics* – it is evident that the industrial (secondary) activities stagnate as well as the development of services (tertiary activities). Tertiary activities are located in buildings in the city center. This requires a satisfactory transportation system for commuters.

- *Change in the city transportation structure* – is reflected in sudden increase in private vehicles which require larger traffic areas than the city can provide. Such development leads to worsening of the living conditions in cities which have inefficient transportation systems, are noisy and have a high emission rate of harmful gases.

Taking into consideration the previous statements the definition of the city itself should be changed so that, according to the new definition, the city includes both the center and all suburban areas as well as small towns gravitating towards the city center. Modern planning discards the concept of the so-called "ideal city" (a city designed for private cars) as a planning concept which is not real, and tends towards the reintroduction of public transportation. According to this new concept, public transportation has advantages over private cars both in the city center and along the main highways in densely populated urban areas.

Hence, private cars could be competitive only in the peripheral city areas and the areas in between the main directions. It is difficult to state precisely whether this reintroduction of the public transportation is more necessary in developing countries or in the paralysed cities of developed countries. There is overall agreement that transportation requirements in the large cities cannot be satisfied exclusively by private cars and that the solution to transportation problems cannot be based primarily on the application of only one transportation technique.

2. Evaluation of investments in traffic systems

All types of investments should yield positive results (exploitation effects). This is particularly important in transportation due to the following reasons:
  - the construction of a traffic infrastructure requires a significant investment with a long-term payback;
  - an increase in traffic leads to congestion and the necessity for expansion;
  - expansion of existing systems, which, as a rule, requires a greater investment, delays the construction of new systems;
  - more expensive technical solutions ensure lower transportation costs, and, vice versa, less expensive technical solutions lead to higher transportation costs;
  - modern equipment also enables an increase in capacity and ensures conditions for more efficient exploitation;

The stated specific characteristics show that there is a connection between the transportation capacity, traffic load and dynamics of its development, investment, exploitation time and costs. The functional connection between these five parameters makes possible to evaluate the investment and the traffic exploitation from the economic standpoint.

The long life of highways and their capacity together with slow return of investment make it necessary to synchronize planning and stress the necessity of long-term planning.

In long-term planning it is possible to make occasional investments in the infrastructure, vehicles and current exploitation. From the economic standpoint, it is important to establish the time and range of these investments since the principle of interest bearing capital illustrates the advantage of delaying the investment.

Among all the known methods for evaluating the investment efficiency, the most suitable one is the method of discounted investment since it connects the efficiency of all five parameters.

This method is suitable for developing a traffic model, i.e. for presenting all transportation investments depending upon the time of the investment.

3. The optimisation model

The city traffic system represents all types of traffic, together with their mobile and stationary capacities, personnel, and traffic flow. Considering the interaction between these branches and in order to ensure systematic organization, they should be divided into several main factors, which from the technological and investment standpoint form large wholes such as: railways, road traffic, tramways or trolleys, subways, etc.

The traffic project should include all discounted investments into highways, traffic hubs, etc during the planning period. Investment into all roads and hubs of one transportation branch represents the branch model, and the basis of the model for each branch constitutes the traffic model of the system.

Investment into new systems and the reconstruction of existing systems should be coordinated with the capacity of the existing roads, depending upon the increased traffic load. Following the same logic it is necessary to plan the purchase of equipment in accordance with an increase in these activities.

Consequently, investment into each traffic project, i.e. into each branch and all branches, represents the basis for the formation of long-term plans for the development of each branch, i.e. the total city traffic system. This approach is efficient since the operation of the systems and the decrease in their capacity represent the basis for establishing the limits for investment terms. Consequently, taking into account this technological interaction, it is possible to establish a closer connection between planning and exploitation, (considering the terms). The application of the method of discounted investment makes it possible to evaluate all investment and exploitation costs considering the time intervals, depending upon the changes in each phase.

For one traffic project total investment during n phases

$$U_{svp} = \sum_{n=0}^{n-1} J_n \eta^{t_n} + \sum_{n=1}^{n} \sum_{t_{n-1}+1}^{t_n} E_{nt} \eta^t \tag{1}$$

providing that $t_0 = 0$, $t_n = t_{sl}$ (≈ 20 years).

Graphical presentation of eqn (1) is given in Figure 1. Figure 1/A presents the time limits of all phases depending upon the decreased capacity of the systems. In eqn (1) the first term represents all discounted investments, and the second term expresses successive investments into exploitation. (The first sum symbolizes one phase, and the second presents the sum within that phase).

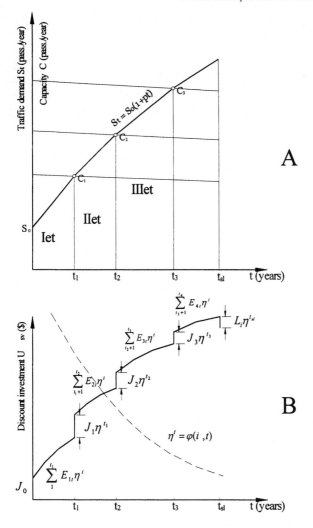

Figure 1: A) Diagram of the traffic load and capacity
        B) Diagram of discounted costs of the construction and exploitation

$\eta = \dfrac{1}{1+i}$ - delay coefficient

η^t - delay parameter

i - discounted rate, i.e. interest rate $i = \dfrac{\Delta E}{\Delta J}$

L_i - liquidation value

In developing countries it can be said that $i = 5 - 8\%$, which depends upon the state on the capital market. Otherwise, a higher rate makes the selection of better investment solutions more difficult.

J_n – investment in the n-th phase for the infrastructure, plants and vehicles.

Considering the calculation of exploitation costs, the limits of the sum of all investments have been moved backward one year, since the system has to be finished earlier and the vehicles were purchased in advance so that they could be used.

Exploitation costs during the n-th phase within the limits of $\left|\begin{smallmatrix} t_n \\ t_{n-1}+1 \end{smallmatrix}\right.$ .contain all costs of passenger (E_{npu}) traffic, related to transportation which are in the n phase for year t

$$E_{nt} = E_{npu} \tag{2}$$

The exploitation costs also include all permanent and variable costs. In our calculations we considered only those permanent costs which, during the whole planning period, were incurred upon the traffic project.

Unlike standard methods for evaluating the investment efficiency, which prevalently have a static character, the discounted investment method includes all dynamic changes in the exploitation period related to the increased traffic.

Hence, if the annual traffic increase along a road with a linear trend is

$$S_t = S_0(1 + pt) \qquad \text{where}$$

S_0 – initial traffic load
p – annual increase rate
t - time/period (year),
then the annual transportation costs are

$$T_{prt} = S_t c(1 + pt) \tag{3}$$

Wherein: c-unit transportation costs ($/km) from the starting point to the last station. This parameter is very important since it contains all specific factors related to the road under consideration: route elements, applied technology, exploitation conditions, etc.

Like exploitation costs, all other costs can be expressed as the same function which is used for expressing the trend of increased traffic. Consequently, for the linear trend, the annual exploitation costs in the *n-th* phase are:

$$E_{nt} = A_n + B_n t \tag{4}$$

For one transportation branch from r facilities, the traffic model is equal to the sum of the discounted investment for all the respective traffic projects.

Subsequently, according to eqn (1) the discounted investment for the railway model is

$$U_{svrw} = \sum_{1}^{r} \left(\sum_{n=0}^{n-1} J_n \eta^{tn} + \sum_{n-1\,t_{n-1}+1}^{n\quad t_n} E_{nt} \eta^t \right) \qquad (5)$$

If the discounted investments are expressed with initial letters for all other possible branches, i.e. U_{svrw} - for railway traffic; U_{svrd} - for road traffic; U_{svtr} - for tramway and trolley transportation; U_{svsb} - for the subway, then the total discounted investment for the entire city for the planning period under consideration are, as follows:

$$U_{svs} = U_{svrw} + U_{svrd} + U_{svtr} + U_{svsb}$$

i. e. for all the four stated city branches

$$U_{svs} = \sum_{s} \left[\sum_{r=1}^{r} \left(\sum_{n=0}^{n-1} J_n \eta^{tn} + \sum_{n-1\,t_{n-1}+1}^{n\quad t_n} E_{nt} \eta^t \right) \right] \qquad (6)$$

Considering an optimal traffic system for the planned period - the total discounted investment for the entire traffic system should tend to be the minimum, i.e.

$$U_{svs} \rightarrow \min. \qquad (7)$$

These conditions can result from two assumptions:
First: if certain financial means are assigned to each branch, in that case investment dynamics, and the resulting exploitation, should give a branch minimum;
Second: with the less strict assignment of investment per branch, it is possible, by iteration, to establish the proportions for the formation of investment U   min.

The first term of the eqn (6) expresses the total discounted investment. If the key of assignment per branch is

$$\alpha_{rw} + \alpha_{rd} + \alpha_{tr} + \alpha_{sb} = 1 \qquad \text{then} \qquad J_{srw} = \alpha_{rw} J_{ss} = \sum_{1}^{t_p} J_{rw} \quad \dots \quad etc.$$

With the analogous assignment of investment to the remaining traffic branches, the total distribution per year and per branch for the planned period of t years is presented in Table 1.

Table 1: Summary review of the investment distribution per year and per traffic branch for the planned time period

t_{year} s	1	2	3	....	t_p	J_s
1 rw	J_{rw1}	J_{rw2}	J_{rw3}	....	J_{rwp}	J_{srw}
2 rd	J_{rd1}	J_{rd2}	J_{rd3}	....	J_{rdp}	J_{srd}
3 tr	J_{tr1}	J_{tr2}	J_{tr3}	....	J_{trp}	J_{str}
4 sw	J_{sw1}	J_{sw2}	J_{sw3}	....	J_{swp}	J_{sw}
Ss	J_{s1}	J_{s2}	J_{s3}	....	J_{sp}	J_{ss}

and finally

$$J_{ss} = \sum_{1}^{t_p}\sum_{1}^{s} J_{st} \qquad (8)$$

Consequently, apart from all combinations of the investment distribution per year and per branch, the planned sum J = const.

In the first revisions of the developmental plans for each transportation branch these sums in the resulting plan do not have to be equal. They can become equal later, by iteration, in the final revision of the total plan.

However, the second term of eqn (5) is not constant without discounting. The only constant per year is the planned traffic volume. On the other hand, it is evident from eqn (3) that the costs of each traffic project depend upon the average costs per travelled kilometre – c ($/tkm), i.e.

$$c = l \cdot c_k \qquad (9)$$

The previously stressed regularities of the structural changes, which occur rapidly in traffic, are influenced more by the liberal market of traffic services than by a tendency to carry out all activities under most efficient economic conditions. The stated changes are not harmless, and if the processes are not controlled, they can lead to hazardous consequences.

The proposed problem of the structural changes can be used as a main indicator for further investigations of the causes of these phenomena, for analyses and for undertaking activities in directing the development of the entire traffic system.

4. Conclusion

Many cities frequently do not have a well-developed traffic system and consequently cannot satisfy increasing transportation demands. Since the spatial development is not consistent, it causes rapid structural changes which are not followed by the respective general socio-economic criteria.

The construction of the infrastructure as the main basis for transportation development requires significant investment which, however, exceeds the financial capacity of the society for such investment.

Consequently, it is necessary to conduct an efficient investment policy which should be based on the following principles: the investment should be repaid as soon as possible by savings during the exploitation phase. This should be considered as a basis for managing the entire city traffic system.

With this objective in view, a method has been developed for establishing a traffic model for each branch, i.e. a traffic system which is based on the prerequisite that the investment in the planned period should be distributed so that the realized investment and the resulting exploitation costs result in a minimum discounted investment.

This method is based upon the application of the method of discounted investment wherein, in the time function, there exists an interaction between the traffic volume, transportation capacity, phase investment and exploitation costs. Consequently, the *time – investment* interaction represents a complete economic category. In addition, the traffic policy possesses a more intense material basis and a guideline pointing when, where and how much to invest and what benefits may be expected.

References

[1] Marušić, D., Stazić, T., Railway as transportation means in urban areas, *Urban Transport VI, Urban Transport and the Environment for the 21st century*, Cambridge UK 2000.

[2] Subotić, U., *Optimisation of investment*, SANU and ANUBiH, Belgrade, 1979.

[3] Camagni, R., (Eds.), *Economia e pianificazione della citta sostenibile*, Bologna, Il Mulino, 1996.

[4] Sheffi, Y., *Urban Transportation Networks*, Prentice Hall, Englewood Cliffs, 1985.

[5] De Serpa, A. C., *A theory of the economics of time*, Economic Journal, vol 81,n. 324, 1971.

[6] Button, K.J., *Transport Economics*, UK, Aldershot, 1982.

[7] Mayers, I., Ochelen, S., Proost, S., *The marginal external costs of urban transport*, Public Economics Research, 51, KA Leuven – CES, 1997.

[8] European Commission, DG XII, Science Research and Development, JOULE, *Externalities of Fuel Cycles.*, report numbers EUR 16520 EN to 16525 EN, 1995. (see website: http://externe.jrc.es/)

[9] Pavalek, J., *Role and importance of public transport in the development and functioning of towns*, 4th International symposium on electronics in traffic, Ljubljana, 1995.

The Bus Rapid Transit System in Taipei City —ridership forecast for the New Light Industrial area in Neihu

S.K. Jason Chang[1] ,James Y.L. Du[2] & C.K. Wang[3]
[1]*Director General, Office of Science and Technology Advisors, Ministry of Transportation and Communications, Taiwan, and Professor of Dept. of Civil Engineering, National Taiwan University.*
[2]*Research Assistant of NTU*
[3]*Graduate Student of NTU.*

Abstract

This paper aims to explore the related issues of Bus Rapid Transit (BRT) and forecast the ridership in the New Light Industrial Area in Neihu, where the BRT will be implemented. First of all, it briefly discusses the current development of BRT system in Taipei City. The performance of BRT system is illustrated based on the figures derived from official reports. Secondly, this paper forecasts a transferring ridership from the MRT to BRT for Neihu, a district of Taipei City using disaggregate model of mode choice. The results show passengers tend to ride the MRT system and transfer to BRT based on a foundation of substantially upgraded bus system performances. Finally, this paper proposes a set of feasible strategies for creating an ameliorated public transportation environment, which will ensure a sustainable transportation development in Taipei City.

1 Introduction: the necessity of building a convenient bus system

Bus systems provide a versatile form of public transportation with the flexibility to serve passengers throughout metropolitan area. However, traffic congestion, urban sprawl, and air pollution have deteriorated the level service, due to the conspicuous traffic growth in Taipei metropolitan area last decade. As a result, fewer passengers would to take buses as the level of service kept declining, due to the cumulative effects of traffic congestion, traffic signals, and long boarding time. Therefore, it is a crucial issue to build up a convenient, high quality public transportation system.

This paper outlines the history and BRT development in Taipei City, and forecast ridership for a new light industrial area in Neihu, a district of Taipei City if the BRT strategy can be implemented there. Finally, a set of a set of feasible strategies for creating an ameliorated public transportation environment is proposed, which will ensure a sustainable transportation development in Taipei City.

2 Current bus system development in Taipei City

The bus system in Taipei used to play an essential role of the public transportation throughout Taipei area. It used to be the most convenient public transportation system in Taipei metropolitan area and reached its peak at 950,114 thousand passenger in 1985, which was 2.6 million passengers on average per day (Table.1). However, the boomed economy and the abolishment of ban on imported automobiles, cause the conspicuous growth of traffic.

Bus Rapid Transit (BRT) network schemes were proposed have been implemented in Taipei City as the concept was drawn as a policy to balance citizens' mode choice in Taipei City. Seven exclusive bus lanes were firstly constructed with great efforts casting various barriers aside (Table 2) in 1996. This policy made bus a more attractive transportation mode by allowing passenger transferring much more conveniently from MTR. It has reduced private mode form 66% in 1996 to 46% in 2000 (Fig.1). An official investigation shows that the bus priority network in Taipei City has successfully drawn back about 13% passengers, and increased the bus driving speed from 5-15 km/hour to 11-20 km/hour on bus exclusive lanes. On other hand, the disorder mixed traffic is greatly improved as the car and bus traffics are separated (Photo1, 2 and3).

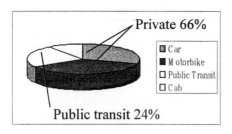

Fig.1. Mode choice of Taipei
City in 1996

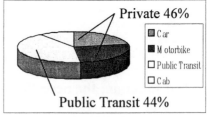

Fig.2. Mode choice of Taipei
City in 2000

Table 1. The capacities of Taipei City Bus system

Items	Total Passenger (thousand)	Average Passenger Per Day
1985	950,114	2,603,053
1991	781,843	2,142,036
1995	640,148	1,753,829
1999	722,607	1,979,745
2000	679,345	1,856,135

Table 2. List of Bus Priority Lanes in Taipei City

Exclusive Bus Lanes	Length	Flows	Dates of Opening
North Sec. of 9th Ave.	1.5km	Concurrent flow	1996.1
South Sec. of 9th Ave.	1.8km	Concurrent flow	1996.6
2nd Blvd.	9.0km	Concurrent & Contraflow	1996.7
3rd Blvd.	6.2km	Concurrent & Contraflow	1996.7
7th Blvd.	8.4km	Concurrent flow	1996.7
9th Blvd.	9.9km	Concurrent flow	1996.8
12th Ave.	3.2km	Concurrent flow	1996.8
4th Ave.	2.0km	Concurrent flow	2001.1
2nd Ave.	1.9km	Concurrent flow	2001.3

Source: http://www.tcc.taipei.gov.tw/index.htm

Photo 1. before   Photo 2. constructing   Photo 3. after

3 Introduction of New Light Industrial District in Neihu

The New Light Industrial Area is in Neihu District of Taipei city. There are several important developed projects, which are in process in this area. Those projects will enable the Neihu Light Industrial Area to be a multi-function commercial area and industrial park, including entertainment and media district, high-tech industrial park, high quality riverside residential area, and warehouse and wholesale district in future.

88.6% bus passengers think the bus service need to be improved, and the items of bus service that need to be improved are:
(1) Arise in the bus frequency (63.8%); (2) Provide door to door service by transferring between MRT station and the destination (54.0%); (3) Increase bus routes (49.7%); (4) Increases mini bus service (20.1%).

Table 3 presents the results of the alternatives priority of the commuters' mode choices. The results show that the most private mode users are willing to choose the public transportation when the private modes are not available.

Table 3 Commuters' Alternatives Priority

Mode Choice	Alternatives Priority		
	1	2	3
Auto	Taxi 31.8%	Bus 29.5%	Motorbike 17.1%
Motorbike	Bus 53.3%	MRT 12.1%	Taxi 12.1%
There are 40%-65% automobile and motorbike users, who are willing to use the transit mode (such as Bus, MRT) when the automobile and motorbike modes are not available.			

4 A disaggregate model of mode choice

The purpose of this section is to develop the basic relation for the mode choice in this area. It primarily identifies the mode choice changes if the BRT strategies are implemented in Neihu Light Industrial District. The results will be used to evaluate the possibility of implementing the BRT strategies. The planning for BRT facilities in this area could take these results into consideration.

4.1 Data collection

The data is derived from two studies, "The Midterm Report of Strategies of Sustainable Transportation for Taipei City—The Case Study of the Light Industrial Area in Neihu" and "the study of Comprehensive Transportation System Planning for Taipei Metropolitan Area." The first report collected questionnaires based on computer-assisted design from a random sample of commuters from the Light Industrial Area in Neihu. The data acquired focus on socioeconomic variables of the commuters in this area, including gender, age, location of home base, and the information on mode choice behavior. The second data source is derived from "The study of Comprehensive Transportation System Planning for Taipei Metropolitan Area, acquired the information on various characteristics for each type of transportation mode, including mode-operating cost per km and average speed in the network of each transportation mode, etc.

4.2 Description of the data

The data verify some of the findings. The mode choice results are shown as Table 4 and 5. The primary and second modes chosen are automobile and motorbike at 65.3 %. The MRT and bus use account for 33.1% of the five-mode total. It is also shown in Table 4 that the taxi, motorbike, and bus modes can be chosen for general work trips to the Light Industrial Area in Neihu. Table 5 shows that there are two or three alternatives for work trips.

Table 4. Actual mode choice market share in Neihu Light Industrial Area

Mode	Actual mode choice	Percentage (%)	Alternatives	Percentage (%)
Auto	113	35.0	131	40.6
Taxi	5	1.6	246	76.2
Motorbike	98	30.3	227	70.0
Bus[1]	76	23.5	258	79.9
MRT[2]	30	9.6	59	18.0
Total	322	100.0	919	284.7

Table 5. Num. of alternative distribution

Num. of Alternatives	Sample size	Percentage (%)
2	110	34.0
3	152	48.3
4	40	14.9
5	10	2.8
Total	322	100.0

4.3 Study method

The paper will forecast the mode choice behavior with five modes by the approach of Multinomial Logit Model. It is the most widely used function for transportation demand analysis, as well as mode choice.

The five alternative modes are considered including automobile, taxi, motorbike, bus (with walking access), and MRT (with bus access). Variables of the model are shown in Table 6. The probability of choosing one mode depends on these explanatory variables. We can get that the utility function of travel time, travel cost, mode dummy variables and the location of passengers' homes. For example, the negative coefficient of travel time indicates that when time spent in a particular mode decreases, the probability of choosing that particular mode increases, while the travel cost stays the same. When the coefficient of travel cost is negative, it means that there is a higher the travel cost and a lower probability of choosing that particular mode. Dummy variables allow attractiveness of a particular mode trip to differ from that of other mode trips for reasons other than travel cost and travel time. The variable of the location of passengers' home measures the effect of the automobile use in CBD. When the automobile is chosen, it causes the roads to be more crowded and increases travel time or travel costs.

Table 6. Explanatory variables in MNL

Variables	Explain
Auto mode constant	= 1 for auto alternatives, = 0 otherwise
Taxi mode constant	= 1 for taxi alternatives, = 0 otherwise
Motorbike mode constant	= 1 for motorcycle alternatives, = 0 otherwise
Bus mode constant	= 1 for bus alternatives, = 0 otherwise
Location of home	If the commuters live in the CBD use auto frequently, it may cause the crowded roads, even increase the travel time and travel cost that auto used will be affected.
Travel time	Minutes one-way from origin to the destination, including in-vehicle time, waiting time and walking time to destination and origin (for auto alternatives)
Travel cost	NT dollars one-way from origin to destination, including transit fare, parking fee, gasoline, or taxi fare for all alternatives

4.4 Result of the estimation

Estimated results are shown in Table 8, in which each variable is discussed. The variables used in the mode choice model are significantly higher in Rho-square value, while travel time, travel cost, and dummy variables are processed.

Travel time is negative; it indicates that an increase in travel time will decrease utility of all alternative modes. The negative sign for the coefficient of the travel cost variable indicates that an increase in travel cost will decrease utility of alternative modes.

Travel time have a high time-value of approximately NT$4.69 per minute. This result indicates that travel time is decisive factor for choosing a transportation mode for work trips.

A dummy variable for the alternatives is notable. The positive sign for the Automobile constant variable indicates that people are more likely to choose automobile as a travel mode. Indeed, those people value the greater comfort, privacy and safety of this mode.

The living environment variables, such as location of home, have negligible effects on mode choice behavior for works trips in this model.

All alternative modes utility functions are shown in (2), (3), (4), (5), (6).

$$U_{auto} = -0.06137 \bullet TT_1 - 0.01245 \bullet TC_1 + DUM_1 \qquad \text{. (2)}$$

$$U_{taxi} = -0.06137 \bullet TT_2 - 0.01245 \bullet TC_2 + DUM_2 \qquad \text{(3)}$$

$$U_{motor} = -0.06137 \bullet TT_3 - 0.01245 \bullet TC_3 + DUM_3 \qquad \text{(4)}$$

$$U_{bus} = -0.06137 \bullet TT_4 - 0.01245 \bullet TC_4 + DUM_4 \qquad \text{(5)}$$

$$U_{MRT} = -0.06137 \bullet TT_5 - 0.01245 \bullet TC_5 \qquad \text{(6)}$$

Table 7. Estimates Coefficients of the MNL

Variable	Coefficient (t-statistic)
Travel time (TT)	-0.0600 (-2.6)
Travel cost (TC)	-0.0128 (-1.6)
Auto mode constant (DUM₁)	0.8571 (2.2)
Taxi mode constant (DUM₂)	-2.032 (-1.8)
Motorcycle mode constant (DUM₃)	-0.8175 (-2.2)
Bus mode constant (DUM₄)	-0.6808 (-1.4)
Location of home (CBD)	0.02465 (0.7)
LL(0)	-328.1868
LL(θ)	-175.2745
LL(M)	-234.2382
ρ^2	0. 4659
ρ_M^2	0. 2517
Sample size	322

Notes: LL(0) = log likelihood at zero
LL(θ) = log likelihood at convergence
LL(M) = log likelihood at constant

ρ^2: = likelihood ratio index $_{1-\frac{LL(\theta)}{LL(0)}}$ ρ_M^2 = likelihood ratio index: $_{1-\frac{LL(M)}{LL(0)}}$

4.5 Test based on conditional choice

The disaggregate model is suitable for forecasting the shifts in mode choice resulting from different policies that have been implemented. We utilized the model of Table 7, and calculated the probabilities of each mode for alternative strategies practiced in the future. These probabilities are summarized in Table 8, while the initial market share we obtained in the sample is on the first row.

Assume that the local government implements the BRT strategies such as exclusive bus way, the bus speed will increase form 11.37 km per hour to 14.27 km per hour. The results are shown in second row (Condition 1). The strong gainers are the bus system and MRT; and the biggest losers are automobile and motorbike. The increase in bus speed is corresponded to a lower probability of choosing either the automobile or the motorbike.

If the BRT strategies are implemented, bus fares will rise from NT$12.7 to NT$14.625. The rate rise from 0.565 NT$/km to 0.845 NT$/km, and MRT and bus fares will be integrated (basic fare is NT$17.1: the rate is 1.81 /NT$/km) as shown in Row 3(Condition 2). The cost to passengers will remain about the same. These conditions also cause the greatest effect on the share of bus and motorbike. Compare the results of the second strategy with the third strategy. The share of bus is reduced by 0.72%, and the probability of choosing MRT will increase by 0.16%.

The empirical results show that the effect of various travel times and travel costs in mode choice. The market share of bus increases by 8%. This illustrates that if the local government implements a public transportation friendly policy in the area, there will be a higher probability of public transit.

The information was derived from the study of Comprehensive Transportation System Planning for Taipei Metropolitan Area. It surveyed bus speed, before and after the transit ways constructed in Taipei city.

Table 8. Market share sensitivities on condition choice (%)

Condition	Auto	Taxi	Motorbike	Bus	MRT
Base case	35.0	1.6	30.3	23.5	9.6
Condition 1	31.98	1.17	24.25	31.56	11.04
Condition 2	32.07	1.2	24.69	30.84	11.2

- MRT Neihu Line will be soon under construction.
- The statistics shown contain mean MRT ridership plus bus transfers.

5 Sustainable Transportation Development Strategies

In this section, a set of Sustainable Transportation Development Strategies is proposed. These strategies can ensure Taiwan urban area to develop toward sustainable transportation.

(1) Public Transit Interchange (PTI)

Through well-designed public transportation interchanges, passengers can rapidly transfer to other transportation modes (Fig.3). As "public transportation" has been adopted as one of the prime policies, we shall pay attention to intermodal transportation linkage. However, poor performance is widely found, as different transportation modes are not integrated due to the rigidity of administrations, as well as departmentalism. Therefore, we are trying hard to encourage different departments work together on establishing PTI, we believe it will make a difference.

(2) Public Private Partnership (PPP)

Due to the difficulties of acquiring sufficient land and considerable capital for transportation systems, PPP has been considered to be one of the best solutions for the public constructions. With teamwork between public and private sectors, efficiency and revenue of operation can be immensely enhanced.

(3) Transferring Bus System

Transferring bus system combined with the MRT line needs to be provided in order to efficiently expand the hinterland service scope of the MRT. Moreover, a convenient feeder bus system can also encourage the usage of public transportation, reduce the car usage at the same time. However, some of the bus routs are still overlapping and competing with the MRT, this causes the inefficiency of source. Therefore, reintegrate the bus routes and MRT is necessary.

(4) Applying Intelligent Transportation System (ITS)

a. Dynamic Information Systems

BRT and feeder bus system facilitated with the renovated Dynamic Information System are able to allow passengers to foresee the arrival time of their buses. It has been a tremendous progress for innovation as it reduces the passengers' perceptional waiting time, while other passengers have to insist waiting without knowing the bus arrival time.

b. Contactless IC Smart Cards Ticketing Systems

Both of the present MRT and bus cards are non-compatible and only suitable individually. Moreover, the present contact cards are neither convenient nor efficient for using in the crowded peak hours due to high transaction time. Accordingly, contactless IC smart cards are more useful in saving transaction time and its convenience will encourage public transportation usage.

(5) Creating Humane Environments for Pedestrians and Cyclists

To promote public transportation, we must provide a door-to-door service by create a comfortable and continuous sidewalk both for pedestrian and cyclist. Taipei City Government is now working hard to sweep away all the barriers including motorcycle parking and vendors on pedestrian sidewalk, and trying to establish a comfortable and continuous pedestrian sidewalk system.

6 Concluding remarks and suggestions

This paper reviews the Bus Rapid Transit development and its achievement in Taipei, and constructs a model forecasting the ridership in Neihu Area, in which light industrial makers and some high tech manufacturers are widely developing.

(1) This study shows that the transportation demand will rapidly grow as soon in the area and private automobile usage will boom, contributed with both the present lack of MRT line and poor bus service during the rush hours. The result of the forecast shows that quite a certain level of drivers would like to give up cars if convenient and rapid public transportation is available.

(2) Departments such as Traffic Planning, Urban Development and Mass Rapid Transit should cast the departmentalism and be more active to coordinate each other in order to cooperate together establishing sustainable environment for the future development. The department should allow denser development and diversify the land use along the public transportation

corridor. The department of Mass Rapid Transit should consider transferring system for passengers, and build up an internalized, comfortable and rapid transferring environment while designing the MRT stations.

(3) This paper also proposes a set of strategies, which can ensure Taiwan urban area to build up a long-term sustainable transportation development. To apply these strategies can also lead Taiwan to gradually develop toward sustainability.

Fig.3. The concept of the PTI

References

[1]   Ya-Lian Consultants Inc., "The Study of Comprehensive Transportation System Planning for Taipei Metropolitan Area," Omitted by Bureau of Transportation Taipei City Government, 1997.

[2]   Duan, L., "NMNL Model of Mode Choice," Transportation Journal Quarterly, Vol.13, No.3, pp.285-308, 1984.

[3]   Lave, C.A. and Train, K., "A Disaggregate Model of Auto-Type Choice," Transportation Research 13A, pp.1-9, 1979.

[4]   Quarmby, D., "Choice of Travel Mode for The Journey to Work," Journal of Transport Economics and Policy 1, pp273-314, 1967.

[5]   S.K. Jason Chang, The Director of the Project, "The Draft of Strategies for Sustainable Transportation in Taipei—The Case Study of Neihu Light Industrial District," Yen Ching-Ling Industrial Research Institute, National Taiwan University, 2001.

[6]   Bonsall, J., "The Busway as Rapid Transit Option," APTA Rapid Transit Conference, 1989.

[7]   Gardner, K. and Cobain, P.A., "Bus Priorities: a solution to Urban Congestion?" 1998.

[8]   Goodman, J., Laube, M. and Schwenk, J., "Issues in Bus Rapid Transit," United States Federal Administration. 2000.

[9]   Hayward, G., "Developing the London Bus Priority Network," 1998

[10] S.K. Jason Chang, S.T. Chien and Y.L. James Du "Transit-Oriented Development Strategies," Raid Transit Systems and Technology, Department of Rapid Transit Systems of Taipei City Government, 2000

[11] S.K. Jason Chang and Y.L. James Du, "Sustainable Development and Green Transportation—Taipei Experience" 9th Symposium of Cross-Strait Urban Transportation, 2001.

Evaluation of a transportation project with the analytic hierarchy process: best parking angle selection

K. P. Anagnostopoulos, B. Stephanis, D. Dimitriou &
A. Vavatsikos
Department of Civil Engineering
Democritus University of Thrace, Greece

Abstract

The design, planning and construction scheduling of the infrastructure works to meet the needs for the Olympic Games of 2004 in Athens are major challenges that the engineers of our country are faced. The location of facilities and the organisation of the transportation system of the capital are prerequisites for the even waging of the Olympic Games. In this paper the Analytic Hierarchy Process is used for the alternatives evaluation for an Olympic transportation project in order to estimate spatial parameters, such as the parking angle, for the facilities of Olympic Tennis Stadium.

1 Introduction

It is well known that the methodological approach for the planning and the operation in Parking Areas constitutes an issue of high scientific and financial interest. When the planning is achieved without methodology, control, rationality and innovations, in specialised subjects important for the regular traffic, such as the pedestrians and vehicles safety, important problems arise [1, 2, 3, 4]. The heavy traffic and the without rules passing of pedestrians and vehicles, the lacks in the labelling are some of them. Planning of parking areas acquires even more interest when it is focused to the case of Stadiums in which the athletic events for the 2004 Olympic Games will take place.

In this paper we are dealing with the planning of a parking area, for the 10.000 spectators Tennis Olympic stadium, defining the principles of planning, and the needs for safety and functional use at the duration of the games. The criteria are determined in order to evaluate the priorities of the alternatives concerning the overall goal, which is the selection of the optimal parking angle of the vehicles parking. The evaluation of the alternatives was based on a multicriteria approach for which the *Analytic Hierarchy Process* (AHP) was used. The AHP has been selected due to its efficacy in analysing a problem by decomposing it into subsystems, its inclusion of possible interactive effects and its power to handle several criteria. The application of the method was supplied by data deriving from a technical study in which the urban, engineering and environmental characteristics of the problem are fully analysed [5]. The hierarchies structuring, the checking of the inconsistencies of the judgments and the sensitivity analyses were realised using Expert Choice 9.0, a software package developed for AHP analysis.

2 The Analytic Hierarchy Process

AHP is a systematic procedure for dealing with complex decision-making problems in which many competing alternatives (projects, actions, scenarios) exist [7, 8, 9]. The alternatives are ranked using several quantitative and/or qualitative criteria, depending on how they contribute in achieving an overall goal.

AHP is based on a hierarchical structuring of the elements that are involved in a decision problem. The hierarchy incorporates the knowledge, the experience and the intuition of the decision-maker for the specific problem. The simplest hierarchy consists of three levels. On the top of the hierarchy lies the decision's goal. On the second level lie the criteria by which the alternatives (third level) will be evaluated. In more complex situations, the main goal can be broken down into subgoals or/and a criterion (or property) can be broken down into subcriteria. People who are involved in the problem, their goals and their policies can also be used as additional levels.

The hierarchy evaluation is based on pairwise comparisons. The decision-maker compares two alternatives A_i and A_j using a criterion and assigns a numerical value to their relative weight. The result of the comparison is expressed in a fundamental scale of values ranging from 1 (A_i, A_j contribute equally to the objective) to 9 (the evidence favoring A_i over A_j is of the highest possible order of affirmation). Given that the n elements of a level are evaluated in pairs using an element of the immediately higher level, an n×n *comparison matrix* is obtained. If the immediate higher level includes m criteria, m matrices will be formed. In every comparison matrix all the main diagonal elements are equal to one ($a_{ii} = 1$) and two symmetrical elements are reciprocals of each other ($a_{ij} \times a_{ji} = 1$).

The decision-maker's judgements may not be consistent with one another. A comparison matrix is consistent if and only if $a_{ij} \times a_{jk} = a_{ik}$ for all i, j, k. AHP measures the inconsistency of judgments by calculating the *consistency index* CI of the matrix

$$CI = \frac{\lambda_{max} - n}{n-1}$$

where λ_{max} is the principal eigenvalue of the matrix.

The consistency index CI is in turn divided by the *average random consistency index* RI to obtain the *consistency ratio* CR.

$$CR = \frac{CI}{RI}$$

The RI index is a constant value for an n×n matrix, which has resulted from a computer simulation of *n×n* matrices with random values from the 1-9 scale and for which $a_{ij} = 1/a_{ji}$. If CR is less than 5% for a 3×3 matrix, 9% for a 4×4 matrix, and 10% for larger matrices, then the matrix is consistent.

Once its values are defined, a comparison matrix is normalised and the local priority (the relative dominance) of the matrix elements with respect to the higher level criterion is calculated. The overall priority of the current level elements is calculated by adding the products of their local priorities by the priority of the corresponding criterion of the immediately higher level. Next, the overall priority of a current level element is used to calculate the local priorities of the immediately lower level which use it as a criterion, and so on, till the lowest level of the hierarchy is reached. The priorities of the lowest level elements (alternatives) provide the relative contribution of the elements in achieving the overall goal.

3 Principles of planning

The diagram of flow, the determination of allowing movements, the traffic lane and the traffic nodes constitute important parts of the road network because its traffic capacity depends on the rational design in order to provide effectiveness, road safety, avoidance of the traffic tails, etc. For these reasons, the traffic regulation plan must satisfy the following parameters:

- Unhindered traffic flow.
- Safe traffic flow in order to separate and ensure the ways for the pedestrians and the vehicles.
- Sufficient traffic capacity in the diagram of flow, the roads, the nodes, the intersections, the parking areas and finally at the checkpoints.
- Acceptable construction and operational cost.
- Satisfactory adaptation in the requirements of Olympic installations, taking into account the existing road network as well as the requirements of the auxiliary tennis stadiums.
- Satisfactory adaptation in the architecture of the stadium and the environment.

The unhindered and safe traffic flow depends on the general regulation of the traffic (diagram of flow, the geometrical design, nodes, pavements, the labelling, etc). The safety of the traffic flow is depending on the system of the providing information to the users of the parking area (particularly to those that have not visited the auxiliaries or the country before) and the providing guidance to the drivers, at the entry and the exit to the space of tennis athletic installations. Taking into account that the arrival of the spectators, journalists and VIP's, is starting only a few minutes before the beginning of the event and the departure is taking place immediately after the end of the game, we should notice that the traffic flow which will be guided at the road network as well as to the pedestrian passages will be increased. As a consequence, the traffic capacity of the road network will be judged from the number of the movements that a driver need in order to park, so that excessive waiting time will not arise in the traffic of the vehicles and the buses as well.

The construction and operational costs are considered as acceptable when the total expenses of construction, operation and maintenance remain in low levels and at the same time it is ensured a high level of safety, traffic capacity and adaptation to the environment.

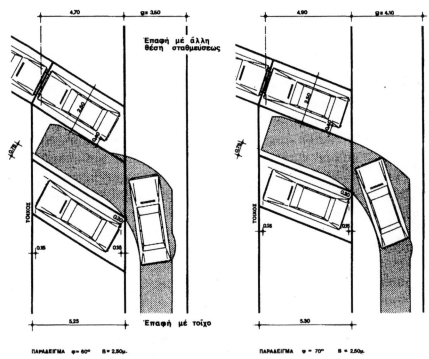

Figure 1: Parking with 60 and 70 degrees angle.

4 Parking angle and parking areas

Parking angle (θ) is defined from the axis of the parked vehicle and the axis of passage access to the parking area (fig. 1). This angle defines the type of the parking area. Thus, accordingly with the values, that the angle receives, the following categories are determined:

- Parallel Parking (θ = 0°).
- Vertical Parking (θ = 90°).
- Parking with angle (45°≤θ<90°).

Angles with values smaller than 45° are not recommended because of the large surfaces of manoeuvres that are created.

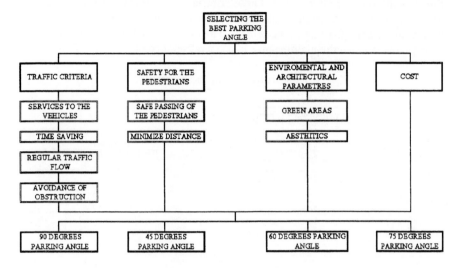

Figure 2: Evaluation hierarchy.

The use of angles in the parking allows increasing the parking ability for every meter in length of kerb. This advantage increases up to the vertical parking (θ = 90°), where 2.5 to 3 times more vehicles are served in contrast with the parallel parking. As long as the parking angle increases, bigger space of road surface is required because of the increase in the parking depth and the manoeuvres needed for a vehicle to park.

In the design of the whole transportation network concerning the spectators' and athletes' displacement from or to the stadiums has taken into account the under study parking area. The dimensions of the parking place are determined from the dimensions of a typical vehicle, the distances between the vehicles and the existing obstructions. The distance between the vehicles ensures a space of safety round the vehicle. This space is essential for the access, door opening and the essential manoeuvres while leaving the stadium.

The choice of width for each parking place is determined by taking into account the types of cars and the needs of persons that are going to make use of the parking area. In Greece it is mentioned that the distance between two vehicles will be 0.70 m. For the determination of depth for each parking place it is essential to determine two depths: one for the case of parking place next to a wall, a kerb or any kind of obstacle and another for the case of parking place next to a neighbouring place in which the depth is limited.

5 The problem hierarchy

The hierarchy in order to approach the problem is structured in four levels (fig.

2). On the first level lies the overall goal, i.e. the selection of the optimal parking angle. On the second level of the hierarchy lie the basic criteria that are used for the evaluation of the alternatives. These criteria are the traffic criteria, the safety assurance of the pedestrian passages, the environmental and architectural component and finally the cost of the project. The cost criterion includes not only the capital cost but also the maintenance and operational costs.

Table 1: Results of the hierarchy.

Criteria	Normalized eigenvectors	Rerative Composite Priorities	Normalized eigenvectors of the scenarios according to the criteria			
			Scenario 1	Scenario 2	Scenario 3	Scenario 4
Traffic	0,511	0,511				
Pedestrians	0,292	0,292				
Enviromental & archt.	0,153	0,153				
Costs	0,045	0,045	0,153	0,372	0,234	0,241
Reliable servise	0,481	0,246	0,500	0,167	0,167	0,167
Time saving	0,073	0,037	0,500	0,167	0,167	0,167
Regular traffic flow	0,078	0,040	0,500	0,167	0,167	0,167
Complications & obstructions	0,368	0,188	0,500	0,167	0,167	0,167
Passing of pedestrians	0,833	0,243	0,400	0,200	0,200	0,200
Minimize distance	0,167	0,049	0,093	0,476	0,254	0,177
Grass places	0,750	0,115	0,141	0,455	0,263	0,141
Aesthtics	0,250	0,038	0,696	0,140	0,082	0,241
		Total Priorities	0,396	0,235	0,193	0,176

The third level is consisted of subcriteria in order to obtain a more comprehensive description of the problem.

In detail, the traffic criterion is formed by:
- The assurance of safety and the reliable service for the vehicles.
- The avoidance of manoeuvres causing the bad positioning of the vehicles in the parking place.
- The assurance of traffic flow under normal conditions into the parking area.
- The avoidance of complications and obstacles to the mass transport system.
  The subcriteria that characterise the safety for the pedestrians are:
- The assurance of safe passages for the pedestrians and handicapped people from/to the stadium and to/from the parking area.
- The minimisation in the walking distance.
  The subcriteria that characterise the environmental and architectural parameters are:
- Green areas.
- Aesthetic parameters and the adaptation to the stadium architecture (circular elements).

The evaluation of the hierarchy parameters is taking place in order to rate the alternative scenarios, which are placed at the last level of the hierarchy. In our model four scenarios are evaluated: scenario 1 ($\theta = 90°$), scenario 2 ($\theta = 45°$), scenario 3 ($\theta = 60°$), and scenario 4 ($\theta = 75°$). The best results are achieved with the use of three main tools. Firstly, the matrices of pairwise comparisons are formed. Secondly, the parameters are evaluated using the Analytic Hierarchy Process weight scale. Finally, the consistency of the pairwise comparison matrices is examinated.

The final ranking of the alternatives is formed by the sum of the relative composite priorities. In order to derive the relative priorities, we multiply the normalised eigenvectors of each scenario by the corresponding relative priority of the subcriteria. From the final ranking of the alternatives (table 1), we conclude that scenario 1 with a total priority of 39,6% is the most preferred.

6 Conclusions

The main objective of this paper is to present the advantages of the multicriteria analysis in the design of engineering projects, especially when it is difficult to obtain a mathematical formulation. Alternative scenarios according the specifications were formed in order to determine the best parking angle. The Analytic Hierarchy Process method was used to modelise the problem and to evaluate the priorities of alternatives according the criteria, which concern the parameters of traffic, security for the pedestrians, vehicles movements, the environmental standards, the architectural design and the cost parameters.

References

[1] Fruin J. J., *Pedestrian, Planning and Design,* Metropolitan Association of Urban Designers and Environmental Planners, INC, 1971.

[2] Frantzeskakis J., Pitsiava – Latinopoulou M., Tsamboulas D., *Traffic Management,* Athens 1997 (in greek).

[3] Frantzeskakis J., *Transportation Design and Traffic Engineering,* Athens 1980 (in greek).

[4] *Parking Principles,* Special Report 125, Highway Research Bord, National Research Council, National Academy of Sciences, National Academy of Engineering, 1971.

[5] Stephanis B., *Transportation Engineering and Design,* Democritus University of Thrace – Xanthi – Greece 1990 (in greek).

[6] Stephanis B. and Dimitriou D., *Design of Traffic Movements for Vehicle and Pedestrian and Design for Parking Areas for the Olympic Stadium of Tennis in Greece,* Athens 2001 (in greek).

[7] Saaty T.L., How to Make a Decision: The Analytic Hierarchy Process, *European Journal of Operational Research,* **48**, pp. 9-26, 1990.

[8] Saaty T.L., Vargas L.G., *Decision Making with the Analytic Hierarchy Process,* RWS Publications, 1994.

[9] Saaty T.L., *Decision Making for Leaders,* 3rd Edition, RWS Publications, 1995.

Simplified land use assessment on car commuting energy

S. Myojin[1] & D. Suzuki[2]

[1]*Faculty of Environmental Science and Technology, Okayama University, Japan*
[2]*The Graduate School of Natural Science and Technology, Okayama University, Japan*

Abstract

The model has three submodels; land use, road and railway network, and commuter trips. The first includes two parameters, residential and workplace with locational densities over the circularized study area. Three kinds of simplified density distributions and the variations are introduced to each resident and workplace, named conic, reverse conic, level and railway-oriented locations, respectively. In the road and railway submodel, the road is defined by traffic lane density distribution, and several simple railway networks are provided. Major parts of the commuter trips submodel are commuter trip distribution, which delivers commuters from residences to workplaces, railway choice and car commuting speed on traffic lane. Energy for car commuting is calculated using energy rate function.

The results are (1) The case without railway; energy is minimized at the combination of conic resident and workplace locations, (2) The case with railway; the effects of railway network and railway oriented relocation on car commuting energy are shown against the combinations of the simplified density distributions. Railway oriented location has characteristic energy use tendency but some details remain to be confirmed.

1   Introduction

The paper is on the line of the authors' interest in assessing energy for urban transportation (Myojin, *et al.*,1999,1999). A model for assessing resident and job locations provided with road with / without railway networks on car commuting energy is dealt with in the present paper. The study area is assumed to be in a circle. Car commuting energy is calculated for those combinations of simplified resident-workplace locations and the variations provided with road with / without railway networks. The results included are some spatial distributions of car commute density over the study area and comparative energy uses resulting from those locational combinations and some railway oriented relocations of the original simplified locations.

2   Modeling

2.1   Definition

The model is outlined in Figure 1. Major parts of the model are resident-workplace location, spatial distribution of commute trip density, commute density distribution on traffic lane, car commuting speed and energy. Assessment is made on energy for car commuting.

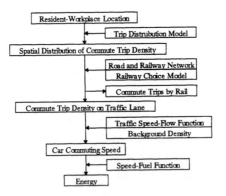

Figure 1: Flow diagram for model description

2.2   Resident-workplace location

Three kinds of simplified density distributions are introduced to each resident and workplace; decreasing, increasing linearly outwards and flat, named conic, reverse conic, level location, respectively. These are called the original simplified locations hereafter in the paper. Every possible set of original simplified locations is alphabetized in Table 1.

A variation is added to the original ones : railway-oriented location. The railway-oriented location finds its local peak density along railway and decreases monotonously off railway line. This will be shown later in further details.

Table 1: Combinations of original simplified locations

workplace density / resident density	(peak)	(flat)	(valley)
(peak)	A	B	C
(flat)	D	E	F
(valley)	G	H	I

2.3 Commute trip distribution

The probability $p(\overrightarrow{P_1 P_2})$ of a commute trip from origin P_1 to destination P_2 is assumed as

$$p(\overrightarrow{P_1 P_2}) = \kappa \, u(P_1)v(P_2)f(l) \qquad (1)$$

where $u(P_1)$ = normalized potential function for commute trip generating that is defined by some parameters at P_1, $v(P_2)$ = normalized potential function for commute trip attracting that is also described by some parameters at P_2, $f(l)$ = commute length distribution in which l = commute length defined by P_1 and P_2, and κ =constant. Integration of the probability $p(\overrightarrow{P_1 P_2})$ by P_2 over the study area, keeping P_1 fixed, must be equal to $u(P_1)$, from which $\kappa = 1/A(P_1)$. So we have

$$p(\overrightarrow{P_1 P_2}) = u(P_1)v(P_2)f(l)/A(P_1) \qquad (2)$$

where $A(P_1) = \int_{P_1} v(P_2)f(l)dP_2$ (integration of $v(P_2)f(l)$ over the whole possible points P_2 keeping P_1 fixed, where P_1, P_2 and l are illustrated in Figure 2 with other notations to appear).

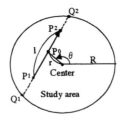

Figure 2: A commute trip from origin P_1 to destination P_2
passing through $P_0(r,\theta)$

2.4 Spatial distribution of car commute density

This is defined by the number of car commutes passing through an infinitely small area. We define a probability $p(r,\theta)$ of a commute trip passing through an arbitrary point P_0 in Figure 2. A brief explanation for the probability $p(r,\theta)$ is as follows;

① Integrate $p(\overrightarrow{P_1P_2})r_c(P_1,P_2;P)$ by P_1 along the line from P_0 to Q_1 after integrating the function by P_2 along the line from P_0 to Q_2 (Fig.2), where $r_c(P_1,P_2;P) = $ car choice ratio of a commute trip from P_1 to P_2, when railway service is available, $P = $ population and Q_1 and $Q_2 = $ intersections of the extended line $\overline{P_1P_2}$ and the periphery, and

② Do the sum of the similar integration by turning the line in 360-degrees round P_0.

Obviously the spatial distribution $p(r,\theta)$ thus obtained is homogeneous on concentric circle only for the original simplified locations without railway network but not so for the otherwise.

2.5 Road and railway network

2.5.1 Road network
Road network in the paper is represented by traffic lane density distribution over the study area. Traffic lane density here is defined by traffic lane length over an infinitely small area. Based on the data from some Japanese local cities having population from 600,000 to 1,000,000, this is assumed by a negative exponential function

$$n_l = \eta e^{-\varsigma r} \tag{3}$$

where r is distance from the center, η and ς are constants that may or may not depend on population. This will be made clear later. Eqn.(3) is based on another assumption that the density is homogenous over concentric circle.

2.5.2 Railway network

Typical but simple railway networks are drawn : one ring and / or four radial lines of equal length meeting at right angles at the center of study area. In the paper, three network patterns are tested, as shown in Figure 3 ; one varying ring, four radial lines of equal varying length and one varying ring on four radial lines of full length.

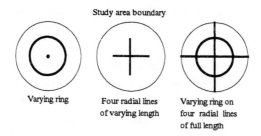

Figure 3: Railway network (heavy line)

2.6 Car commuting speed

This means traffic speed on lane through the hours (peak hours in the morning , because just commute to work is regarded). This is calculated using so called speed-density relation in which background car trip density is also regarded on the data from traffic census in Japan.

2.7 Energy for car commute

Car commuting energy is calculated by

$$E = \int_0^R \int_0^{2\pi} d_1(r,\theta;P)e(r,\theta)rd\theta dr \qquad (4)$$

where $e(r,\theta)$ = energy rate (kcal/car trip-km) converted from fuel-speed function identified for Japanese passenger cars on the data from the late Ministry of Transport.

3 Calculation

3.1 Preparation

3.1.1 Railway-oriented locations

Figure 4 illustrates railway-oriented location. Railway-oriented location is given by a conditional relocation of the original simplified location. That is made in the way that, for example by the radial railway line, the locational density is conserved on every concentric circle throughout the relocation, conversely, no local centralization and / or decentralization of the original density should take place through the modification. The density conservation in the case of four radial railway lines is illustrated in detail in Figure 4, where the figures $ABCD$, $A'B'CD$ and $A''B''C$ are equal in area each other and of course the area of $ABCD$ is defined by the original simplified locational density, that is uniform over a circle, and the $A'B'CD$ and $A''B''C$ by the relocated ones. The height DA or DA' is the density at D lying on a line dividing the area contained between adjacent radial lines into two equal territories. Another modified density is drawn symmetrically on the other side of the radial line.

A measure is introduced to define the extent to which the relocated density is inclined to railway line. For example, the relocated density $A''B''C$ is more inclined to the line than the $A'B'CD$, while no inclination is found in the original density $ABCD$. Thus the density subtracted the original one (CB) from the relocated one (CB' or CB'' etc.) at point C that lies on railway line, divided by the original one, may be most preferable as the measure because it, being defined simply and commonly throughout railway line and of physical meaning, can meet the requirements as above. It is easy to see that it ranges from zero to infinity.

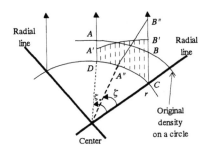

Figure 4: Illustrative railway-oriented locations

3.1.2 Commute length distribution

Following function is introduced

$$f(l) = \gamma \, l^{\alpha} e^{-\beta r} \tag{5}$$

where α, β and γ are constants. The function finds its peak at $l = l_p = \alpha / \beta$. The peak position is estimated, for example, at $l_p = 1.8$ kilometers ($\alpha = 0.735$ and $\beta = 0.407$) based on the data from trip survey in Okayama where the authors live and work. In the present paper, however, $l_p = 2.0$ is assumed. Normalization factor γ is evaluated in due result.

3.1.3   Railway choice

Railway choice ratio, instead of car choice one, is assumed as a linear function ;

$$r_i(l, l_a, l_i) = a + bl + cl_a + dl_e \tag{6}$$

where l = commute length, l_a (l_e) = access to (egress from) the nearest railway, and a, b, c and d = constants. Based on the data from trip survey in some Japanese local cities of 600,000~1,000,000 population, the constants were estimated at $a = 0.0981$, $b = 0.00269$ and $c = d = -0.0103$. Car choice ratio r_c is given by

$$r_c = r_c(P_1, P_2; P)$$

$$= 1 - r_i(l, l_a, l_e) = 1 - \{0.0981 + 0.00269l - 0.0103(l_a + l_e)\} \tag{7}$$

where $600,000 \leqq P \leqq 1,000,000$, and l, l_a and l_e depend, of course, on P_1 and P_2. The ratio is applied to the cases with railway network.

3.1.4   Total commute trips

The percentage of the total number of trips to work to the city population proved nearly constant ranging from 35.8 to 38.1% despite of population. So the total peak hour trips to work is assumed here as

$$T_{com} = 0.37P \tag{8}$$

3.1.5   Spatial distribution of traffic lane density

Through testing based on road network data from some Japanese local cities, the constants in eqn. (3) were estimated at $\eta = 7.283 + 0.07P$ and $\varsigma = 0.325$, which means traffic lane density is distributed in proportion to population.

3.1.6   Other factors

These are estimated on the data from traffic census and trip survey in Japanese cities : $g = 29.5$, $h = -1.20$ and $\varepsilon = 1.37$ in eqns (4) and (6), respectively. No statistical significance was found of correlation of ε with population.

3.2   Results

The following is some typical results obtained so far;

3.2.1   Spatial distribution of car commute density

Figure 5 shows spatial distributions of car commute trip density resulting from the original simplified locations (without railway) A,B,C and I. Car commute trip density is divided by the corresponding traffic lane density to get spatial distribution of car commute density on traffic lane.

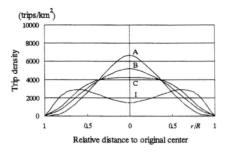

Figure 5: Spatial distribution of commute trip density
(original simplified location)

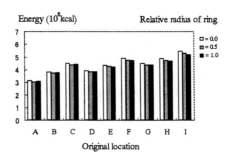

Figure 6: Energy use (original simplified locations with one varying ring
on four radial lines of full length)

3.2.2 Mixed effects
Original simplified location with railway

Figure 6 shows comparative energy use from the original simplified locations provided with railway networks, one ring on four radial lines of full length, in which $R = 9.7$ km is given to the relative radius of ring line R_r / R. Relative radius = 0, for example, means original simplified location provided only with four radial lines of full length.

Figure 7 shows the marginal effects of ring line in terms of the percentage of energy reduction by ring line to the energy use resulting from the original simplified locations provided with the four radial lines of full length.

Railway-oriented location

Figure 8 shows energy use resulting from relocation of the original simplified locations A, B, C and I provided with full length radial lines. Horizontal axis is named railway-oriented gradation, the measure for railway-orientedness of the relocated density. By definition, each corresponds to that from the original simplified location only when the gradatiton = 0.

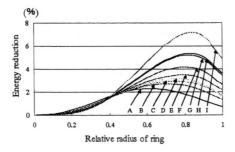

Figure 7: Energy reduction by varying ring line on four radial lines of full length (original simplified locations)

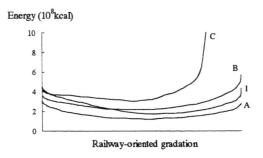

Figure 8: Energy use (railway-oriented locations)

3.3 Examination and discussion

Spatial distributions of car commute density resulting from the original simplified locations without railway are, as a matter of course, grouped into three patterns; bell, plate and plateau (Figure 5). Most of these spatial distributions, divided by the traffic lane density distribution given, are transformed to a certain distribution of car commute density on traffic lane, having a bottom at the center and a concentric peak density moving outwardly in alphabetical order of the locations. This comes mostly from an exponentially decreasing tendency of traffic lane density distribution used.

Energy use from the original simplified locations without railway has a clear tendency to increase toward south-east corner of locations in Table 1. Location A is the most centralized while I is the most decentralized. It is noteworthy that, with the conditions attached in the paper, energy use from I is round 1.8 times as much as that from A.

The maximum percentage of incremental energy reduction by varying ring line, set on full length radial lines provided for the original simplified locations, to the energy use form those without ring line falls within 2.5 and 7.0%, corresponding to locations A and I, respectively. The ring lines to give peak reduction grow up roughly in alphabetical order.

respectively. The ring lines to give peak reduction grow up roughly in alphabetical order.

The results from the railway-oriented locations are partly true to our expectations but partly not so. As is expected, car commuting energy decreases slowly with the railway-oriented gradation but it is, unexpectedly, reversed slowly and rapidly after that. This unexpected behaviors of A, B and C is characterized by the existence of minimum energy use where two conflicting effects of energy use of growing car trip density in the area along railway, are balanced. The former surpasses the latter to the left of the balancing graduation but is surpassed by the latter to the right where sharp increase in energy use is caused by higher traffic density. Remarks on an uncertain behavior of relocation of I will be made at the end of the following section.

4   Conclusions

Energy use for car commuting is minimized by given by the location A given by a combination of conic resident and workplace locations, while maximized by I given by a combination of the reverse conic locations. This is attributed to the fact that the location A is most centralized among resident-workplace locations given but I most decentralized. Level locations of resident and / or workplace give of course moderate energy use for car commuting.

On the whole the effect of railway line, provided on the original simplified location, on reducing energy for car commute is larger in reverse conic location than in the conic. This may be attributed to the nature of reverse conic location likelier to generate long commute which is likely to make railway choice. On the other hand, however, reverse conic location is most energy consumptive for car commuting.

The railway-oriented location is defined by a conditional relocation of the original simplified location. The results from the relocations are to and at the same time against our expectations. A certain result so far is that car commute energy decreases slowly with the railway-oriented gradation so long as it is not higher.

The model might have been successful in the sense that we could get general understanding of energy use for car commute generated from several typical simplified locations of resident and workplace. Several problems, however, are left for examination for further improvement of the model. These are related to; (1) traffic speed function, (2) trip length distribution and traffic lane density distribution and (3) railway choice model. The following are remarks for model improvement: (1) Traffic speed function assumed in the paper is so called speed-flow relationship estimated for existing traffic lane. We applied it to calculate traffic speed at an arbitrary point by substituting the flow at an infinitely small area including the point. But the relationship for lane might not necessarily give traffic speed at point. This will be improved by calibrating the estimated speed-flow relationship so that special distribution of calculated speed may fit good to the observed which is easy to find using traffic census data. (2) The distributions used were estimated for existing Japanese local cities where resident and workplace are located nearly conicly, that is, these might be specialized to location A for example, but not to location I for example. Widely useful distributions for various locations are needed. Firstly for traffic lane density distribution, one of the promising ways will be found by introducing new function of resident and workplace density together with some other variables if useful. One of these functions will be expressed by linear combination of those variables. It is of course identified on existing data. Secondly for trip length distribution, the problem, if any, may be related not to the function itself but to the values of constants included because the function has been accepted widely for its flexibility coming from the two key constants α and β. Fluctuation analysis of α, β and α/β for various existing cities may suggest need/no need for revised values for reverse-conic locations. (3) Railway choice model will be polished by introducing service frequency, fare and capacity parameters. This may be achieved by analyzing commuters' mode choice in various cities. Data from person trip survey are available for the analysis. Finally for an uncertain behavior of energy use for relocation of I, our attention for improvement will be focused on calculation program for processing projectingly high density of car trip on lane that might cause sharp special fluctuations in traffic speed leading to missing calculation of energy use.

The author would like to express their gratitude to anonymous referees for their instructive comments. They are also grateful to Stacey Hobbs for her assistance. Revision of the paper could not be completed without her.

References

[1] Myojin,S., Abe,H., Urban Transportation Energy in Japan and Residential Location Assessment on Work Trip Energy, Selected proceedings of the 8th World Conference on Transport Research, Vol.4, pp.228-239, 1999.

[2] Myojin,S. Abe,H. and Nakamichi,K., Commuting Energy Assessment Through Simplified Resident Workplace Location, Modelling and Management in Transportation, Vol.2, pp.67-73, 1999.

S.A.T. project: tetra-re-dimensioning of urban space.

J. Serrano, N. A Pecorari & V. Serrano
Serrano Pecorari & Assoc. Buenos Aires, Argentina.

Abstract

Based upon a conceptual-statistical urban analysis regarding the critical situation found in modern cities/mega cities (saturation, pollution, degradation and lack of interrelation), a diagnosis was achieved posing the 'bi-dimensional use' of present urban settlements. As a response, the concept of an 'urban re-structure' became our hypothesis. We developed a Project that proposes the 'tetra-re-dimensioning (4D) of urban space'. To achieve this, we had to create and design a 'tool' (S.A.T.), that would, upon its implementation in cities, allow the following: decrease urban pollution standards; decrease the rate of urban accidents; lead to a decongestion of obstructed neuralgic areas; reduce the pace of urban life; promote optimisation of time; generate 'architectural mutations', breaking-up the present 'vertical-function' dependency; increase security standards in case of natural or manmade catastrophes, promote a wider range of options regarding access/evacuations means; transform existing means of transport; generate the increase of green public spaces; avoid wounds in the urban-grid; regenerate residual-urban spaces; use economical resources efficiently.

S.A.T. (Sistema Autónomo de Transporte - undergoing Patent registration) creates the first steps towards the 'breaking-up' of the 'static-way of use' in contemporary cities. It is an electric-private/public transport-system for people and/or freight. It works under different directions of movement such as horizontal, vertical and on a gradient. Its main characteristic derives from the possibility it has of connecting different spaces that are to be found, not under the same geometrical plane, but under different-direction axis (x, y and z), belonging to different planes of use. In this way, it would generate and define a 'tetra-dimensional' liveable space. The S.A.T. project is an innovation that could act in a catalytic way, towards the overall improvement in life-quality in present urban areas, drawing a trend towards 'sustainability'.

1 Present city-profile, urban crisis

In order to define our Project background we must place ourselves on a scale of megacities, such as Tokyo, New York, Seoul, Sao Paulo, Shangai, among others. The concept of mega-cities, which arose in the last period of the 20th century, involves several yet unsolved issues regarding our present and future life as citizens. The visible consequences that define the present situation that cities are submerged in were taken into account. Themes such as sound and visual contamination, pollution, increasing worldwide migrations towards cities, inadequate use of land, low proportions of inner-city green public spaces in metropolitan areas, saturation of means of transport, inflexibility of public-service systems or the lack of optimisation regarding time-lost periods generated by the unsystemic use and development of modern cities. Worldwide urban policy appears then, as a main significant factor on which to focus our attention in order to consolidate future sustainable urban settlements.

Statistics show urban populations expanding at a high rate (more than 6% annually), therefore the conformation of megacities is a main issue. Faced therefore with such a contrasting reality, we should immerse ourselves in the idea that we do not live in cities; cities make us live the way we do. There is a role-player problem, therefore, who is the actor and who plays the scenario? Have we become stunts in our own drama of life? Can we find common denominators in everyday life in present urban areas, without considering their geographical location? If this is so, how many of us arrive at work, to start a productive day and have already faced a one-hour drive? How many of us spend hours that transforms into days, on a highway, or stopped in a traffic jam? How many of us believe in achieving better quality-of-life standards? How many of us realize that the increase of inner-residual spaces leads to greater insecurity, more garbage-lots and increase social-rejection?

A conceptual reading of the developing process found in some of our contemporary metropolis shows a clear physical fragmentation, of continuous and discontinuous and a lack of compatibility between time and speed. We recognize the modern urban city as a multiplicity of fragments, which is distant from acting as a whole. We can qualify them as constantly spreading and dismembering, an addition of unconnected spaces.

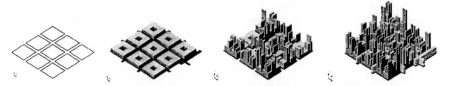

Figure 1: Urban densification and suffocation.

Does the human being play the main role in the life he lives in these cities? Nothing so obvious (in theory) and so improbable (in practice)... In early times man acted as the measurement unit and reference pattern in the development of human settlements, concept now lost in our present cities and societies. We are no longer the rulers of our 'space'. We are not the ones to define our scenery (urban landscapes). Further more, we becomes mere 'players' in it (pre-established game with rules to be followed).

2 Urban-geometry (structure): Diagnosis

Several trends towards sustainability are, nowadays, taken into consideration. For instance, the promotion of compact-urban developments, creating therefore high-density urban realms avoiding travel distances (but increasing congestion and pollution). On the other hands, others that promote extended (sprawling) urban landscapes, responding to low-density settlements 'sustained' under a rigid road based structure (promoting long-travel distances as well as fragmentation, not encouraging the appearance of mixed-use areas). These main trends make contact in a common denominator (our Diagnosis) that could take their theoretical-basis to collapse. Therefore, by reading how cities are 'used' we are able to understand their structure (geometrical at first, and then organizations and uses).

If we analyse the role of urban space, we notice that it should constitute the supporting space of the city's activities, promoting its organization and structure. The fact of being undefined and not qualified makes it impossible (in spite of exceptions) for interactions to occur. We see then that the three-dimensionality of the city, in relation to its function, appears conceptually represented on only a two-dimensional sense (actions taking place only on the plan-level at 0.00 m, ground zero). Therefore, the city-structure is shaped by a single main public-plane, in charge of 'absorbing' every function generated in the city, although it is already saturated. The overlapping of these functions (ironically on a 'same plane') generates the chaotic situation found in present urban cores. We find mere connections, only 'materialized' in it. Realty makes us see the saturation level it possesses, and since we talk about absorption, we talk about saturation (i.e. measurements of traffic jam in the City of San Pablo show statistics such as: 292 km of traffic queues existing simultaneously in the city). Therefore, the "non-use" of this space for interaction, is what keeps this ground level in its chaotic state.

A City could be, functionally represented then, from a bi-dimensional scheme of uses (i.e. the Urban Code), which regulates and organizes urban structure-conformation (defining commercial areas, residential areas, public-green areas, among others). Therefore, we pose as our Diagnosis then, that cities work as entities deriving from a conceptual-construction in 2D. Why make such a statement? Given the fact that spaces are being defined by areas.

 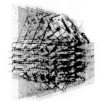

Figure 2: Urban code, conceptual progression from 2D to 3D.

This implies two things, first that spaces lose representation in one of their dimensions (taking what is conceptually attached to them) and in the second place that breakdowns occur, due to the limited flexibility they have to respond to each element that requires a 'piece of it' to develop. Therefore, fragmentation appears. For instance, the existence of a continuous-grid ruling this space, generated by vehicular circulation, affects the development of human activity, subjected to implicit laws of modern human-slavery vs. vehicle domain, constituting a sectorisation and atomisation of the use of space itself, in its real-three dimensional sense.

3 Hypothesis: Tetra-re-dimensioning of urban space

As a response to the Diagnosis obtained, the concept of an urban re-structure (producing mutations and changes under dimensional/functional features by altering spatial geometrical-conception and order) became our hypothesis. Understanding now the bi-dimensional (2D) functionality of existing cities and their consequences, we set up as a main objective: the tetra-re-dimensioning of urban space (4D). We believe that the close future will manifest itself based on these relationships, where the three dimensions (3D) won't be taken by default (tacit, expressed in vertical projections over a plan-structure) and the fourth dimension not taken theoretically but as a real one (TIME). Time, as a concept, shapes to what we understand nowadays as optimisation, taken as the measurement-unit, in the development of urban life. Thus, we pose the re-conformation of cities under the concept of a time-space integrated vision (this being our field as designers and our environment as citizens). It should be 'sustained' from the construction of Urban and Property Legislation Codes, making it possible to verify this concept in them, finding that at present this situation, definitely does not occur.

The tetra-re-dimensioning of urban space proposes then the 3D-use of our cities, optimised with time-factor. To achieve this; we had to create a 'tool': S.A.T. (a Project in itself) that upon its implementation in urban landscapes would allow this to happen, drawing a trend towards sustainability.

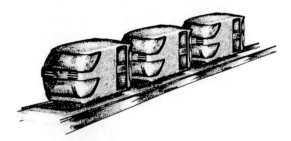

Figure 3: S.A.T. convoy.

S.A.T. Project, named under Sistema Autónomo de Transporte, (undergoing Patent Registration), creates the first steps towards the breaking-up with the bi-dimensional use of modern cities. The system has the special feature of working under different directions of movement such as horizontal, vertical and on a gradient (three direction-axis that shape and limit urban space). It conforms a private public transportation system because of the possibility of interacting under different urban scales, from one smaller and private (given for instance in one building or in a building complex) to a larger one, involved in the conformation of urban environment and being public. S.A.T.'s main characteristic resides in connecting different spaces that are to be found not under the same geometrical plane (buses, undergrounds, cars, elevators, trains, etc), but under different direction axis (x, y, z), belonging to different planes-of-use. In this way, therefore, S.A.T. would generate and define a 'tetra-dimensional-4D' (3D + time), liveable space. It would develop mainly in an urban and metropolitan environment, in the 'open' or trespassing the 'solid', not depending on 'tops' or 'bottoms'. The tetra-dimension concept proposes, to sustain the 3D-use and function of existing cities, therefore its way of transportation in/through them. S.A.T. would therefore, generate an interrelation between different heights, levels and directions, opening a random game of multiple commuting-options. We would start travelling through space, in a continuous uninterrupted change of levels. To give 'man' the wings he lacks, redefining his pedestrian role, returning his freedom to move in his own cities.

The structure of the system is a three dimensional one, generating a volumetric virtual-grid of organization and uses, that becomes more important thanks to the possibilities of interaction with itself (on different scales) and with other means of transport. Geometrical relationships therefore are created, based on a 3D-virtual-grid; in charge of defining the way we use, no longer our base-plan (ground-zero); but our space. Why do we talk about three dimensions then? All means of transport, work under a two-dimension structure, in only one plane-of-use (either xy-plane, finding buses, undergrounds, cars, etc; or under the xz-plane, in which the elevator is situated, therefore to be considered a vertical mean of transport, always inscribed under the same co-planar axis). S.A.T. works under three directions of movement, being able to move horizontally, vertically and on a gradient, as an ordinary displacement. Therefore, we can say that interactions do appear between different planes xy, xz and yz.

The main characteristic resides in that conceptually S.A.T. allows us to connect different spaces-of-use that are to be found, not on one same plane-axis, but under different direction-axis belonging to different planes of use, in different geometrical planes. We therefore generate a 3D-network, where optimisation given by the latter would, consequently, generate and define a 4D-habitable space.

4 S.A.T Project (Sistema Autonomo de Transporte)

The system is designed for the transportation of people and/or freight (around 15-20 passengers per unit). It consists of unitary electric-vehicles that would move along two tracks. Its cabin maintains its horizontal-level position regardless of changes in track direction or even height-levels. It is powered by an electric engine (DC 220v), which is also used to reduce speed and to regenerate energy, without producing noise or pollution by fuel-combustion. Its implementation will not create damaging electric fields. The tracks are modular structures in the form of suspended tubes, requiring minimum supports. On these, vehicles will run on tracks, made of materials that will absorb vibrations and provide adherence in every track section. The weather does not affect its deployment (rain, snow, wind, etc.). Several vehicles (units or in convoys) are able to circulate on one track, in its different displacement directions either in suspension or held in place. The duct is the space or path where the S.A.T runs, containing the guides. If the line develops outdoors, it will become virtual; but it will become blind inside a building (complemented by a security system against fire or accidents). The System is to be supervised by a Central Control Station, which may programme the route to be followed by convoys within intervals, on a same track, adding or withdrawing different vehicles from different routes. This will allow parked vehicles to be incorporated into the network as required (i.e. rush-hours). In case of accident, the CCS will be able to inject rescue or security forces (ambulances, fire-fighters, etc.) to the system for emergency attention, allowing free routes and permitting evacuation upon changes in directions generated by tracks by-passes. It will generate high-efficiency upon low speed.

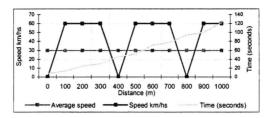

Figure 4: S.A.T. Performance

The geometrical structure of the system does not develop as a simple series of overlapping transportation planes. Our system is dynamic. It will, consequently, act as a catalytic tool towards the re-defining of urban space, generating mutations on architectural morphology and typologies. Interactions will appear between the urban grid (public) and buildings (private).

When we think of its implementation in the Cities, we can imagine a three-dimensional network, conformed by S.A.T. routes, the latter working on two tracks. We could find them externally attached to buildings, circulating internally, on underground levels, in trenches (entrenchment), at ground level, on a third or a fifth level or supported by columns, etc. It will never be evident on solid lateral or lower planes. Everything would be 'ethereal, virtual' and vehicles that roll on tracks, will appear unexpectedly due to their silent movement, only revealed by shadow projection.

Cities are 'organic' entities. Organic because they are in constant movement, in constant change and defined by a continuing mutating-structure. Progressive growth, densification, partial obstructions or inner-migration, generate these changes. Thus, S.A.T. is conceived as a system that could cover the necessities of urban-transportation, and would possess the required versatility to absorb this changing behaviour.

S.A.T acts, as its name implies, as a system; therefore it responds to a systemic-structure. It is conformed by 'circuits', each of them acting as a sub-system working under a holistic view. They have the special feature of being 'open-circuits'. This means that they could change, expand or alter their original direction or destination, depending on passenger demand or requirements created upon changes in temporal periods given in the City's rhythm (i.e. rush-hours, accidents, natural or manmade catastrophes). This becomes possible owing to the existence of a nexus between circuits. These are known as dynamic-terminals, and would act as automated interconnection-gateways between open-circuits. From the existence of these 'nodes', it is that we define the system as a continuous and integrated circuit. In the latter, convoys could be detained or detoured, controlling frequencies between stations, quantity of passengers being transported or amount of vehicles within a convoy. Dynamic-terminals increase under a geometrical-progression, the functionality of the System. Here we will be able to recognize the tetra-dimension of public/urban spaces, due to versatility and optimisation. For instance, using a ground area of approximately 1000 square meters, creating three functioning-levels, we could manage 18 S.A.T. lines or routes (with their combinations), transporting around 2 million people per day, relating main and secondary routes, integrating the 18 lines among themselves (vertical liaisons).

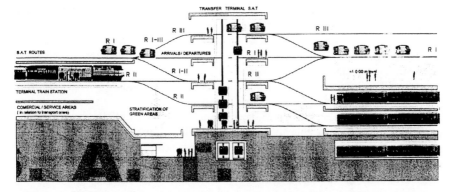

Figure 5: Dynamic terminal: systemic transformation of mass means of transport.

The systemic-structure is carried out by the interactions achieved by the different types of stops. They could be classified as passive, active or multiple stops. Passive stops correspond to common stops; passengers will use them as their chosen destination. Active stops, act as terminals, generating loops to close or derive a circuit, returning over it (in the same geometrical-plane axis). It will develop either below or above the former circuit lane; to be implemented in urban contexts where the lack of space generates the requirement of minor-scale terminals. Finally, when several circuits overlap or meet, ordinary stops become transfer centres, named as multiple-stops, where connexions are generated among them, allowing passengers to interact between different circuits, activating the plurality of ways in which the network could be used. Here, passengers are the ones making connections or interactions between circuits (as a difference from the automated dynamic terminals); therefore, ramps, escalators and elevators will be part of this sub-system. It acts as a connection stop, evidently situated in dense areas. Its main objective is to avoid the congestion or saturation at ground zero, with movements generated by the freight transport or migration of people.

5 Heading towards a sustainable future

The development of the S.A.T. Project (taking it only as a new 'tool') appears to provide the answer to existing limitations found in present urban settlements. For instance, the increase in height-limits found in present buildings and the tendency to maintain this trend in the future, makes the elevator (its inner mean of transportation) likely to become obsolete to fulfil its requirements. Also, time lost periods are generated in our cities, due to non-effective transportation, seen at neuralgic-overcrowded centres at inner-cores, generating a decrease in economical benefits, non-optimisation of natural resources, risks to health, chaotic 'construction' of our urban environment, etc). The S.A.T. project also responds to an increase in transportation security standards, implemented under two main parameters: a private and a public one. In natural or manmade catastrophes and accidents, we find inexistent emergency pathways or even an inefficient evacuation network. Deficient connection is shown between public services (firemen-ambulances-policemen, etc) and private property (dwelling/ office buildings, corporation-blocks or commercial centres). Inefficiency is caused by relying on daily urban transit flow (special reserved lanes, so called, but with no special features, depending on probable obstructed arteries, on contact with other means of transportation, on climate influence, etc.), far from guaranteeing a free-flow, connecting a specific spot to the corresponding emergency services (hospital / fire-department, etc). Other limitations correspond to the fact of not being able to find today public means of transport that could compete with the freedom and reliability (time, comfort, scale) provided by private transportation (car).

If S.A.T. is to be installed in cities, architectural mutations will definitely occur breaking up the vertical functioning-dependency that is present in today's city medullar-structure. A new freedom will be achieved by the promotion of social-equity by creating public-transport systems that will flow through the city nourishing public-spaces, green areas, and private sectors. Public routes will connect different buildings transporting either passengers or freight. These prolongations (pathways) will go from buildings towards public networks that do not act as simple virtual channels, but create spaces as habitable as the ones working on ordinary plan levels. These pathways and their morphology will become not only possible structural entities towards other buildings or to the urban environment, but create optional evacuation pathways, to encourage the migration of residents from a building to its neighbours, or to specific secure spots in the public network. Interrelations are generated between different zone areas according to their densities, creating sectors of higher or lower compactness in its structure. Acting as a system, it transforms the existing means of transport towards not self-sufficient services, but inter-dependent (in relation to others) forcing them to act also under this systemic-organization. The transportation structure shows its complexity when trying to manage the overlapping functions generated in city-cores. Incompatibilities manifest themselves between public, private and freight-transportation.

Its implementation acts as a catalytic tool forcing unconnected isolated elements to plug-into the network (system). This is its methodology. Regulations determining this plugging-in and out, or inner-relations, responds to its dynamic and organic structure as expressed previously. S.A.T. promotes then, a tetra-dimensional structure, forcing the city to work based on in its three-dimensions, heading towards sustainability. The concept of intranet-internet appears as an example from which to explain the conformation of S.A.T. as a private-public transportation system. This interrelation will be generated between possible private-convoys, corresponding to industrial complexes or multinational enterprises (i.e. public, private or freight transportation), that will upon plugging-into the network, promote the opening of their domain over public realms. For instance, they could reach massive transport terminals or convey employees to parking lots in urban peripheries. Therefore, private convoys will travel through the city showing their distinctive logo. These relationships will contribute to economical benefits promoting cooperation between private and public sectors. This will show the dynamic configuration of circuits, switching from private to public domain, according to temporal periods. Dynamic terminals will determine the relationships and connections between public, semi-public, private and semi-private routes, each one maintaining its attributes, or interconnecting them. S.A.T., as a public-transportation system, will be in charge of creating new connections home/work or generate tours around the city, probably proposing new perspectives from which to recognize the urban scenery (aerial views, crossing lakes, or sea-shores, etc.). Due to its high safety standards (no possible physical contact with other means of transportation or invulnerability regarding climate phenomena) and its security measures, promotes social equity towards elderly or disabled passengers. Freight transportation, for instance in the City of Buenos Aires, is carried out when the city is asleep, having therefore a limited time to develop its duties. This is owing to the fact that it shares the same area as public and private transportation. Therefore, S.A.T. as a freight-transportation system will allow a continuous feeding-net, with no interruptions. Dangerous or fragile materials could be handled, without requiring human contact. The functional-stratification in levels (connecting underground with different aerial ones) could be appreciated, interacting with each other, but behaving individually at the same time.

We could define main and secondary routes within the network (without worrying about their direction of movement, horizontal, vertical or sloped). The main ones could develop, for instance, between airport and industrial areas or downtown areas, financial sectors, corporation settlements or cultural centres. We could find also 'alternative or secondary' routes, which due to transfer stops, could deliver us to residential areas, in fact, arriving even at our specific floor-level (home). Therefore, in a few words, the airport (as an example) could be connected (plugged-in) to different attraction centres, without any interruption generated at ground zero, transforming it, consequently, into man's domain. If we focus on the interior of buildings, as it does not depend on cables, we do not have height limits. Several vehicles or convoys could simultaneously function under one same channel, promoting optimisation in travel-time-periods and flexibility of use. We could define also, resting-secondary channels, were several units could be waiting to be coupled to the system, when they are needed; or under the by-pass function, to detour high-speed units, in rush hours or emergencies.

Figure 6: S.A.T. implementation in the city.

Spatial-relationships will become efficient, were upon concentration generate an abrupt growth, decreasing or absorbing urban sprawl, producing a re-organization and re-structuring of the obsolete concept of presently verticalism. Consequently, we discover a new-morphological-spatial conception, promoting an increase in height and based on a 3D-interrelation, in terms of space and fluidity, what we define as interactive-verticalism.

6 S.A.T.'s implementation in cities, will allow us to:

- Return man's pedestrian freedom in present-day saturated cities.
- Decrease life's rhythm, reducing the pace of urban life.
- Decrease urban pollution (such as air, visual, vibrations, sound contamination).
- Generate an increase in open green public spaces.
- Transform, all current means of ground transportation.
- Increase urban traffic average speed.

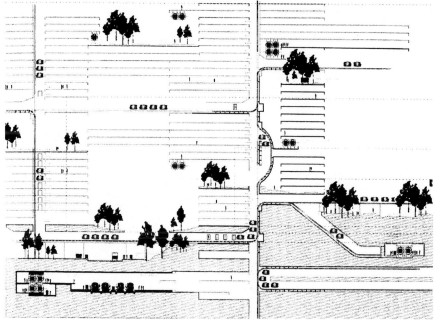

Figure 7: Tetra-dimension of Urban Space

- Promote optimisation of time, regarding time lost due to traffic and transport bottlenecks.
- Allow the recovery of creative leisure time.
- Tetra-dimensional use of our space, not creating barriers for man's mobility.
- Be a catalyst towards systemic.
- Hierarchy Individual scales in a massive media.
- Improve public health.
- Not only, avoid creating wounds in the urban-grid, but healing of existing ones.
- Re-generation of residual-urban spaces.
- Promote an efficient use of economical resources.
- Generate 'architectural mutations', breaking up the 'vertical-functioning dependency' of present buildings + spaces, due to the plurality of directions, the infinite combination of possible routes, crosses and gradients created under immeasurable options of degrees and directions that it will create.
- Create new connections between already built volumes (not depending or relying on the ground level where all public/private connections are generated), translating this into economic benefits, due to optimisation of time travel, transportation wages, etc
- Generate a city with an ecological concern.

The tetra-re-dimensioning (3D+Time) generated by S.A.T. proposes to draw a trend towards the conformation of sustainable cities, promoting man to become the reference-pattern in our contemporary and future urban landscapes.

Investigating the possibility of a coordinated goods delivery service to shopping centres in Uppsala city to reduce transport intensity

G. Gebresenbet & D. Ljungberg
Dept of Agricultural Engineering, Swedish University of Agricultural Sciences, Sweden

Abstract

The current paper reports the results of the investigation made to determine the possibilities of promoting a coordinated goods delivery system to various galleria, located in the city centre, to reduce congestion and environmental impact.

Uppsala is the 4th biggest city in Sweden and has a very narrow city centre. Increasingly frequent goods delivery performed by less than half-loaded distribution vehicles lead to the consequences of congestion, traffic accidents, and pollution, particularly in the city centre. It was assumed that a co-ordinated distribution system is among the plausible strategies to address the current problem.

The objective of the work is investigate the possibilities of a co-ordinated distribution system in Uppsala city using a *'city goods terminal'*, which should be located at the suburb of the city. To reach the objective, the activities performed were: (a) mapping out goods flow to the four main galleria that are located in the city centre, (b) conducting a demonstration trial of coordinated distribution, and (c) determining constraints and possibilities of coordinated goods distribution.

97 transport companies delivered goods to these galleria. 15 to 60 deliveries were performed per day to each galleria and intensive deliveries were made before and during lunch. About 43% of the delivered goods were food including bread, brewery and dairy products, fruits and vegetables and about 69% of food deliveries were made before 11 a.m. Queue time was significant and the actual unloading time was found to be less than 50% of the duration of the delivery.

Nine boutiques participated in the small-scale demonstration trial on coordinated goods delivery from the terminal to galleria and it continued for a year. Goods were first delivered from suppliers to the terminal that was situated at the suburb of the city and thereafter to the galleria according to the time specified by the retailers. The result of the mapping activities indicates that transport system can be effective through coordination. The practical demonstration also confirmed this. In the current trial, the number of deliveries reduced by 40% through coordination.

The main conclusion of this work is that information, communication and change of attitude play central roles to promote coordination, and dialog between retailers, distributors and suppliers is necessary and essential.

1   Introduction

Transport plays an important role in stimulating economy. However, transport activities are among the major factors that contribute to problems associated with environment (in the form of pollution), health and traffic safety. In accordance with international directives, the Swedish government has decided to reduce CO_2-emissions by 25% by year 2010, or should remained at the level of CO_2 during 1990. However, CO_2 emission from transport has been increased by 20% in Uppsala from 1990 to 1999.

Uppsala is the 4th biggest city in Sweden and it has a very narrow city centre. Besides the local wholesalers, many other suppliers are distributing their goods in Uppsala. Currently, it is very common that half or less loaded vehicles from different transport companies are queuing up in front of shops or at shopping centres to deliver specific goods in time. Traffic intensity increases steadily in the city (increased by 10% between 1990 to 1999), and many of the retailers are concentrated in and around shopping centres in the city centre. As a consequence, congestion in the centre of the Uppsala is increasing.

To break such a tendency, the promotion of a co-ordinated goods distribution through application of the third party terminal with effective utilisation of IT is among the plausible strategies to attenuate the transport work in the goods distribution sector.

Coordinated transport within health sector in Borlänge administrative region in Sweden reduced the number of vehicles from 204 to 68, while the possibility to transport individuals increased by 30% [1]. After conducting field measurements and simulation, Gebresenbet [2] reported that the number of vehicles that distributed food in Uppsala region could be almost halved in case of coordination. However, the main constraint when implementing coordination was un-willingness to change the system. The study made in the city centre of Göteborg [3] in Sweden concluded that unless forced measures were associated, coordination couldn't be implemented.

The objective of the work is to investigate the possibilities of a co-ordinated goods distribution system in Uppsala city using '*city goods terminal*' which should be located at the suburb of the city.

2   Method

To reach the objective, the activities performed were: (a) mapping out goods flow to the four main gallerias that are located in the city centre, (b) conducting a demonstration trial of coordinated distribution, and (c) determining constraints and possibilities of coordinated goods distribution.

A questionnaire, concerning the current distribution system, was distributed to 89 retailers at the initial phase, and measurements of goods delivery were made at four galleria for 174 hours and 508 deliveries were registered. The field trial was depending on the retailers' voluntary participation. They were offered coordinated distribution via a terminal at no extra cost. They only had to change their delivery address when ordering goods and inform the terminal of their participation, address and desired time of delivery. To attract the shops to participate in the system, a marketing campaign was carried out. The campaign was built mainly on personal contacts, per telephone, visits and information meetings. The primary targets for the marketing activities were the local shop owners and representatives, but also chains and dealers' associations were contacted. Interviews were made with the locally based transport companies, to obtain information on their distribution systems and their opinions on transport coordination. After the field trial interviews were made with all the participating retailers and the involved staffs at the terminal.

3   Results

3.1   Questionnaire and interview study

The average response frequency of thequestionnaire study was 29%. The responseshowed that the retailers were generally satisfied with the current goods delivery system. However, the problems noted were delivery at non-suitable time, very frequent delivery, queues, and air pollution at the delivery points. The timing of deliveries caused problems since the staff often had to leave the shop to receive goods during the busiest lunch-hours. The large number of small deliveries were also mentioned as a problem. Environmental issues were seen important, but not as important as quality and safety of the delivery service. Suggestions to improve the delivery service included improved goods tracking possibilities, faster delivery, better service and delivery at fixed times.

The interview investigation showed that most of the transport companies were positive for the development of a coordinated goods delivery system in the city. However, most transport companies tended to valuate their own distribution system as rather effective.

3.2   Measurements at the delivery points

During the measurements at the delivery points of four shopping centres, a total of 508 deliveries and 62 vehicle stops for other reasons were observed. Goods delivery was done in different ways according to delivery contract. However, the most common sequence were as follows: *arrival – queue – parking – contacting the addressee – unloading – delivery signature – loading of return goods and packaging – departure.*

Most remarkable were the bread deliveries, as the drivers occupied the delivery bay while price marking as well as placing the bread on shelf inside the shop. This had a major impact on the duration of delivery, and it will be presented later in the text.

3.2.1 Amount of goods

The four shopping centres, mentioned above, received between 14 and 44 goods deliveries per day during the observed period. Average daily deliveries are described in Figure 1. In general, the deliveries were rather small. Packages accounted for the major part of the number of deliveries even though pallet and cage deliveries provided the goods volume. Among the package deliveries, the smallest deliveries were the most common. The mean size of package deliveries was 5.4 packages. Deliveries of less than 5 packages accounted for two thirds of the number of package deliveries, yet only 27% of the total number of packages delivered (Figure 2).

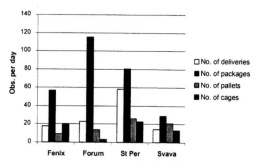

Figure 1: Average number of deliveries and goods by different loading units, per day

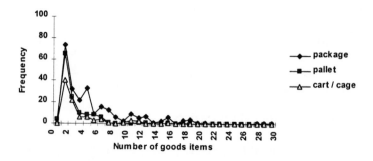

Figure 2: Delivery size distribution for different loading units

3.2.2   Frequency and duration of deliveries

The goods deliveries were concentrated to morning and lunchtime and 58% of the deliveries arrived before noon. The St Per galleria received much more deliveries than the others, and most of them in the morning hours. Forum had also most of its deliveries in the morning, while Fenix and Svava had their peaks during lunchtime (57% of the deliveries to Fenix arrived between 11 a.m. and 2 p.m.). Especially, grocery distribution was highly concentrated to the morning hours, 69% arriving before 11 a.m.

The mean duration of delivery was 13.4 minutes, varying widely between 1 and 82 minutes. Bread deliveries had a mean duration of over 18 minutes and were the most common over 50 minutes. No significant correlations between amount of goods and delivery duration were seen. During the observations in Fenix, the time used for different activities of each delivery were registered and it was shown that the actual unloading activity was responsible for only 43% of the total delivery duration. The time used for unloading, contacting boutiques' staffs and other activities accounted for 4.2, 3.6, and 1.9 minutes, respectively. No queues occurred during the observations.

The concentration and duration of deliveries resulted in queues, frequently observed at the delivery points. Using the registered times of arrival and departure to determine if queues occurred, and comparing the duration of delivery with and without queue, queues were found to have an impact on the duration of deliveries (Figure 3).

3.2.3   Transport companies

A total of 97 transport companies performed the 508 observed deliveries. These transport companies are displayed in order of frequency in Figure 4. Most companies,were observed only at one single delivery.

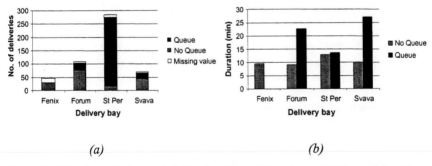

(a)   *(b)*

Figure 3:   Number of observed deliveries (a) and duration of delivery (b), with and without queue

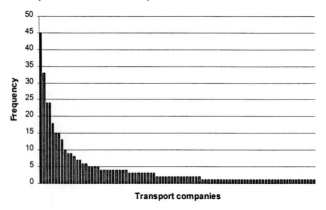

Figure 4: Number of observed deliveries per transport company (each bar represents one transport company)

3.2.4 Load rate

The load rate distribution varied widely, ranging from 5% to 100%, with an average at 40% (Figure 5). The observations of load rate were based on occupied floor space in the vehicles.

3.3 Coordination field trial

The response to the marketing activities for the coordination field trial was mainly positive. However, when requested to come up with a decision, most of them choose to wait for various reasons, and the most common expressions were as follows:

> *"We would like to see the system functioning in practice first", "We would participate, if only the others in the galleria also joined", "It sounds good, but we are quite content with the current system, and therefore don't want to risk it", "Yes, fine, but we're quite busy at the moment, please come back in a couple of months",* etc.

At the end, 9 shops actually joined the demonstration.

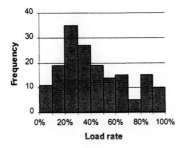

Figure 5:   Load rate before delivery (based on used floor space, observed at
Fenix, Forum and Svava shopping centres)

3.3.1   Participants' opinions and experiences

The pilot demonstration study went on from May 2000 until May 2001. The participating shops joined successively during the period. One of them, however, withdrew after only a few weeks due to the reduced interest from the surrounding shops.

The predominant reason for participation in the trial was that the participants expected improvement of the delivery service, in terms of fewer deliveries at fixed times and avoiding lunchtime deliveries. Environmental concern was also mentioned as another reason for participation. According to interviews made with the participants, the deliveries actually were improved during the trial, mainly due to reduced number of deliveries. Even though the shops did not have all their deliveries coordinated, an average reduction of 40% was achieved.

Some problems also occurred during the field trial. Delays were rather frequent during the first one or two months and the promised delivery time windows were not kept. Moreover, problems with delays of more urgent deliveries occurred. Later on during the trial, the participating retailers experienced that the service successively improved.

3.3.2   Opinions and experiences of staffs at the terminal

It took some time for the terminal staff to adjust their routines so that the coordination could run smoothly. That was why it was impossible to avoid delays and at the same time deliver within desired time windows. After some time, however, the routines were adjusted, deliveries from the suppliers could be better predicted and the system performance improved.

4 Discussion and concluding remarks

Very few comparable studies of goods distribution have been conducted earlier. and therefore, this study made a valuable contribution to the field of distribution logistics. The different parts of the study contributed to a clearer picture of the system as a whole. The mapping showed that the existing delivery service was not very effective. A very large number of transport companies were involved in the distribution and a small goods volume accounted for a large proportion of the number of deliveries. Queues were frequent at the delivery points. The utilisation levels of vehicles were as low as in the previous investigations made by Gebresenbet [2], Kristiansson & Pettersson [3] and others. On the other hand, the shops would prefer fewer delivery stops, shorter time of delivery and fixed times of delivery. These findings put focus on the need, interest and possibilities for a coordinated goods distribution service in Uppsala city. Possible improvements to be achieved are:

- More effective use of vehicles through reduced numbers of delivery stops and vehicles, increased loading rate and shorter transport distance
- More efficient delivery through fewer and larger deliveries, on fixed times. Queues at the delivery points are avoided and the total time for delivery is reduced, to benefit of both shops and transport companies.
- Traffic and environmental improvements through reduced vehicle emissions, congestion and noise, improved traffic security and accessibility, which is a benefit for the shops.

The field trial was carried out successfully and showed that the proposed model for coordinated distribution is possible to realise. The coordination did function and no advanced technology was needed. At the same time, it was obvious that the approach to attract participants was not successful. Thus, the problem is rather social than technological. On the basis of the experiences from both the terminal staffs and participating and not participating shops, it could be concluded that for the coordination scheme to be successful, it is needed to address the following constraints:

- *Support* – involvement and interest from all relevant actors,
- *Extent* – enough goods volume incorporated to fill one vehicle per day,
- *Communication* – to enhance goods flow planning,
- *Flexibility* – possibilities to make exceptional arrangements for urgent deliveries, and
- *Competition* – transport companies operating under market conditions.

The main actors' considered in the transport system all have benefits to gain from coordinated goods distribution, and they also have the possibilities to initiate the process. Transport companies may lower their distribution cost through initiating cooperation with other transport companies. Shop owners have the possibility to initiate the kind of coordination used in this study, while financing the local distribution has to be dealt with in cooperation with the involved transport companies who would also gain from making the system more effective. Official instances may also invoke coordinated distribution, through measures of control such as city centre zones with entrance fees or other restrictions.

The result of the mapping activities indicates that transport system can be effective through coordination. The practical demonstration also confirmed this. In the current trial, the number of deliveries reduced by 40% through coordination. The retailers were satisfied in general, but a few complained of delay of delivery. Improving communication between the terminal, boutiques and transporters may solve such a problem.

Coordination may promote the retailers so that they receive their goods at the specific time with reduced number of deliveries, and this could reduce staff resource requirement at goods reception/delivery point. However, they have not shown sufficient interest to be the driving force to initiate coordination.

A small number of companies control a major part of the goods flow. It will be possible to control a significant part of goods flow by co-ordinating the delivery system of these companies. To include others (many deliveries but smaller in volume), the retailers need to influence both the transport companies and goods producers (and wholesalers).

Possible arrangements for coordination are presented in Figure 6. While the ideal situation would be to have all goods coordinated at one single terminal (case b), this seems at the moment impossible to realise without forced measures. A more realistic scenario would be coordination involving a number of terminals (case c), at the same time improving the conditions for economic competition.

The main conclusion from the current work is that information, communication and change of attitude play central roles to promote coordination, and dialog between retailers, distributors and suppliers is necessary and essential.

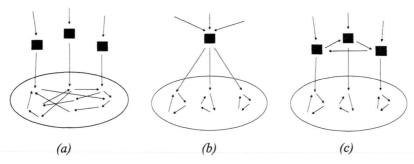

(a)   *(b)*   *(c)*

Figure 6: (a) Today's terminal distribution, (b) coordinated distribution with a single terminal, (c) coordinated distribution using multiple terminals; ■, terminal; →, transport

5 References

[1] Mattsson, B. 1996. Samverkan mellan logistik och fordonskrav vid upphandling av transporter [Joint effect of logistics and vehicle criteria at transport purchase]. Borlänge Municipality, Sweden
[2] Gebresenbet, G. 1999. Promoting effective goods distribution through route optimization and coordination to attenuate environmental impact – the case of Uppsala. Report 240. Swedish University of Agricultural Sciences, Department of Agricultural Engineering. Uppsala, Sweden
[3] Kristiansson, L. and Pettersson, M. 1996. Varudistribution i innerstad. Möjligheter och hinder för en samordnad livsmedelsdistribution [Goods distribution in city centre. Possibilities and hindrances forcoordinated grocery distribution]. Dep. of City- and Traffic planning, Chalmers University of Technology, STACTH-report 1996:6, Göteborg, Sweden

The tram-train: Spanish application

M. Novales, A. Orro & M. R. Bugarín
Transportation Group, Technical School of Civil Engineering, University of La Coruña, Spain.

Abstract

The tram-train is a new urban transport system that was originated in Germany in the 1990's, and which is undergoing a great development at the moment, with studies for its establishment in several European cities.

The tram-train concept consists of the operation of light rail vehicles that can run either by existing or new tramway tracks, or by existing railway tracks, so that the services of urban public transport can be extended towards the region over those tracks, with much lower costs than if a completely new line were built.

The authors are developing a research project about the establishment of such a system in Madrid, which would involve the construction of a new light rail system in a suburban zone of the city, which could connect with Metro lines or with suburban lines of Renfe (National Railways Company). In this way, better communications would be achieved from this area towards the city centre.

During the development of this project we have studied the European systems that are in service at the present time, as well as those that are in construction, in project, or in preliminary study phase. So, we have determined which are the critic issues of compatibilization, and from these issues we have studied the particular characteristics of the Spanish case.

The aim of this paper is to carry out a brief summary of tram-train systems in operation nowadays, after which we explain the main advantages of this system, to pass later on to a deeper description of the Spanish case, with a discussion about the best solutions to each problem that has arisen in the development of this kind of system.

1 Introduction

The tram-train concept was born in Germany, in the city of Karlsruhe, in 1992, year in which several lines of the railway network were connected to the tramway network of the city (Griffin [1]). A new light rail vehicle was made to run through this new extended network, with some adaptations to be compatible with the infrastructure of the two systems, each one with different characteristics.

The main difference between light rail and conventional rail systems is that in the first ones the vehicle runs "on sight", and are either integrated or separated from urban traffic, while in the second ones the vehicle running is controlled by a signalling system, and the tracks are generally completely separated, and very rarely interface with other transport systems (with the exception of level crossings) (UITP [2]).

2 Existing systems nowadays

A brief summary about the main systems of tram-train that are in service or in construction nowadays, is presented bellow:

2.1   Karlsruhe (Germany)

As it has been discussed above, the first tram-train system was established in Karlsruhe in 1992. Several measures had to be taken for it: the development of a vehicle compatible with the two kind of networks; the compliance of regulations over the building and operation of trams (BOStrab) and railways (EBO); the physical connection between both networks; and the construction of further stops along the existing conventional railway lines, which could be used without increasing journey times thanks to the improved acceleration and braking performances of light rail vehicles with regard to conventional railway vehicles (EAUE [3]).

The main technical problems that arose in Karlsruhe, and the answers to them, were as follows:

2.1.1   Electrification
The tracks of the national railways of Germany (DB) are electrified at 15 kV 16 2/3 Hz, while the urban tram lines are supplied at 750 V DC. The solution adopted was the use of a dual voltage vehicle, equipped with a transformer and a rectifier. All the additional equipment is fitted above the roof or under the floor, and does not therefore reduce the space available for passengers (Drechsler [4], Ludwig [5]).

The change from a voltage to another is made in a transition section, in which the vehicle automatically detects the new voltage and adapts accordingly, whilst the driver only have to put the controller in neutral position (Drechsler [4], Ludwig [5], Hérissé [6]).

2.1.2   Structural strength
The Karlsruhe vehicle has a structural strength of 600 kN, instead of 1500 kN minimum required in the UIC leaflets for conventional railway vehicles (Griffin [1], UITP [2]).

2.1.3   Safety and communication systems
The Karlsruhe light rail vehicles are provided with two different safety systems: the Indusi system, DB signalling repetition system; and the IMU system, with automatic stopping, corresponding to the transport services of the city of Karlsruhe (AVG). The radio system is duplicated too (Ludwig [5], Hérissé [6]).

2.1.4   Tyre profile
It is necessary that the wheel profile of the light rail vehicle be compatible with the rail profile and geometry of the DB points and crossings, as well as with the rails and track material of the tram network. To get this, it was necessary to develop a special tyre profile, whose operation can be seen in figure 1 (Griffin [7]).

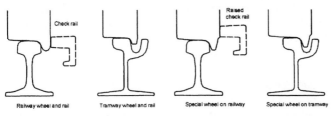

Figure 1: Use of raised check rails and special wheel profiles

2.1.5   Passenger access
Other problems are the co-existence of high platforms on conventional railway lines (height of 380, 550 and 760 mm over top of rail) and the low city platform (200 mm), as well as the fact that the body of light rail vehicles is narrower than that of conventional railways, that is why there is an excessive horizontal gap between the vehicle and the platform in railway stations. In order to solve these problems, the vehicle is fitted with retractable steps, which adapt the vehicle access height and gap according to the type of area it is in.

2.2   Saarbrücken (Germany)

The first stretch of line with shared tracks in Saarbrücken was opened in 1997.

The technology used in the case of Saarbrücken is basically the same as that used for Karlsruhe, but with two main differences: on the one hand, the fact that trams had not been in use in Saarbrücken since 1965, reason why lines of new construction would be used, thereby avoiding the need to take the characteristics of existing trams into prior consideration; on the other hand, the use of a low floor vehicle. The low floor does not imply any problem regarding to the DB structural gauge, because the lower part of the vehicle is 75 mm over the track.

2.2.1 Electrification
The question of electrification was solved in the same way as in the case of Karlsruhe, except that the length of the neutral section is 80 m, instead of 170 m in Karlsruhe.

2.2.2 Structural strength
Regarding to the structural strength of vehicles, it was adopted the same reasoning as in Karlsruhe.

2.2.3 Safety and communication systems
The tram-train runs mainly on run on sight, without signalling, which only exists on single track stretch, that is still operated as a conventional railway line, fitted with classical DB signalling (main and advanced signals), and with train detection by means of axle counter devices (ScanRail [8], Krempper [9]).

2.2.4 Tyre profile
As the Saarbrücken light rail is a completely new system, it has been possible to select a tyre of the type traditionally used on the German railways, thereby avoiding problems of compatibility with DB infrastructure. So, the system was fitted with a wide grooved rail, which allows railway wheels to run over it (Krempper [9], Kendel [10], Veinnant [11]).

2.2.5 Passenger access
In urban zone the platform heights are of 350 or 200 mm (in case that the stop is shared with the bus). On the railway sections, the platforms are at a height of 380 mm, but there is a horizontal gap of 275 mm, because the light rail vehicle is narrower than conventional rails. This gap is covered by a retractable step of 197 mm, thereby reducing the gap to around 78 mm (ScanRail [8], Krempper [9]).

2.3 Kassel (Alemania)

The main particularity of the tram-train of Kassel is the way to solve the passenger access from railway platforms, that consists of diverting the tram line from the track axis, nearing it to the platform, in that way that it produces a four rail section (Catling [12]).

2.4 Sunderland (England)

In Sunderland they are going to extend the existing metro system, making a conection with Newcastle, using the railway lines of the Railtrack between Pelaw and Newcastle, and serving this section with metro vehicles (ScanRail [8]).

The metro gauge is 1435 mm, while the Railtrack gauge is 1432 mm. It is expected that this minimum difference will not cause any problem in operation, although a speed limitation will exist in the connection zone (ScanRail [8]).

The electric supply will be done by 1500 V DC catenary system.

The conventional railway is to be fitted with TPWS (Train Protection and Warning System), and the Indusi inductive loop protection system will be installed for the metro cars. It will have an integrated radio infrastructure in order to enable staff at Railtrack's IECC (Integrated Electronic Control Centre) to talk to all vehicles on the line, both metro and conventional trains (ScanRail [8]).

3 Main advantages of the tram-train concept

The tram-train system has several advantages, some of them are discussed below:

3.1 Financial advantages

❑ Existing traditional railway infrastructure can be used, thereby reducing the amount of investment necessary in new infrastructure.
❑ The need to build long sections of new track necessary for new lines is avoided, thereby offering considerable cost savings compared with completely new light rail systems.
❑ Increases in passenger numbers provide extra income, thereby reducing subsidies on annual operational costs. The increase in passenger numbers is the result on the one hand of additional stations, improved links with the urban system and more direct links with residential and business areas. On the other hand, this increase is also due to the improved quality and image of the light rail system, encouraging private car users to change to this mode of transport without any sensation of "quality loss".
❑ Vehicle composition may be adjusted during periods of low traffic density (evenings, Saturdays and Sundays), thereby reducing total running costs.
❑ Operation costs for this kind of vehicles are lower in comparison with conventional rolling stock.

3.2 Advantages for passengers

❑ Public transport users save time, as the tram-train can reach speeds double those of buses. Door to door travelling time is comparable with that of the private car, as running times between stations are reduced thanks to the braking and acceleration values of light rail vehicles in comparison with traditional trains. Stopping times at stations are also shorter, thanks to improved passenger access due to the number of side access doors. Finally, waiting times between different modes of transport are reduced.
❑ Direct access from the region to the main business and shopping centres, without the need to change to another mode of transport, as occurred before the introduction of these services.
❑ Punctuality rates are extremely high, as this means of transport is not affected by road traffic incidents.
❑ Greater comfort, due to an increased number of larger seats in each car and their improved dynamic features, which make for a smoother journey.

❑ The system is easy to use, as its introduction is usually accompanied by improved passenger information systems, with electronic information devices at stops, normally operated from the control centre, specifying the arrival time of the next vehicle, as well as the stops along the route and waiting times.

❑ Integrated pricing, due to the fact that an operating company is normally set up to take charge of planning and co-ordinating the timetables and prices of both urban and regional public transport in order to make it user-friendly.

❑ An increase in the number of stops on the routes previously covered exclusively by trains entails that stations are now closer to potential users, which makes the system more accessible.

❑ Greater frequency of light rail services compared with traditional rail services, thereby reducing waiting times at stops.

3.3   Non-user benefits

❑ Reduced congestion on motorways and local roads
❑ Reduction in the need for investment in road building and maintenance.
❑ Lower environmental impact
❑ Savings on parking costs.
❑ Savings on costs arising from accidents.

4 Spanish application

The possible solutions for each one of the technical problems that arise when a light rail vehicle is going to run over rail tracks or metro tracks in the Spanish area are shown below:

4.1   Electrification

If we want to do compatible a light rail system, usually under 750 V DC, with the Metrosur system in Madrid, with 1500 V DC power supply, or with the suburban railways of Renfe, with 3000 V DC power supply, we have the following options:

❑ Use of a dual voltage vehicle, either 750-1500 V DC, for the case of Metrosur, or 750-3000 V DC, for the case of suburban railways.
The case of 750-1500 V DC has already been developed technically, and it does not have too many problems, because the ratio between the voltages is 2, and the change from one to another can be obtained by connecting the electric motors in series or in parallel. The case of 750-3000 V DC would be technically more complicated.

❑ Use of a light rail system that runs under 1500 V DC through the streets, in that way that the connection with Metrosur will be direct. In the case of the connection with suburban railways, it would be necessary to use a dual voltage vehicle of 1500-3000 V DC, but this is easy to do because the voltage ratio is 2.

This solution seems to be the more technically acceptable, although it is not usual to establish systems under 1500 V DC in urban environment, sharing the way with road traffic. Nevertheless, there is examples of cities with this kind of operation, as the city of Kyoto, in Japan, in which the conventional heavy rails share the way with the road traffic in a stretch of 600 m, under 1500 V DC. Other examples are the lines Aigle-Sépley-Diableretes and Aigle-Leysin, of the company Public Transports of the Chablais, in Switzerland, that run under 1500 V DC through the cities without protection.

❑ Use of a diesel-electric vehicle, that runs in the Metrosur network under 1500 V DC, but that use the diesel group through the city. The same approach can be applied for suburban railways of Renfe, but in this case it would be with 3000 V DC in its network.

This solution has the problem that the passengers are used to the idea of the light rail as a very high environment quality, so that it would not seem acceptable to them that in the urban zone, which is the most affected by the atmospheric pollution, the vehicle runs under diesel traction.

❑ Use of a vehicle with accumulators, batteries, or other similar devices.

Generally, these solutions imply a very important weight penalty, and they are not profitable unless the stretches to share are very short.

❑ Use of a vehicle that runs with fuel cells traction.

This solution is too premature, because the fuel cells have not still been used in rail vehicles. Nevertheless, with the great development that this technique is undergoing, it seems very probable that this is a feasible option in the future.

Among the solutions that have been presented, it is recommended like the optimum nowadays the second one, that is, running through the streets under 1500 V DC, with a direct link to the Metrosur line, and with change of electric motors connection in series or in parallel, to link with Renfe.

4.2   Track gauge

The problem is due to the fact that light rail systems use to have a track gauge of 1435 mm, while Metrosur system has 1445 mm, and suburban railways of Renfe have 1668 mm.

For the case of Metrosur, it is recommended that the light rail system is built with the Metrosur gauge, that is, in 1445 mm, which is not a problem for manufacturers of vehicles or for the street infrastructure.

For the case of Renfe, there are several solutions:

❑ Construction of the light rail system in 1668 mm gauge, establishing the lines through the cities with this gauge.

This solution has the problem that the negotiability of sharp curves can be reduced, but a vehicle of the Saarbrücken type, adapted to this gauge, would be able to negotiate curves of radius 25 m, and less value can be obtained varying the bogie and box pitch.

❑ Light rail system in 1435 mm gauge, and adaptation of Renfe lines that are to be used by means of three-rail tracks.

This system has the characteristic problems of a three rails track: the complexity of points and crossings, with lower reliability, and greater seriousness of derailments; greater impact of the failure of rolling stock, due to the use of vehicles of different gauges and the decentred position of the couplers; duplication of space in the workshops; complexity of the signalling system; dissymmetry of loads and decentred position of the contact wire.

❑ Light rail system in 1435 mm gauge, and adaptation of Renfe lines that are to be used by means of four rails tracks.

This solution avoids some problems of the three rails track, like the impact of the failure of rolling stock, the dissymmetry of loads and the decentred position of the contact wire, but adds greater complexity to all of the others. Moreover, due to the short distance between rails, the feet of the two rails of each stretch of rails do not fit completely, reason why they must be cut, and this results in a weakening of rails, and in the need of establishing a special system of fastening, which increase the price of the solution.

❑ Vehicles with variable gauge.

This solution does not exist nowadays in the tram market, and this has some inconvenients like: technical difficulties for its development; great complexity and loss of reliability; and considerable increase of expenses of vehicle production and maintenance.

Among the solutions that have been presented, it is recommended the use of vehicles of 1445 mm gauge for the connection with Metrosur, and the use of vehicles of 1668 mm gauge for the connection with Renfe.

4.3   Structure gauge

In principle, there might not be problems with structural gauge, because light rail car bodies are narrower than those of heavy rail vehicles (conventional rail and metro). Nevertheless, the structural gauge of the lower parts of the vehicle must be checked, because in the case of use a low floor vehicle, may cause some problem.

4.4   Rail type / tyre profile

The problem of the tyre profile consists of the difference between wheels of rail and tram vehicles, with narrower tyres and flanges in the case of tram. This fact can cause problems of guidance when running over turnouts or crossings, as the size of the crossing nose gaps and check rails do not guarantee that the axles will be guided safely, due to the reduced thickness of the flange wheel (Griffin [1], UITP [2]).

This problem can be solved in two opposed ways:

❑ Use of a modified tyre, of Karlsruhe type, adapted to the running over tram sections with narrow groove, and to the running over railway lines. This solution implies the raising of the check rails in railway deviations.

❏ Use of a typical railway tyre, like in the case of Saarbrücken. This solution can only be adopted in the case that the light rail network is of new construction.

Therefore, the recommended solution is the Karlsruhe type, in the case that the light rail system is going to use existing tram lines, and the Saarbrücken type, in the case that the light rail network is of new construction.

4.5 Structural Strength

The problem in this case is due to the impossibility of building light rail vehicles which met railway crashworthiness standards (structural strength of 1500 kN according to UIC leaflets). This impossibility is due to the requirement that the driver have a clear view of the street traffic around him, and to the variations in floor height and vehicle size regarding to a conventional railway vehicle (Griffin [1]).

The solution recommended to this problem is the European one, that consist of accepting that light rail vehicles that are going to share tracks have a intermediate structural strength (of 600 kN), improving their performances in active safety (protection against accidents by means of signalling systems and acceleration and braking characteristics).

4.6 Safety and communication systems

The solution to this problem consist of the duplication of systems, that is, the vehicle must be fitted with compatible systems in both operation areas, and must be noticeable by the two kind of equipments. It must be checked the existence of operation problems (as interferences) between both systems.

4.7 Passenger access

In this case the problem is double: on the one hand, it is the smaller width of light rail vehicles relating to conventional railways; on the other hand, it is the differences between platform heights in urban and rail zones.

The possible solutions to each of these problems are:

❏ Smaller width of light rail vehicles: this can be solved by means of retractable steps, like in Karlsruhe and Saarbrücken, or by means of a deviation of the tramway track axle in the stations, like in the Kassel case.

❏ Different platform heights: this can be solved by means of retractable steps, double-height platforms, double-height doors, modification of the track height, etc.

4.8 Vehicle functional compatibility

Finally, for each individual case it will be necessary to study several specific aspects of the light rail vehicle which must be adapted to enable it to run on shared track. Some of these aspects are listed below:

- Pantograph: this must allow current collection both in an urban context (normally through trolley wire) and in the conventional railway context (through a catenary system).
- Coupling: In the event of a breakdown, the vehicle must be adapted for coupling with a conventional rail vehicle.
- Vehicle signalling: Vehicle lights must be compatible with those required by the railway authority owning the shared track.

5　Acknowledgements

The authors thank to the Spanish Inter-ministerial Commission for Science and Technology (Comisión Interministerial de Ciencia y Tecnología) for the financial support they have offered through the Technological Research and Development Project TRA99-0291.

6　References

[1]　Griffin, T., "Inter-operable urban rail transport", *Institution of Mechanical Engineers*, pp. 109-118, 1996.

[2]　UITP, Light Rail Committee, *Track sharing* (working document), Montpellier, 2001.

[3]　"Karlsruhe: The Karlsruhe model of a dual-mode railway". (1996). <http://www.eaue.de/winuwd/85.htm>. Page of the European Academy of the Urban Environment (EAUE).

[4]　Drechsler, G., "Light railway on conventional railway tracks in Karlsruhe, Germany", *Proceedings of the Institution of Civil Engineers – Transport*, London, 2, pp. 81-87, 1996.

[5]　Ludwig, D., Brand, W., Wallochny, F., Gache, A., "En matière de transports urbains et regionaux: Karlsruhe, un exemple a méditer...", *Chemins de Fer*, Paris, 422, pp. 8-16, 1993.

[6]　Hérissé, P., "Le tramway à la mode de Karlsruhe", *La Vie du Rail*, 2377, 7, pp. 12-20, January 1993.

[7]　Griffin, T., "Light rail transit sharing the Railtrack system", *Proceedings of the Institution of Civil Engineers – Transport*, London, 2, pp. 98-103, 1996.

[8]　ScanRail Consult, DK, *Integrating local and regional rail, incl. cross-border aspects*, GROWTH Project GRD1-1999-10843 of FP5, 2001.

[9]　Krempper, M., "Où en est le Tram-train de Sarrebruck?", *CDR – Connaissance du Rail*, Valignat, 210, pp. 11-17, January 1999.

[10] Keudel, W., "La Saarbahn – Le nouveau système de transport urbain et régional sur voie ferrée de la région de Sarrebruck", *Transport Public International*, Paris, 4, pp. 25-31, 1998.

[11] Veinnant, B., Cacciaguerra, F., "Un tram-train nommé succès: l'exemple de Sarrebruck", *Revue genérale des chemins de fer*, Paris, 11-12, pp. 35-42, 1998.

[12] Catling, D., Guillossou, M., Rovere, G., Stefanovic, G., *Ease of use of light rail systems*, UITP, Paris, 1995.

On board system model for road intelligent transport system

C. García, F. Alayón, E. Fernández & P. Medina
Department of Computer Science and Systems, University of Las Palmas de Gran Canaria, Spain.

Abstract

In this paper we describe a model to implement on board systems for road passengers transport in the intelligent transport system context. In this model we propose the use of some new technologic advances to achieve a proper integration of the on board information systems, traditionally weakly integrated. This model integrates all the on board elements needed to give us useful information (communications, positioning, sensors devices and ticketing).

1 Introduction

This work belongs to Intelligent Transport System field. Here we describe the information mobile system architecture to install in the buses fleet of a passengers public transport company by road. We can develop it by the use of news elements of the information technologies, specifically: industrial computers, mobile computing and communications infrastructure. Using this architecture we can develop on board information systems that are integrated in the overall company information system in a proper way, García [1]. In this point, we must say that frequently the on board system are less developed than the rest on the information system of the company, this is due to economical and reliability factors. Nowadays the technology offers us products and services that permit us overcome these unsuitable. An illustration of this opinion is the system that we have developed based on this architecture; this system has been installed in a 200 buses fleet. In this paper we describe the architecture by the explanation of the following aspect: first, the design principles (motivations, goals, requirements and technological art state). In second place, we explain the architecture (hardware/software elements and the connexions between them). Finally we resume the main conclusions of the work.

2 Motivation

The main development goal is to enhance the transport corporation production by improving its on board information mobile systems. Specifically, the aspects to improve are:
- The user service quality.
- The assignation of resources (vehicles and workers)
- The corporation situation in relation with on board system suppliers.
- The technological development possibilities.

The first and second goals can be achieved by the quality information use produced in the fleet on aboard systems. In our opinion, in this context, quality information means information obtained at the time, in the quantity and with the format needed by all the information processes executed in any place of the transport corporation, and the way to achieve it is by properly on board system integration in the corporation information system. Basically, our goal is to obtain all the needed information, originated in the fleet operation, for the decision making short-dated, middle-dated and long-dated. The decision making short-dated is related with the time tables fulfilment and by these decisions we can resolve isolated planning exceptions, middle-dated decision is related with service planning changes (changes in routes, vehicles and drivers assignation, etc.) and long-dated decision is related with the design of the corporation production planning. Nowadays, the action capacity of the companies is limited by the slight information generated in the on board systems, due to the technological limitations of these systems. Our proposal is to improve these systems by using these new technological advances that can support the special environment of the buses. About the last two goals, these can be achieved by using standard technology and design methodologies oriented to open systems.

3 Functionalities and requirements

The architecture must permit the system development with the following capacities:
- It is able to know at every time the time table fulfilment levels.
- It integrates all the devices that can provide useful information .related to: passengers, mechanical , electrical, environment and dynamic.
- It integrates all man-machine interfaces which enhance the driving security and the vehicles comfort.
- It must permit the access to any relevant information generated in on board system by any department of the company in a proper way.

Talking about system requirements, these are the following:
- It must support the special environments conditions producing on board system.
- Economic interest.
- The elements must be connected in order to facilitate on board installation and maintenance.

- It must use the communications in an efficient way, specially the long distance communications.
- It must be scalable in order to permit the incorporation of new functionalities in a non traumatic way.

4 Technological art state

To apply this architecture to the on board systems, it is necessary that the technology supplies us the needed elements. Fortunately the current technology can give us these elements. Specifically, in our opinion the critic technical elements are the following:

- Industrial computing. It provides the required hardware elements to build systems that can operate with the vehicles special environment conditions (temperature, vibrations, shocks, electrical power, noise, etc). Nowadays, there is a wide offer, but there are two types of industrial specifications that can achieve our requirements: PC-104 system and CompactPCI. The first is a ISA system evolution to industrial environments IEEE [2], this kind of devices can work in a higher temperature range than ISA systems. A second advantage is that the device connexions are more robust, because of the short dimensions of the PC-104 devices and the connector structure. The ComactPCI devices are the newest industrial systems PCI [3] and maybe they are the substitutes of the VME devices (the best from a technological point of view but with a high cost), the CompactPCI devices have suitable characteristic such us: higher temperature range of operation, physical connexion without loose margins and the possibility of hot-swap connexion. But there are two unsuitable: the high price and the short offer of devices.

- Mobile computing. It is an aspect of the information technologies that have been developed very much in the last years and the predictions are that this development will continue with the mobiles communications. To illustrate it, nowadays we have mobile computers with similar capacity of processing and storage than no mobile computer. Some aspects that were being improved are: the storage devices (capacity and reliability), the CPUs (higher processing capacity with less consumption requirements) and wireless communication devices (higher band wide and standard specifications). At present the mobile computer is a technology of wide use, thus the price will be cheaper each time.

- Long distance communication systems, such us mobile telephony and radio systems, offering better services with low prices.

- Vehicles mechanics state integration. Intelligent vehicles are more frequent; these vehicles have systems to control the mechanical and safety, so these systems could inform us about relevant aspects of the vehicle. At present there are specifications standards that permit us to integrate this kind of system, for example CAN bus, Philips [4].

5 System architecture

It plays a critic role in the system development. The system architecture specifies the elements (hardware and software), the relations and the connexion existing between them, and the techniques and tools used in the development. Assuming this concept about system architecture, we describe our architecture using these topics. From a functional point of view, the system is configured by the following devices or subsystem:

- On board computer. It is the main element and it has access to any device of the system. Basically it is configured by a CPU of low power, 64 Mbytes of main memory, disk to storage all the data and programs (5 Gbytes), PC-104 expansion bus, PC-104/PCMCIA adapter and serial communications ports (RS-232 and RS-485).
- Positioning subsystem. This is configured by all the elements that provide us dynamic information of the vehicle (position, velocity, etc). In our case a GPS receptor and a digital tachometric unit form this subsystem. The GPS provide us a reliable and common time reference for all the vehicles fleet.
- Communication subsystem. It permits us transmitting receiving information from outside (voice and data) and from on board systems (data). The long distance communications are supported by public infrastructure (radio, mobile telephony) or by private infrastructure (normally radio systems), in the case of data long distance transmission, the information travels by short packet of data associated to relevant events. To transmit great amount of data between on board systems and the company information system we use a wireless local net, this element any on board system can be accessed in any place of the corporation.
- Ticketing subsystem. It is configured by the entire element required to pay on board, normally: a driver console and reader/writer magnetic card. This subsystem stores the events associated with passengers movements.
- Sensors subsystem. By these elements the on board system can access to critic parameters related to: mechanicals (for example: oil level, motor temperature, refrigerant liquid level, etc), safety of the vehicle (for example open doors alarm), electrical (for example battery voltage level) or environment (for example temperature).

The connexions schemes deal about the resources, communications specifications and protocols used in the system devices connexions. This aspect is critic in the architecture because it affects to:

- Autonomy level of the different devices and subsystems.
- Complexity and cost of the installation and maintenance of the on board system.
- Data communications reliability.
- New elements integration capacity.

In figure one, we show a connexion scheme between the different elements of the system. We can observe that the connexion topology is a star where the main element is the on board computer. To simplify the connexions and to achieve an autonomous operating of some subsystems, specifically the ticketing subsystem and sensors subsystem, we use in these elements an internal multipoint bus, in the case of the ticketing subsystem we achieve it by a RS-485 connexion and in the case of the sensorial subsystem by CAN bus.

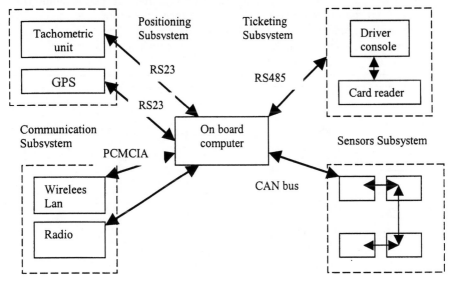

Figure 1: Connexion scheme and subsystems

About software elements to fulfil the specified requirements, like hardware elements, the software plays a critic role. From the on board software point of view the following aspect are important:
- The basic software (operating system). In this point the question is if we choose a proprietary basic software (very common in the technology for road transport) or a wide availability product. Obviously if we want to fulfil the standardization and scalability requirements the option is clear; we must choose a software of wide use. In our development we use a UNIX system for on board computer and for the data communications we use a protocols family TCP/IP.
- Possibility of using free or/and shareware software. Nowadays is a phenomenon which affects the software industry in a critic way. If we use this kind of software the cost of the system decreases substantially. In our case, we use a linux system.
- Design model. Using a wide availability basic software we can use tools and methodologies of design which facilitate fulfilment of the requirements, specifically in our development we applied the hierarchic, Client/Server and object oriented model.

The software structure is developed in a layered way in order to build a modular, flexible and scalable system. The layered structure is configured by three levels: level 0, basic software, it is formed by the operating system and basic communication services, level 1, devices abstraction level, responsible of integrating all o board system hardware devices (for example: GPS, mobile radio system, magnetic card reader, user information panels, power and temperature monitor device, etc.) and level 2, applicative server and exceptions monitor, in this layer all the on board specific company processes (applicative server) and the exception monitor (it process all the relevant events) are executed. Figure two shows us this layered design and the relations between levels.

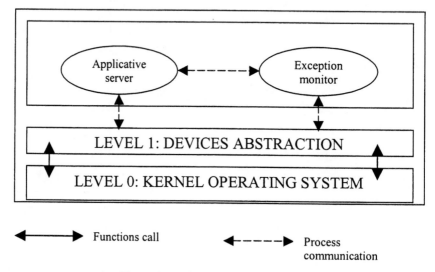

Figure 2: Software design structure

6 Conclusions

At present the new information technologies help us to develop on board system in the context of intelligent systems for a passengers road transport company. These technological advances permit us integrating the mobile information system in the information system of the transport company in a proper way; so we can access to the on board system like any station of the corporation net. We have implemented a architecture for on board system based on some products of the new information technologies, this implementation achieves all the goals describe in Wall [5], these are:
- Company requirements.
- It is integrated properly with other information subsystem of the company.
- The cost is competitive.
- It has a high functionality, usability and scalability.
- It is based on standard technology that will enable reusing the existing design and facilitate competitive purchase.

Our implementation permits the transport company to improving the service quality and the resources assignment. The architecture explained has been implemented in the Global Salcai-Utinsa transport company (it operates in Gran Canaria, Canary Island, Spain) , this company has a fleet of 300 buses and an annual overage of 17.000.000 of passengers . Actually, our implementation is installed in 200 buses and in the next year will be installed in the complete fleet.

References

[1] Garcia, C. et al, "Architecture of an integral information system for public road transport of passengers", Advances in Transport, vol. 6, pp. 95-102, 2000.

[2] IEEE, "Compact version of the IEEE P996. Electrical and mechanical standard specification. 1990.

[3] PCI Industrial Computer Manufactures Group, "CompactPCI short form specifications. 1995.

[4] Phillips, "CAN Specification", Philips Semiconductors Unternehmensbereich der Philips GmbH, 1991.

[5] Wall, N. "System architecture and communications", Advanced Technology for road Transport, pp. 17-47, 1994.

To construct urban light rail with the idle assets of railway hub

Y. Jinying
Economics and Planning Research Institute,
Ministry of Railways, China.

Abstract

In the course of China's urbanization, more and more serious traffic jams and environmental pollution hinder urban modernization. Urban light rail, which is characterized by its large transport volume, high speed, little pollution, and traffic safety is becoming the shining spot in China's urban traffic construction. The railway corporations occupy favourable positions in the planning, constructing and running of urban light rail because railway has many similarities with urban light rail in technology, equipment and management. For many reasons, a large part of the assets of railway hubs are set aside over a long period of time in China. Owing to the superiority of geographical position, resources and technology, these assets contain large potential value in the development of urban light rail. From the point of the development of China's urban light rail in future, this thesis analyses the superiority of the assets of railway hub in the construction of urban light rail, and studies the concrete ways of utilizing the idle assets of railway hub to construct urban light rail on this basis.

1 Introduction

With the development of China's economy, more and more people will move from rural areas to cities. According to the estimates of Chinese government, China's urban population will grow to 400 million by the end of 2000 and 600 million by the year 2010[1]. The rapid growth of urban population causes the problems of traffic jams and congestion, the deterioration of transportation environment, and the increasing of road accidents in the cities of China. Urban transportation bottlenecks will no doubt restrain economic development, and will be obstacles to efforts to improve the environment and the living quality of the urban population.

Light rail which is an effective urban transport vehicle to reduce the conflict of transport supply and demand in larger cities, to improve urban environments, and to increase transport safety and transport efficiency, has been listed as an important part of China's urban infrastructure construction[2]. However, the shortage of capital and land together with the great quantities of demolition and migration limit the development of urban light rail. By sharp contrast with the deficient resources for constructing urban light rail, a large number of assets have been left unused in China's railway hubs. As the consequence, utilizing the idle assets of railway hub to construct urban light rail is a good choice.

2 The idle assets of railway hub

Railway hub, which usually consists of a marshaling yard, a few passenger and freight stations, some storehouses, and several contact lines, is the center of linking up main lines and branch lines. It is generally situated in larger city. According to the data provided by China's government[3], by the end of year 1999, 75 cities which each has an urban population of more than 500,000 are all served by railway, and 46 cities, 61.3 percent of them, have formed railway hubs. At the same time, 29 among 32 cities which its population exceeds 1 million in every city also have formed railway hubs in China.

Over a long period of time, railway hubs had been playing important roles not only in national economic development but also in the development of the cities they are located in. But in recent years, owing to the adjustment of city's manufacture distribution, the expansion of urban district, and the transformation of railway itself, many railway hubs are falling into difficult positions in management. The utilizing rate of their assets declines remarkably.

2.1 The idle assets caused by the adjustment of city's manufacture distribution

The adjustment of city's manufacture distribution as the results of local economic development, industrial structure alteration, and the strengthening of environmental protection sense, changed the conditions on which railway hub depended for existence. The original function of railway hub degenerated. Its assets, such as branch line, contact line, special line, goods yard, storehouse and so on, are unable to be fully utilized, even in an idle state. For instance, Wanghe (Wangjing--Hepingli) branch line, the important component part of Beijing railway hub, was a special line for freight completed by the end of 1960s. Its main line was 9.8 kilometers in length. Besides serving the special line, Hepingli Station, the terminus of Wanghe branch line, possessed a comprehensive goods yard and handled containers. In accordance with the stipulations provided by Environmental Protection Act, however, most of factories served by it had been removed to outskirts in recent years, and the rest would be accomplished the migrating in the coming future. As a result, the utilizing rate of overall Wanghe branch line dropped to a much lower extent, and its assets had been set aside for a long time. The same case occurred in Xihuang branch line, the component part of Beijing railway hub.

2.2 The idle assets caused by the expansion of urban district

Owing to the expansion of city, the railway hub that was situated in outskirts now is encircled tightly by urban district. Its original function has been restrained seriously, and its assets have been left unused in a certain degree. The cases of Shanghai railway hub give the glaring example. With the expansion of Shanghai city proper from 350 square kilometres in 1950s to 1050 square kilometres at present[4], the assets of Shanghai railway hub including Songhu branch line and Huhang branch line which were located in suburbs sink into the hinterland of urban district. Songhu line, 8.47 kilometres in length, and Huhang line, 14.74 kilometres in length, have 48 crossings in urban district which not only restrain seriously the normal business of railway but also become the main reason of traffic jams and road accidents. Nanhe branch line, which passes through Putuo, Baoshan, Hongkou, Wusong, Yangpu District, and Xinri branch line that cuts through Xuhui District, are facing the same problems.

2.3 The idle assets caused by the reform of railway

To accompany the reform of railway including the adjustment of transport distribution, the changing of transport route, the transformation of former line, and the completion of new line, the original function of railway hub has been altered. The decreasing of freight volume makes the assets of railway hub in an idle state. The lines, goods yards, and buildings in urban district, even have been listed the plans of demolition by the local government. Pumei branch line and Ningxi branch line of Nanjing railway hub have been claimed to demolish for many times because they can not play their proper roles.

3 The potential superiority of the idle assets of railway hub

Although the assets of railway hubs are left unused, they have enormous potential value in fact, especially in the construction of urban light rail. Because there are many similarities between urban light rail and railway on technical standards, facility requirements, management and administration, etc., the idle assets of railway hub have much superiority in constructing urban light rail.

3.1 Position superiority

The assets of railway hub are located mainly in urban district, even at the key junction. The areas that they occupy usually are golden section. For example, the 4 railway stations of Beijing railway hub, such as the West, the North, the South, and the Beijing Station, not only link up many railway lines but also lie in the downtown district. Furthermore, most of them are connected with other traffic modes such as bus, metro, etc., so it is easy for passengers to change to other vehicle. These characteristics of railway hub are suited to the requirements of urban light rail on geographical position.

3.2 Asset superiority

Urban light rail and railway because of their similar technical requirements can use the similar facilities. Therefore, many assets of railway hub, such as rail tracks, communication lines, power supply system, etc., are able to be used in the construction of urban light rail after being remade. It will bring about double benefits: on one hand, the idle assets of railway hub can be reanimated, and on the other hand, the investment can be saved in the constructing of urban light rail. At the same time, it also can accelerate the development of urban light rail. One successful example is that Shanghai Bright Pearl light rail has been completed in a short time by utilizing the idle assets of Songhu line and Huhang line.

3.3 Technological superiority

The urban light rail has the same technological fundamentals with railway. As a result, the Railway Corporation possesses the professional superiority on the research, design, planning, construction, and repair of urban light rail. So railway corporations have no technical obstacles and can directly participate in the construction of urban light rail. In the course of constructing Shanghai Bright Pearl light rail, the Shanghai Railway Group provided lots of technical assistance and played an important role for the successful completion of this project. At the research stage of Beijing U-shape light rail, Beijing Railway Group also played a spectacular role[5].

3.4 Human resource superiority

Human resource is the important superiority of the Railway Corporation in the construction of urban light rail. In recent years, the idleness of railway hub's assets causes not only the income of railway staffs to decrease but also the personnel to spare. However, the construction and running of urban light rail demand lots of workers who have professional knowledge or rich experience. The superiority of railway hub staff is absolutely obvious. The professional person of railway hub can be directly engaged in the planning, design, and management of urban light rail. Similarly, the ordinary workers can be employed as the skilled workers. The Urban Light Rail Company can benefit from the saving of new staff's training-cost, and the Railway Corporation can well arrange its staff.

4 The ways of operation

Although the idle assets of railway hub have much potential superiority in the construction of urban light rail, it is more important that the potential superiority can be turned into the real superiority in practice. In the course of concrete operation, the following ways have proved valid.

4.1 Replacing property rights

The Railway Corporation can invest in urban light rail with the idle concrete assets. By transferring the property rights of its idle assets, the Railway Corporation will hold the relevant shares in the new Light Rail Company. This is an effective way of reanimating the idle assets of railway hub along with promoting the rapid development of urban light rail. In the construction of Bright Pearl light rail in Shanghai, Shanghai Railway Group invested in Bright Pearl Light Rail Corporation with Songhu branch line and Huhang branch line, which belonged to Shanghai railway hub and were 23.21 kilometres in total length. After replacing the property rights, Shanghai Railway Group held 18.5% of total shares in the Bright Pear Corporation, and became the second shareholder. By this way, the idle assets of Shanghai Railway Group had been put into use, and at the same time, the investment of Bright Pear Corporation also had been reduced.

4.2 Selling the idle assets

The Railway Corporation can solve the problem of idle assets by selling them to Urban Light Rail Company. This way was used in the construction of Beijing U-shape light rail[6]. Wanghe branch line, the component part of Beijing railway hub, was set aside over a long period time because of little freight volume and hopeless technical innovation. After fair evaluation, Beijing Railway Group sold Wanghe line and its subsidiary facilities at RMB 310 million yuan to Beijing Light Rail Corporation. Both the seller and the buyer profited a lot from this deal.

4.3 Opening up the right of use

This way is specially suited to the service line that is mainly used to self-service by Railway Company. Over a long period of time, service line has not been paying enough attentions in China. Although most service lines of railway hub are situated in suburbs or even in urban district, they have not been listed into the overall plans of urban transportation and city's development. Its utilizing rate has been in a much lower level, and most of its assets have been set aside. In fact, service line can be linked up with the urban light rail and become the component part of urban light rail network. By opening up its partial rights of use to urban light rail, the transport capacity of service line can be fully utilized. On the basis of meeting the self-service needs of Railway Company, it can accelerate the development of urban light rail.

In conclusion, to construct urban light rail with the idle assets of railway hub is a good pattern in China. In the course of its operation, the Railway Corporation and the local government should act in close cooperation. It should accord with the demands of railway's development as well as should be coordinated with the urban overall plan.

References

[1] The Comprehensive Transport Research Institute of the State Development Planning Commission. The suggestion about accelerating the development of urban rail transport in China. *Economic reference materials*, 20, pp. 16-22, 1999.

[2] Yu Xinan. Thinking about developing urban rail transport in China. *China Railway*, 1, pp. 21-24, 2000.

[3] Transport Bureau of the Ministry of Railways. *The chart of China's railway hub*, The Railway Press, pp. 33-45, 1998.

[4] Liu Xiaohong, Luo Yang, & Hu Ling. The enlightenment from the constructing of Shanghai Bright Pearl Light Rail to develop urban passenger transport market of railway. *China Railway*, 3, pp. 38-48, 2000.

[5] Guo Chunan. The planning and the developing tactics of Beijing urban rail transport network. *China Railway*, 2, pp. 24-28, 2000.

[6] Wang Tieke. The project of the first light rail in Beijing started. *Railway Knowledge*, 1, pp. 10-11, 2000.

Light rail transit is on the right way

R. Christeller[1] & H. Schaffer[2]
[1] Products and Bids Manager, Alstom Transport
[2] Senior Mobility Consultant

Abstract

The advantages and use of Light Rail Vehicles for clients, politicians and the public in general are demonstrated by use of concrete, manufactured examples such as CITADIS Montpellier, Dublin, Melbourne....

The following paper will deal with a variety of subjects such as :
- Why should a tram be used instead of a car?
- How to integrate a Light Rail Vehicle perfectly in the image of a city without destroying it?
- The investment for a tram system is very heavy and the construction causes a lot of trouble in a city
These questions which concern both the end user and the client are answered and supported by real examples.

The answers and arguments will demonstrate that the Light Rail Vehicle is a comfortable and modern way of traveling, that it underlines the spirit of a city and enriches it by linking different districts until then completely separated. New technologies in the construction of tramway lines lead to shorter lead-times, more cost-efficiency and less disturbance in city centers.

1. The right choice

A city lives when people meet and discover all the various possibilities for contact in an environment that encourages encounters. Mobility allows the people to meet each other, but except for pop-concerts, sporting events, love-parades etc. people usually meet in small groups, often only in twos or threes.

The roads enter the cities radially, and in many cases, they extend out into the countryside or are even motorways. A radial road network naturally becomes narrower as it progresses in towards the centre, streets are merged, and the traffic concentrates into fewer lanes. There are many points where the streets are restricted in width, for example bridges, but also crossroads, and of course the old, historic centres of the cities.

Thus, the completely wrong signals are given. The journey begins without problems, and it only becomes difficult near the destination: A driver will have managed to get rapidly almost to the destination, but then draws the wrong conclusions from bad experience of the traffic situation for the last part of the journey, that is to say: the authorities have failed, the restrictions have to be eliminated right now. But never that he has chosen the wrong means of transport.

The multi-lane motorways, the flyover junctions, and tunnels with buildings constructed over them lead the roads in a straight line and quickly, bring us to the proximity, but rarely to the final destination, whether the cinema, shops or a small bistro, where it is comfortable and people can relax.

When many people all wish to get to the same destination at the same time, then the car as a means of transport has a major problem, because there will never be enough streets and parking spaces for all the people who want to meet there.

If a city wants to give back to people some living space then efficient and effective means of mass transport have to be created, which will enable the number of cars to be limited , but without restricting the mobility of the people. Shortly after the opening of the eagerly awaited new tram system in the French city of Montpellier, 65,000 people were using it on a daily basis.

2.   Better use of space

Does that mean that some of the surface area now used by traffic should be reclaimed for people, instead of using it more intensively for cars? Are there any really attractive alternatives to the private car?

On average, each person makes about a thousand journeys per year, each time making a new decision about mobility based on experience, knowledge, expectations and the availability of different means of transport.

These individual decisions of mobility must be influenced by:

- Reducing the contrasts between the private car and public transport and

- Making available, combined, associated and attractive alternative and/or supplementary systems, which enable an equivalent or even better mobility than can be achieved by private car.

With such "inter-modality", it is actually a case of re-organisation of the traffic in the cities.

3. Improving the city environment

But this would mean that tomorrow's mobility must be more oriented towards the service offered rather than the means of transport. The pollution from cars must be reduced by the best possible integrated use of cars and other means of transport. And the introduction of a tram system allows city politicians to apply in parallel urban improvement measures to embellish their city as was done by Orleans in 1999, and planned by Bordeaux over the next two years.

The focus must not be on the means, but on linking the different elements in the transport chain without problems, for which
- Attractive systems of public transport must form the backbone of the inter-modality and be efficiently combined with each other,
- Innovative supplementary products must be proposed which cover the lack of offer of public transport and
- Harmonious integration with the individual traffic is guaranteed.

4. Transport Management

If the problems of mobility are to be permanently resolved, then the preoccupation with the means of transport, which is dominating today's thinking must be replaced by a new philosophy for mobility, the inter-modality.
Inter-modality clearly means much more than eliminating bottlenecks to maintain the traffic flow. The authorities must manage transport to provide road users with a sensible choice between means of transport, which can at first be stimulated by an attractive offer of public transport, successful "inter-modality" is based on well developed and attractively built public systems.

The technical comparison between systems, shows that electrically operated railroad systems offer the best efficiency. Tramway systems are flexible and environmentally friendly.

5. Intermodal transport

The objective should actually be a sensible sharing of tasks and co-operation between public and individual means of transport, by making the right means of transport with the least ecological damage available for each mobility requirement.

ALSTOM sees this in the same way. In the centre of the city predominant use of the public transport should be the objective. In the suburban environment, bus feeder systems can bring people to efficient railroad systems, or park-and-ride facilities (P+R) should be provided, for greater distances from the centre, the use of a private car can present an alternative, but it should end at the nearest P+R-installation.
A modern tramway system can be considered appropriate, especially for medium size cities, and it may also be sensible in large cities to supplement the existing underground and the suburban railway systems. The latest technology makes it even possible to operate vehicles that can run as trams in cities, and speed up to 100km/h in the countryside.- The Tram-Train.

6. Financial aspects

But tramways require high investment and have a long construction time. Is this justifiable in terms of business management?

It is exactly these problems which can be resolved with the modern tramway. Construction proceeds by stages with the integration in existing roads, and operation of a tramway can start rapidly by sections. Modern civil engineering techniques give a drastic reduction in the disturbances caused by tramway construction. For these reasons, the costs are also significantly lower than for underground systems. A city can also purchase a turnkey system, which minimises the difficulties for the city authorities, and afterwards such tramway systems become also attractive for Public Private Partnership (PPP)-solutions. And if more passengers than expected wish to use the tramway, then modern vehicles can now be easily lengthened by adding an extra car module

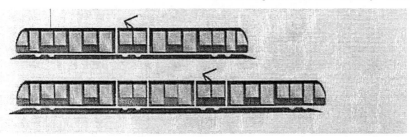

7.   Practical issues

Tramway systems must nevertheless fulfil a series of conditions if the investment shall find expression in market success. Unlike a car, where the driver can determine and influence the departure time, and travel by himself, the passengers of a public transport systems depend on timetables being kept. The reliability must be assured by three measures:

- Segregated lanes for the tramway to ensure a journey without hindrance between the stops. This will range from protected lanes in the road system up to sections in tunnels.
- For systems that mainly mix with normal traffic, it is crucial that they are treated with priority at crossroads with traffic light installations that allow trams through without loss of time.
- Hold-ups should be avoided if possible, and if they occur, they should be cleared as quickly as possible.

8. Reliability

Reliability is the key to succes. Modern technologies are required to meet the high demands of customers. But it is worthwhile. Modern tramway systems have a great impact in urban areas. And due to modern technologies the overall annual operating costs are decreasing whilst the reliability is increasing

9. Life along a tramway line

But doesn't a tramway destroy the cityscape and make living along the tracks a misery!

On the contrary, there is no other traffic system, which is able to combine efficiency and urban acceptability to the same extent as a tram system. Tramways can be integrated into pedestrian precincts without problems. By this capability of integration and not least by the modern design of vehicles, and the individual aesthetics that can be defined by each city, the value of whole streets and even districts can be improved with the introduction of a new tram systems. It is even possible to replace the catenary system by other means of electric power supply in order not to disturb the view of valuable historic buildings as is being done in Bordeaux. This allows for a completely new perception of the city environment and an impression of transparency. ALSTOM has proved that, with modern technology in the vehicles, the noise pollution can be much lower than with road traffic having a comparable efficiency.

10. Comfort and security

In other cities customers complain that they feel uneasy in the light rail vehicles. They are uncomfortable and the atmosphere is often unbearable.

These are images from the fifties of the last century. The progress in vehicle technology has lead to a significant increase in attractiveness in recent years: modern and pleasant materials and design elements, the increase in safety due to inflammable or incombustible construction materials, the lowering of energy consumption thanks to new power systems and economy in weight. The creation of generous space for passengers and the possibilities for passage between the vehicles in the train formation have improved the openness and therefore the subjective sensation of security of the passengers. The introduction of low-floor vehicles with entrances without steps have facilitated the access for disabled persons to surface public transport systems. Moreover, modern vehicles have comfortable seats, large windows and are air-conditioned, like the private car. If this is not an alternative...?

 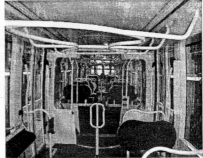

11. Discussion

More and more cities have recognised that they cannot resolve their traffic problems only with the car. At the beginning we agreed that integrated mobility must be the model of future, that is to say, everyone can choose the means of transport, which is the most appropriated.

The tramway can, in the framework of such systems, play a decisive role in most cases. To use it shows that you are ahead of your time. The modern design of new systems underlines the avant-gardisme of their users. People of the 21st century can finally afford to leave their car at home and feel comfortable when going out. Is there a better contribution to maintaining the cities as somewhere worth living than to use the trams in these cities?

References : Conferences and publications by Horst Schaffer

- "Lineamenti per una moderna vettura tranviaria per la citta di Zurigo: tram 2000". Congress Report "Materiale mobile per metropolitana leggera" Torino 1978
- "Vom Sprechfunk zur automatischen Betriebslenkung". VDI-Fortschritt-Bericht. Reihe 12, Nr. 38,1979.
- "Platzbedarf (Clearance) von Normal- und Gelenkbussen in engen Kurven". Strasse und Verkehr 4/81 and Verkehr und Technik 2/1981.
- "Kommentar zu den Ausführungsbestimmungen der Eisenbahnverordnung, Lichtraumfragen". Budesamt für Verkehr, Bern, 1984
- "Zürichs erste Stadtbahnstrecke". Verkehr und Technik, 9/1986
- "Kriterien für die Wahl von Stadtbahnsystemen" UITP Report for the UITP Congress in Budapest 1989
- "Die VBZ Züri-Linie. Unterwegs vom Amt zum Unternehmen". Der Nahverkehr, 1/1991
- "Quality-Management: Brückenschlag zwischen Kostensteuerung und Marketing". Der Nahverkehr, 12/1994
- "Five rules for successful light rail systems". Tramways & Urban Transit, October 1999.
- "Policies for sustainable mobility. Complementarity between Modes and New Mobility Products". Report for the UITP Conference „The Challenge of Urban Mobility" in Mexico City. April 2000, published by UITP.

Section 3:
Traffic control

Adaptive traffic signal control for the fluctuations of the flow using a genetic algorithm

S. Takahashi[1], H. Nakamura[1], H. Kazama[2] & T. Fujikura[2]
[1] *Department of Electronics and Computer Science,*
College of Science and Technology,
Nihon University, Japan.
[2] *Kyosan Electric Manufacturing Co., Ltd., Japan.*

Abstract

This paper describes adaptive traffic signal control for the fluctuations of flow using a genetic algorithm (GA). The target of signal control parameters for this study is offset that is difficult to optimize because of its variety of combinations. Offset optimization using GAs has been investigated in previous studies. Most of them however, focused on signal control in a condition where the traffic flow was fixed. In a practical scene, the rate of flow changes as time passes, so that offset-optimization considering these fluctuations of flow is required. As a case study, an urban traffic route in a city of the Chubu region in Japan, with twenty-one signalized intersections, was tested. To perform offset-optimization by a GA, offset values were represented in a chromosome having the same number of genes as the signals. Two different conditions of traffic flow, slow monotonous and rapid increase, were chosen for the simulation. The results show that the offset optimization technique used in this study was a valuable one for efficient signal control.

1 Introduction

The traffic signal control has been recognized as an important means of solving various traffic problems such as traffic congestion. Among the various signal control parameters such as cycle length or green split, offset is one of the most important yet most difficult to optimize.

In a practical traffic scene, offset based on a very simple algorithm has

Figure 1: The schematic diagram of the target route.

Table 1: Signal parameters for the route.

Signal No.	1	2	3	4	5	6	7
Link [m]	0	215	295	500	450	300	650
Split [%]	67	75	56	54	75	75	69
Signal No.	8	9	10	11	12	13	14
Link [m]	500	405	450	495	430	370	530
Split [%]	68	57	63	62	76	68	62
Signal No.	15	16	17	18	19	20	21
Link [m]	495	430	370	530	400	100	350
Split [%]	62	76	68	62	71	71	50

been used for traffic signal control. However, the offset using the present method is not guaranteed to be an optimum parameter. In addition, it takes enormous time to test all offset patterns because of their variety of combinations. To find an optimal offset, a genetic algorithm (GA) (Goldberg [1]), which is a search/optimization algorithm, is valuable technique.

Offset-optimization using GAs has been investigated in previous studies (Park [2], Goto [3]). However, most of them focused on signal control in a condition where the traffic flow was fixed. In a practical scene, the rate of flow changes as time passes, so that offset-optimization considering the fluctuations of flow is required.

In this study, we investigate adaptive offset optimization by a GA-based program designed to take into account the fluctuations of the traffic flow.

2 Target route

As a target for computer simulation, an urban traffic route, with twenty-one signalized intersections in a city of the Chubu region in Japan, was selected. Figure 1 shows the schematic diagram of the target route. The route is 8,305 meters long, and consists of twenty-one signal intersections shown as numbered circles in the Figure. The distance between the 19th and the 20th signals is short, so they are controlled together.

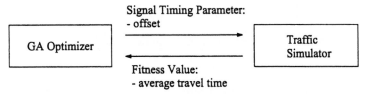

Figure 2: Concept for GA-based program.

In this study, the parameter of offset is optimized for traffic signal control. The other parameters, cycle length and green split, are fixed. The cycle length for all signals is 130 seconds, and the green splits and the link length between signals are displayed in Table 1.

3 Genetic algorithm-based program

3.1 Concept

In order to find a near-optimal offset, we make a genetic algorithm-based program. The genetic algorithm-based program consists of two main components: a GA optimizer and a traffic simulator. The concept for our GA-based program is shown in Figure 2. The GA optimizer produces randomly a certain number of individuals (offset) as the initial generation. Each individual offset is evaluated by the traffic simulator which then returns a fitness value (average travel time) to the GA optimizer. The GA optimizer will evolve the next generation based on fitness values obtained from the traffic simulator. Evolution is continued until the specified number of generation is achieved.

3.2 Genetic algorithm optimizer

To perform offset-optimization, offset values have to be coded as a gene value of a chromosome. The basics of genetic algorithms use binary strings to represent solutions. In this study, integers from 0 to 99 are used as a gene value to code an offset value that is a percentage of a cycle length. Each chromosome has the same gene value for the offset values of the 19th and the 20th signals for the reason described in the section of the target route. An example of a chromosome representing an offset is shown below:

{15:93:7:86:34:53:87:51:65:83:6:33:38:17:1:12:92:79:29:29:0}

Table 2 shows the parameters for the GA optimizer. The size of chromosome is the number of signals in the route. A pair of mates is picked from

Table 2: Parameters for the GA optimizer.

Number of individuals	30
Size of chromosome	21
Crossover rate	0.8
Mutation rate	0.5
Number of generation	250

Table 3: Parameters for a vehicle.

Acceleration [m/s^2]	1.4
Deceleration [m/s^2]	1.7
Maximum speed [km/h]	60

the population by using the roulette wheel selection, and crossover is performed with two-point crossover operation. The number of generations is set at 250 because this is enough for the GA optimizer to find the individual having the best fitness value in an optimization trial.

In this research, we are investigating adaptive offset control for fluctuations of traffic flow. The GA-based program will start when the traffic flow level changes to a different one. Therefore, the population of individuals (offset) at the initial generation contains the optimal offset for the previous traffic flow level. This prevents the GA optimizer from producing more recessive offset than for the previous traffic level. In addition, this suppresses dispersion of the best solution for each optimization trial.

3.3 Traffic simulator

The traffic simulator is a part of the GA-based program for providing fitness values. In the simulator, vehicles are generated at the 1st intersection for an up flow and the 21st intersection for a down. Losses of vehicles turning left or right are not taken into account in this simulator. A traffic flow level can be set as the degree of saturation for an up and down flow separately. The parameters for a vehicle are shown in Table 3.

The fitness value provided from the simulator is a reciprocal number of average travel time, the average of travel time for all vehicles. The travel time for each vehicle includes the number of stops $\times$ 30 seconds.

Table 4: Average travel time for five different flow levels.

	U10D5	U15D5	U20D5	U25D5	U30D5
Average [s]	548.2	547.3	554.8	556.2	575.5
Previous [s]	553.4	547.9	563.8	566.2	601.7

4 Adaptive offset control

To evaluate adaptive offset control for fluctuations of traffic flow, two different conditions of flow were tested. These were slow monotonous, and rapid increase in flows.

4.1 Slow monotonous increase in flows

4.1.1 Offset optimization
For the first condition of a flow, five different flow levels were selected. The degree of saturation for a down flow was fixed to 5 % for all flow levels. The degree of saturation for an up flow increases from 10 % to 30 % in 5 % stages. Thus, the five different flow levels are U10D5(up 10%, down 5%), U15D5, U20D5, U25D5 and U30D5.

Ten optimization trials by the GA-based program were carried out for each flow level in order to find the best offset. To perform optimization for each flow level, the population of individuals at the initial generation contained the best solution of the previous flow level. In the case of U10D5, the previous flow level was U5D5. The results of optimization for five flow levels are displayed in Table 4. 'Average' means the average of average travel times (ATTs) for ten trials. 'Previous' indicates the ATT obtained by using the best offset for the previous flow level. For example, Previous 563.8 [s] for the flow level U20D5 is the ATT under the condition of U20D5 by using the best offset for the previous flow level U15D5. The results show that Average and difference between Average and Previous increase with the rise of traffic flow levels.

4.1.2 Evaluation
To evaluate the offset control using the offsets optimized the GA-based program, the effect of changing or unchanging offset with the rise of a traffic flow was examined by a traffic simulator. The effect is measured by the transition of 'moving average travel time' (MATT), which is the average of travel times for vehicles that started in the past six cycles (780 [s]).

Figure 3 shows the typical transitions of MATT for four different conditions of flows. The first flow level lasts for fifteen cycles, then the second flow level continues for thirty cycles (e.g. U10D5 → U15D5). In the case of changing offset, the new offset for the second flow is set with the rise of a traffic flow. In the low flow levels, the loss of MATT occurs only for

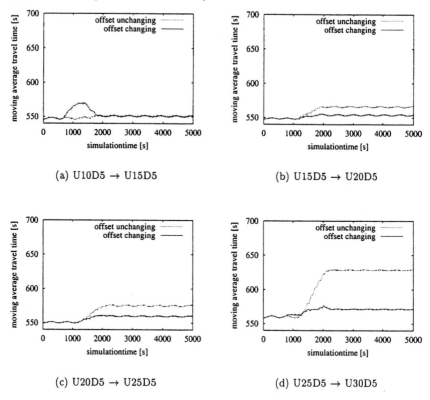

(a) U10D5 → U15D5

(b) U15D5 → U20D5

(c) U20D5 → U25D5

(d) U25D5 → U30D5

Figure 3: Transition of MATT for slow monotonous increase in flows.

changing offset (Figure 3(a)), and as the flow level becomes higher, the gain of MATT increases (Figure 3(b)-3(d)).

4.2 Rapid increase in flows

4.2.1 Offset optimization

For the second condition of a flow, rapid increase in flows was tested. A traffic flow level rises rapidly from U5D5 to U25D5. Because a loss can be expected with the change of an offset, reduction of the loss should be considered. To find an optimal offset without change of the loss, a distance between new and previous offsets was incorporated into a fitness value provided from the traffic simulator. The distance between the offsets can be a parameter to represent ease of changing offset. The distance between the

Table 5: Typical results for different c_d values.

c_d	0.0	0.5	1.0	2.0
ATT	559.5	562.0	571.5	578.5
$D_{offsets}$	100.51	13.45	8.66	6.86

offsets is determined as follows,

$$D_{offsets} = \sqrt{\sum_i (o_i^{Prev} - o_i^{New})^2} \tag{1}$$

where

$o_i^{Prev} = i_{th}$ offset value of a previous offset (U5D5)

$o_i^{New} = i_{th}$ offset value of new offset (U25D5).

The fitness value for the GA-based program is now given by the following equation:

$$Fitness = \frac{1}{ATT + c_d \times D_{offsets}} \tag{2}$$

where

ATT = average travel time [s]

c_d = contribution rate of $D_{offsets}$ to a fitness value

Four different c_d values were chosen, and ten optimization trials were carried out for each value. The typical results with ATT and $D_{offsets}$ for the different c_d values are shown in Table 5.

4.2.2 Evaluation
The effect of changing or unchanging offset was examined with the optimized offsets providing the results in Table 5. The procedure for evaluation was the same as for slow monotonous increase in flows described in 4.1.2. Figure 4 shows the transition of MATT for the offsets with different $D_{offsets}$. Although the MATT for changing offset grows slightly, the offset with small $D_{offsets}$ values gives the more efficient control.

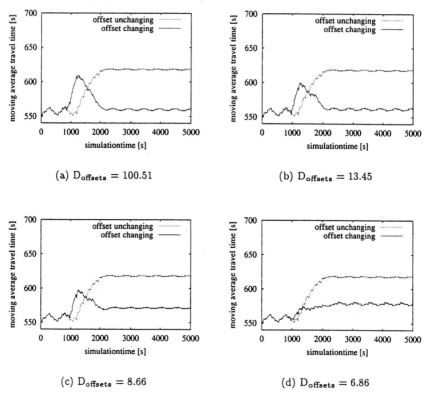

(a) $D_{offsets} = 100.51$

(b) $D_{offsets} = 13.45$

(c) $D_{offsets} = 8.66$

(d) $D_{offsets} = 6.86$

Figure 4: Transition of MATT for the offsets with different $D_{offsets}$.

5 Discussion and Conclusions

In a practical scene of traffic flow conditions, the rate of flow changes as time passes. Therefore, it is important that an optimized offset considering these fluctuations of flow can be found within a useful time. In this study, we have investigated adaptive offset control for two different conditions of flows, slow monotonous, and rapid increase. The results presented in this article indicate that offset-optimization by a genetic algorithm (GA) gives valuable solutions for efficient offset changing.

In a condition where the traffic flow increased slowly, the optimized offsets found by the GA for the new flow gave shorter average travel time than did offsets for the previous flow, without serious loss occuring with offset changing. However, in the low flow level where the average travel time for offset changing was greatly close to one for offset unchanging, only the loss with offset changing was observed. This suggests that in the low flow level, imprudent change of offset should be avoided.

On the other hand in a condition where the traffic flow increased rapidly, although the optimized offsets found by the GA gave good average travel time, the loss occuring with offset changing was serious. This problem could be solved by incorporating a parameter of the distance between new and previous offsets into a fitness value for the GA. The offset with an appropriate small distance value gave efficient control without serious loss.

The results in this study are for the target route with twenty-one signalized intersections under the typical conditions of traffic flow. More research should be done to investigate other routes having different networks and various conditions of traffic flow.

References

[1] Goldberg, D.E., Telles, J.C.F. & Wrobel, L.C., *Genetic Algorithms in Search, Optimization, and Machine Learning*, Addison-Wesley Publishing Company, Inc., 1989.

[2] Park, B., Messer, C.J. & Urbanik II, T., Traffic Signal Optimization Program for Oversaturated Conditions, *Transportation Research Record*, **1683**, pp. 133-142, 1999.

[3] Goto, Y., Komaya, K. & Fukuda, T., A Simulation Experimental Study of Traffic Signal Control by Using Genetic Algorithm, *Trans. of IEE Japan*, **115-D**, No. 6, pp. 784-792, 1995 (in Japanese).

Guided corridor development for sustainable urban transport

P.S. Rana
Housing and Urban Development Corporation, India

Abstract

The rail-based systems in urban areas are highly capital intensive and the cost is much higher than road-based systems in the early stages. However, when the traffic volume along a particular corridor increases, the cost for road based systems increases exponentially.

Establishing a fresh set of rail based infrastructure, although more efficient than any road based solution, is highly capital intensive and involves large amount of difficult land acquisition. On the other hand, if existing rail corridors were utilised for guiding future urban development, the system would be efficient as well as cost effective. National Capital Region in India provides an opportunity to utilise the existing railways lines. This available infrastructure and its potential can be exploited to the maximum extent. Various corridors with high growth potential can be prioritised and the one with highest potential can be prepared for future urbanisation. Even one corridor fully developed on these lines can take care of future urbanisation of the capital city of Delhi. The corridor consisting of railway, pipeline, highway, H. T. power line and communication lines would form the infrastructure spine.

1 Introduction

The world population projections indicate that India's total population will almost double during the next century. During the third decade of the next century, India will become the most populous country of the world. Whatever efforts are made for controlling the population growth, the next three decades are the most crucial for planning and development of human settlements and provision of the required infrastructure.

Although the rate of urbanisation in India has been quite moderate during this century due to a low level of urbanisation (Table 1), and large population base there has been a rapid growth of urban population. Over the last 50 years, the urban population has been doubling itself every twenty years. In spite of such a rapid growth rate, the urban population accounted for 25.72 per cent of the total population in 1991. The past experience clearly indicates that Economic Growth and Urban Development go hand in hand. Therefore, the rate of urbanisation in India in coming decades is likely to increase. This will put an unprecedented demand for growth of urban areas.

In India and most of the developing countries, the urban development is mostly uncontrolled. The development planning and control mechanisms in our cities are either absent or so ad-hoc that the unplanned urban extensions are being added to each city without any infrastructure. Transport as well as other service Infrastructure try to keep pace with the development resulting into a vicious circle which leads to perpetual scarcity and shortage.

In such an uncontrolled scenario, the right type of infrastructure cannot be planned or provided. By the time an Infrastructure is provided to meet the present demand, it is already over-loaded and hence in need of further expansion. Such flexibility could be provided by the road based systems predominated by personalised modes for transportation and individual arrangements for water supply and sanitation. And that is what has been happening in all our cities. But such a system is neither cost effective nor it can make optimum use of resources. Due to perceived lower marginal costs of meeting incremental demand, all our larger cities have grown into nightmares. If we want to make optimum use of our urban Infrastructure, it should precede development and act as a catalyst for development in a desired pattern. Long-term measures are, therefore, to be taken without further loss of time to meet the demand of further urbanisation and reverse the migration to our mega cities.

2 Urbanisation trends and economic growth

When India got independence in 1947, about 85 per cent of its population was living in rural areas and only 15 percent in urban areas. The rate of urbanisation in the preceding decades had been very slow. The urbanisation increased from 10.81 percent in 1901 to 11.99 percent in 1931 and 13.86 percent in 1941. After independence, the urban growth was accelerated and registered the highest decadal growth of 46.14 per cent during 1971-81. During the last five decades (1941-91) the urban population has increased from 13.86 percent to 25.72 per cent. The urban population growth in India is a result of pull as well as push factors i.e. attraction of better employment opportunities in urban areas and labour force rendered surplus due to the limited capacity of the rural economy to accommodate the increasing population.

In a developing economy, urbanisation is a necessary and desirable phenomenon. The cities are considered as Engines of Economic Growth and 'Wealth of a

Nation'. The urban and rural share of Gross Domestic Product (GDP) over last four decades is illustrated in Table 1. Urban contribution to GDP has increased from 30 percent in 1950-51 to 60 percent in 1990-91 i.e. 25.72 percent of urban population contribute 60 per cent of GDP. Per capita GDP contribution by urban and rural sectors in 1990-91 were Rs. 10.844 and Rs.2.997 respectively. In other words the urban sectors' contribution per capita was 3.62 times more than the rural sector.

Table 1: Urban / Rural Shares of GDP

Year	GDP at factor costs at current prices (Rs. Billion)			Per Capita GDP (Rs)		Ratio of Urban/ Rural Per Capita GDP
	Urban	Rural	Total	Urban	Rural	GDP
1950-51	27	67	94	422	225	1.97
1980-81	673	759	'433	4222	!449	2.91
1990-91	2355	1570	3925	10844	2997	3.62

Source:
I. Planning Commission, Task Force Reports on Urban Development, 1983
2. Planning Commission. Eighth Five-Year Plan, Vol. II Ch. 13
3. Mulkh Raj, Urbanization. Infrastructure and Besieged Growth Potential (mimeo), 1993.

3 Urban infrastructure and resource utilisation

Urban utility infrastructures required for efficient functioning of an urban area are Transportation, Water Supply and Sanitation, Power Supply and Communication

Optimisation leads to optimum use of resources to create most favourable conditions for the best trade off between the opposing tendencies. The basic resources utilised in provision of urban Infrastructure are: -
Space   Energy   Time   Capital   Manpower   Environment.

Thus, for overall cost effectiveness optimisation needs to be achieved in totality involving all the above resources.

The cost of development, operation and maintenance of urban Infrastructure depends upon the location, size and structure of a city. Transportation, water supply, sewerage, drainage and solid waste disposal in particular are highly influenced by the city size and location. An attempt is being made to identify the parameters, which are conducive for optimisation of these sectors of urban Infrastructure, and to suggest the ways to obtain the conditions to achieve the same.

4 Transportation

4.1 Travel demand

The size and structure of an urban area considerably influence per capita travel demand as well as total demand for the area. A report of Working Group on Transportation, Government of India indicated that the average per capita trip rate is higher and the average trip length longer in the larger cities.

4.2 Selection of mode

A study conducted by TRRL in three medium cities namely Vadodara, Jaipur and Patna indicates a uniform pattern in selection of modes for similar travel distances. The average distance for walk and cycle were 1.2 and 3.1 km. respectively. When travel distance increases further, the choice shifts to motorised private and public modes. (TRRL, New York. 1987)

4.3 Space/Energy requirements

Considering the PCU equivalent and their occupancy, cars and scooters require about 3 times more space on roads per passenger, as compared to the public bus transport for movement alone. In addition, the parking requirement of these vehicles, particularly in central areas is phenomenal.

Table 2: Capacities of various modes per lane

System	Heavy rail	LRT	Metro	EMU	Double Decker	Std. Bus	Mono Rail	Mini Bus	Car / Scooter
Capacity (PPHPD) in '000	105	72	63	58	35	30	20	15	10

The rail-based system provides 2 to 3 times the Crush Capacity of Buses. The capacities of various modes per lane are given in Table 2.

The capacity of each road-based mode is the maximum capacity with crush loads on an exclusive lane used for the particular mode.

The energy required for personalised modes is 4 to 5 times higher than the road based mass transport and about 100 times higher than a rail based system. These values are based on the use of petrol/diesel for road modes and the use of electricity for rail modes.

5 Urban form and cost of infrastructure

Regarding transport, it is a known fact that the road-based systems have been the most traditional, most conventional and most convenient modes of transport over the ages. Once a paved/unpaved road is available, the choice of vehicle, time of journey and destination is quite flexible. However, with development of other specialised means of transport, more efficient and more cost effective systems such as railways, pipelines and communication are now available for certain specialised needs. To get the maximum out of these specialised systems, certain prerequisites are to be fulfilled through a coordinated effort. For example, for local travel in a small town walk/ cycle are most cost effective but with increase in travel distance or density of travel, these modes are no more convenient or cost effective. On the other hand for short distance and low density, railways are very expensive. Railways become cost effective only for mass movement.

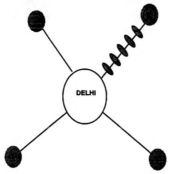

Figure 1: Satellite towns vs. corridor concept

6 Satellite towns vs. corridor concept

Although incremental cost of accommodating additional population in an existing city are generally lower for small increments as compared to setting up a new town. In the long run, the congestion costs overtake and the overall cost becomes very high. P.V. Inderesan has recommended an annular city based on a circular bus route. For minimizing local travel, he suggests a mixed land use along a ring road with a hollow core for energy efficiency and ecological balance. Another alternative could be with a high-density core surrounded by medium and low-density development with each town having its own character. The flexibility of shape and structure for such a medium city is unlimited based of local geographical, cultural and economic parameters.

It seems impossible to control the growth of cities, particularly large ones due to their own momentum and economic forces. A via media has been attempted in several countries by developing satellite towns around large metropolitan cities. The concept has not lived up to expectations. In my opinion, this concept cannot be cost effective and generally proves counter-productive in achieving the laid down objectives. Several towns developed along the same corridor will be more cost effective than developing satellite towns in different directions as shown in Fig: 1. By this approach, high-density corridors along railways will be conducive for high capacity rail systems.

When we try to decongest a metro through satellite towns, we end up increasing travel distances. When we do that through corridor planning, we achieve same result with lesser distance to travel. Density pattern of the resulting urban form matches the transport network pattern.

On the accessibility front, there has been a system in India for last 50 years of independence of chalking out successive nation-wide 20-Year transportation plans and implementing them to a satisfactory level as well. Thus, the problem is not so much of the 'connectivity' now, but more of 'mobility'. Although there is accessibility for most of the villages and towns, the level of mobility available to its inhabitants is generally low. Therefore, what we aim for now is higher level of mobility with minimum investment.

Since transportation is a network type of service, it is more efficiently utilised if it is provided in an aggregated manner. Urbanisation provides this level of aggregation, necessary for the efficient provision of transportation services.

It is very costly to develop new rail corridors in our large cities but it is quite easy to develop our new cities along existing railways. A ten kilometre wide corridor along part of our National Rail Network could be declared as the most preferred zone for future urban development. Availability of local water sources and railway should be necessary attributes for inclusion into this zone.

7 National capital region of India – a case study

The Government of India in 1961 set up a board to look after the need of the National Capital Region (NCR). Further, the Town and Country Planning Organisation started work on the preparation of Regional Plan in late sixties, which ultimately led to the creation of NCR Planning Board by parliament enactment and concurrence of adjoining states of Haryana, UP, and Rajasthan. NCR now covers an area of more than 30,000 sq. km. consisting of about 13,500 sq. km. from Haryana, 10,000 sq. km. from UP, 5000 sq. km. of Rajasthan and about 1500 sq. km. of Delhi at the centre.

A regional plan was drafted in 1989 with a perspective year 2001. This was aimed at reducing the pressure of population on Delhi and achieving a balanced and harmonised development of the region. At the time of preparation, Delhi had about 9.5 million of population and about 40% of Delhi's area was built-up (almost three times of what it was in 1960).

The plan envisaged that in 2001, the 11 million projected population of Delhi would be housed in less than 43% of Delhi's area and another two million will choose adjoining towns within NCR instead of coming to the heart of Delhi.

Today, it is estimated that Delhi's population will be about 15 millions in 2001 and about 20 millions in 2011. Either the projections underestimated the growth rate or the theory of arresting migration in the adjoining NCR towns did not materialise. Probably both are valid explanations.

8 Existing scenario of NCR

Officially, latest documents and reports from the NCR Planning Board argue that the problem has essentially been of relationships. The core Delhi extracts economic surplus of the NCR's periphery and whatever development takes place in the periphery mostly reflects the expanding needs of the core. Several other reasons have been put forward such as the tax differentials and availability of better social and physical infrastructure, which has influenced the decision of people locating industries and trading houses. Added to these is the fact that Delhi, being the national capital, is government's and bureaucracies headquarter and place of final decision-making.

While many factors have been attributed to the rapid growth of Delhi over the last decades, its transportation network is blamed for assisting and accelerating this growth. This is so as Delhi is a hub where five National Highways (India's arteries for regional traffic) and eight rail transport corridors converge. These rail lines serve 350 passenger and 40 goods trains per day with just three main termini. Delhi also has a permanent container depot and several other customhouses and warehouses.

Existing policies of the NCR Planning Board continue to be based upon the induced growth of eight Priority Towns at the periphery of the region. This involves integrated townships centred on core economic activities to be relocated out of Delhi as part of its dispersal strategy. Higher order social facilities are

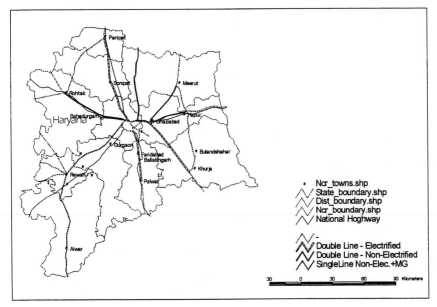

Figure 2: National Capital Region – Transportation Network

also proposed to be dispersed. Major infrastructure works such as expressways, widening and laying of new rail lines are proposed in all directions to serve these dispersed activities. These capital intensive works will have to be taken up in all directions as the Priority Towns which they are meant to serve are spread all over the region.

Since transportation is a network type of service, it will be more efficiently utilised if it is provided in an aggregated manner. Urbanisation provides this level of aggregation, necessary for the efficient provision of transportation services. Through corridor planning, we can accentuate this aggregation and, in addition, match the density pattern of the population with the density pattern of transport infrastructure, ultimately resulting in lesser distance to travel. The next section elaborates this idea in the context of National Capital Region of India.

9 Sustainable urban transport in NCR

Cost of development, operation and maintenance of four basic infrastructure networks, namely, railway, highway, pipeline, power grid and communication are highly sensitive to the location and structure of cities. A spinal type of linear corridor development along the existing rail lines in the NCR would prove to be the most cost effective and environment friendly pattern for urban development of the region than the existing strategy of having priority towns all over the region.

This available infrastructure and its potential must be exploited to the maximum extent. Corridors with high growth potential can be identified and prepared for future urbanisation. Even if one corridor out of eight rail line spreading out from Delhi is developed, it will be enough to take care of future growth. A typical

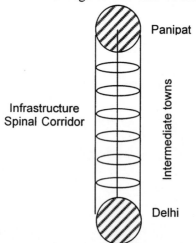

Figure 3: Recommended Urban Development and Infrastructure for NCR

corridor of about 100 km connecting Delhi with a major town would be ideal for this purpose. The corridor consisting of railway, pipeline, highway, H. T. power line and communication lines would form the infrastructure spine, as shown.

A corridor width of 4 to 5 km on either side of the spinal corridor should be reserved for planned and guided urban development. A railway station every two km can be developed as a centre supporting a population of about two lacs. Initially, these towns may function as the dormitory to the major cities at the ends of the corridor and later developed into self-contained towns for most of the functions. The series of such towns will function as complimentary and supplementary to each other providing the economy of scale for all types of specialised activities that a mega city can support. At a gross density of 10,000 persons per sq km i.e., 100 persons per hectare one such corridor of 100 km can support an urban population of one crore. This can easily take care of population growth of next 20 years.

The infrastructure spine of 100 km length supporting a population of about one crore will generate the demand volumes justifying high capacity systems and also ensure their optimum utilisation. The unidirectional tidal flows which are common in suburban commuter systems will be balanced due to the presence of major cities at either end and the inter town movement along the corridor. This would. However necessitate a four-track system to meet the high demand volumes and the operational necessities to provide differential speeds.

By confining the width of the corridor the rural hinterland is available within a couple of km. The supply of various consumables produced in the rural hinterland (particularly the perishable items) and disposal of the various types of wastes generated in the town will be much more economical. This concept offers the advantages of a mega city as well as the benefits of a small town for maintaining ecological balance and environmental quality

We can also extend this scheme to connect at-least three towns in a triangular fashion so that the hinterland trapped inside the triangle gets mobility from the triangular urbanisation and also serves it as its immediate hinterland. (Figure 4)

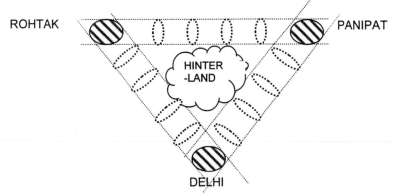

Figure 4: Application of corridor concept on regional level

Three sides of this triangle will not only form high-density urban areas but also high capacity infrastructure spines. As one goes towards the centroid of the triangle, the density as well as capacity of transportation links will start decreasing, making way for more land-intensive uses such as horticulture, arboriculture, poultry etc. These areas will help serve the urban areas on the triangle sides.

10 Conclusions

1. With the increase in size of a city travel distances increase even faster
2. Increase in travel distance results in change of mode from walking and cycling to motor vehicles private and public.
3. Personalised fast modes make inefficient use of space and energy. They are also highly polluting.
4. Each mode has a range of a capacity when it is more cost effective as compared to other modes.
5. Rail based systems require minimum space and manpower for providing a particular level of capacity and these are most reliable and time saving.
6. Walking cycling and rail-based systems are highly energy efficient, least polluting and most cost effective.
7. A narrow corridor surrounded by rural hinterland helps in reducing the cost of water supply, disposal of wastewater, sewer and solid wastes.
8. Perishable consumer items like fruits, vegetables, milk and poultry products etc. can be supplied economically.
9. The regional rail network operated by the Indian Railways is a potential resource that can: be exploited to provide future urban transport infrastructure.
10. Corridor development along an infrastructure spine can help optimum utilisation of infrastructure and achieve sustainable development.
11. The high rate of urbanisation throws a challenge but it also provides an opportunity to achieve the desired urbanisation pattern for optimum use of urban Infrastructure.

11 Recommendations

1. Identify key corridors based on primary parameters and supplementary services mentioned above and carry out pre-feasibility studies
2. Notify a band of five kilometres on either side as potential urban areas along the corridors under the Town Planning or UD Acts/ legislations of the respective govt.
3. Projectisation of corridors for necessary infrastructure development
4. Create SPVs or nominate one of the existing agencies as a nodal agency for developing infrastructure spinal corridors
5. Invite developers, (govt. agencies, PSUs, private entrepreneurs) for taking up development along the corridor.
6. Ministry of Railways may be requested to include these sectors in their plan for up gradation of service levels on priority

Design and evaluation of traffic calming schemes in urban areas – the case of the city of Larissa

C.Taxiltaris, S.Basbas & M.Miltiadou
Aristotle University of Thessaloniki, School of Technology
Faculty of Rural & Surveying Engineering,
Dept. of Transportation & Hydraulic Engineering, Greece

Abstract

Within the framework of this paper, the design and evaluation of a comprehensive scheme concerning a variety of traffic management measures, and especially traffic calming measures, like woonerf, 30 km/h zones, bus priority measures, routes for cyclists, interventions at intersections, pedestrian facilities etc., aiming at the improvement of traffic and associated environmental conditions are presented and discussed with reference to the center of the city of Larissa in central Greece. The evaluation of these measures is based on the use of both qualitative and quantitative criteria, which were selected in accordance with the objectives and type of the proposed measures. Examples of such criteria are the geometric characteristics of traffic lanes and sidewalks, the strict use of bus lanes by authorized vehicles, the degree of use of the respective infrastructure by the pedestrians, the parking rules violations, the degree of use of the respective infrastructure by cyclists, speed, the overall perception of the environment as a safe one by the road users etc. The results presented are quite revealing about the effectiveness of traffic calming measures in central areas of medium size Greek cities, but there is a lot to be done yet concerning the research on the evaluation process of such measures.

1 Introduction

Most urban areas in the E.U. and in other countries all over the world suffer from the private car domination. The extensive use of cars results in a number of undesired effects such as environmental pollution, low safety levels, visual intrusion, and in general degradation of quality of life. These traffic-related problems continue to increase as a consequence of both high mobility and increasing car ownership. At the same time it has been recognized that increased supply of road infrastructure cannot really offer a solution to this problem. On the contrary it promotes the use of private cars in the long run. In order to deal with this issue, transport planners have come with a variety of Transport Demand Management (TDM) measures. A rather exhaustive list of TDM measures can be found in many transport books as well in several research reports and papers [1].

Traffic calming has been always an efficient TDM measure. It discourages car users from using the car in certain areas and thus it reduces drastically traffic flows and speeds in these areas. Traffic calming are combinations of physical and/or regulatory measures that impose certain restrictions allocated in space and/or in time, In fact traffic calming measures have been mainly associated with constructions of road surface humps or thumps, street narrowing, alignment changes, use of coloured materials for surfacing, elevated (humped) pedestrian crossings, creation of lay-bys for parked vehicles and other similar constructions.

Examples of traffic calming measures can be found in many books, articles, and research reports from E.U. projects [2,3,4]. The Danish Road Directorate has issued a manual on Speed Management [5] that contains useful examples and practices for this purpose, where traffic calming is one of the most promising interventions and also a manual concerning the framework for the planning and evaluation process for speed management measures in urban areas [6].

The majority of Greek cities of large, medium and even small size experience nowadays a situation where traffic and associated environmental problems exist and seriously affect people's life. Many attempts have been made in the past to overcome these problems but with limited success. Specialized studies about traffic calming measures concerning the urban road network are not a common situation in Greece. Therefore, most of the traffic calming measures which were proposed and implemented until now, are part of short-term traffic management schemes dealing –among others– with pedestrians, traffic flows, road infrastructure, public transport, safety, parking, environment etc.

Quite recently, the implementation of traffic calming measures has been proposed within the framework of such studies, basically aiming at the improvement of road safety level and the environmental conditions at urban areas in Greece. The availability of experience and the positive results arising from the implementation of such measures abroad was a decisive factor to implement traffic calming measures in Greek cities too. Based on the examination of the alternative traffic schemes which were proposed and partially implemented [7] in various municipalities in Thessaloniki Metropolitan Area, the following measures can be classified as traffic calming measures: pedestrianisation with no vehicle access, pedestrianisation with limited vehicle access, plateau, speed humps, changing street alignment, woonerf, street narrowing and 30km/h zones. The above measures were implemented in different timings during the period 1991-99.

The city of Larissa in central Greece is also considered to be a good reference point because it was the first major city in Greece (together with the city of Heraklion on the island of Crete) where a master plan was designed and partially implemented at the end of '80s. An extensive pedestrian network was also designed and implemented in the city center and its greater area. The Municipality of Larissa participates in the European Network "Car Free Cities" and in other programs concerning exchange of experiences (PACTE) together with the Municipalities of Edessa, Graz and Leeds. Within the framework of this paper, the design and evaluation of a comprehensive scheme concerning a variety of traffic management measures, and especially traffic calming measures, aiming at the improvement of traffic and associated environmental conditions are presented and discussed with reference to the center of the city of Larissa.

2 Trips characteristics in the city of Larissa

Within the framework of the research project which was carried out in the city of Larissa by the Aristotle University of Thessaloniki in 1997 [8], an extensive questionnaire based survey was included. The survey consisted of a total number of 913 questionnaires (2.938 residents) and the study area was divided into 20 traffic zones. It must be mentioned at this point that the city population, according to the 1991 national census, was 110.116 residents (33.659 households). The estimation for the population for the year 2001 is 119.107 residents. The most important results of this survey are presented hereinafter in order to provide a clear image of the traffic characteristics in the study area before going to the proposed traffic calming measures. More specifically, the vehicle ownership index for various vehicle categories is presented in Table 1.

Table 1: Vehicle ownership indices in the city of Larissa

Number of vehicles	Bicycles (%)	Two-wheels cycles (%)	Private cars (%)	Rural engines (%)	Other vehicles (%)
0	65,2	81,1	28,9	96,4	18,1
1	24,8	17,7	65,6	3,2	41,9
2	6,2	1,1	5,0	0,3	22,6
3	3,8	0,1	0,4	0,1	10,6
4-	-	-	-	-	6,8
Proportion	153 per 1.000 residents	64 per 1.000 residents	241 per 1.000 residents	13 per 1.000 residents	-

The private car ownership and the mobility of households are presented in the following Table 2.

Table 2: Car ownership and mobility of households in the city of Larissa

Number of private cars per household	Trips per household (average value)	Trips per member of the household
0	2,26	1,49
1	3,59	1,61
2	4,17	1,94
Total	3,23	1,59

The frequency of trips to and from the city center is as follows: two or more trips per day: 52,6 %, once a day: 18,0 %, not very often: 29,4 %. The frequency of trips made to and from the city center by different modes is presented in Table 3.

Table 3: Frequency of trips made to and from the city center by different transport modes

Frequency of trips	Walking trips and bicycle trips	Trips made by Public Transport buses	Trips made with private cars, taxis & two-wheel cycles
Very often	62,3 %,	12,5	25,1 %
often	10,4 %,	14,0	16,7 %
not so often	6,0 %,	5,5	13,3 %
rarely	9,5 %,	19,9	26,0 %
never	11,7 %.	48,0	18,9 %

The trip duration to the city center (average value from all twenty traffic zones) is 13,1 minutes for walking), 15,7 minutes for bicycles, 13,1 minutes for two wheel cycles, 16 minutes for private cars, 13,5 minutes for taxis and 26,2 minutes for public transport buses. Trip distribution per mode and average trip duration are presented in Table 4:

Table 4: Trip distribution per mode and average trip duration

Transport mode	%	Average trip duration (minutes)
Walking	42,1	13,1
Bicycle	4,6	15
Two wheel cycle	4,9	12,1
Private car	32,3	19
Taxi	2,2	16,8
Public Transport bus	12,3	26
Special bus	1	-
Truck, semi truck	0,5	-

Trip purposes are as follows: Return to home: 48,5%, Work: 17,5%, Education: 6,5%, Shopping: 8,3%, Recreation: 10,4%, Other: 8,8%.

Regarding the above presented data it seems that every resident makes, in general, two or more trips per day to and from the city center. The residents usually walk or use their own bicycles for their trips to and from the city center. The high number of bicycles, although no adequate infrastructure exists for them, gives a strong indication about people's will to further use environment friendly transport means when such an infrastructure will be available. The use of Public Transport is not at desirable level due to various reasons (e.g., bus stop at a long distance from point of trip origin, expensive fares, long duration of trips by bus, insufficient scheduling etc.). Finally, one out of four residents use either its own private car/ two-wheel cycle or a taxi for trips to and from the city center.

3 Proposed traffic calming measures

The proposed traffic calming measures in the city of Larissa include changes in the physiognomy of the road network and their main objective is to reduce the speed of vehicles and to improve the overall traffic and environmental conditions in the central area. They also include reduction in the width of a road, creation of dead ends, construction of mini roundabouts etc. It is known that traffic calming measures aim at the improvement of road safety, the protection of pedestrians, the upgrade of local streets, the creation of an environmental friendly urban area, the reduction of visual intrusion, the reduction in noise levels, the reduction in vehicle emissions etc. Therefore all these measures serve the overall target which is the improvement of the traffic and environmental conditions in the city center. This center according to the results of the trip characteristics survey plays an important role in the overall transportation system of the city.

More specifically the regulatory and physical measures proposed for the city center include the following (measures refer to the Public Transport system support the traffic calming measures since they affect modal split) :
Upgrade and improvement of the Public Transport system
  i.   Incorporation of new bus lines in order to serve the city center and also the interurban bus terminals
  ii.   Buslanes along the main arterial network
  iii. Reformation of the existing exploitation system including the transformation of through bus lines to radial ones
Construction of woonerf (priority given to pedestrians)
Implementation of 30 km/h traffic zones
Changes in the geometric characteristics of the road network
  i.   Widening of sidewalks
  ii.   Discontinuation of road alignment
  iii. Elevated pedestrian crosswalks
Interventions at junctions
  i.   Simplification of turning movements

ii.   Design of pedestrian crossings at an angle of 90° (vertically) to the road alignment
iii.   Settlements for the restoration of visibility
iv.   Incorporation of roundabouts

Development of transition areas (from pedestrian streets to ordinary urban streets)
Constructions on the sidewalks for the incorporation of on street parking (e.g., recess areas)
Construction of bicycle lanes or cyclists routes
Installation of proper signing (vertical and horizontal)

The master plan of these measures is presented in the following Map 1. It must be mentioned at this point that, in the framework of the efforts made by the municipality of Larissa for the improvement of the environment for the pedestrians, the city authorities decided to participate in the European Car Free Day (E.U. car free cities network) in 22-9-2000. Within the actions taken for that day the following are included:

a) distribution of relevant printed material (e.g., brochures etc) concerning the "Car Free Day", b) meetings and other events with school authorities and city officials in order to disseminate information, c) design and production of maps with the bicycle network for that day. A number of 650 bicycles were distributed to school students. A number of 300 bicycles were available to all residents at central points. d) the bus operator has agreed to issue a rebate ticket of approximately 0,3 Euros for that day. Students made their trips by bus free of charge.

The area of 2.200 hectares in which "Car Free Day" program is implemented is presented in Map 1. The following vehicle categories were allowed to enter this area during that day: Public transport buses, school buses, emergency vehicles, vehicles belong to people with special needs, vehicles belong to administration (central/local), police vehicles, vehicles belong to press (permission holders only), vehicles to/from hotels, vehicles of parents transporting children to kindergarten and taxis for emergency purposes only.

4 Evaluation methodology and results

The evaluation of traffic calming measures is based on a number of criteria that are related to the expected effects of the measures. The most common of these criteria are the following: traffic flow, vehicle speed, traffic accidents or road safety, pollutant emissions, noise levels. Other criteria may also be used such as drivers and pedestrians' behaviour in the area or other subjective ones such as opinions or attitudes. A questionnaire based survey was conducted in Thessaloniki in order to evaluate the effects from the implementation of speed humps on a road in front of a school area. According to the results of the survey [9] people who lived in the area before the implementation of the traffic calming

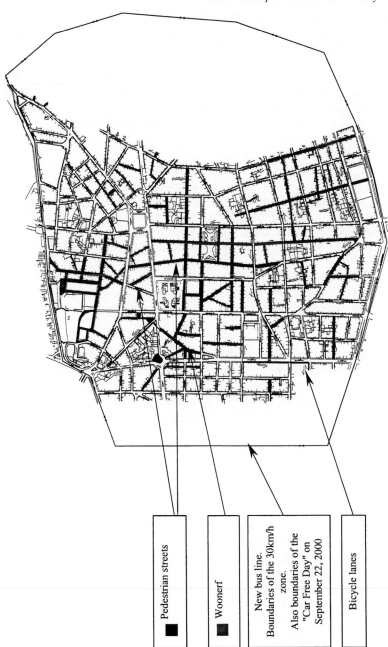

Map 1: Master plan of traffic calming measures in the city of Larissa

Pedestrian streets

Woonerf

New bus line.
Boundaries of the 30km/h zone.
Also boundaries of the "Car Free Day" on September 22, 2000

Bicycle lanes

measures seem to be more sensitive concerning road safety. It must be mentioned at this point that such surveys are not very common in the areas of traffic calming measures in the country.

Economic criteria can be also employed such as commercial value of residences and/or shops. The success or not of the measures will depend on the values of certain indices that are used to measure the change achieved in these criteria. In the case of Larissa there were no data available for all the above mentioned criteria in order to perform a complete "before" and "after" evaluation.

Therefore, quantitative criteria apply only to the Public Transport system of the city and to the road geometrical characteristics where a rearrangement took place, while qualitative criteria apply to all the rest measures. In Table 5, the results of the evaluation of the traffic calming measures are presented, following a "before" and "after" approach. It should be mentioned at this point that driving behaviour, and also pedestrian behaviour, are not at desirable level in the country. This affects the success of the measures but it is not easy to be quantified. The Ministry of Transport and Communications has recently, started a big effort in the field of drivers' behaviour and emphasis has been given on the design and operation of drivers' education and examination centers in the country [10].

In order to perform the evaluation, observations, measurements, on site visits and expertise were made in the city center. Modern technology was used (or will be used in next evaluation steps) like GPS, speed-radars, digital video and photo cameras. As a result of the above mentioned process a clear image of the implementation impacts of traffic calming measures (and not only) has been obtained, with emphasis given to the impacts for pedestrians and generally the vulnerable road users (aged people, students, people with special needs, cyclists).

5 Conclusions

As a result of the above findings there is need for better enforcement in bus lanes and construction of physical separation due to illegal entrance of unauthorized vehicles. Running times of buses in bus lanes were significantly reduced in some cases but there are no available results about the effect on modal split. Woonerf were not implemented so far. Shopkeepers or residents usually react in the idea of loosing their parking places in woonerf and sometimes, due to such reactions, local authorities postponed their plans. The positive effect of elevated crosswalks in intersections is sometimes limited due to improper implementation. In any case, illegal parking seems to be eliminated in these intersections.

Problems appear to continue with illegal parking on sidewalks, unless special measures are taken. Changes in road alignment seem to have a positive effect towards the creation of a safe environment for the pedestrians. Finally it seems that only the provision of the adequate infrastructure does not necessarily means

Table 5: Evaluation of traffic calming measures in the city of Larissa

Thematic areas of measures	Type of measure	Objectives	Quantitative Criteria	Before	After	Rate	Qualitative Criteria	Before	After	Rate	Comments on the "after" situation
Public Transportation System (not traffic)	Bus lanes	Change in modal split in favor of Public Transport; Traffic separation	Number of buses per 3 hours for two bus lanes	83	82	+	Strict use of bus lanes by authorized vehicles e.g. buses, ambulances etc.	Not applicable	Illegal use of bus lanes by unauthorized vehicles	-	Need for better enforcement. Need for physical separation of bus lanes
				81	79	+					
		Increased reliability and efficiency of the Public Transport System	Running times for two bus lanes (minutes)	395	300	+	n.a.	n.a.	n.a.	n.a.	
				46	45	+					
	New bus line on the perimeter of the city center	Elimination of through traffic	n.a.	n.a.	n.a.	n.a.	n.a.	n.a.	n.a.	n.a.	Not implemented yet. Proposed in combination with 30km/h zones in the city center
Woonerf	Change of local streets to Woonerf	Speed reduction; Acceptable safety level for the pedestrians; Improvement of the environment (noise level, emissions from traffic etc.)	n.a.	n.a.	n.a.	n.a.	n.a.	n.a.	n.a.	n.a.	Not implemented yet. Speed limit: 15 km/h. Use of special material for pavements. Use of obstacles (physical and other). Changes in alignment. Provisions for people with special needs. Proper signing
intersections between local streets and pedestrian streets or Woonerf	Construction of elevated crosswalks	Speed reduction	n.a.	n.a.	n.a.	n.a.	Use of activated traffic lights by the pedestrians	Limited	Limited	±	Coloured bricks have been used in crosswalks. Elevation is not easily understood by the drivers (they do not decelerate). Inadequate vertical signing
	Installation of effective traffic light system (activated)	Priority to pedestrians; Improvement of safety level	n.a.	n.a.	n.a.	n.a.	Illegal parking	At the pedestrian zones' entrances	No	++	
Redesign of intersections layout (for the rest of intersections in the center)		Illegal parking elimination; Comprehensive understanding of the intersection layout; Adequate visibility conditions; Improvement of safety level	n.a.	n.a.	n.a.	n.a.	Environment	Unsafe	Safe	++	Need for extra protective measures in order to fully eliminate illegal parking on sidewalks
							Illegal parking	On crosswalks	On sidewalks	+	
30km/h zones	Implementation of 30km/h speed limit within the city center	Improved safety environment for pedestrians and drivers; Protection of neighborhoods	n.a.	n.a.	n.a.	n.a.	n.a.	n.a.	n.a.	n.a.	Not implemented
Redesign of street layout (Including all remaining streets in the center)	Change of alignment; Sidewalks widening; Parking control	Speed reduction; Improved safety environment for pedestrians and drivers	Traffic lanes width	3,6-4,3m	Standard 3,5m	++	Environment	Unsafe	Safe	+	Pedestrians use sidewalks only. Speed reduction achieved. Parking is adequately controlled
			Sidewalks width	1,5-2,2m	1,7-3,6m	+	Pedestrians	Forced to walk on the pavement	Use the sidewalks	++	
			Available parking lots	125	83	+	Speed	High (>50km/h)	Low	++	
							Parking	Illegal	Legal	+	
Bicycle lanes	Exclusive infrastructure for bicycle users	Promotion of the use of environment friendly transport means; Improved safety environment for cyclists	n.a.	n.a.	n.a.	n.a.	Bicycles volume in the same infrastructure with the rest of the traffic	Large	Large	±	Satisfactory level of separation. Small number of bicycles use the same bicycle lane. Improper use of the bicycle lane by the pedestrians
							Environment	Unsafe	Unsafe	±	

n.a.: not available data, ++ : Improved, + : Better, ± : The same, - : Not improved, -- : Worse that a cyclist will not continue to use the traffic lanes for the vehicles. Therefore there is need for changing cyclists' behaviour through proper educational programs. This may also apply in the case of pedestrians who continue to use, in the "after" situation, the infrastructure made for the cyclists. Finally it became obvious that a standard evaluation framework is needed in order to enable objective and subjective evaluation of traffic calming measures in the country.

References

[1] AIUTO Project, Assessment of Innovative Urban Transport Options, Deliverable D1, International Survey of TDM Policies and Innovative Systems, Project Co-ordinator MIP, Milano, Italy, 1996.

[2] Wouters P., Urban Safety Management in Europe: an overview of current practice in nine countries in the context of DUMAS project, Report on DUMAS project, WP1, SWOV Institute for Road Safety Research, The Netherlands.

[3] ADONIS project, Analysis and development of new insight into substitution of short car trips by cycling and walking, Project Co-ordinator RfT, Transport Research, 4th Framework Programme, Urban Transport, Office for the official publications of the European Communities, 1998.

[4] CROW, Bicycle Parking in the Netherlands, Report, The Netherlands, 1997.

[5] Danish Road Directorate, Ministry of Transport, Speed Management – National practice and experience in the Netherlands and in the United Kingdom, Report no.167, 1999.

[6] Danish Road Directorate, Ministry of Transport, Speed Management IN urban Areas – A framework for the planning and evaluation process, Report no.168, 1999.

[7] Papaioannou P., Basbas S., Mintsis G., Taxiltaris C., Evaluation of traffic calming measures in Thessaloniki Metropolitan Area, *Proc.of the ICTCT workshop on Traffic Calming*, satellite workshop to the 5th World Conference on Injury prevention and Control, International Cooperation on Theories and Concepts in Traffic Safety, New Delhi, India, 2000.

[8] Aristotle University of Thessaloniki, Faculty of Rural and Surveying Engineering, Department of Transportation and Hydraulic Engineering, Evaluation of structural and functional elements of the Larissa transportation system. Design of prototype short and long term measures, Project Co-ordinator Taxiltaris C., Final Report, Larissa, 1999.

[9] Pitsiava-Latinopoulou M., Tsohos G., Basbas S., Dimoula S., Traffic calming measures. The experience of their implementation in urban areas in Greece, *Proc.of the International Conference Traffic Safety on Three Continents*, Pretoria, 2000.

[10] Aristotle University of Thessaloniki, Faculty of Rural and Surveying Engineering, Department of Transportation and Hydraulic Engineering, Determination of the structural and operational elements of traffic educational parks and examination centers for candidate drivers, Project Co-ordinator Mintsis G., Final report, Thessaloniki, 1998.

Evaluating access road network structures for built-up areas from a sustainable transport perspective

J. Krabbenbos, M.F.A.M. van Maarseveen & M.H.P. Zuidgeest
Department of Transportation Engineering & Management,
University of Twente, the Netherlands.

Abstract

The relation between motor traffic and liveability in residential built-up areas is usually rather strained. Separation of terminating traffic from through-traffic by infrastructural measures is often difficult to realise without causing a decline in the accessibility of the area. On the other hand, a good accessibility might generate substantial through-traffic with all its adverse impacts on liveability and traffic safety.

Within the framework of the sustainable safety program, a study has been carried out to analyse the impact of various elements of a road network structure in a built-up area on accessibility, liveability and traffic safety. The elements of the network structure are: the number and distribution of access roads, the number and distribution of access directions, and the type of linking to the external road network. A simulation study for a large number of synthetic network structures shows that the impact of access directions is much larger than that of access roads, since it affects route choice more substantially. In addition, the amount of through-traffic is very sensitive to the type of linking to the external network. The simulation study clearly demonstrates the divergent and partly opposite impacts on accessibility, liveability and traffic safety.

The relationship between the number of access directions and accessibility has also been tested in an empirical case study for four different built-up areas in the city of Enschede, the Netherlands. The results of the field study confirm the simulation results.

The implications for the (re)design of access road network structures for built-up areas are discussed. In addition, recommendations for future research are provided.

1 Introduction

Notions of sustainable development have evolved in recent years preceded by the appearance of the 'Our Common Future' report (WCED [1]) and international agreement conform 'Agenda 21' (UNCED, [2]). A wide array of issues and public policy concerns resulted.

In the transportation field the concept of sustainable development gave rise to conceptions as sustainable transportation, sustainable cities etc. Topics as the role of transportation in ensuring future availability of petrol, urban air pollution, traffic congestion and traffic safety are addressed frequently since.

Liveability of residential built-up areas is closely connected to discussions on sustainability. It is here, where the dichotomous concept of sustainable development, indicating an apparent, inherent contradiction, becomes clear. On the one hand accessibility is highly valued, indicating the ease of physical movement in built-up areas, whereas on the other hand there is the search for a liveable environment in built-up areas, in other words a built-up area with limited danger or nuisance by motorised traffic, a place where children can safely play and cross streets and a place where social interaction is possible etc.

The residential street environment is a matter of continual concern to residents living in it, but of only fleeting interest to the passing driver. Therefore, there is a strong argument that it should be designed in a way that living and driving are in balance. It is only then that *function – form – use* of the built-up area are in balance for both drivers as well as people residing in the area.

This paper discusses the relationship between characteristics of the residential transportation network versus its performance in terms of liveability, safety and accessibility. First traffic liveability is discussed based on the conceptual ideas preceding this research, followed by a simulation study, where elements of road structures in a built-up area are systematically varied. In addition, the ideas have been tested in a case study for the city of Enschede, the Netherlands. Finally, some lessons are drawn in the conclusions and recommendations.

2 Characteristics of built-up areas

2.1 Traffic liveability

Liveability is a very wide concept. It refers to human well-being. In this research, the term liveability is narrowed to traffic liveability, which is indicated in terms of liveability, accessibility and traffic safety (figure 1).

Liveability then refers to the amount of through-traffic and the crossability of streets. From the perspective of liveability, through-traffic in built-up areas is undesirable. Air pollution, noise nuisance and perceived traffic unsafety caused by traffic have a negative influence on the well-being of the local residents in the built-up area. Even though all traffic influences liveability, through-traffic can be seen as avoidable traffic in built-up areas in particular.

In addition, liveability refers to the crossability of streets. In order to be able to cross a street, a minimum acceptable gap in the traffic flow of at least the crossing time needs to occur. As traffic flow increases such gaps occur less often. The crossability decreases at two-direction flows of more than 500 veh/h (ASVV [3]). Furthermore, Miedema and Van der Molen [4] demonstrated that lower traffic flows influence the experience of the residential environment positively.

Accessibility of a built-up area can be derived from the average car trip length, relative to the size of the built-up area. The average car trip length denotes the generalised cost of reaching the point of destination from the road surrounding the built-up area.

Traffic safety is the product of exposure and risk. Exposure is derived from traffic performance, which can be expressed in vehicle kilometres. The *roads* surrounding the built-up area have different characteristics than *streets* in built-up areas, therefore risk on roads and streets differ.

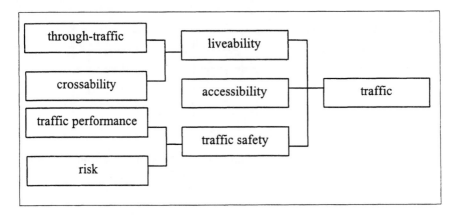

Figure 1: Elements of traffic liveability

2.2 Elements of road network structures

In this study, elements of a road network structure that influence the route choice of motor traffic have been taken into account. These elements are: (1) the number and distribution of access roads, (2) the number and distribution of access directions, and (3) the type of linking to the external road network (Janssen [5], Cerwenka [6], Van Minnen [7]). These elements are illustrated in figure 2. For structures (1 – 4) the type of linking is kept constant at the corners, i.e. traffic enters the network structure in the corners instead of centrally, as in structure (5). For example, figures 2-2A and 2-2B have an equal number of access roads, i.e. 2, but differ in the direction, i.e. West and South vs. North and South. The impact of these elements has been analysed systematically in a theoretical study.

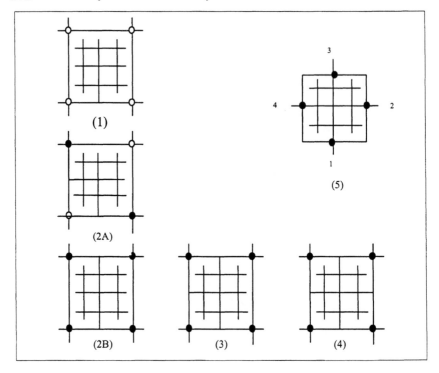

Figure 2: The number and distribution of access roads and directions for corner-type of linking (1-4) to the external road network as well as centrally (5).

3 Simulation study

3.1 Simulation lay-out

To assess the impact of (1) the number and distribution of access roads, (2) the number and distribution of access directions and (3) the type of linking to the external road network, a simulation study was carried out (Krabbenbos [8]). The microscopic simulation model Getram/AIMSUN2 [9] has been used. In the model, a hypothetical built-up area, including the outer (surrounding) road structure was built. A square built-up area with a grid road structure of about 41 hectares was simulated. The housing density and the trip generation were assumed to be equally divided over the built-up area. The basic premise in the route assignment is the assumption of a rational traveller, i.e. one choosing the route which offers the least perceived travel time, as in the so-called 1st equilibrium of Wardrop (see Ortúzar and Willumsen [10]), so delays caused by congested traffic may affect route choice. Therefore, two scenarios, one with a low level of congestion at the outer structure and one with a high level of congestion at the outer structure were carried out. A large number of synthetic network structures were simulated while systematically varying the elements of road structures.

3.2 Simulation results

Figure 3 shows one of the results for the high level of congestion scenario. Because of the congested situation at the outer structure one can expect through-traffic within the built-up area. In this example the linking to the external road network is in the corners of the network structure as in figure 2 (structures 1-4).

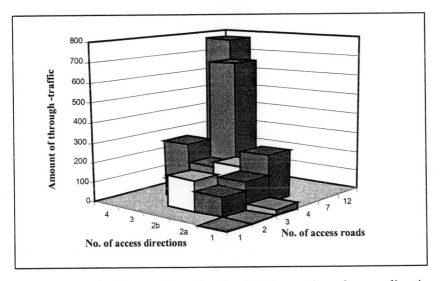

Figure 3: Amount of through-traffic related to the number of access directions and number of access roads.

The simulation study shows that:

- The impact of access directions is much larger than the effect of the number of access roads, since it affects route choice more substantially. The addition of an extra access road, preferably in a new direction and an equal distribution of the access roads over the directions appears to be most effective in terms of access;
- The amount of through-traffic is very sensitive to the type of linking to the external network. Congested traffic causes delays making built-up areas an attractive alternative for through-traffic. Too much through-traffic has a negative influence on liveability;
- The crossability of streets is another measure for liveability. Avoiding through-traffic increases crossability of streets. Adding more access roads, preferably in different directions and an even distribution over the sides of the built-up area, divides traffic more equally over streets. A side-effect of building more access roads can increase through-traffic, which influences crossability in a negative way;
- Accessibility refers only to trips terminating in the built-up area and is therefore independent of the outer network. Accessibility increases by

increasing the number of access directions, the number of access roads and an equal distribution of these access roads.

To estimate the effect of road network structure on traffic safety, not only the built-up area has been taken into account, but also the surrounding structure. Increasing the number of access roads may decrease trip length and therefore traffic performance. But if this leads to more through-traffic in the built-up area, risk can increase, as *function – form – use* of the streets are not balanced anymore. As the relation between flow and risk is depending on the detailed situation and external factors a general conclusion concerning the influence on traffic safety cannot be given. Although traffic safety has been researched in this study, the results are not discussed here, as further research needs to be done to estimate the relation between flow and risk on streets and roads more exactly. For the preliminary results the reader is referred to Krabbenbos [8].

The simulation study clearly demonstrates the divergent and partly opposite impacts on accessibility, liveability and traffic safety. More access roads, preferably distributed equally over the various sides of the built-up area, increase the crossability of streets and the accessibility of destinations in the area. The amount of through-traffic and traffic safety restrains the maximum number of access roads.

As every situation is unique, it is not possible to give general conclusions concerning the optimal number and distribution of access roads and access directions, because this also depends on the other factors like the internal road structure and the amount of through-traffic around the built-up area (the external road structure). The amount of through-traffic is very sensitive to the type of linking to the external network.

4 Case study

4.1 Introduction

The relationship between the number of access directions and accessibility has been tested in an empirical case study. Therefore a comparative study has been carried out. Four built-up areas in the city of Enschede, the Netherlands have been selected. These built-up areas have respectively one, two, three and four access directions. Figure 4 shows the road network structures of the selected areas.

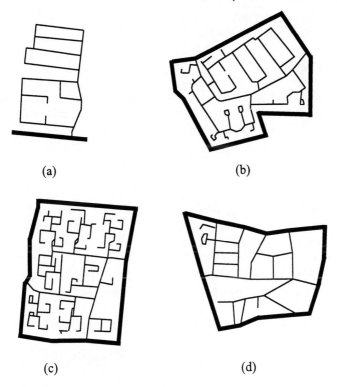

Figure 4: Road network structures of the selected built-up areas in Enschede: (a) Voskamp, (b) Stroinkslanden, (c) Wesselerbrink, (d) 't Zeggelt, with numbers of access directions varying from 1 to 4.

4.2 Method

In order to assess the relationship between the number of access directions and accessibility, accessibility is defined as the distance inhabitants of the built-up area have to travel in order to reach their point of destination. A method has been developed to derive this distance. It is measured by the internal car trip length (L_{trip}), which is the distance travelled on streets by terminating traffic. The average internal trip length was derived using the following formula:

$$L_{trip} = \frac{\left[\sum_i (L_i \cdot i_i)_{total} - \sum_i (L_i \cdot i_i)_{through} \right]}{N_{hb}} \tag{1}$$

with:

L_{trip} = internal car trip length
L_i = length of street link i

i_i = flow on street link i
N = number of terminating trips

4.3 Data collection
The length of the streets (L_i) was derived from the National Road Database. Flows on streets and the number of through-traffic vehicles were obtained by carrying out a traffic counting survey. To make a distinction between terminating traffic and through-traffic, a licence plate survey was performed. The data was collected on workdays (Monday, Tuesday and Thursday) between 15:30 and 17:30.

4.4 Results
For every built-up area, the average trip length for terminating traffic was calculated. Due to differences in size (A) of the areas the average trip length (L_{trip}) has been adjusted by dividing the trip length by the root of the size of the built-up area $(L_{trip}/\sqrt{A})$ in order to make the results comparable. This results in an adjusted average internal trip length (table 1). In figure 5 the adjusted internal car trip length for terminating traffic is shown graphically.

Table 1. Characteristics of built-up areas and the average internal car trip length.

	Voskamp	Stroinkslanden	Wesselerbrink	't Zeggelt
access directions	1	2	3	4
access roads	1	2	3	9
area size (A)	9	28	40	28
L_{trip} unadjusted [m]	447	574	838	414
L_{trip} adjusted [-]	146	114	88	80

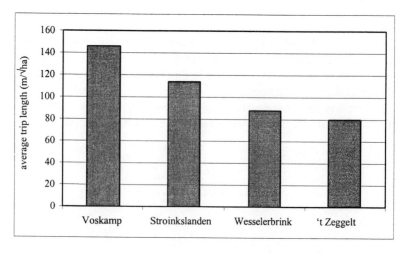

Figure 5: Adjusted average internal car trip length.

The results show that, after adjusting for the size of the built-up area, the average internal car trip length for terminating traffic decreases with the number of access directions. The results of the field study confirm the simulation results.

5 Conclusions and recommendations

As the number of possible network structures is unlimited in practice, it is not possible to give the optimal number and distribution of access roads and access directions for the different structures. However, this research hopes to have revealed at least the notion that liveability and accessibility of built-up areas are sensitive to the type of linking to the external network, the amount and direction of access roads and the congestion level at the outer structure.

It has been shown that the effect of the direction of the access roads is more important than the number of access roads. Furthermore, the amount of through-traffic is highly dependent on the amount of access roads, since through-routes are shortened. On the contrary, an increase in the number of access roads and an equal distribution in the direction improve the crossability of the streets, because of a more homogenous distribution of traffic in the network, and therefore an increased number of minimum acceptable gaps.

Most of these simulation results are also revealed in the Enschede case-study. An increase in the number of access roads leads, indeed, to a decrease in the average travel distance for terminating traffic in the built-up area.

In order to avoid through-traffic in the built-up areas one could consider increasing speeds at the roads, whereas decreasing speeds at the streets. This could also be done by enlarging the length of built-up area streets and, of course, by lowering the number of access roads.

With the results in mind traffic professionals should now be able to see what kind of measures taken to the built-up area network structure as well as to the outer structure have what kind of effect. Examples of these measures for (re)design of access road network structures are given in table 2.

Further research should be conducted to the relation between traffic unsafety versus flow on both the streets as well as roads in the area under consideration.

6 Acknowledgements

The authors wish to express their gratitude to the Institute for Road Safety Research (SWOV), Leidschendam, the Netherlands for their valuable remarks and help in the research, as well as the financial means to conduct the case-study. Furthermore, the traffic department of the Municipality of Enschede is acknowledged for their help in the case-study.

Table 2. Examples of measures taken to decrease the number of through-traffic.

Measure	Method	Examples
Increase speed at roads	Improve throughput at major intersections	• Optimise traffic control design • Roundabout
	Divert through-traffic	• Ring road
Decrease speed at streets	Speed measures	• Traffic humps • Narrowing streets • Intelligent Speed Adaptation (ISA)
Increase length of through-route	Change internal network structure	
	Change distribution of access roads compared to the outer structure	
Decrease number of access directions		

References

[1] World Commission on Environment and Development (WCED). *Our common future*,. Oxford University Press, Oxford/New York, 1987.

[2] United Nations conference on environment and development (UNCED). *Agenda 21: programme of action for sustainable development*, Rio de Janeiro, 1992.

[3] Information and technology centre for traffic and transportation (CROW) *Recommendations for traffic provisions in built-up areas*, Ede, 1998.

[4] Miedema, B., Molen, H.H. van der, *Veiligheidsbeleving voor en naherinrichting van tien verblijfsgebieden* [In Dutch]. VK-83-09. Centre for environmental and traffic psychology, University of Groningen, 1983.

[5] Janssen, S.T.M.C., *Demonstratieproject herindeling en herinrichting van stedelijke gebieden (in de gemeenten Rijswijk en Eindhoven)* [In Dutch]. R-84-28 I., Institute for road safety research (SWOV), Leidschendam, 1984.

[6] Cerwenka, P. & Henning-Hager, U. *Verkehrssicherheit in Wohngebieten; Einflußgrößen Bewertung und Planungshinweisen* [In German]. Forschungsbericht 99, Federal highway research institute (BASt), Bergisch Gladbach, 1994.

[7] Minnen, J. van, *Geschikte grootte van verblijfsgebieden* [In Dutch]. R-99-25. Institute for road safety research (SWOV), Leidschendam, 1999.

[8] Krabbenbos, J. *Verkeersleefbaarheid in woongebieden – Een modelstudie naar de relaties tussen kenmerken van ontsluitingsstructuren en verkeersleefbaarheid met toetsing aan de praktijk* [In Dutch]. M.Sc.-thesis, University of Twente, Enschede, 2000.

[9] Getram/AIMSUN2, Transport simulation systems (TSS), Barcelona.

[10] Ortúzar, J. de D. and Willumsen, L.G., *Modelling transport.* John Wiley & Sons, Chichester, 1990.

Impact of telework and flexitime on reducing future urban travel demand: the case of Montreal and Quebec (Canada), 1996-2016

Y. Bussière[1] & P. Lewis[2]
[1] INRS-UCS (Urbanization-Culture-Society), University of Quebec, Canada
[2] Urban Planning Institute, University of Montreal, Canada,

Abstract

A research completed in 1999 for the Quebec Department of Transportation on the impact of telework (telecommuting and autonomous telework) and flexitime on future travel demand in the urban areas of Montreal and Quebec concludes that on the long term we can expect that the combination of these three forms of work could induce a reduction in the range of 6% of morning peak work trips.

1 Introduction

This paper presents the results of a research completed for the Quebec Department of Transportation in 1999, by a team from three universities (University of Quebec, University of Montreal and Laval University) to measure the impact of telework (telecommuting and autonomous telework) and flexitime (flexible hours and compressed work schedule) on reducing future travel demand in the urban areas of Montreal (population of 3.7 million) and Quebec (0.7 million).

2 Methodology

The study consisted of surveys and modelling for both cities, proceeded by an extensive review of the literature. The (near) absence of literature on the Canadian scene made these surveys essential. On flexitime and telecommuting, the surveys consisted in 3 parts: a pre-survey by telephone to give a preliminary evaluation of the phenomenon, a face-to-face survey of selected enterprises and organisations which offered some form of flexibility, and a survey of workers in these enterprises to get a profile of mobility patterns of employees using some form of flexibility. A separate survey was also done on a sample of autonomous workers (Figure 1).

Figure 1: Summary of surveys in Montreal and Quebec

Impact on long term transportation demand (1996-2011-2016) from surveys in Montreal and Quebec:
- Flexible hours
- Flexible week (compressed work schedule)
- Telecommuting
- **Enterprises**: telephone and person to person interviews of directors of personnel from a sample (Quebec: 55; Montreal: 76)
- **Workers**: From a sub-sample of the previous enterprises, a sample of workers (Montreal: 20; Quebec: 23) with a self-administrated questionnaire (Montreal: 98; Quebec: 101).
- **Autonomous workers**: From a large sample autonomous teleworkers (workers who used telecommunications technologies to complete their work)
- Self-administered questionnaires: 97 workers
- Detailed interviews on a sub-sample of the workers: 15 workers

These surveys permitted us to draw profiles of various types of flexibility offered by the enterprises in various sectors of activity and a profile of mobility patterns of the workers (salaried and autonomous). From this data we were able to model future travel demand, as described below.

3 Results

3.1 Flexitime and telecommuting
The review of the literature shows that the proportion of telecommuters in industrialised countries is still less than predicted (Claisse and Rowe, 1995), between 10 and 15% of the work force, even if we add various types of telecommuting and autonomous workers. The proportion is lower than some expected, partly because of the resistance shown by employers (Mokhtarian, 1998). For flexible hours, the proportion of workers affected is much larger – around 20% to 25% of the work force in Canada and USA - , even if most of those working regular hours still start work between 6:30 and 9:30 AM.

In Montreal and Quebec, according to our analysis, the level of telework was lower, in proportion to the global labour force, with around 7% in 1999 (2% for the salaried workers and an additional 5% for autonomous workers). The reorganization of the work schedule (flexitime) is much more frequent with about 20% of the labour force on flexible schedules, but most of them still arrive at work morning during peak hours. Compressed work weeks (for instance a 5 days work in 4 days) account for less than 5% of the work force.

For a better understanding of the level of flexible work in the enterprises of our sample, Table 1 presents basic data on the actual implementation of different forms of flexible work arrangements of various sectors of economic activity surveyed. This data has been disaggregated into 3 forms of flexibility:

- the proportion of enterprises which offer flexibility (FLEX1);
- the proportion of employees to whom it is offered (FLEX2);
- the proportion of employees who accept flexibility (FLEX3).

The total impact (FLEXT) is the proportion of employees who are touched by some form of flexibility (which is the filtering result of multiplying the ratios of the 3 forms of flexibility). A close examination of Table 1 leads to four conclusions:

(1) It is flexible hours which are the most offered by enterprises in the Montreal and Quebec regions: 88% of the enterprises offer flexible hours, the proportion being lower for the compressed week (70%) and still lower of the telecommuting (56%).

(2) The proportion of employees who have access to flexitime is lower, more so for compressed week and telecommuting: 75% of the employees have access to flexible hours, 39% to flexible week and, finally, 25% to telecommuting.

(3) It is the employees to whom telecommuting is offered who, the most, accept this possibility (68%), comparatively to 60% for variable hours and only 18% for the compressed week. The low rate of acceptance of compressed week reflects its relative unpopularity, probably due to the loss of revenue that it generally induces. However, telecommuting and variable hours are more popular.

(4) The variable hour affects sensibly a higher proportion of workers (between 35% and 40%) than the compressed week (3% to 5%) or even telecommuting (5% to 10%), a more recent phenomena.

An analysis by sectors of economic activity adds more nuances to these results as Table 1 shows. By sectors of activity the profiles of the regions of Montreal and Quebec are quite similar, even though we noted two main dissimilarities:

(1) The impact of flexible hours is more important in Montreal (48%) than in Quebec (36%), mainly because more employees accept it in Montreal.

(2) The level of telecommuting is more important in Montreal than in Quebec, where it is very low for most sectors, except for the education sector.

Table 1: Level (1) of flexitime in the enterprises of the survey, for various sectors of activity, Montreal and Quebec, 1999(*)

Sector of activity (***)	Nb. (**)	Flexible hours (2)				Flexible week (3)				Telecommuting (4)			
		FLEX1	FLEX2	FLEX3	FLEXT	FLEX1	FLEX2	FLEX3	FLEXT	FLEX1	FLEX2	FLEX3	FLEXT
Communications and other public services	4	50%	79%	81%	32%	75%	27%	85%	17%	50%	2%	0%	1%
Financial services and insurance	6	100	99	61	60	100	94	2	2	67	9	100	6
Manufacturing sector	4	50	50	100	25	25	2	0	0	100	41	37	15
Hotels/restaurants/others	13	100	97	53	51	62	74	5	2	77	52	60	24
Education services	2	100	95	20	19	0	0	0	0	50	74	61	23
Government services	12	100	64	84	54	92	57	23	12	17	N/D	N/D	N/D
Transportation and storage	1	100	6	67	4	100	16	100	16	0	0	0	0
Others	1	N/D	N/D	N/D	N/D	N/D	N/D	N/D	N/D	100	N/D	N/D	N/D
Total	43	88	75	60	40	70	39	18	5	56	25	68	10

Source: Survey on enterprises. (*) The survey over-sampled enterprises offering flexibility. An overall estimation of the economy of Montreal and Quebec would give 2% of salaried workers with flexible hours, 15% with flexible week and 2% for telecommuting. (**) Number of enterprises in the survey. (***) FLEX1: Enterprises who offer it; FLEX2: Employees to whom it is offered; FLEX 3: Employees who accept it; FLEXT: Employees touched by flexitime.

Notes: (1) Due to the small size of the samples, these tables intend primarily to give a global idea of the phenomenon. (2) Flexible hours: Of the 43 enterprises contacted, 38 answered positively, 3 negatively and 2 had no availability. (3) Flexible week: Of the 43 enterprises contacted, 30 answered positively, 11 negatively and 2 had no availability. The flexible hours seem to be a very common practice, in all sectors of activity. (4) Telecommuting: Of the 43 enterprises contacted, 24 answered positively, and 10 negatively.

To sum up, the enterprises are very open to flexible hours and such measures are widely spread in most sectors of economic activity and very popular among employees. The flexible week is more recent, less developed, and less popular among employees. Telecommuting is less developed; it is still a new phenomenon in front of which the enterprises are often hesitant but generally favourable to its implementation (Mokhtarian, 1998). However it is very popular among employees who often use it when it is offered.

3.2 Autonomous work

Autonomous work is much more widespread and we can expect it to continue growing. According to census data it represented, in 1991, 8.9% of the total work force in Quebec and 8.4% in Montreal (Roy, 1997). Our survey showed us, furthermore, that the level of education of the autonomous workers is rather high with (Montreal and Quebec combined) 18.5% with college education and 66% with some form of University degree (from Bachelor to Ph.D.). The number of autonomous workers grew rapidly during the 80s, when the labour market was difficult to enter; this is confirmed by our survey: 37% (28.3% in Montreal and 51.5% in Quebec) of respondents became autonomous workers because they had not been able to find a job. The other main reasons were: "I wanted to be my own boss" (26%) and "I wanted more autonomy" (22%). Table 2 illustrates the modal choice of the autonomous workers. We can see that they are mainly auto-drivers (78.3%), but that transit is still important (23%), mainly in Montreal (32%), where transit supply is much higher than in Quebec, because of the presence of an efficient metro system in the central area.

We can also note that autonomous workers travel generally outside peak hours. As is shown in Table 3, more than 40% travel during peak hours only once or twice a week and around 30%, never during peak hours. We can therefore expect a certain impact of autonomous workers on trip reducing during peak hours.

4 Method of forecasting

The question asked was to what extent will the observed proportions change in the future and what could be its impact on morning peak hours travel demand by mode for Montreal and Quebec metropolitan areas.

4.1 Forecasting of the impact of flexitime and telecommuting

For flexible hours and telecommuting, from the data collected in the surveys and the review of the literature, and travel data from O-D surveys, we constructed a model to simulate the actual impact on reducing travel demand, and we elaborated various scenarios to measure its probable impact on future demand in the morning peak hour.

Table 2: Distribution of autonomous workers in function of the choice of mode for travelling, Montreal and Quebec, 1999 (%)

	Montreal	Quebec	Total
Auto-driver (alone)	68.3%	96.9%	78.3%
Auto-driver (with passenger)	1.7	0.0	1.1
Auto-passenger	1.7	0.0	1.1
Public transport	31.7	6.3	22.8
Walking	10.0	6.3	8.7
Other	8.3	0.0	5.4

N = 92 Source: Survey on autonomous workers.
Note: more than one mode could be given for trips.

Table 3: Distribution of autonomous workers in function of their trips during peak hours, Montreal and Quebec, 1999 (%).

	AM			PM		
	Montreal	Quebec	Total	Montreal	Quebec	Total
5 times a week	14.0%	15.6%	14.6%	14.0%	18.8%	15.7%
3 or 4 times a week	14.0	9.4	12.4	14.0	3.1	10.1
1 or 2 times a week	43.9	46.9	44.9	36.8	43.8	39.3
Never	29.8	25.0	28.1	33.3	28.1	31.5

N = 89 Source: Survey on autonomous workers.

The data used were the following:

(1) Distribution of employment by industry and by zone in both cities in 1995 (from 1996 census data), for poles of attraction.
(2) Pre-survey on enterprises (141 enterprises: 87 in Montreal and 54 in Quebec).to measure to presence of flexitime.
(3) Survey in enterprises (total of 42 in Montreal and Quebec).
(4) Survey on workers on a sub-sample of the previous enterprises (98 workers in Montreal; 101 in Quebec).
(5) O-D surveys of Montreal (1993) and Quebec (1996).

The model incorporated four main dimensions:

(1) Employment and flexibility. Estimation of the attraction of workers touched by flexibility (variable hours and telecommuting) by sector of activity and zone with employment data of 1995. As discussed above,

flexibility was disaggregated in the 3 dimensions of flexibility, where total flexibility is equal to: FLEXT = FLEX1 x FLEX2 x FLEX3; the enterprises of the pre-survey were selected in various sectors of activity in areas susceptible to offer flexibility. This permitted to elaborate a sample of enterprises for direct interviews. This pre-survey was used for a first calibration of FLEX1, which was complemented with a Delphi method consisting of a cross-examination of the coherence of the rates observed with the review of the literature. Since the sample was small, and since the sector of activity appeared determinant in the presence of some form of flexibility, we supposed that the level of penetration by sector was the same in both cities as well as by zone. The impact by zone would therefore be a direct function of the type of activities by zone. The next step consisted in the estimation of the number of "flexible" jobs which would induce a diminution of trips during the morning peak hour (6h to 9h AM in Montreal and 7h to 9h AM in Quebec). The ratios used for these calculations were drawn form the surveys of enterprises. These ratios were then applied to travel trips by mode (auto-driver, auto-passenger, transit, other) and by O-D pairs.

(2) Variation of flexibility according to various scenarios. We supposed that one flexible employment corresponds to a diminution to one travel trip during the morning peak period.

(3) Variation of trips. For each scenario we translated the variation of trips of dimension (2) to the matrix of O-D trips for work, morning peak, by O-D pairs, by mode and by zone. This permitted to generate rates of variation of travel demand.

(4) Calculation of the total impact of the various effects.

4.2 Various scenarios

For each type of work mode, disaggregated in FLEX1, FLEX2 and FLEX3, various scenarios were constructed: a reference scenario (1996-99); a low-growth scenario, and a high-growth scenario, supposing substantial growth of flexibility. Let us briefly present the results of the impact of various forms of flexibility for the reference scenario (1996-99) and the strong scenario at the horizon 2016.

For various forms of flexibility, the hypothesis we the following:

- Autonomous workers would increase by 100% over a period of 20 years.
- Flexible hours (FLEXT) would increase by 25%. This reflects an increase of 10% of FLEX 1, 10% of FLEX 2 and 10% of FLEX 3, with a constraint of a maximum of 100%.
- Telecommuting would increase by 62% in Montreal and 66% in Quebec, and reach respectively 3.3% and 3.6% of salaried workers (from 2.1% in

Montreal and 2.2 in Quebec in 1996) with more telecommuting in the centre than in the outer suburbs (i.e., 3.1% compared to 1.8% in Montreal). This represents an increase of 100% in FLEX1, 10% in FLEX2 and 10% in FLEX3, with a constraint that FLEX1, 2 or 3 cannot surpass 80%.

Table 4 summarizes the impact of the various scenarios. These results will vary by mode and destination. The diminutions of trips will be slightly higher for auto-driver than for public transport and for destinations to the centre of the city. Globally, over the long term (defined here as 20 years) the diminution in morning peak work trips would be, respectively in Montreal and Quebec, of 2.9% and 2.8% for autonomous workers, 1.1% and 0.6% for flexible hours and 2.3% and 2.5% for telecommuting. Over the period studied, this gives a total impact of 6.3% in Montreal and 5.9% in Quebec. Among the measures, flexible hours will have the least effect.

Table 4: Impacts of different forms of flexible work arrangements on AM peak hour travel demand for work, Montreal and Quebec, 1996-99 and 2016, and annual growth rate 1996-2016 (%)

	Montreal		Quebec	
	1996-99	2016	1996-99	2016
Autonomous work	-2.9%	-2.9%	-2.8%	-2.8%
Flexible hours	-3.0	-1.1	-1.7	-0.6
Telecommuting	-0.4	-2.3	-0.4	-2.5

Finally, Table 5 (below) gives detailed projections by mode for flexible hours and telecommuting in Montreal and Quebec, and translates in annual rates the long term global impact on a 16 years period (1996-2011) or a 20 years period (1996-2021).

5 Conclusions

The impact of telework and flexitime on future travel demand will depend on their development in various economic sectors, but also on the reaction of workers to the possibilities. In the past, the progression of autonomous work and flexible hours had a significant impact on the reduction of peak travel demand (and the spreading out of peak hours), and much less so, telecommuting which is still a new phenomenon. However, telecommuting is perceived positively as a technological solution for the future, by employers and employees, as well as transportation networks' managers. If full-time telecommuting was to develop as many have predicted, it could induce a certain diminution of travel demand.

Table 5: Impact of telework and flexible hours on AM peak work trips, Montreal and Quebec, 1996-2011-2016 (strong scenario)

	Montreal		Quebec	
Total variation on the long term				
	Flexible hrs	Telecom.	Flexible hrs	Telecom.
Auto-driver	-1.14%	-2.29%	-0.62%	-2.58%
Auto passenger	-1.13	-2.28	-0.59	-2.44
Public transport	-1.07	-2.21	-0.55	-2.19
Other modes	-1.16	-2.34	-0.59	-2.40
All modes	-1.12	-2.27	-0.61	-2.52
Total variation: annual growth rates over 16 years (1996-2011)				
	Flexible hrs	Telecom.	Flexible hrs	Telecom.
Auto-driver	-0.072%	-0.145%	-0.04%	-0.16%
Auto passenger	-0.071	-0.144	-0.04	-0.15
Public transport	-0.067	-0.140	-0.03	-0.14
Other modes	-0.073	-0.148	-0.04	-0.15
All modes	-0.071	-0.144	-0.04	-0.16
Total variation: annual growth rates over 21 years (1996-2016)				
	Flexible hrs	Telecom.	Flexible hrs	Telecom.
Auto-driver	-0.055%	-0.110%	-0.03%	-0.12%
Auto passenger	-0.054	-0.110	-0.03	-0.12
Public transport	-0.051	-0.107	-0.03	-0.11
Other modes	-0.056	-0.113	-0.03	-0.12
All modes	-0.054	-0.109	-0.03	-0.12

In the future we can expect autonomous work to continue its expansion as well as telecommuting, but much less so for flexible hours. Compressed week schedule does not seem to be expanding much in the future and the reduction of travel demand that it would induce is mostly concentrated on Fridays, and would have little impact on traffic congestion the other days of the week. On the long term we can expect that the combination of autonomous workers, flexible hours and telecommuting could induce a reduction in the range of 6% of morning work peak travel trips, which is significant in the context of scarce resources for new infrastructures.

References

Bussière, Y., Lewis, P., Thomas, C., with the collaboration of M. Lee-Gosselin, M. , Villeneuve, P.-Y. and others, « L'impact du télétravail et de la réorganisation du temps de travail sur la mobilité dans les régions de Québec et de Montréal: Analyse prospective », Montreal, Quebec Department of Transportation, 3 vol., 1999.

Claisse, G. and Rowe, F., "Télécommuniquer dans trente ans : incidences sur la mobilité?", in *Se déplacer au quotidien dans trente ans. Éléments pour un débat*, Paris, La documentation française, pp. 125-138, 1995.

Mokhtarian, P.L., "A synthetic approach to estimating the impacts of telecommuting on travel", *Urban studies*,35: 2, pp. 215-241, 1998.

Roy, G., *Diagnostic sur le travail autonome, version synthèse*, Montréal, Société québécoise de la main-d'œuvre, 81 p., 1997.

The schedule-based dynamic modelling for public transport networks: a new approach in path choice and assignment

A. Nuzzolo[1] F. Russo[2] & U. Crisalli[1]
[1] *"Tor Vergata" University of Rome - Department of Civil Engineering Italy*
[2] *"Mediterranea" University of Reggio Calabria – Department of Computer Science, Mathematics, Electronics and Transportation Faculty of Engineering, Italy*

Abstract

This paper presents a general overview of the schedule-based approach in dynamic path choice and assignment models for transit networks. The first part describes different specification of path choice models in relation to different user and service characteristics. The latter deals with a classification of assignment models.

1 Introduction

Public transport networks are usually modelled using the *frequency-based approach*, which considers services in terms of lines. In this case run scheduled times are not considered explicitly, but the time dimension is considered through the service frequency (inverse of the line headway), from which the name of the approach derives. The most used frequency-based models refer to the concept of hyperpath or optimal strategies (Nguyen and Pallottino [8], Spiess and Florian [17]). The main hypothesis of the hyperpath model is that users choose the line in an indifferent adaptive way, that is they board the first arriving run belonging to their line choice set, defined as the set of lines that minimises the expected total travel time. The underlying hypotheses that allow such results are that vehicles arrive at stops in a random way and that users arrive at stops with constant rate. In recent years deterministic and stochastic equilibrium models have been presented in order to take into account congestion and perception errors of path attributes (De Cea and Fernandez [3], Wu et al. [20], Lam et al. [7]). The above described hypotheses are fully acceptable for services with high frequency, very low punctuality and low user information, but can generate considerable approximations when used in different contexts, in particular when ITS (Intelligent Transportation Systems) are present, or in the case of low-frequency services. For this reason in the last ten years a new approach, called *schedule-based approach*, has been developed; it refers to services in terms of runs, using the real vehicle arrival/departure time at stops to obtain attributes that can be explicitly considered in run choice modelling. As it will be better described in the following sections, this approach allows us to take into account the evolution in time both of supply and demand, as well as run loads and level of service attributes. Hence this approach is also called *dynamic*.

The core of the assignment modelling is the path choice that allows, in addition to a supply/demand interaction procedure, vehicle loads of transit services to be obtained. Transit path choice models can be differently specified according to user behavioural hypotheses that depend on specific user and service characteristics.

The service characteristics affecting user behaviour in path choice are *frequency, regularity* and *information* available to users.

Service *frequency* can be directly related to the frequency of line l in the reference period (i.e. the number of runs belonging to line l connecting the *od* pair in such a period) or, for overlapping lines, to the cumulative frequency (i.e. the sum of the frequencies of all "attractive" lines connecting the *od* pair). Usually service frequency is defined high if the average headway of vehicles is less than 12-15 minutes, while frequency is defined as low if the average headway exceeds 15 minutes.

Service *regularity* is a measure of to what extent the schedule is observed. If regularity is used to make assumptions on user behaviour in line-based systems, such as buses and trains, deviations from the schedule should be related to the average headway of runs belonging to the same line. Usually regular services are associated with low-frequency systems, typical of extraurban services. On the other hand, irregular services generally refer to high-frequency systems as in urban or metropolitan areas.

Pre-trip and/or en-route real-time *information* on services can be available to users in different places (for example at stops or at home) and concerns at least waiting times of arriving vehicles at the chosen access stop, while more advanced information systems could give information on travel times and on-board occupancy, too. Static information on run schedule is traditionally available with timetable. Intelligent Transportation Systems (ITS) have significantly expanded the range of information available to the traveller through Advanced Traveller Information Systems (ATIS). ITS also improves the performance of transit services, in terms of regularity, through the use of Advanced Public Transportation Systems (APTS).

As regards user characteristics, the main difference to consider concerns whether they are frequent or occasional users. *Frequent users* travel frequently and know routes and scheduled timetable as well as the real system functioning based on previous experience. *Occasional users* use sometimes transit services, so they only know some line routes (the most important) and their scheduled timetable.

One of the first schedule-based path choice models was the one introduced for high-frequency transit services by Tong (described in Wong and Tong [18,19]), even if the schedule-based approach was initially developed for low-frequency transit systems, allowing the explicit consideration of the early/late schedule penalties, which play a key role in path choice for extraurban services. Nuzzolo and Russo [11], Carraresi et al. [1], Nguyen et al. [9], Florian [4] specified deterministic path choice models, while Nuzzolo and Russo [11], Cascetta et al. [2], Nielsen and Jovicic [10], Nuzzolo et al. [13] defined stochastic path choice models.

Recently the schedule-based approach was proposed for urban transit systems in order to consider more coherent user behavioural hypotheses in relation to service characteristics. Hickman and Wilson [5], Hickman and Bernstein [6], Nuzzolo and Russo [12], Wong and Tong [18,19] presented within-day dynamic path choice models that allow time variation in supplied services to be considered. They have been specified for regular and irregular high frequency services, with or without information systems to users at stops. The Nuzzolo and Russo [12] path choice models were extended in a doubly dynamic stochastic path choice model (Nuzzolo et al. [14,16]) that explicitly considers the within-day and day-to-day variations of services and user learning on attributes. The extension to different user classes, considering explicitly frequent and occasional users, was presented in Nuzzolo et al. [15].

In the following sections the scheduled-based approach is dealt with. Section 2 and 3 describe the path choice and assignment models developed in the literature, while section 4 ends the paper with some considerations about the application fields of the traditional frequency-based and the new schedule-based approaches.

2 Schedule-based path choice models for transit services

User behaviour hypotheses and path choice models are specified in the framework of the (random) utility theory, in which users are assumed rational and behave with the aim of maximising their perceived utility.

User decisions can be classified according to two types of choice behaviour:

- *pre-trip choice behaviour*, which underlies user choices before departure. It includes the comparison of possible alternative paths and the choice of one of them on the basis of expected values of attributes. Pre-trip choices are analogous to those assumed for path choice in road networks;

- *en-route choice behaviour*, which underlies user choices during the trip. This behaviour describes how users respond to unknown or unpredictable events.

The type of en-route choice behaviour can be defined as *indifferent* (if users board the first arriving vehicle belonging to the set of alternatives) or *intelligent* (if users, when a vehicle belonging to the path choice set arrives, compare the disutility of the arriving vehicle with the disutility of the next arriving vehicles belonging to the path choice set).

As the main factor that greatly affects user behaviour is service frequency, the following sections will describe path choice models for both high and low frequency services.

2.1 Path choice models for high-frequency services

In relation to the high frequency of services we can assume that the origin departure time coincides with the desired origin departure time, so user arrival at the stop is not related to run departure scheduled times. Furthermore, it is assumed that users do not have full information before starting their trip and they follow a mixed pre-trip/en-route choice behaviour. En-route choices occur at stops and are relative to the decision to board a particular run or to wait for another run of the choice set. The choice of boarding stops is considered before starting the trip, since it is not influenced by unknown events.

In the sphere of the schedule-based modelling approach for *high-frequency services*, as this kind of services are typical of urban areas, generally several boarding stops can be reached for the same origin and departure time and, even if considering the same user arrival time at stop, many runs can be available. Thus path choice implies choice of access stop and choice of run (or sequence of runs) leading users to their destination.

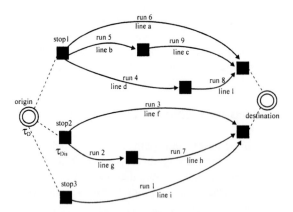

Figure 1: Example of path choice set

Figure 1 reports an example of path choice set: considering the origin departure time τ_{Di}, three different access stops are available, from which different runs of different lines can be used to reach the destination (e.g., from stop *2*, run *3* of line *f* or the combination of run *2* of line *g* and run *7* of line *h* can be considered).

In the schedule-based approach a path between origin o and destination d, departing from o at a given time τ_{Di}, is defined by the space-time sequence which includes: origin o with origin departure time τ_{Di}, access to access stop s with relative arrival time τ_{Dis}, run (or sequence of runs) with run departure time from access stop and run arrival time to egress stop s', egress from stop s' to destination d with relative arrival time at destination.

The probability $p_{od}[r,s|\tau_{Di}]$ of choosing a path including run r at boarding stop s, given the od pair and the origin departure time τ_{Di}, can be written as

$$p_{od}[r,s|\tau_{Di}] = p_{od}[r|s,\ \tau_{Dis}]\ p_{od}[s|\tau_{Di}] \tag{1}$$

which is the product of the probability of choosing run r at stop s, given the arrival time at stop τ_{Dis}, by the probability of choosing stop s, given the origin departure time τ_{Di}. In the following the index od, when not reported, is understood.

The probability $p[r|s,\tau_{Dis}]$ of choosing the arriving run $r \in K^s$ at stop s can be expressed as:

$$p[r|s,\tau_{Dis}] = prob(U_r > U_{r'})=prob(V_r + \varepsilon_r > V_{r'} + \varepsilon_{r'}) \qquad r' \neq r,\ r,r' \in K^s \tag{2}$$

where the perceived utility U_r of the generic run r, belonging to the choice set K^s, can be expressed as

$$U_r = V_r + \varepsilon_r = \textstyle\sum_j \beta_j \cdot X_{jr} + \varepsilon_r \tag{3}$$

in which β_j are the weights of attributes X_{jr}, which make up the systematic utility V_r, and ε_r is a random residual. Attributes X_{jr} usually considered are: waiting time, on-board time, transfer time, number of transfers, "route" on-board comfort (function of on-board crowding on the following links), "stop" boarding comfort (function of on-board crowding at the stop), monetary cost.

The run choice model can be deterministic (Hickman and Wilson [5]) or stochastic (Hickman and Bernstein [6], Nuzzolo and Russo[12], Wong and Tong [18,19], Nuzzolo et al. [14,15,16]) if random residuals ε_r are assumed null or otherwise, and different random utility models (logit, probit, etc.) can be specified according to the distribution of random residuals ε_r.

The random residuals ε_r usually take into account aggregation errors (e.g., zoning, network model), missing attributes (e.g., scenic quality, habit), dispersion of user behaviour (e.g., value of time) and user perception errors (e.g., travel time). Moreover, some models include in the random terms some aspects they do not consider explicitly, like service irregularity.

Users assess in different ways attributes of eqn (3) if they are frequent users or occasional ones, and if a user information system, especially on waiting time of arriving runs, is available at stops. Users typically forecast attributes at the time in which they decide on the basis of available information and past experience. Anyway, if a user information system is working, some attributes can be assessed directly through real-time information at stops (e.g., the waiting time of next arriving runs provided to users). Moreover, in the case of high-frequency services, sometimes there is a substantial difference between real arrival/departure times of vehicles at stops and scheduled times (irregular services). This aspect, jointly with the type of user (frequent or occasional), leads to considerable different run choice mechanisms. As above described, in the framework of run choice, three types of behaviour are possible: pre-trip, intelligent en-route, indifferent en-route.

For irregular services with user information at stops about waiting times, considering frequent users, the run choice at stop is typically en-route and can be simulated through a sequential mechanism that considers an intelligent en-route choice behaviour. When a run r of the path choice set K^s arrives at stop s, the user chooses to board r if the perceived utility U_r is greater than the utility $U_{r'}$ of all other runs $r' \in K^s$ yet to arrive.

In this case, $U_{r'}$ includes the waiting time of the next run r', given by the difference between the arrival time of run r' and the arrival time of run r (supplied by the user information system), while in U_r the waiting time of run r is replaced by the time already spent at the stop (equal to the difference between arrival time of run r and the user arrival time τ_{Dis} at stop s) simulating a possible "impatience effect". Other attributes of eqn (3) are considered as previously described.

Of course, if the user does not choose run r, the choice is reconsidered when the next run arrives and so on (*sequential run choice mechanism with intelligent en-route behaviour*). Occasional users behave in the same way, but they consider a reduced run choice set (i.e., they only consider the most important runs connecting the *od* pair).

For irregular services without information, frequent users consider a run choice set that minimise their average perceived cost, within which they choose comparing the first arriving run with the others belonging to the run choice set on the basis of the further expected waiting times, in addition to the other level of service attributes (*intelligent en-route behaviour*). If no information is provided and services are irregular, occasional users do not have enough experience of system functioning and board the first arriving run belonging to their run choice set (*indifferent en-route behaviour*). For frequent users, if vehicle arrivals are random as Poisson process, the indifferent en-route behaviour can also be assumed.

Finally, one of the most important classification parameter in path choice modelling is the dynamic characteristic of the model. In the sphere of schedule-based approach, path choice models consider at least the within-day dynamic, which allows the system evolution (level of service attributes) within the reference period to be taken into account. Schedule-based path choice models can also consider the day-to-day dynamic (i.e., the evolution of system characteristics from one day to another) if they include a learning process on attributes of eqn (3). Path choice models that consider both the within-day and day-to-day dynamics are usually referred in literature as doubly dynamic path choice models (Nuzzolo et al. [16]).

For what concerns the stop choice, it is usually assumed to be fully pre-trip, as no real-time information is typically available at origin. The probability $p[s | \tau_{Di}]$

of choosing the boarding stop s, within a choice set of boarding stops, S_{od}, can be expressed as

$$p[s|\tau_{Di}] = prob(U_s > U_{s'}) = prob(V_s + \varepsilon_s > V_{s'} + \varepsilon_{s'}) \qquad s' \neq s, s,s' \in S_{od} \qquad (4)$$

where U_s is the perceived utility, sum of the systematic utility V_s and of a random residual ε_s. The systematic stop utility is a function of stop-specific attributes (e.g., access or egress times, presence of shops, etc.) and "inclusive utility" expressing the average utility associated with all runs available at stop s. As described for the run choice, deterministic or stochastic stop choice models can be specified according to the assumptions on random residuals ε_s.

2.2 Path choice models for low-frequency services

From a practical point of view, *low-frequency services*, as regional bus and intercity railways, are usually characterised by *regular* service functioning and we hypothesise users have full information before starting their trip. In this case there is no difference in user behaviour for frequent and occasional users, and the presence of user information is unnecessary to support user choices, assuming that they at least know routes and timetable. Furthermore, as low-frequency services are typical of extraurban areas, it is common that only one access terminal as well as a single egress terminal are available, so stop choice can be easily simulated. The run choice is assumed fully pre-trip and, in addition to the other service attributes, we need to consider the disutilities that occur because of the difference (that can be considerable) between desired user departure time and vehicle scheduled departure time or between desired user arrival time at destination and run scheduled arrival. In the literature, this difference is called *early schedule penalty* or *late schedule penalty* (Nuzzolo et al. [15]).

The probability $p[r|\tau_{Di}]$ of choosing run r, given the *od* pair and desired departure time τ_{Di} (or desired arrival time τ_{Ai}) can be expressed as

$$p[r|\tau_{Di}] = prob(U_r > U_{r'}) = prob(V_r + \varepsilon_r > V_{r'} + \varepsilon_{r'}) \qquad (5)$$

where the systematic utility V_r is a linear combination, through β_j parameters, of attributes X_{jr}. A set of attributes that can be considered (Nuzzolo et al. [13]) are: access and egress times and costs, on-board times, transfer times, number of transfers, monetary cost, comfort, early/late schedule penalty.

Most of schedule-based path choice models for low-frequency services take into account user target times (desired departure times at origins or destination arrival times at destinations), considering as path choice set alternatives the two "nearest" paths in terms of minimum early and late times with respect to the user target time (Nuzzolo and Russo [11], Cascetta et al. [2], Nielsen and Jovicic [10], Nuzzolo et al. [13]). Florian [4] considers maximum earliness and lateness values to define a time slice around user target time (see figure 2), within which the path choice set is defined, while Carraresi et al. [1] and Nguyen et al. [9] consider only the late alternative with respect to the origin target time or the early alternative in the case of desired arrival time at destination. If the path choice model is deterministic, the minimum disutility alternative is considered, while if it is stochastic a certain probability to all alternatives of the choice set, calculated through eqn (5), is associated.

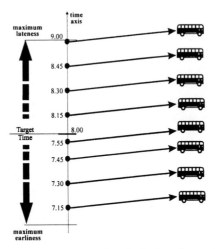

Figure 2: Example of path choice alternatives

Deterministic (Carraresi et al. [1], Nguyen et al. [9], Florian [4]) and *stochastic* (Nuzzolo and Russo [11], Cascetta et al. [2], Nielsen and Jovicic [10], Nuzzolo et al. [13]) path choice models can be specified according to the hypothesis of null ε_r or otherwise. Assuming ε_r different from zero, different random utility models can be specified. In particular, in the case of multi-class multi-service transit systems (e.g., railways), the existing correlations between alternatives have to be taken into account, and nested-logit or probit models should be used (Nuzzolo and Russo [11], Nuzzolo et al. [13]).

Moreover, considering a learning process on attributes of V_r, *day-to-day dynamic* schedule-based path choice models for low-frequency services can be specified to take into account the day-to-day evolution of on-board loads and level of service attributes.

3 Schedule-based assignment models for transit services

Assignment models allow the on-board load of transit vehicles to be obtained. Using a *schedule-based approach*, in which all runs of the transit services are explicitly considered, it is possible to obtain very detailed results in terms of on-board loads and level of service attributes for each vehicle.

The classification of assignment models usually refers to the classical one adopted in road network modelling, in which different assignment models can be specified according to the type of behavioural path choice model (deterministic or stochastic), the type link performance functions (flow-dependent or otherwise, which lead to uncongested or congested networks), the assignment approach (network loading, user equilibrium, dynamic process, etc.), and the dynamic evolution (within-day and/or day-to-day) they take into account.

Table 1 reports the classification parameters of assignment models for transit networks. In particular, for uncongested transit networks, both AoN (All or Nothing) and SNL (Stochastic Network Loading) assignment models can be considered to calculate on-board loads, as well as DUE (Deterministic User Equilibrium) and SUE (Stochastic User Equilibrium) assignment models can be specified for congested transit networks.

Table 1: Classification of schedule-based transit assignment models

Transit network	Assignment approach	Path Choice Model	
		Deterministic	Stochastic
uncongested [c=cost]	Network Loading	AoN	SNL
congested [c=c(f)]	Equilibrium	DUE	SUE
	Dynamic	DDP or SDP	DDP or SDP

AoN=All or Nothing; SNL=Stochastic Network Loading; DUE=Deterministic User Equilibrium; SUE=Stochastic User Equilibrium; DDP=Deterministic dynamic process; SDP=Stochastic dynamic process.

For what concern the dynamic evolution, as in the schedule-based approach the timetable is explicitly considered, the within-day dynamic is a native characteristic of the schedule-based approach, in the sense that all schedule-based assignment models are at least within-day dynamic. Moreover, considering a learning process on attributes, the day-to-day dynamic can be also considered, leading to doubly dynamic (within-day and day-to-day dynamic) assignment models. The dynamic evolution can be simulated by dynamic process models, both stochastic and deterministic.

All above described assignment models can be specified in the case of regular service functioning or otherwise, considering the randomness of on-board loads in relation to the randomness (irregularity) of transit services.

4 Conclusions

In the last ten years the improvements in computer science and the increasing computation capacity have allowed the schedule-based approach to be developed and applied. The schedule-based approach was initially developed for low-frequency systems and has recently been proposed for urban transit systems in order to consider more coherent user behavioural hypotheses in relation to user and service characteristics.

Frequency-based models are suitable to be used when a high degree of detail is not necessary and aggregate results can be obtained with few input data. For example in the case of the strategic planning of a new transit network, we need to specify only the line paths and stops in addition to service frequencies, and the average line loads, obtained as output, are sufficient for the aims of the project. In this case, the definition of the timetable, required by the schedule-based approach, and the output in terms of load for each run is not consistent with the level of detail of the other components of the simulation models, and is not necessary. By contrast, in the sphere of operative planning (e.g., with the aim of supporting the definition of a new timetable or to assess the introduction of ITS systems) we need more precise and detailed results that can be obtained only through a schedule-based approach.

Further developments are in progress and mainly regard the use of the schedule-based approach in applications, as the estimation of transit O/D matrices from traffic counts and the transit network design.

References

[1] Carraresi, P., Maluccelli, F., & Pallottino, S., Regional Mass Transit Assignment with resource constraints. *Transportation Research,* vol. 30B, pp. 81-98, 1996.

[2] Cascetta, E., Biggiero, L., Nuzzolo, A., & Russo, F., A System of Within-Day Dynamic Demand and Assignment Models for Scheduled Intercity Services. *Proceedings of 24th European Transportation Forum Seminar D-E,* London, England, 1996.

[3] De Cea, J., & Fernandez, E., Transit Assignment for Congested Public Transport System: An Equilibrium Model. *Transportation Science,* vol. 27, pp. 133-147, 1993.

[4] Florian, M., Deterministic time table transit assignment. *Preprints of PTRC seminar on National models,* Stockholm, 1998.

[5] Hickman, M.D. & Wilson, N.H.M., Passenger travel time and path choice implications of real-time transit information. *Transportation Research,* C3, N.4, pp. 211-226, 1995.

[6] Hickman, M.D., & Bernstein, D.H., Transit service and path choice models in stochastic and time-dependent networks. *Transportation Science,* 31, 129-146, 1997.

[7] Lam, W.H.K., Gao, Z.Y., Chan, K.S., & Yang, H., A Stochastic User Equilibrium Model for Congested Transit Networks. *Transportation Research,* vol. 33B, pp. 351-368, 1999.

[8] Nguyen, S. & Pallottino, S., Equilibration Traffic Assignment for Large Scale Transit Networks. *European Journal of Operational Research,* vol. 37, pp. 176-186, 1988.

[9] Nguyen, S., Pallottino, S., & Gendreau, M., Implicit enumeration of hyperpaths in logit models for transit networks. *Transportation Science,* 1997.

[10] Nielsen, O.A., & Jovicic, G., A large scale stochastic timetable-based transit assignment model for route and sub-mode choices. *Proceedings of 27th European Transportation Forum, Seminar F,* Cambridge, England, pp. 169-184, 1999.

[11] Nuzzolo, A., & Russo, F., Departure time and path choice models for intercity transit assignment. *Proceedings of 7th IATBR Conference,* Valle Nevado, Cile, 1994.

[12] Nuzzolo, A. & Russo, F., A Dynamic Network Loading model for transit services. *Proceedings of TRISTAN III Conference,* San Juan, Puerto Rico, 1998.

[13] Nuzzolo, A., Crisalli, U., & Gangemi, F., A behavioural choice model for the evaluation of railway supply and pricing policies. *Transportation Research,* 35A, pp. 211-226, 2000.

[14] Nuzzolo, A., Russo, F., & Crisalli, U., A doubly dynamic assignment model for congested urban transit networks. *Proceedings of 27th European Transportation Forum, Seminar F,* Cambridge, England, pp. 169-184, 1999.

[15] Nuzzolo, A., Russo, F. & Crisalli, U., Doubly dynamic path choice models for urban transit systems. *Travel behaviour research. The leading edge,* Ed. D. Hensher, Pergamon, pp.797-812, 2001.

[16] Nuzzolo, A., Russo, F., & Crisalli, U., A doubly dynamic schedule-based assignment model for transit networks. *Transportation Science,* vol. 35, pp. 268-285, 2001.

[17] Spiess, H., & Florian, M., Optimal strategies: a new assignment model for transit networks. *Transportation Research,* vol. 23B, pp. 83-102, 1989.

[18] Wong, S.C., & Tong, C.O., A stochastic transit assignment model using a dynamic schedule-based network. *Transportation Research,* vol. 33B, pp. 107-121, 1999.

[19] Wong, S.C., & Tong, C.O., Planning an urban rail transit system using a schedule-based network model. *Proceedings of 9th WCTR Conference,* Seoul, Korea, 2001.

[20] Wu, J.H., Florian, M. & Marcotte, P., Transit Equilibrium Assignment: A Model and Solution Algorithms. *Transportation Science,* vol. 28, pp. 193-203, 1994.

The pricing measures to manage urban traffic: a preliminary survey in a medium-sized town

C. Pronello & F. Iannelli
Department of Hydraulic, Transport and Civil Infrastructures,
Turin Polytechnic, Italy

Abstract

The objective of the research is aimed at understanding which is the effect on peoples habits of TCMs as pricing measures. In particular it is important to know how the people change their behaviour in function of the cost of accessibility to some defined areas. To catch this goal, an overview of the experiences carried out in the world concerning road pricing is presented and a deep analysis of them is given to understand their effectiveness in terms of reduction of traffic.

Subsequently, a survey in a medium-size Italian town was carried out, focused to understand the willingness of people to pay to enter into urban areas subjected to pricing. The results have emphasised that the people are sensible to the problems that traffic causes to the environment, but their sensibility is totally given up by their behaviour: 59% are not disposed to pay anything to use the roads. The most significant variables influencing the willingness to pay of the people are the home location, the necessity and the number of times to go to the centre. Who lives in the very central zone is well-disposed to pay until 2 € (about 1.8 USD).

The results of the survey seem to confirm the behaviour of the people that is experimenting the road pricing in some cities of the world.

1 The objectives of the research

One of the major problems in our cities is the management of traffic in such a way to reduce congestion and air/noise pollution. The typical actions carried out by the towns are the improvement of the pedestrian and biking infrastructures and of public transport, the parking management, the freight traffic management, the pedestrianization of some areas and, less used, the pricing measures, either road pricing or other taxation systems (on emissions, fuel, etc.).

A general overview of the road pricing applications in the world is presented and the different experiences are analysed to understand their efficacy in term of traffic reduction (demand restriction) and, hence, change of people bahaviour.

The objective of this research concerns with the question if the traffic control measures (TCMs) really favour a traffic reduction. Has the literature already answered to this question ?. From this basic hypothesis, the objectives come out:
1. to find out which are the effects of TCMs as pricing measures;
2. to investigate either the effect on people behaviour of TCMs as pricing measures or the consciousness of motorists regard the cost they charge on community entering in determined areas of the territory.

The second point has been caught by a survey regarding the willingness to pay of people to enter in urban areas subjected to pricing. It has allowed to define the threshold values over which is possible to define a taxation scheme to be applied in a medium-sized town.

2 An analysis of the main road pricing policies in the world

Here, an overview of road pricing experiences in the world is presented, to understand the level of implementation of pricing measures. So, it is important to find out which are the studies carried out, but, mainly, which of them have been adopted. In addition, to better understand the general framework, the road pricing policies have been clustered in function of the variables characterising them:
- the scheme adopted: area or single facility;
- the technical system adopted: paper permit system or any not electronic system (in table is mentioned as manual), electronic road pricing (ERP);
- the reason of the road pricing adoption: to fund maintenance and construction of infrastructures, to reduce congestion, to reduce environmental impacts.

  Inside this classification, a further split can be considered: the real cases operating today; the case studies planned, but never operated; the case studies where a study is in progress to implement a pricing policy.

This split is important to distinguish the cases by the data availability, to understand the real effects of such a policy in term of change of people behaviour and so of demand elasticity. The cases not operated cannot give any indication about the effects of the implemented policies, but only hypotheses based on forecast.

A cross of the mentioned variables produces the scheme presented in table 1 where the different cases in the world find their position.

As depicted in table 1, there are a lot of cases of road pricing in the world, but the majority is only under study. In this last case, in some towns a long debate has been already done and consistent studies have been carried out while in the other ones a very preliminary phase is in course.

In table 1 it is possible to observe that the road pricing cases concerning area schemes are the most spread over the world; some of them are already in place, as Singapore, Norwegian towns and Melbourne, the others are in study: Cambridge, Hong Kong, Stockolm, London, Randstad, Dublin and the cities participating to the European projects named PRIMA and PROGRESS.

The toll on highways is present in a lot of countries and it has been using till today, while the congestion pricing regarding single facility is less spread.

Table 1. Cases of road pricing either adopted or studied in the world

	In place (starting date)		Under study	
	Manual	ERP	Manual	ERP
Area scheme				
Central area	Singapore (1975)	Singapore (1998) Melbourne (2000)	Cambridge Milan [#]	Hong Kong
		Bergen (1986) Oslo (1990) Trondheim (1991) Stuttgart (1994-95)	Bristol [#] Copenhagen [#] Edinburgh [#]	Stockolm
			Bern* Zurich*	Dublin ° Rome # Genoa # Gothenburg # Helsinki #
Area-wide			London Randstad	
Single facility	Barcelona (1970) Autoroute A1 (1992) Marseille (1993) Lyon (1997)	State Route 91 California (1995) Interstate 15 California (1996)	Rotterdam	

* road pricing is avoided by national legislation
° an electronic system is preferred, but nothing has been decided
this studies are in a very initial phase and technical choices are not yet taken

▭ congestion pricing

▮ financing infrastructures

▮ behavioural test

One case is in France, the Autoroute A1, and two cases in USA, State Route 91 and the Interstate 15 in California. The other cases mentioned in table 1, concerning Barcelona, Marseille and Lyon are, really, under study for a road pricing implementation while, nowadays, they are experiencing tolls on tunnels and expressways, very close to the normally adopted concept of highways' pricing in a lot of European countries.

In this paper only in place cases will be analysed because the aim of understanding the effects on traffic and, hence, people behaviour. The only exception is the case of Melbourne, in Australia, where the very recent implementation (December 2000) does not allow to have traffic data to be analysed (see Melbourne City Link Authority [11]).

For the other cases under study see Small, Ibañez [16] and, in particular: Hong Kong (Transpotech, Ltd. [18]); Cambridge (Sharpe [15]), (Ison [7]); Dublin (Faber *et al.* [4]), (Gibbons, O'Mahony [5]); Randstad (Dutch Minister of Transport [3]), (Verhoef [19]); London (May [10]), (London Planning Advisory Committee [9]), (Alt-transp [1]); Milan (Corriere della Sera [2]); Barcelona,

Lyon, Marseille Oslo, Stockolm, Randstad, Rotterdam, Bern, Zurich: for these towns see the European project PRIMA (PRIcing Measures Acceptance) (PRIMA project [12]); Bristol, Copenhagen, Edinburgh, Genoa, Gothenburg, Helsinki, Rome, Trondheim: for these towns see the European project "PROGRESS (Pricing ROads use for Greater Responsability, Efficiency and Sustainability in citieS) and the European Transport Pricing Initiative (ETPI) CUPID (PROGRESS project [13]).

3 Findings

The analysis of the experiences in which road pricing has been adopted shows that the road pricing policies can determine:
- a redistribution of traffic volumes in different periods than peak hours, overall in the very first period of system implementation. Think about the results observed in Singapore and Autoroute A1 in France.
  - In Singapore a consistent decrease was observed in the first year (1975) in the morning peak period (- 30%) and a slight increase before it (+ 1.3%). In 1989, with the extension of the taxation, only 7% decrease was registered in the morning peak period while a 28% decrease on the evening peak period. In addition, among commuter to jobs in the restricted area, the share commuting in cars with less than four passengers dropped from 48 to 27% and the combined modal shares of carpool and bus rose from 41 to 62%. While traffic speed inside the area increased, outside the zone the congestion became worse and the average travel time increased from May to September 1975 (Watson, Holland [20]). The electronic road pricing (ERP) replaced the road pricing scheme (RPS) on the East Coast Parkway (ECP) on the first of April 1998. On ECP the traffic monitoring showed a traffic decrease of 15% and an increase of average speed from 55 to 60 km/h. In Singapore the effect was noticeable because the taxation policy varied by time period and place in function of congestion level. The toll ranges from 0.50 to 3 USD on expressways and from 0.50 to 2.50 USD on arterial for passengers cars (Land Transport Authority [8]).
  - On the Autoroute A1 a decrease by 4% was recorded during the red tariff, but an increase by 7% on the green one; so, in general a traffic increase occurred. The normal tariff from Paris to Lille is 9.88 USD while on Sunday decreases to 7.41 USD during the green hours and increases to 12.35 USD during the red hours (Small, Ibañez [16]);
- a general traffic growth due to induced traffic on new toll roads, usually less congested, has been recorded as also an increase of solo drivers. This behaviour seems to be typical of single facilities and it has been observed in California (USA), on State Route 91 (SR 91) and Interstate 15 (I-15). The traveller's decision to use toll lanes is very closely related to hour-by-hour variations in traffic conditions and demand is moderately price-sensitive, which demonstrates substantial scope for fine-tuning hourly demand through time-variables tolls. So, this kind of value-priced facilities seems to be

financially successful in a carefully selected market.

- On State Route 91, two lanes were added in each direction along a 16-km stretch in Orange County (in 1995). The original freeway lanes remain untolled while the users of the new 91 Express Lanes must pay a fee, except for motorcycles and high-occupancy vehicles (HOVs) with three or more passengers. In 1998 the Eastern Toll Road (ETR) was opened. The final report on SR 91 (Sullivan [17]) showed that the opening of SR 91 Express Lanes (1995) and ETR (1998) were both accompanied by significant jumps in peak period traffic, in which the single occupant vehicle (SOV) component was the largest part. However, high occupancy vehicle use also grew significantly during the same period, with HOV-2 traffic increasing a little, and HOV-3+ traffic increasing dramatically.

  About the traffic growth on the charged lanes, the average daily traffic (ADT) increased 14% in the first year following opening (1995) of the toll lanes. It is estimated that 21% of the jump in SR 91 ADT experienced during the few months are commuters who had previously used parallel city streets but who returned to the freeway or express lanes because of substantially improved travel conditions. The 59% of the first year growth in ADT (equivalent to 8% of the previous ADT level) appears to be induced traffic associated with the dramatically improved corridor travel conditions. Most of this induced traffic are trips for non-work purposes.

  Throughout the study period, traffic volumes remained stable in the SR 57/60 freeway corridor located roughly parallel to SR 91, about 16 km to the north. The influence of the toll lanes, while locally important, did not influence detectable traveller route shifts at the regional scale.

  The introduction of a more differentiated toll structure in September 1997, with tolls varying by the hour, had little effect on the sharpness of the overall afternoon time of day distribution for the corridor. Until September 1997 the maximum fee on SR 91 was 2.75 USD, then increased to 2.95 USD from September '97 to April '98, to 3.20 USD from April '98 to January '99, to 3.50 from January '99 to March 2000 and to 3.75 USD from March 2000 to January 2001.

- The Interstate 15 Congestion Pricing Project is a three-year demonstration that allows single occupant vehicles (SOVs) to use the I-15 high occupancy vehicle lanes, known as the I-15 Express Lanes, for a fee. The pricing project operated in two phases. During the first phase, ExpressPass (2/12/1996 to 30/03/1998), participants were charged a monthly fee for unlimited use of the Express lanes. During the second phase, FasTrakTM (30/03/1998 to 31/12/1999), participants were charged a dynamic per-trip fee that varied based on total vehicles in the Express Lanes and time of day (SDSU [14]). An eight-miles section of I-8, an east-west commuter route, located approximately the same distance from downtown San Diego as the I-15 Express Lanes, was identified as the control corridor for the evaluation.

  The traffic study has shown, for both I-15 and I-8, the changes from the pre-project period (Fall 1996) to Phase I (Fall 1997) and to the Phase II

(Fall 1998) to evaluate the program's traffic impacts.

Overall daily traffic volumes in the I-15 study corridor (both the I-15 main lanes and Express Lanes) remained virtually unchanged from Fall 1996 to Fall 1997, but increased substantially from Fall 1997 to Fall 1998. The values in the two peak periods, a.m. and p.m., are quite different and, normally, the greatest changes occurred in the morning peak (Table 2). The greatest change really occurred on I-15 Express Lanes in the morning peak where an increase by about 20 percent was recorded.

Table 2. Changes in overall daily traffic volumes in the I-15 and I-8 corridors

	a.m. peak period		p.m. peak period	
	Fall '96-'97	Fall '97-'98	Fall '96-'97	Fall '97-'98
I-15 study corridor	+ 0.7%	+ 7.5%	- 1.3%	+ 5.0%
I-15 Express Lanes	+ 19.8%	+ 20.9%	+ 11.6%	+ 8.0%
I-15 main lanes	- 1.6%	+ 5.5%	- 3.2%	+ 4.5%
I-8 control corridor	+ 7.5%	- 5.5%	+ 8.0%	n.a.

I-15 ExpressPass/Fastrak users were found to be travelers who drive alone virtually every day for work-related purposes. Dynamic analysis showed that the prior mode of the Fastrak users was primarily solo driving and not carpooling. From Spring 1998 to Fall 1998, the number of trips made by Fastrak users on the I-15 Express Lanes increased significantly by 0.5 trips per week.

Compared with Fastrak, the fixed monthly ExpressPass pricing program was not able to redistribute traffic volumes towards the shoulders of the peak periods. The maximum toll, during the peak hours is 4 USD;

- the toll rings are mainly able to increase the revenues of the Municipality, but they are not effective in traffic decrease and fight against pollution.

In Scandinavian toll rings a quite modest decrease (5-10%) of traffic has been recorded, but the tolls are low, between 0.70 to 1.75 USD per entry and they do not change significantly during the day. Here the benefits are the revenues used to fund road maintenance and construction (Small, Ibañez [16]);

- the behavioural tests are useful to understand people reaction, as in Stuttgart, but a permanent system might elicit some additional responses that a limited-duration experiment does not (Small, Ibañez [16]).

A not consistent traffic decrease was observed also in the Stuttgart experiment. This one concerned 400 volunteer motorists agreed to subject themselves to charges. They paid fully for any trip taken and, in return, they received three weeks later a block allocation of funds that was intended to more than cover expected charges. The 12.5 percent of sample switched to cheaper routes when the charge was 2.50 USD greater compared to the other ones. Similarly for large price differentials over time. The next common responses were to shift to public transport or to carpool. The first ones varied over the five different charging schemes from 3.4 to 5.9 percent of participants' total weekday trips. Carpooling was a small but steadily increasing response, with participants reporting by the end of the experiment that about 7 percent of their trips were in newly formed carpools.

Another considerations has to be done. In the cases under study the forecast are probably optimistic compared to the results of in place cases; in the area-wide scheme of Randstad a 50% decrease was hypothesised while in London the study carried out in 1975 calculated 40% decrease and a more recent study (1988) spoke about 10-12 percent decrease. In 1985, at Hong Kong, a 20% traffic decrease was forecasted (Small, Gomez-Ibañez [16]).

In-depth studies of public concerns about proposed road user charging schemes have revealed a number of issues, ranging from the reliability of the technology to a lack of acceptance of the principle of direct charging. However, the most pervasive and deep-seated concerns relate to the 'fairness' of the scheme (Jones [6]).

Of course could be affirmed, based on the real case studies, that the road pricing could be a relief of congestion in peak hours, redisributing the travels, but it does not seem to be strongly effective in term of environmental improvement or traffic reduction and mode diversion.

It seems that the real problem is the entity of the fee; only a high charge could reduce traffic and create a real mode diversion, but the problem of equity is consistent and the management of public opinion too.

At this aim, a survey has been carried out in a medium-size town in the north-west of Italy, Vercelli, located between Turin and Milan, to understand a possible threshold over which the people is not willing to pay for entering in a charged area.

4 The case study

During the closing of the 22nd of September 2000 (during the European initiative "in the city without my car") a survey addressed to the people present in the centre of the city of Vercelli was carried out. A questionnaire was prepared, so organised:
- a first part aimed to understand where the interview had place and where the answering person lived and worked;
- the first three questions were focused to know the origin and destination of the trip of the interviewed people and the scope of his/her trip (study, work, shopping and other);
- the questions from 4 to 8 were finalised to know the opinion of people regarding a traffic control measure as the closing of the city centre: if they are well-disposed to this one; if this favours or damages themselves; which variables it influences (air pollution, noise, safety; good living, etc.);
- then the following questions were aimed to understand if the people need to go to the city centre anyway, how many times they go to the centre and how much is their willingness to pay to go the centre;
- at the end, the last question was focused to know if the people have adopted some protections against the noise in their home.

The sample interviewed was formed by 241 units; 71% of the people was interviewed on the road, in the station, at university, etc; the others at home (8%), at office (11%) and in the shops (10%).

The descriptive analysis of the data has shown that the 86% of the people were conscious of the closing, also because this initiative was well advertised by the media and by the Municipality: as overall in Europe the 22nd of September was the "European day: in the city without my car".

This could explain the decrease of traffic recorded along some entries in the city in 1999; in 2000, in a road on the limit of the closed area, a 25% of traffic decrease was recorded. It seems that the people have changed their behaviour in this occasion; unfortunately, the noise levels have recorded a very contained improvement (about 1 dBA) outside the closing area while only in the protected one the noise is strongly decreased (till 10 dBA). Anyway, where an intensive human activity has taken place, the improvement is negligible, because the traffic noise is replaced by the "human noise".

The answers of the people to the questionnaire have emphasised that the people think that a similar initiative is good for a day (73%), but less if it is permanent (52%). This could explain the sudden reaction of people, well-disposed to not use the car for a day, but it is an indicator about the elasticity of the demand relative to this kind of traffic control measures. It is likely that the people, in the medium-long term, get used to the changes, overall when the new configuration requires a payment. This is proved by a lot of initiatives carried out in Italy regarding the parking. In a lot of towns the parking in the central area (and not only) are on payment; in the first days a lot of not occupied parking there were, but after a short period every place was again used as before. The people have internalised this "tax" as one of the many existing taxes. This consideration seems to be confirmed by the results of the questionnaire, as explained at a stretch.

Really, it seems that the people are conscious that the traffic causes a lot of problems to the environment (air pollution, noise) that confirm the people sensibility versus the environment; but this is totally disavowed by their behaviour: the 86% of people have not taken any protection against the noise in their homes and the 59% are not disposed to pay anything to use the roads.

So, there is the awareness of the damage produced by the use of the private vehicles to the environment and, hence, to ourselves, but there is not the real consciousness of its broadness and, anyway, there is not the willingness to pay for the damage they produce either to the environment or to the other people for the loss of time because congestion. The people think that to use their car is a right and not a choose that has to be influenced by its sustainability.

Really, about the well-disposition to the traffic closing, a lot of people said that they would use anyway the car, rounding the centre and, perhaps, with the results of having more vehicles miles travelled. The people is not disposed to leave their car and, so, it would be easier to "avoid the obstacle" or to pay than to choose another mode of transport.

The data analysis has shown that the most significant variables influencing the willingness to pay to enter in the city centre are the home location, the necessity to go there and, overall, the number of times the people go.

The people living in the city are more available to pay in respect to ones living outside and, amongst them, who lives in the very central zone is well-disposed to pay until 2 € (about 1.8 USD).

Really the people is not well-disposed to pay to use the roads; the 59% of people are not disposed to pay anything to access to the city centre, the 16.6% is disposed to pay 0.5 Euros (€) (about 0.45 USD)and, amongst the others, the 7.5%, the 8.7% an the 8.3% would pay, respectively, 0.75, 1.5 and 3 € (about, respectively, 0.68, 1.36, 2.72 USD).

The necessity to go to the centre is also very important because the people that need always to go to the centre are disposed to pay more than four times in respect to the opposite group. These results seems to confirm that the people really interested to go to the centre would be available to pay for that and perhaps only a very strong taxation could induce them to change mode of transport.

The results of the survey seem to confirm the behaviour of the people that is experimenting the road pricing in some cities of the world.

5 Conclusions

The analysis of the road pricing policies adopted in the world seems to emphasise a redistribution of traffic volumes in different periods than peak hours, overall in the very first period of system implementation. The decrease of traffic is visible (-17%) on area-scheme congestion pricing as Singapore where the tolls are extensive and variable during the day; the decrease is less consistent (- 5 to 10%) in Scandinavian towns where the tariffs are lower and the aim is to finance the infrastructures. A different effect occurs in single facility pricing where a generalised increase of traffic is recorded, because the induced traffic by toll roads in spite of the charge.

It is very important, hence, to understand the people behaviour in function of external interventions on traffic to individuate the best policy in function of the desired objective: to finance infrastructures, to reduce congestion during the peak hours, to have lower travel time, to have a general traffic reduction, to decrease air and noise pollution.

The survey carried out in the Italian town of Vercelli has been focused to understand what the people think about the use of the cars in their towns, their effects and the people availability to renounce using private vehicles to enter in the city centre. The answers have emphasised that the people are sensible to the problems that traffic cause to the environment, and they are favourable to initiatives regarding the traffic closing of the city centre. But the people sensibility versus the environment is totally disavowed by their behaviour: the 86% of people have not taken any protection against the noise in their homes and the 59% are not disposed to pay anything to use the roads.

The most significant variables influencing the willingness to pay of the people are the home location, the necessity and the number of times to go to the centre. Who lives in the very central zone is well-disposed to pay until 2 € (about

1.8 USD). The results of the survey seem to confirm the behaviour of the people that is experimenting the road pricing in some cities of the world.

References

[1] Alt-Transp, Londra: il nuovo sindaco promuove il congestion pricing, 2000 http://digilander.iol.it/webstrade/CASI-STUDIO/Londra/congestion-pricing.htm

[2] Corriere della Sera, Soste e ingorghi, la città chiede la linea dura, 29/09/2001.

[3] Dutch Minister of Transport, Contours of implementation of congestion charging (Rekening Rijden), Abstract of a Letter to Parliament from the Minister of Transport, 23 June 1995.

[4] Faber, O., Goodbody, TSRG, TORG, A study of Road Pricing in Dublin, http://www.environ.ie/press/ocarexsum.html, 1999.

[5] Gibbons, E., O'Mahony, M., Transport policy prioritisation for Dublin, *Transportation*, **27**, pp.165-178, 2000.

[6] Jones, P., Addressing Equity Concerns in Relation to Road User Charging, http://www.transport-pricing.net/jonel.doc, 2001.

[7] Ison, S., Pricing road space : back to the future ? The Cambridge Experience, *Transport Reviews*, **16 (2)**, pp.109-126, 1999.

[8] Land Transport Authority, Singapore, http://www.gov.sg/lta/index.htm, 2000.

[9] London Planning Advisory Committee, Strategic Planning Advice for London, London, 1988

[10] May, A.D., Supplementary licensing: an evaluation, *Traffic Engineering and Control*, **16**, pp.162-167, 1975.

[11] Melbourne City Link Authority, http://www.citylink.vic.gov.au/pages/home.html, 2001.

[12] PRIMA project, http://www.certu.fr/internat/peuro/prima/pridev.htm, 2000.

[13] PROGRESS project, http://www.progress-project.org/, 2000.

[14] SDSU (San Diego State University Foundation), I-15 congestion pricing project monitoring and evaluation services – Phase II year two overall report, 2001.

[15] Sharpe, J.M., Demand management: The Cambridge approach, Transp. Studies, Cambridgeshire County Council, Cambridge, UK, 1993.

[16] Small, K.A., Gomez-Ibañez, J.A., The equity impacts of road pricing (Chapter 10). *Road Pricing, traffic congestion and the Environment*, K.J.Button, E.T.Verhoef, Edgar Elgar, 1998.

[17] Sullivan, E., Continuation Study to Evaluate the Impacts of the SR 91 Value-Priced Express Lanes, Final Report, December 2000.

[18] Transpotech, Ltd., Electronic Road Pricing Pilot Scheme: Main Report, Report prepared for the Hong Kong Government, pp. 269-279, 1985.

[19] Verhoef, E., Economic Efficiency and Social Feasibility in the Regulation of Road Transport Externalities, PhD Dissertation, Free University of Amsterdam, 1996.

[20] Watson, P.L., Holland, E.P., Relieving Traffic Congestion: The Singapore Area License Scheme, World Bank Staff Working Paper No. 281, p.85, pp.41-133, Washington, DC, 1978.

Section 4:
Simulation

The experiences in evaluating the multicriteria traffic environmental impacts in urban road networks using SIMESEPT

P Klungboonkrong[1] & MAP Taylor[2]
[1] *Department of Civil Engineering, Faculty of Engineering*
Khon Kaen University, Thailand
[2] *Transport Systems Centre, University of South Australia, Australia*

Abstract

Spatial Intelligent Multicriteria Environmental Sensitivity Planning Tool (SIMESEPT) is a microcomputer-based decision support system that was developed to evaluate traffic environmental impacts of urban road network. SIMESEPT integrates various advanced information technologies (eg GIS and KBES), some MADM methods, and some traffic environmental impact evaluation models. SIMESEPT can efficiently be used to evaluate both separate and multiple criteria environmental impacts at the local (link-based) level, identify and rank the environmental problem locations, and specify the possible causes (criteria) and key contributing factors to those problems. In addition, it was found that the TAHP method and the FMADM method illustrates the similar capability in differentiating links according to their composite environmental impacts characteristics, and both of them perform better than the FCAHP does. However, the latter can be used as conservative decision-making tool when considering only the most critical environmental criterion. Sensivity analysis was also conducted to examine the influences of the variation of relative weights of each environmental criterion in each land use type.

1 Introduction

The estimation and assessment of safety, amenity, and environmental degradation caused by road traffic is difficult and complex. This is because although some aspects can possibly be quantified (eg air pollution and noise level), others can only be qualitatively gauged (eg social severance, visual intrusion, fear and intimidation). Furthermore, both qualitative and quantitative environmental impacts normally vary, ranging from annoyance effects to direct health hazards. Consequently, the development of a decision support tool is needed to estimate and evaluate the traffic environmental impacts. Such tools are of particular importance in prioritising the special attention and investigation for roads indicated as problematic sites, establishing appropriate functional road hierarchy classes, and allocating limited government funds for the implementation of the suitable traffic calming schemes.

Spatial Intelligent Multicriteria Environmental Sensitivity Planning Tool (SIMESEPT) can be utilised to evaluate both separate and multicriteria environmental impacts at the local (link-based) level, identify and rank the environmental problem locations in the urban road network, and specify the possible causes (criteria) and key contributing factors to those problems. SIMESEPT has been applied to several areas (eg the City of Prospect in Adelaide, South Australia, the Geelong City in Victoria, Australia, and the City of Unley, South Australia, Australia). In this paper, SIMESEPT is applied to investigate and evaluate the environmental impacts characteristics of the Khon Kaen road network in Thailand. This paper is organised to present the following topics: (i) fundamental structure of SIMESEPT; (ii) environmental sensitivity method (ESM); (iii) the Khon Kaen case study; (iv) future devlopment and finally (v) the conclusions.

2 The Fundamental Structure of SIMESEPT

SIMESEPT is a microcomputer-aided system. SIMESEPT is an integration of the traffic environmental impacts evaluation methods (Environmental Sensitivity Method, ESM) [1] and the Mathematical Modeling Method (MMM)), the Multiattribute Decision-Making (MADM) methods (Analytic Hierarchy Process (AHP) [2] and Fuzzy Multiattribute Decision Making (FMADM) method [3]), Fuzzy Set Theory (FST), the Knowledge-Based Expert System (KBES) approach, and the Geographical Information System (GIS) technology. Currently, SIMESEPT can be applied to estimate and assess three important environmental criteria: difficulty of access, noise pollution, and pedestrian safety. The Composite Environmental Sensitivity Indices (CESI) obtained from the use of KBES (based on the ESM concept) and MADM methods are suitable for gauging the traffic environmental sensitivity (preliminary traffic environmental effects), while the Composite Environmental Consequences Indices (CECI) values derived from the use of the MMM and the FMADM methods are appropriate to measure the more accurate traffic environmental impacts of the urban road network. The detailed discussion was given in [4]. The fundamental structure of SIMESEPT is illustrated in Figure 1.

The KBES, the MADM, and the MMM components of SIMESEPT were developed entirely within the KPWin programming environment. For KBES, the rule-based structure was used as a knowledge representation. The inference mechanism used in this research is the backward chaining method. The user interface efficiently provides interactive two-way communication between the user and SIMESEPT. For MMM, three mathematical models have been developed in SIMESEPT to estimate the traffic environmental impacts for difficulty of access using the Troutbeck's model [5], noise pollution using CoRTN [6], and pedestrian safety using the Song's probabilistic model [7]. These mathematical models can explicitly incorporate the influences of both the road physical and land use characteristics and traffic conditions. This method can provide some advantages over the ESM concept that will be described in the next section.

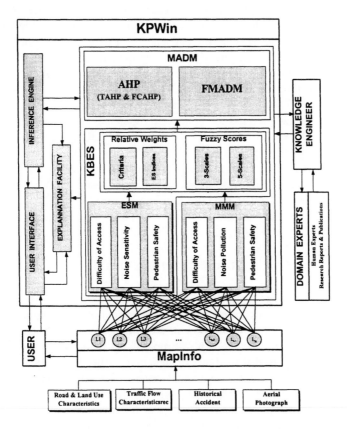

Figure 1: The Fundamental Structure of SIMESEPT.

In practice, it is common to combine several separate environmental impacts estimated for different criteria of a given link to enable assessment and comparison of the composite traffic environmental impacts of separate links in an urban road network. Such composite environmental impacts can be utilized to disclose the ranking order of different links according to the degree of composite environmental impacts. Typical Analytic Hierarchy Process (TAHP), Fuzzy Compositional AHP evaluation method (FCAHP) [8], and the Fuzzy Multiattribute Decision-Making (FMADM) methods [3] have been developed and utilized to handle this difficulty. Each of these methods was described in details in [9]. The theoretical foundation of TAHP that is the ordinary AHP methodology using the principle of hierarchical composition, and FCAHP that is the ordinary AHP methodology using the fuzzy compositional evaluation method were described in [8]. Because of the limited space, the AHP theoretical foundation will not be elaborated in this paper. For the FMADM methodology, the general calculating procedures are almost identical to TAHP, except the numerical values of each ES index for all criteria. The Simple Additive Weight (SAW) is used as the MADM method and the Fuzzy Scoring method [3] is adopted to convert the linguistic terms (eg low, medium, and high) to the corresponding numerical values. The detailed discussion of the FMADM methodology can be found in [10].

All SIMESEPT components are designed and organized as separate files (modules) and these modules are connected, operated, and interacted with each other through the use of a Graphical User Interface (GUI). The GIS (MapInfo) package was mainly used as the database management system and map-displaying tool. A GUI module (developed by using the MapBasic programming language) was designed to manipulate the communication between the GIS and other modules residing within the KPWin environment. The details of each component and the operational procedures of SIMESEPT can be found elsewhere [10].

3 Environmental Sensitivity Method (ESM)

ESM was developed to evaluate the environmental sensitivity induced by road traffic in urban road network for the three important criteria, including difficulty of access, noise sensitivity, and pedestrian safety. The ESM assumed that the physical and land use characteristics of a particular road section can be utilized to determine the ES of that road due to vehicular traffic. In the ESM procedures, a number of appropriate environmental criteria were firstly selected and key factors contributing to each criterion were then identified. The road network in the study area was divided into a number of homogenous links. Then the road physical and land use data relevant to the contributing factors for each criterion of each link were collected. These measured values of each contributing factor for each criterion were then compared with the corresponding measuring scales and a score of each factor was assigned accordingly. For each criterion, all derived scores of each factor were used to determine the ES indices (in terms of low, medium, and high) by using an established system for combination. Finally, the ES indices of different links for each criterion were then plotted separately.

4 The Khon Kaen Case Study

4.1 Data Collection and Presentation of the Khon Kaen Road network

Khon Kaen is located in the central north eastern region of Thailand and in 1994 contained a population of approximately 1.7 million of which 172,000 live in the Muang district. Khon Kaen is currently one of the fastest growing cities in the Northeast due to its geographical location and government promotion of the city as a gateway to Indochina. Khon Kaen has been designated a regional institutional center and is one of the nine main industrial cities in the country [10]. The Khon Kaen CBD road network was adopted as a case study area with its road network in a grid-based system as shown in Figure 2. This case study is concentrated on the determination of the traffic environmental impacts of all road links on the residents, pedestrians, and visitors who live or undertake their activities in the abutting land uses along these links. Difficulty of access, noise sensitivity, and pedestrian safety are selected as the important criteria for the case study. Eleven major roads were selected and divided into 39 homogenous links consistent with the method used by [1]. The categories of the data used in the Khon Kaen case study include road physical characteristics, availability of pedestrian facilities, nature of parking restrictions, types and practicality of land use access, land use categories, existence of the opposite building facade, traffic conditions, and traffic management schemes. The database was generated, integrated, and stored in a GIS (MapInfo) environment as shown in Figure 2.

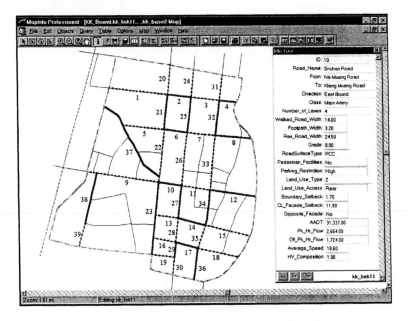

Figure 2: The Khon Kaen CBD road network study area.

4.2 The Modeled Results of Khon Kaen

Given the required data of road physical and land use characteristics of any road links, the KBES component (based on the ESM concept) of SIMESEPT was used to determine the appropriate ES indices of each link for difficulty of access, noise sensitivity, and pedestrian safety. As an illustration, Figure 3 shows the output window presenting all necessary data required for determining the ES index for pedestrian safety, the fired rule to derive the final outcome and its relevant explanation.

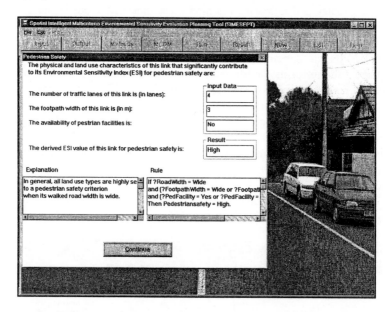

Figure 3: An example of the output window of pedestrian safety.

As an example, the spatially distributive patterns of all ES indices of each links for pedestrian safety is illustrated in Figure 4. All links identified as the "High" ES index can be considered as the potential problem sites in the Khon Kaen road network for the pedestrian safety criterion. Special attention and/or investigation regarding the pedestrian safety aspect may be needed for these links. The key factors contributing to any problematic link for each criterion can be identified from the road physical and land use characteristics data of that link.

The estimated CESI values can be used to determine the composite environmental sensitivity of each link for multiple criteria and identify potential problem locations in the urban road network. In addition, these CESI indices can also be utilized to reveal the ranking order of all links according to the magnitudes of their CESI values. All CESI values estimated for all links in the

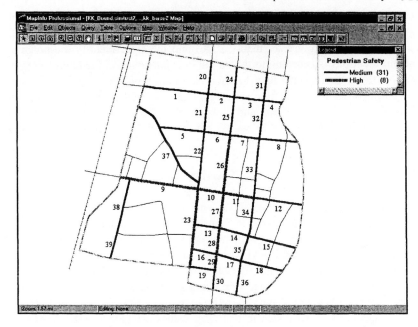

Figure 4: The ES indices of all links in the Khon Kaen road network for pedestrian safety.

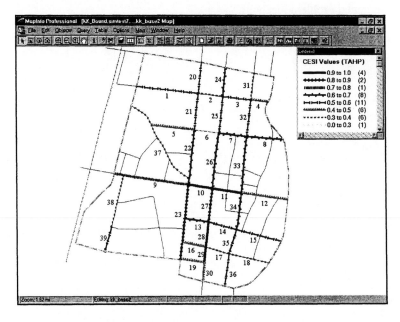

Figure 5: The estimated CESI values (based on the TAHP approach) of all links in the Khon Kaen road network .

Khon Kaen road network were grouped into eight intervals and displayed in Figure 5. The CESI values of seven links (link numbers: 9, 10, 11, 23, 27, 28, and 29) are high (say greater than 0.7000) and therefore identify the potential problem locations. According to the output data contained in the output file, the rank of these links according to the magnitudes of their CESI values in descending order are: link numbers 10, 11, 28, and 29 (CESI = 1.000), link numbers 23 and 27 (0.840), and link number 9 (0.700). In addition, the numerical composition of CESI values can be used to determine the potential causes of the problems for each link.

4.3 Comparisons among TAHP, FCAHP and FMADM Approaches

The estimated CESI values of all links using TAHP and FMADM methods, and FCAHP methods were illustrated in Figure 6. It was clearly that the TAHP and the FMADM methods perform better in terms of differentiating capability than FCAHP. While TAHP and FMADM takes all criteria into account, the FCAHP will take only the most critical criterion into consideration. Therefore, the latter can be used as a conservative decision-making approach. However, as shown in Figure 6, the FCAHP can generally capture a number of very high and very low CESI values which well match to the CESI values estimated by the TAHP and the FMADM methods. Based on the findings derived from this study and elsewhere [8], the FCAHP method can possibly be used as a screening approach for preliminarily detection of the candidates of road links that show the potential environmental problem locations.

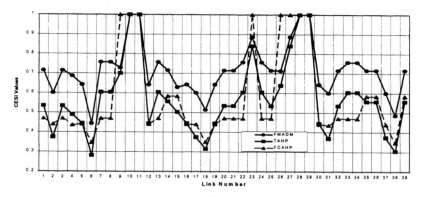

Figure 6: Comparisons of the CESI values based the TAHP, FCAHP, and FMADM methods

4.4 Sensitivity Analysis

The sensitivity analysis of the CESI values of all road links of the Khon Kaen road network with respect to the variations of the relative weights of each criterion for each land use type was conducted in this research. In the Khon Kaen case study, only land use types 1 and 2 were presented. Therefore, the sensitivity analysis for land use types 1 and 2 was done. For each land use type, any links having identical ES indices for each criterion will be grouped as the same link. Therefore, the sensitivity analysis will be concentrated only on the variation of the CESI values of links in each land use type. The following analysis will utilise the results of the sensitivity analysis of the CESI values of all links by varying the relative weight of pedestrian safety for land use type 1 as an example.

As an example, Figure 7 illustrates the results of the sensitivity analysis of the CESI values of all links (in land use type 1) of the Khon Kaen road network with respect to pedestrian safety. While the relative weights of pedestrian safety increase, the CESI values of link number 18 and link number 26 increase. The CESI values of all remaining links decrease. Link number 26 is highly sensitive to the variation of the relative weights of pedestrian safety. Link number 4, link numbers 14, 35, 36, and 39, and link number 15 are moderately sensitive to such variation, while link number 18 and link number 31 are less sensitive to such changes. If the relative weights of pedestrian safety are greater than 0.42, the ranking order of all links remains constant. The ranking order of all links in this land use type is varied according to the changes of the relative weights of pedestrian safety when such relative weights are less than 0.42. It was found that most links in both land use types 1 and 2 are generally sensitive to the changes of the relative weights of each criterion in terms of the alterations of their CESI values and their ranking order.

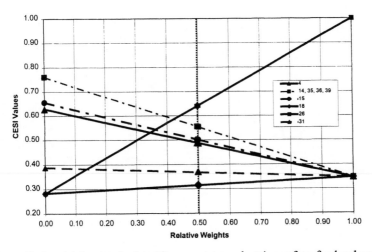

Figure 7: Sensitivity Analysis with respect to pedestrian safety for land use type 1 (the Khon Kaen case study)

5 Future Development

SIMESEPT has been improved by including more modeling components. Air pollution, pedestrian delays and others are being developed and then added into the existing SIMESEPT. In addition, the available traffic environmental impacts evaluation modules such as noise levels, pedestrian accident risk and difficulty of access have been expanded to incorporate more applicable models for each criterion. For example, for traffic noise levels, the ROADNOISE software package is being developed at Transport Research Center (TRC), Department of Civil Engineering, Faculty of Engineering, Khon Kaen University (KKU), Thailand by including four traffic noise prediction models (eg CoRTN [6] and etc.) These models are currently validated by using the field data of the Khon Kaen City case study for their appropriateness and applicability. Also KKU-TAPP have been developed at TRC by incorporating four air emission models (eg Taylor [11] and etc.). However, the Khon Kaen University Traffic Air Pollution Prediction (KKU-TAPP) model are being improved by the inclusion of emission dispersion model based on the Guassian Dispersion theory. Figure 8 illustrates two main windows of both ROADNOISE and KKU-TAPP packages.

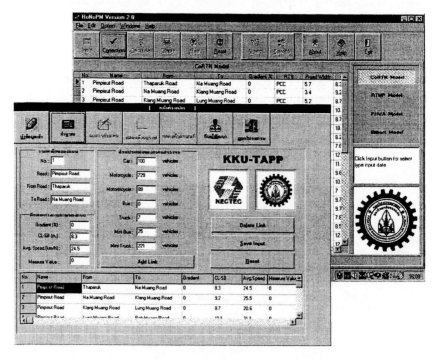

Figure 8: Main windows of ROADNOISE & KKU-TAPP software packages

In addition, the on-going research at TRC, KKU is to develop the knowledge-acquisition tool for extracting the knowledge and expertise of both experts and people who live and undertake their activities in different land uses adjacent to various road types in urban areas in terms of their perception and attitudes towards the relative importance of a variety environmental criteria (eg traffic noise levels, air pollution, pedestrian safety, pedestrian delays, difficulty of access, etc). The derived research findings will be stored in the existing knowledge module of SIMESEPT and will finally be used to determine the CESI and CECI values and enhance the accuracy of SIMESEPT.

6 Conclusions

This paper described the fundamental structure and the application of the SIMESEPT model for evaluating the multicriteria ES of the Khon Kaen road network, Thailand. The results of the case study indicate that the SIMESEPT package can be used to determine, understand, and evaluate both the separate and multicriteria environmental impacts of road traffic on urban road networks at the local (link-based) level, identify and prioritise problem locations in the road networks according the degree of their environmental impacts, and specify the possible causes (criteria) and factors contributing to those problems. It was also found that the TAHP and the FMADM methods appear to be more powerful in differentiating links according to their combined ES characteristics than FCAHP. However, the latter can be used as a conservative decision making tool when considering only the most critical environmental criterion. It was found that most links in both land use types 1 and 2 are generally sensitive to the changes of the relative weights of each criterion in terms of the changes of their CESI values and ranking order.

7 References

[1] Singleton, D. J. and Twiney, P. J. Environmental sensitivity of arterial roads. *Proceedings 10 th Australian Transport Research Forum* 10(2), pp. 165-182, 1985.

[2] Saaty, T. L. *The Analytic Hierarchy Process: Planning, Priority Setting, Resource Allocation.* McGraw-Hill International Book Company, 1980.

[3] Chen, S J and Hwang, C L *Fuzzy Multiple Attribute Decision Making – Methods and Applications,* Springer-Verlag, Berlin, 1992.

[4] Klungboonkrong, P. A microcomputer-aided system for the multicriteria environmental impact evaluation: The City of Unley case study, Australia. *Journal of the Eastern Asia Society for Transportation Studies (EASTS): Environment & Safety, 3* (1), Taipei, Taiwan, pp.99-114, 1999.

[5] Troutbeck, R J Average delay at an unsignalized intersection with two major streams each having a dichotomised headway distribution, *Transportation Science, 20(4)*, pp. 272-286, 1986.

[6] UK DoT *Calculation of Road Traffic Noise (CoRTN)*, Department of Transport (Welsh Office), HMSO, London, 1988.

[7] Song, L, Black, J and Dunne, M Environmental capacity based on pedestrian delay and accident risk, *Road & Transport Research*, 2 (3), pp 40-49, 1993.

[8] Klungboonkrong, P. and Taylor, M. A. P. An integrated planning tool for evaluating road environmental impacts. *Journal of Computer-Aided Civil and Infrastructure Engineering, 14*, pp. 335-345, 1999.

[9] Klungboonkrong P *Development of A Decision Support Tool for the Multicriteria Environmental Impact Evaluation of Urban Road Networks*, Unpublished PhD Thesis, Transport Systems Center, School of Geoinformatics, Planning and Building, University of South Australia, Adelaide, SA, Australia, 1999.

[10] Klungboonkrong, P. A decision support tool for the fuzzy multicriteria environmental sensitivity evaluation of urban road networks. *Journal of the Eastern Asia Society for Transportation Studies (Spatial Analysis, Environment, & Financing)* 2(6), pp. 1961-1980, 1997.

[11] Taylor, M A P Incorporating environmental planning decision in transport planning: a modeling framework, In Hayashi, Y and Roy, J R (Eds), Land Use and the Environment , Kluwer, Dordrecht, pp. 337-358, 1996.

On a simulation model for merging traffic management evaluation

Y. Makigami[1], T. Isizuka[2] & M. Hori[2]
[1]Professor, Civil and Environmental Systems Engineering,
Faculty of Science and Engineering, Ritsumeikan University,
Kusatsu, Shiga, Japan
[2]Graduate Student, Civil and Environmental Systems
Engineering, Ritsumeikan University, Kusatsu, Shiga, Japan

1 Abstract

Traffic conditions in Japanese urban districts are becoming worse every year and the congestion along urban expressways develops from many bottlenecks, which bring adverse effects on urban social, economical and industrial activities. Therefore attention is being given to physical design and network improvements such as bypass constructions and widenings as well as to quick effective operational measures such as ramp metering. Especially attention is being given to operational countermeasures on the merging zones along a congested route of an urban expressway because electric toll collection system is going to be installed on the Metropolitan Expressway in Tokyo as well as the Hanshin Expressway in Osaka and Kobe. Those operational countermeasures possibly applicable to the Hanshin Expressway include ramp metering, lane changes restriction between through lanes near merging zones as well as installation of lane dividers on the merging zone which lets merging drivers make single merge only.

This paper describes the model structure, computation logic as well as application results of a computer simulation model hereafter called " Merging Traffic Simulation Model" developed to evaluate the effectiveness of the above mentioned operational countermeasures for the urban expressway merging zones.

2 Objectives and assumption for the model

In order to predict the traffic conditions and evaluate the effectiveness of the design and operational improvement for a merging section, a merging traffic simulation model was developed based on the results of a traffic survey. The merging traffic simulation model is a kind of microscopic model treating the merging traffic flow as compressible fluid. The assumptions for the model structure are as follows;

(i) Traffic is treated as a compressible fluid. Each vehicle is regarded as an integral part of the fluid and is not considered individually. Furthermore, a linear relationship is assumed between the average running speed and the traffic density in that compressible fluid.

(ii) Within a given time interval, traffic flow remains constant and does not fluctuate over that time interval. In order to simulate traffic demand fluctuation, traffic demands are input to the merging zone as a step function over the entire time period under consideration.

(iii) The lane changing maneuvers between neighboring lanes in the merging zone occur according to the lane changing ratio determined for each section from the collected data for congested and non-congested flow conditions.

(iv) Even if the lane traffic volume calculated with input lane traffic volume and lane change ratio exceeds the lane capacity of a certain location of a lane or lanes for the first time, the lane traffic volume for each   location of each lane is calculated using the lane change ratio for the non-congested flow conditions. However the lane changes to the congested area is considered to be zero and the lane changes to the neighboring lanes from the congested area is reduced considering merging probability for the given conditions.

3 Logic in the computation process

3.1 Free merging flow model

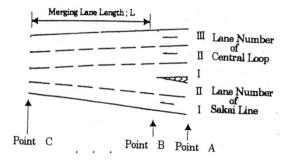

Fig.1: Geometric structure of merging section

The lane traffic volume for each lane is calculated using the lane change ratio indicating lane use transmission between the speed measurement locations, and the average running speed on the normal lane is calculated following the assumption of a linear speed and density relationship.

On applying the speed density relationship to the merging lane which has a variable lane width from a double lane width at the upstream end of merging point to a single lane width at the downstream end, as shown in Fig.1, the speed density relation is to be transformed directly proportional to the width of the merging lane location under investigation using the following equation:

$$v = v_f - \frac{v_f}{k_j(1+\alpha)} \cdot k \quad \text{and} \quad v' = v'_f - \frac{v'_f}{k'_j(1+\alpha)} \cdot k' \tag{1}$$

Where α is the ratio of the length from the downstream end of the merging lane to the point of investigation (x) to the total merging lane length.

Now once the calculated lane volume exceeds the lane capacity at any point of a lane (or lanes) in the merging area, the congestion starts extending upstream from the excessive demand location, the Congested Flow Model checks the demands and of the capacity at any location in the merging zone, then the model pursues the behavior of a shock wave.

3.2 Congested Merging Flow Model

The congested model first compares the lane capacities with the lane traffic volumes, which are given as the output of the Free Flow Model for every location of each lane in order to find the locations with excess demand. If two or more excess demand locations are found, it is assumed that the congestion starts upstream from the point with the minimum capacity among those excess demand locations. Following this assumption, the congestion usually starts forming at the downstream end of the merging lane.

The lane traffic volume of the congested merging lane and the neighboring lanes are adjusted according to the following procedures:
i) Vehicles in the lane neighboring the congested merging lane do not make lane changes to the congested part of the merging lane, instead, keep running straight downstream.
ii) Vehicles in the congested merging lane make a lane change to the non congested neighboring lanes with the congested period lane change ratio multiplied by the

merging probability calculated based on the above mentioned adjusted neighboring lane traffic volume.

iii) If the excess demand calculated by the free flow model disappear as a result of the above mentioned adjustment process, then the lane traffic volumes are determined according to the adjustment process, and the average running speed and traffic density are calculated using the continuation equation and the speed density relationship.

iv) If an excess demand still remains after the above mentioned adjustment process, the behavior of the tail of congestion is pursued based on the excess demand and the density difference between congested and non congested flow using the equation as shown below:

$$s' = \frac{q - q'}{k - k'} \tag{2}$$

Where s' is the speed of the tail of congestion, or shockwave speed and q_r as well as k, k' are merging traffic flow and density in non-congested and congested conditions respectively. The traffic volume at the down stream section from the section with the excess demand is replaced by the flow rate of the capacity flow rate after congestion starts.

v) With the development of congestion toward upstream, lane change from the neighboring lanes to the congested lane with the excess demand become zero, consequently, the lane traffic demands to the congested region decrease.

3.3 Jam propagation model to the merging lane upstream

Congestion developed from the merging section usually propagates upstream beyond the merging nose. At this stage the congestion propagate upstream along the shoulder lane to which the on-ramp merges forming the merging section.

And not a few vehicle make lane change to the non congested median lane from the congested shoulder lane or from the upstream non congested shoulder lane avoiding the congestion. Then congestion starts on the median lane because of the traffic concentration, and the congestion propagates quickly upstream. The Jam propagation model was developed to evaluate the delicate performance of the congestion corresponding the various aspects of merging control process such as introduction of the lame change prohibition and placement of lane dividers. Assumption for the Jam propagation model is almost same except the following description

The development of the congestion beyond the merging nose is traced lane by lane.

The amount of merging traffic is fixed to the predetermined rate of on-ramp traffic flow for the case of the present traffic conditions, and to the rate of flow determined from the single merging probability for case of lane divider installation. The merging traffic is to be included in the merging traffic lane volume. The shoulder lane traffic volume (q_1) approaching to the tail of the congestion is to be the lane traffic volume calculated by multiplying the input traffic demand from the upstream of the congestion by the lane distribution rate to the shoulder lane.

Now suppose that the congestion developing from the taper end of the merging lane exceeds the upstream end of the range of the merging model and keeps developing upstream for the time sequence of t seconds forming the total length of the congestion of $x(t)$. Furthermore suppose the rate of lane changes from the congested shoulder lane is to be l_e for the unit length of the congested lane and the unit time, and further suppose that the maximum flow rate of the congested merging lane is q'_1, and the traffic density of the congested and noncongested shoulder lane are to be k'_1 and k_1 respectively. By the way, q'_{1c} is to be the sum of the maximum flow rate of the congested merging lane and the number of lane changing traffic vehicles. The input ramp demand is denoted by q_r as shown in Fig.2.

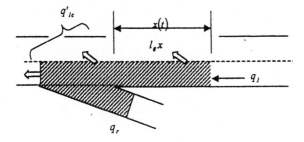

Fig. 2 Variables of gap propagation model

Since the running sped of the merging lane can be calculated using the QV relationship determined based on the previous survey results, the traffic density at the merging nose (k'_0) can be determined by the running speed calculated from the QV relationship corresponding the flow rate of $(q'_{1c}-q_r)$. Therefore the congested flow rate and the congested density at the tale of the congestion are

$$q'_{1c}-q_r+\frac{1}{2}l_e p_0 t^2 x(t) \text{ and } k'_0-l_e p_0 t \text{ respectively. Here, } p_0 \text{ is the}$$

single merging probability.

Assuming that the running speed and the traffic density in the free flow side at the congestion tail are q_1 and k_1 respectively, and that $q'_{1c} - q_r - q_1 = \Delta q$ and $k'_1 - k_1 = \Delta k$, the propagation speed of the congestion s_1 is given by

$$s'_1 = \frac{dx(t)}{dt} = \frac{\Delta q_1 + \frac{1}{2} l_e p_0 t^2 \cdot x(\tau)}{\Delta k_1 - l_e p_0 t} \tag{3}$$

This is a first linear differential equation. However there are items that can not be integrated in the solution. Therefore, the correction items in the numerator and denominator in equation (3) is replaced by

$$\tfrac{1}{2} l_e \wp_0 x(t) \qquad \text{as well as} \qquad \tfrac{1}{2} l_e \wp_0$$

considering the average number of lane change during one simulation period of τ

Then,
$$\frac{d(x)}{dt} = \frac{\Delta q_1 + \frac{1}{2} l_e \upsilon p_{0 \cdot x(t)}}{\Delta k_1 - \frac{1}{2} l_e \wp_0} \tag{4}$$

Now, let

$$\frac{\frac{1}{2} l_e \tau P_0}{\Delta k_1 - \frac{1}{2} l_e \tau P_0} = c_1 \qquad \frac{\Delta q_1}{\Delta k_1 - \frac{1}{2} l_e \tau P_0} = c_2$$

Then,
$$x(t) = exp\left(\int_0^t c_1 dt \right) \left[\int_0^t c_2 \cdot exp\left(\int_0^t -c_1 dt \right) dt + c \right]$$
$$= \frac{c_2}{c_1} \left(1 - e^{c_1 t} \right) = \frac{\Delta q_1}{l_e} \left(1 - e^{\frac{l_e}{\Delta k_1} \cdot t} \right) \tag{5}$$

On the other hand, the lane traffic volume in the median lane at the merging nose of the merging section at time $t(q_2(t))$ is given by the following equation.

$$q_2(t) = q_2 + \frac{1}{2} l_e p_0 t^2 x(t)$$

Therefore, from the timing when $q_2(t)$ given by the above equation exceeds the maximum flow rate at the median lane, calculation process to chase the congestion propagation along the median lane starts. The lane by lane congestion propagation calculation is to be conducted until the congestion tail overpasses the congestion in the shoulder lane. After that the congestion propagation calculation is continued using a simulation model described below.

3.4 Through traffic-jam simulation model

The objective of the through traffic jam simulation model is to simulate the traffic flow and to follow the behavior of traffic in the congested region on an expressway section between interchanges with two or more bottlenecks on it. In order to ensure a meaningful relationship between traffic volume and the average running speed, the expressway section is divided into several homogenous subsections with constant capacity over their length. Those subsections are numbered 1, 2,... n from upstream to downstream. The basic assumptions for the model are same as those for the merging traffic model except the traffic demand is input as a form of OD table that makes it possible to evaluate the effect of on-ramp volume fluctuation due to each merging traffic management procedure. The propagation speed of the tail of the congestion in subsection $i\{s'_j(i)\}$ is calculated using equation 2 and the development and dispersion of the congested region in the time and space field is traced by calculating the time for the tail of congestion to reach the upstream end of subsection $i\{t(i)\}$ by equation 6 under the condition that the congestion starts at the upstream end of subsection j, and that length of subsection k is $l(k)$.

$$t(i) = \sum_{k=j-1}^{i}\left[\frac{l(k)}{-s'_j(k)}\right] \qquad (6)$$

The total travel time at subsection i at time period T [$TTr(i)$ in vehicles hours is computed by multiplying the area of congested and uncontested regions in the time and space field by the corresponding traffic density as follows:

$$TTr(i) = k'(i)l(i)\left[\tau - \frac{t(i+1)+t(i)}{2}\right] + k(i)l(i)\frac{t(i+1)+t(i)}{2} \qquad (7)$$

Where $k'(i)$ and $k(i)$ is the density of subsection i under congested and non-congested flow conditions respectively.

Then traffic stream characteristics of subsection i such as average travel time, average running speed and average traffic density are calculated in the same way,

4 Outline of traffic survey and application of the model

4.1 Outline of traffic survey

A series of traffic surveys were conducted to evaluate the adaptability of the model to the study section and to collect basic data to prepare input date for the merging traffic management evaluation. The survey contains two data collection stages ; 1) survey for the traffic stream characteristics on the merging section and 2) lane change measurements between on and off ramps. The date and location of the traffic surveys are summarized in table –1 and Fig. 3. All the traffic flow during the survey periods were recorded in the video tapes by video cameras set up on the top of

Table 1: Outline of Traffic Survey

Date and Year	Lacation
Sep.17th-18th 1998 Sep. 1st- 3rd 1999 Sep. 18th-20th 2000	A: Minatomachi B:Tsukamoto, C: Kashima, D: Toyonaka South The same as The oboe

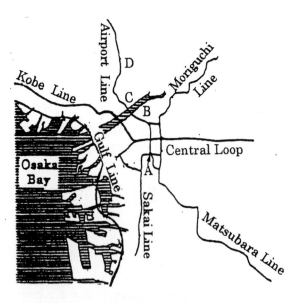

Fig.3 Network of the Hanshin Expressway

neighboring buildings as well as TV cameras in the suitable locations among those of the traffic surveillance and control system of the Hanshin Expressway System. The five minutes lane traffic volume, lane change measurements between each lanes, running speed as well as gap distribution on the merging nose were manually obtained from the played back video screen. The collection of traffic operation data from the Hanshin Expressway Surveillance and Control System includes the output from all detectors along the study section, congested region fluctuation patterns on the time and space field developed from the detector outputs.

4.2 Application of the model

4.2.1 Merging model

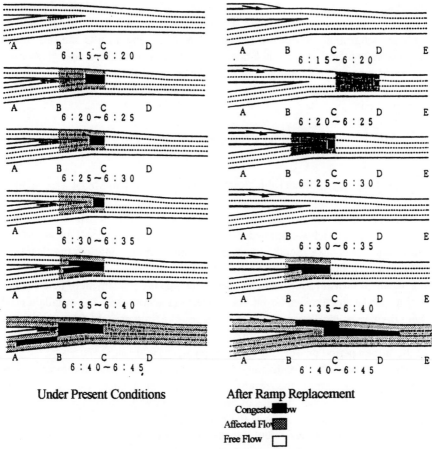

Under Present Conditions   **After Ramp Replacement**

Congested Flow ■
Affected Flow ▓
Free Flow □

Fig.4 Fluctuation of congested area from simulation output

In order to check the reliability and usability of the merging traffic simulation model the model was applied to an improvement plan for a merging section called the Minatomachi ramp where the ramp traffic merge into the upstream section of a merging section between the Central Ring and a radial route called Sakai line of the Hanshin Expressway in Osaka. Hanshin Expressway Public Corporation is now considering an improvement plan in which the Minatomachi on-ramp will be relocated from the present location to the shoulder side of the Sakai Line. The merging traffic simulation model was applied to simulate the traffic flow to see the change in the traffic after the relocation of the Minatomachi on-ramp. Fig.4 shows that congestion appears from the point one block downstream at the initial stage of congestion development at 6:15 and 6:25 AM comparing from the present conditions, since the lane changes to the right-hand side lanes are assumed to shift toward downstream flocks to avoid the conflicts of merging traffic between the Central Loop and the Sakai Line. However, congestion is decreased as a whole as indicated during the five-minutes interval without congestion between 6:25 and 6:35 AM. The results indicate quite reasonable outcome of the simulation. The merging simulation model gives very appropriate and reliable results indicating the effect of the improvement plan for reducing traffic congestion. It is considered that the ramp relocation improvement.

4.3 Application of Jam Propagation and Through Traffic jam Simulation Model

The Jam Propagation Model and Through Traffic Traffic-jam Model were applied to confirm the possibility to apply the Jam-propagation and Through Traffic-jam Simulation model to evaluate the effectiveness of margin traffic management measures. The model was applied to the inbound traffic between Tsukamoto on-ramp and Toyonaka South on-ramp on the Airport line of the Hanshin Expressway using the results of traffic survey described in section 4-1. The management measures for the investigating include the implement of lane change prohibition at the Tsukamato on –ramp merging section and the installation of lane- dividers at the Toyonaka South on-ramp. The time period for the simulation includes the beginning of the morning period starting from 6:00 PM to 9:00 PM of the survey period on Tuesday 19th of September 2000.

Fig.5 shows the results of the simulation for the development of the congestion. From the result for the implementation of lane change prohibition, any distinct changes of the congestion evolution are not observed. It is considered that this is because the number of lane change on the Tsukamoto merging section are very few for the moment. On the other hand, it is noticed that the lane dividers at the Toyonaka South on-ramp decrease the congestion length starting from both the Tsukamoto and the Kashima on-ramp. Whereas the development of congestion from the Toyonaka South on-ramp is fairly slow because the forced single mergers reduce the capacity of merging traffic flow. Those results indicate that the Jam-propagation and Through Traffic-jam Simulation Model have definite possibility to evaluate the effectiveness of merging traffic management measures.

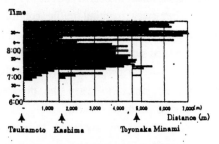

Fig. a   Results for Present Conditions

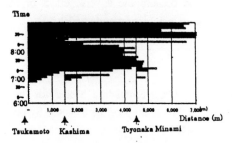

Fig. b   Results for Lane Charging Prohibition

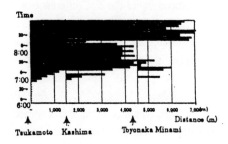

Fig.5 Output of Jam Propagation Model

5. Conclusion and future study

The merging traffic evaluation method based on the simulation models developed in this study shows definite possibility to evaluate the effectiveness of the merging traffic management measures. The subjects for future study are as follows.

i)   The conclusion described above is based on the results of the simulation applied the three consecutive on-ramps on the Airport line of the Hanshin Expressway in Osaka for the first time. Therefore it is considered important to bring the reliability and usability by applying the process to the different locations and other management measures such as ramp metering.

ii)   The evaluation of expressway merging traffic control measures must be conducted considering the effect of the measures not only on the expressway itself but also on the related surface street network. Therefore it is considered necessary to widen the range of investigation towards the connected surface streets especially surface streets to carry the diverted traffic from the expressway on-ramp under control measures.

iii)   It is considered more and more important to develop theoretical and philosophical back ground to investigate the ramp control method on the consecutive on ramp because the adverse effect of the control method is considered to bring on social issues quite widely.

References

[1]   Yasuji Makigami etal ; On a Simulation Model for the Traffic Stream in a Freeway Merging Aera, Proceedings of the 8th Inter. Symp. on Transportation & Traffic Theory, pp.426-451 1981.

[2]   Yasuji Makigami etal ; Traffic Stream Characteristics on the Merging Area of Expressway Junctions, Proceeding of the 8th Conference of Road Engineering Ass. of Asia & Australia, pp.234-247

[3]   Yasuji Makigami etal ; MergingLane Length for Expressway Improvement Plan in Japan, Journal of Transportain Engineering. Vol.114, No.6, American Society of Civil Engineers, pp.714-734

[4]   Yasuji Makaigami and Takeshi Matsuo; A Merging Probability Calculation Method Considering Multiple Merging Phenomena, Proceeding of the Eleventh International Symposium on Transportation and Traffic theory, Yokohama, pp.21-38, 1981.

[5]   Yasuji Makigami etal; Evaluation on Outside and Inside Expressway Ramps Based on Merging Probability, Journal of Transportation Engineering Vol. 117, No.1 American Society of Civil Engineers, 1982.

[6]   Yasuji Makigami etal; Evaluation on Weaving Traffic Using Merging Probability ; Elsvier, Transportation and Traffic Theory, 1993

[7]   Yasuji Makigami and Kyoichi Kasama ; Study on the Evaluation of Merging Traffic Stream on the Urban Expressway in Osaka WIT Press. Urban Transport and the Environment for the 21st Century IV, pp.137-148, 1998.

Parking search modelling in freight transport and private traffic simulation

J. Muñuzuri[1], J. Racero[1] & J. Larrañeta[1]
[1]Department of Industrial Organisation, School of Engineering,
University of Sevilla, Spain.

Abstract

This paper presents the work carried out in order to achieve better approximation to reality in traffic simulation. It is embedded within a line of research in the Organisation Department of the University of Seville aimed at developing a microscopic traffic simulator to use as a tool for urban planning issues related to freight transport and private traffic.

For private traffic, the simulator uses traffic assignation algorithms which, from an O-D matrix, give the input to generate the route that each vehicle will follow through the links of the city network. Then, real-time movement algorithms calculate the actual movement of the vehicle through each link, interacting with the other vehicles present in the simulation. The model presented in this work is used for representation of the parking procedure at the end of the vehicle's route.

For freight transport, the shortest path algorithm was used for direct calculation of routes for freight vehicles. Knowing the different delivery stops that have to be made by the vehicle, the algorithm calculates the links that form the shortest route between each pair of consecutive stops. Then, when the freight vehicle arrives to a link where it must stop, the parking search model examines the parking spaces available, and determines which is the best one according to its distance to the final delivery point. That best parking space is then assigned to the vehicle.

1 Introduction

Models that represent the movement of vehicles through a network (acceleration models, turning models, generation models...) are widely studied and present in the literature (May, [1]). However, the development of the microscopic traffic simulator TRAMOS (Traffic Analysis, Modelling and Optimisation Simulator) in the University of Sevilla (Eguía, [2]) found the need to create a model for the extraction of vehicles from the network: a parking search model, according to which vehicles would determine when and where to park. This model would also have to include freight delivery vehicles, to illustrate their routes and delivery stops along the network.

This paper describes the general operating principles of the parking search model, as well as a test run carried out after implementing it in the simulator TRAMOS.

2 Microscopic traffic simulation

This section describes briefly the sequence of procedures followed in a microscopic traffic simulation.

2.1 Initial input

In order to start the microscopic simulation, several input data is required:
- Network data: all the links and nodes of the network, distributed in zones, and including the capacity functions for all links.
- An O-D matrix, needed to determine how many vehicles are generated in each zone of the network.
- A previous four-step macroscopic traffic assignment, in order to determine flow volumes for each turn in the network.

2.2 Microscopic simulation models

All the different models included in microscopic traffic simulation are described here, as well as showing an overview of the general simulation procedure. The models are (Yang, [3]):

- **Vehicle generation model**: this model is used to incorporate vehicles to the network. It consists of a probability distribution that spreads vehicle generation over the simulation period for each origin zone. Private vehicles are thus generated randomly in each zone, with a uniform probability distribution that depends on the number of trips generated in each zone, extracted from the O-D matrix.

- **Follow-up model**: this model establishes dynamically the reference for the movement of each vehicle, that is, the input used by that vehicle to adjust its speed. This reference can be either the vehicle driving in front of it, the end of the link in case there is no such vehicle, or, if the vehicle is to park in the current link, the parking space assigned to it (Gipps, [4]).

- **Overtaking model**: model used to make vehicles change lanes within a link when the lane they are in is moving too slow, or when they need to be in a certain lane to make the next turn, or when they are approaching a parking space. Every time a vehicle changes lanes, its reference changes.

- **Acceleration model**: this model, for each simulation instant, receiver as input the position, speed, acceleration and reference of each vehicle in the previous instant. The output is the new acceleration, which then is used to determine the new speed and position.

- **Intersections model**: this is the model used to simulate the movement of vehicles from one link to the next one in their route (in TRAMOS, it considers "give way" priorities and traffic light regulations). Private vehicles move randomly through the network, keeping in mind the fact that flow volume proportions must be maintained for all turns in the network. Every time a vehicle reaches the end of a link, the model retrieves the number of vehicles that follow each one of the possible turns, data obtained from the macroscopic traffic assignment. These proportions are then used as probabilities, which will determine the next link to be entered by the vehicle.

To simulate the parking process both for private vehicles and for freight transport vehicles, the two following models were developed for TRAMOS:

- **Parking search model**: this model is used for determining whether vehicles are going to park in the link they are entering, and to assign parking spaces to them. The next sections will focus on carrying out a deeper description of this model, both for private vehicles and for freight delivery vehicles.

- **Parking model:** when a vehicle is approaching thane assigned parking space, its reference is set to it, which makes the vehicle change lanes and reduce speed until it stops in front of the space. Then the vehicle is extracted from the simulation after a certain time (parking manoeuvring time).

The integration of all these models, which results in the microscopic traffic simulation procedure, is represented on figure 1.

3 The parking search model

The parking search model for the microscopic traffic simulator reflects the process followed by a vehicle, whether private or for freight delivery, to choose a parking space in a certain link. The parking search model is used:

- To determine, when a vehicle enters a link, whether it is going to park in it
- To assign parking spaces to vehicles: after it has been determined by the model that the vehicle will park in the link, it scans all available parking spaces in the link and assigns the best one for the vehicle to park in it.

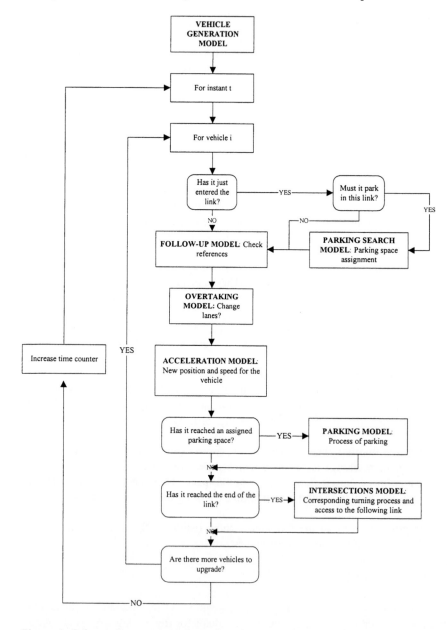

Figure 1: Schematic representation of a microscopic traffic simulation algorithm.

For description of the parking search procedure, the different types of parking spaces existing in the network will be described in the first place, and after that the specific parking characteristics of both private vehicles and freight transport vehicles will be shown.

3.1   Types of parking places

When a certain vehicle enters a link in which it has to park, it searches for available parking spaces and chooses the one that best meets its needs, depending, among other aspects, on the type of parking spaces available. These different types of parking spaces that can exist in a link are:

- *Normal* parking space: available for all types of vehicles.
- *Load/unload* zone: available only for freight delivery vehicles, during certain periods of time.
- *Double-parking*: illegal parking space, which blocks the corresponding lane.
- Parking on *sidewalk*: illegal parking procedure that does not block the lane. It is frequently used for freight delivery stops, hence its introduction in the model.

Normal and *load/unload* parking spaces exist in the network a priori (that is, every link must have all these parking spaces assigned before the simulation starts). On the other hand, *sidewalk* and *double-parking* spaces are generated automatically every time they are needed by a freight transport vehicle (they will not be used by private vehicles) in front of their delivery destination point. The vehicle will then stay in parked for a given time length (necessary for delivery), and then continue the route, with the illegal parking space eliminated from the network.

It is possible to eliminate the possibility of generating *sidewalk* parking spaces in a link (to represent streets where parking on the sidewalk is not possible). In that case, *double-parking* would be the only illegal possibility for freight delivery vehicles to park close to their destination points.

When the vehicle enters a link where it has to stop, it compares the weights of the available parking spaces with the weight that would have *double-parking* or *sidewalk* parking in front of the delivery point. In case this type of parking had the highest weight, the *double-parking* or *sidewalk* space would be generated, and assigned to the vehicle for parking.

3.2   Private vehicles

Private vehicles will only park once during the simulation period, because private traffic assignments only consider routes between an origin and a final destination. Thus, in the simulation, every private vehicle is generated in a certain link of the network (origin) and, after finishing its route, will search for parking in another link (destination), and will exit the simulation after parking. This is why illegal parking (*double-parking* and *sidewalk*) will not be allowed for private vehicles (a possible extension of the work would include developing a model for *double-parking* of private vehicles, to illustrate the capacity reduction in urban networks due to irregular parking patterns).

The decision to park for a private vehicle depends on the total distance covered since it was generated at its origin, estimating the maximum trip length typically as 1.25 times the width of the network. Then, every time the vehicle enters a certain link, the probability of parking in it is determined from a function like the one shown in figure 2, that takes a value 0 when the vehicle is generated and 1 for the maximum trip length.

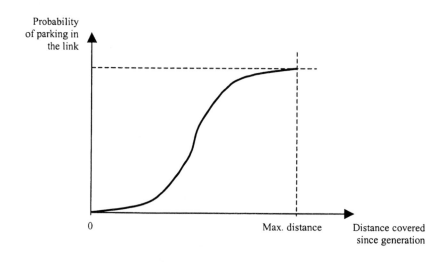

Figure 2: Probability function for private vehicle parking.

By calculating a random number between 0 and 1 and comparing it with the parking probability, the decision of whether to park or not is made. Then, two scenarios can occur:

- There are parking spaces available in the link: the vehicle will choose the first one it finds and park there.
- There are no parking spaces available in the link: the vehicle will continue its route and park in the first available space it finds.

3.3 Freight delivery vehicles

Freight delivery vehicles, on the other hand, do not park only once, but several times along their route, depending on the different delivery points spread throughout the network. These vehicles do not move randomly through the network, but the following data must be assigned to each one of them before the simulation starts:

-   Origin link.
-   Stops (link, position in the link and time spent at each one of them). The route that the vehicle will follow between them is then calculated via a shortest path algorithm.
-   Destination link (which can be the same one as the origin, in case the vehicle follows a circular route).

At each stop, the freight delivery vehicle will search for the most suitable parking space available, including all different types of parking spaces. The choice will be made according to the type of parking spaces available and their distance to the final destination point in the link, represented as a series of weighing functions. These weighing functions were estimated according to the following assumptions:

-   Legal parking is preferred to illegal parking: a *load/unload* parking space 20 meters away from the destination point will be equally preferred to a *sidewalk* parking right in front of it.
-   Load/unload parking is preferred to normal parking: a *load/unload* parking space 15 meters away from the destination point will be equally preferred to a *normal* parking right in front of it.
-   The choice between *sidewalk* parking or *double-parking* depends on the number of lanes in the link:
    -   3 or more lanes: *double-parking* is always preferred to *sidewalk* parking.
    -   2 lanes: a *sidewalk* parking space 15 meters away from the destination point will be equally preferred to *double-parking* right in front of it.
    -   1 lane: *double-parking* in front of the final destination only when there is no other space available in 50 meters.
-   For long distances to the destination point, the type of parking space is irrelevant, the closest one to the destination will be chosen.

Following these assumptions, the weighing functions shown below were estimated. It is important to note that the actual weight value for each parking space is not relevant, but the choice will be made depending on the relative values for all the available parking spaces in the link. That is why the coefficients in the weighing functions could take different values, as long as their relative proportions were the same.

The parking space weighing functions (y) depending on the distance to the final destination point in the link (x) are:

- *Load/unload* zone parking: $y = 9,5 \cdot e^{-0,001 x^2}$

- *Normal* parking: $y = 8,0 \cdot e^{-0,001 x^2}$

- *Sidewalk* parking: $y = 6,5 \cdot e^{-0,001 x^2}$

- *Double-parking* (for single-lane links): $y = 1,0 \cdot e^{-0,001 x^2}$

- *Double-parking* (for two-lane links): $y = 5,0 \cdot e^{-0,001 x^2}$

- *Double-parking* (for three or more lanes in the link): $y = 7,0 \cdot e^{-0,001 x^2}$

These expressions are shown graphically on figure 3:

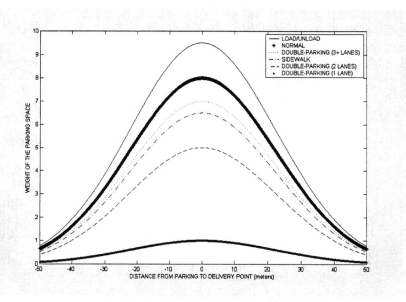

Figure 3: Weight of the different types of parking spaces depending on their distance to the final delivery point (the distance takes positive and negative values to account for the fact that the parking space can be located before or after the delivery point in the link).

4   Test run

The work concludes with an illustration of the model operation, once it has been implemented in the TRAMOS simulator. To this effect, the test network represented on figure 4 was generated.

Three vehicles participated in the test, all of them generated at the beginning of link 1:

- Freight delivery vehicle F1, generated at simulation instant 0.5
- Freight delivery vehicle F2, generated at simulation instant 0.5
- Private vehicle P, generated at simulation instant 4

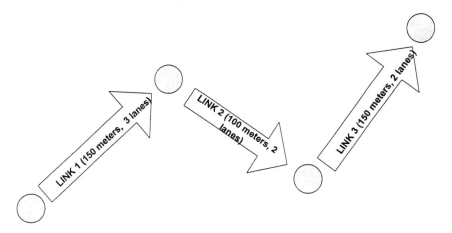

Figure 4: Test network for the experiment (3 links and 4 nodes).

The network characteristics in terms of predefined "legal" parking places, and the scheduled stops for the two freight delivery vehicles, are represented in tables 1 and 2. With respect to the private vehicle P, it has an assigned maximum route length of 250 meters.

Table 1: Parking spaces defined in the test network

LINK	POSITION	TYPE
1	35	Load/unload
	90	Load/unload
	100	Normal
2	35	Normal
	80	Load/unload
3	10	Normal
	100	Load/unload

Table 2: Scheduled stops for freight delivery vehicles

VEHICLE	LINK	POSITION	TIME LENGTH
F1	1	30	15 sec
	2	40	10 sec
	3	120	10 sec
F2	1	50	10 sec
	1	120	5 sec
	3	20	15 sec

The results of the test run carried out using TRAMOS are shown in table 3. It can be seen how the private vehicle (P) does not park in the first link, but chooses to park in the second one, in the existing normal parking place. The first freight delivery vehicle (F1) makes its first stop at a load/unload zone, which is very close to its destination, but for the other two stops chooses to park in front of them on the sidewalk. The other freight delivery vehicle (F2) makes its two first stops with double-parking, since the first link has three lanes. For its last stop, it uses a normal parking space close to its delivery destination.

Table 3: Actual parking spaces chosen by the vehicles during the test run.

VEHICLE	LINK	POSITION	TYPE
F1	1	35	Load/unload
F2	1	50	Double-parking
P	2	35	Normal
F2	1	120	Double-parking
F1	2	40	Sidewalk
F2	3	10	Normal
F1	3	120	Sidewalk

References

[1]   May, A.D. Traffic flow fundamentals. Prentice Hall, 1990.

[2]   Eguía, I., Canca, D., Racero, J. & Larrañeta, J. Un nuevo modelo para la simulación del tráfico en entornos urbanos. Departamento de Organización Industrial y Gestión de Empresas, 1999. Escuela Superior de Ingenieros, Universidad de Sevilla.

[3]   Yang, Q. & Koutsopoulos, H.N. A microscopic traffic simulation for evaluation of dinamic traffic management system. Transportation research, vol 4; p. 113-129.

[4]   Gipps. A behavioural car following model for computer simulation. Transportation research, vol 158; p. 105-111.

The effect of multi-combination freight vehicles in urban traffic

M. Lake[1], L. Ferreira[1] & D. Stewart[2]
[1]*School of Civil Engineering, Queensland University of Technology, Australia.*
[2]*Queensland Department of Main Roads, Australia.*

Abstract

The use of heavy vehicles that are capable of carrying increased loads has continued to increase rapidly. Such vehicles, such as B-Doubles, Road-Trains and other large sized vehicles, are termed here as Multi-Combination Vehicles (MCV). Significant economic benefits result from the use of such innovative vehicles, which are able to carry up to twice the payload of standard semi-trailers. Those benefits, however, need to be traded-off against the potentially negative impacts on other road users, such as additional delays in urban areas.

The research detailed here will deliver an increased understanding of some of those impacts by investigating models which can be used to estimate delays to other road users. Preliminary results from adding small numbers of MCV for a freeway section and an intersection demonstrated a significant adverse impact on the performance of the network. These results imply higher passenger car equivalent values than those commonly used for MCV. Further research is being conducted, including calibrating the input parameters and performing the same network simulations on other microsimulation packages to compare the results.

Introduction

Road freight transport plays a major role in the Australian economy. This influence is unlikely to decrease, with freight transport increasing 4% annually between 1970 and 1990 in Australia [1]. Freight movement within urban areas is a very significant part of the total freight task.

In Australia, vehicles meeting current limits of 42.5 tonnes gross vehicle weight, 19.0 metres overall length, regularly operate on major urban routes.

Road trains weighing 115 tonnes, 53 metres in length, operate in remote locations. The trend is for increasing load limits and truck size, with the transport industry continuously seeking to increase productivity through increasing load carrying space, mass or access [2].

This paper is organised as follows: the next section discusses impacts of MCV on other road users and the community, in terms of delays, accidents and environmental consequences. This is followed by a discussion of the use of microsimulation modelling to estimate MCV impacts, including some preliminary results. Finally, some conclusions are given in the last section.

MCV impacts on traffic

General

There are two main traffic related issues associated with MCV in urban areas, namely: delays that they may cause to other vehicles and safety related impacts. These are interrelated in urban areas, as accidents involving MCV create delays, while congestion affects the probability of accidents. Other considerations of MCV in urban regions include: efficiency; contribution to the national and local economy; and environmental effects.

Three factors contribute the effect of heavy vehicles on roads: the large size of trucks; the operating capabilities of trucks that are inferior to cars; and the physical impact on nearby cars and psychological effect on the drivers of those cars [3]. It has been suggested by a number of authors that the presence of a truck in front of a passenger car may result in the driver being more cautious due to the large size of the vehicle and the diminished sight distances. Thus, the headways of the cars (not just the headways of the heavy vehicles), in mixed traffic may be larger, effecting congestion, delays and capacity [4] [5]. Other research has concluded the concluded the reverse, that the average headways of passenger cars and heavy vehicles in mixed traffic are independent of the type of vehicle immediately ahead [6] [7].

The issue of MCV accidents and incidents on urban freeways is a vital concern, with public awareness is heightened because of the rise in MCV volume, the interaction of these large vehicles with the traffic and the publicity given to major MCV accidents [8]. Crashes involving heavy trucks also tend to have more severe consequences for the other involved road users, as a result of the size and mass difference [9]. Urban crashes represent a significant proportion of truck crashes, with 50 to 75 percent of all serious rigid truck crashes and 25 to 50 percent of serious articulated vehicle crashes occurring in urban areas [10].

Before implementing a MCV management strategy, investigation should be conducted on the current effects of the MCV, to allow the most cost-effective and efficient solution to be implemented. Despite this, a field survey showed that the majority of the 15 states in the US that implemented lane restrictions for trucks, applied these restrictions without detailed evaluation plans or before and after studies [8]. In addition, large truck restrictions have been proposed to improve air quality and reduce congestion, however, there is actually little hard evidence as to their impact on either [11].

The costs of large MCV negotiating urban traffic, such as adverse effects on traffic speeds and capacity, need to be weighed against the economic benefits of requiring fewer vehicles to move the same quantity of freight

Congestion impacts

An approach which has been widely used in analytically modelling traffic with more than one class is to represent the other classes in terms of passenger car equivalents (PCE's) or passenger car units (PCU's).

The extensive research into PCE's for the movement of heavy vehicles at signalised intersections is reviewed by Lake and Ferreira [12]. Recent research aims to incorporate the delays to other vehicles, with Benekohal and Zhao [13] presenting a method for calculating PCE's for heavy vehicles at signalised intersections in under-saturated conditions based not only on headways, but the delay caused to the rest of the traffic stream. The resulting delay-based PCE are not constant and depend on traffic volume, truck type and truck percentage. A large body of research also exists on calculating PCE's for freeway sections, as detailed in Lake and Ferreira [12]. Fisk [14] found that the PCE approximation could lead to erroneous predictions, mainly because for uninterrupted flow, the different performance characteristics of the two classes are not taken into account.

The second approach that has more recently been applied is the use of simulation models to examine actual effects of heavy vehicles on a simulated road network. This method is considered to be superior to the PCE technique, as the different characteristics that cause the effect of the heavy vehicles on the surrounding traffic, such as performance characteristics, size and driver behaviour, can be explicitly modelled. The use of microsimulation models is discussed in a later section of this paper.

Safety related impacts

Despite the fact that the public overwhelmingly considers MCV to be unsafe [15], the available evidence does not support this perception for urban environments. The data, internationally and nationally, has shown that heavy vehicle involvement in collisions is more of an issue in rural areas than urban environments. A review of the research in this area can be found in Lake and Ferreira [12]. In addition, in multi-vehicle accidents involving heavy vehicles, the majority are the fault of the other vehicle. This does not mean that the effect of safety should be discounted in urban areas, given the potential loss of life. In addition, all crashes impact on the performance of an urban road network.

Environmental impacts

Gurney [16] found that the main environmental impacts, as perceived by the local urban community, are lack of safety, noise/vibration and air pollution, with heavy vehicles considered to be major contributors to these impacts. Attributed to air pollution are a number of serious long-term effects on people and the environment. From the studies, a review of which can be found in Lake and Ferreira [12], heavy vehicles contribute significantly to emissions from traffic. The potential impact of diesel vehicles on health is of particular concern due to the significant contribution of those vehicles to the total amount of particle matter emitted from road transport. Therefore, heavy vehicles are extremely important to predicting or reducing the effects of transport emissions on the environmental and human health. In addition, heavy vehicles also contribute significantly to noise pollution.

Microsimulation models

A number of commercially available packages have the ability to define different classes of vehicles with different operating and size characteristics. In principle, these models are suitable to examine the effects of heavy vehicles on congestion/delays in urban areas. In addition, as the acceleration and deceleration of the vehicles are simulated, it could be possible to generate the emissions from the vehicles, and therefore determine the environmental effects. Although, crash rates cannot be predicted using a simulation model directly, the areas of conflict that could result in a crash may be could be identified through simulation. This would highlight the major safety risks with regard to the interaction of heavy vehicles with urban traffic. In addition, an incident could be simulated to view the effect of this on the network.

Model testing

There is a lack of understanding of how MCV affect traffic flow in individual manoeuvres, in terms of the delays they may cause to other traffic and the link and intersection capacity implications. Micro-simulation models are usually used to evaluate the performance of a general traffic stream made up primarily of passenger cars. This paper reports on a preliminary analysis using the microsimulation model AIMSUM2 (Advanced Interactive Microscopic Simulator for Urban and Non-Urban Networks), which has been selected as one of the most commonly used models. AIMSUN2 is one of a number of microscopic simulation traffic models in common use by traffic engineering professionals world wide. As a microsimulation model, the behaviour of every single vehicle in the network is continuously modelled throughout the simulation period, using several driver behaviour models including car following, lane changing and gap acceptance. Any number of different types of vehicles can be simulated by defining the vehicle in terms of the parameters used by the underlying vehicle behavioural model, such as acceleration, deceleration, and maximum speed.

The degree to which this package can be used to model the interaction between MCV and other traffic is assessed using test data for a section of freeway and for a signalised intersection. These two networks, which are detailed below, are used to investigate the effect of the MCV on the performance of the network, therefore primarily the impact of delays. Future research could involve examining other effects such as environmental and safety impacts. In addition, future work will involve conducting the same network simulations on different models to compare the results.

Freeway network

A model of a 13.2km section of the inbound carriageway Pacific Motorway in Brisbane, with five off ramps and 6 on ramps, is used for the initial tests. The section is modelled during AM peak flows from 06:00 to 09:00 when the route is very congested, with much of its length operating in stop start conditions for at least part of this time. The model used is that of the motorway prior to the 2001 opening of a 5km Transit Lane now operating in the section. It should be noted that the operation of this network relied heavily on the operation of the merges, the modelling of which is one of the most difficult challenges for a microsimulation model. While the overall journey time through the network predicted by the model compared favourably with surveyed results, the delay in various sections of the network showed some discrepancies. The model is considered to be calibrated as well as could be expected with the given data and suitable for the purpose of examining the effects of varying the number of MCV.

Intersection network

A small model of a traffic signal intersection on an arterial road, the intersection of River Road and Brisbane Road in Dinmore, an outer western suburb of Brisbane, was used. As Brisbane Road is the main link between Brisbane and the predominantly industrial town of Ipswich, it was considered to be suitable to test the impact of varying numbers of MCV on the road network. The model consisted of the traffic signal intersection on Brisbane Rd and a closely coupled intersection on River Rd together with associated approach roads. The approaches are modelled for 200-400m to ensure that queues from the traffic signals would be contained in the model. The PM peak hour was modelled, with volumes based on 1999 traffic counts factored to account for growth to 2000. With these flows the intersection was undersaturated with a reserve capacity of about 40%. The saturation flow across a simple stop line was tested with the same parameters used in this model to ensure that the calibration was acceptable.

Initial results

All results presented are the average of 12 separate simulations. The MCV added are 19m in length, which corresponds to a number of heavy vehicle combinations in Queensland, Australia, including truck-trailers, prime mover semi-trailers and 19m B-Doubles [2].

The performance measures of the traffic for the freeway traffic, with 0, 10, 30 and 100 MCV per hour, are given in Table 1. The results indicate that the introduction of relatively small numbers of MCV has a significant adverse impact on the performance of the network. The additional delay is especially significant as the freeway is quite long, at 13.2 km, with a freeway throughput of approximately 4,400 vehicles per hour and a total network volume of 9,900 vehicles per hour. The introduction of 30 MCV increased the total delay in the network by approximately 116 vehicle hours per hour. This may be related to the highly congested state of the network used. To investigate the effect of differing levels of saturation on the results, the passenger car volumes in the intersection network are altered.

Table 1: The traffic characteristics with varying numbers of MCV

MCV (vph)	Density (v/km)	Speed (km/hr)	Travel Time (sec/km)	Delay Time (sec/km)	Stopped Time (sec/v/km)
0	33.6	50.7	93.3	52	21.4
10	33.8	50.3	93.9	53	21.8
30	34.6	48.8	96.5	55	22.3
100	35.0	46.0	101.8	60	24.4

To investigate the effect of MCV on a signalised intersection, a single intersection is used, so that signal coordination and other such factors do not affect the results. As the intersection is initially under saturated, the effects of the MCV on the differing levels of intersection saturation are investigated by increasing the passenger cars flows on the arterial road by 25% and 50%. Figure 1 gives the average vehicle speeds on the network for different levels of passenger car and MCV flows. Adding 100 MCV to the base case reduced the average speed by 2.0km/hr, more than adding 650 extra passenger cars (25%), which decreased the average speed by 1.6 km/hr from the base case. This implies the MCV has a PCE of greater than 6.5 in unsaturated conditions, well in excess of the usual estimates for signalised intersections, which show a maximum of 4.5 [12].

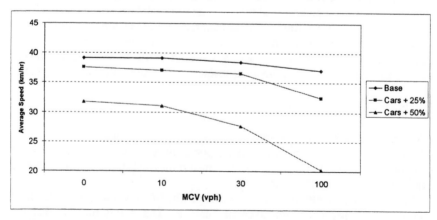

Figure 1: The average vehicle speed varying the passenger vehicle volumes

The effects of the MCV are more pronounced as the network becomes more saturated. The difference in average speed for the additional 100 MCV for the highest level of saturation simulated is 11.5km/hr, which is considerably higher than the 2.0km/hr for the base case. As microsimulation models commonly report the performance of the network in terms of average vehicle speed and average vehicle delay it may be difficult to see the impact of small numbers, for example 30 MCV per hour, of MCV in an undersaturated network. In a saturated network the impact of the same number of vehicle may be more pronounced and thus identifiable in the results reported by the model.

The simulations, however, do imply a high PCE value even at low saturation levels, which could be the result of one of the following:

- The input parameters for the MCV could be incorrect;
- The microsimulation model may not be representing the MCV accurately;
- The values of PCE commonly used underestimate the effect of MCV.

To examine the first of these options, that is the sensitivity of the microsimulation model to the input parameters, a number of the characteristics of the MCV were altered for the intersection. Sensitivity analysis also indicates the importance of obtaining the actual values versus using estimates or default parameters for the microsimulation model. Changing the acceleration of the MCV produced the largest impact on the network, but only at the highest level of MCV simulated, as shown in Figure 2. The values simulated in m/sec^2 were 0.75, 1 and 1.25, in contrast to the acceleration of passenger cars at 2.20 m/sec^2.

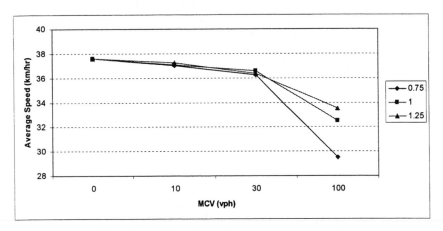

Figure 2: The average speed with varying MCV acceleration

The length of a MCV was increased to 25m (equivalent to a B-Double) and decreased to 12m (a rigid truck) for alternate simulations. Adjusting the length of the MCV, as for the acceleration, only had an effect for the highest level of MCV simulated (100 vph). The average speeds in the network are shown in Figure 3. The normal and maximum deceleration values for MCV were also simulated at ±0.25 m/sec^2, however, these did not produce any significant effect on the performance of the network.

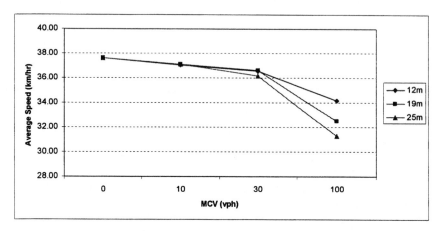

Figure 3: The average speed with varying MCV lengths

The results for the analysis indicate that the model is only sensitive to certain input parameters, and only at higher saturation levels. This indicates that incorrect input parameters are not likely to be the cause of the implied PCE values at low saturation levels. To ensure that the values used are accurate, however, research is being performed in another project at QUT to calibrate the MCV input parameters. To examine whether representation of the MCV and the surrounding traffic network by AIMSUN2 is accurate, different microsimulation models will be used to compare the results for the same networks and input parameters.

Conclusions

There are two main traffic related issues associated with MCV in urban areas, namely: delays that they may cause to other vehicles and safety related impacts. Other considerations of MCV in urban regions include: efficiency; contribution to the national and local economy; and environmental effects.

The degree to which a microsimulation package (AIMSUN2) can be used to model the interaction between MCV and other traffic was assessed in this paper using test data for a section of freeway and for a signalised intersection. These networks were used to investigate the simulation of the effect of the MCV on traffic congestion, however, future research could involve examining the other effects such as environmental and safety.

Preliminary results imply a higher PCE value even at lower saturation levels for an intersection than the values commonly used for MCV. Further research is being conducted to establish the causes of this, including calibrating the input parameters and performing the same network simulations on other microsimulation packages to compare the results.

Acknowledgments

The research reported here forms part of a joint program of research initiated in 2000 under the Memorandum of Understanding between the Queensland Departments of Transport and Main Roads and the Queensland University of Technology. The views expressed in this paper are, however, solely those of the authors.

References

[1] McRobert, J. Greenhouse Emissions and Road Transport. *Research Report ARR 291*, ARRB Transport Research: Vermont South, Australia, 1997.

[2] Bruzsa, L. Initial results of the B-Triple trial in Queensland, *Proceedings of the 5th International Symposium on Heavy Vehicle Weights and Dimensions.* Australian Road Research Board: Melbourne, Australia, pp. 279-302, 1998.

[3] Krammes, R. and Crowley, K. Passenger Car Equivalents for Trucks on Level Freeway Segments. *Transportation Research Record,* **1091**, pp. 10-17, 1987.

[4] Molina, C. Development of Passenger Car Equivalencies for Large Trucks at Signalised Intersections. *ITE Journal,* November, 1987.

[5] Kockelman, K. and Shabih, R. Effect of Light-Duty Trucks on the Capacity of Signalised Intersections. *Journal of Transportation Engineering,* **126(6)**, pp. 506-512, 2000.

[6] Kimber, R., McDonald, M. and Housell, N. Passenger Car Units in Saturation Flows: Concept, Definition, Derivation. *Transportation Research B,* **19(1)**, pp. 39-61, 1985.

[7] Tsao, S. and Chu, S. Adjustment Factors for Heavy Vehicles at Signalised intersections. *Journal of Transportation Engineering,* **121(2)**, pp .150-157, 1995.

[8] Fitzpatrick, K., Middleton, D. and Jasek, D. Countermeasures for Truck Accidents on Urban Freeways: A Review of Experiences. *Transportation Research Record,* **1376**, pp. 27-30, 1992.

[9] Smith, K. Trucks and Road Trauma. *Proceedings of the Transportation 2000 AITPM International Conference,* Australian Institute of Traffic and Management Inc.: Thornleigh, Australia, pp. 221-232, 2000.

[10] Sweatman, P. and Ogden, K. Urban Truck Crashes - What Really Happens. *Road Transport Technology 4,* ed. Winkler, C. University of Michigan Transportation Research Institute: Ann Arbor, pp. 537-541, 1995.

[11] Campbell, J. Using Small Trucks to Circumvent Large Truck Restrictions: Impacts on Truck Emissions and Performance Measures. *Transportation Research A,* **29(6)**, pp. 445-458, 1995.

[12] Lake, M. and Ferreira, L. Towards Quantifying the Impacts of Multi-Combination Vehicles in Urban Traffic. *Physical Infrastructure Centre Research Report 01-05,* School of Civil Engineering, Queensland University of Technology: Brisbane, Australia, 2001.

[13] Benekohal, R. and Zhao, W. Delay-Based Passenger Car Equivalents for Trucks at Signalised Intersections. *Transportation Research A*, **34(6)**, pp. 437-457, 2000.

[14] Fisk, C. Effects of Heavy Traffic on Network Congestion. *Transportation Research B*, **24(5)**, pp. 391-404, 1990.

[15] Mingo, R., Esterlitz, J. and Mingo, B. Accident Rates Of Multiunit Combination Vehicles Derived From Large-Scale Data Bases. *Transportation Research Record,* **1322**, pp. 50-61, 1991.

[16] Gurney, A. Perceptions of the Environmental Impacts of Heavy Vehicles. *Heavy Vehicles and Roads: Technology, Safety and Policy*, eds. Cebon, D. and Mitchell, G. Thomas Telford Services Ltd: London, UK, pp. 25-29, 1992.

A simulation procedure for the assessment of traffic management impacts on urban road safety

A. Nuzzolo & P. Coppola
Department of Civil Engineering, University of Rome "Tor Vergata", Italy

Abstract

Recent statistics and research projects have shown that road accidents are one of the greatest cause of death in Europe. Moreover, almost half of these deaths takes place in urban areas, where the conflicts between different traffic components (i.e. vehicles, pedestrians, cyclists, etc.) are bigger. One of the levels which local authorities can handle to contain the phenomenon is Traffic Management, i.e. the set of all those measures reducing traffic volumes and conflicts among traffic streams, reducing vehicles speed and so on.
Models and simulation procedures have been proposed in the literature to predict the risk and/or the rate of accidents on the elements of a road network. However, very few of them have been calibrated in urban contexts. In this paper, we present a simulation procedure for the assessment of the impacts of traffic management measures on urban road safety. The procedure consists of two main modules: the former aiming at the estimation of traffic flow on links and at junctions, the latter estimating by means of performance functions of urban road safety, the accident frequency on each element of the network given the average daily traffic flows. Specification and calibration results of road safety functions based on data gathered in the urban area of Rome (Italy) are presented. Preliminary applications of the procedure to the case study are discussed.

1 Introduction

The enormous welfare costs related to deaths and injuries in road accidents, have led in the last years to a great number of studies and research projects focusing on road safety. It has been estimated that road accident deaths are the eighth cause of death in the World and could become the third one in the future if any prevention policies will not be undertaken (World Health Organization, 1996).

In 1997 the European Commission has endorsed the program "Promote road safety in the EU: the program 1997-2000" [7] aiming at reducing road accident deaths of 40% within the year 2010. As a consequence, in many European countries road safety programs started up, supported both by local authorities (e.g. [5]) and by the European Commission itself (e.g. [6]).

The results of such researches show that it is not possible to isolate single specific causes of road accidents, but it is rather a combination of factors, namely the complex system "Vehicle-Driver-Environment" (Figure 1), which determine the higher or lower probability of accident on a given element of the network. Therefore, an integrated approach consisting of strategic actions aiming at removing relevant factors is needed to improve road safety in an efficient and effectiveness way.

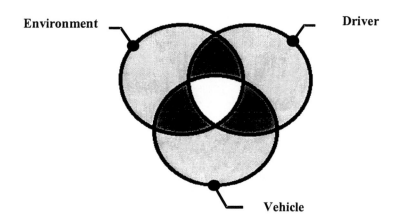

Figure 1: Road accident factors.

It has also emerged that in EU countries (see Table 1), on the average, the 66% of road accidents happens in urban context due to mainly two reasons. On the one hand, on urban roads, conflicts between traffic streams are bigger then on extra-urban roads, and, on the other hand, in urban network, typically, different traffic components (e.g. pedestrians, cyclists, motorists, automobiles, etc.) are promiscuous. Thus, an effective strategic-plan to improve road safety cannot avoid to facing the problem in the urban context. Here, the main factors of road accidents are the "driver" and the "environment" components. These can be handled by means of reducing the exposition of people to the risk of accident, (i.e. reducing the vehicleKm's on the network), by reducing the conflicts among traffic streams and traffic components, promoting educational campaign and so on. In general, four classes of road safety measures (i.e. set of actions of the same typology) can be identified. These can be outlined according to the following topics:

- *Emergency*, including the set of measures aiming at improving the first-aid medical services in case of accident (e.g. first-aid patrols, direct-communication-line to hospitals, etc.);

- *Enforcement*, including the set of actions enforcing the respect of driving rules (e.g. speed limits, priority rules at junctions, etc.) and/or enforcing the control of drivers psycho-physical status (e.g. use of drugs or alcoholics);

- *Education-Encouragement*, including the set of measures aiming at sensitizing people on road safety phenomenon (e.g. educational campaign, radio and television program, etc.

- *Engineering*, including the set of actions aiming at reducing the risk of accident by means of interventions on Traffic Management and on road infrastructures.

Table 1: Urban road accidents in European Union in year 1995 [5].

	Number of urban road accident	Total number of road accidents	%of urban road accident
Austria	23,344	38,956	59.9%
Belgium	27,509	50,744	54.2%
Denmark	5,140	8,373	61.4%
Finland	4,639	7,812	59.4%
France	91,088	132,949	68.5%
Germany	246,617	388,003	63.6%
Greece	Not available	22,800	n.a.
Ireland	4,818	8,117	59.4%
Italy	133,851	182,761	73.2%
Luxembourg	Not available	5,500	n.a.
Holland	6,334	11,437	55.4%
Portugal	Not available	48,300	n.a.
United Kingdom	173,945	237,168	73.3%
Spain	46,369	83,586	55.5%
Sweden	9,015	15,626	57.7%
EU	**772,669**	**1,165,532**	**66.3%**

Traffic Management measures for road safety in urban areas consist of measures oriented both to the demand and to the supply. The former ones aim at improving road safety by diverting the demand on collective modes of transport from individual ones. In this respect, Travel Demand Management (TDM) policies (e.g. parking policies, pedestrian zones, etc.) as well as those policies aiming to improve the quality of collective transport modes, can be outlined as road safety measures "demand-oriented". On the other hand, examples of road safety actions oriented to transportation supply typically are the modification of ways of circulation aiming at reducing conflicts at junctions, the identification of ranking among network links so to identify priority rules, and so on.

Typically the modeling tools for the assessment of the impacts of traffic management policies, with only very few exceptions (see, for instance, the software-package *SafeNET* [10]), do not allow for the explicit simulation of the phenomena related to road accidents, they rather make use of parametric and qualitative analysis. In facts, it is common practice to assume road accidents as proportional to the total number of vehiclesKm's, albeit, in some cases, this could lead to erroneous evaluation.

In the next sections, a simulation procedure for the assessment of the impacts of traffic management measures on urban road safety is presented. This procedure consists of two main modules. The former aims at the estimation of traffic flow on links and at junctions given the transportation network supply and the travel demand. The latter allows to estimating, by mean of performance functions of urban road safety, the frequency of accidents on each element of the network given the traffic flows.

The paper is organized as follows. In section 2 the overall modeling framework is presented. Section 3 reviews the state-of the-art of urban road safety modeling. Section 4 reports on the calibration results of the performance functions estimated for the case study of Rome and presents preliminary results of applications of the simulation procedure to the case study. In Section 5 conclusions are drawn and the perspectives of future research are discussed.

2   The proposed simulation procedure

The simulation procedure proposed for the assessment of the impacts of traffic management measures on urban road safety consists of two main modules: the transportation system module and the road safety module (Figure 2).

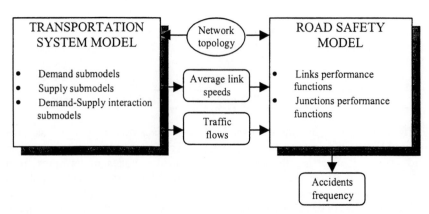

Figure 2: Schematic representation of the simulation procedure proposed.

The transportation system module consists of:

- a demand model simulating drivers travel choices such us trip frequency, destination, mode and path and allowing to estimating the O-D trip-by-car matrix for given reference periods (i.e. the morning peak hour and the average working-day of the year);
- a supply model simulating road network topology and traffic performances at link and junction level;
- a demand-supply interaction model which allow to estimate average daily total (ADT) traffic and the hourly-base peak traffic flows for each link and for each turning movement at junctions.

In the following sections, the focus is on the road safety module. For sake of brevity, the transportation system module [4] will be not described.

Given the ADT traffic flows the road safety module allows to estimating the accident frequency on each link and at each junction of the network. To this aim, performance functions of urban road safety are adopted. These are described in the next section.

3   Performance functions of Urban Road Safety

The performance functions of urban road safety are the main components of the Road Safety module (Figure 2). This section reports on a review and a classification of the Urban-Road-Safety (URS) functions proposed in the literature.

In recent years, different model specifications to estimate the number of accidents in urban networks have been proposed. These, albeit limited in number if compared to the ones relative to extra-urban roads, allow to identifying common elements of classification.

Firstly, urban road safety models can be classified according to the output variables. We can distinguish among *accident-frequency* and *accident-rate* models: the former estimating the average number of accident in a given reference period (typically a year); the latter estimating the average number of accidents per million or per thousand of vehicles. In general, most of the model specifications proposed in the literature are of the first type (i.e. accident-frequency models), however, examples of accident-rate models have been developed in Sweden [2] and in Denmark [3].

Moreover, we can distinguish between *macroscopic* and *microscopic* models. The macroscopic models [1] link the number of road accidents in a given study area, typically on a year base, to urban "macro-variables". These variables can be related, on the one hand, to the transportation system (e.g. the average speed on the road network, the total number of junctions, etc.) and, on the other hand, to population and/or activity system (e.g. the distribution of population over age classes, car availability, etc.). These models can be specified by means of regression analysis but in general result not transferable to contexts different from those for which they have been calibrated.

On the other hand, microscopic models consider explicitly the single elements of the road network, namely links and junctions, and estimate the number of road accidents based on traffic speeds and flows on each element. In doing so, they require a higher degree of complexity in specification and calibration, and a greater computational effort in validation and application. However, they result more easily transferable since they do not depend on attributes, specifics of the study area on which they have been calibrated.

Microscopic models can be specified both for links and junctions. Link models mainly relate the number of road accidents to traffic volume and to average speed on the link [12]. Junction models, on the other hand, express the number of accident as a function of traffic flows on the turning movements at junction. In doing so, different typologies of urban junctions can be considered: priority crossroads and staggered junctions [9]; 4-arms signalized junctions [8]; 3-arms signalized junctions [13]. In some cases, the average speeds on the arms approaching the junction are also considered [10].

Junction models can be further distinguished according to the traffic component considered (e.g. only vehicle flows or vehicle plus pedestrian flows), and according to the level of aggregation of the turning movement at the junction. Following the research studies carried on at the TRL (Transport Research Laboratory, UK) two levels of modeling specification can be identified.

At the first level, traffic flows approaching a given junction from the different arms are aggregated. Accordingly the proposed functional form of accident-frequency is the following one:

$$A = k[Q_V]^\alpha [Q_P]^\beta \tag{1}$$

where:
- A represents the accident frequency at the junction;
- Q_V is the total vehicles flow, given by the sum of the flows on all the traffic streams approaching the junction;
- Q_P is the total pedestrian flow, given by the sum of the pedestrian flows crossing the arms of junction;
- k, α and β are duly calibrated parameters.

Second-level road accident models do not treat the junction as a whole but make distinction among different turning movements. Groups of turning movements, which could be involved in a given *accident-scenario* are identified. For each scenario, i, the accident-frequency, A_i, is estimated by means of a specific model. The global accident-frequency at the junction is finally given by the summation of the accident frequencies over all the groups of turning movements (i.e. the accident-scenario, i) identified:

$$A = \sum_i A_i \tag{2a}$$

$$A_i = k_i [Q_{V,i}]^{\alpha_i} [Q_{P,i}]^{\beta_i} \qquad (2b)$$

An examples of an accident scenario for a 3-arm junction is depicted in Figure 3. Here the "conflicting" turning movements belonging to the given scenario are highlighted using bold lines. A comprehensive set of accident-scenarios and the relative calibrated parameter can be found in [8] and [9] for 4-arms junctions and in [13] for 3-arm junctions.

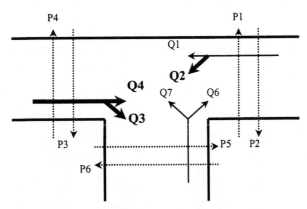

Figure 3:   Turning movements (depicted in bold) belonging to a given *accident-scenario* for a 3-arm junction.

4   The case study of Rome

For the case study of Rome, the observed accident-data available were relative to a temporal interval that resulted to be inadequate to estimating models of the second-level type. Therefore, only first-level accident-models (see equation 1) have been calibrated. The results are reported in Table 2 for four typologies of junctions.

Table 2:   Estimates of the parameters of the first-level URS-functions calibrated for the city of Rome.

Typology of junction	k	α
3-arms not signalized	0,425	0,629
3-arms signalized	0,014	1,496
4-arms not signalized	0,310	0,625
4-arms signalized	0,048	1,350

As it can be seen, the magnitude of the parameter k (see equation 1) for not-signalized junctions is one order higher than for signalized junctions.

Conversely, the power α of the total flow of vehicles, Q_V, results bigger than 1 for signalized junctions and lower than 1 for not-signalized ones. Note that pedestrian flows are not considered in the specification since observed data on such typology flows were not available.

For preliminary applications, two functional specifications have been outlined: the "first-level" (see equation 1) and the "second-level" models (see equations 2) previously introduced. As a matter of facts, the first-level models are those calibrated *ad hoc* for the study area whose parameters are reported in Table 2; the second-level models are those calibrated on data relative to United Kingdom cities, whose functional specification are reported in [8], [9] and [12].

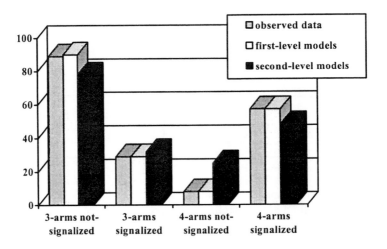

Figure 4: Comparison between observed and estimated number of accidents (case study: V distric of the city of Rome – Year 2000).

The histograms depicted in Figure 4 report a comparison between the observed number of accident in the year 2000 and the estimates provided by the models adopted. As it can be seen, the first-level models reproduce the observed data better than the second-level models. This result was to be expected since the second-level models have not been calibrated on observed data specific of the city of Rome, but in a different urban context (i.e. UK cities).

A second set of application has been carried on in order to evaluate the response of the models to Traffic Management policies. In doing so, the network topology of the study area has been modified. In facts, in order to reduce the number of conflict points at junctions, one-way links have been created and traffic lights have been introduced for some junctions. As consequence, the total number of vehicleKm's does increase. Thus, a traditional parametric analysis, according to which the number of accident on the network is proportional to vehiclesKm's, would estimate an unreliable increase of the accident frequency. Surprisingly, such a result is obtained also using the first-level models: an increase of about 5% of accident frequency is estimated, as reported in Table 3. This is due the very nature of first-level models, which do not take into account of the conflicts between traffic streams at junctions, but consider only total traffic volumes.

Table 3:   Urban Road Safety models response to Traffic Management policies.

	N. of accidents	% changes
Base scenario	183	-
Traffic management policies (first-level URS-models)	192	+4.9%
Traffic management policies (second-level URS-models)	165	-9.8%

As a matter of facts, owing to the changes in network topology introduced, a reduction of accident frequency has to be expected. In facts, this happens when second-level URS-models, which explicitly consider conflicts among traffic streams at junctions, are applied. Indeed, using such models a reduction of about 10% in accident frequency is estimated (see Table 3).

5   Conclusion and further research perspectives

In this paper, a simulation procedure for the assessment of the impacts of Traffic Management measures on urban road safety has been presented. The procedure consists of two main modules: the Transportation System module and the Road Safety module. The Transportation system module consists of demand, supply and demand-supply interaction models, which allows to estimating traffic flows on links and at junctions for the average day of the year. The Road Safety module consists of performance functions of road safety that provides the accident frequency on each element of the network, given the average daily total traffic flows.

Urban Road Safety (URS) models, proposed in the literature, have been reviewed and some classification criteria have been introduced. According to such criteria, distinction is made between "first-level" models, which treat the traffic flows at junctions as a whole, and "second-level" models, which explicitly consider conflicts among traffic streams at junctions.

The calibration results of first-level accident models for four typologies of junctions, based on data gathered in the fifth district of the city of Rome, have been presented.

Accident estimates using the calibrated "first-level" models match the observed data better than the "second-level ones which have been simply transferred from UK cities contexts for which they have been originally calibrated. An analysis of the response of such models with respect to Traffic Management measures (e.g. modification of network topology, introduction of priority rules, modification of the traffic light setting at junctions, etc.) has then been carried on. Preliminary results show that "first-level" URS-models appear to be inadequate to evaluating the impact of Traffic Management measures on accidents frequency, since they do not take into account of traffic streams conflicts at junctions. On the other hand, "second-level" models give reasonable response with respect to Traffic Management policies: a decrease of about 10% of the frequency of accidents with respect to the Traffic Management measures introduces, has been estimated. An improvement of the "second-level" models for the case study of Rome constitutes, therefore, the core of further work.

6   Acknowledgments

The authors wish to thank Stefano Giovenali and Roberto Gigli (S.T.A. - Rome) for having allowed the access to the accidents data by means of which the models presented have been calibrated.

7   References

[1] Baruya A. and D. J. Finch. Investigating of traffic speeds and accidents on urban roads. Proceedings of the 22th European Transport Forum (Seminar J), 1994.

[2] Brude U.,J. Larsson & K. Hedman. Design of major urban junction accident prediction model and empirical comparisons. VTI EC Research 3, 1998

[3] Brude U., K. Hedman, J. Larsson & L. Thuresson. Design of major urban junction comprehensive report. VTI EC Research 2, 1998

[4] Cascetta E., A. Nuzzolo and P. Coppola. A system of mathematical models for the simulation of land-use and transport interactions. In 6th *Urban Transport* Brebbia C. and Sucharov L. Eds., WIT Press, 2000.

[5] Cascetta E., P. Giannattasio, A. Montella and R. Polidoro. Un approccio integrato per il miglioramento della sicurezza stradale. Italian National Research Council, CNR-PFT2, Rome (Italy) 1999.

[6] Directorate General for Transport of the European Union (EU-DG VII). The DUMAS project research report. 2000.

[7] Directorate General for Transport of the European Union (EU-DG VII). Promote road safety in the EU: the program 1997-2000. Com. 131, 1997.

[8] Hall R.D. Accident at four-arm single carriageway urban traffic signals. TRRL Contractor Report 65, 1986.

[9] Layfield R.E, I. Summersgill, R.D. Hall and K. Chatterjee. Accident at urban priority crossroads and staggered junctions. TRL Report 185, 1996.

[10] *SafeNET* User Guide. Transport Research Laboratory Application Guide 34, TRL, Crowthorne, 1999.

[11] Stark D.C. Relating speed to accident risk at priority junctions. Proceedings of the 22th European Transport Forum (Seminar J), 1994.

[12] Summersgill I. and Layfield R.E. Non-junctions accidents on urban single-carriage-way roads. TRL Report 183, 1996.

[13] Taylor M. C., R.D. Hall and K. Chatterjee. Accidents at 3-arms traffic signals on urban single-carriageway roads. TRL Report 135, 1996.

Traffic flow in dense urban areas by continuum modelling

F.G. Benitez & L.M. Romero
Transportation Engineering
School of Engineering, University of Sevilla, Spain

Abstract

This paper considers a new approach for modelling the traffic flow in dense urban areas by using a mathematical continuum model, which needs information data from a very limited number of points from the network. The purpose of this communication is to provide a mathematical foundation for the study of this approach. This methodology can speed up the computation of relevant values concerning the time evolution of traffic on a city network.

1 Introduction

The modelling of traffic systems is, at present, mainly based on discretizing the region to be analyzed by a discrete network. This approach might be valid and convenient for the study of not very extensive regions and/or not very road-dense zones. In case the real road and street network are complex (the number of roads is large enough, the density of roads impedes a proper and reliable modelling, the origins and destinations are difficult to be precisely pointed out, etc.) the network theory method would not be an adequate tool. The errors made in the modelling of the network itself (roads not considered, missing interconnection, crossings not well defined, etc.) will introduce a savage uncertainty on the results obtained by solving problems based on this model. Moreover, the more precise the model is defined the larger its size becomes, making the algorithms used for the solution impractical from a computational point of view. In these cases it might be more convenient to model the region to be studied under a continuum representation.

In the last 25 years several researchers have proposed different methods for dealing with the traffic distribution in dense urban regions. We should acknowledge the works by Vaughan [1] and Newell [2]. More recently Yang,

Yagar and Iida [3] published a work on the solution of the traffic assignment problem in a congested city composed of many trip origins and a single trip destination by using the finite element method (FEM).

In this paper we advance in this direction substituting the finite element method by the boundary element method (BEM), which presents some very well known advantages usually emphasized in text books. The purpose here is to develop a practical method to solve problems of continuum modelling in traffic networks, Benitez [4], ready to be implemented for obtaining the solution of practical scenarios.

2 Basic concepts on traffic flow

The first investigators who formulated the equation for traffic flow, from a macroscopic continuum modelling point of view were Lighthill and Whitham [5]. The only equation formulated in this model is that of continuity in a onedimensional space:

$$\frac{\partial K(x,t)}{\partial t} + \frac{\partial Q(x,t)}{\partial x} = \Theta(x,t), \tag{1}$$

which expresses the balance between the number of vehicle's growth rate (traffic density or concentration K) in a road section, the net flow ($Q = K \cdot V$ - density times speed -) across the section and a trip generation function (Θ). In this model, the *Simple Continuum Model*, the mean space speed is supposed to be dependent on traffic density.

The above expression can be extended to two-dimensional regions based on the concepts defined in the works of Dafermos [6] and Newell [7] on dense urban street grids. In traffic theory we named dense grids to a grid of roads and streets packed enough to assume that the spacing between them and the length of any one of them are small compared to the whole region analyzed. Such a grid can be approximated by a continuous space with appropriate characteristics. On such a continuous space the orientation of roads will depend on the zone being observed. Thus, if a zone has roads in almost any orientation, this zone will be considered an isotropic-road area, on the other hand if a zone has roads orientated in almost only two directions this is to be assumed an orthotropic-road zone. In general, any spatial region can be divided, according to the orientation of the roads and streets, into different zones, with isotropic, orthotropic or anisotropic geometric characteristics.

In an isotropic-road zone $\Re \in E^2$ the traffic flow of a single-commodity, only one pair O/D, would satisfy the conservation equation:

$$\frac{\partial \phi(\mathbf{x},t)}{\partial t} + \nabla \cdot \mathbf{f}(\mathbf{x},t) = \rho(\mathbf{x},t), \tag{2}$$

where $\mathbf{x} = (x, y)$, t the time coordinate and $\mathbf{f}(\mathbf{x}, t)$ stands for the traffic flow (vehicles per unit of time and unit of length) vector function (f_x, f_y), $\boldsymbol{\rho}(\mathbf{x}, t)$ the generating function ($\boldsymbol{\rho}(\mathbf{x}, t)$ will be positive if flow is originated at $\mathbf{x}$ or negative when it is absorbed), and $\phi(\mathbf{x}, t)$ the traffic density or concentration (per unit of surface area).

This model was first postulated by Michalopoulos, Beskos and Yamauchi [8] for the particular case of describing flow along two or more homodirectional lanes.

By presuming that the traffic flow is not only function of velocity and density but function also of density gradient, one can write (Benitez [4]):

$$\mathbf{f}(\mathbf{x}, t) = -\mu \nabla \phi(\mathbf{x}, t) + \mathbf{u}(\mathbf{x}, t) \phi(\mathbf{x}, t), \tag{3}$$

where $\mathbf{u}(\mathbf{x}, t) = \left[u_x, u_y \right]$.

Assumption (3) neither violates the behaviour or forces the dependance of traffic flow on density and speed in accordance to the physical problem, as it is expected that the flow decreases/increases not only as a result of a decreasing/increasing of speed and/or density but also as due to an increasing/decreasing in the density space gradient; this hypothesis is also in accordance to that proposed by Whitham [9]. The magnitude of the variation of traffic flow related to density gradient is defined in the model by the scalar parameter μ, which depends of all usual factors present in urban traffic (city planning, road design, weather conditions, drivers behaviour, etc).

3 Formulation of one-commodity two-dimensional flow by boundary integral equations

Substituting (3) into (2), the following transient equation is obtained:

$$\frac{\partial \phi(\mathbf{x}, t)}{\partial t} - \mu \nabla^2 \phi(\mathbf{x}, t) + \nabla \cdot \left[\mathbf{u}(\mathbf{x}, t) \phi(\mathbf{x}, t) \right] = \boldsymbol{\rho}(\mathbf{x}, t). \tag{4}$$

As the velocity $\mathbf{u}$ varies in space, assuming that this variation is small in the neighbourhood of an equilibrium speed, we can write:

$$\mathbf{u}(\mathbf{x}, t) = \bar{\mathbf{u}}(t) + \tilde{\mathbf{u}}(\mathbf{x}, t), \quad \nabla \cdot \bar{\mathbf{u}} = 0 \tag{5}$$

Substituting (5) into (4), and applying a weighted residual technique to the above equation over the whole region $\Re$, using as weighting function the fundamental solution of the steady-state equation:

$$\mu \nabla^2 \psi(\mathbf{x}, \xi, t) + \bar{\mathbf{u}}(t) \cdot \nabla \psi(\mathbf{x}, t) = -\delta(\xi), \tag{6}$$

and by integrating the following expression is obtained:

$$\phi(\xi,t) + \mu \int_{\partial\Re} \left[\phi(\mathbf{x},t) \frac{\partial \psi(\mathbf{x},\xi,t)}{\partial \mathbf{n}} - \psi(\mathbf{x},\xi,t) \cdot \frac{\partial \phi(\mathbf{x},t)}{\partial \mathbf{n}} \right] d\Gamma +$$

$$+ \int_{\partial\Re} \phi(\mathbf{x},t) \psi(\mathbf{x},\xi,t) \cdot \bar{\mathbf{u}}_n(t) d\Gamma = \tag{7}$$

$$= \int_{\Re} \left[\frac{\partial \phi(\mathbf{x},t)}{\partial t} - \rho(\mathbf{x},t) + \nabla \cdot \left[\bar{\mathbf{u}}(\mathbf{x},t)\phi(\mathbf{x},t) \right] \right] \psi(\mathbf{x},\xi,t) d\Re$$

where $\bar{\mathbf{u}}_n(t) = \bar{\mathbf{u}}(t) \cdot \mathbf{n}$, being $\mathbf{n}$ the unit outward normal vector to $\partial\Re$, being $\partial\Re$ the boundary of $\Re$.

Integral equation (7) is valid for any point within the domain ($\xi \in \Re$) and on the boundary ($\xi \in \partial\Re$), where the integrals are defined in the sense of Cauchy Principal Values and $c(\xi)$ is given by $\frac{\omega}{2\pi}$, being ω the internal angle at point ξ in radians. It is noteworthy that all integrals, except the one on the right hand side of (7) are boundary integrals. If the domain integral is transformed into boundary integrals, the numerical evaluation of preceding equation is facilitated. In what follows this transformation is undertaken.

4 Dual reciprocity transform

To obtain a boundary integral, corresponding to the domain integral of the kernel terms, in (7), regarding the partial derivative of density $\phi(\mathbf{x},t)$ respect to time, the generating function $\rho(\mathbf{x},t)$ and the divergence term $\nabla \cdot \left[\bar{\mathbf{u}}(\mathbf{x},t)\phi(\mathbf{x},t) \right]$, the following approximations are taken:

$$\frac{\partial \phi(\mathbf{x},t)}{\partial t} = \sum_{k=1}^{M_1} \alpha_k(t) f_k(\mathbf{x}), \ \rho(\mathbf{x},t) = \sum_{k=1}^{M_2} \beta_k(t) r_k(\mathbf{x}), \ \nabla \cdot \left[\bar{\mathbf{u}}(\mathbf{x},t)\phi(\mathbf{x},t) \right] = \sum_{k=1}^{M_3} \lambda_k(t) s_k(\mathbf{x}), \tag{8}$$

where the functions $f_k(\mathbf{x}), r_k(\mathbf{x}), s_k(\mathbf{x})$ are particular solutions of the equation :

$$\mu\nabla^2(\zeta_k, \vartheta_k, \lambda_k)(\mathbf{x},t) - \bar{\mathbf{u}}(t) \cdot \nabla(\zeta_k, \vartheta_k, \lambda_k)(\mathbf{x},t) = (f_k, r_k, s_k)(\mathbf{x}). \tag{9}$$

M_1, M_2 and M_3 are the number of interpolating points used for defining the DRM transforms of the cited functions.

Coefficients α, β, λ are obtained by:

$$\{\alpha\} = \left[F^{-1} \right] \left\{ \frac{\partial \phi(\mathbf{x},t)}{\partial t} \right\}, \ \{\beta\} = \left[R^{-1} \right] \{\rho\}, \ \{\lambda\} = \left[S^{-1} \right] \{\nabla \cdot [\bar{\mathbf{u}}\phi]\}. \tag{10}$$

5 Boundary and internal points integral equation

Under the DRM assumptions, for the numerical solution of expression (7), the boundary $\partial\Re$ is replaced by a complete set of patches, the so called *boundary elements*. The boundary data is then interpolated over each boundary element. Therefore, the integrals over the boundary are approximated by a summation of integrals over individual boundary elements, abstracted to the following simple expression:

$$w(\xi,t) = \int_{\partial\Re} f(\mathbf{x},t)\kappa(\mathbf{x},\xi,t)d\Gamma = \sum_{e=1}^{NE} \int_{\partial\Re_e} f(\mathbf{x},t)\kappa(\mathbf{x},\xi,t)d\Gamma = \sum_{e=1}^{NE} w_e(\xi,t), \quad (11)$$

where $\mathbf{x} \in \partial\Re_e \subset \partial\Re$ and NE stands for the number of elements into which the contour is discretized.

The variation of the generic function $f(\mathbf{x},t)$ within each element is approximated by interpolating from the values of this function at certain element nodes. For a generic case of an element defined by N_e nodes, any function $f(\mathbf{x},t)$ defined on it will be approximated by:

$$f(\mathbf{x},t) = \sum_{n=1}^{N_e} \Phi^n(\mathbf{x})f^n(t), \quad (12)$$

where $\Phi(\mathbf{x})$ are interpolation functions.

Following the above philosophy, eqn (7) can be discretized, for a given boundary node i $(\xi = x_i)$. If the boundary elements in which the contour is discretized include N nodes, a collocation technique of equation (7) applied to these nodes will yield a system of N equations of the form:

$$[\mathbf{H}]\cdot\{\phi\} - [\mathbf{G}]\cdot\{\mathbf{q}\} =$$

$$\sum_{k=1}^{M_1}\alpha_k(t)\cdot\left([\mathbf{H}]\cdot\{\zeta_k\} - [\mathbf{G}]\cdot\left\{\frac{\partial\zeta_k}{\partial\mathbf{n}}\right\}\right) -$$

$$\sum_{k=1}^{M_2}\beta_k(t)\cdot\left([\mathbf{H}]\cdot\{\vartheta_k\} - [\mathbf{G}]\cdot\left\{\frac{\partial\vartheta_k}{\partial\mathbf{n}}\right\}\right) + \quad (13)$$

$$\sum_{k=1}^{M_3}\lambda_k(t)\cdot\left([\mathbf{H}]\cdot\{\gamma_k\} - [\mathbf{G}]\cdot\left\{\frac{\partial\gamma_k}{\partial\mathbf{n}}\right\}\right),$$

and where $[\mathbf{H}]$ and $[\mathbf{G}]$ are $N\times N$ matrices and $\{\phi\}, \left\{\mathbf{q} \equiv \dfrac{\partial\phi(\mathbf{x},t)}{\partial\mathbf{n}}\right\}$, $\{\zeta_k\}, \{\vartheta_k\}, \{\gamma_k\}, \left\{\dfrac{\partial\zeta_k}{\partial\mathbf{n}}\right\}, \left\{\dfrac{\partial\vartheta_k}{\partial\mathbf{n}}\right\}, \left\{\dfrac{\partial\gamma_k}{\partial\mathbf{n}}\right\}$ are vectors of length N.

Matrices $[\mathbf{H}]$ and $[\mathbf{G}]$ are evaluated numerically using a Gaussian integration.

By incorporating eqns (10), expresión (13) yields

$$[\mathbf{B}]\cdot\left\{\frac{\partial\phi(\mathbf{x},t)}{\partial t}\right\}+[\mathbf{H}]\cdot\{\phi\}-[\mathbf{G}]\cdot\{\mathbf{q}\}+[\mathbf{Z}]\cdot\{\nabla\cdot[\tilde{\mathbf{u}}\phi]\}=\{\mathbf{d}\}. \qquad (14)$$

In order to solve the preceding equation system, any standard direct time-integration scheme can be used to obtain a solution. A valid scheme would use a linear approximation for the variation of ϕ and q between two consecutive time steps m and $m+1$:

$$\{\phi\}=\left(1-\theta_{\phi}\right)\{\phi\}^{m}+\theta_{\phi}\{\phi\}^{m+1},$$

$$\{\mathbf{q}\}=\left(1-\theta_{q}\right)\{\mathbf{q}\}^{m}+\theta_{q}\{\mathbf{q}\}^{m+1},$$

$$\{\nabla\cdot[\tilde{\mathbf{u}}\phi]\}=\left(1-\theta_{Div}\right)\{\nabla\cdot[\tilde{\mathbf{u}}\phi]\}^{m}+\theta_{Div}\{\nabla\cdot[\tilde{\mathbf{u}}\phi]\}^{m+1}, \qquad (15)$$

$$\left\{\frac{\partial\phi(\mathbf{x},t)}{\partial t}\right\}=\frac{\{\phi\}^{m+1}-\{\phi\}^{m}}{\Delta t},$$

where θ_{ϕ}, θ_{q} and θ_{Div} are parameters of the approximation. Substituting (15) into (14), the following expression is obtained:

$$\left[\hat{\mathbf{H}}\right]\cdot\{\phi\}^{m+1}-\left[\hat{\mathbf{G}}\right]\cdot\{\mathbf{q}\}^{m+1}+\left[\hat{\mathbf{Z}}\right]\cdot\{\nabla\cdot[\tilde{\mathbf{u}}\phi]\}^{m+1}=\{\hat{\mathbf{d}}\}. \qquad (16)$$

The right hand side of the above expression is always known, since it involves values that have been calculated previously or which have been specified as initial conditions. From the boundary conditions at time $(m+1)\Delta t$, the values of ϕ are prescribed over part of the contour $\partial\mathfrak{R}_{\phi}$ where q are unknown, along the rest of the contour $\partial\mathfrak{R}_{q}$ occurs the opposite. The values of $\nabla\cdot[\tilde{\mathbf{u}}\phi]$ are unknown on the boundary, therefore there are $2\times N$ unknowns in the equation system (16), defined by only N equations.

6 Density gradient and laplacian integral equation

Differentiating (7), with respect to the coordinates of the source point ξ, transforming the domain integrals into boundary integrals, and using a numerical approximation under the same scheme developed in 4, we get:

$$\nabla \phi_i = -\left[\mathbf{D}_i\right]^{-1} \cdot \{\nabla \mathbf{h}_i\}^T \cdot \{\phi\} + \left[\mathbf{D}_i\right]^{-1} \cdot \{\nabla \mathbf{g}_i\}^T \cdot \{\mathbf{q}\} + \left[\mathbf{D}_i\right]^{-1} \cdot \{\nabla \mathbf{b}_i\}^T \cdot \left\{\frac{\partial \phi}{\partial t}\right\} - \left[\mathbf{D}_i\right]^{-1} \cdot \{\nabla \mathbf{Z}_i\}^T \cdot \{\nabla \cdot [\tilde{\mathbf{u}} \phi]\} + \left[\mathbf{D}_i\right]^{-1} \cdot \nabla d_i,$$ (17)

valid for $\xi \in \Re$.

Expression (17) provides the values of $\nabla \phi$ at any time for any domain or boundary point from the known values of densities, derivative of densities respect to normal and time derivative of densities at the boundary.

Differentiating (7) twice, with respect to the coordinates of the source point ξ, and following the same steps than for inferring the gradient integral equation, the following expression is obtained:

$$\mathbf{e}_i \nabla \phi_i = -\{\nabla^2 \mathbf{h}_i\}^T \cdot \{\phi\} + \{\nabla^2 \mathbf{g}_i\}^T \cdot \{\mathbf{q}\} + \{\nabla^2 \mathbf{b}_i\}^T \cdot \left\{\frac{\partial \phi}{\partial t}\right\} + \nabla^2 z_i \cdot \{\nabla \cdot [\tilde{\mathbf{u}} \phi]\} + \nabla^2 d_i,$$ (18)

valid for $\xi \in \Re$.

Multiplying the gradient equation (17) by the vector $\mathbf{e}_i$, equating to eqn.(18), grouping terms, and introducing the scheme defined in (15) the following system of equations is reached:

$$\left[\hat{\mathbf{H}}\right] \cdot \{\phi\}^{m+1} - \left[\hat{\mathbf{G}}\right] \cdot \{\mathbf{q}\}^{m+1} + \left[\hat{\mathbf{Z}}\right] \cdot \{\nabla \cdot [\tilde{\mathbf{u}} \phi]\}^{m+1} = \{\hat{\mathbf{d}}\}.$$ (19)

The above expression provides a new relationship between boundary densities ϕ and flows q with vector $\{\nabla \cdot [\tilde{\mathbf{u}} \phi]\}$. It defines a system of N equations with $2 \times N$ unknowns, which can be solved simultaneously with the system defined by (16).

The right hand side of the above expression is always known, since it involves values that have been calculated previously or which have been specified as initial conditions. From the boundary conditions at time $(m+1)\Delta t$, the values of ϕ are prescribed over part of the contour $\partial \Re_\phi$ where q are unknown, along the rest of the contour $\partial \Re_q$ occurs the opposite.

Introducing the boundary conditions into (19) and arranging the system by moving known terms to the right hand side, we can write:

$$[\mathbf{A}] \cdot \{\mathbf{x}\} = \{\mathbf{y}\},$$ (20)

where $\{\mathbf{x}\}$ is a vector of unknown boundary values of ϕ and q, and $\{\mathbf{y}\}$ is a load vector. This system can be solved by using a standard direct procedure like Gauss elimination.

7 Numerical algorithm

The following steps constitute the algorithm to be observed in order to solve the boundary of a continuum region. The results provided by this scheme are *density*, *flow* and *speed* for all boundary nodes and internal points. A general scheme may be stated as next:

Step 1.   General definition of the problem to be solved.

   Substep 1.1 Define the geometry of the discretized boundary, comprising N nodes and NE parabolic elements.

   Substep 1.2   Define internal points coordinates.

   Substep 1.3   Define time parameters:

   (i)   Time-integration parameters: θ_ϕ, θ_q and θ_{Div}

   (ii)   Time-step size: Δt

   (iii)   Time-interval: (t_0, t_∞) with $t_m = t_0 + m\Delta t$

Step 2.   Define the initial time step $m = 0$.

Step 3.   Define the data available for the ongoing time step.

   Substep 3.1 Data corresponding to the boundary conditions, concerning densities, of the region analyzed:

   (i)   Boundary conditions of Dirichlet type: $\{\phi\}^m$

   (ii)   Boundary conditions of Neumann type: $\{q\}^m$

   (iii)   Boundary conditions of Robbins type: $\{\phi\}^m$ on $\partial\Re_\phi$ and $\{q\}^m$ on $\partial\Re_q$

   Substep 3.2   Data corresponding to the boundary conditions, concerning either flow or speed, of the region analyzed:

   (i)   Flows of, all or some, boundary nodes: $\{f\}^m$ on $\partial\Re_f$.

   (ii)   Speeds of, all or some, boundary nodes: $\{u\}^m$ on $\partial\Re_u$.

   Substep 3.3 Data corresponding to the domain and boundary conditions, concerning trip generation/attraction values, of the region analyzed: $\{\rho\}^m$.

   Substep 3.4 Data corresponding to the variation with respect to time of density for all boundary nodes: $\{\dot{\phi}\}^m$.

Step 4. Define estimate values of $\bar{u}$ for the time step m: $\bar{u}^m$. An initial estimate of $\bar{u}^m$ might be obtained averaging the speed u from the boundary nodes wherein this data is known:

(i) $\bar{u}^m \equiv \bar{u}(t^m) = E\left[u(x,t^m)\right]$ $x \in \partial\mathfrak{R}_u$, where $E[\ ]$ stands for the statistical mean value.

Step 5. Solve system (16), (19) obtaining the unknowns terms of $\{\phi\}^m$ or/and $\{q\}^m$ and $\{\nabla \cdot [\bar{u}\phi]\}^m$ not available from the boundary data.

Step 6. Using equation (13), particularized for internal points, determine $\phi(x,t^m)$ for all internal points of interest.

Step 7. From expression (17) determine the density gradient $\nabla\phi(x,t^m)$ for all boundary nodes and for all internal points of interest.

Step 8. Using equation (3) determine the speed u, corresponding to the active time step m, for all boundary nodes and for all internal points of interest wherein this data is unknown:

(i) $\bar{u}^m(x,t^m) = \dfrac{1}{\phi(x,t^m)}\left(f(x,t) + \mu\nabla\phi(x,t^m)\right).$

Step 9. Re-estimate the equilibrium speed by averaging the speed u of all boundary nodes and internal points:

$\bar{u}^m = \bar{u}(t^m) = E\left[u(x,t)\right]$ $x \in \partial\mathfrak{R} \cup \mathfrak{R}$.

Step 10. Compare $\bar{u}^m$ obtained from the boundary nodes and internal points with the initial estimation:

Substep 10.1 If $\bar{u}\big|_{\partial\mathfrak{R}\cup\mathfrak{R}}$ differs appreciably from $\bar{u}\big|_{\partial\mathfrak{R}_u}$, re-estimate the equilibrium speed by averaging the speed u of all boundary nodes and internal points and go to *Step 4*.

Substep 10.2 If $\bar{u}\big|_{\partial\mathfrak{R}\cup\mathfrak{R}}$ does not differ appreciably from $\bar{u}\big|_{\partial\mathfrak{R}_u}$, go to *Step 10*.

Step 11. Define a new time step $m \equiv m+1$ and go to *Step 2*, till $t_m \geq t_\infty$.

Several other algorithms, based on the above one affected by minor modifications, can be formalized. The efficiency of them depend on factors such as the way the code is written, the machine-dependent characteristics used for implementing it, etcetera, as it is usual in computer numerical analysis.

8 Conclusions

On the basis of the model that have been developed a completely new approach based on the technique of Dual Reciprocity Boundary Element Method (Partridge et al. [10]) for the analysis of two-dimensional traffic flow has been presented.

The architecture presented is only valid for problems with only one pair origin-destination.

Certainly, this approach sacrifices a great deal of realism in particular in the use of some assumptions, i.e. approach of some field functions by series of term products of separable functions of geometry and time. However, although this model contains several hypotheses that might be under a ban, the methodology presented outlines a new horizon which may lead to a better handling of dense networks. Besides, we are conscious that further research is needed to resolve some outstanding issues. First, empirical studies of the various approaches. Second, further modelling work is required to investigate the robustness of the method.

References

[1] Vaughan, R. *Urban Spatial Traffic Patterns*. Pion Ltd., London, 1987.

[2] Newell, G. F. *Traffic Flow in Transportation Network*. MIT Press, Cambridge, Ma, USA, 1980.

[3] Yang, H., Yagar, S. & Iida, Y. Traffic assignment in a congested discrete/continuous transportation system. *Transportation Research*, 28B, 161-174, 1994.

[4] Benitez, F.G. Traffic flow in dense networks. *World Transport Research. Modelling Transport Systems*. (Ed. D. Hensher, J. King, T. Oum), Pergamon, 153-166, 1996.

[5] Lighthill, M. J. & Whitham, G. B. On kinematic waves: A theory of traffic flow on long crowded roads. *Proceedings of the Royal Society*, Series A, 229, 317-345, 1955.

[6] Dafermos, S.C. Continuum modeling of transportation networks. *Transportation Research*, 14B, 295-301, 1980.

[7] Newell, G. F. Flow around distortions in a dense rectangular grid road network - I. Theory. *Transportation and Traffic Theory* (Ed. C. F. Daganzo), Elsevier, 1-15,1993.

[8] Michalopoulos, P. G., Beskos, D. E. & Yamauchi, Y. Multilane traffic flow dynamics: some macroscopic considerations. *Transportation Research*, 18B, 377-395, 1984.

[9] Whitham, G.B. *Linear and Nonlinear Waves*. Wiley-Interscience, USA, 1974.

[10] Patridge, P.W., Brebbia, C.A. & Wrobel, L.C. The Dual Reciprocity Boundary Element Method. Computational Mechanics Publications, Southampton, U.K, 1992.

A qualitative decision-making tool for transport planners, assessing urban pollution due to traffic

M.Mavroulidou, S.J.Hughes & E.E.Hellawell
School of Engineering, University of Surrey, UK

Abstract

A qualitative approach is presented, which can be used as a preliminary decision tool for assessing air quality related to traffic. It is based on the interaction matrix method, originally developed for rock engineering systems. The method incorporates a total systems approach, which identifies and quantifies interactions between the various parameters involved in a particular system.

The paper demonstrates how the methodology could be applied to urban air quality related to traffic, using an interaction matrix with a reduced number of variables. Possible ways of obtaining weighting factors for the variables are discussed. The subsequent necessary stages for the implementation of the technique (i.e. the computer coding of the interaction matrix, and the use of a Geographic Information System (GIS) to produce vulnerability maps) are also explained.

The technique shows promise for the development of a simple, versatile and fast qualitative decision tool, which can be used by transport planners to assess current air quality, and to perform easily and fast what-if-scenarios for future transport planning.

1 Introduction

Growing concerns about health and environmental issues are leading to new ideas for traffic routes, which would not only optimise throughput, but which would also minimise air pollution. The design of such routes requires an understanding of how airborne pollutants are dispersed around roads, cities and the surrounding environment as well as an awareness of the influence of local factors such as topography, meteorological conditions and chemical interactions between the pollutants and the atmosphere. A description of such phenomena, related to a wide range of disciplines, is extremely complex. While techniques modelling separate mechanisms become gradually more sophisticated, a complete understanding of air quality related problems requires a synthesis of information resulting from all the different specialities.

Due to the complexity, uncertainties and costs involved in a thorough modeling of pollutant dispersion in urban areas, local authorities and transport and urban planners are growingly asking for easy-to-use, versatile qualitative tools, to assess existing routes, and, more importantly, to assist in the initial planning stages of future developments.

This paper presents a methodology, which can be used to develop simple and versatile preliminary decision tools for assessing air quality related to traffic. It is based on a total systems approach, initially developed for rock engineering applications (Hudson and Harrison [1], Mazzoccola and Hudson [2]).

The technique identifies the main variables involved in a particular system and quantifies their interactions through an interaction matrix. In such a matrix, the principal variables involved in the system being analysed (in our case, the urban system, with reference to traffic-induced air quality) are presented as the leading diagonals of the matrix, from which the cumulative effect of all the interactions on a given parameter can be determined. The interaction of variable A on variable B and of variable B on variable A (which constitute the off-diagonal boxes of the matrix) are then evaluated and assigned a value (see Figure 1).

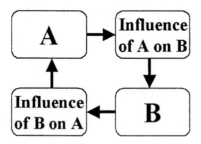

Figure 1: Schematic representation of a two-dimensional interaction matrix

The difficulty arises in determining a numerical value of the influence of A on B and vice versa. This is usually achieved using constant values based on engineering judgment. In this study, however, semi-empirical relationships were used, where possible, to determine the off-diagonal elements in the matrix. Moreover, the matrix is now formulated computationally, so that the values of the interaction weightings for different conditions can be obtained automatically and then introduced in a Geographic Information System (GIS) to express the results spatially (in order to create vulnerability maps). Anticipated advantages of the methodology thus implemented include an increased versatility and the ability to provide visual assessments of vulnerability at greatly reduced computing times and complexity.

2 Methodology

The first stage in the development of the method consists in the selection of the key variables involved in a system. For demonstration purposes, five key variables influencing urban air quality were selected and placed on the leading diagonal of a 5x5 matrix. An interaction matrix was developed to assess qualitatively the interaction between these five key variables influencing urban air quality when air quality is poor. The matrix that was thus obtained (Table 1) accounts for 20 possible interactions between the variables (subsequently, the matrix can obviously be extended to include many more factors associated with air quality). The variable constituting the focus of the study was set as the last (i.e. in our case, fifth) element of the leading diagonal of the matrix. Note that the matrix was constructed to account for air quality with respect to a primary pollutant (CO in this case). Moreover, a static urban system was assumed.

Table 1: An example interaction matrix for urban air quality

Emissions from Traffic	0	0	0	-0.375
0 (for this wind range)	Wind speed	-0.5	0	-0.7
0	-1.41	Atmospheric Stability	0	-0.43
0	-0.31	0 (based on Pasquill-Briggs stability categorisation, initial state F)	Roughness	0.78
0 (for a static system)	0	0	0	Air Quality

To quantify the interactions between variables, the following semi-empirical relationships were used:

a)   For the last column of the interaction matrix, related to the variable 'air quality', a Gaussian line source equation was assumed to provide an acceptable model for all interactions. The equation is expressed as:

$$C(x, y, z) = \sqrt{\frac{2}{\pi}} \frac{Q}{U\sigma_z} \exp\left(-\frac{z^2}{2\sigma_z^2}\right) \tag{1}$$

where Q is the emission rate per unit length, U the wind speed at the effective emission level, z the receptor height and σ_z the vertical dispersion parameter. Note that Eqn (1) assumes a wind normal to the source. The fact of not accounting for the effect of wind direction is not very significant here, since an urban scale is considered (the roads in an urban scale are at random directions with respect to the that of the wind).

The values of σ_z are calculated from Pasquill-Briggs relationships (Briggs [3]) for urban and rural conditions respectively. An additional turbulence term is assumed to account for initial dilution due to car-induced turbulence.

The wind speed U at the effective emission level (assumed to be 2 m) is calculated by a power law relationship, namely:

$$U(z_e) = U_{10}\left(\frac{z_e}{10}\right)^p \tag{2}$$

in which z_e is the emission level, $U(z_e)$ and U_{10} are the wind at emission level and at 10m respectively; the parameter p varies as a function of atmospheric stability and roughness length z_0 according to relationships provided by Irwin [4].

b) The non-zero interactions in column 2 (i.e. the effects of the stability and roughness on the wind speed at emission level) are calculated according to equation 2.

c) The non-zero interactions in column 3 (i.e. the effects of the wind and roughness on atmospheric stability) are calculated according to Pasquill's tables, relating wind speed values to atmospheric stability classes (Pasquill and Smith [5]).

d) The rest of the parameter interactions (i.e. where empirical expressions were not available/known) were given values based on engineering judgement (e.g. the influence of the wind on the emissions).

The above-mentioned relationships were used to calculate the value of each interaction, i.e. the slope of the curve showing the variation in the values of each variable for a step variation in the values of the other variables (changing one at a time). Note that the resulting variation in the variable values was normalised with respect to the maximum expected value of each variable within the whole system (or with respect to the difference between the maximum and the minimum expected values, where the latter value was non-zero). Coded in this way, this particular interaction matrix accounts for a worst (rather than average) case situation.

As an example of how the total weightings for each variable are calculated, we refer to the matrix in Table 1. The interaction values in this matrix are based on a variation from the initial values of the variables of the system, consisting of a 20% of range reduction on a linear scale for the source term and stability category (A to F) and on a logarithmic scale for the roughness, and a 20% increase on a logarithmic scale for the wind speed. The initial values assumed were: Q=20g/km/s, U_{10}=2m/s, Pasquill stability category F, and a roughness length z_0=1m (urban).

Two different ways of calculating the overall weightings of each variable may be used, depending on the purpose of the study:

a) One can assign the values with respect to a particular engineering objective only. For instance, if this objective were to achieve good air quality, the signs of the interactions should be allowed to vary (i.e. be positive or negative), according to whether they worsen or improve air quality (which is manifested by an increase or a decrease in concentrations respectively). This type of coding (with the particular objective to improve air quality), is shown in the Table 1.

b) One may want to view the system as a whole, with potential conflicting partial objectives. In this case it may be more appropriate to use the absolute values of the interactions, in order to find which variables are bound to have a greater overall impact on the system (i.e. to investigate the sensitivity of the overall system to changes in each particular variable).

Based on the interaction values, the weighting of each variable in the overall system can be obtained by summing the individual row and column containing that variable and expressing this sum as a percentage of the total sum of all interaction values. This final weighting determines the relative significance of each variable. For instance, based on the absolute values of the interactions figuring on Table 1 and viewing now the total system vulnerability (rather than focusing on air quality only; i.e. ignoring positive and negative effects), a variation of 20% in the initial assumed value of the parameters gives the following weighting for the wind:

$$W_{wind}(\%)=100*(\Sigma I_{i2}+ \Sigma I_{2j})/(\Sigma\Sigma I_{ij}+\Sigma\Sigma I_{ji})=100*(1.72+1.2)/(2*4.505)=32.41\%$$

The bar chart in Figure 2 represents the weighting for each variable, calculated from the absolute values of the respective interactions in Table 1. These weightings show that, as it stands, the system is of low interactivity.

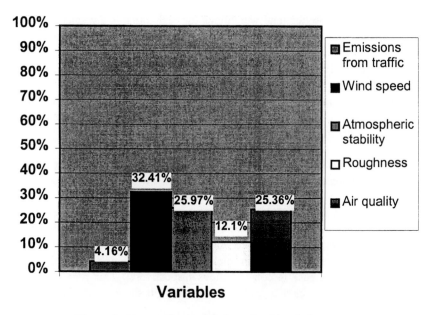

Figure 2: Interaction weightings for the whole system

Since the weightings of the variables vary according to the variable value ranges, some automation is needed in order to obtain the weightings at each range of variation. A computer program was written for this purpose. The output is expressed in such as form, so that it can be readily usable in a GIS.

In order to apply the weightings to a certain area, spatial datasets of the selected variables must be obtained (i.e. in this case, surface roughness, weather data and traffic-emissions information). The final stage of the analysis is to apply the weightings of each variable to the GIS datasets. First, the spatial datasets for each variable need to be normalised with respect to the maximum and minimum values. We suggest that they are then assigned a value between 0 and 5, according to their original magnitude. These normalised datasets are then multiplied by the respective weightings, for each range of values. The resulting weighted datasets with spatially varying values can then be overlaid in the GIS, in order to produce vulnerability maps.

3 Discussion

Some explanation is needed for the value of certain interactions and their respective weightings, which may seem surprising at first sight. For instance, the low relative effects of the emissions on air quality shown on Table 1, and the low overall weighting of the emissions on the system (see Figure 2) would not have been expected, since traffic is the only pollution source considered here. Also, from Eqn (1) a factor of -1 (rather than -0.37) would have been expected, since the relationship between concentrations and CO emissions is directly proportional. The low interaction value is due to the fact that the concentration variation was normalised with respect to the maximum concentration within the whole system. This maximum concentration corresponds to sub-urban or rural locations. When accounting for the effect of a 20% reduction in the emissions, the urban roughness conditions were used instead (i.e. the base roughness conditions used in the parametric studies), which yield lower concentrations than the respective rural conditions. Note also that, if a future situation were considered, where emissions may have increased, the sign of the interaction would be positive, showing an increase with respect to the current maximum concentrations (used to normalise the concentration results).

The matrix shows correctly that, at least for this range of values, changing the factors affecting pollutant dispersion has a greater impact on air quality than changing the emissions by the same relative amount. This explains the low overall weighting of emissions within the system.

The matrix presented in this paper, was used for demonstration purposes in order to explain how the methodology could be applied to air quality problems. It was therefore based on a minimum number of key variables involved in urban air quality. For this reason, the interactivity of the variables considered was rather low (see Figure 2). An increased number of variables would increase the interactivity of the system. The matrix shown in Figure 2 mainly incorporates natural factors, with a given range of values, difficult to alter (at least at the scale of effects considered here). If perturbations to the natural system due to man-induced causes (other than just the pollution sources) are accounted for, then the interplay of the variables increases and optimisation techniques may be needed to control potential knock-on effects onto the system. For instance, if the variable 'roads' were considered in the matrix, instead of the variable 'emissions', then a number of effects of this variable may have to be considered: if the design of new roads is anticipated, these roads may alter air quality not only due to extra pollutant emissions (according, e.g. to interaction I_{15}). They may also induce further interference due to engineering works (e.g. modification of local topography due to road embankments, cuttings etc, interfering with pollutant dispersion).

Thus, the proposed method becomes of interest when a large number of interacting variables are considered. In such cases, the complexity and uncertainties involved are too high to allow for a thorough and at the same time quick 'conventional' assessment of the situation. Conversely, the proposed methodology provides a convenient way of depicting, handling and assessing the impact of a large number of interacting variables, while providing a synthesis of information from different fields of expertise. The results obtained in terms of vulnerability maps constitute an easy way of visualising the effects of traffic-induced emissions. At the same time, they provide a better understanding of the interplay of a number of variables, involved in a given urban system. As in the case of the simple interaction matrix used here, the methodology may provide a useful depiction of how a modification in traffic emissions would work in combination with other factors influencing pollutant dispersion. It may thus be used to point at areas of expected adverse conditions to pollutant dispersion, where an increase in traffic flow should be avoided, and to help finding alternative routes for the excess traffic, where factors favouring pollutant dilution are stronger. The vulnerability model thus obtained can be used as a simple preliminary decision tool for transport planners, considering pollution levels related to current or future transportation strategies. It can point at potential problem areas where further, more sophisticated investigation (e.g. using numerical or physical modeling) may be necessary.

The present interaction matrix was constructed in such a way so that it could be as general and flexible as possible (e.g. by selecting equations whose parameter values can be modified according to different conditions, or constant values based on engineering judgment which can be straightforwardly changed to adapt to a new situation). However, it suffers the limitations of the underlying assumptions involved in the equations (e.g. a Gaussian dispersion model, Pasquill-Briggs curves to express atmospheric stability etc). For this reason, when the situation is totally dissimilar to the assumptions on which the present matrix is based, further changes may be needed to obtain some of the interaction weightings. Improved expressions may be introduced to quantify interactions between the variables of the system. However, for a qualitative tool, such refinements may not be necessary, or even justified in terms of increased complexity (especially when a large number of interacting factors need to be considered).

4 Conclusions

The paper presented a methodology aimed at predicting urban air quality related to traffic through the production of GIS vulnerability maps. Once fully developed, the technique can be used as a decision tool for transport planners. The method is fast and simple enough to be easily used for what-if scenarios for preliminary assessment of future transportation strategies, with a considerable reduction in computing time and complexity. It can also be used to indicate locations susceptible to air pollution due to current traffic where more detailed air quality monitoring measurements may be needed. The technique is quite general and versatile and can be extended to include a large number of variables. Further anticipated advantages of this methodology over conventional numerical modelling, include a holistic approach to urban planning, and the use of spatially distributed input parameters.

5 Acknowledgements

Financial support for this work was provided by the UK Engineering and Physical Sciences Research Council (EPSRC).

References

[1] Hudson J.A., and Harrison, J.P. A new approach to studying complete rock engineering problems, *Quarterly Journal of Engineering Geology*, vol 25, pp. 93-105, 1992

[2] Mazzoccola, D.F. and Hudson, J.A., A comprehensive method of rock mass characterization for indicating natural slope instability, *Quarterly Journal of Engineering Geology*, vol 29, pp. 37-56,1996.

[3] Briggs, GA., *Diffusion estimation for small emissions in environmental research laboratories, air resources atmospheric turbulence and diffusion laboratory*. ADTL Contribution file No. 79, Air Resources Atmospheric Turbulence and Diffusion Laboratory, NOAA, Oak Ridge, Tennesee, USA, 1973.

[4] Irwin, J.S., A theoretical variation of the wind profile power law exponent as a function of surface roughness and stability, *Atmospheric Environment*, vol 13, pp. 191-194, 1979.

[5] Pasquill F. and Smith, F.B., *Atmospheric Diffusion*, (3rd Ed), Ellis Horwood, Chichester, UK, 1983.

Travel time predictions in urban networks

A.G. Hobeika
Department of Civil and Environmental Engineering
Virginia Tech, USA

Abstract

In-vehicle information, collective and individual dynamic route guidance, congestion management, and incident detection are all systems requiring predictions of short-term link travel times. Hobeika et al. (1993) were among the early researchers who provided a complete approach for predicting travel times in urban networks under incidents based on anticipatory traffic conditions. This paper extends the early work to include travel time predictions under lane(s) closure for construction and maintenance. The algorithm for lane closure relies on the real time dynamic data obtained from sensors and uses a macroscopic traffic input-output model for calculating delays and consequently travel times. The algorithm has been tested and verified using the well-known CORSIM simulation model developed by Federal Highway Administration.

1 Introduction

The prediction of travel times in urban road networks is a basic component of many traffic monitoring and control systems. In-vehicle information, collective and individual dynamic route-guidance, congestion management and incident detection are all systems requiring predictions of travel times on the given network. Such predictions could also make a useful contribution to bus management and passenger information systems.

Historically, most forecasting models in the transportation area have tended to focus on short-term traffic-flow prediction for use in the operation and control of traffic signals and ramp meters (Okutani and Stephanedes, 1984; Davis and Nihan, 1991; Dougherty and Kirby, 1993). Since the late 1980s, the estimation and prediction of short-term link travel times has become increasingly important. This is in recognition of the fact that for distributed Route Guidance Systems (RGS) to be successful, the calculated routes should be based not only on historical and real-time travel time but also on anticipatory link travel time information.

Hobeika, A.G., et al. (1993) were among the early researchers who provided a complete approach for predicting travel times in urban networks under incidents based on anticipatory traffic conditions. The approach encompassed three levels of analysis. At level 1, the incident clearance time and the total vehicular delays are estimated based on incident characteristics and on real time traffic data obtained from surveillance systems after the incident is detected and verified. If the delay estimation is beyond a certain threshold, the approach activates level 2 analysis, which searches for the best candidate routes to divert the drivers onto based: 1) on the best feasible diversion routes, 2) on the anticipated demand in the next one hour, and 3) on the traversed travel times on each of the candidate routes under future traffic conditions. Once the diversion route(s) is selected and the route advisory to the public is provided, the traffic control strategies on the arterial system are optimized to take care of the diverted traffic. These last actions are conducted at the level 3 analysis.

The focus of this paper is to present the procedure for determining travel times in an urban network under the incident/lane closure situation. The incident/road closure algorithm is based on the 6-year research conducted at Virginia Tech, which resulted in the Wide Area Incident Management System (WAIMS). WAIMS builds on the 3-year data collection efforts of incidents conducted in Northern Virginia with the help of local and state police and VDOT personnel. The collected data provided an important component of the travel time prediction algorithm, which is the time needed to clear an incident based on incident characteristics and emergency response personnel and equipment. The collected data, which contained 3,000 incidents, has been classified using the Classification and Regression Tree (CART) statistical package, and its outputs for determining clearance times were documented in 1996 [1].

The prediction of clearance time feeds into the macroscopic input-output model developed by Morales (1987) and Lindley (1987) and represented here in Figure 1. The figure is used as a basis for delay and travel time estimations. It shows the constriction of flow due to an incident at a highway link as indicated by the decrease in roadway capacity (C2), where C2 is less than C1, and C1 represents the normal capacity flow of the roadway. This reduction in capacity stays until the incident is completely cleared, at which time the get away capacity of the roadway returns to its normal capacity C1.

During the incident response and clearance times, the queue of traffic builds up and stays that way until the incident is cleared. After that, the queue starts to dissipate until the time to normal flow is reached, which is at the end of the recovery period. The difference between the arrival rate of flow and the departure rate of flow gives the number of vehicles in the queue and also estimates the individual delay experienced by a driver as shown in Figure 1.

2 The bottleneck algorithm

The bottleneck algorithm deals with traffic conditions under lane closure and under reduction in lanes due to incidents and other constrictions due to geometric features. In order to understand the development of the algorithm, figure 2 is prepared to show the bottleneck condition on a freeway and the definition of the symbols used in deriving the algorithm.

2.1 Algorithm procedure

The procedure for finding out travel times when there is a lane closure is applicable when the number of lanes downstream of a section of road is less than the number of lanes upstream of that section. Under such circumstances there is not enough room for vehicles to flow freely and a reduced speed section is created upstream due to conflict from merging traffic. This affects the traffic upstream of the bottleneck and consequently a queue builds up on the freeway. The boundary between the queuing traffic and the arriving traffic, known as 'Shockwave' will move upstream against the direction of the traffic. The higher the difference between the vehicular flows at upstream and downstream sections, the greater will be the shockwave speed. The lower the difference between densities at these two sections, the higher will also be the shockwave speed.

A description of variables used in the algorithm is provided here first. The detectors are named DT in Figure 2 and there are five of them. These are the detector on link $(i-1)$, detector on link $(i+1)$ and three detectors on link i. The link i is assumed to have three detectors, one at the upstream section, one at the start of the bottleneck and one at the end of the link. The flows are designated in the figure by 'q' and the densities by 'k'. The three links in consideration are link $(i-1)$, link i, and link $(i+1)$ which are respectively the upstream link (i.e. link $(i-1)$), the link for which travel time is being calculated (link i) and, the downstream link $(i+1)$. The number of lanes is designated by 'N'. The subscripts to the symbols refer to the link which they represent and the location of the detector on the link. First we determine what data from detectors should be used in the algorithm based on their availability. From Figure 2, assume that

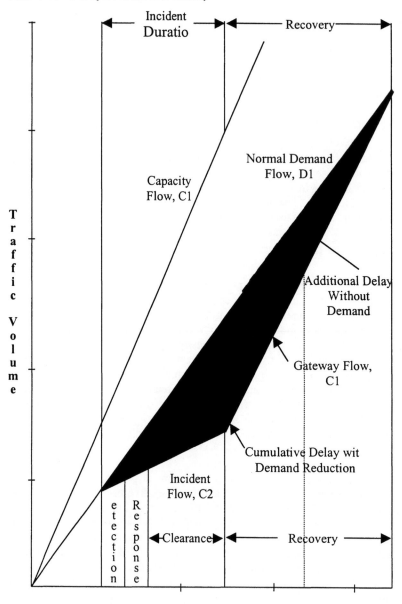

Time

Figure 1: Delay Calculations

upstream detector DT_{i_u} is available and functioning, and, either of downstream detectors DT_{i_b} or DT_{i_d} is available and functioning.

Then, if at time $= t_0$; (assuming $\bar{q}_{i_b}$ is available)

If, $\bar{q}_{i_u} \times N_{i_u} \leq \bar{q}_{i_b} \times N_{i_b}$ i.e., departing flow is less then the arriving flow, then, no congestion is imminent since approaching flow is less than departing flow. We use the normal travel time estimations as for no closure and no incident case. Also, if $\bar{q}_{i_b}$ is not available, then if

$$\bar{q}_{i_u} \times N_{i_u} \leq \bar{q}_{i_d} \times N_{i_d} \text{ (usually } \bar{q}_{i_b} \times N_{i_b} = \bar{q}_{i_d} \times N_{i_d})$$

no congestion is imminent.

If at time $= t_0$

$$\bar{q}_{i_u} \times N_{i_u} > \bar{q}_{i_b} \times N_{i_b} \quad \text{or} \quad \bar{q}_{i_u} \times N_{i_u} > \bar{q}_{i_d} \times N_{i_d}$$

then, congestion is imminent as the number of vehicles approaching is higher than number of vehicles departing. We use this algorithm to determine the expected travel times, under a bottleneck condition.

Note that if Detector at the bottleneck DT_{i_b} does not exist or is malfunctioning, we can estimate the flow at the bottleneck as a proportion of the flow at the downstream detector.

We use: $\bar{q}_{i_b} = \dfrac{\bar{q}_{i_d} \times N_{i_d}}{N_{i_b}}$ if downstream detector DT_{i_d} is functioning, and

If DT_{i_d} is also missing or not functioning we use $\bar{q}_{i_b} = 2000 \text{ vphpl}$, (practical capacity of a freeway lane) and $\bar{K}_{i_b} = 120 \text{ vpmpl}$, (Jam density).

(At no time should $\bar{K}_{i_b}$ be less than 120 vpmpl in the travel time estimation equations under congestion conditions even if the detector DT_{i_b} indicates differently).

If downstream detector DT_{i_d} also does not exist or is malfunctioning, then we substitute $\dfrac{\bar{q}_{i_d}}{\bar{K}_{i_d}} = V_f$, where V_f is link free flow speed from link attributes, or free flow speed from the detector DT_{i_d} before it malfunctioned. If Detector DT_{i_u} also does not exist or is malfunctioning; then use $\bar{q}_{i_h}$ and $\bar{K}_{i_h}$ from historical archived data for the same day type and the same time period. However; if $\bar{q}_{i_h} > \bar{q}_{i-1}$ then use $\bar{q}_{i-1}$ and $\bar{K}_{i-1}$ from the detector in the upstream link (i-1). Now that required flows and densities are determined from

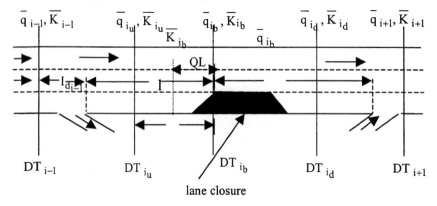

lane closure

DT   = indicates the detector location on the freeway

$\bar{q}$ = is the average flow (vehicle per hour per lane, vphpl) at that detector location

$\bar{K}$ = is the average density (vehicle per mile per lane, vpmpl) at that location . It is calculated as: density (k) = 2.4 Occupancy (OCC). In the QL area It is 120vpmpl.

N_{i_b} = number of available traffic lanes downstream from the start of the bottleneck on link (i).

N_{i_d} = number of available traffic lanes downstream of the bottleneck on link (i)

N_{i_u} = number of available traffic lanes upstream of the bottleneck on link (i)

$N_{(i+1)}$ = number of available traffic lanes upstream of link (i) on link (i+1)

$N_{(i-1)}$ = number of available traffic lanes downstream of link (i) on link (i-1)

I_d = the distance in miles from the start of the bottleneck to the downstream node (end node of link (i))

l_u = the distance in miles from the start of the bottleneck to the upstream node (end node of link (i)

= the distance in miles from the start of obstruction to the location of the upstream detector on link (i).

$l_{d_{i-1}}$ = the distance in miles from the detector DT$_{i-1}$ to the downstream node (end node of link (i-1)

l_{i-1} = the distance in miles of link (i-1)

Figure 4 Bottleneck Condition

The following are the various steps in the algorithm:

Step 1
Determine the backward forming shock-wave velocity upstream of bottleneck in (mph). Shockwave is the interface between the queuing flow and the free flow. It moves against the direction of traffic as long as the queue is building up. Hence, it is always negative in the queue building case.

$$W_u = \frac{\bar{q}_{i_u} \times N_{i_u} - \bar{q}_{i_b} \times N_{i_b}}{\bar{K}_{i_u} \times N_{i_u} - \bar{K}_{i_b} \times N_{i_b}}$$
W_u is negative since the denominator is negative indicating the backward movement of the shock wave (1)

then, the Queuing Rate (QR) (veh/hr) is:

$$QR = \frac{dn}{dt} = \left(\bar{q}_{i_u} \times N_{i_u} - \bar{q}_{i_b} \times N_{i_b} - W_u \times \bar{K}_{i_u} \times N_{i_u} \right) \quad (2)$$

Step 2
Determine the number of vehicles in queue (Q) at time $(t_0 + n\,\Delta t)$ where Δt is the time interval for travel time update on this link (i) (considered in this analysis to be 5 minutes), and n is the number of update cycle from time t_0.

$$Q_n = QR \times \Delta t_n \qquad \text{where } n = 1, 2, 3...m \quad (3)$$

'm' is reached when $\bar{q}_{i_u} \times N_{i_u} \leq \bar{q}_{i_b} \times N_{i_b}$ i.e. when the approaching flow rate becomes less than the departing flow rate. Repeat for every interval and estimate the total number of vehicles in queue using the following expression.

$$Q_m = \sum_{n=1}^{m} Q_n$$

Step 3
Now, we determine the average travel time $\left(\overline{tt}_{b_n} \right)$ in hours in the congested region. This is estimated based on the following logic. For Q_m vehicles to leave the queue at a rate of $\bar{q}_{i_b}$ vehicles per hour from N_{i_b} lanes, the average time required would be

$$\overline{tt}_{b_n} = \frac{Q_m}{\bar{q}_{i_b} \times N_{i_b}} \times \frac{1}{2} \qquad \text{hours, for } n = 1, 2, 3...m \quad (4)$$

This is based on the assumption that the downstream flow remains constant.

Step 4
Determine the Queue Length (QL) in miles from the start of the bottleneck:

$$QL = \frac{Q_m}{\bar{K}_{i_b} \times N_{i_u}} \quad (5)$$

The above equation is valid as long as QL < s.

If QL $\geq$ s, but $\leq l_u$, then substitute $\overline{q}_{i_u}$, $\overline{k}_{i_u}$ with $\overline{q}_{i_h}$, $\overline{k}_{i_h}$ which are the historical flow and densities for the link 'i', if $\overline{q}_{i_u} < \overline{q}_{i-1}$ to determine the flow and density of approaching traffic on link (i) in the next update cycle.

Where, $\overline{q}_{i_h}$ = The mean historical flow for that day type and time period

$\overline{k}_{i_h}$ = The mean historical density for that day type and time period

$\overline{q}_{i-1}$ = The flow on the immediately upstream link (i-1)

However, if $\overline{q}_{i_u} \geq \overline{q}_{i-1}$, then use $\overline{q}_{i-1}$ and $\overline{K}_{i-1}$ as the flow and density of the approaching traffic on link (i) in the next update cycle.

Now,

If, $\quad l_u \leq QL \leq l_u + l_{d_{i-1}}$, then $\qquad\qquad$ (6)

use $\overline{q}_{i-1}$ and $\overline{K}_{i-1}$ as the flow and density of the approaching traffic
on link (i) in the next update cycle.

If, $\quad QL > l_u + l_{d_{i-1}}$, then $\qquad\qquad$ (7)

use $\overline{q}_{i-1_h}$ and $\overline{K}_{i-1_h}$ as the historical flow and density
values for link (i-1) in the next update cycle.

Repeat (6) and (7) for link $l_{i-2}, l_{i-3}, l_{i-4}$ and so on if necessary.

In general, if N_{i_u} differs upstream use the average length of queue in each link weighted by the different number of lanes on each link.

Step 5

Determine the total travel time (TT_i) in hours on the link (i);

If equation (5) is valid here, i.e. QL < s then the travel time on the link i is split into three components. First, the travel time upstream of the shockwave, second the travel time in congested region and third the travel time downstream of the congested region. The travel time upstream of the congested region is estimated by dividing the length of the un-congested section by the average speed in the un-congested section. The average speed in the un-congested region is found by dividing the flow by the density. The travel time in the congested region is found as described in equation (4). The travel time downstream of the congested region is again determined by dividing the length by the average speed.

$$TT_i = \left(l_u - QL\right)\bigg/ \frac{\overline{q}_{i_u}}{\overline{K}_{i_u}} + \overline{tt}_{b_n} + l_d \bigg/ \frac{\overline{q}_{i_d}}{\overline{K}_{i_d}} \qquad (8)$$

or, if $s \leq QL \leq l_u$,

and if $\overline{q}_{i_u} < \overline{q}_{i-1}$ then;

$$TT_i = \left(l_u - QL\right) \bigg/ \frac{\overline{q}_{i_h}}{\overline{K}_{i_h}} + \overline{tt}_{b_n} + i_d \bigg/ \frac{\overline{q}_{i_d}}{\overline{K}_{i_d}} \tag{9}$$

or, if $\quad q_{i_u} \geq \overline{q}_{i-1}$, then;

$$TT_i = \left(l_u - QL\right) \frac{\overline{q}_{i-1}}{\overline{K}_{i-1}} + \overline{tt}_{b_n} + l_d \bigg/ \frac{\overline{q}_{i_d}}{\overline{K}_{i_d}} \tag{10}$$

if $QL > l_u$, i.e
equations (6) and (7) hold true, then travel time on link (i) has only two
components. The travel time in congested region and the travel time
downstream of the congested region:

$$TT_i = \overline{tt}_{b_n} \times \frac{l_u}{QL} + l_d \bigg/ \frac{\overline{q}_{i_d}}{\overline{K}_{i_d}} \tag{11}$$

In this case the travel time on link l_{i-1} can be calculated as follows:

If $\qquad QL - l_u \leq l_{d_{i-1}}$

$$TT_{i-1} - \overline{tt}_{b_n} \times \frac{QL - l_u}{QL} + \left[l_{i-1} - \left(QL - l_u\right)\right] \bigg/ \frac{\overline{q}_{i-1}}{\overline{K}_{i-1}} \tag{12}$$

otherwise; If $QL - I_u > l_{d_{i-1}}$

$$TT_{i-1} = \overline{tt}_{b_n} \times \frac{QL - l_u}{QL} + \left[l_{i-1} - \left(QL - l_u\right)\right] \bigg/ \frac{\overline{q}_{i-1_h}}{\overline{K}_{i-1_h}} \tag{13}$$

Step 6
Repeat steps 1 to 5 for the next update cycle 2 of Δt (Δt is chosen here to be 5
minutes) and so on until the cycle is reached where; $\overline{q}_{i_u} \times N_{i_u} \leq \overline{q}_{i_b} \times N_{i_b}$ then
execute the forward shockwave condition which is a repeat of the above steps
where the shockwave is positive now.

3 Conclusions

The algorithm has been tested on freeway I-66 in Washington, D.C., where
several sensors are available on several adjacent links of the freeway. The
results were compared to the outputs obtained from the simulation of the same
stretch of road using the CORSIM simulation package. The algorithm travel
time estimates were in general 5% greater than those obtained from the
simulation model. This is attributed to the macro-modeling approach used in this
algorithm compared to the micro-simulation approach used in CORSIM. The
results were very encouraging and the author is currently pursuing
implementation of the algorithm in a real world Traffic Control Center.

References

[1] Kan Ozbay, (PhD.), "A Framework for Dynamic Traffic Diversion During Non-Recurrent Congestion: Models and Algorithms", April, 1996, Virginia Tech

[2] Jeff A. Lindley "Urban Freeway Congestion: Quantification of the Problem and Effectiveness of Potential Solutions", ITE J., December, 1987.

[3] J.L. Morales "Analytical Procedures for Estimating Freeway Traffic Congestion", ITEJ, January, 1987.

[4] I.Okutani and Y.J. Stephanedes "Dynamic Prediction of Traffic Volume through Kalman Filtering Theory", Transportation Research, Part B, 18(1), 1984.

[5] A.G. Davis and N.L. Nihan " Nonaparacuchic Regression and Short-term Freeway Traffic Forecasting", J. Trans. Eng'g, ASCE, 117(2), 1991.

[6] M.S. Dougherty and H.R. Kirby "The Use of Neural Networks to Recognize and Predict Traffic Congestion", Traffic Eng'g and Control, 34(2), 1993.

[7] A. G. Hobeika et al, "A Real Time Diversion Of Freeway Traffic: A conceptual Approach," Journal of Trans. Eng'g., ASCE Vol. 119(4), July 1993.

Empirical modeling of automobile dependence in the Boston area

M. Zhang
Department of Landscape Architecture & Urban Planning, Texas A&M University, USA

Abstract

The public concern over automobile dependence is not the automobile itself, but the overuse of and dependence on it. Measuring automobile dependence properly is essential to better understanding the nature and causes of automobile dependence, and to identify and evaluate effective policy strategies to overcome automobile dependence. This paper complements existing studies by analyzing automobile dependence from the perspective of individuals' travel choices. Applying logit captivity modeling, the study quantifies the degree of automobile dependence as the likelihood of an individual becoming captive to driving. The study shows that, in the Boston area, there are 16% and 86% chances that the urban and suburban travelers, respectively, are captive to the automobile. The estimated automobile dependence indices for the non-work trips are generally greater than for the work trips. Surprisingly, the lower income drivers have a stronger tendency to be dependent on the automobile than the higher income. The study suggests that policy making should be aimed to increase viable travel choices. Achieving the goal requires a combination of complementary strategies including land use planning and design, alternative transportation supply and automobile pricing.

Introduction

The issue of automobile dependence has raised increasing public concern because the automobile-dominated travel and the automobile-oriented built-environment have come along with many undesirables. For example, road congestion, air pollution and over consumption of energy and land resources.

There are growing efforts both in academia and in practice to identify or to implement effective policy strategies to overcome automobile dependence [1], [2], [3], [4], [5], [6]. On the other hand, the automobile as a means of transportation offers convenience, flexibility, comfort and privacy and provides a great deal of personal mobility and accessibility; these are important aspects of quality of life. A worldwide trend is evident towards higher motorization as income rises [7], [8].

The issue of concern on automobile dependence is not the automobile and its use *per se*. Those who have strongly advocated reducing automobile dependence have also emphasized that the problem is "not the automobile in itself but an overuse of and dependence on it." [5], p.60. The current level of automobile use is economically inefficient and socially unequal; they are the outcome of the distorted transportation and land use markets [4]. Thus, presumably, there is a normal, optimal level of automobile use. Existing vehicle travel has gone beyond that optimal point and into the region of overuse of and dependence on the automobile.

A question arises immediately: what is the optimal level of automobile use? The question is of both theoretical and policy importance and has been a focal point of recent national transportation conferences and journal discussions, e.g. [9], [10]. To fully address the question, however, a critical methodological question to be answered first is how the degree of automobile dependence can be measured.

Most existing studies use aggregate indicators. For example, automobile dependence has been typically characterized as: (1) low land use density averaging 20 persons or less per hectare and large downtown and suburban parking supply; (2) high car ownership at about 400 or more cars per thousand people; (3) large energy consumption at an annual average of 40 gigajoules per capita; and (4) low transit utilization with less than 10% of total motorized passenger miles made by transit [1], [5]. These indicators show the overall intensity of revealed or required vehicle travel. Still, it is difficult to apply these normative measures to assess automobile dependence to reflect the local variations in income and economic development, in social and demographic characteristics, and in vehicle and fuel technologies, which are also important factors affecting automobile use [11].

This paper complements the existing studies by addressing the issue of automobile dependence from the perspective of individuals' travel choices. In essence, automobile dependence means having no options but driving, for subjective and practical reasons. Accordingly, in this study, automobile dependence is defined and measured as the likelihood of an individual becoming captive to driving. That is, the likelihood that the automobile is the only element in the individual's feasible set of mode choices. Within this conceptual framework, automobile dependence is investigated through the analysis of the process of choice set formation involved in an individual's travel decision.

The rest of the paper contains three parts. First it presents an analytical framework of modeling automobile dependence. It defines automobile dependence in a mode choice context and describes the choice model used to measure automobile dependence. The next part reports the results of the empirical modeling of automobile dependence in the Boston area, and highlights the study findings. The final part draws policy implications and discusses the areas for future research.

The analytical framework

In this study, automobile dependence is interpreted from the behavior of individuals' mode choice. According to the basic economic choice theory [12], an individual's mode choice behavior consists of a two-stage sequential process: 1) choice set formation, and 2) mode choice from a feasible choice set. The first stage serves as a screening stage in which the individual appraises what modes are available. In the second stage, mode choice decision is made based on the screening results. Automobile dependence can be analyzed through the process of choice set formation, i.e. which set of modes becomes the feasible set to the individual.

A travel mode becomes feasible to an individual when the mode is perceived and considered available by the individual. A group of feasible modes comprises the individual's feasible choice set from which the individual compares all feasible modes and chooses the one that brings the greatest benefits. When an individual has only one mode, i.e. the automobile, in his/her feasible choice set, the individual becomes captive to driving, i.e. s/he is automobile dependent.

Obviously, to a specific traveler, which mode(s) comprise his/her feasible choice set depends on a variety of constraints s/he faces. These may include social and economic resource constraints, transportation service constraints, informational constraints, and attitudinal or self-imposed constraints. People's reliance on their automobile in their daily activities can be attributed to some or all of these constraints. For example, it may be simply because driving is inexpensive relative to the income. It may be due to the fact that there is no other viable alternative near where people live and work. People may have family commitments (such as taking children to and from daycare centers) that cannot be feasibly fulfilled with other travel modes. They may lack sufficient knowledge or information about alternative travel modes (such as transit station locations at destinations, service routes, frequencies and operating hours). Their (mis)perceptions of the service quality, safety, and reliability of other modes may exclude the consideration of these alternatives at the outset of their travel decision process. Some people may self-impose certain restrictions when deciding how to travel due to, for example, the concern about their social status and image, since transit is often portrayed as an inferior mode both technically and socially (for instance, the notion of 'transit is to serve the poor'). Still others rely on the automobile because of their attitudes—they simply enjoy driving and will drive anyway regardless of the existence and viability of alternatives.

In analyzing the mode choice behavior, the analysts usually do not have sufficient information about individuals' feasible sets of travel modes. This is because the choice set formation under the internal and external constraints is a subjective, latent process specific to each individual. What is observed is the actual, discrete mode choice outcome, i.e., either driving, or transit, or other modes being chosen for a trip. Lack of certain information on individuals' perception and consideration of what modes comprise their choice sets leads to the treatment of the choice set formation as a probabilistic process. Accordingly, *automobile dependence can be expressed as the likelihood that a choice set contains a single element, driving.*

The lack of observable indicators on individuals' feasible choice sets also means that the process cannot be empirically modeled *independently and directly*. Nevertheless, the data on the observed choice outcome can be utilized to estimate, *jointly* with the mode choice modeling, the probabilities of the pre-defined choice sets being the actual choice sets considered by travelers. This is achieved by employing the *captivity logit modeling* method, an extension of the conventional multinomial logit (MNL) modeling. The model is expressed in the following form:

$$P(i) = \frac{d_i}{1+d} + \frac{1}{1+d} P(i \mid C) \tag{1}$$

where d_i is the odds that the individual is captive to i, and d is the sum of d_i for all modes i. $P(i)$ is the probability of an individual choosing mode i. $P(i|C)$ is the conditional probability of an individual choosing mode i given the choice set C. The first term on the right hand side is the probability of being captive to mode i, whereas the first part of the second term is the probability of the individual being free to choose from set C.

The single indicator d_i in eqn (1) gives the quantification (the odds) of the degree of automobile dependence when i represents the driving mode. The model is generally referred as *the single coefficient captivity logit model*. It was initially derived and tested by Gaudry and Dagenais [13] and Gaudry and Wills [14] aiming to relax the strict IIA (Independence from Irrelevant Alternatives) assumption imposed by the conventional MNL models. The theoretical and behavioral foundations of the model have been shown by McFadden [15] and by Ben-Akiva [16].

Automobile dependence in the Boston area

This section reports the results of applying the modeling framework described above to measure the degree of automobile dependence in the metropolitan Boston region. To reduce computational complexity (without losing the essence of the analysis), the multi-mode choices observed in the sample are congregated into two modes, driving and non-driving. Driving includes driving alone or car-pool, whereas non-driving includes rail, bus, taxi, biking and others.

The empirical modeling of automobile dependence utilizes the 1991 Trip Diary Survey for the Boston area. There were 3,854 households surveyed, with a total of 9,281 persons who made 39,373 trips. The sample used in this study contains 7,158 trips made by those who had driver's licenses or had access to private vehicles. The statistical package used for the modeling is Stata 7.0.

In total there are eighteen models estimated with the full sample or with the sub-samples of specific market segments stratified by income and geographic locations of residence and travel destinations. For the comparison purposes, the same model specifications are maintained across all models. Variables are kept in the models even though in cases they enter as statistically insignificant. The focus of the interpretation and discussion is primarily on the magnitude and statistical importance of the driving captivity coefficients in these models.

Table 1. The Boston automobile dependence modeling by geography

	Region-wide		Suburb-to-Suburb		Urban-to-Urban	
	Coef.	*z-test*	*Coef.*	*z-test*	*Coef.*	*z-test*
Driving						
Driving Time	-0.124	-17.11	-0.107	-3.19	-0.183	-13.32
Driving Cost	-0.108	-4.89	19.032	0.01	-0.073	-4.61
Trip Distance	0.123	6.82	0.221	2.69	0.140	2.66
CBD	-1.527	-6.74			-0.934	-3.7
Vehicles per Worker	1.008	7	0.564	1.88	1.306	6.32
Full Time Worker	0.712	4.49	1.015	2.45	0.609	2.74
Housing Owner	0.452	3.06	1.138	2.29	0.016	0.08
Constant	3.071	10.08	1.395	1.53	3.251	7.18
Non-Driving						
Trip Time	-0.026	-5.97	-0.013	-1.29	-0.045	-5.71
Trip Cost	-0.079	-4.68	-0.024	-0.65	-0.102	-3.94
Age 60 or Older	0.468	2.23	0.673	1.32	0.674	2.3
Age 30 or Younger	1.089	6.9	1.818	3.61	1.370	6.26
Transit Seat Supply	0.043	5.51	-0.001	-0.03	0.039	3.61
Captivity Coefficient	0.292	6.46	5.987	1.90	0.193	5.02
[Auto. Dep. Index]	0.23		0.86		0.16	
Number of obs	7158		3636		2464	
Wald chi-squared	470.39		22.84		244.19	
Prob > chi-squared	0.000		0.001		0.000	
Log likelihood	-1230.11		-294.69		-623.68	
Note: The automobile dependence index (ADI) is derived from the odds ratio with the following formula: ADI = Probability = odds / (1+ odds)						

The Region-wide model shown in Table 1 represents the base model estimated with the full sample. The estimated captivity coefficient has a value of

0.292 at the 99% significance level. It reads that, in the Boston area, the odds are 0.292 for an average individual being captive to the automobile in travel for all home, work and leisure activities. The automobile dependence index, or ADI, is derived from the odds ratios and expressed in the probability terms. A value of 0.23 means that, on average, a Bostonian has 23% chances being captive to driving. With a simple generalization, in aggregate, 23% of some four million people in the Boston area are automobile dependent.

The Suburb-to-Suburb model estimates the automobile dependence of those who's work and non-work activities all take place in the suburb. (In this study the suburb refers to the cities and towns outside Route-128, or the areas beyond the second ring defined by the Boston MPO, see [17]). That is, they live in the suburban area, commute to work in the suburban area, and go shopping or eat-out in places all located in the suburb. The odds that they are captive to driving are 5.987 (The estimate is statistically significant at 90% confidence level). In other words, there are 86% chances that the suburban Bostonians depend on automobiles for their daily activities. They have no options, don't know other possible travel alternatives, or don't like other means to travel regardless.

In contrast, the Urban-to-Urban model estimates the automobile dependence of those who's work and non-work activities all take place in the urban area. As the model estimate shows, the odds that they are captive to cars are 0.193. In other words, there are 16% chances that the urban Bostonians depend on automobiles for their daily activities. Given the fact that urban Boston has a quite extensive and efficient public transportation system, the urban Bostonian's 16% degree of automobile dependence is unlikely due to the lack of travel alternatives. Other factors such as family constraints, perception, information, and/or habits may dominate.

Table 2. Automobile dependence indices in the Boston area

	All Trips	Work Trips	Non-Work Trips
Region-wide	0.23	0.18	0.36
Suburb-to-Suburb	0.86	0.95	0.79
Urban-to-Urban	0.16	0.09	0.27
High Income (>$90,000/yr)	0.09	*0.04*	*0.17*
Med. Income ($30,000~$90,000/yr)	0.22	*0.08*	0.45
Low Income (<$30,000/yr)	0.21	0.24	0.23
Note: In italic are the estimates not significant at the conventional confidence level.			

The modeled automobile dependence indices obtained from other fifteen models are reported in Table 2. Major findings are highlighted below.

1) A pattern is evident that the automobile dependence indices for the suburban travelers are consistently greater than those for the urban travelers. It portrays a picture of the real world: the suburban residents are more dependent on automobiles than the urban residents. It also indicates a correlation between the automobile dependent travel behavior and the land use patterns, given that in

the suburb the density is typically low and alternative travel (e.g. by biking and transit) is largely not viable.

2) For the suburb-suburb work trips, the magnitude of the ADI indicates that the suburb-to-suburb commuting shows the strongest dependence on private vehicles, with a measured dependence index of 0.95. It means that, for an average traveler, there are 95% chances being captive to driving.

3) The estimated ADIs for the non-work trips are generally greater than those for the work trips. For example, region-wide, the ADI for the non-work trips is 0.36, whereas for the work trips, the index is 0.18. The result conforms to the common knowledge that people tend to rely more on private travel means for their non-work activities because these activities take place at various destination locations (as a result of functionally-segregated land use development), and are relatively easily served by private transportation means.

4) A result contradictory to the general perception is that, in the Boston area, the level of automobile dependence does not necessarily increase with income. For all trips, the higher income is moderately captive to the automobile, with a probability of 9% (statistically significant at the marginal level). On the other hand, the probabilities of being captive to the automobile for the medium and the low income drivers are 22% and 21%, respectively. For the commuting trips, the high and medium income groups do not appear captive to driving, whereas the low income drivers do, with an index of 0.24. For the non-work travel, the medium income group is most likely to be dependent on the automobile, with a captivity probability of 45%, and the lower income drivers have 23% chances being captive to driving. On the other hand, the high income group does not show measurable dependence on automobiles.

Conclusions

This paper has offered a behavioral interpretation of automobile dependence and presented a disaggregate modeling framework to investigate automobile dependence. Defining automobile dependence as the likelihood an individual being captive to driving, the study explicitly models and quantifies the degrees of automobile dependence of different population groups in the commuting and non-work travel in the Boston area. The single coefficient captivity logit models have demonstrated the empirical advantages in quantifying the intensity of automobile dependence. The relatively simple formulation makes it convenient to compare and contrast the varying degrees of the automobile dependent travel by those with different income and in the suburban and urban locations. The findings of the study provide important insights into the understanding of the nature of automobile dependence.

A sharp image is depicted by the modeled automobile dependence indices, showing the suburban Bostonians' overwhelmingly dependence on private vehicles for their daily activities. One explanation is that the public transportation system, particularly the rail transit, in the Boston region has been historically developed in a radial network pattern, better serving the suburb-to-downtown travel. The suburb-to-suburb transit service is rather rare. When there are no viable alternatives, the suburban residents have no choice but driving. This raises an important question to transportation policies that are aimed to reduce automobile dependence. One highly recommended policy strategy is pricing, i.e. increasing the costs of driving through increased tolls, higher parking charges and larger fuel taxes. Will the pricing reduce automobile dependence? It is unlikely to have significant effects unless desirable alternatives exist. Responding to higher costs of driving imposed by the pricing, people may drive less by making travel more efficient, for instance, by combining trips. It is also very likely that they continue to drive but taking the no-toll routes (although longer), negotiating with the employers for parking subsidies, or using more fuel-efficient vehicles. From the travel choice perspective, when there are no feasible options, they still have to depend on their automobiles in their daily life, possibly ending up with even a larger portion of income and time spent in driving.

Therefore, public policies aiming to overcome automobile dependence should emphasize the first at providing travel alternatives. The policy goal should be to offer more choices with improved and diversified transit services and with pedestrian- and biking-friendly working and living environments.

The challenge is that the current suburban land use patterns do not offer favorable conditions to providing alternative transportation services. For example, the suburban density is too low to enable transit services to be efficient and cost-effective; health care and other services are so scattered that driving is the only feasible choice for a working mother; roads and streets are designed for swift vehicle movement, making biking and walking unsafe.

Hence, the precondition of overcoming automobile dependence is to re-plan and re-design the built environment to make alternative travel more viable. This is the rationale on which many planners have recommended the land use-based strategies such as densification, mixed development, and pedestrian-friendly design to overcome automobile dependence. To this end, the role of land use as a mobility tool is to facilitate alternative travel supply, which in turn helps reduce dependence on vehicle travel.

There is a legitimate question to ask: even if travel alternatives are provided, will it guarantee that people switch from driving to non-driving, or drive less? The answer is it depends: some may and some may not. The sources of automobile dependence are complex and diverse, varying among people differing in travel purposes, income, family structure, and residential locations. It is therefore important to emphasize that overcoming automobile dependence requires a combination of complementary policies including land use, transportation supply, and automobile pricing. Each is designed to deal with one or more aspects of automobile dependence while all needs to work together. Land use and alternative travel supply are to provide more choices, whereas the pricing strategies are to harness the excessive demand growth of driving.

The empirical modeling in the Boston area reveals that the lower income drivers are more dependent on automobile than the higher income, a result contradictory to the general perception. This is an area that warrants rigorous study in the future, because whether it is the case will have very different policy implications. One direction to investigate further is to look at the job market or the occupational characteristics of the drivers in different income categories. Several studies have suggested the great importance of the automobile in accessing jobs for the low income, minority people [18], [19], [20]. It may be hypothesized here that a significant portion of the lower income drivers works on the part-time jobs or the jobs with multiple locations (e.g. cleaning, delivery). These jobs demand frequent and flexible travel typically in the non-peak hours when public transportation services, if any, are less available. Private transportation means thus becomes a necessity. On the other hand, the higher income people typically have stable jobs with regular work hours at rather fixed locations, for example, in the downtown CBD. These trips having certain spatial and temporal regularities are well served by the subway, the commuter rail, and the bus systems. If this is indeed the situation in the Boston region, pricing strategies recommended to reduce automobile dependence should be re-examined and carefully designed to avoid any unintended social consequences.

This study can be extended in several other directions. Firstly, the automobile captivity coefficient in the single-coefficient logit model can be parameterized to allow simultaneous controls for the effects of various factors pertaining to travel mode choice, and thus to explicitly account for the sources of automobile dependence. (The extended work in the Boston case has been done and reported in a separate paper.) Secondly, for computational convenience, the modeling structure in this study is simplified into a binary formulation, that is, driving vs. non-driving. The analysis can be expended into three or more modes to examine the captive travel behavior associated with transit or other modes, in addition to driving. Finally, the analytical framework can be applied to other metropolitan areas to understand the regional variations in the nature and causes of automobile dependence. It will better inform the transportation and land use policy making to reduce the undesirable social and environmental consequences associated with excessive automobile use, and to improve the quality of urban and suburban life at large.

References

[1] Newman, P. & Kenworthy, J., *Cities and Automobile Dependence: An International Sourcebok,* Aldershot: Gower, 1989.

[2] Holtzclaw, J., *Using Residential Patterns and Transit to Decrease Auto Dependence and Costs*, Natural Resources Defense Council: San Francisco, CA, 1994.

[3] Pivo, G., *Land Use Trends Affecting Auto Dependence in Washington's Metropolitan Areas*, Olympia, Washington: Springfield, VA, 1995.

[4] Litman, T., *The Cost of Automobile Dependency and the Benefits of Balanced Transportation*, Victoria Transport Policy Institute: Vancouver, B.C., 1999.

[5] Newman, P. & Kenworthy, J., *Sustainability and Cities--Overcoming Automobile Dependence,* Island Press: Washington, D.C., 1999.

[6]   City of Toronto, *Reduce Car Dependence -- Transportation Options for the City of Toronto*, Transportation Planning, Urban Development Services, City of Toronto, 2001.

[7]   Lave, C., Cars and demographics, *Access*, 1, pp. 4-11, 1992.

[8]   Ingram, G. & Liu, Z., Determinants of motorization and road provision (Chapter 10). *Essays in Transportation Economics and Policy: A Handbook in Honor of John R. Meyer*, ed. J. Gomez-Ibanez, J. & W. Tye, Washington, DC: Brookings, pp. 325-356, 1999.

[9]   TRB (Transportation Research Board), *Automobile Dependency: Debating the Optimal Level of Automobile Use*, TRB Annual Meeting, Sessions 21 & 58, January 9-11, Washington, D.C., 1999.

[10] Transportation Quarterly, Optimal level of automobile dependency: a TQ point/counterpoint exchange with Peter Samuel and Todd Litman. *Transportation Quarterly*, **55(1)**, pp. 5-32, 2000.

[11] Gomez-Ibanez, J.A., A global view of automobile dependence. *Journal of the American Planning Association*, **57**, pp. 376-9, 1991.

[12] Manski, C., The structure of random utility models. *Theory and Decision*, **8**, pp. 229-254, 1977.

[13] Gaudry, M.J.I. & Dagenais, M.G., The dogit model. *Transportation Research B*, **13B(2)**, pp. 105-111, 1979.

[14] Gaudry, M.J.I. & Wills, M.J., Testing the dogit model with an aggregate time-series and cross-sectional travel data. *Transportation Research B*, **13B(2)**, pp. 155-166, 1979.

[15] McFadden, D., *The Multinomial Logit Models When the Population Contains 'Captive' Subpopulations*, working paper: MIT, MA, 1976.

[16] Ben-Akiva, M., *Choice Models with Simple Choice Set Generating Processes*, working paper: MIT, MA, 1977.

[17] CTPS (Central Transportation Planning Staff), *Boston MPO Transportation Plan, 2000-2025*, CTPS: Boston, MA, 1999.

[18] Taylor, B. & Ong, P., Spatial mismatch or automobile mismatch? an examination of race, residence and commuting in US metropolitan areas. *Urban Studies*, **32**, pp. 1453-1473, 1995.

[19] Ong, P., Work and car ownership among welfare recipients. *Social Work Research*, **20**, pp. 255-262, 1996.

[20] Shen, Q., Location characteristics of inner-city neighborhoods and employment accessibility of low-wage workers. *Environment and Planning B*, **25(3)**, pp. 345-365, 1998.

Section 5:
Information systems

Modelling effects of logistical matching systems on transport

E. Taniguchi[1], T. Yamada[2] and Y. Naka[3]
[1,3] *Department of Civil Engineering, Kyoto University, Japan*
[2] *Department of Social and Environmental Engineering, Hiroshima University, Japan*

Abstract

This paper presents a model for evaluating the effects of logistical matching systems on transport. The logistical matching systems have become popular in the logistics industry. The systems provide a market through the Internet for shippers who offer their goods to be carried and freight carriers who offer a space in their trucks to carry goods. These systems are useful to efficiently use the vacant space in the trucks. The model application to a small road network showed that the systems are effective to reduce the freight transport costs as well as the total running times of pickup/delivery trucks.

1 Introduction

Recently logistical matching systems have become popular in the logistics industry[1]. This is an e-commerce of logistical transaction between shippers and freight carriers via Internet. Shippers will offer their goods to be carried and freight carriers will offer a space in their trucks to carry goods. If they agree on the price for carrying goods, they make a contract. The procedures in the matching systems include:
(a) Offering jobs by shippers and freight carriers
(b) Showing jobs available and vacant space in trucks on the systems
(c) Bidding the price by reverse auction or negotiation of price

(d) Making contract between shippers and freight carriers

Recently many of web sites provide these systems in Japan, Europe and US. Normally only designated members are permitted to use these systems and the system operators identify the membership requirements. In most cases these systems are used for a spot market rather than daily freight transport. There are some methods for determining the price for carrying goods. (1) Shippers will offer the price with information of the contents and weight of goods, the origin and destination of transport, etc. and freight carriers who are interested in the job will talk with shippers for the contract based on First-in-first-service. (2) Reverse auction will be used to identify the lowest price based on bidding of freight carriers. (3) The system operator will give an appropriate price based on the market price and then freight carries who are interested in the job will talk with shippers.

The main merit for shippers is that they can find good freight carriers with cheaper price. The merit for freight carriers is that they can efficiently use their space of trucks that might be vacant without finding any goods in the matching systems. The system operator normally imposes some handling charge including insurance both on shippers and freight carriers.

If the matching systems work well, freight carriers can efficiently use their trucks, which will lead to the reduction of number of trucks for carrying same amount of loads. Therefore the matching systems will produce positive effects on transport by alleviating traffic congestion and improving the environment.

This study tries to clarify how much the matching systems can contribute to reduce the total costs and improve the environment by reducing running times of trucks. We developed mathematical models for evaluating the effects on transport of the matching systems. The models were applied to a test road network.

2 Models

2.1   Formulation of models

A mathematical model was developed for vehicle routing and scheduling with time windows based on previous studies in this area by Taniguchi *et al.* [2]. The problem can be defined as follows. A depot and a number of customers are defined for each freight carrier. A fleet of identical vehicles collects goods from customers and delivers them to the depot or delivers goods to customers from the depot. For each customer a designated time window, indicating the desired time period to be visited is also specified. For example, in the case of collecting goods, vehicles depart from the depot and visit a subset of customers to pick up goods in sequence and return to the depot to unload them. A vehicle is allowed to make multiple routes per day. Each customer must be assigned to exactly one route of a vehicle and all the goods from each customer must be loaded on the vehicle at the same time. The total weight of the goods for a route must not exceed the capacity of the vehicle. The problem is to determine the optimal assignment of vehicles to customers and the departure time as well as the order of visiting customers for a freight carrier.

We formulated the vehicle routing and scheduling problems with time windows to minimise the total costs that are composed of the fixed costs, the operation costs and the early arrival and delay penalty.

Minimise

$$C(t_0, \mathbf{X}) = \sum_{l=1}^{m} c_{f,l} \cdot \delta_l(\mathbf{x}_l) + \sum_{l=1}^{m} C_{t,l}(t_{l,0}, \mathbf{x}_l) + \sum_{l=1}^{m} C_{p,l}(t_{l,0}, \mathbf{x}_l) \quad (1)$$

where,

$$C_{t,l}(t_{l,0}, \mathbf{x}_l) = c_{t,l} \sum_{i=0}^{N_l} \left\{ \overline{T}(\overline{t}_{l,n(i)}, n(i), n(i+1)) + t_{c,n(i+1)} \right\} \quad (2)$$

$$C_{p,l}(t_{l,0}, \mathbf{x}_l) = \sum_{i=0}^{N_l} \left[c_{d,n(i)} \cdot \max\left\{0, t^a_{l,n(i)}(t_{l,0}, \mathbf{x}_l) - t^e_{n(i)}\right\} + \right.$$

$$\left. c_{e,n(i)} \cdot \max\left\{0, t^s_{n(i)} - t^a_{l,n(i)}(t_{l,0}, \mathbf{x}_l)\right\}\right] \quad (3)$$

Subject to

$$n_0 \geq 2 \quad (4)$$

$$\sum_{l=1}^{m} N_l = N \quad (5)$$

$$\sum_{n(i) \in \mathbf{x}_l} D(n(i)) = W_l(\mathbf{x}_l) \quad (6)$$

$$W_l(\mathbf{x}_l) \leq W_{c,l} \quad (7)$$

$$t_s \leq t_{l,0} \quad (8)$$

$$t'_{l,0} \leq t_e \quad (9)$$

where,

$$t'_{l,0} = t_{l,0} + \sum_{i=0}^{N_l} \left\{ \overline{T}(\overline{t}_{l,n(i)}, n(i), n(i+1)) + t_{c,n(i+1)} \right\} \tag{10}$$

where,

$C(t_0, \mathbf{X})$: total cost (yen)

t_0 : departure time vector for all vehicles from the depot

$$t_0 = \left\{ t_{l,0} \mid l = 1, m \right\}$$

$\mathbf{X}$: assignment and order of visiting customers for all vehicles

$$\mathbf{X} = \{ \mathbf{x}_l \mid l = 1, m \}$$

$\mathbf{x}_l$: assignment and order of visiting customers for vehicle l

$$\mathbf{x}_l = \left\{ n(i) \mid i = 1, N_l \right\}$$

$n(i)$: i th customer visited by a vehicle

$d(j)$: number of the depot (= 0)

N_l : total number of customers visited by vehicle l

n_0 : total number of $d(j)$ in $\mathbf{x}_l$

m : maximum number of vehicles available

$c_{f,l}$: fixed cost for vehicle l (yen /vehicle)

$\delta_l(\mathbf{x}_l) := 1$; if vehicle l is used

$\qquad = 0$; otherwise

$C_{t,l}(t_{l,0}, \mathbf{x}_l)$: operating cost for vehicle l (yen)

$C_{p,l}(t_{l,0}, \mathbf{x}_l)$: penalty cost for vehicle l (yen)

$c_{t,l}$: operating cost per minute for vehicle l (yen /min)

$t_{l,n(i)}$: departure time of vehicle l from customer $n(i)$

$\overline{T}(\overline{t}_{l,n(i)}, n(i), n(i+1))$: average travel time of vehicle l between customer

$n(i)$ and $n(i+1)$ at time $\bar{t}_{l,n(i)}$

$t_{c,n(i)}$: loading/unloading time at customer $n(i)$

$c_{d,n(i)}(t)$: delay penalty cost per minute at customer $n(i)$ (yen/min)

$c_{e,n(i)}(t)$: early arrival penalty cost per minute at customer $n(i)$ (yen/min)

N : total number of customers

$D(n(i))$: demand of customer $n(i)$ (kg)

$t'_{l,0}$: last arrival time of vehicle l at the depot

t_s : earliest time for starting truck operations

t_e : latest time for starting truck operations

$W_l(\mathbf{x}_l)$: load of vehicle l (kg)

$W_{c,l}$: capacity of vehicle l (kg)

2.2 Models for matching systems

We assume that multiple freight carriers exist within the road network. They have their own depot and plan vehicle routing and scheduling with time windows for visiting their customers.

It is assumed that there are two types of customers: (a) regular customers and (b) chance customers. Regular customers already made contract with the freight carrier and they do not use the matching systems to ask other freight carriers to transport their loads. Chance customers are new customers who will use the matching systems to find appropriate freight carriers to make a contract with. They can ask any freight carriers who are interested in the job based on some methods. The following three cases were examined for choosing the freight carrier who will carry the loads of chance customers.

Case 1: The system operator makes decision for identifying the freight carrier who will carry the loads of chance customers in order to minimise the increase of running times of pickup/delivery trucks by visiting the new customers. In this case it is assumed that the system operator takes into account the alleviation of traffic congestion.

Case 2: A freight carrier who can minimise the increase of total costs by visiting the new customers can take the job. In this case the freight carrier can bid the minimum price in the reverse auction, since his cost increase is minimum among all freight carriers.

Case 3: A shipper will give a job to freight carriers who will less likely be late at the designated time as well as bidding the minimum price. Therefore in this case a freight carrier whose delay in arrival time at customer is minimum will take the job. If the delay time is same for some freight carriers, one of those who can minimise the increase of total costs will be chosen.

A case without the matching systems was also considered to evaluate benefits for using the matching systems. In the case it is assumed that chance customers make fixed contract with freight carriers.

2.3 Flow of matching

Firstly a freight carrier within the road network makes a vehicle routing and scheduling plan for regular customers. The number of trucks is assumed to be unlimited on this step. Then the calculated optimal number of pickup/delivery trucks can be the number of trucks that the freight carrier owns. On further steps involving chance customers, the vehicle routing and scheduling problem will be optimised within the limitation of this number of pickup/delivery trucks.

When the first chance customer comes into the matching systems, a freight carrier will be identified based on rules in three cases described in the previous section. Then the second chance customer comes into the matching systems and this job will be given to a freight carrier in a same manner as the first one. Thus whenever a new customer comes into the matching systems, decision-making is undertaken sequentially.

3 Problem definitions

Figure 1 shows a test road network with 25 nodes and 40 links. The average travel times on each link are assumed to be constant with time. There are three freight carriers, Carriers A, B and C within the network. Each carrier has a single depot and 10 regular customers whose location is illustrated in Figure 1. The symbols A, B and C in Figure 1 specify the location of regular customers for freight carriers A, B and C, respectively. We examined two cases with a single chance customer and three chance customers. Figure 1 indicates the location of a single chance customer "1". In this study pickup/delivery trucks only collects goods at customers and come back to the depot to unload them.

The loads of customers to be transported varied between 250 kg and 2,000 kg with the increment of 250 kg. The location of customers was randomly determined on the network. Time windows were given such as the starting time will be between 9 a.m. and 4 p.m. and the ending time will be between 10 a.m. and 5 p.m. The width of time window was at least one hour.

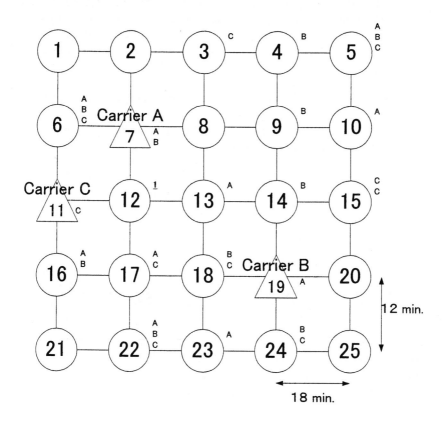

Figure 1: Test road network

4 Results

Table 1 shows the comparison of total costs and running times with and without the matching systems. The required number of pickup/delivery trucks was 3, 2 and 3 for Carriers A, B and C, respectively. Without the matching systems, Carrier A was to transport loads of the chance customer 1. In Case 1 the increase of running times by taking the chance customer 1 was 36 min., 0 min. and 0 min. for Carriers A, B and C, respectively. Therefore Carrier B or C should be chosen, since they have the minimum increase of running time. Table 1 (a) shows the case that Carrier B took the new customer. In this case the total cost for Carrier A decreased by 840 yen and that for Carrier B increased by 840 yen and the sum of total costs for 3 carriers remained at same level. Note that only the operation costs changed whereas the fixed costs and delay penalty did not change. However, the total of running times for 3 carriers reduced by 36 minutes. As a whole using the matching systems is beneficial to reduce the total running times with the same freight costs. It is interesting that Carrier B was successful to visit 11 customers (10 regular customers and 1 chance customer) in the same running times of visiting 10 regular customers by optimising the visiting order of customers.

For Case 2 the increase of total costs was 840 yen for both Carriers A and B, and 224 yen for Carrier C. Then Carrier C should take the job, since it can bid the lowest price for carrying the loads. As a result both the total costs and the running times reduced by 616 yen and by 36 minutes, respectively.

Table 1: Change of total costs and running times with and
without matching systems
(a) Case 1

Carrier		With matching systems	Without matching systems	Change	Change (%)
A	Total cost (yen)	41,810	42,650	−840	−1.97
	Running time (min.)	552	588	−36	−6.12
B	Total cost (yen)	32,428	31,588	840	2.66
	Running time (min.)	576	576	0	0.00
C	Total cost (yen)	45,506	45,506	0	0.00
	Running time (min.)	792	792	0	0.00
Total	Total cost (yen)	119,744	119,744	0	0.00
	Running time (min.)	1,920	1,956	−36	−1.84

(b) Cases 2 and 3

Carrier		With matching systems	Without matching systems	Change	Change (%)
A	Total cost (yen)	41,810	42,650	−840	−1.97
	Running time (min.)	552	588	−36	−6.12
B	Total cost (yen)	31,588	31,588	0	0.00
	Running time (min.)	576	576	0	0.00
C	Total cost (yen)	45,730	45,506	224	0.49
	Running time (min.)	792	792	0	0.00
Total	Total cost (yen)	119,128	119,744	−616	−0.51
	Running time (min.)	1,920	1,956	−36	−1.84

Since no delay was observed for Case 3, if any of carriers took the chance customer 1, Carrier C took the new customer based on the minimum increase of total costs. It means that the result was the same as Case 2.

Table 2: Change of total costs and running times with and
without matching systems (Average of 10 cases)
(a) A single chance customer

| | Total costs (Japanese yen) | | |
| | With matching systems | Without matching systems | Change (%) |
Case			
1	143,920	144,178	−0.18
2	143,706	144,178	−0.33
3	143,706	144,178	−0.33

| | Running times (minutes) | | |
| | With matching systems | Without matching systems | Change (%) |
Case			
1	2,063	2,086	−1.10
2	2,065	2,086	−1.01
3	2,065	2,086	−1.01

(b) 3 chance customers

| | Total costs (Japanese yen) | | |
| | With matching systems | Without matching systems | Change (%) |
Case			
1	171,930	172,212	−0.16
2	160,605	161,875	−0.78
3	160,584	161,875	−0.80

| | Running times (minutes) | | |
| | With matching systems | Without matching systems | Change (%) |
Case			
1	2,138	2,198	−2.73
2	2,123	2,180	−2.61
3	2,123	2,180	−2.61

Table 2 represents the average of 10 cases in terms of the comparison of total costs and running times with and without the matching systems. These 10 cases contain randomly variable demands and location of customers. Without the matching systems, Carrier A is to transport loads of the chance customer 1 for a single chance customer case. For 3 chance customers case, Carriers A, B and C are to transport loads of each of 3 chance customers.

Table 2 indicates that the matching systems are effective to reduce the sum of total costs and running times for 3 carriers. Cases 2 and 3 are obviously suitable for decreasing the total costs and Case 1 is suitable for decreasing the running times. When 3 chance customers come into the matching systems, more reduction in the total costs as well as the running times are observed.

5 Conclusions

This paper presented a model for evaluating the effects of logistical matching systems on transport. Case studies for a test road network indicated that the logistical matching systems are effective to reduce the total of running times of freight carriers who participate in the systems as well as the total costs of freight carriers. It was also recognised that the more users come into the matching systems, the larger benefits of using the matching systems will be produced.

For further studies it is required to modify the model to be able to incorporate delivering and collecting goods in the same routing. Another improvement of model may introduce the reverse auction for identifying the freight carrier to take a new customer.

References

[1] Visser, J., Nemoto, T. and Boerkamps, J., E-commerce and city logistics, In: E. Taniguchi and R. G Thompson (Eds.) *City Logistics II*, Institute of Systems Science Research, Kyoto, pp.35-66, 2001.
[2] Taniguchi, E., Thompson, R. G, Yamada, T. and van Duin, R., *City Logistics--- Network Modelling and Intelligent Transport Systems*, Pergamon, Oxford, 2001.

User-based definition of higher-order decision constructs to model preferences for P&R transfer points

D.M. Bos[1], E.J.E. Molin[1] & R.E.C.M. van der Heijden[1,2]
[1]*Transport Policy and Logistics' Organisation, Faculty of Technology, Policy and Management, Delft University of Technology*
[2]*Nijmegen, School of Management, Nijmegen University*

Abstract

To achieve a reduction in the number of cars entering the city centre, transfer points (P&Rs) at the city edge should be realised where car users can switch to public transport. However, recently realised P&Rs in the Netherlands do not attract many car users. The planning of more frequently used P&Rs obviously requires a better understanding of the car users' preferences. For this purpose, the hierarchical information integration (HII) method will be used.

HII requires relevant attributes to be clustered into decision constructs. To the best of our knowledge, the researcher has so far always performed this. This might result in decision constructs that do not reflect the grouping process of travellers. Hence, to attain potentially more valid results the grouping of attributes should be based on empirical data. In this paper, we develop and apply such an empirically based grouping procedure and present the results of an Internet-based survey completed by potential users of P&Rs.

1 Introduction

Cities in industrialised countries are increasingly confronted with the negative consequences of car use growth, resulting in traffic jams and parking problems in and around the cities. City authorities therefore pursue a reduction of the number of cars entering the city centre. One way to achieve this is to realise high-quality public transport to the city centres. P&Rs could combine the advantages of public transport with those of the car. However, recently realised P&Rs in the Netherlands do not attract many car users. The planning of more frequently used P&Rs obviously requires a better understanding of the car users' preferences.

When describing P&Rs many aspects need to be taken into account. The traveller is confronted with those aspects from entering the P&R from the motorway until the departure from the P&R with public transport. First, the traveller may be informed about the attractiveness of the P&R, its location and the number of parking places. Of course, the P&R should be accessible. Arrived at the P&R, the traveller will consider the quality of the P&R. This involves the chance of finding a free parking place, parking costs, the liveliness at the car park, the distance between the parking place and public transport, and the fact whether this route is roofed over. Arrived at the platform the traveller has to wait a certain time. Travellers can fill in this waiting time by using additional facilities, such as heated waiting rooms, kiosks or supermarkets. Finally, characteristics of the public transport are relevant, for example the type of transport, frequency, costs, reliability and comfort. These aspects are announced attributes for the rest of this paper.

To trace the preferences of the car user, often the stated preference (SP) approach is applied (e.g. Davidson [1]). Following this approach, an individual evaluates a number of hypothetical choice situations by giving a rate or making a choice. From these evaluations, the contribution of the part utility of each attribute level to the total utility of an alternative can be derived.

However, a traditionally stated preference experiment can only handle a limited number of attributes. One of the methods, which takes a large variety of attributes into consideration, is the hierarchical information integration (HII), proposed by Louviere [2]. The advantage of HII is that this method is theoretically well funded (Oppewal [3]). The assumption of the HII-method is that individuals firstly cluster the attributes in higher order decision constructs, then evaluate each decision construct separately and finally integrate these evaluations into an overall preference or choice (Louviere and Timmermans [4]). Consistent with these assumptions an experiment will be conducted for each decision construct separately, within only the attributes that define the construct. Parallel to this, a so-called bridge experiment will be carried out, in which all the decision constructs will be compared to obtain an overall evaluation or choice.

The grouping of attributes into decision constructs has so far always been performed by the researcher. This may result in decision constructs that do not reflect the grouping process of travellers. Hence, to attain potentially more valid results the grouping of attributes should be based on empirical data.

The goal of this paper is to make a contribution to the development and application of a method that clusters pre-selected attributes into decision constructs needed to apply the HII method. Therefore, an Internet-based questionnaire was developed. In this questionnaire thirty pre-selected attributes are shown separately to the respondent in a randomised order. The respondents are asked to group these attributes into clusters, which contain similar attributes. An available method to analyse these clusters of attributes is Multidimensional

Scaling (MDS) (Louviere [2]). MDS allows transforming these forthcoming similarity judgements to distances represented in a multidimensional space (Kruskal and Wish [5]).

This paper is organised as follows. Section 2 explains the theory behind the MDS method. Section 3 discusses the research design. In section 4 the results are presented and finally in section 5 some conclusions are drawn.

2 Theory Multidimensional Scaling

The goal of Multidimensional Scaling (MDS) is to transform respondents' judgements of similarity or preference of objects into distances represented in a multidimensional space. If two arbitrary objects are judged to be most similar compared with all other possible pairs of objects, the MDS-method positions these objects so that the distance between them in multidimensional space is smaller than the distances between any other two pairs of objects. The most often-used measure of dissimilarity is the Euclidean Distance (Chatfield and Collins [6]). The resulting perceptual map shows the relative positioning of all objects. Statistically, it is not only possible to find an MDS solution in a two or three-dimensional space, but also in a more-dimensional space. Hence, the interpretation of this solution is more difficult by increasing the dimensionality.

The number of dimensions refers to the number of coordinate axes, that is, the number of coordinate values used to locate a point in the space (Kruskal and Wish [5]). The determination of the number of dimensions represented in the data is generally reached by using the stress measure, which indicates the proportion of the variance of the disparities (differences in the computer-generated distances representing similarity and the distances provided by the respondent) not accounted for by the MDS model. The stress is minimised when the objects are placed in a configuration so that the distances between the objects best match the original distances. Stress always improves by increasing the dimensionality. A scree plot of the R^2 measures supports making a trade-off between improving the fit of the solution and reducing the number of dimensions.

3 Research design

Several choices are made to derive the clustering of attributes. To start, attributes which can influence the choice behaviour of the traveller are selected. This selection procedure was as follows. First, a list of attributes was obtained by analysing the successes and failures of already existing P&Rs from the literature (e.g. Ministry of Transport [7]). This list contained 60 attributes, which were tested in a pre-questionnaire test that consisted of two rounds. In the first round ten respondents were asked to evaluate the importance of 60 attributes on a scale from one (the attribute does not influence the choice behaviour at all) to seven (the attribute certainly influences the choice behaviour). The respondents were also asked to add some additional attributes, if any, which influenced their choice behaviour. In the second round, ten other respondents tested these additional attributes. In both rounds the respondents were also asked to sort cards with the attributes into stacks so that all the cards in a stack represented similar attributes according to the respondent.

After testing it was obvious that the respondents could not handle the clustering of 60 attributes. Therefore, the number of attributes was reduced to 30, based on two criteria. Attributes with too much overlap were combined to form a new attribute. Attributes which received very low importance scores and are not really prominent in the literature were also excluded from further analyses. Finally, a list of 30 attributes was obtained, which is described in Table 2.

In spite of the reduction of the number of attributes, it was obvious that the clustering of attributes with cards would be too time and costs consuming as it required interviewers to explain and supervise the task. Therefore, interactive software was used to carry out this task. This also provided the possibility to use the Internet for deriving respondents and collecting data easily. Making use of the computer, the task was simplified by showing the attributes separately to the respondent, thus making it possible that the respondent could place these attributes into one of six boxes with a click of the mouse. Accordingly, respondents could define a maximum of six groups, because these could clearly be arranged on the computer screen and from preliminary research it was observed that respondents hardly ever formed more clusters. After placing the attribute shown in one of the six boxes, the next attribute appeared. The order of showing the attributes was randomised for each respondent. By doing this, the chance of inaccurately classifying attributes because of fatigue effects is equal for each attribute. This means a minimalisation of the aggregated error. This process was repeated until all attributes were grouped into clusters. It was also possible to introduce some changes by dragging the attribute in question to another box.

The questionnaire consisted of three parts. The first part included questions about personal aspects and a filter question to reach the target group. The respondents who never used the car were thanked for their contribution and their questionnaires were excluded from the analysis. In the second part the respondents were asked to indicate the importance of all the thirty attributes given. The value attached to the attribute indicates the measure of influence of the attribute regarding the choice behaviour of the respondent concerning the decision whether to use the P&R or not. The order of the attributes presented was also randomised for each respondent. Placing this task before the clustering task has the advantage that the respondents have seen the attributes already before they have to group them into clusters. The third part of the questionnaire was the clustering task.

To reach the target group, a link to the Internet page with the questionnaire was included in the electronic newspaper of *snelheidscontrole.com* e-mailed on 9 June and 16 June. This newspaper contains the expected speed checks in the Netherlands. The Dutch car users among the subscribers to this newspaper belong to the target group. Furthermore, a link was established in the daily electronic newspaper of *kranten.com*, e-mailed from 25 June until 28 June (from

Monday to Thursday); the link was also advertised on the site of *kranten.com* from 25 June until 1 July. On this site the most prominent news is presented from national leading newspapers.

558 Respondents filled in the questionnaire completely; 424 (76.0%) males and 134 (24.0%) females. The fact that men use the car more frequently than women (Lucassen [8]) is an explanation of the overrepresentation of men.

Looking at the age groups, 45.9% of the respondents are younger than 30, 47.3% of the respondents are between 30 and 50 years of age and 6.8% of the respondents are older than 50. The small number of respondents older than 50 can be explained by the fact the Internet is less widely available to this group,

Finally, the level of education was examined. A majority (74.6%) of the respondents had a bachelor's or master's degree; 25.4% had received lower or intermediate education. The number of highly educated respondents is explainable because of the fact that people with a bachelor's degree or higher have a higher availability of the Internet (Bosveld and Greven [9]). Looking at the percentages, the response group is not representative when taking into account the three aspects mentioned above. Therefore, the differences between the categories of these aspects need to be analysed.

4 Clustering of attributes in decision constructs

The input of the MDS calculations is a 30-30 data matrix with the dissimilarity data in the cells. These values are calculated as follows: the maximum possible number of times that attribute pairs can be grouped in the same cluster (i.e. 558 times) minus the real number of times that the attribute pair in question has been grouped in the same cluster. The dissimilarity data obtained are of ratio level. Indeed, the lowest value in the matrix is zero, which is reached when all respondents group the attribute pair in question in the same cluster; the highest level is 558, which is reached when none of the respondents group the attribute pair in question in the same cluster. The calculations are made with the help of the ALSCAL procedure in SPSS [10].

SPSS allows determining a solution containing one to six dimensions. The more dimensions, the better the distances of the observed similarities can be presented. However, the more dimensions, the more difficult it is to understand the solution as well. Therefore, a well-balanced solution has to be found which is interpretable.

To determine the dimensionality of the solution, it is not only possible to study Kruskal's stress measure for each dimensionality; it is also possible to apply the R^2 (explanatory variance) as well. Table 1 gives both values for each dimensionality. The solution obviously improves when including one to two dimensions as is indicated by the decrease of the stress and the increase of the R^2 value. The change from two to three dimensions also leads to a better solution, but to a lesser degree, although the increase of the R^2 value is still present. The improvement of the solution is substantially smaller when a change is made from three to four dimensions. After studying the two and the three-dimensional solution, the three-dimensional solution was chosen because this solution allows a more sophisticated interpretation.

Table 1: Stress and R^2 values for each dimensionality

Dim	Stress	Decrease stress	Dim	R^2	Increase R^2
1	0.49	0.51	1	0.60	0.60
2	0.31	0.18	2	0.80	0.20
3	0.23	0.08	3	0.89	0.09
4	0.17	0.06	4	0.92	0.03
5	0.13	0.04	5	0.94	0.02
6	0.10	0.03	6	0.95	0.01

To interpretate the three-dimensional solution three plots are made: the x-coordinates of the solution against the y-coordinates, the x-coordinates against the z-coordinates and finally the y-coordinates against the z-coordinates. This results in Figure 1, Figure 2 and Figure 3. In other words, these three figures are the two side-views and the view from above of a cube. Thus, the figures have to be interpretated as such. In these figures, the numbers of the attributes (see Table 2) have been chosen so that the numbers support the interpretation of the solution.

Attributes in the same cluster are more similar to each other than to those in other clusters. Therefore, these attributes belong to the same decision construct. Based on the solution, the attributes can be grouped in the following five main clusters, also represented in Table 2: public transport, time, parking, costs and staying at the P&R. From the plots it can be seen that the cluster *public transport* can be grouped again into two subclusters, *reliability* and *comfort of the public transport*. The attributes within the cluster *time* are positioned a little further away from each other, but nevertheless a clear cohesion can be seen. However, all attributes within the cluster *parking* are situated very closely to each other. Hence, a dichotomy can be distinguished: on the one hand the information aspects, on the other hand the facilities about parking. The three attributes within the cluster *costs* are positioned close to each other. Furthermore, it is noteworthy that the other attributes are positioned far away from this cluster. Finally, the attributes within the cluster *staying at the P&R* have been positioned remarkably close to each other, except for attribute 30, *the possibility to rent a bike*. This is explainable given the fact that the remaining ten attributes are truly about *staying at the P&R* whereas attribute 30 is seen as an additional provision which does not directly have anything to do with *staying at the P&R* itself. The remaining attributes can be grouped into subclusters that are about *safety, human contact* and *additional provisions*. The classification, which has been measured with data derived from a great number of possible transferring travellers, deviates from the respondents' original thoughts about clustering attributes concerning *information, costs* and *time*. While initially a separate cluster *information* was considered, the respondents appear to combine the aspects of information with the different parking aspects.

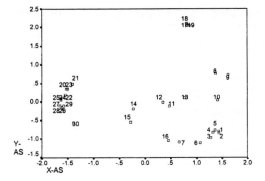

Figure 1: X-axe en Y-axe of the three-dimensional configuration

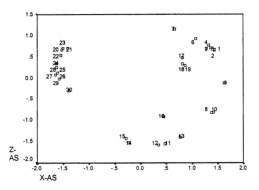

Figure 2: X-axe en Z-axe of the three-dimensional configuration

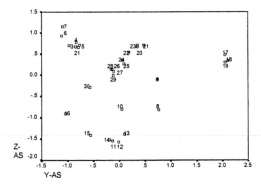

Figure 3: Y-axe en Z-axe of the three-dimensional configuration

Table 2: Clusters of attributes with values of influence on choice behaviour

No	Attribute	Importance
	1 Public transport (PT)	*4.8[1]*
	Reliability	**5.0[2]**
1	Number of transfers until destination	5.3
2	Frequency (number of departures per hour) of PT to the city	5.5
3	Separate free (bus) lane for PT to the city	3.8
4	Punctuality of PT from P&R (deviating from the time table)	5.3
5	Number of destinations in the city to be reached without transferring	4.9
	Comfort	**4.2**
6	Transport to city also possible by rail	3.8
7	Certainty of seat in PT to the city	4.5
	2 Time	*4.7*
8	Time needed to look for a parking place at destination	4.9
9	Amount of traffic toward/in the city	4.8
10	Extra travel time from principal road to P&R	4.4
	3 Parking	*4.0*
	Information	**4.3**
11	Information on the way about travel time per P&R and per car	3.7
12	Information on the way about occupancy of the parking place of the TP	4.2
13	Chance to find a parking place at the P&R	5.1
	Facilities	**3.7**
14	Possibility to reserve a parking place at the P&R	3.2
15	Parking lane to bring and meet travellers at the P&R	3.3
16	Walking distance from parking place at the P&R to platform PT	4.5
	4 Costs	*4.3*
17	Total costs of transferring (costs parking + costs PT)	4.9
18	Costs road pricing (per car kilometre) after passing the P&R	3.5
19	Parking costs at destination	4.6
	5 Staying at the P&R	*3.1*
	Safety	**3.8**
20	Supervision at the P&R	4.1
21	Surveyable, lighted pedestrian route from parking place to PT	3.8
22	A good state of repair P&R (clean, no graffiti, paved parking place)	4.2
23	Liveliness at the P&R	3.1
	Human contact	**2.8**
24	Manned ticket service	2.8
25	Manned information desk at the P&R	2.8
	Provisions of P&R	**2.8**
26	Heated waiting room	3.2
27	Kiosk	2.4
28	Toilet	3.0
29	Additional provisions (eg. dry cleaner's, supermarket, filling station)	2.6
	Extra	**2.2**
30	Possibility to rent a bike at the P&R	2.2

[1] Average importance score of the cluster *(in italics)*
[2] Average importance score of the subcluster **(in bold)**

Furthermore, initially the costs of for instance parking at the P&R and parking at the destination were expected to be grouped into a variety of quality aspects of the P&R and the destination. However, the empirical data clearly reveal that the clustering is based on the consideration between the different aspects of costs. This suggests that the aspects of costs have to be grouped into one cluster. The same argumentation applies to the aspects of time.

As mentioned above, the response group is not completely representative of the population. Therefore, a comparison was made of choices of males and females, of younger and older respondents and of respondents with an intermediate and higher level of education. This comparison produced no significant differences. Therefore, the solution found is not susceptible for disfigurements of the representativity.

Before the clustering task the respondents were asked to evaluate the attributes concerning the influence of the choice behaviour on a scale from 1 to 7. In the last column of Table 2 the average importance scores are given not only for the single attributes but also for both each cluster and each subcluster.

Table 2 shows that the *reliability* within the cluster *public transport* is considered most relevant. The respondents especially consider the frequency of the public transport to be important. Furthermore, the cluster *time* is important to the respondents, especially the accessibility of the city, that is the time needed to find a parking place in the city itself and the traffic density of the city. Furthermore, the costs are important, primarily the comparison between the costs of the transfer and the costs of parking at the destination. Road pricing is less relevant in this cluster. The cluster parking is considered less relevant, but the information offered is more significant in this cluster than parking facilities. The chance of finding a parking place is very relevant as well as the information offered about free parking places. Finally, the whole cluster *staying at the P&R* is considered less important. Within this cluster the subjective safety is relatively the most important subcluster. In the other subclusters only a heated waiting room is somewhat appreciated.

5 Conclusion

The planning of more frequently used P&Rs obviously requires a better understanding of the car users' preferences. Often, the stated preference method (SP) is used for tracing those preferences. However, the number of attributes that influence the choice behaviour of the traveller is too large for using the traditional SP method. As a solution to this problem, the Hierarchical Information Integration (HII) method has been developed in the past. Accordingly, an experiment will be developed for each decision construct, which requires attributes to be grouped to define that construct. In this paper, a procedure was developed to define these constructs on the basis of the perceptions of potential users of P&Rs. This clustering of attributes was performed in an Internet-based questionnaire.

The grouping made on the basis of the empirical data is the clusters containing aspects about public transport, time, parking, costs and staying at the P&R. This deviates from the original thoughts about clustering attributes in terms of information, costs and time. Whereas initially separate cluster *information* was considered, the respondents appear to combine the aspects of information with the different parking aspects. Furthermore, initially the costs of for instance parking at the P&R and parking at the destination were expected to be grouped to a variety of quality aspects of the P&R and the destination. Nevertheless, the empirical data clearly reveal that the clustering is based on the consideration between the different aspects of costs. This suggests that the aspects of costs have to be grouped into one cluster. The same argumentation applies to the aspects of time. The evaluations of respondents how the thirty attributes influence their choice behaviour regarding the use of P&R show that the *reliability of the public transport* is quite important. Furthermore, *time* and to a lesser degree *costs* considerably influence a traveller's decision to use the P&R or not. The parking aspects are less important, except for the information aspects about parking. Finally, respondents evaluated the attributes about *staying at the P&R* as least important.

In this research the influences of each attribute were measured separately. However, it is not certain what influence these attributes have on travellers' real behaviour towards P&Rs. This will be examined in an additional study with the help of the HII method. The decision constructs will be defined based on the clusters found in this paper and attributes which were found to be of lesser importance will be excluded from further analyses. The results of this additional study will also be published.

References

[1] Davidson, J.D. (1973), Forecasting Traffic On STOL, *Operations Research Quarterly*, **24** (4), 561-569.
[2] Louviere, J.J. (1984), 'Hierarchical information integration: a new method for the design and analysis of complex multiattribute judgement problems' in *Advances in Consumer Research*, **Volume XI** Ed. Th. C. Kinnear (Association for Consumer Research, Provo) pp 148-155.
[3] Oppewal, H. (1995), *Conjoint experiments and Retail Planning; Modelling Consumer Choice of Shopping Centre and Retailer Reactive Behaviour*, Faculteit Bouwkunde, TU Eindhoven (dissertation).
[4] Louviere, J.J. and H.J.P. Timmermans (1990), 'Hierarchical Information Integration Applied to Residential Choice Behavior' in *Geographical Analysis*, **22**, No. 2, pp 128-144.
[5] Kruskal, J.B. and M. Wish (1978), *Multidimensional Scaling*. Sage University Paper Series on Quantitative Applications in the Social Sciences, 07-011, Beverly Hills, Calif.: Sage.
[6] Chatfield, C. and A.J. Collins (1980), *Introduction to Multivariate Analysis*, University Press, Cambridge.
[7] Ministry of Transport (2000*), Transferia: een handreiking bij voorbereiding en realisatie*, Den Haag (in Dutch).
[8] Lucassen, S. (1999), Mobiele vrouwen, *Index* **6**, CBS, p. 10-11 (in Dutch).
[9] Bosveld, W. and J. Greven, Internet en klassieke methoden van marktonderzoek, *Onderzoek* **11**, p. 26-28 (in Dutch).
[10] SPSS (1990), *SPSS Reference Guide: SPSS Inc.*, 444 N. Michigan Avenue, Chicago, Illinois 60611.

This paper proceeds from the research programme Seamless Multimodal Mobility of TRAIL (Research school of TRAnsport, Infrastructure and Logistics).

Section 6:
Finance and planning

The use of mechanism design in the regulation of congestion

O. Kveiborg

National Environmental Research Institute, Department of Policy Analysis, Denmark.

Abstract

Since Pigou [3] it has been known that tax levels equal to marginal external costs give the most efficient social outcome. However, to be able to use these results the social planner has to know the value of the congestion costs in order to determine the size of the Pigou tax. Newer economic theory suggests that it may not be necessary to calculate the value of the external costs. The theory concerns the implementation of socially desired outcomes (e.g. the most efficient level of transport in a road network). In relation to internalisation of externalities, and also in relation to congestion, the Compensation Mechanism implements the outcome reached using Pigou taxes in an economy with externalities – that is, the economic efficient outcome. The mechanism implements this result by having each individual announce the amount (of money) he will pay in compensation for the delay he causes, and the amount he should receive in order to compensate him for the delays generated by other commuters.

The practical uses of mechanisms have been few, and no examples in transport settings have been seen. This paper demonstrates the important elements of the Compensation Mechanism and discusses some of the problems this new methodology rises.

1 Introduction

Congestion is one of the major problems in most major urban areas. In some cases congestion leads to a complete halt of the vehicles. Transport economist has favoured the use of the so-called marginal cost pricing as a solution to this problem. Ever since Pigou [3] focus has been on the benchmark case where a social planner levies a tax equal to marginal disutility incurred by other drivers due to one additional vehicle using the road. This has been so in spite of the many practical difficulties this approach has had. Two major difficulties are the asymmetric information that makes the task of finding optimal Pigou taxes very difficult. Moreover it is recognised that whenever small changes to the system occurs then the taxes must actually be changed in order to retain optimality.

In this paper we look at some of these difficulties and propose the use of a new economic theory that solves these problems. This is done in Section 2. In Section 3 we translate this theory into a transport setting in which congestion occurs, and demonstrate how the methodology can come up with the same efficient solution as will be reached using Pigou taxes. We further demonstrate that loosening the assumption of perfect information does not alter the conclusion of the analysis in Section 3. This is done in Section 4. In the final section we give a short conclusion.

2   The implementation of socially desired outcomes

Since late 60'ties a new theoretical approach to the problem of ensuring the implementation of outcomes desired by a society has been developed. This theory is called *Implementation theory*, and the specific suggested solutions are *Mechanisms* or *Mechanism Design*. For a review of the development see Hurwich [1], and for a description of the main theoretical elements see e.g. Corchón [2]. However, we will in this paper not go into details on these theories and results, but instead discuss the implication of this new theory in a general sense.

The overall problem a society faces when it consists of a given number of individuals (call these commuters in a transport network for simplicity) having some (unknown) preferences, is to ensure that a desired outcome is implemented given these preferences. In our case of transport this could be ensuring efficient use of a given transport network. In order to obtain this the planner must know the preferences and provide incentives that ensures that only the drivers having the highest need (e.g. *value of time*) for use of the infrastructure actually use it. One way of doing this is levying a congestion tax equal to the marginal delay one additional commuter causes in the optimal (efficient) level of congestion. This tax is equal to the famous Pigou Tax [3].

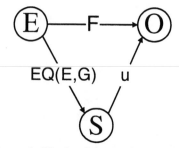

Figure 1: The implementation triangle.

The overall problem can be described using the *Implementation Triangle* shown in Figure 1. Starting in the upper end of the triangle this is the desires and needs of the individuals. In the upper left the E symbolises an economy consisting of the individuals and their preferences (e.g. value of time as described above). The upper right is the outcomes that we wish given a specific set of preferences; that is, we wish to ensure the implementation of a social choice correspondence F, which link preferences with outcomes.

The transport system defines a set of game rules G, which also consists of the regulation instruments introduced by a social planner (e.g. the Pigou tax mentioned above). Given these rules, the economy, E, and a common equilibrium concept, EQ, a set of possible strategies, S, is defined. The strategies in a transport system are choices of mode, departure time, route etc. An equilibrium is found when e.g. nobody can obtain more without somebody loosing some. Translated into a transport system with congestion this is when nobody can reduce his delay without someone incurring an increased delay. Finally, from the set of possible strategies defined by the equilibrium concept, the economy, and the game rules individuals choose strategies that maximise their preferences, or in a commuting setting ensuring them the fastest journey.

If the game rules are optimally specified the outcome will be equal to the desired outcomes. Unfortunately this not an easy task. As already mentioned this would mean that a planner has to assess the individual preferences and design appropriate regulatory rules according to this. In our transport setting this corresponds to measuring the value of time for each individual and calculating the optimal Pigou tax. It is well known that the assessment of individual values of time is very difficult. Almost any transport conference has a number of papers devoted to the value of time assessment. E.g. at the European Transport Conference 2001 at least 4 papers ([4], [5], [6], [7]) were devoted to this specific task. Furthermore, as the economy is subject to changes all the time through e.g. new commuters, change in jobs, locations etc. new taxes must be applied all the time. Hence the task of monitoring and adjusting is enormous.

The problem calls for another solution. The solution is quite simple in its abstract form. Simply apply game rules that are independent of the individual preferences and the economy as such. Hence, the rules do not have to be changed every time the economy changes and the planner does not have to assess the preferences in order to design the rules and set the appropriate taxes. The idea resembles that of heat regulation. In the old days the temperature in a room was regulated by opening the radiator when the temperature was too low, and turning it of again and opening the windows if the temperature got to high. This is the manually method a planner uses in the regulation of transport (traditional welfare economics). The introduction of thermostats made the problem much easier to handle. Simply define the temperature you want and the thermostat automatically takes care of the rest. The described mechanism design solution corresponds to the thermostat.

The solution is almost to simple to be true, but it is shown that such general rules do exist for specific equilibrium concepts (see Maskin [8], and Moore &

Repullo [9]). The general results are very abstract and do not relate to any real world situation. However, for specific problems simpler solutions do exist.

3 A simplified example solving the congestion problem

The general idea presented in the previous section may be very difficult to comprehend in a specific context as in the problem of relieving congestion. In this section we will describe a simple model of congestion (or externalities in general), and demonstrate how a mechanism can be designed so that the externalities are internalised in the decisions made by the individuals. The simple model can easily be generalised, and the solutions can be demonstrated to hold also in very general settings. This is done in Kveiborg [10]. However, for the understanding of the methodology this simple set-up is adequate, and the specific mechanism chosen is actually the same. The mechanism was originally proposed by Varian [12] for a general solution to the problem of externalities. Kveiborg [10], [11] generalise some of the results and analyse them in a transport related context.

3.1 Traditional welfare solutions to the problem of congestion

Consider a small economy of three commuters competing for the use of one road. The road is such that if any other driver is on the road there will be delays, which is perceived negatively by any of the commuters. The preferences of the three commuters are illustrated by the utility functions:

$$u_1 = A_1 x_1^{\alpha} - B_1 x_2 - C_1 x_3 + z_1 \tag{1}$$

$$u_2 = -A_2 x_1 + B_2 x_2^{\beta} - C_2 x_3 + z_2 \tag{2}$$

$$u_3 = -A_3 x_1 - B_3 x_2 + C_3 x_3^{\gamma} + z_3, \tag{3}$$

where x_i is transport demanded by commuter i, and z_i is demand for other goods, which can be transferred from one individual to another. Transport on the other hand is personal and cannot be transferred or substituted from one commuter to another.

In an ordinary approach individuals maximise utility given some budget constraint. For commuter 1 this constraint would be

$$p_i x_i + t_i x_i + q z_i \leq y_i, \tag{4}$$

where p_i is the price on transport by individual i (e.g. fuel and other variable expenses), t_i is a tax levied on driving by individual i (e.g. a Pigou tax), q is the price on good z, and finally y_i is income for individual i.

In the choice made by each commuter the influence the choice has on the other commuters does not enter. Hence, there is an incentive to overuse the road, unless the tax is correctly specified. This is an issue we will return to in a little while. On aggregate this lead to inefficient use, which the social planner wants to solve. The way this can be done is to maximise overall utility, or maximise one individual's utility given that the other individual's utilities do not decline. This lead to the famous result that the congestion tax, t_i, must be set equal to the marginal disutility of the other commuters in order to ensure efficient usage of the transport system. In our case this corresponds to setting $t_1=A_2+A_3$, where A_2 is the marginal disutility to commuter 2 of commuter 1's choice of transport. In this case this disutility is fixed irrespective of the level of transport, but this is not crucial for the results. In other words the optimal (Pigou [3]) tax is equal to the sum of the marginal disutilities of the other commuters.

Note that this corresponds to the static situation where preferences and number of commuters are fixed from period to period. As mentioned above this is not likely to be the case. Preferences change due to e.g. new job, children etc. Hence, in our simple case this corresponds to a change in A_i. The problems for the planner is that she must assess A_i for each consecutive repetition of the choices (e.g. once per day) in order to levy the optimal tax. But A_i is private information not necessarily known by the social planner. One way of assessing the A_i's is to conduct a RP or SP survey. But in such a survey the individuals have incentives to misrepresent their true values. If they state a value above A_i they can induce less transport by the others and thus face less delay. But if they all do that, the road will be underused.

3.2 Using mechanism design to solve the problem of congestion

An alternative way of solving the problem is to use the *Compensation Mechanism* proposed by Varian [12]. Instead of levying a tax on commuting, which is dependent on the actual preferences, we assign more general game rules. The Compensation Mechanism consists of two stages.

In the **first stage** each individual must announce two sets of taxes (compensations). First, a compensation that he will pay to the others for the delays he is causing them, call this t^i_{ji}. Secondly, a compensation that he should receive from the others for the delay they are causing him, call this t^i_{ji}. Hence, in our simple model each commuter has to announce 4 compensations.

In the **second stage** of the mechanism each individual maximise utility given a slightly changed budget constraint. The additional terms in the budget are what we termed "the additional game rules" in the previous section. The new budget constraint commuter 1 faces is

$$p_1x_1 + (t^2_{21} + t^3_{31})x_1 + qz_1 \leq y_1 + t^2_{12}x_2 + t^3_{13}x_3 + (t^1_{21} - t^2_{21})^2 + (t^1_{31} - t^3_{31})^2 , \tag{5}$$

and similarly for the other two commuters.

There are three additional terms in this constraint. The first is a term that resembles the tax introduced in eqn (4), $(t^2_{21} + t^3_{31})x_1$, the second is the compensation that commuter 1 receives from the other commuters, $t^2_{12}x_2 + t^3_{13}x_3$.

This second term is thus a supplement to the ordinary income. The final change is a penalty term that must be paid if announcements differ, $\left(t_{21}^1 - t_{21}^2\right)^2 + \left(t_{31}^1 - t_{31}^3\right)^2$.

Note that individual 1 does not himself decide the tax he has to pay or the compensation that he receives. On the other hand he decides (part of) the tax the other commuters must pay. In this way he can induce the other commuters to travel less by rising the announced compensations. However, as he also demands other goods, z, he would like to get the supplementary money from the other commuters, which mean that he cannot set the compensation too high. The optimal announcement is actually to announce the marginal disutility he suffers from the choices made by the others, which we demonstrate analytically below. The other thing to notice is that it is also optimal for the individuals to announce a tax equal to the one the affected commuters has announced ($t_{ji}^i = t_{ji}^j$) so that no penalty must be paid.

To solve the problem analytically we look at commuter 1. The problem is similar for the other two commuters. The problem is solved backwards. First step is to maximise utility (1) constrained by eqn (4) taking the announced compensations as given. This gives the following reaction function

$$x_i = \exp\left(\frac{\ln\left(\left(p_1 + t_{21}^2 + t_{31}^3\right)/qA_1\alpha_1\right)}{\alpha_1 - 1}\right), \tag{6}$$

and similarly for the other two commuters. Inserting the three reaction functions into the utility functions (1), (2), and (3) and maximising for the choice of t_{21}^1 and t_{12}^1 gives us

$$\frac{\partial u_1}{\partial t_{21}^1} = 0 = 2(t_{21}^1 - t_{21}^2) \Rightarrow t_{21}^1 = t_{21}^2 \tag{7}$$

$$\frac{\partial u_1}{\partial t_{12}^1} = -\frac{B_1 x_2}{(\beta - 1)(p_2 + t_{12}^1 + t_{32}^3)} = -\frac{\lambda t_{12}^2 x_2}{(\beta - 1)(p_2 + t_{12}^1 + t_{32}^3)} \tag{8}$$

Eqns (7) and (8) gives us that $t_{12}^1 = t_{12}^2 = B_1$, which is the marginal disutility for commuter 1 of transport by commuter 2. Solving this for all three commuters gives us that optimal announcements are exactly the marginal disutility of transport chosen by the other commuters.

We have found that using the Compensation Mechanism instead of having a social planner levying the optimal Pigou taxes, we obtain exactly the same efficient outcome. The main difference is that we did not have a social planner to assess individual preferences and define appropriate taxes, the individuals themselves accomplished this. Furthermore, if preferences for some reason change, then it will benefit the commuters to alter their announcements and thereby change the outcome of the system. This is the automation that we discussed in Section 2.

4 Some properties of the proposed solution

The suggested solution described in the previous section does have a number of problems. In this section we will mention a few of them, and focus specifically on one particular problem related to the information requirements. But first let us look at some other problems that can be found.

It is immediately clear that as the system increases the number of announcements will tend to be prohibitively large. In a system of N individuals, each must announce $2N$ compensations. In a real world situation this cannot be accomplished, moreover how should any one individual be able to distinguish each of the N-1 other commuters and take each of their individual preferences for transport into account when making announcements. One thing worth mentioning in relation to this is that when N goes to infinity the total compensations to be paid are equal. Hence, there may be a potential reduction in the number of announcements, which are required for the mechanism to work. However, this is an issue that has not been solved yet.

In order to find optimal announcements, the individuals were assumed to know the reaction functions of all the other individuals, which in a general setting is equal to possessing perfect information. Hence, instead of only having one individual (the social planner) assessing the preferences we now have that all individuals are supposed to do that. However, the proposed mechanism is an incentive scheme that induce the individual commuters to actually announce their true preferences, which as was argued above they did not have in the original situation.

In relation to the problem of imperfect information it is very likely that the commuters will make inefficient announcements in the first repetitions of the system. Whether this is a major problem can be analysed through the stability of the system. If the efficient equilibrium is stable, then the announcements will approach the optimal announcements over time. To analyse this problem a few additional assumptions must be made. First, which part of the system is suffering from imperfect information, and secondly, which adaptation procedure do the commuters use. Before we continue a small remark on the repetition should be made. If we consider a system of commuters there will gradually be some accumulation of knowledge contained in the different commuters. This knowledge about e.g. the size of the congestion problem can be utilised in the announcements of the taxes. The commuting situation is not very different for the commuters from one day to the next. Hence, we can consider the system of commuting as a repetition of (almost) the same case for every repetition.

Conditions for stability would involve two difference equations in a discrete setting. First it is recognised that an individual will try to ensure that penalties are not paid. Hence this lead to the condition

$$t_{21}^1(k) = t_{21}^2(k-1) \tag{9}$$

where k indicates the round of repetition. In equilibrium this condition ensures that no penalties are paid. The second observation is that uncertainty about the reaction function of the other agents prevails. Hence, uncertainty about the announcement of t_{12}^1 is of interest. If optimal announcements are made then $t_{12}^1(k) = t_{12}^1(k-1)$. However, when uncertainty about x_j prevails, there is also uncertainty about the value of the marginal disutility. This leads to the following condition

$$
\begin{aligned}
t_{12}^1(k) \quad &= t_{12}^1(k-1) + \kappa_i \left(\frac{\partial u_1/\partial x_j}{\partial u_i/\partial z_i} - t_{12}^1(k-1) \right) \\
&= t_{12}^1(k-1) + \kappa_i \left(\frac{\partial u_1/\partial x_j}{\partial u_i/\partial z_i} - t_{12}^1(k-1) \right)
\end{aligned}
\tag{10}
$$

where κ is an adjustment parameter. Analyse the stability of this system of difference equations is thus equivalent to analysing the convergence to the efficient solution of the transport system described in the previous section.

The system is stable if the eigenvalues of the following matrix are smaller than 1.

$$
\begin{bmatrix}
\dfrac{\partial t_{21}^1(k)}{\partial t_{21}^1(k-1)} & \dfrac{\partial t_{21}^1(k)}{\partial t_{21}^2(k-1)} \\[2ex]
\dfrac{\partial t_{21}^2(k)}{\partial t_{21}^1(k-1)} & \dfrac{\partial t_{21}^2(k)}{\partial t_{21}^2(k-1)}
\end{bmatrix}
=
\begin{bmatrix}
0 & 1 \\
-\kappa_1 & 1
\end{bmatrix}
\tag{11}
$$

The eigenvalues are

$$\lambda = \tfrac{1}{2} \pm \sqrt{1/4 - \kappa_1} \tag{12}$$

It can then easily be shown that the system is stable if $\kappa_1 \in (0;1)$.

Hence, generally the announcements will converge to the efficient announcements. This is demonstrated in Figure 2 for a specific combination of marginal disutility ($B_1=1$) and adjustment parameter ($\kappa_1=0.75$). The figure shows the evolution from inefficient initial announcements of $t_{21}^1 = 0$ and $t_{21}^2 = 2$ towards equilibrium and stability. The values are chosen a bit extreme in order to illustrate the point more clearly.

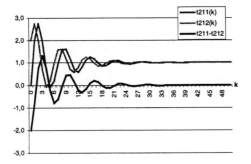

Figure 2: The evolution of the system described by eqns. (9) and **(10)**, when $\kappa_1=0.75$ and $B_1=1$.

The adaptation procedure described above is quite simple and only information from the previous period is taken into account in the updatings. However, it may be more realistic to allow for usage of even more information in the updatings. This would *ceteris paribus* lead to an even faster adjustment.

In conclusion there is a tendency that over time equilibrium will be found. This also suggests that it may not be necessary for the commuters to assess the delays on a daily basis, but only make announcements if something has changed.

5 Conclusions

In this paper we have discussed a new theoretical method that can possible be utilised to solve the problems of externalities. The discussion has been carried out firstly in a very general and abstract setting using the implementation triangle. However, in specific settings things can be formalised and simplified. We have done this using a very simple set-up with only three commuters having very specific utility functions. However, it should be clear that the methodology carries over to much more general settings as illustrated in [10]. We have demonstrated that using the Compensation Mechanism we can actually obtain the same efficient benchmark case as is found using traditional Pigou taxes.

There are several practical problems related to the use of Pigou taxes, some of those are solved using the proposed methodology. On the other hand this methodology rises new problems. A few of these have been touched in the paper, and arguments trying to overcome the stability problem have been provided.

It remains to be seen whether this methodology actually has a potential use in relation to congestion pricing and transport in general. However, the paper has demonstrated that it is not an artefact that the traditional welfare approach should always be used, there may be other solutions to be found in the economic theories.

References

[1] Hurwich, L., Economic design, adjustment processes, mechanisms, and institutions. *Economic Design,* **1**, 1-14, 1994

[2] Corchón, L., *The Theory of Implementing Socially Optimal Decisions in Economics.* MacMillan Ltd. London, 1996

[3] Pigou, A., *The Economics of Welfare.* (4th edition, 1950) MacMillan Ltd., London, 1920

[4] Shepherd, S.P., May, A.D., Milne, D.S. & Sumalee, A., Practical algorithms for defining optimal cordon pricing locations and charge. *Procedings of the ETC 2001.* CD-Rom, PTRC, London, UK, 2001

[5] Gunn, H., The value of small travel time savings, - some new evidence. *Procedings of the ETC 2001.* CD-Rom, PTRC, London, UK, 2001

[6] Jara-Díaz, S., A closer look at the value of leisure behind travel time savings. *Procedings of the ETC 2001.* CD-Rom, PTRC, London, UK, 2001

[7] Mackie, P., Fowkes, T., Wardman, M., & Whelan, G., Three controversies in the valuation of travel time savings. *Procedings of the ETC 2001.* CD-Rom, PTRC, London, UK, 2001

[8] Maskin, E., Nash Equilibrium and Welfare Optimality. MIT Mimeo, 1977, reprinted in updated version in *Review of Economic Studies.* **66**: 23-38, 1999

[9] Moore, J. & Repullo, R., Subgame Perfect Implementation. *Econometrica* **56**: 1191-1220

[10] Kveiborg, O., Modern welfare economics in transport. *Proceedings of 4th. KFB Conference, Cities of Tomorrow.* Gothenburg, 23-24 August 2001.

[11] Kveiborg, O., The use of mechanisms in congestion pricing. *Procedings of the ETC 2001.* CD-Rom, PTRC, London, UK, 2001

[12] Varian, H. R., A solution to the problem of externalities when agents are well-informed. *The American Economic Review*, **84**, 1278-1293, 1994.

Application of the European standards to the Local Public Transport (LPT)

R. Bozzo[1], G. Dellepiane[2], G. Pizzorno[3], G. Sciutto[1], A. Traverso[2]
[1] *Sciro S.r.l., Genoa, Italy*
[2] *CIRT, Centro Interuniversitario Ricerca Trasporti, University of Genoa, Italy*
[3] *AMT, Genoa, Italy*

Abstract

The objective of the paper is to analyse the process of reforms in the urban public transport which has been going on in some EU member states (Italy, Spain and Germany). How some countries are proceeding in transferring the sector competence from the central governments to the local authorities; how the direction, legislation and programming functions are separated from the management ones in transforming a monopolistic market into a competition-driven one, is going to be evaluated, considering the dispositions and guidelines issued by the European Union. The analysis shows that the legislative environment of the Union leaves ample space to discretion, thus encouraging different action, depending on the national peculiarities, and producing widely differing results.

1 Introduction

In the early 80's it became clear that the LPT was required to plan a mobility system capable of reducing the traffic congestion of urban areas and to guarantee the mobility and health rights to the citizens. In those years some important problems related to the serviced demand, to the economic imbalance of the service suppliers and to the production efficiency were raised. Based on these elements, the EU had deemed necessary to regulate the service by downsizing the role and power of the public body and trying to direct the service toward higher quality and efficiency.

The Union legislation (regulations No. 1191/69, 1893/91 and directives No. 34/96, 4/98 and 440/91) has regulated the LPT, although it limits itself to guidelines. It has introduced two basic concepts in the field of public transport:

1. the competent authorities may impose on the operators the obligation to provide public service where this is required to guarantee the sufficient level of transport services;
2. a gradual transformation from the monopolistic market into a competitive one must be enforced.

The first point indicates the legislator's intention to separate the public transport planning from the operation management. The public service contract in which the relevant authority defines the sufficient "service level" to the patronage specifies:

- the characteristics of the offered services with the indications of service continuity, regularity, capacity and quality;
- the price of performance with the indication of tariffs and conditions to be applied for some passenger categories and some routes;
- the period of validity of the contract;
- the sanctions in case the contract is not honoured.

This means that it is not up to the transport companies to define the service levels and the conditions offered because these strategic indications are defined by the regulating body on a preliminary basis. As to the opening of the market, the EU orientation stated in the Green Paper 1995 proposes an intermediate solution between the planned and market systems. It is recognised that, although the planned system is hardly stimulating and penalising for quality and efficiency, the market system dos not consider sufficiently the integration of different transport modes and the goals of the economic and social policies. The best solution is therefore the assignment of exclusive rights through tenders, in such a way as to encourage the operators to enhance the standards of service. The application of these dispositions within the Union has left ample space for discretion of the member States, as appears from the analysis developed in three states: Italy, Spain and Germany.

2 Italy

The reform of the LPT takes place in the 90's by means of some legal instruments intended to surpass the existing legislation and to adopt the Union provisions on the matter. Up to that time the lack of common rules, the inadequacy of standards and the lack of a system have determined poor efficiency. The LPT had been offered for long time as monopoly: the state and the local authorities guaranteed by means of the mechanism of concession, the exclusive rights to a company to the routes where it provided service. As an alternative to the company monopoly, the laws contemplated the foundation of the transport activity by the administrations themselves. The goals of the reform which was regulated by the framework rules set by the Legislative Decrees 422/97 and 400/97 may be summarised as follows:

- administrative decentralisation;
- efficiency of companies restored;

- separation of roles between Government and companies.

The administrative decentralisation has taken place by assigning all tasks and functions related to the local and regional public transport services to the regions and local authorities. This is especially true of the programming and planning of the service. It is expected that the regions themselves will transfer such powers to the local authorities (provinces and municipalities) in accordance with the principle of subsidy, if the service is not of regional interest. This is a new element: to date the LPT companies have been owned by the local authorities or have operated in concession arrangements granted by the latter, covering both programming and production roles. The regions share the responsibility of defining the "minimum service levels" with the local authorities, i.e. the sufficient quality and quantity of service to satisfy the need of citizens for mobility. The costs of such service are borne by the regions. The new rules redefine the roles of companies: to acquisition of the right to operate, organisation of personnel and fleets, the management of the service offer remain their duties. In order to overcome the monopolistic settings, introduce the competition rules and push the sector toward better efficiency, the legislation includes provisions for tendering procedures in selecting the service operator. The criterion of assignment is correlated to the economic conditions and to the proposed service performance. By conferring to regions, the decree starts the process of reforms and traces its completion through the regional legislation. This has brought about the differentiation among regions and more competition due to the need of companies to contain expenses and keep up the market quality standards. The process of adoption by the regions of the Legislative Decree 422/97 may be considered completed, despite the fact that the programming and regulation activities (approval of the service and network planning instruments, tariff integration, reinforcement of the administrative structures for the former, service contracts and tenders for the latter) have not yet started, despite the considerable differences among the various local situations. The regulatory authorities - regions and local authorities - must complete in the transition period (before the end of 2003) the approval of programming acts defined by the national and regional legislation and prepare the instruments for the future service assignment. After the transformation process from the formerly municipality-based transport companies into the capital companies or limited-liability co-operatives which should take place before the end of 2001, they must also start the process of aggregation in order to reach the market as strong entrepreneur subjects and participate in the first tenders announced by the regulatory authorities. Currently, the activities appear very diversified and unsystematic; this is due to the fact that the subjects identified as regulatory authorities of such activities seem unprepared for their task since for decades they have delegated the task to the service operator companies. It is interesting to analyse case studies such as the reform processes started by the Region Liguria and the Municipality of Rome.

2.1 Liguria

The Region Liguria has established by its law No. 31/98 that the procedure for the stipulation of new contracts for the assignment of the public transport on tire (after the tender) must be finished before Dec. 31, 2001. The reform process involves the provinces of Genoa, Imperia, La Spezia and Savona and the Municipality the region capital. Such provisions adopt the reform with a two years' advance over the law 422 of 1997. The service levels and its characteristics were established by the region in agreement with the local authorities, as defined in the Legislative Decree 422/97. The financing of the activity takes place through the establishment of the Regional Transport Fund which is fed from its own resources and with transfers from the State. It must be emphasised that the service contract is stipulated following the net cost principle. The assignment of the service for the period of 5 to 9 years (in Genoa it will be probably for 6 years) follows a tendering procedure which selects the economically most favourable offer and it covers the whole territorial unit (the Municipality of Genoa is the first one to tender the whole service, not only some parts or routes). It must be added that a regulatory and guarantee authority for the LPT shall be established.

2.2 Rome

Another significant example is the City of Rome which remains the only one to have assigned a part of the service network through tenders during the transition period. The reform features may be summarised in the following points:

1. the services tendered are the additional ones, even if they involve the already operated routes. The personnel and vehicles already used by Trambus on the assigned lines are transferred to other lines. In this case it is not necessary to transfer the personnel and vehicles from one operator to another;
2. the service contract with the new operator is based on the gross cost, therefore he will not collect fares, but a fixed amount to cover the costs, thus keeping only the production risk;
3. STA SpA, the agency for mobility of the City of Rome, was established with the public participation majority and the task of planning and designing traffic and mobility and keeping up with the innovation and information services.

3 Spain

Starting the analysis from the legal point of view, the absence of a reform of the Local Public Transport in Spain promoted by the European Union may be noted. There is a framework law No. 16 dated July 30, 1987, titled L.O.T.T. (Ley de Ordenacion de los Transportes Terrestres) which defines the land transport. It dedicates only 10 to 12 articles to the urban and local transport and has limited value as it was challenged in the Spanish Constitutional Court which has accepted the appeal. At present there is no National law which regulates the service organisation and operation of the public transport in cities and in metropolitan areas. Despite that, the companies members of ATUC, an association of approx. 90% of the operators, public and private, in the field of local public transport which transport 80% of passengers in buses and 100% of passengers in the metro networks, have decided to follow the overall indications of the LOTT. The LOTT sets the duration of a concession assigned by tendering at 15 years; it is not clear what is the value of that law, whether its provisions may also be applied to the LPT and if it will be superseded by the Union directives, as the interviewed operators fear. The reason for feeble interest for privatisation is that there have always existed private companies in the local public transport industry and there were no problems of coexistence or of service organisation. Until 1959 the surface transport in Barcelona has been privately run and since that year a transition to the public operation was made and it has lasted ever since. Currently, the single regional administrations propose to regulate the assignment of concessions to private companies which have had privileged treatment since the company which traditionally operated a service on a route had its concession automatically renewed if it complied with certain service levels and agreements. As far as the service programming is concerned, in bigger areas there is a government authority for the public mobility which co-ordinates both public and private companies providing the transport service in the urban and metropolitan centres; in smaller areas , e.g. Valencia, there is no such entity, the responsibilities between public and private sectors are clearly defined and the market is divided by territory and/or by line. From that point on, the responsibility and the real weight of the government authority on LPT in the two outlined cases are different: ATM of Barcelona limits itself to study the tariff integration and to provide strategic indications; CRTM of Madrid plans the services of all the participating companies which do not have such a function within their structures.

3.1 Barcelona

In the Barcelona Metropolitan region there are both public and private operators. To manage the transport offer in such a vast and densely populated area, a government authority on public mobility named ATM had to be instituted. As set in its statute, the Authority for the Metropolitan Transport (ATM) is a voluntary inter-administrative consortium assembling the public administrations running the public transport services in the Barcelona metropolitan area. The administrations participating in this Consortium are: Generalitat de Catalunya (51%), Municipality of Barcelona (25%) and Entitat Metropolitana del Transport (EMT) which encompasses 18 municipalities (24%), with the intention to include other administrations appointed for the public transport services. Note that the General State Administration is also present in the consortium as an observer. The goal of ATM is the co-ordination of the public authorities appointed for the transport services and infrastructure in the Barcelona area. Beside that, ATM manages the economic and financial agreements among authorities (e.g. State/RENFE) which are involved with LPT at any level. The founding of ATM is a decisive step for the planning and management of different networks within the public transport in Barcelona; moreover it gives the opportunity to study the tariff integration of different modes of transport and among different transport companies. Through the "agreed planning" instrument, the Barcelona transport authority set as its goal the improvement and advancing of the service by doing their best in trying to meet the needs of the 21st century mass public transport users. The main ATM functions may be tabulated as follows:

Table 1: Main ATM functions

PLANNING FUNCTION	planning of new investments in infrastructure for the local passenger public transport by defining their characteristics and investment programs in order to achieve financial agreements preparation and approval of a common tariff plan which sets the level of costs to be covered by the fares and an integrated fare system
CONTROL FUNCTION	project supervision in order to verify that the planning goals are achieved monitoring of the LPT market evolution, especially regarding the efficiency of the private transport sector

3.2 Madrid

The Madrid metropolitan area is operated by the public and private operators co-ordinated by CRTM. They provide public transport in the whole region. Madrid is the only area where the metropolitan region coincides with the administrative one, due to the special status of the Nation's capital. The CRTM (Consorcio Regional de Transportes de Madrid) was founded in 1985 as a result of the Law No. 5 dated May 16, 1985 and it consists of 120 persons, including economists, lawyers, engineers and sociologists; it was constituted in 1986 in order to concentrate the efforts of public and private institutions related to the public transport and having a goal of improving and co-ordinating the services, transport networks and fares so that a better capacity and quality of transport can be offered to the public. The CRTM plans the interurban and urban public transport of the municipalities within the Madrid metropolitan region. The Consortium acts in the role of the only authority in the public transport section and it has sufficient representatives and technical capacity to operate in the following functions:
1. global planning of the transport infrastructures;
2. co-ordination of operation programs for all transport modes;
3. introduction and management of an integrated fare system;
4. creation of an image of uniqueness for the transport system.

The Consortium does not limit the estate autonomy nor does it change the legal aspect of the its member transport companies, public or private, which are required only to comply to the Consortium's common directives. By the end of 1998 the Consortium had 169 member municipalities from the Madrid province which represent practically the whole Madrid population. Beside dealing with the global strategic planning and with the modal integration, the CRTM plans the activities of single members in order to co-ordinate their efforts.

4 Germany

As far as the public transport is concerned, before the reform the general trend of losing public transport passengers to advantage at individual transport took place in Germany, due to the absence of competition and the regulation of the service being mostly in the public subject domain. In the nineties the legislation regarding the LPT was thoroughly renewed; the reform has been originated by the National law for the reform of the railways. Based on this, the Local Railway Transport (LRT), consisting of urban, suburban and regional services, has been recognised as an important part of the local transport. Moreover, the railway transport regional organisation law has set the legislative definition of the LPT for the first time, corresponding with the one adopted in Italy, thus casting the foundation for a systematic evaluation of the industry and for the co-operation between the Federation and Länder. This made it possible to avoid the weak spots in the system resulting from the splitting of responsibilities. For these reasons a close examination of the regulatory system of the Local Public Transport cannot leave aside the main contents of the Law on the regional organisation of railways. The Law foresees that the responsibilities for the National transport be maintained by the Federal government, whereas the political responsibility for the local transport is transferred to the Länder; the Länder have the duty of acting in the field of harmonisation of the planning, organisation and financing methods for the whole LPT system. As far as the regional legislation has set, the Länder had to face both urban and suburban transport. The amendment of the Law on the Passenger Transport (PbefG), being part of an ample context of the reform of railways, has brought about thorough changes to the LPT by acting on the non-rail urban line transport. The main amendment contents are:

- institution of the co-ordinating body (transport authority) nominated by the territorially competent Land; it is responsible for the organisation of the LPT in the area it has been assigned;
- introduction of the local transport plan drawn up by the co-ordinator according to the contents and criteria set by the Land;
- introduction of new procedures for the assignment of service along one or more lines based on the competition principle;
- the release of a formal authorisation for the service operation from a specific body;
- the limiting of the public financing to cover the balance losses.

The procedures for the assignment of the transport service are under the jurisdiction of the co-ordinator who has the duty to promote them by selecting among the forms defined by the national Law, which are of three types: public tender, restricted tender, by appointment. In case of tendering, the co-ordinators must keep one part of the service subject to tendering to medium and small-size companies, so that the access of private companies is assured. The appointment takes place in two cases:

1. each time when the service may be operated by a company which declares itself completely self-financed and whose activity would not burden the public balance for subsidies to cover the balance losses; the co-ordinator should avoid the tendering, or invalidate it if already started;
2. when, at license expiry time, the call for tender constitutes a risk of fragmentation of timetables and fares, the co-ordinator may reconfirm the current operating company in the public interest, without proceeding with tenders. In such cases the transport performance is referred to as "imposed performance".

The transport performance is operated by operator companies. The essential condition for the not self-financed companies to obtain service assignment is that the costs charged to the public are as low as possible; the limitless coverage of balance deficit by the public administration no longer exists and the road opens to the competition in the industry. The principle used to identify the lowest cost for the public to be applied in the evaluation of tendered offers is set in a dedicated decree of the Federal Ministry of Transport. In large urban agglomerates where the mobility issues are critical and require a consistent offer for transport, the public companies are authorised to use the profits coming from the involved service companies (e.g. the power, gas, water utility companies) to cover the loss generated by the public transport service. The authority which issues authorisations, operating in co-ordination with the co-ordinating body, must check that within the appointed service company exist the conditions to meet the planned requirements of efficiency. In case of public companies the authorisation is denied if there is no documentation to prove the declared costs or if the equal opportunity principle is violated. Based on the applied rules, the following considerations may be made:

- only in few cases the desired unification of all the responsibilities within the sector has been completely achieved;
- in cases where the public territorial body covers both the roles of co-ordinating body and the owner of the LPT company there is the risk of a suboptimal use of resources and of the conflict of interests during the tendering phase;
- the possibility to cover the deficit with the revenues of involved companies leaves open the possibility for the public companies to avoid tendering, thus bypassing the competition in service contracts.

The study of the LPT of two important cities, Frankfurt/M. and Berlin, has shown the management of the LPT over three levels.

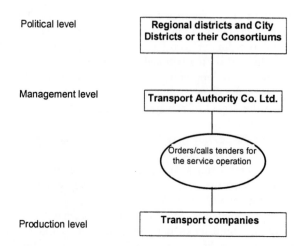

Figure 1: LPT management levels in Frankfurt/M. and Berlin

The first level has the role of establishing the level of service offer and assure its financing, the management level takes care of the offer development and guarantees the competition among parties and the production level deals with the personnel programming and the use of vehicles, management of revenue and quality control. Summarising the situation in the two sample cities, the following has been found:

- an overall high quality level of service;
- better efficiency and higher level of advancement in the development of some initiatives, especially those related to the modal and fare integration achieved by RMV (Frankfurt/M. Transport Authority) and by the LPT companies related to it as opposed to what was found in Berlin-Brandenburg;
- the greater dynamism of the VBB (Berlin Transport Authority); despite the very difficult initial operating situation because of the consequences of the reunion, in 10 years it has achieved the efficiency levels comparable to those of the western territories;
- failure to build an effective competition system due to the conflict of interests generated in the tendering location by the co-ordinating authority which is entirely public property, just as the described transport companies.

Conclusions

The above analysis shows that the service regulatory efforts in the three countries covered are very diversified. In all analysed cases the separation of programming powers and operation management has been formally accomplished through the founding of competent authorities. Beside that, the open market was introduced through the assignment of services by tendering. Nevertheless, the National provisions differ considerably and contain some drawbacks. For instance, it is emphasised in Italy that the reform has some weak points:

- art.18 of law No.422/97 gives competitivness strong constraints and limits the possibility partecipation of operator companies, which already have direct assignments, in tenders;
- corrent regulations does not rule staff and equity management if service is assigned to a new operator
- it does not encourage the real fare integration mechanism;
- it does not introduce independent subjects of tender regulation and of service contracts, leaving the public administrations in the double role of the interested party and of the controller, with the evident conflict of interests.

These aspects show how the real status of the reform of the LPT is linked to the regional provisions and their will to review the service organisation. The Spanish reform has accomplished some important objectives; the transport authorities are actually independent and an effective separation between the functions of programming and operation has already taken place. Moreover, the service quality is high, the transport companies are efficient and an excellent modal integration has been achieved, especially in large cities. In Germany the reform may be considered partial, since there was no real market opening and almost all operators are public property. Although the reform process has been started, the achieved level of competition and efficiency is still not sufficient to overcome the previous situation.

References

[1] World Bank, Sustainable Transport, Priorities for Policy Reform, 1996
[2] European Commission, "The Citizens' Network – Fulfilling the potential of public passenger transport in Europe", Office for Official Publications of the European Communities, 1996
[3] TIS, "ISOTOPE, Improved structure and organisation for urban transport operations of passengers in Europe", 1997, Transport Research Fourth Framework Programme, Urban Transport, Office for Official Publication of the European Communities, 1997
[4] EEC provisions Nos. 1191/1969 and 1183/1991
[5] EU Directives Nos. 34/1996 and 4/1998
[6] Proposal for the regulation of the European Parliament and Counsil COM (212/2000)

For Italy

[7] Law No. 142/1990, Legislative Decree No. 422/1997, Legislative Decree No. 400/1999

For Spain

[8] Framework law No. 16 dated July 30, 1987 (LOTT)
[9] ATM Statute, CRTM Statute

For Germany

[10] AEG (Allgemeine Eiesenbahngesetzt – General railway law)
[11] PbefG (Personenbeforderungsgesetzt – Law on the reform of the Passenger Transport)

The perception of network congestion by using parking fees

M. Migliore
Institute for Transport Studies, Palermo University, Italy.

Abstract

A lot of work has been produced in order to internalise the external effects of road transport in the user perceived cost by using traffic fares. In the traffic engineering practice only a few links can be charged by a toll system.

The principal aim of this work has been the calculation of parking fees able to take into account the congestion cost generated by road users in the network and in the parking areas.

The simulation of the transport system has not considered crossover traffic and it has supposed the presence of a public transport system, which could meet a higher level of demand.

It has been proved that the calculated parking fees are a local maximum of the non-convex function estimating the social surplus generated by parking fees.

The existence of the solution of the fixed-point problem has been proved by the Brower theorem and an algorithm to solve it has been proposed. The demand elasticity for modal split has been taken into account.

A simulation of the method has been carried out in a part of the real network of Palermo (the principal town of Sicily). A comparison between the proposed method and an optimisation algorithm able to search a local maximum of social surplus function, taking into account the equilibrium between transport demand and supply, has been carried out.

1 Introduction

Congestion pricing is a particular form of road pricing that imposes higher charges on motorists who travel at times and places where the road system is congested. Higher charges are justified because travel in congested periods or places imposes high costs on society; these costs take the form of either expensive additions to roadway capacity or delays to other motorists. Rather than spreading the charges for road use evenly across all users, congestion pricing targets those who cause the greatest problem or expense. Road pricing can be implemented in any of a wide range of forms that vary in their degree of complexity, financial arrangements, and technology [6].

The methodological idea is founded on the welfare-economics principle of marginal pricing, stating that, when external effects are present, an optimal equilibrium is achievable, from a social point of view, by charging each decision-maker the differences between marginal social costs and average individual costs. Within the transportation field, this idea has been firstly applied to the equilibrium assignment problem in Beckmann [1], where it is shown the optimally of marginal pricing with respect to total user costs in a mono-user and mono-modal deterministic context with rigid demand and separable link cost functions. In Bellei [2] this idea has been extended in a multi-user and multi-modal stochastic context with elastic demand for the mode choice.

Because implementing the marginal pricing solution to the toll optimisation problem requires charging each link of the network any real valued toll, which is not realistic, then it is worth addressing the problem with reference to specific pricing schemes. In the traffic engineering practice, in fact, only a few of links can be charged by toll system.

The principal aim of this work has been then the calculation of parking fares able to take into account the congestion cost generated by road users in the network and in the parking areas.

The simulation of the transport system has not considered crossover traffic and it has supposed the presence of a public transport system with reserved lanes, which could meet a higher level of demand.

2 The marginal pricing applied to parking areas

Parking fares should be the differences between marginal social costs and average individual costs.

At the equilibrium between demand and supply of the transport system,

$$D_x = \sum_{O_i Z_i} \sum_j d^{O_i Z_i, j, x}$$

represents the total number of parking users, desegregated by origin (O_i), destination (Z_i), category (j), parking area (x).

The marginal cost of the x parking user is:

$$c_{mx} = \frac{dc_T}{dD_x},$$

where

$$c_T = \sum_a t_a \times f_a + \sum_k t_k \times D_k$$

and

t_a is the running time on the link a;

t_k is the waiting time on the k parking area;
f_a is the flow on the link a.
Then we can write:

$$c_{mx} = \frac{d}{dD_x}\left(\sum_a t_a \times f_a + \sum_k t_k \times D_k\right) = \sum_a \frac{d(t_a \times f_a)}{dD_x} + \sum_k \frac{d(t_k \times D_k)}{dD_x} \quad (1),$$

where $t_a = t_a(f_a)$ and $t_k = t_k(X_k)$ are continuous (and their first derivative) and monotone increasing functions [3], [5].
For the waiting time at the parking areas, the following composite function [7] could be used:

$$t_k(X_k) = t_o \times (X_k)^{\left(\frac{T_n \times C}{2 \times N \times t_o}\right)} \qquad \frac{T_n \times C}{2 \times N \times t_o} > 1 \qquad \text{if } 0 \leq X_k < 1$$

$$= t_o + (X_k - 1) \times \frac{C}{N} \times \frac{T_n}{2} \qquad \text{if } X_k \geq 1,$$

where:
t_o is the waiting time when the parking is empty;
X_k is the occupancy rate of the k parking area;
T_n is a fixed period of time;
C is the capacity of the k parking;
N is the number of vehicles going out of the parking during T_n.
We can also write:

$$\frac{d(t_a \times f_a)}{dD_x} = \frac{dt_a}{df_a} x \frac{df_a}{dD_x} x f_a + t_a x \frac{df_a}{dD_x},$$

$$\frac{df_a}{dD_x} = P_{ax}$$

where P_{ax} is the link flow rate going to the x parking; and so we obtain:

$$\frac{d(t_a \times f_a)}{dD_x} = \left(\frac{dt_a}{df_a} x f_a + t_a\right) x P_{ax}.$$

$$\frac{d(t_k \times D_k)}{dD_x} = \frac{dt_k}{dX_k} \times \frac{dX_k}{dD_x} \times D_k + t_k \times \frac{dD_k}{dD_x} \quad (2)$$

where

$$X_k = X_k(T_{n-1}) + \frac{D_k}{C_k} - \frac{U_k}{C_k}$$

and U_k represents the number of users going out of the parking during T_n.

If $x \neq k \Rightarrow \frac{dX_k}{dD_x} = 0, \frac{dD_k}{dD_x} = 0$;

if $x = k \Rightarrow \frac{dX_x}{dD_x} = \frac{1}{C_x}, \frac{dD_x}{dD_x} = 1$

and then the eqn (2) can be written as follows:

$$\frac{d(t_k \times D_k)}{dD_x} = \frac{dt_x}{dX_x} \times \frac{D_x}{C_x} + t_x$$

Finally the eqn (1) can be written as follows:

$$c_{mx} = \sum_a \left(\left(\frac{dt_a}{df_a} \right)_{f_a} x f_a + t_a \right) x P_{ax} + \left(\frac{dt_x}{dX_x} \right)_{X_x} \times \frac{D_x}{C_x} + t_x .$$

The average individual cost is:

$$CMV_x = \sum_a t_a \times P_{ax} + t_x$$

and then:

$$c_{mx} - CMV_x = \sum_a \left(\left(\frac{dt_a}{df_a} \right)_{f_a} x f_a x P_{ax} \right) + \left(\frac{dt_x}{dX_x} \right)_{X_x} \times \frac{D_x}{C_x} .$$

Then we obtain:

$$p_x = \sum_a \frac{\sum_m a_{xa}^m \sum_j \left(F_m^j \times \tau^j \right)}{f_x} \times \left(\frac{dt_a}{df_a} \right)_{f_a} \times f_a$$

or:

$$p_x = \sum_a \sum_m a_{xa}^m \sum_j \left(F_m^j \times \tau^j \right) \times \left(\frac{dt_a}{df_a} \right)_{f_a} \times \frac{f_a}{f_x} \tag{3},$$

where:

a_{xa}^m is 1 if the link x (the x parking) and the link a are part of the same path; 0 otherwise;

F_m^j represents the number of m path users of the j category;

τ^j is the value of time of the j category user;

computing:

$$\left(\frac{dt_x}{dX_x} \right)_{X_x} \times \frac{D_x}{C_x} = \frac{\sum_m a_{xx}^m \sum_j F_m^j}{f_x} \times \left(\frac{dt_x}{df_x} \right)_{f_x} \times f_x ,$$

being $f_x = D_x$ and $\sum_m a_{xx}^m \sum_j F_m^j = D_x$.

As a result, the eqn (3) represents the functional link, $\mathbf{p} = f(\mathbf{F}_m^j)$, between parking fares and path flows.

3 Combined mode and route choice using a multi-user model

Fixed the fares for the parking areas, these will influence, before, the costs of the paths and, later, the generalised cost of the private vehicle. In order to estimate the path flows, a combined mode and route choice logit model can be used.

In particular, we can write:

$$F_m^j = \sum_{OD} \frac{D^{0j}{}_{ODcar}}{\left(1 - P^{0j}{}_{ODcar}\right) \times e^{-\Delta w_{OD}^j} + P^{0j}{}_{ODcar}} \times \frac{e^{V_m^j}}{\sum_{k(OD)} e^{V_k^j}} \quad (4)$$

where
$D^{0j}{}_{ODcar}$ is the initial value of the car demand of the j category between the origin O and the destination D;
$P^{0j}{}_{ODcar}$ is the rate of $D^{0j}{}_{OD}$ using car;

$\Delta w_{OD}^j = \beta * [\log\left(\sum_k V^k\right) - w^{oj}{}_{OD}]$ is the variation in the user satisfaction function of the car users between O and D of the j category;
$w^{oj}{}_{OD}$ is the initial value of the user satisfaction function;
V_k^j is the utility function of the k route and j category, being k the alternative routes for each couple O/D.
As a result, the eqn (4) represents the functional link, $F_m^j = f(p)$, between the path flows and the parking fares.
We have obtained a fixed-point problem defined by the system:
$p = f(F_m^j)$;
$F_m^j = f(p)$.

4 The existence of the solution for the fixed point problem

The fixed-point problem has a solution at least. In fact, the route choice function $p_{od} = p_{od}(V_{od}(p, F_m))$, the satisfaction function $w_{OD} = \log(\sum_k e^{Vk})$, the demand function $D_{OD} = D_{OD}(s)$ and the parking fare function $p = f(F_m)$ are continuous in their definition region. The composite function $F_m^j = f(p(F_m^j), F_m^j)$, where the solution at equilibrium F_m^{j*} is a fixed point, is a continuous function defined in the S_F region, not empty (being the network connected), compact and convex. The function $F_m^j = f(p(F_m^j), F_m^j)$ has real values only in the S_F region.
Therefore, all the hypothesis of the Brower theorem are satisfied and then the existence of the solution for the fixed-point problem is demonstrated [4].

5 The algorithm to solve the fixed-point problem

In order to solve the fixed-point problem, the method of the successive averages (M.S.A.) can be used.
Initialising the path flows using the network equilibrium flows when the parking areas are free, $F_m^{j\,0}$, and initialising the counter k =0, it is possible to start the algorithm iterations as follows:
step 1) k = k + 1
$p^k = f(F_m^{j\,k-1}, t(F_m^{j\,k-1}))$
$F_m^j = f(p^k, t(F_m^{j\,k-1}))$

If for each j and for each m $\dfrac{\left|F_m^j - F_m^{j^{k-1}}\right|}{F_m^{j^{k-1}}} < \varepsilon$ then **stop** otherwise

$F_m^{j\,k} = F_m^{j\,k-1} + 1/k\ (F_m^j - F_m^{j\,k-1})$
then back to step 1.

6 The marginal pricing: an optimal solution of the parking fare design problem

The present study represents a classical problem of transport system planning.
In such case, we want to maximise the social surplus function intentionally avoiding to calculate all that factors (environmental, ethical, social) not monetary.
The design variables are the fares to apply to the parking areas, really because easier and immediate application in comparison to the fares to be applied on all the links of the network (feasible only through vehicle electronic control systems).
The conditions of the problem are:
• parking fares ≥ 0;
• the congruence between costs and flows on the network and, therefore, the respect of the equilibrium between demand and supply.
The transport supply is represented using a graph simulating the road network and the parking areas.
The transport demand is supposed multi-user and elastic for the mode choice.
The social surplus function can be written:

$$S_S = \sum_{O-D}\sum_j \frac{1}{b^j} \cdot \int_{w_{OD}^{oj}}^{w} D_{O-D}^j(w)\,dw + \sum_j\sum_k p_k \cdot D_k^j,$$

where:

$\sum_j\sum_k p_k \cdot D_k^j$ is the parking fare revenue;

p_k is the k parking fare;
D_k^j is the parking demand of the j category going towards the k parking;

$\sum_{O-D}\sum_j \int_{w_{OD}^{o}}^{w} D_{O-D}^j(w)\,dw$ represents the user surplus, S_u;

b^j is the income marginal utility of the j category;

$D_{O-D}^{\ j}$ is the transport demand of the couple O-D and j category;

$w^j_{OD} = log(\Sigma e^V)$ is the value of the user satisfaction function (if the Logit model is used for the user route choice) of the car users between O and D and of the j category;
w^{oj}_{OD} is the initial value of the user satisfaction function.
The design problem can be set as:

$\mathbf{p} = \max_{\mathbf{p}} S_S(\mathbf{p})$

$p_x \geq 0 \ \forall x$

$\mathbf{F} = \mathbf{D}(\mathbf{C}(\mathbf{F})) * \mathbf{P}(\mathbf{C}(\mathbf{F}))$ \hfill (5)

The function $S_S(\mathbf{p})$, as it has been defined, is not convex, in fact its Hessiano could be negative, and therefore many local maximum could be found.

It is possible to express the conditions of the first order that guarantee the existence of a local maximum for the function S_S.

We can write:

$$\forall x \ \frac{\partial S_S}{\partial p_x} = 0$$

and so follows:

$$\frac{\partial S_S^j}{\partial p_x} = \frac{1}{b^j} \frac{\partial S_u^j}{\partial w} \frac{\partial w}{\partial p_x} + \sum_k \left(\frac{\partial p_k}{\partial p_x} \cdot D_k{}^j \right) + \sum_k \left(p_k \cdot \frac{\partial D_k{}^j}{\partial p_x} \right) = 0$$

$$\frac{\partial w}{\partial p_x} = \frac{-b^j (e^{V_1^j} + \ldots + e^{V_k^j})}{\sum_i e^{V_i^j}} = -b^j \cdot \sum_m P_m^j,$$

where P_m^j represents the choice probability that the j category of users goes through the m path including the x parking.

Following with the demonstration, we can write:

$$\frac{\partial S_u^j}{\partial w} = D^j(w);$$

therefore:

$$\frac{1}{b^j} \frac{\partial S_u^j}{\partial w} \frac{\partial w}{\partial p_x} = -D_x^j.$$

It is also:

$$\sum_k \frac{\partial p_k}{\partial p_x} \cdot D_k^j = D_x^j.$$

If we consider that:

$$\frac{\partial S_S}{\partial p_x} = \sum_j \frac{\partial S_S^j}{\partial p_x} = 0 \quad \forall x,$$

we can write:

$$\sum_j \sum_k p_k \cdot \frac{\partial D_k^j}{\partial p_x} = 0 \quad \forall x. \hfill (6)$$

The parking fares, in order to be a local maximum of the problem, should satisfy:

the condition $\displaystyle\sum_j \sum_k p_k \cdot \frac{\partial D_k^j}{\partial p_x} = 0 \quad \forall x$; \hfill (7) the condition $p_x \geq 0 \ \forall \ x$ (8)

the equilibrium between demand and supply. (9)

In the paragraph related to the marginal cost pricing, it is occurred that, for the respect of the condition of marginal cost pricing on the network, has to result:

$$p_k = \frac{dC_T}{dD_k} - CMV_k$$

Setting such value of p_k in (6), it results:

$$\sum_j \sum_k \left(\frac{\partial C_T}{\partial D_k} - CMV_k \right) \cdot \frac{\partial D_k^{\,j}}{\partial p_x} = \sum_j \sum_k \left(\frac{\partial C_T}{\partial D_k^j} \cdot \frac{\partial D_k^{\,j}}{\partial p_x} \cdot \frac{\partial D_k^{\,j}}{\partial D_k} \right),$$

$$- \sum_j \sum_k \cdot \frac{\partial \left(CMV_K \cdot D_k^{\,J} \right)}{\partial p_x} = \sum_K \frac{\partial C_T}{\partial p_x} - \sum_K \frac{\partial C_T}{\partial p_x} = 0 \qquad \text{c.v.d.}$$

Being besides $p_k \geq 0 \ \forall k$, results that the system constituted by the eqns (7), (8), (9), it is equivalent entirely to the system of equations individualised in the marginal cost pricing. Then we reduce the optimisation and the assignment problem to an assignment problem.

7 The application in Palermo

An application of the methodology has been carried out in a part of the historic centre of Palermo (the principal town of Sicily). The area is 471.500 squared meters and its perimeter is 2.830 meters. Many commercial and business activities are present inside the area. The level of congestion in the network is high and the parking areas are saturated for many hours.

A specific survey has been carried out in order to determinate the characteristics of the road network and the parking supply.

The parameters calibrated in the Urban Planning Study of Palermo have been used for the demand model and for the cost functions of the network links.

In order to carry out a comparison between different techniques, different methodologies have been implemented to design parking fares in this area.

After the marginal pricing, optimisation algorithms (Conjugate Gradient Descent before and Gauss-Newton later) have been used in order to optimise the social surplus function, taking in account the congruence between costs and flows on the network and, therefore, the respect of the equilibrium between demand and supply. In particular, the algorithm can be written as follows:

$k = 0$

step 1) $k = k + 1$

$p^k = \max_p S_S(p^k)$

$p_x \geq 0 \ \forall x;$

obtaining p by optimisation algorithms, we can calculate:

$F_m^j = f(p^k, t(F_m^{j \, k-1}))$ and then:

if for each j and for each m $\dfrac{\left| F_m^j - F_m^{j\,k-1} \right|}{F_m^{j\,k-1}} < \varepsilon$ then **stop** otherwise

$F_m^{j\,k} = F_m^{j\,k-1} + 1/k\,(F_m^j - F_m^{j\,k-1})$

then back to step 1.

Finally, it has been implemented another algorithm adding to the previous algorithm the condition in the optimisation process:

% $occ_x \leq 100$ $\forall x$ (limit of capacity for the parking areas).

In the table 1 are reported the results of the simulation.

Table 1: the parking fares obtained using different techniques

Parking areas	Initial conditions		Marginal park pricing		Optimisation algorithm and M.S.A with the limit of capacity	
	fare (euros)	% occ	fare (euros)	% occ	fare (euros)	% occ
1	0,52	113	0,46	113	3,52	100
2	0,52	112	0,74	111	3,25	100
3	1,03	179	1,57	139	2,47	100
4	0	225	1,23	148	2,31	100
5	0,52	159	0,97	144	2,96	100
6	0,52	203	1,53	158	3,03	100
Social surplus function (euros)	964,84		1012,30		527,47	

The simulations have shown that the results obtained from the marginal pricing method and the optimisation algorithm with the method of successive averages are the same. However the marginal pricing method has been less time consuming (about 80%) than the competitive technique.

The increasing of the social surplus function has been about 5 % and the congestion peaks in the parking areas have been cut. In particular the results of the simulation have shown a strong reduction of the long-lasting parking.

Finally, the last technique has been used in order to obtain parking fares able to contain the parking demand under the limit of the capacity.

The results of this simulation have shown a strong reduction of the social surplus function. This suggests the adoption of different solutions in order to reduce the level of congestion in the urban areas. Road pricing can be a way in order to optimise the transport system and its performance but cannot be the solution of the problem.

8 Conclusions

In this paper the marginal pricing applied to parking fares has been used in order to internalise the network congestion costs in the user perceived costs.

It has been proved that the calculated parking fares are a local maximum of the non-convex function estimating the social surplus generated by traffic fares.
The existence of the solution of the fixed-point problem has been proved by the Brower theorem and an algorithm to solve it has been proposed.
Then, the optimisation and the assignment problem has been reduced to an assignment problem.
An application has been carried out in a part of the real network of Palermo and the results have shown a strong reduction in the computing time in comparison to competitive techniques. The results have also shown the increasing of the social surplus function and the decreasing of the levels of congestion.
In the next steps of the research the elasticity of the demand for the time departure and the environmental costs generated by transport system users will be taken in account.

References

[1] Beckmann M., McGuire C., Winsten C., *Studies in the Economics of Transportation,* Yale University Press, New Haven, CT, 1956.

[2] Bellei G., Gentile G., Papola N., Ottimizzazione del trasporto urbano in contesto multiutente e multimodo mediante l'introduzione di pedaggi, *Modelli e Metodi per l'ingegneria del traffico* (a cura di) Cantarella G. E., Russo F., Ed Franco Angeli, Milano, Italy, pp.347-370, 2000.

[3] Bifulco C., A Stochastic User Equilibrium Assignment Model for the Evaluation of Parking Policies, *Ejor*,**71**, pp. 269-287., 1993.

[4] Cascetta E., Teoria e Metodi dell'Ingegneria dei Sistemi di Trasporto, UTET, Torino, 1998.

[5] Festa D.C., Nuzzolo. A., Analisi sperimentale delle relazioni velocità-flusso per le strade urbane, *Le strade*, **1226**, pp. 459-464, 1990.

[6] Gomez-Ibanez J.A., Small K.A., Road Pricing foe Congestion Management: A Survey of International Practice, NCHRP Synthesis 210, *Transportation Research Board*, National Academy Press, Washington D.C., 1994.

[7] Migliore M., Un modello d'ottimizzazione domanda-offerta nella sosta, *Proc. 3rd Conf. Rilievi, modellizzazione e controllo del traffico veicolare,* Rende (Italy), 1998.

Induced development in the transportation investments corridors - the probability appearance appraisal method based on the land use profiles

V. Depolo

Urban Land Development Public Agency, Belgrade, Yugoslavia

Abstract

Transportation system investments (Infrastructure and/or Public Transport Subsystem) produce the redistribution of existing (short-term effect) and generate the new travel demand (long-term impact of investment). The induced development is the key factor of new demand generation. The probability of induced development appearance appraisal method, developed by the author, is based on the use of the *Land Use Profiles*, defined for three basic land uses: housing, commercial activities and industry/storehouse, based on two criterion sets.

Forecasts based on the *Land Use Profiles* are evaluated by the use of experts' interview for real estate, whose estimates are in the range between 5 to 25 % (in some specific sites the percentage is even greater) compared to the existing/planned volume of development. This is equal with forecasts performed on the basis of the method and can be interpreted as an evidence of forecasting results.

The essential importance of the authors' work is that it describes *adjustment process* in the investment-influenced area. It also represents one step towards the induced demand forecasting method improvements, whose existence, despite evidences, was neglected by the part of the professional community.

1 Problem definition

In the previous period transportation system impacts were examined by land-use/transportation relationship. The goal was reaching balance, in steps and in the cycles, by defying middle / long - term programs of development. Each cycle defined a new state of balance. The state of balance in relation with the land-use/transportation replaced the state of imbalance and vice versa thus creating the conditions for stimulating the new development/investment. The influence of cumulative (economic development and superstructure construction) and stabilization factors (infrastructure investments) are occurred in cycles.

When urban transportation infrastructure investments are in question, measurement of economic benefits is accompanied by the complex conceptual and the practical problems. The questions concerning social values and social welfare are in the first line. The influence of indirect, especially external effects has been insufficiently researched. As far as transportation investments are in question, positive external effects, especially those connected with induced development phenomena and following form of appearance are of particular importance. In the past 10 - 15 years research efforts have been more intensive, but still there is a need for new methods of research.

From the present theoretical and practical works in the field of urban transportation investments impacts analysis come that positive externalities arise as consequence of infrastructure offer.

In some circumstances, efficient means of the state intervention/regulation is represented by appropriate rules - in urban agglomeration urban planning appears as regulation. By land use and appropriate standards one can influence the demand elasticity, the quality of offer, and the land parcel values. But, because of the imperfect mechanisms in location quality measurement, the biggest rate of increased land value is internalized[1] by owners/tenants.

When public land use is concerned (for example, infrastructure corridors), standards directly influence on the investment costs. If positive effects of agglomeration process (for of social benefit) are researched, appropriate development programs in the infrastructure investment corridor can help its efficient realization.

Existence of social benefits, positive externalities as consequence of infrastructure offer/development and their different shapes of appearance[2], are sometimes neglected by the part of the professional community (Button K, Quinet E, [1]). The reason is, after all, insufficient research of these phenomena[3]. Having in mind these facts, the research of social benefit generated by transportation infrastructure influence, especially in urban agglomeration, has the essential importance in minimum two reasons:

1. Assessment of investment efficiency is more complete;
2. Possibilities for analysis and managing of cyclic changes are created with respect of the relation between the transportation system and the catchments

---

[1] Internalization of external effects is the procedure by which one can reach balance of economic and social optimum. For each external effect quantification method, there is an appropriate internalization procedure. It can be said that every method of external effect quantification is based on corresponding internalization procedure. In practice, command and control instruments of internalization are often used. They do not represent strict internalization, but have the character of quasi internalization procedure - state intervention.

[2] On broader plan it is the matter of undeveloped regions progress, and in the urban areas, this relate to the activity, employment and development inducement, etc.

[3] Once the benefit has been detected, it is natural to internalize it, which is one of the reasons of dispute. Because of this, external benefits of significant intensity appear in proportionally shorter period than the investment life period, and they are evident in the field of land for development.

area (shifting of state of balance and unbalance), in other words, possibility for defining of the role of cumulative (induced development) and stabilization (investment) factors relationship.

Decisions connected with the social effects request more complex methodologies which integrate all known methods and techniques of analysis, forecasts, and assessment, and evaluation of impacts of transportation system to the environment, approved in current practice of transportation engineering. In that context, request for further improvement of transportation investment evaluation methodologies appears, especially when concerning cumulative influences, which stimulate secondary (induced) development.

The basic task of the investment impact analysis is identification of all potential influences that will be generated by the investment corridor, in other words, stimulation of the positive influences by which its entire efficiency will increase. Traffic generated as consequence of (induced) development is of special concern.

2 Research methodology

In the literature, induced development of superstructure objects, in terminological and essential meaning is treated in different ways. It is a process induced by direct investment influence on the level of accessibility. The inducement process takes time; it has a long-term character. Attractive location stimulates development, strengthening the "pressure" for its activation. This pressure manifests through the location prices or the other demand aggregates, and directly influences generation and intensification of imbalance between transportation system (offer) and transport needs (demand). It is, therefore, secondary consequence of investment and since it is not directly connected with physical presence of investment but with effects of functioning, it is considered as external effect.

The problem of the state of balance between transportation system and transportation demand (which comes from space distribution, structure and intensity of urban functions) definition is question constantly present in theory and engineering practice. However, the point is the process that has its continuity of life in observed urban area, in which there is a permanent change of states of balance and imbalance under the influence of cumulative and stabilization factors. Since in the process of adjustment between transportation system and its environment occurs "pressure" for development of new space of superstructure, it exerts influence on the continual increase of transportation demand.

In ideal circumstances this "pressure" originates from induced development, and in the course of time, creates such level of social costs, which require new investment cycle. Because of this, it is socially suitable, in the phase of creating each development cycle of urban transportation system, to clearly identify and define levels of acceptable deviations of balance, and, create measures for establishing "quasi" state of balance. In other words, this means establishment of marginal level of balance deviation. When transportation system and its environment reach these marginal conditions of imbalance, new investment/development cycle starts. Described flow has analogy with Hirshman's thesis of continuing state of imbalance, as condition of progress.

Research of transportation investments impacts on the induced development is carried out through identification and systematization of impact components, their quantification, with parallel process of formulation appropriate stimulant measurers and evaluation of possible solutions by which stimulant measures could be reached.

Specialties of basic land uses (housing, industrial/warehouse development and commercial land development) have influence on the choice of methods for impact quantification, that is, on the techniques for induced development allocation. The estimations are to be performed in two steps. The first one, net increase of development inside urban area is calculated, and distributed between potential locations planned for development and area of investment influence. When one researches influence of transportation investment on the location decisions in economy, specifically in commercial and industrial activities, number of models based on accessibility and transportation costs are in disposal; certain number of this models are also useful for distribution of housing space inside urban area (Banister D, Berechman Y, [2]). In the second step, appropriate net increase of corridor is allocated to the locations inside the corridor. In that step, factors generating induce development come into focus, and the analyzed locations are ranged according to the probability of attracting the induced development and then, the possible volume of development is calculated. Potential for acceptance of certain volume and structure of induced development is defined by location profiles, which plays the key role in this phase. Insufficient empirical research connected with induced development, cause that methods and techniques for second analysis step are based on analogy.

2.1 Location profiles

Two clusters of criteria are used in accessing the probability that certain location situated in investment corridor will attract corresponding volume of induced development: limiting and stimulating criteria. They are adapted to the type of investment, i.e., they are different slightly if investments are in streets from those in public transport.

Criteria that limit the probability of induced development involve: technical - function characteristics of investment corridor, and land use characteristics in area of influence (disposed locations, type of ground, urban limits, etc.). Quoted characteristics belong to the domain of state intervention instruments by which the emission of external effects is regulated. Marginal planned levels of development increase by locations are defined by estimation of indicators from this cluster of criteria. Criteria that stimulate the probability of induced housing development involve: location of corridor in relation to the city center network and posts of employment, and the potential of economic life[i]. Housing locations are analyzed on the basis of corresponding location profiles (Holm T,ationsare analyzed on the basis of corresponding location profiles (Holm A, Stavanger A.V, [3]). Profiles of locations position related to the city center network Pc, is defined by cluster with elements "accessibility quality" - C_i^j for which the function of common feature $P(RI^j)$ exists, that is:

$$Pc=\{C_i^j|P(RI^j)\} \tag{1}$$

Where:

Pc -   Profile locations position related to the city centre network,

C_i^j -   "Accessibility quality" of location j related to the centre belonging to class i

RI^j Change of accessibility index of location j, calculated by relation: Ip^j_{inv}/Ip^j, where:

Ip^j_{inv}-   Value of accessibility index of location j for network with investment

Ip^j -   Value of accessibility index of location j for network without investment

"Economic life" profile Pe of housing location is defined in the similar way, i.e., it represents cluster with elements "relative price" of apartment/house of class i, on the location j, Rc_i^j, with common feature function $P(RI^j)$. That can be expressed by:

$$Pe=\{Rc_i^j|P(RI^j)\} \tag{2}$$

Where:

Pe -   Economic life profile of location in investment corridor,

Rc_i^j -   Relative price of apartment/house of class i (i=1,2,....,m) on the location j (j=1,2, ..., n) in the zone of influence of investment in relation to the accessibility index change by influence of investment, that is, $Rc_i^j=f(RI^j)$, where:

RI^j Change of accessibility index of location j, calculated by relation: Ip^j_{inv}/Ip^j, where:

Ip^j_{inv}-   Value of accessibility index of location j for network with investment

Ip^j -   Value of accessibility index of location j for network without investment

Both profiles are de facto two-dimensional matrices - i*j.

Allocation of net increase of industrial/warehouse space performs on the basis of accessibility profiles and mobility profiles. Before defining of those profiles, locations must be systematized by type, i.e., by a characteristic that represents transportation volume intensities (Depolo V, [4]).

The induce criteria that are used for commercial space analyzing involve: agglomeration potential and economic life potential.

Basic element in agglomeration potential analysis is corridor absorption power of demand. Key indicator for calculations of absorption power of demand is frequency of commercial space user (expressed by number of users in given time period). When daily needs of consumer space are concerned, the systematization of frequencies in appropriate clusters is performed owing to the satisfactory number of valid results of empirical research. The clusters are called "absorption power profiles" - Pam (Depolo V, [4]). They enable the determination of agglomeration of induced development probability for locations, which is

---

[4] The probability for investment in housing stock of certain type is to be more profitable in shorter period of time than it is its economic lifetime comparing the same investment in any other part of urban area is calculated.

proportional to its accessibility, in comparison with the same ones in investment corridors. Possible volume of induced development is determinate by:

$$Pam = \{AM_k^j | D(FU_k)\} \tag{3}$$

Where:

Pam -   Absorption power profile of commercial locations,
AM_k^j -   Absorption power of commercial space class k (k=1,2, ... m) on the location j (j=1,2,......n) in the investment corridor
D -   Common feature function, by which frequency of users of commercial space class k is performed, that is, $FU_k = f(d)$, where:
FU_k-   User frequency of commercial space class k in the investment corridor (on the location j), in function of distance of commercial space from demand zone middle-point.

User frequencies, systematized in relation to the accessibility of the commercial space, are also used for potential of economic life Pe^k, which is represented by cluster of elements R^k_{FU} - relative frequencies with common feature function F_r^k represented by relation of users frequencies of commercial k in the investment corridor, and same class space frequencies on locations sited anywhere inside urban area (and/or defined by normative frequencies). This can be also described as:

$$Pe^k = \{Pe^j_k | F^k_U(F^K_R) \tag{4}$$

Where:

Pe_k -   Economic life profile of commercial space class k inside investment corridor
Pe^j_k -   Economic life of commercial space of class k on the location j inside investment corridor
F^k_U -   Common feature function of cluster element Pe^j_k whose volume is calculated for each element of cluster from ratio of frequencies of commercial space of class k in investment corridor and same ones located anywhere in urban area - F^k_R, that is, normatively defined. Value of function F^k_U can be:
$F^k_U > 1,0$
$F^k_U = 1,0$ i
$F^k_U < 1,0$
Locations with value of function greater than 1,0 are potentially attractive for induced development.

2.2 The probability of induced development appearance

In second phase, estimates are performed and locations in investment corridor are ranked according to the probability of induced development to be attracted. Probability assessment are estimated by adapted multicriteria analysis method and using location profiles.

For the inducement of housing and commercial spaces, one can measure characteristic of location in regard to the real estate investment efficiency. The comparison of economic life potentials of certain locations with the average ones for urban area shows the potential of investment efficiency in commercial space n the investment corridor.

Each industrial and warehouse location profile is labeled with corresponding probability of the induced development attraction of complementary production/warehouse land uses, by using accessibility profiles.

Volume of induced development quantification by locations was performed by the use of distribution factors related to the change of accessibility index influenced by investment, i.e., probability of attracting the same.

Test results show that there is a high correlation between the location induced development probability and its estimated volume. In absence of recent concrete empirical evidence[4], confirmation was obtained by inquiry of experts for superstructure development. The result of inquiry approved that volume of induced development is frequently greater than 20% in comparison with the planned one, which was also approved by the use of quantification method described above.

2.3 Induced development time scenario

As far as the description of time scenario by which agglomeration process is performed, there is no evidence in sufficient volume to perform scientific analysis. On the basis of terrain inquires performed for impact analysis of public transport terminus zones on the commercial space agglomeration process (Depolo V, [5]), it can be described by "S" curve with two asymptotes; the first one represents the existing level of developed commercial space, and the other is proportional to the market potential of terminus gravity area:

Phase I: Gradual start of agglomeration process; slow tempo of development (on the example of analyzed terminus, the tempo was about 9% of average annual increase of development in the first five year period;

Phase II: Dynamic tempo of induced development with high value of annual rate of development (at analyzed terminus zone example, the rate of development reaches value of 20% annually in the second five years period), and

Phase III: The process gradually slows down and the process of induced development stops. New level of transportation demand generated by process of inducement needs adaptation of transportation system. Depending on the established criteria, new transport system investment cycle begins in this phase.

One of the opened questions concerning the described flow is connected with the problem of determination of its starting point[5]. This is essential from standpoint of economic benefits estimation of new investment.

---

[5] In the case study for the city of Belgrade, evidence of development changes in the corridor investments which was used, were generated by synergetic influence both planned location development and investment. As it is the matter of investment dated from earlier period, it was not possible to delimit clearly influence of two factors (because the existence of development plan stimulates itself a part of induced development). According to this, author preformed method of real estate expert inquiry, as a method of result approval.

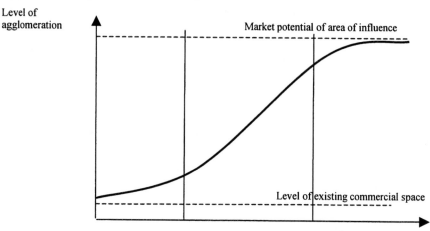

Figure 2 - Commercial space agglomeration process phases at the public transport terminus zone

3 Concluding considerations

Are the evidences about induced development existence under the influence of investment obtained?

Before answering, one brings out the opinion that divides professionals and scientists dealing with this matter into two diametrically opposite groups:

- The first state that appearance of induced development and thus induced transportation demand can be attributed to inadequate forecast methods, unproved development hypothesis, etc.
- The second one doesn't find that the existing forecasts methods are inadequate, but think that they produce reliable results to the extent in which relevant development tendencies are included and profiled. They consider that induced development exists and that in creating new methods and improvements of existing ones more effort should be taken.

From the point of view of this work, both groups are right. Namely, if procedures and methods are inadequate, and accordingly, development tendencies are

---

[6] Location selection represents, as a rule, act of rational judgment about advantage of one compared to an other potential possibility, no matter if professional or "unqualified" individual brings the decision. Then, "perception" factor of potential benefits from transport infrastructure investment comes in focus. Someone will anticipate advantages at the very beginning (project design phase), and others will need more evident and tangible proof. By the described behavior of potential demand, one can support arguments for proposed flow chart of induced development, represented by "S" curve. The empiric research will define the slope of curve and points of its changes.

without arguments, proposed method gives possibility for improvement of the existing procedures. On the other hand, advocates of induced development existence are given certain contribution to its arguments, and offered procedure for possibility assessment and estimation of induced development volume. Location profiles, as induce components of the probability assessment of induced development, show that there is possibility for location ranking according to its potential for inducement generation. Profiles are connected with the changes of transportation variables so they are under the influence of investment. *Is the reliability of results, by offered methodology and methods of quantification ensured?*

Empirical results, which present strong evidence of result reliability, are not numerous. One of the analogous examples that has very important influence on this work is based on the extensive research of Goodwin and associates, from SACTRA, who researched induced traffic phenomenon at new road network in Great Britain (Goodwin P.B, 1996, pp 53 [6]). In the resume of research, author quotes: "... the balance of evidence reasonably clearly indicate that additional traffic may be induced by the provision of extra road capacity, as result of combination of wide variety of different behavioral responses. ... the amount of extra traffic will vary according to the specific circumstances, ... In UK conditions, an average result ... may be of the order of 10% in the short run and 20% in longer run, with a range of 0-20% in a short run and 0-40% in the longer run ... these effects take place over time, with relevant period of several years for behavioral changes and possibly longer for land - use changes..."

Research conducted in this work confirms the existence of the planned volume of development violation, which is proportionally greater in the zones of higher accessibility. The calculations of induced development appearance probability show that locations in the investment corridor demonstrate different intensities of inducement. They are under the strong influence of the accessibility changes. By varying the criterion weights in the final estimate of probability of both clusters, starting from greater significance of limit criteria (measures of state intervention concerning external effects), to the predominantly greater share of stimulate criteria (where significance of investment influence increase through change of accessibility attributes) which is by its nature closer to the market principles, it was shown that final estimate, by rule, is connected with the criteria in which accessibility is essential indicator. This proves that the investment influence on the process of development inducement is essential. The volume of the induced development greatly corresponds to the results concerning induced transport demand on the roads in Great Britain.

What is the specific contribution of this work?

One of the most important findings is connected with the quantification of "push" (induce) criteria, especially in the fields of housing and commercial activities. Available evidences, which are used for relative price of housing development model, are limited to the estimation of, so called one-time effects. Existence of evidences concerning rent prices on the rent market[6] enables, by the similar procedure, relation definition of relative rent in function of relative change of accessibility caused by investment influence. That is how it will also be possible to calculate the "repeated" effects transferred through life time period of transportation investment.

As far as commercial use location, by means of common feature function in the economic life profile (or absorption power) new characteristic of profile can be determinate. Owing to increase of location accessibility, absorption power of commercial space increase. Locations with greater value of absorption power in comparison with average conditions for the whole urban area are proportionally profitable, or, time of return for invested money is shorter - they have greater economic life potential. This characteristic of locations is attributed to the influence of positive external effects of transportation investments.

The research field started with this work (in Yugoslavia), and with the offered methodology, the space for its improvement in future is opened. Methodology is very important for interpretation of agglomeration processes that are significant for urban growth. It is also important, from the point of new improvements of methodology for urban transpiration investment evaluation.

References

1. Button K, (1994): *Overview of Internalizing the Social Costs of Transport*, Internalizing the Social Costs of Transport, OECD/ECMT, Paris
2. Banister D, Berechman Y, (1996):*Transport and The Environment: The Role of Infrastructure and Physical Planning*, paper prepared for the VSB Farewell-Dialog Seminar on Transport and Environment, Amsterdam
3. Holm A., Stavanger A.V., (1997): Using GIS in Mobility and Accessability Analysis, ESRI User Conference, California, USA
4. Depolo V (1999a): *Uticaj tokova saobracaja na indukovanu izgradnju komercijalnog prostora u zonama terminusa javnog gradskog i prigradskog prevoza putnika*, Tehnika, Saobracaj 1, SITJ, Beograd
5. Depolo V, Vukanovic S, (1999): *Traffic Follows Impacts on the Induced Commercial Space Development in the Public Transport Terminus Zones - Case Study of Belgrade*, International Conference: 20th Century Urbanization and Urbanism, Urbanisticni Institut Republike Slovenije, Bled, Slovenija
6. Goodwin P.B, (1996): *Extra traffic induced by road construction: empirical evidence, economic effects and policy implications*, European Conference pf Ministers of Transport, Round table Conference 105, on "Infrastructure-induced mobility", Paris

---

[7] This market is, in the most developed countries, especially in Europe, partially under the influence of state intervention mechanisms (rent maximization). This is the evidence of the strong influence of external effects.

Section 7:
Emissions

Comparison of diesel and hybrid vehicle emissions by computer modelling

M. Ackerman, T. Davies, C. Jefferson, J. Longhurst & J. Marquez
*Faculty of Computing, Engineering and Mathematical Sciences,
University of the West of England, Bristol, UK*

Abstract

Regional passenger transport is a rapidly growing market in Europe, as a result of the need to minimise pollution in cities by reducing the demand for personal transport. Persistent requirements for mass transport include:

- Reduction in investment cost;
- Minimisation of emissions;
- Reduction of maintenance costs;
- Improvements in energy efficiency.

As the cost of electrification is often unacceptably high, diesel-powered vehicles are still the only remaining alternative. However, the maintenance costs associated with the diesel engine are very high, while frequent stop/start cycling on suburban routes results in high levels of noxious emissions and reduced energy efficiency.

This paper describes a hybrid power train simulation model, in which an electric vehicle's operational performance has been set up to generate input data to a hybrid and a diesel vehicle model. Those models behave as independent vehicles predicting fuel consumption and emissions to be compared to each other running in identical traffic conditions.

1 Introduction

A realistic scenario between 2000 and 2005 has been drawn by government authorities and environmental protection agencies in order to reduce emissions in urban centres because of the risk to human health and the need to preserve global and urban environment[1].

The vehicle industry is therefore mobilising effort and resources to reach environmental parameters established by Europe and the USA in order to help meet CO_2 reduction target[2][3].

Programmes have been sponsored by government funds with the objective to measure and analyse the effects of new fuel properties and vehicle technology on the exhaust emissions from gasoline, light-duty diesel and heavy-duty diesel vehicles. As a result of this effort, to accelerate the emissions reductions overall, Europe and the USA (since the early 1990's) have introduced emission standards now accepted world-wide[4].

2 Ultra low emission vehicles

Recently a new concept of vehicles has been researched and hybrid electric vehicles (HEVs) have been gradually introduced into the world market to achieve those emissions standards, for private and public transport[5].

These types of vehicle do not need overhead wires making them flexible and autonomous due to the fact that they generate their own energy. HEVs are provided with a gas turbine, fuel cell or diesel engine big enough to drive a generator and an energy storage system, which can be a battery, flywheel or ultracapacitor to provide energy to the electric traction motors[6].

3 Vehicle simulation

A simulation model has been developed in order to predict and compare the performance of a conventional diesel vehicle to that of a hybrid electric one operating on identical duty cycle. The hybrid electric vehicle model is shown in figure 1.

Matlab using Simulink[7] tools have been used to model the vehicle and its components allowing accurate analysis of results. Simulink is a program that runs as a companion to Matlab. Simulink and Matlab form a package for modelling dynamic systems. Simulink provides a graphical user interface that is used in building block diagrams, performing simulations, as well as analysing results. Results are displayed by numeric oscilloscope or output on the Matlab work environment. It is also possible to integrate a Matlab program inside a Simulink model to use the wide range of functions this provides.

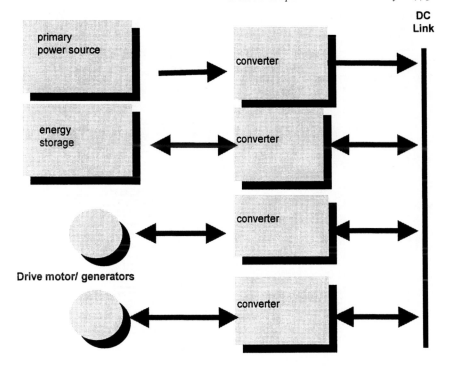

Figure 1: Hybrid vehicle transmission system

Figure 2 shows the model where each system box models and check vehicle performance through graphical displays.

The flexibility in the design of hybrid vehicles comes from the ability of the controller to manage how much power is flowing to or from each component. In this way, the components can be integrated in accordance with a control strategy to achieve the optimal design for a given set of design constraints[8]. There are many, often conflicting, objectives desirable for HEVs, the primary ones being:

- To minimise fuel consumption
- To minimise emissions
- To minimise propulsion system life cycle costs
- To improve performance.

The model is designed to be as generic as possible, and can be adapted to any kind of configuration of motor, engine or storage energy unit, and any type of vehicle, road or rail.

**VEHICLE MODEL
READING
DRIVE CYCLE**

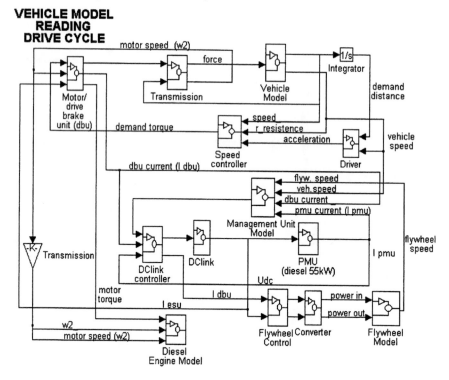

Figure 2: Model of simulation of a hybrid and diesel vehicle

4 Simulation of driver operation

Once the vehicle drive cycle has been specified, including distance to be covered, the driver action can be modelled by means of a driver subsystem model, shown in figure 3, which sets the acceleration, maximum speed and the point where deceleration must begin. The driver model thus works as any human driver in a real system, checking speed and distance, and accelerating and decelerating as necessary. Inside the driver model there is a drive cycle sub-system, which has been created to update the demand distance database so that multiple drive cycle can be simulated. This also determinates the stop-time during which passengers would get on and off the vehicle. At this point the demand distance for the next cycle is updated.

The drive cycle input data is generated by a VISSIM model[9], which simulates the stochastic aspects of traffic flow in real time including vehicle behaviour.

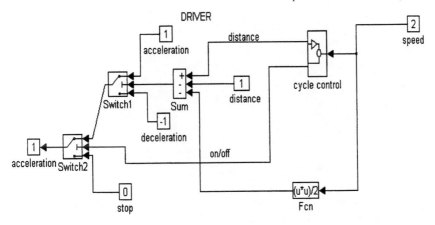

Figure 3: Driver subsystem model

Thus, the choice of the area to simulate the hybrid and diesel vehicles is very critical because the result validity depends from this decision. The first requirement was to choose a busy lane in the city centre, which suffers from pollution. The Bristol City Transport Department has been contacted to obtain information related to pollution in the entire Bristol road network, taking into consideration that Bristol is one of the most polluted cities in the South West of England. VISSIM can thus be used to generate realistic urban drive cycles.

As an example a road including a bus lane in Bristol, UK, shown in figure 4, has been modelled. Buses, private cars and other vehicles subjected to a fixed sequence of traffic lights and bus stops could be simulated.

Figure 5 shows the generated drive cycle of a specific bus. Distance, speed and acceleration data are saved in a suitable file extension, which can be read in Matlab. The driver model (fig 6) is able to read speed and acceleration demands given by Vissim generating fuel consumption and emission in real time in a specific route in Bristol. The Simulink vehicle model can thus predict fuel consumption for the HEV and diesel vehicle under this driving condition.

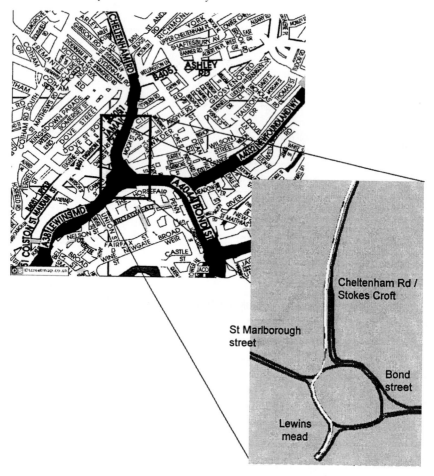

Figure 4: VISSIM Model - Bristol City Centre

5 Fuel consumption and emissions modelling

The model can also predict fuel consumption and emissions for the hybrid electric and equivalent diesel powered vehicle operating over the same duty cycle. The diesel vehicle was assumed to be powered by a conventional 150 kW diesel engine using a measured fuel consumption map based on engine speed and power shown in figure 7[10].

N° Vehicle	Distance	Speed	Acceleration	Lane
0	307.00		302 0 0	
553	33.73	4.53	-0.18	1
548	57.11	1.96	-0.93	1
543	68.20	3.77	2.65	1
521	89.76	5.53	-0.22	2
540	140.07	9.36	-0.07	1
535	158.27	8.85	0.21	1
534	181.01	8.08	-0.84	1
511	233.02	3.05	-1.06	1
0	307.00		301 0 0	
562	4.36	0.00	-0.43	2
558	15.46	0.00	0.00	2
526	233.22	5.25	-0.91	1
0	307.00		202 0 0	
547	64.17	9.21	-0.14	2
520	640.92	8.75	0.14	1
514	720.60	9.68	0.22	1
0	307.00		201 0 0	
530	130.48	6.34	-0.12	1
518	334.83	7.28	0.28	1

Before being filtered

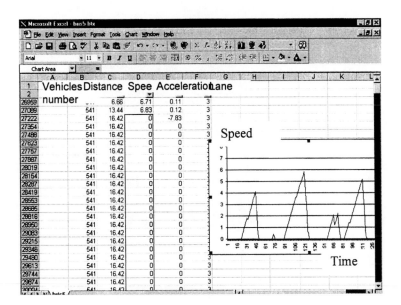

After being filtered

Figure 5: Vehicle performance data generated by VISSIM

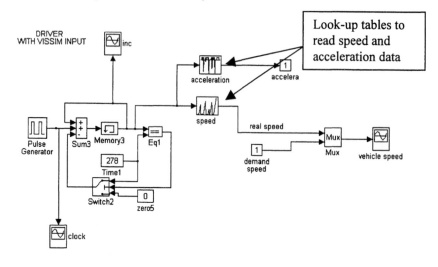

Figure 6: Modified drive model

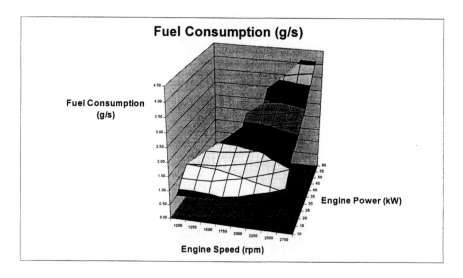

Figure 7: Fuel consumption map

This map was obtained from static measurements on a 1.9 litres turbo diesel engine and scaled up as required. The model can also predict emissions of CO, NOx, HC and Particulates, in the same way, using emission maps obtained from the same source[10].

The diesel engine model incorporated a conventional gearbox and automatic gear changing routine with assumed transmission efficiency of 85%. The hybrid vehicle PMU was assumed to be powered at constant level of 40 kW by an equivalent diesel engine operating at its optimum efficiency.

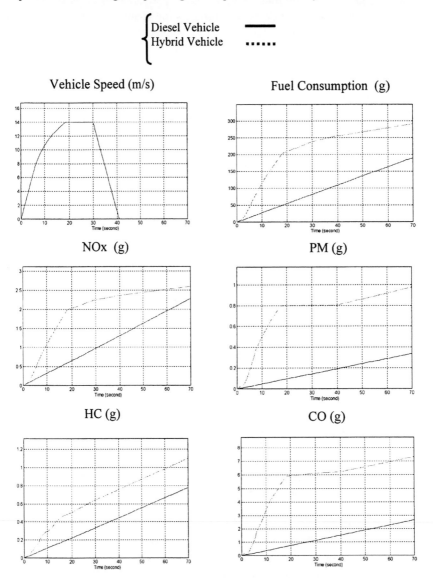

Figure 10: Model results for fuel consumption and emissions

Figure 10 shows the fuel consumption and emissions with each vehicle running within a generic drive cycle.

8 Conclusions

A comparison between hybrid electric and a diesel vehicle has established that, assuming both vehicles are running on the same particular operational and route conditions, using the model described, predicts the following reductions in fuel consumption and emissions due to hybrid vehicle operation compared with diesel operation:

- 35.7% fuel savings
- 63% CO
- 15% NO_x
- 36% HC
- 70% Particulate emissions.

These results indicate the potential environmental benefit of a change from diesel to hybrid propulsion in urban transport.

References

1. **Emissions standards: Europe and USA for heavy-duty diesel truck and bus engines-** http://www.dieselnet.com
2. Haus R, Wilkinson R, Heland J, Schaefer K –**Remote sensing of gas emissions on natural gas flares** –Pure Appl. Opt. 7 – pages 853-862 – 1998
3. Wellburn, A - **Air Pollution and Climate Change: The Biological Impact** - 1994
4. Jefferson C ; Ackerman M - **Global Emissions due to Urban Transport and the Potential for their Reduction** – Urban Transport IV, Lisbon – pages 339-348 - 1998
5. Appleby AJ – **Electrochemical energy** – progress towards a cleaner future: lead/acid batteries and the competition – Journal of Power Sources – vol 53 – pages 187-97 – 1995
6. Gutman G. – **Hybrid electric vehicles and electrochemical storage systems a technology push-pull couple** – Journal of Power Sources 84 – pages 275-279 – 1999
7. **Simulink User's Guide** - The Math Works Inc. - March 1992
8. Jefferson CM, Ackerman M – **A flywheel variator energy storage system** – Energy Convers Mgmt – vol 37 N.10 – pages 1481-91 – 1996
9. **Vissim User's Manual - Program Version 3.50 -** PTV system software and Consulting GmbH - July 1998
10. Private Communication between UWE, Bristol and Imperial College London

The impact of road pricing and other strategic road transport initiatives on urban air quality

G.Mitchell[1,2], A.Namdeo[1], J.Lockyer[1] and A.D.May[2].
[1] School of Geography, University of Leeds, United Kingdom.
[2] Institute for Transport Studies, University of Leeds, United Kingdom.

Abstract

The UK National Air Quality Strategy (NAQS) recognises road transport as a principal source of urban atmospheric pollution, hence an objective of the 1999 Transport White Paper was to reduce air pollution through better management of urban road traffic. Whilst there are numerous policy options available for managing urban traffic their air quality implications at the city scale are largely unknown. This paper presents preliminary results from the application of a chain of dynamic simulation models of traffic flow (SATURN, SATTAX), pollutant emission (ROADFAC) and dispersion (ADMS-Urban), integrated within a geographic information system model (TEMMS) to assess the impact of alternative transport scenarios on air quality for the city of Leeds, UK.

The scenarios addressed include "business as usual" traffic growth to 2015; network development; road pricing with cordon charging; road pricing with distance charging; and the wider adoption of clean fuel vehicle technology. The impact of these developments on air quality (nitrogen dioxide, particulates and sulphur dioxide), including exceedence of air quality standards is identified. Finally, differences in the spatial distribution of air quality (as NO_2) between scenarios are highlighted, in light of their significance to social equity concerns.

1 Air quality review and assessment

Over the last few decades significant improvements in urban air quality have been made in many countries, yet in 1998 the European Environment Agency (EEA) concluded that significant problems remain, particularly with nitrogen oxides, sulphur dioxide, carbon monoxide and particulates, all of which sometimes exceed World Health Organisation guideline values. The EEA [1] estimate that in the EU's 115 largest cities, 40 million people experience at least one exceedence of a health based air quality standard every year.

These problems have fuelled the demand for a coherent regulatory framework for the management of atmospheric emissions and air quality at local, regional and national levels. In the UK, government passed the 1995 Environment Act stating national policy concerning air quality.

The Act required the development of a National Air Quality Strategy (NAQS) to enable the UK to achieve its air quality objectives, and meet it's international commitment's, including those of 1996 EU Air Quality Framework Directive (96/62/EC) and subsequent daughter directives. These directives set legally binding limit values for a range of pollutants, and the target dates by which these standards must be met, but it remains the responsibility of member states to decide how best to achieve the objectives set by the directives.

The NAQS, published as a consultation document in 1997, and formally adopted in 2000 (DETR [2]) defines UK policy, tasks and responsibilities for achieving ambient air quality objectives. A major task is the review and assessment of urban air quality, where local government must determine if ambient air quality is likely to meet EU standards by the target date of 31 December 2005.

The NAQS recommends a three phase assessment approach, with the final phase employing detailed modelling if the earlier screening phases indicate the possibility of standard exceedence(s). If this stage 3 assessment confirms this possibility, then local government has the power to designate air quality management areas (AQMA's), which must be supported by an air quality management action plan detailing measures that the authority intends to pursue to ensure that the air quality objectives for that location are met in time.

In Western Europe road transport has overtaken industrial processes and coal combustion as the main source of atmospheric emissions (EEA[1]), and for most UK cities, it is the main source of NO_2 and PM_{10} pollution (Carruthers *et al.*,[3]; Stedman, [4]) Thus while air quality management action plans will address a range of sources, it is has been suggested that management of urban road transport will be key to ensuring that air quality objectives are met.

To support air quality management action planning, we investigated the impact of several strategic road transport scenarios and policy options on urban air quality, through application of a series of linked dynamic models. The research addressed Leeds, UK, a large (562 km^2) metropolitan district with 740,000 residents.

Leeds has experienced strong economic growth since 1981, second only to London, and forecasts indicate this growth is likely to continue. Car ownership has also risen, by 11% in the last decade, and net in-commuting is predicted to grow 50% in the next (LDA, [5]). Such rapid growth suggests that air quality in 2005 may be at risk of failing the directive standards. However, this growth also makes Leeds an ideal city to study the air quality implications of alternative road transport 'futures' and management options, as the results can give advance notice of likely outcomes in comparable but less rapidly growing cities.

2 The transport-air quality modelling system

2.1 Overview and traffic modelling

Central to the integrated transport-air quality model system is TEMMS (Traffic Emission Modelling and Mapping Suite), a GIS-model using network link-based data on vehicle flow and speed as an input, to produce link based emissions in a format suitable for entry to an atmospheric dispersion model. Namdeo *et al.*, [6] give a detailed description of TEMMS development and application.

To date, TEMMS has been exclusively applied in conjunction with SATURN, a widely used interactive simulation and assignment model (Van Vliet [7]), although any source of link flow data can be used.

Using a fixed trip (origin-destination) matrix and description of the network, assignment and simulation procedures run iteratively, until an equilibrium point is reached at which costs (e.g. times) are optimised. These procedures consider parameters of minimum gap acceptance, junction type, number of lanes, turn data, traffic signal stages and cycle rate, which all impact upon time spent at junctions, the key parameter fed back to the cost optimising routine. The final result is a detailed spatial representation of traffic flow (PCU's) and mean speed for each link of the network for a specified period such as the morning peak.

2.2 Emission modelling

Using its integral model ROADFAC, TEMMS calculates link based emissions of NO_x, CO, CO_2, SO_2, PM_{10}, $PM_{2.5}$, VOC's, benzene and 1-3 butadiene. In addition to the link flow and speed data (from SATURN), ROADFAC requires data on fleet composition and speed dependent emission factors, both of which are drawn from MEET (EC [8]). The fleet is described according to vehicle type, gross weight, engine capacity and type, fuel and emission control technology used, giving 72 sub-classes with characteristic emission rates. Data is based on vehicle sales, with projections for future years based on historical trends in vehicle ageing, and scheduled emission control legislation.

Speed dependent emission factors for each vehicle class are developed from chassis dynamometer tests simulating observed drive cycles of differing mean trip speeds. Additional emissions from acceleration and queuing at junctions are therefore included, but these emissions are allocated evenly to the whole link, and not apportioned using a junction weighting. ROADFAC uses CORINAIR methods to estimate the additional emissions resulting from cold start motoring.

For each link, a composite emission factor is determined from the fleet data, vehicle class emission factors, and mean link speed. Total link emissions are the product of this composite factor and link flow. Speed and flow data from SATURN relate to a short period only (e.g. AM peak), hence to calculate emissions through 24 hours, time variant emission correction factors must be applied to the modelled short period emission. These correction factors are developed from time variant data, using observed vehicle count and speed data collected hourly throughout the week, and for a range of road types.

2.3 Air quality modelling

For the work reported here, TEMMS was applied in conjunction with ADMS-Urban (CERC [9]), a commercial dispersion model formally recognised by the NAQS as being suitable for assessing compliance of urban air quality to standards. ADMS-Urban uses boundary layer similarity profiles to parameterise variation in turbulence with height within the boundary layer, and uses a skewed-Gaussian distribution to determine the vertical height of pollutant concentrations in a plume under convective conditions. Boundary layer stability parameters are calculated from wind speed, surface heat flux and boundary layer height.

Emission from sources other than vehicles were derived from the local government stationary source emission inventory, which quantifies pollutant annual mass emission and ADMS-Urban required parameters (stack location and height, gas exit velocity and temperature) for the 416 regulated point source emissions in the city. Minor point (< 0.1 tonne/yr) and other area source emissions are addressed through consideration of background concentrations (using observed concentrations from an upwind rural monitoring station) and via calibration of modelled and observed data.

ADMS-Urban was applied to Leeds using surface roughness default values to represent topography, and the Generic Reaction Set model to calculate NO_2 concentration from NO_x emission. We used sequential (hourly) meteorological data for 1999 which is a close approximation to the long run (1990-99) average, has a time step corresponding to that used in modelling mobile emissions, and which gives better estimates of peak values than statistical meteorological data.

In hourly steps, the model simulates a full year of atmospheric pollutant concentrations from which compliance to the prevailing air quality standards is assessed as annual mean and percentile standards (Table 2). For example, the NO_2 1 hour mean must not exceed $200\mu g/m^3$ more than 18 times a year, which is the 99.8[th] percentile of one year of hourly values. Emissions were modelled for a 30 x 25km box centred on Leeds, and concentrations simulated for a 12 x 12km box covering the entire built urban area, at a spatial resolution of 200m.

2.4 Model Calibration and Validation

Namdeo *et al.*, [6] note that the likely error of the constituent models are c. ±12% for SATURN vehicle flows, ±4-35% for the emission factors, ±5-10% for fleet composition, and ±20% for the dispersion model, suggesting that the system should be capable of predicting pollutant concentrations within about 40-75% of observed concentrations, which NAQS guidance indicates is acceptable for conducting strategic level statutory air quality assessments.

To calibrate the system we modelled 1993 air quality, the only year for which we had corresponding SATURN matrices, meteorological and observed pollutant concentration data (NO_2, PM_{10}, SO_2 from the Leeds central AUN station). A calibration factor was derived by comparing observed mean concentrations (Jan-June) with modelled values for the same location. Application of the calibration factor to the modelled data (July-Dec) gave calibrated means within 4% of the observed. Ideally, this procedure would be conducted over a wider spatial area using data from multiple monitoring stations, but this data is not available.

3 Development of road transport and emission scenarios

We investigated the air quality implications of five strategic transport and emission scenarios with potential city wide effects, including 'business as usual'; network development (new roads); road user charging using distance and cordon charges; and the introduction of clean fuel vehicle technology. These scenarios address strategies that are underway (new roads), under consideration in the local transport plan (road pricing), or promoted nationally (clean fuels).

3.1 Network development

The impact of major road schemes on air quality was investigated through three Leeds SATURN networks. The first represents the network as it was in 1993, with 10,250 links, 1314 intersections, 327 priority junctions and 17 roundabouts. For the morning peak simulation, over 85,000 trips between 370 zones are simulated. The second represents the network in 2005, with the minimum of major road schemes implemented (and >102,000 trips). This 'Do-Min' network includes the A1-M1 link road (opened in 2000), a motorway skirting the city to the south east, linking two existing regional motorways. The third network (2005 'Do-All') additionally includes 3 km of inner-city dual carriageway that completes the inner ring road, and is expected to remove much city centre through traffic, and the east Leeds link road, 4 km of dual carriageway intended to relieve congestion and promote economic regeneration in east Leeds.

3.2 'Business as usual'

The effect of a 'do nothing' strategy was assessed for 1993 (standard network), 2005 and 2015 ('Do-Min' network). For each simulation year, traffic volume, and fleet characteristic data are required. Traffic volume (PCU's / link) for 1993 and 2005 are output by SATURN, and the 2015 link flows obtained by applying a growth factor to the 2005 flows. The Leeds factor was derived from TEMPRO 3.1, the UK national trip-end forecast model (HMSO [10]). This predicted a growth of 17.3% (2005-15), which we understand forthcoming TEMPRO 4 projections will show are conservative. From 1993-2005 trips grew by 21%, and total vehicle/kms travelled by 34%. For all years, observed or predicted UK fleet composition and emission factors were obtained from MEET (EC, [8]).

3.3 Road user charging

Under the Transport Act 2000, UK local government has the power to implement road user charging to tackle congestion and traffic pollution. To date, only London has made a firm commitment to road pricing, but 24 other UK local authorities, including Leeds, consider its implementation in their local transport plans for 2000-2005.

We assessed possible impact on air quality of road pricing using cordon and distance charging. Cordon charging was selected as it is proven technologically (Singapore, Norway), and hence of most interest to local authorities. However, from an assessment of network performance (generalised cost, trip time and distance, total trips) under road pricing, May and Milne [11] found that cordon pricing was the least effective regime, although it is very sensitive to cordon location. They concluded that, given concerns over added driver risk taking and the uncertain charge per trip associated with time and congestion charging, future road pricing work could usefully focus on distance based charging.

All our road pricing tests were conducted on the 2005 'Do-Min' network, using SATTAX (Milne and Van Vliet [12]), a module of SATURN that uses the SATEASY elastic assignment algorithm to model trip demand in response to generalised cost. Cordon charging is represented by adding the crossing toll to the generalised cost for that link, and distance charging by adding a fixed km cost for all links that fall within the charge area. The model response is then to transfer trips off the network (switch mode, travel at other times or not at all) and to modify route choice. Table 1 details the tests and associated trip suppression.

Table 1: Road user charge scenarios, trip and total distance travelled suppression

Road user charging (2005 'Do-Min')	% Reduction in trips [and v/kms]
City centre (inner orbital) cordon : £3	7.0 [2.0]
Distance charge : 2p/km	8.8 [11.1]
Double cordon : £2 inner and £1 outer	18.5 [17.2]
Distance charge : 10p/km	47.0 [46.1]
Distance charge : 20p/km	62.5 [55.7]

The inner cordon charge was set to £3, deemed politically acceptable by the local government, but below the £5 toll fated for London in 2003. A second test splits this fee over two cordons, which increases trip suppression as more trips are affected by the outer cordon. Using real monetary values in SATEASY, a revenue of £97,000 for 470,000 PCU kms travelled is generated. From this a 20p/km toll is derived that is consistent with tests elsewhere (May and Milne [11]) but gives a trip suppression likely to be far from the economic optimum, even if externality effects were valued highly. Additional distance charges were thus set at half the 20p/km charge, and at an order of magnitude lower, the latter giving a trip suppression similar to the initial inner cordon charge. All charges were levied according to PCU's with no attempt to differentiate by vehicle type.

3.4 Clean fuel vehicle technology

Finally, we investigated the air quality implications of growth in clean fuel vehicle (CFV) use, addressing technologically viable fuels with proven emission benefits promoted through the government's 'Powershift' programme: liquefied petroleum gas (LPG) and electricity. For 2015, fleet composition was adjusted to include 2% electric vehicles, 3% hybrid, 1% fuel cell and 5% LPG. For electric vehicles we used the MEET (EC [8]) high growth forecasts. These are based on evolutionary not revolutionary market changes, and hence are very speculative. MEET has no UK LPG use forecasts, so we chose a value consistent with MEET forecasts for the Netherlands and Italy, which exhibit strong LPG growth.

Emission factors were also drawn from MEET (EC [8]), although the data is sparse and are meant only as a guide. For electric vehicles (hybrid and methanol fuel cell), emission factors are not speed dependent, and are given for three classes only: passenger cars, light duty vans and buses. Emissions from battery operated vehicles are assumed to be zero at point of use. For LPG, factors relate only to vehicles <2.5 tonnes, and only address uncontrolled and Euro I standards. Euro I LPG factors were therefore applied for Euro II-IV vehicles.

4 The impact of strategic road initiatives on urban air quality

Results from the study are summarised in Table 2 for nitrogen dioxide (NO_2), particulates (PM_{10}) and sulphur dioxide (SO_2). Results are given city wide for all three pollutants (annual mean, 1 or 24 hour mean, and number of sites exceeding the standard) and also for a single city centre location for NO_2.

Under the 'business as usual' scenario, 1993-2015, there is a great reduction in city wide annual mean NO_2 (by 42%, P<0.001), a small (1%, P<0.001) reduction in PM_{10}, and no significant change in SO_2. The NO_2 reduction is driven by a rapidly declining fleet weighted emission factor, c. 90% over the forecast period. For PM_{10} and SO_2 the comparable emission factor reductions are c.10% and 2% respectively, insufficient to offset additional emissions arising from an increased trip volume. The modelling forecasts no NO_2 standard exceedence by the NAQS 2005 target year, and a few exceedences for SO_2 and PM_{10}. These exceedences are largely attributable to point sources, that typically account for 40% of all NO_x emitted, 76% of PM_{10} and 93% of SO_2 (i.e. NO_x is most sensitive to road traffic).

The planned Leeds network developments reduce air quality city wide for all three pollutants, as under the 'Do-All' scenario, trips increase by 2.4%, and vehicle kilometres by 4.2%, raising total emissions. The additional capacity reduces the generalised cost for some O-D pairs, bringing additional trips onto the network via the elastic assignment procedure, and causing re-routing of some trips to longer, but faster routes. City wide, the air quality differences are not statistically significant, but there is a significant spatial redistribution, with air quality reduced around the new links and their feeders, but improving elsewhere.

City wide, road pricing lowers NO_2 concentrations (P<0.001), reduces PM_{10} under the 10p/km and 20p/km charges only (P<0.001), and has no effect on SO_2. Effects are greatest for NO_2, which is most sensitive to road emissions, and least in SO_2, where total emissions are dominated by point sources. Each pricing regimes has a different effect. City wide, NO_2 is reduced by just 0.7% under a single cordon, 4% under a double cordon, and 3%, 12% and 15% under the 2p, 10p and 20p per km charges respectively.

Table 2: Nitrogen dioxide, PM$_{10}$ and SO$_2$ concentrations (μg/m³) modelled for Leeds, UK.

Scenario [1]	NO$_2$ at city centre AUN site		City-wide (12x12km) [Number of site exceedences in brackets] [2]			
	Annual Mean	1 hr mean 99.8th centile	NO$_2$ Annual Mean	PM$_{10}$ Annual Mean	24 hr mean PM$_{10}$ 90.41th centile	1 hr mean SO$_2$ 99.72th centile
Air quality standard	40	200	40	40	50	350
Business as usual						
1993 network	39.36	146.72	29.24 [260]	28.65 [24]	42.88 [92]	288.20 [13]
2005	24.04	110.43	19.68 [0]	28.71 [24]	42.94 [91]	288.24 [13]
2015	21.99	107.99	17.09 [0]	28.38 [24]	42.59 [80]	287.95 [12]
Network development						
1993 network	39.36	146.72	29.24 [260]	28.65 [24]	42.88 [92]	288.20 [13]
2005	24.04	110.43	19.68 [0]	28.71 [24]	42.94 [91]	288.24 [13]
2005 Do-All	23.82	110.43	19.74 [0]	28.72 [24]	42.99 [92]	288.25 [13]
2015	21.99	107.99	17.09 [0]	28.38 [24]	42.59 [80]	287.95 [12]
2015 Do-All	19.59	106.87	18.49 [0]	28.77 [24]	42.99 [92]	288.28 [13]
Road pricing [3]						
Zero toll	25.75	112.83	20.05 [0]	28.78 [25]	43.02 [95]	288.27 [13]
Single cordon £3	24.38	111.67	19.92 [0]	28.76 [25]	42.99 [93]	288.26 [13]
Double cordon £2+£1	24.02	111.45	19.25 [0]	28.66 [24]	42.89 [91]	288.22 [13]
2p/km distance toll	24.63	110.99	19.44 [0]	28.68 [25]	42.92 [94]	288.23 [13]
10p/km distance toll	20.05	107.39	17.69 [0]	28.41 [24]	42.66 [81]	288.12 [13]
20p/km distance toll	17.58	107.25	17.12 [0]	28.33 [24]	42.58 [81]	288.09 [12]
Clean fuel vehicles						
2015 Do-All	19.59	106.87	18.49 [0]	28.77 [24]	42.99 [92]	288.28 [13]
2015 Do-All Clean fuels	21.83	107.91	18.48 [0]	28.70 [24]	42.93 [91]	288.25 [13]

1. Networks 2005 Do-Min unless otherwise stated; 2. 3600 sites at 200m intervals; 3. Modelled SATURN demand flow, not SATURN 'actual' flow

These changes in NO_2 correlate highly with change in total vehicle kms travelled (Table 1). All pricing regimes reduce this distance. Under the single cordon, distance is reduced more strongly via trip suppression, with mean distance per trip increasing 6%, indicating re-routing to avoid the cordon. This is clearly seen in an NO_2 map, where a redistribution from the city centre to the cordon exterior occurs. The 2p/km regime is arguably most efficient from an air quality perspective: NO_2 reduction is comparable to that of the double cordon but at a fraction of the toll (mean trip fee is c. 20p), and with only 2.5% of locations experiencing increased NO_2 (cf. 0.4% double cordon, 24% single cordon).

Strongly growing the use of clean fuels produces a minor and statistically insignificant improvement in city-wide air quality. The proportion of the fleet as CFV's in 2015 is still small compared to conventional vehicles, and so might be expected to have a minor impact, but it is the crude CFV emission factors that underpin these results. In particular, emissions from LPG Euro I vehicles are greater than from petrol Euro II-IV vehicles, giving an elevated fleet weighted NO_x emission at lower speeds typical of city centre traffic. Thus to assess the effect of CFV's on city air quality much improved emission factors are required.

5 Conclusions

The study has shown that air quality in Leeds is generally good, with forecast exceedences of PM_{10} and SO_2 standards attributed largely to point sources, not road traffic. Management of road traffic does, of course, modify air quality. The network development for Leeds is likely to degrade NO_2 as the added capacity increases trips and hence emissions. The drop in air quality is most noticeable close to the new roads, particularly the radial East Leeds link route, but also occurs widely across much of the eastern suburbs. However, the associated re-routing effect also leads to an improvement in air quality in the south of the city, where air quality is currently poorest due to the urban motorways.

Implementation of road user charging also has strong implications for the redistribution of air pollution. The single cordon in particular reduces pollutant concentrations significantly in the city centre, but does so at the expense of all areas immediately surrounding the cordon. Road pricing only brings major improvements in air quality ($> 1\mu g/m^3$ NO_2 reduction) under high distance charges. However, considering the overall impact and distributional effects, a modest distance charge appears to be most efficient in reducing concentrations.

The clean fuel analysis demonstrates a need for much improved CFV emission factors. However, Euro II-IV vehicles have very low emissions so it is difficult to make an air quality case for CFV's at the strategic level. They may of course have a role to play in tackling local pollution hot spots (which we confirmed are more numerous under street canyon than flat terrain modelling), in low emission zones (LEZ) for example. But even ambitious LEZ's only achieve the gains which will arise by 2005 through natural fleet renewal (Carslaw and Beevers [13]). From an air quality perspective, the lesson is to ensure effective control of point sources, and adopt 'do nothing' strategic traffic management. Reducing congestion (where emissions are poorly modelled) is also likely to be important.

Acknowledgements

We are indebted to David Cherry, Richard Crowther, David Gilson, Chris Hill, John McKimm, John Tubby and Graham Wilson (Leeds City Council), for essential guidance and material support, and to David Milne (ITS) for the SATTAX application. We gratefully acknowledge the financial support provided by the EPSRC-DETR Future Integrated Transport programme.

References

[1] EEA. *Europe's Environment: The Second Assessment*. European Environment Agency, Copenhagen, 1998.
[2] DETR. *The Air Quality Strategy for England, Scotland, Wales and Northern Ireland: Working Together for Clean Air*. Department of the Environment, Transport and the Regions, London, 2000.
[3] Carruthers, D., Edmunds, H., King, H., Lester, A., Nixon, S. *Dispersion Modelling of Emissions in an Urban Area*. Report to the Department of the Environment, Transport and the Regions, Cambridge Environmental Research Consultants Ltd., 1998.
[4] Stedman, J.R. *Revised High Resolution Maps of Background Concentrations in the UK: 1996*. NETCEN report to the Department of the Environment, Transport and the Regions, Abingdon, UK, 1998.
[5] LDA. *Leeds: A Summary*. Leeds Development Agency, 2000.
[6] Namdeo, A; Mitchell, G. and Dixon, R. TEMMS: an integrated package for modelling and mapping urban traffic emissions and air quality. *Journal of Environmental Modelling and Software*, In press.
[7] Van Vliet, D. SATURN: a modern assignment model. *Traffic Engineering and Control*, **23** (12) pp. 578-581, 1982.
[8] European Commission. *MEET: Methodology for Calculating Transport Emissions and Energy Consumption*. Office for Official Publications of the European Communities: Luxembourg, 1999.
[9] CERC. *ADMS-Urban*, Cambridge Environmental Research Consultants Ltd., Cambridge, 1999.
[10] HMSO. *Design Manual for Roads and Bridges*, Vol. **12 (2)**, 3, 1997.
[11] May, A.D. and Milne, D.S. The effects of alternative road pricing systems on network performance. *Transportation Research*, **34(A)**,6, pp. 407-436, 2000
[12] Milne, D and Van Vliet, D. *Implementing Road User Charging in SATURN*. Working paper **410**, The Institute for Transport Studies, University of Leeds, 1993.
[13] Carslaw, D.C. and Beevers, S.D. The efficacy of low emission zones in central London as a means of reducing nitrogen dioxide concentrations. *Transportation Research*, **D (7)**, 49-64, 2002.

Emissions of mopeds and motorcycles in Belgium

E. Cornelis, I. De Vlieger & L. Int Panis
Vito, Flemish Institute for Technological Research

Abstract

In this paper we report our estimates for the total emission of CO, NO_x, VOC and CO_2 of mopeds and motorcycles in Belgium and indicate confidence intervals.

Data on the fleet of motorcycles are readily available from registration records, but the number of mopeds had to be estimated. Different sources were evaluated to obtain a best estimate for the yearly mileage and a distribution over rural, urban and highway roads. Most emission factors used were provided by MEET. Emission factors for CO and VOC are much higher than the factors of modern petrol cars.

When compared to the total Flemish road transport emission (1999) it turns out that mopeds and motorcycles can no longer be neglected. They are responsible for 11% (58ktonne; 7-15%) of the CO emission and 25% (22ktonne; 15-35%) of the VOC emission. These shares have doubled over the last decade. This can be explained by their success, but also by the introduction of environmentally friendly cars since the beginning of the nineties and the fact that more stringent emission regulations for mopeds and motorcycles came into force in 1997.

When compared to the total emission of Flanders in 1999, the mopeds and motorcycles are responsible for 6.6% of the total emission of CO and 6.9% of the total emission of NMVOC, or, weighted to the capacity to produce ozone, of 3.7% in the total emission of ozone precursors.

An attempt to quantify the noise emission by mopeds and motorcycles failed due to a lack of data.

1 Introduction

Despite their recent success, mopeds (scooters included) and motorcycles are often excluded from environmental and mobility studies in Belgium, because so little is known about them. Today this lack of knowledge is seriously hampering a range of environmental and mobility studies.

The last survey of the emissions of these vehicles in Belgium dates from 1995 [1]. It showed that in 1990 mopeds and motorcycles accounted for 5.5% of the total emission of CO by road transport and 11% of the total emission of VOC. In 1993, these shares had increased to 7.0% and 13% respectively.

In the meanwhile, powered two-wheelers gained popularity; the number of motorcycles has more than doubled from 1990 to 2000 and sales figures of new scooters rose from 5,000 in 1990 to 27,000 in 1999. An update of their impact on the environment is hence needed.

In this paper, the emissions of mopeds and motorcycles are calculated for the year 2000 and compared to the national emission inventory. Attention is also paid to noise pollution caused by these vehicles.

2 Methodology

The general formula for calculating emissions is:

$$\text{emission [tonne/year]} = \text{number of vehicles} \times \text{activity} \times \text{emission factor}$$

This formula is applied for four types of emissions:
- tail-pipe emissions,
- extra emissions at start,
- hot soak emissions,
- diurnal breathing emissions.

In the case of tail-pipe emissions, the activity refers to the average mileage [km/year] of the vehicles. For calculating the extra emissions at start and hot soak emissions, the number of starts are taken. Diurnal breathing emissions are evaluated per day.

Tail-pipe emission factors [g/km] were found in literature for CO, CO_2, NH_3, N_2O, NO_x, PM and VOC and extra start emission factors [g/start] for CO, NO_x and VOC. Hot soak emissions [g/stop] and diurnal breathing emissions [g/day] are only calculated for VOC.

Out of the CO_2 emissions, the fuel consumption and emissions of lead and SO_2 are derived based on fuel characteristics. The VOC emissions are split up into emissions of CH_4, NMVOC, benzene, toluene and xylene with constant fractions.

The accuracy is assessed for each of the factors in the general formula, allowing the determination of a confidence interval for the calculated emitted quantities.

3 Available data

3.1 Number of mopeds and motorcycles in Belgium

Motorcycles with a cylinder content exceeding 50cc are registered and their exact number - 277,838 in 2000, compared to 139,170 in 1990 - is hence known [2].

For the sake of accuracy, this fleet has to be split up in different segments according to the type of engine (two-stroke or four-stroke), cylinder capacity (less than 250cc, 250-750cc, higher than 750cc) and according to the emission legislation they comply with.

Little information is available about the size of each segment. A share of 4% for two-stroke motorcycles is assumed, based on advice from representatives of manufactures and suppliers. Following MEET [3], 65% of the fleet is believed to be conventional, whilst the rest complies with the European directive 97/24/EC. The classification according to cylinder content – 14% < 250cc, 51% between 250 and 750cc and 35% > 750cc – is derived from sales figures.

Mopeds are not longer registered since 1986, so their present number has to be estimated. Based on sales statistics and an estimated lifetime, a number of 400,000 ± 15% for 2000 is derived, which is about one fourth more than in 1990. The proportion of conventional mopeds (69%) and moped complying with 97/24/EC Stage 1 (17%) and Stage 2 (14%) is taken from MEET [3].

3.2 The activity of mopeds and motorcycles in Belgium

An assessment revealed that the mean yearly mileage for Belgian motorcycles is 6,400 km/year (± 15%) and for mopeds 4,600 km/year (± 15%) [4]. The mileage for motorcycles is corrected for cylinder capacity, based on the results of a Swiss survey [5]. Light motorcycles (<250cc) are believed to have a mileage which is 30% lower than average (4,500 km/year), heavy motorcycles to have a mileage which is 25% higher than average (8,000 km/year).

The mileage travelled with powered two-wheelers is distributed over highways, rural and urban roads. For each of these conditions, a fraction of peak traffic is assumed and a mean speed is allocated [4], see table 1.

Table 1:   distribution of the mileage over different traffic conditions with the corresponding mean speed

Location	Traffic condition	Moped		Motorcycle	
		fraction	speed	fraction	speed
Highway	normal	0%	-	16%	110 km/h
	peak	0%	-	4%	25 km/h
Rural	normal	45%	36 km/h	45%	51 km/h
	peak	5%	25 km/h	5%	25 km/h
Urban	normal	35%	31 km/h	21%	25 km/h
	peak	15%	25 km/h	9%	15 km/h

A mobility survey carried out in Flanders, Belgium, revealed that the average length of a trip with a motorcycle is 12km and with a moped 4.6km [6]. This allows us to calculate the number of starts and stops.

3.3 Emission factors for mopeds and motorcycles

The tail-pipe emission factors for CO, CO_2, NO_x and VOC were taken from MEET [3].

Figure 1, showing the emission factors for mopeds, indicates that the combustion of fuel is more complete for Stage 2 mopeds compared to Stage 1 mopeds. This is in turn more complete than the combustion for conventional mopeds, as the latter ones emit relatively more VOC and CO and less CO_2 than the former ones.

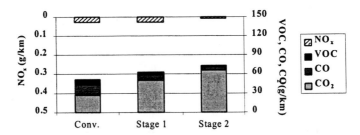

Figure 1: Emission factors for NO_x (left axis), CO, CO_2 and VOC (right axis) for different categories of mopeds

This applies also to motorcycles. The conversion of the fuel to CO_2 is more complete for motorcycles, complying with 97/24/EC compared to conventional ones, regardless whether they are driven by a two-stroke of a four-stroke engine, see Figure 2.

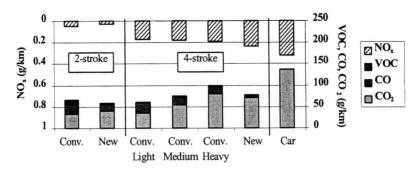

Figure 2: Emission factors for NO_x (left axis), CO, CO_2 and VOC (right axis) for different categories of motorcycles (New: complying with 97/24/EC – Light: <250cc, Medium: 250-750cc, Heavy: >750cc) and an Euro1 small petrol car at a speed of 51 km/h

Figure 2 clearly demonstrates that motorcycles emit substantial amounts of CO and VOC, compared to an average small Euro1 petrol car.

The NO_x emissions of a four-stroke motorcycle are lower than those of a petrol car and in turn higher than those of a two-stroke motorcycle. This phenomenon is due to the high amount of residual burnt gas in the cylinders, acting as an internal exhaust gas recirculation.

An uncertainty interval for tail-pipe emission factors of 40% was assumed for mopeds and 15% for motorcycles.

Emissions factors for hot soak and diurnal breathing evaporative emissions are also given by MEET [3]. The emissions factors for extra emissions at a start were taken from EPA [7], as no factors could be found in a European source.

For particulate matter, N_2O and NH_3 are only indicative emission factors available [8, 9].

4 Results

Table 2 shows the calculated emissions of various pollutants and the fuel consumption of mopeds and motorcycles in Belgium in 2000.

The confidence intervals are a result of a combination of the confidence intervals of the number of vehicles, their activities and of the emission factors. No confidence interval was calculated on the emitted quantities of N_2O, NH_3 and PM_{10}, as only rough, indicative emission factors could be found.

Table 2:   emissions and fuel consumption of mopeds and motorcycles in Belgium in 2000

		Mopeds		Motorcycle		Sum	
Benzene	tonne	680	± 50%	340	± 50%	1,000	± 50%
CH_4	tonne	1,000	± 50%	520	± 50%	1,500	± 50%
CO	tonne	25,000	± 35%	33,000	± 40%	58,000	± 38%
CO_2	ktonne	60	± 40%	144	± 40%	200	± 40%
N_2O	tonne	9.2		8.9		18	
NH_3	tonne	3.7		3.6		7.2	
NMVOC	tonne	14,000	± 50%	7,000	± 50%	21,000	± 50%
NO_x	tonne	53	± 40%	360	± 40%	420	± 40%
Pb	kg	96	± 50%	230	± 50%	330	± 50%
PM_{10}	tonne	74		210		290	
SO_2	tonne	5.5	± 50%	13	± 50%	19	± 50%
Toluene	tonne	1,800	± 50%	900	± 50%	2,700	± 50%
VOC	tonne	15,000	± 40%	7,500	± 40%	22,000	± 40%
Xylene	tonne	1,600	± 50%	820	± 50%	2,500	± 50%
Fuel	TJ	860	± 50%	860	± 50%	2,900	± 50%

The confidence intervals are very broad; for mopeds is this mainly due to the low accuracy of their number and of the emission factors, for motorcycles is this mainly a consequence of assumptions on the geographical distribution of the mileage and the composition of the fleet.

The figures in table 2 concern the emissions of the four types considered in this study. Figure 3 splits the VOC emissions of motorcycles up according to the type.

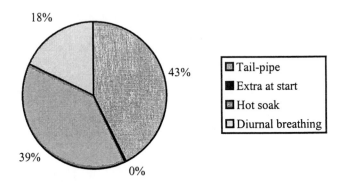

Figure 3: Contribution of every type of emission to the overall VOC emission by motorcycles in Belgium

The extra emissions at start can be neglected compared to the tail-pipe emissions. This is not the case for the hot soak and diurnal breathing emissions; according to the calculation results, they may account for more than half of the total VOC emissions.

However it is quite likely that the evaporative emissions are overestimated, as every stop was assumed to lead to a complete cooling of the motorcycle and as no seasonal influences were included into the calculation. Nevertheless figure 3 reminds us that evaporative emissions of powered two-wheelers should not be neglected.

The figures in table 2 were compared with national emission levels and fuel consumption. However, due to a lack of a national inventory of the emissions for the year 2000, these figures were compared, after correction for the number of mopeds and motorcycles, with the emitted quantities in Flanders for 1999 [10], see table 3.

Within the road transport sector, powered two-wheelers seem to be an important source of pollution, especially for CH_4, CO and NMVOC.

Even when compared to the total emissions of these pollutants in Flanders, table 3 reveals that mopeds and motorcycles account for about 7% of the CO (4-9%) and the NMVOC (3-10%) emissions. Hence, powered two-wheelers cannot longer be neglected as a source of these pollutants in Flanders or Belgium.

When the emissions of CH_4, CO, NMVOC and NO_x are weighted for their capacity to form ozone, the contribution of mopeds and motorcycles to the emission of ozone precursors by the road transport is 8.8% (4.8-13%) and by all sources in Flanders 3.7% (2.0-5.6%). The contribution to photochemical smog by mopeds and especially motorcycles might exceed the contribution to the emission of ozone precursors, as their activity in summertime is higher than in wintertime.

Table 3:   Contribution of mopeds and motorcycles (M&M) to the emission and fuel consumption by road transport and to the total emission and fuel consumption in Flanders, Belgium in 1999

		M&M	Total road transport		Total Flanders	
		Emission	Emission	Contrib. M&M	Contrib. road trsp.	Contrib. M&M
CH$_4$	tonne	880	2,838	31%	1%	0.2%
CO	tonne	33,000	288,939	11%	58%	6.6%
CO$_2$	ktonne	120	14,633	0,8%	22%	0.2%
NMVOC	tonne	12,000	49,518	24%	28%	6.9%
NO$_x$	tonne	230	82,382	0.3%	53%	0.1%
SO$_2$	tonne	11	3,977	0.3%	3%	<0.1%
VOC	tonne	13,000	52,356	25%	10%	2.5%
Fuel	PJ	1.7	198.6	0.9%	22%	0.2%

The results from this study can be compared with those of the previous survey in Belgium [1], see table 4.

Table 4:   Share of mopeds and motorcycles in the Belgian fleet of road transport vehicles and their contribution to the emission of CO and VOC by road transport in Belgium in 1999

	Number of vehicles	CO emission	VOC emission
1990	9.3%	5.5%	11%
1993	9.1%	7.0%	13%
1999	11%	11%	25%

The CO and VOC emission of mopeds and motorcycles have increased with 60%, resp. 70%, in absolute figures from 1990 to 1999. The contribution of these vehicles to the road transport emissions however has doubled and has risen more than their share in the national fleet of road transport vehicles. This is not because powered two-wheelers nowadays are more polluting than ten years ago, but because cars and trucks became much cleaner under pressure of various European directives, which came into force at the beginning of the nineties.

Mopeds and motorcycles did however not escape the European Commission's notice completely, but the emission standards they have to meet only came into force at the end of the nineties. One might hence expect that, unless the number of powered two-wheelers continues to grow, the contribution of these vehicles to the pollution of road transport would drop in future.

5 Noise pollution

Motorcycles and especially mopeds are a known source of noise pollution. A Dutch survey revealed that mopeds are the most predominant source of annoyance and disturbed sleep. Motorcycles occupy the third place with regard to annoyance and the eighth with regard to sleep disturbance [11]. Similar results might be expected for Belgium.

However, a literature research failed in providing noise emission factors. Only rough noise emission levels for motorcycles could be traced, indicating that an average motorcycle is almost twice as loud as an average car and almost as loud as an average lorry [12]. As a consequence, the noise impact of mopeds and motorcycles could not be assessed. Further research is hence needed to fill the gap.

6 Conclusion

In this paper we have presented estimates of the emissions of mopeds and motorcycles in Belgium.

A lot of information regarding these vehicles is missing and if some data can be found, it often lacks accuracy. Most striking among the gaps in knowledge is the unknown number of mopeds in Belgium. Also the lack of detail regarding the composition of the fleet of mopeds and motorcycles was hampering this study.

Further research is needed to provide emission factors with a higher degree of accuracy than present. Attention should first be addressed to evaporative emissions.

Despite these shortcomings, this study revealed that mopeds and motorcycles should no longer be neglected as an important source of CO and NMVOC pollution, as they contribute about 7% to the overall emission levels in Flanders, Belgium. When the emissions are weighted to their capacity to form ozone, mopeds and motorcycles contribute about 3.7% to the overall emission level.

According to the calculation results, more than half of the VOC emitted originates from evaporative emissions, both of hot soak emissions and of diurnal breathing emissions. This might be an overestimation, but highlights that this type of emission should not be overlooked.

Mopeds and motorcycles emitted about 60 to 70% more CO and NMVOC in 1999 than in 1990, but their contribution to the emission by road transport has doubled. This is a result of the emission reduction strategy implemented on passenger cars and trucks since the beginning of the previous decade. European directives, aiming at reducing emissions of powered two-wheelers, only came into force at the end of the nineties.

This study also attempted to quantify the noise impacts of mopeds and motorcycles, but failed due to a lack of data. This is striking as, in other countries, mopeds - and motorcycles to a lesser extent - are recognized as the most predominant source of annoyance and sleep disturbance. Further research is hence needed.

References

[1] De Vlieger, I. *Wegverkeersemissies in België: Evolutie 1990-1993*, Report ENE.RA9511, Vito, Mol (B), pp. 36-41, 1995 (in Dutch).

[2] NIS, *Vervoersstatistieken: Motorvoertuigenpark op 1 augustus 2000*, Ministry of Economical Affairs, Brussels (B), p. 7, 2001. (In Dutch).

[3] EC. *MEET - Methodology for calculating transport emissions and energy consumption.* Office for official publications of the European Communities, Luxembourg (GDL), pp. 73-74, 108, 121-124, 1999.

[4] De Vlieger, I., Van Poppel, M. *External Costs of Transport in Belgium, Overview Input Data and Assumptions for Emission Assessment.* Report V&M/N5560/IDV/99.081, Vito, Mol (B), 1998.

[5] André, M., Hammerström, U., Reynaud, I. *Driving Statistics for the Assessment of Pollutant Emissions from Road Transport*, Report LTE 9906, Inrets, Bron (F), pp. 170-172, 1999.

[6] Hajnal, I., Miermans, W. *Onderzoek Verplaatsingsgedrag Vlaanderen, Eindverslag.* Provinciale Hogeschool Diepenbeek, Diepenbeek (B), p. 54, 1996. (in Dutch)

[7] EPA. Highway Mobile Source Emission Factors Table (Appendix H). *Compilation of Air Pollutant Emission Factors, Volume II: Mobile Sources (AP 42)*, pending 5th edition, US EPA, 2000.

[8] Wee van, G. P., Waard van der, J. *Verkeer en vervoer in de nationale milieuverkenning 3 en de SVV-verkenning 1993*, Report 251701014, RIVM, Bilthoven (NL), 1993.

[9] Keller, M., et al. *Handbuch Emissionsfaktoren des Strassenverkehrs*, Version 1.2 (CD-ROM), BUWAL, Bern (CH), 1999.

[10] VMM, *Lozingen in de lucht 1980-1999*, VMM, Aalst (B), pp. 56-108, 2000. (in Dutch)

[11] Jong de, R.G., Steenbekkers, J.H.M., Vos, H. *Hinder en andere zelf-gerapporteerde effecten van milieuverstroring in Nederland, Inventaris verstoringen 1998,* Report PG/VGZ/2000.012, TNO Preventie en Gezondheid, Leiden (NL), pp. 28, 45, 2000. (in Dutch)

[12] Sandberg, U. Report by the International Institute of Noise Control Engineering Working Party on the Effect of Regulations on Road Vehicle Noise. *Noise/News International*, **3(2)**, pp.85-113, 1995.

Fuel cell bus Berlin, Copenhagen and Lisbon: A sustainable and environmental technology for the urban passenger transportation sector

T.L. Farias

Instituto Superior Técnico, Portugal

Abstract

The main objective of the present paper is to present a sustainable and environmental alternative solution for the passenger transport systems. The solution is based on the fuel cell technology and will be presented under a Thermie demonstration project sponsored by the European Union entitled "Fuel Cell Bus Berlin, Copenhagen and Lisbon". The project involves the design and construction of a completely new bus by MAN that will use stacks of fuel cells supplied by Air Liquide. The fuel selected for operating the bus is liquid hydrogen stored in a cylindrical vessel at –253° C. The bus will be monitored by a team of Instituto Superior Técnico, Lisbon and demonstrated for several months in three major cities of Europe: Berlin, Copenhagen and Lisbon. Demonstrations will be executed using the local main transportation companies that will incorporate the fuel cell bus into their normal lines. The bus will be tested initially by the Berlin Bus transportation company - BVG in the city of Berlin on the route between the airport and the city center. The bus will also undergo test runs in Copenhagen operated by HT and in Lisbon operated by CARRIS. Of special interest in these test runs will be how factors such as climate and geography (e.g. flat/hilly terrain) can influence the fuel cell bus performance. The project will demonstrate advantages of fuel cell buses compared to conventional diesel buses. The performance of the test runs will by analyzed in relation to inner city conditions. Economic data such as vehicle reliability, technology, operation and fuelling will be gathered as part of a process to establish the market viability of this technology. The project will be accompanied by a comprehensive measurement program which will clearly show the environmental benefits to be gained from the introduction of a technology which provides a 100% reduction in emissions.

Aim of the project

The project "Fuel Cell Bus for Berlin, Copenhagen, Lisbon" aims to demonstrate the first European implementation of a fuel cell bus using liquefied hydrogen in an inner city situation. The demonstration of the innovative fuel cell propulsion system will clearly outline not only the benefits to be obtained from a zero emission fuel, but also the advantages of this type of bus from a design point of view. Fuel cell battery technology is very much at the cutting edge of vehicle design and the project aims to show how its wider market introduction in the long term could have major environmental benefits in urban applications, see Hart and Bauen [1]. Urban traffic managers are constantly seeking new ways to improve the local air quality of our towns and cities through changes in passenger trends. Vehicle pollution is a major contributor to environmental impairment, see Taschner [2]. By demonstrating the use of a non-fossil, zero emission fuel it is expected that the market response will encourage manufacturers and urban planners to view fuel cell technology as the way forward. The use of this technology will show how European dependency on foreign energy sources can be decreased and also show the longer term benefits of lower emissions and less noise pollution. It is hoped that the project will provide guidance for manufacturers and researchers on further need for action regarding fine-tuning.

Description of the projects and the demonstration locations

The project consists, in the first instance, of the demonstration of one fuel cell bus in three inner urban applications, namely the cities of Berlin, Copenhagen and Lisbon. The bus will be tested initially by the Berlin Bus transportation company - BVG in the city of Berlin on the route between the airport and the city center. The bus will be based at the BVG depot in Usedomer Strasse in the Wedding district of Berlin. This will also be the location of the mobile filling station. The bus will also undergo test runs in Copenhagen operated by HT and in Lisbon operated by CARRIS. Of special interest in these test runs will be how factors such as climate and geography (e.g. flat/hilly terrain) can influence the fuel cell bus. The project will demonstrate advantages of fuel cell buses compared to conventional diesel buses. There are no local emissions since the fuel cell only emits water steam, i.e. no CO_2. An operation plan will be set up and implemented in each city. The bus will be integrated within the respective bus fleets during the demonstration period. The performance of the test runs will by analyzed in relation to inner city conditions. Economic data such as vehicle reliability, technology, operation and fuelling will be gathered as part of a process to establish the market viability of this technology. The project will be accompanied by a comprehensive measurement program which will clearly show the environmental benefits to be gained from the introduction of a technology which provides a 100% reduction in emissions. This will help to convince potential users of fuel cell technology of its benefits in inner urban applications. In line with the THERMIE objective of promoting clean and alternative fuels this project will demonstrate how this innovative technology, in comparison to other clean technologies and conventional technologies, e.g. diesel, is an appropriate choice for urban mobility.

The fuel cell system

The actual fuel cell technology to be implemented in this project has been designed by Nuvera (former DE NORA). who have been developing the technology for almost a decade. In this project the fuel cell technology uses liquefied hydrogen. Hydrogen is one of the most widely available chemical elements in the world. However, it is predominantly found in a combined form which prevents it from being used directly as a fuel. Nonetheless, hydrogen can be produced, for example, through the input of electricity from electrolysis or through re-formed vapor from natural gas, see Cunha and Azevedo [3] (and references cited therein). A fuel cell is a static device for the generation of electric power - see Leo and Mugerwa [4]. It converts the chemical energy of the fuel and oxidant directly into electricity. Hydrogen fuel and air react at low temperature (130^0C max.) thus producing electric power and pure water only as a by-product. Its energy efficiency is high, typically above 40% over a wide range of loads (50-100%). The absence of moving parts reduces to a minimum maintenance, manpower requirements and down-time. The low operating temperature allows for a fast start-up. It responds well to thermal cycling and to vibration. Fuel cells are inherently modular in their configuration. The intrinsic advantage of a fuel cell over an internal combustion engine is clear.

The fuel cell has numerous advantages over the most advanced batteries currently available. The fuel cell provides a higher power density and power volume solving problems of space constraints. It does not require re-charging since it operates as long as fuel is available and it has a much longer operating life in comparison to other batteries available. It employs no corrosive liquid electrolytes and has no moving parts. Its components can, therefore, be easily recycled at the end of its operating life, thus avoiding the environmental problems associated with battery disposal. These extremely favorable characteristics of the fuel cell technology allow applications where intermittent operation is required and where safety and reliability must be enhanced. These factors make it an ideal technology for use in all types of road vehicles, especially heavy trucks and buses.

The fuel stacks from Nuvera are integrated by the French company Air Liquide DIA within a power module whose net power is 120 kWmax. Air Liquide was responsible for of the integration of the power module. The approx. 120 kW net power module will consist of three 100-cell stacks systems, as these systems are developed already in other projects. Each system will contain the integrated following main items: an air compressor, directly connected to the stack; a fuel cell stack; a water recovery system; an hydrogen recirculating mechanism; a primary demi-water cooling loop including water/water heat exchangers. The produced heat will be evacuated by a common freezing proof secondary loop, which will contain a fan and an air heat exchanger. The power modules are placed in dedicated places in the rear part of the vehicle. The power module is fed by hydrogen at the required flow pressure and temperature and delivers non-converted current, the specification of which results from the stack assembly. Energy for the compressor and the power module auxiliary is operated in a generally steady condition, controlled locally within the power module.

Preliminary experimental results obtained from a tested 100 kW fuel cell system are presented in Figure 1. These curves giving efficiency, voltage and net power without the cooling fan consumption that must be subtracted, has supported the option for a 120 kW system to be installed in the bus.

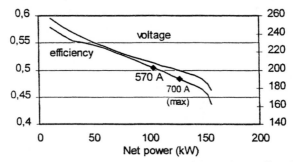

Figure 1: Net efficiency and power without the cooling fan.

The fuel cell bus

The basic vehicle to be used is a new generation, MAN low-floor bus fitted according to the specifications of the Berlin public transport company, the BVG. The vehicle is noted for its low-floor technology throughout which permits "step-free" boarding. The vehicle powertrain is composed by two electrical drives including three-phase induction motors of Siemens VI, each one with a rated power of 75 kW. Induction motors are linked via a mechanical summation gearbox with the serial rear axle. Electrical drives also include power electronics inverters feeding directly the induction motors. They are supplied from the direct current intermediate circuit that provides electrical energy for all the bus.

With the omission of the diesel engine, all the required vehicular auxiliary energy such as electricity for the 24 volt on-board computer, compressed air for the brakes/suspension, hydraulic energy for vehicle steering and powering the water pumps must be supplied by this electric circuit from the fuel cells. For the required tank range of approximately 400 km per re-fuelling, the liquid hydrogen storage unit located on the vehicle roof should, according to preliminary estimates, have a capacity volume of approximately 600 liters hydrogen. The electric drives including induction motors, power electronics converters and control were defined according to the voltage level supplied by the fuel cell unit. Figure 2 shows the complete bus including the components of tanks and the cooling system.

Liquefied hydrogen as a fuel

One innovative aspect in test in this project is related to the fact that the fuel cell technology uses liquefied hydrogen as combustible. This option fulfills the bus operators' demand of at least four hundred kilometers per tank for normal urban application. Comparing different solutions, liquid hydrogen storage systems are more efficient as far volume and weight are concerned. The hydrogen storage system contains one 600 liter hydrogen thermo insulated bottle from Linde. The hydrogen will be stored at a temperature of -253^{0}C and has a lower weight and system volume than gaseous hydrogen. The shut-off and safety equipment is situated on the roof of the bus. The bus will have a capacity for about 70 to 75 persons, approximately 40 seats will be available.

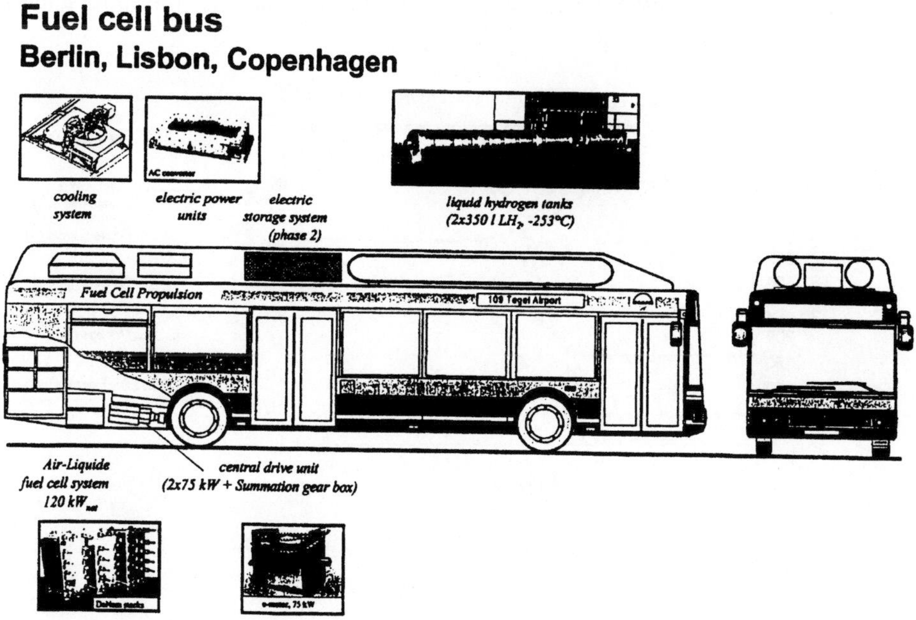

Fuel cell bus
Berlin, Lisbon, Copenhagen

Figure 2: The MAN Fuel Cell Bus and main components.

Complementary electric energy storage system

Preliminary results of the fuel cell behavior allow confirming expected results of its limited dynamic performance. Figure 3 shows the experimental results of a transient demand from 50 to 550A at the fuel cell output.

This dynamic result confirms that the energy demanded, for instance, in a sudden acceleration could not be obtained directly from the fuel cell imposing the need of a complementary electric energy storage system. For the provision of these transient or peak energy demands several options for the are possible and in analysis by the project such as battery, flywheel and supercapacitors. Moreover, during the bus braking operation, an electrical storage system must be capable of dynamically recovering electrical energy from the electrical driven powertrain. Batteries and supercapacitors are particularly suitable options for this task. In addition, it is planned to store energy in a flywheel system, composed by a high-speed rotating mass with a non-frictional supporting system enabling the greatest possible loss-free energy storage. An innovative superconduting magnetic bearing will be tested in order to implement the loss free, self-stabilizing supporting system of the rotating parts of the flywheel system. Figure 4 show the basic layout of the flywheel system and presents the superconduting magnetic bearing. A previous calculation and design by computer simulation is testing all the different possible options for the complementary electric energy storage system and for the energy management system. A second step will test the different components in a test bench, allowing to obtain the results for the most suitable system that will be installed in the bus.

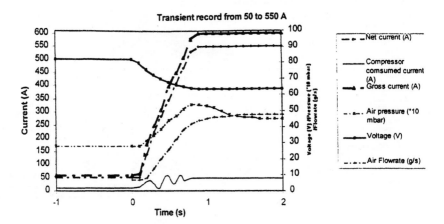

Figure 3: Transient record from 50 to 550 A.

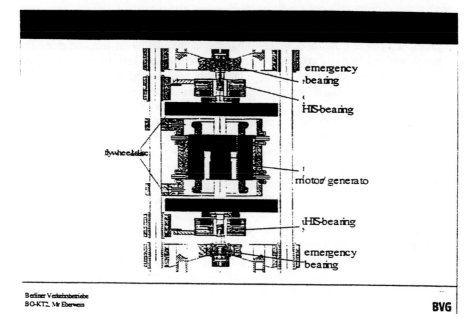

Figure 4: Flywheel system.

Monitoring and measuring systems

IST is responsible for monitoring the fuel cell bus. Properties to be monitored include the actual position of the fuel cell bus as well as analogue and digital signals sent by different sensors distributed throughout the bus components. The bus monitoring system uses the GSM/SMS network in order to establish real time communication between a control station PC and the fuel cell bus.

The system to be used includes a cellular phone installed in the fuel cell bus responsible for collecting data from an Input / Output box where a GPS can be plugged in. The collected data containing the speed of the bus as well as the position are compacted into a SMS message and sent on a regular basis (defined by the user) to a cellular phone installed in the central station PC. Also in the central station PC is a software responsible for decoding the messages and transforming them into a readable format.

Modeling program

IST is also responsible for developing a model capable of anticipating the required power by the bus powertrain for different working conditions. Factors in analysis can be the bus current occupation, the topography of the course, use or not of air conditioning, or the acceleration desired. This numerical model will help the partners involved in the technical specifications of the bus as well as the end-users partners when selecting the most appropriate running conditions. This aspect is of particular importance for the test cases in Lisbon where the course includes several hills, and air conditioning is mandatory in the summer. The problems that initially arose were linked to the possible lack of nominal power that the electric motors will develop. In fact, buses running within CARRIS fleet are equipped with Diesel engines that have a maximum net power above 200 HP. The fuel cells will produce ca 120 kW but after introducing the energy required for the different auxiliary equipment this value will be considerably lower. Therefore the energy required to supply the Siemens electric motors (producing a nominal power of 150 kW) will have to come from additional sources to complement the fuel cell system. Therefore the super capacitors and the fly wheel systems will be of utmost importance to guarantee maximum power in peak running conditions while absorbing energy during normal or breaking running conditions.

The software developed will be used to investigate these effects, namely comparing the performances of a fuel cell bus (with an electric power train) with a Diesel standard version exhibiting a larger maximum net power as well as investigating the improvements in bus dynamic due to the additional energy sources such as the fly wheel system.

The code, denominated ECOGEST (Silva and Farias [5]), will calculate the power required by the bus as a function of travelling position for a variety of variables such as course selected; topography; bus weight (number of passengers, quantity of fuel in the tanks); outside temperature; i.e. use of air conditioning; accelerations desired to achieve the estimated performances; type of engine; type of gear box.

Summary and conclusions

The potentialities of a bus powered by a fuel cell system have been described. The bus currently being built by MAN under the scope of as European Union Thermie project entitled Fuel Cell Bus Berlin, Copenhagen, Lisbon has been presented. The bus, to be inaugurated during December of 2001 will run during several months in the cities of Berlin, Copenhagen and Lisbon. The project involves several partners including IST from Lisbon that is responsible for the monitoring and modeling programs. These programs were also represented in the current paper.

Acknowledgements

This work has been supported by the THERMIE A Demonstration European project entitled Fuel Cell Bus Berlin, Copenhagen, Lisbon.

References

[1] Hart, David and Bauen, Ausilio., *Fuel Cells – Clean power, clean transport, clean future*, FT Energy, London, 1998.

[2] Taschner, K., Need for drastic changes in transport to improve air quality. *5th International Conference on Technologies and Combustion for a Clean Environment*, Vol. III, p.1, 1999.

[3] Cunha, J. and Azevedo, J. L. T., Modeling the integration of a compact plate steam reformer in a fuel cell system. *Journal of Power Sources.* in press, 2000.

[4] Leo, J. M. J. Blomen and Mugerwa, Michael N., *Fuel Cell Systems,* Plenum Press, New York, 1993.

[5] Silva, C. M., Farias, T. L., Effects of the driving behavior on the emissions and fuel consumption of vehicles equipped with gasoline internal combustion engines. *Proc. of the Clean Air VI - sixth international conference on Technologies and Combustion for a Clean Environment,* Porto, 9-12 Julho, 2001.

Policy options for transport to reduce CO_2 and tropospheric ozone

I. De Vlieger, A. Colles, J. Duerinck & S. Verbeiren
Vito – Flemish Institute for Technological Research, Belgium.

Abstract

Within the Belgian national programme 'Sustainable Mobility' Vito carried out a multidisciplinary study. Twelve policy options within transport were selected and evaluated on their effectivity to reduce CO_2 and tropospheric ozone, and their techno-economic and social feasibility. It was found that individual policy options affect the emissions of CO_2 and ozone precursors, and the ozone concentration in the atmosphere only in a small degree compared to trends set under Business-As-Usual scenario. Obviously large policy efforts are required to achieve more sustainable mobility. Although enhanced use of public transport seemed to be the most socially feasible option, this option did not fall within the best scoring options: (a) advanced introduction of environmentally friendly conventional vehicles, (b) enhanced inspection and maintenance, (c) reduced passenger car use through more car pooling and teleworking. The worst scoring options were enhanced replacement of old passenger cars and introduction of electric passenger cars.

1 Introduction

In Belgium, as in many countries, growing traffic has raised concerns about air pollution. In 1999 the amount of vehicle kilometres driven on Belgian roads increased by 30% compared to 1990. This is a tripling compared to 1970 [1]. All these activities in transportation have a negative influence on the environment and public health.

In 1999 transport was responsible for about 22% of the carbon dioxide (CO_2) emission, which still is the most import greenhouse gas. The contribution of traffic to the main precursors of ozone, in particular nitrogen oxides (NO_x) and non-methane volatile organic compounds (NMVOC) was respectively 53% and 31% [2].

Within the national programme 'Sustainable Mobility' (1996-2001) Vito worked on a project focussed on the possibilities to reduce CO_2 and tropospheric ozone. It is interesting to evaluate the opportunities within transport to help fulfil international agreements on environmental problems. Within the Kyoto Protocol Belgium agreed to reduce the emission of greenhouse gases by 7.5 % averaged over the period 2008-2012 compared to 1990. The European NEC (National Emission Ceilings) Directive sets national emission limits on NO_x, SO_2 (sulphur dioxide) and VOC for 2010. In Belgium those limits were translated to emission limits for transport: 68 kton NO_x, 2 kton SO_2 and 35.6 kton VOC.

In this perspective, it is essential to inform policy makers about the possible policy options within transport to work out emission reduction strategies for CO_2 and tropospheric ozone.

As the methodology and tools used within the above-mentioned study have already been described elsewhere [3], the rest of this report will mainly consider assumptions being made and final results.

2 Approach

On the basis of an inventory of measures within transport to deal with the CO_2 and ozone problem, 12 policy options were defined (Table 1). These policy options were investigated for their effectivity in reducing CO_2, NO_x, VOC and ozone concentrations, and their techno-economic and social feasibility.

In the techno-economic feasibility, assessments were made for the costs and benefits at national level of the different policy options. In the social feasibility, the policy options were evaluated on their social desirability and political feasibility.

Table 1: Overview of the 12 policy options.

	Evaluated policy options
1	Advanced introduction of environmentally friendly conventional vehicles
2	Advanced introduction of environmentally friendly alternative vehicles
3	Enhanced replacement of old passenger cars
4	Conversion of vehicles to more environmentally friendly alternatives: retrofit
5	Introduction of electric passenger cars
6	Enhanced inspection and maintenance
7	More environmentally friendly driving style
8	Reduce passenger car use through more car pooling and teleworking
9	Reduce passenger car use through more public transport
10	Reduce passenger car use through more cycling and walking
11	Reduce road freight traffic through rail transport
12	Reduce road freight traffic through inland shipping

The results of the effectivity and feasibility studies formed the basis for a multiple criteria analysis (MCA). Twelve decision-makers were involved by means of the organisation of two consultation workshops. For each decision-maker the ranking of the policy options was determined. Subsequently, the individual rankings were processed to the 'best' group ranking. Eight criteria were used within the evaluation and ranking of the policy options (Table 2).

Table 2: Overview of criteria used within the MCA-exercise.

N°	Criterion
1	Cumulative* CO_2 (carbon dioxide) emission reduction
2	Cumulative* NO_x (nitrogen oxides) emission reduction
3	Cumulative* VOC (vol. org. comp.) emission reduction
4	AOT40° – threshold guarding vegetation
5	AOT60° – threshold guarding public health
6	National cost
7	Social desirability
8	Political feasibility

* Cumulative emission reduction = the total emission reduction during the period 2001-2012.

° AOT = Accumulated (ozone) exposure Over a Threshold of 40 or 60 ppb (parts per billion). 40 ppb = 80 $\mu g/m^3$.

Finally policy recommendations were formulated based on the group ranking of the different policy options, as well as on the specific findings resulting from the individual disciplines.

3 Scenarios

3.1 Business-As-Usual scenario

A reference scenario assuming policy is left unmodified, i.e. Business-As-Usual or BAU scenario has been designed. Hereby, account was taken of the expected developments in technology, economics and mobility. Technological measures taken until mid 2000 – even when the implementation starts after this date - were taken into account. The agreement of the European Commission and the automotive industries to reduce average CO_2 emission from new cars was also integrated in BAU scenario. Table 3 shows an overview of the assumed annual mobility growth for the different vehicle categories.

Table 3: Annual mobility growth in <u>percentages</u>.

Transport mode	1999-2010	2011-2012
Road traffic*		
PC	2.68	2.28
LDP	2.68	2.28
HDP-buses	- 0.46	- 0.46
HDP-coaches	- 0.70	- 0.70
LDG	3.4	3.0
HDG	3.4	3.0
Rail traffic		
Persons	1.22	1.03
Goods	2.95	2.50
Inland shipping	2.57	2.17

* PC =passenger cars, LDP = light duty persons, HDP = heavy duty persons, LDG = light duty goods, HDG =heavy duty goods.

3.2 Policy options

For each of the 12 policy options (Table 1) model runs have been performed for a realistic implementation level of the measures. Input data and boundaries for these scenarios were selected based on a questionnaire on the assessments of the economical and social acceptation for each option. First an internal Vito working group came to a consensus to fill in this questionnaire. These results were then discussed during a workshop with external experts.

3.2.1 Policy option 1: environmentally friendly conventional vehicles
Once a new technology leading to more environmentally friendly conventional vehicles than prescribed in applied emission legislation is available; it was assumed that 75% of the users opt for this new technology when they buy a new vehicle. A transition-period of two years was taken into account. Furthermore, it was presupposed that no surplus costs are involved with the new technology. Therefore, government has to draw up supporting measures (e.g. fiscal advantages).

3.2.2 Policy option 2: environmentally friendly alternative vehicles
In the short term not all brands will have alternative vehicles in their spectrum. Furthermore, the willingness to opt for alternative vehicles is smaller than for conventional. Once alternative technologies are available without a additionalcost, it was expected that about 55% of the users choose an alternative technology. This has to be seen within a time frame of 5 to 10 years.

3.2.3 Policy option 3: replacement of old passenger cars
By analogy to measures taken in France and Greece [4], a two year lasting action programme (2001-2002) to replace old passenger cars - not complying with the European emission Directive 91/441/EC (= Euro 1 from 1993 on) - was

evaluated. The willingness to opt for enhanced replacement of old passenger cars was expected to be 17.5%.

3.2.4 Policy option 4: retrofit

For passenger cars and LD vehicles it was assumed that retrofit equipment is installed during the first two years after more stringent emission regulation (Euro 3 and Euro 4) come into force for new vehicles. It was expected that about 20% of cars eligible for conversion to more environmentally friendly vehicles would be converted. Furthermore, vehicles were believed to be converted only once in a lifetime and to be driven at least three years after conversion.

HD vehicles are converted between their 6th and 21st year of usage. After retrofit the vehicles still have to be used for at least 5 years. Conversion of HD vehicles can be carried out during revision of the vehicles. It was believed that with the right supporting measures the willingness to opt for more environmentally friendly technologies during revision is 50%. A vehicle is converted only once in its lifetime.

3.2.5 Policy option 5: electric passenger cars

Within a timeframe until 2010 it was expected that only small petrol-fuelled passenger cars (city traffic) would be replaced by electric cars. The willingness to buy an electric car will rise in the coming 10 years from about none nowadays to about 5%, taking into account the hypothesis that the surplus cost will be 5 to 10%.

3.2.6 Policy option 6: inspection and maintenance

Instead of inspection after 4 years, new passenger cars have to be inspected after 2 years. Emission factors for passenger cars increase during their lifetime. This is taken into account by using ageing factors. The effect of enhanced inspection affects these ageing factors. From the results of an extensive European study [5], a correction factor for enhanced inspection for petrol-fuelled cars were deduced. This factor was 0.73 and has to be multiplied with the ageing factors of the BAU for CO, NO_x and VOC. Except for CO and PM (particulate matter), inspection of diesel cars only affects emissions in a small extent [6].

3.2.7 Policy option 7: more environmentally friendly driving style

The potential to reduce CO_2 emissions from petrol and diesel cars was estimated at respectively 15 and 5% [7]. For NO_x and VOC only rough data were available in literature, not making difference between fuel types. Potential reduction through adapted driving style was estimated at 49% for NO_x and 22% for VOC [8]. In reality it was expected that the willingness of drivers to adapt their driving style is 10% and take 4 years to get that level: 0% in 2000, 1% in 2001, 3% in 2002, 6% in 2003 and 10% in 2004.

3.2.8 Policy option 8: more car pooling and teleworking
In Belgium the amount of teleworkers will increase from 5% in 2000 to 27.5% in 2015 [9]. From 2001 until 2005 teleworkers will be working one day a week outside their office (at home or satellite offices). From 2006 until 2010 there will be an annual rise of 0.1 days. In 2011 and 2012 the number of teleworking days stays constant at 1.5 days. It was assumed that the average teleworker lives about four times further away from work than an average employee (single trip about 17 km [10]) who drives to work by car.

It was expected that more carpooling results in a reduction of car commuting traffic equal to about 44% of the reduction due to teleworking [9]. It was assumed that 35% of car traffic is commuter traffic. By 2012 more carpooling and teleworking reduce kilometres driven by cars with about 10% compared to the total passenger car kilometres under the BAU scenario in 2012.

3.2.9 Policy option 9: more public transport
The number of commuter kilometres driven by cars is held constant during the period 2001-2012. The remaining passenger car kilometres rise annually by 2.5% instead of 2.68% under BAU. At the field this implies a substitution of 15 billion passenger kilometres by passenger car through bus and train. It was assumed that the number of vehicle kilometres covered by bus and train annually rise by 5%. Furthermore, the seat occupancy of busses and trains has to double. Busses are responsible for about 1/3 of the substitution.

3.2.10 Policy option 10: more cycling and walking
The amount of passenger car kilometres driven for short trips (≤ 10 km) was estimated to be 10% of the total amount of kilometres driven by the passenger car fleet. It was assumed that 50% of the kilometres for short trips could be substituted by cycling or walking. But due to the willingness of car users, this 50% will not be met. In 2001 10% of this 50% will be substituted, in 2006 this will be 30% and in 2012 60%. For the other years a linear extrapolation exercise has been done. In 2012 passenger car kilometres decreased by 3% compared to BAU 2012.

3.2.11 Policy option 11: reduce road freight traffic through rail transport
Compared to the BAU the annual growth in vehicle (trucks) kilometres was reduced. This has been carried out in 4 phases of 3 years: within the first phase annual growth was 2.27%, 1.17% in the second, 1.09% in the third to stagnate in the last phase.

For LD vehicles average loading capacity is 1 ton, whereas for HD vehicles this is 15 ton [11]. Average loads were expected to be 40% of the maximum [12]. For LD avoided kilometres are due to improved co-ordination of traffic streams and higher average loads.

In 2012 these assumptions result in a doubling of the total ton-kilometres transported by railway compared to 2012 BAU.

3.2.12 Policy option 12: reduce road freight traffic through inland shipping

An analogous reduction of tonkm by road transport is assumed as in policy option 11, but instead of a shift to railway a shift to inland shipping was supposed. In 2012 this results in a rise of the total ton-kilometres transported through inland shipping by a factor 2.4 compared to 2012 BAU.

4 Results and Discussion

4.1 Observed criteria values

Table 4 gives an overview of the values of eight criteria (Table 2) for each policy option. Those values are the results of the activities within the different disciplines in the project.

Table 4: Values of the criteria for the 12 policy options.

Option	Criterion							
	CO_2 [kton]	NO_x [kton]	VOC [kton]	AOT40 [ppm]*h	AOT60 [ppm]*h	6 [1]	7 [2]	8 [3]
1	1 200	47.4	18.6	7.22	0.982	[]	+	[]
2	1 060	36.2	13.9	7.23	0.985	--	+	[]
3	150	9.3	16.7	7.23	0.975	--	-	-
4	0	42.4	25.3	7.24	0.991	-	+	[]
5	800	~0	3.9	7.25	0.984	--	-	[]
6	0	39.6	39.3	7.19	0.962	--	+	[]
7	1 620	18.7	4.7	7.25	0.984	[]	+	[]
8	10 700	12.9	6.0	7.24	0.978	+	+	[]
9	9 190	0.2	3.9	7.25	0.984	+ , -	++	+
10	3 680	9.9	5.3	7.25	0.984	+	+	+
11	9 470	16.9	7.5	7.24	0.982	[] , -	+	[]
12	8 220	10.8	8.2	7.24	0.978	[] , -	+	[]

[1] National cost: '--' stands for very expensive (> 500 million euro); '-'stands for expensive (> 50 million euro); '[]' stands for not expensive, moderate benefits; '+' stands for significant benefits. Due to the big uncertainty on the capital outlay for rail transport and inland shipping, an assessment of the lowest and highest value has been integrated. A sensitivity analysis has been done to evaluate the effect of the capital outlay and the ranking of the policy options.

[2] Social desirability: '-' stands for moderate; '+' stands for high '++' stands for very high.

[3] Political feasibility: '-' stands for unlikely; '[]' stands for probable; '+' stands for very probable.

A better insight into the values of criteria 1 to 5 could be gained by comparing them with reference values. In 1998 CO_2 emission from transport amounted to 24 090 kton, for 2010 it was estimated to be 30 120 kton under BAU. In 1998 NO_x and VOS emissions were respectively 147 kton and 103 kton, assessments for 2010 resulted in respectively 71 kton and 61 kton. The average AOT40 and AOT60 values (2005 and 2010) under BAU scenario were estimated to be respectively 7.25 ppm*h and 0.98 ppm*h.

The best options to reduce CO_2 are modal-shift to public transport and freight transportation by rail or inland shipping. Over the period 2001-2012 a CO_2 reduction of 30 to 40% of average (1998 and 2010) annual emitted CO_2 by transport is gained. This is only a low reduction on a yearly basis. Except for option 3 and 5, technological measures are more effective in reducing NO_x. Except for electric cars, technological measures are also more effective in reducing VOC.

AOT40 and AOT60 values decrease only marginally regarding the individual policy option. The most pronounced reduction, still low at only 3%, has been noted for AOT60 for enhanced inspection and maintenance.

In earlier publications it was already stated that for CO_2, NO_x, VOC, AOT60 and AOT40 trends set by the BAU scenario are only effected in a small degree by the individual policy options. Current understandings show that international objectives concerning CO_2 and NO_x from transport will be difficult to meet [3,13].

4.2 Importance of the criteria

Figure 1 shows the importance of the different criteria according to the twelve decision-makers (d), including policy makers. All decision-makers considered CO_2 and VOC as important. CO_2 has had the two highest gradings: extremely and very important. VOC the three highest: extremely, very and moderately important. For the criteria related to the effectivity to ozone, the economic and social feasibility there was disagreement. NO_x fell in the middle.

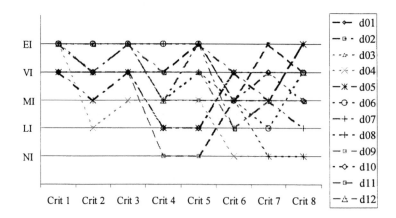

Figure 1: Importance of criteria according the 12 decision-makers.
(EI = extremely important, VI = very important, MI = moderately important,
LI = little important, NI = not important)

4.3 Ranking of the policy options

Taking into account all eight criteria, the integrated evaluation of the policy options results in to the following ranking using the ARGUS multiple criteria analysis:

Policy options which scored 'good':
- Advanced introduction of environmentally friendly conventional vehicles;
- Enhanced inspection and maintenance;
- Reduce passenger car use through more car pooling and teleworking.

Policy options which scored 'moderate to good':
- Reduce passenger car use through more public transport;
- Reduce road freight traffic through rail transport;
- Reduce road freight traffic through inland shipping.

Policy options which scored 'very moderate to moderate':
- Conversion of vehicles to more environmentally friendly alternatives: retrofit
- More environmentally friendly driving style;
- Reduce passenger car use through more cycling and walking;
- Advanced introduction of environmentally friendly alternative vehicles.

The two worst scoring policy options, were:
- Enhanced replacement of old passenger cars;
- Introduction of electric passenger cars in city traffic.

The low order in ranking for the option 'retrofit' can be explained by the fact that this option has no or only little influence on CO_2 emissions. Note that the evaluation of the effectivity to reduce particulate matter fell outside the scope of this study. However particles seem to be the most important impact factor of traffic on public health [14]. So retrofitting of diesel vehicles may not be excluded in policy strategies.

Though an adapted driving style has a large emission reduction potential, the option 'More environmentally friendly driving style' scored very moderately. Changing people's behaviour is difficult. Furthermore, this measure was only calculated for passenger cars. An extension to the other vehicle categories should result in higher emission reductions. If one wants to change driving style, this should most probably happen indirectly by technological measures, such as in-car devices (speed-limiting device, cruise control, black boxes) and ISA (Intelligent Speed Adaptation). However, the cost of those technological solutions is higher than for a driving course. Attention given to advice for adapted driving style could decrease, especially some years after the training.

The moderate score for the option 'Reduce passenger car use through more cycling and walking' could be explained by the small amount of passenger car kilometres that could be substituted (about 3% by 2010).

The 'Enhanced replacement of old passenger cars' is not an interesting policy option for Belgium. This option works only during a short period. Also, the economic and social feasibility of this option appeared to be very low.

Furthermore, the study has shown that within a global policy (on international, federal and regional level) with respect to the reduction in CO_2 and ozone from transport, introduction of electric vehicles is not a suitable policy option within a time horizon of 2010 or 2012. To what extent electric vehicles on local level could contribute to other specific objectives (noise reduction, emissions of particles, ...) was not studied.

5 Conclusions and recommendations

The most efficient way to reduce the negative effects of traffic on the environment and public health is to move and travel less with motorised vehicles. In accordance with policy, measures to control mobility demand are of high importance. The disconnection between economical growth and mobility demand has to be pursued. Policy has to pay attention to measures stimulating teleworking, an option that scored well within the study. At the same time measures have to be worked out to minimise the fill up of avoided kilometres.

If one has to move anyway, then this has to be done in the most environmentally friendly way: even better in the most sustainable way. Shifts in transport modes have to be stimulated. According to the study it seems that substitution of passenger traffic through public transport is the most socially feasible. Furthermore, also technological measures could be taken, such as the promotion of more environmentally friendly vehicles and the drawing up of an adapted inspection and maintenance programme for vehicles.

Moreover our personal perception according to how we deal with and act in traffic, plays an important role in the whole traffic business and its consequences. Policy initiatives also have to be directed towards changes in behaviour of drivers (purchasing behaviour, driving style, use of luxury accessories).

Obviously large policy efforts are required to achieve more sustainable mobility. The different policy levels have to focus their efforts on a common target. Starting from a European policy receiving maximal support from the member states, efforts at federal, regional and local level have to be well-tuned into one another and be co-ordinated. Furthermore, there is a need for a policy that integrates environmental interests and other aspects of sustainability to the decision-making regarding transport and related policy. An optimal tuning of policy towards environment, mobility, town and country planning and infrastructure planning must be targeted.

Acknowledgements

The multidisciplinary study was commissioned by the OSTC (Federal Office for Scientific, Technical and Cultural Affairs), within the national programme 'Sustainable Mobility' (1996-2001).

References

1. Traffic countings 1999 (Nr. 17) (*in Dutch: Verkeerstellingen 1999*), Ministry of Transport and Infrastructure, Bestuur van wegverkeer en Infrastructuur, Dienst Wegennormen en Wegtoegankelijkheid, Brussels, August 2000.
2. Discharges in the air 1980-1999 (*Dutch: Lozingen in de lucht 1980-1999*), VMM-rappert D/2000/6871/037, Erembodegem, 2000.
3. De Vlieger I., Berloznik R., De Keyser W., Duerinck J. & Mensink C., Multidisciplinary study on reducing air pollution from transport – methodology and emission results, *Urban Transport VII, Urban Transport and the Environment in the 21ˢᵗ Century, (Editors: L.J. Sucharov and C.A. Brebbia)*, pp. 429-440, ISBN 1-85312-865-1, WIT Press, Southampton, 2001.
4. Second National Communication of France under the Climate Convention, November 1997.
5. JCS-study, The Inspection of In–Use Cars in Order to Attain Minimum Emissions of Pollutants and Optimum Energy Efficiency, DG XI, DG VII and DG XVII of the European Commission, May 1998.
6. De Keukeleere D., Cornu K., De Vlieger I. & Van Poppel M., Evaluation of reduction potential of new measures within the field of environmentally friendly vehicle technologies and fuels, *Vito report (in Dutch)*, under contract of the Flemish Government (Aminal), January 2001.
7. De Vlieger I., De Keukeleere D. & Kretzschmar J., Environmental Effects of Driving Behaviour and Congestion related to Passenger Cars, *Atmospheric Environment*, 34, pp. 4649-4655, 2000.
8. Van Beukel J., Van Dongen J.E.F., Pulles M.P.J., Steenbekkers J.H.M. & Van der Vliet J.M., Driving styles: how to minimize fuel consumption and emissions, *TNO-IMW Report R 9/0943*, P.O. Box 6033, Delft, Netherlands, 1993.
9. 2020: Mens en Samenleving zijn mobiel als nooit tevoren!, *Febiac Info (in Dutch and French)*, pp. 4-9, Brussels, March 2000.
10. Pollet I., National inquiry upon mobility of housholds, *Proceedings OSTC workshop Sustainable Mobility (in Dutch and French)*: De enquêtes: een kijk op mobiliteit en de bezigheid van de mensen, pp. 18, 30 March 2000.
11. TRITEL, Flemish Mobility Plan (in Dutch) Mobiliteitsplan Vlaanderen, Fase 2: Modelopbouw – evaluatie trendscenario (1), *Report ½: Final report*, under contract of the Flemish Government, Departement Environment and Infrastructure, Mobiliteitscel, Brussels, July 1998.
12. Mailbach M., Peter D. & Seilen B. Ökoivertar Transporte, SPP Umwelt, Modul 5, INFRAS. –
13. De Vlieger, R. Berloznik, A. Colles, K. Cornu, J. Duerinck, C. Mensink, W. Van Aerschot, M. Van Poppel & S. Verbeiren, Measures in transport to reduce CO_2 and tropospheric ozone, Final report 2001/IMS/R/139, under contract of OSTC, August 2001
14. Int Panis L, De Nocker L., Torfs R., De Vlieger I. & Wouters G., External environmental costs of transport in Belgium, A report for OSTC, Vito, 2001.

EcoGest - Numerical modelling of the dynamic, fuel consumption and tailpipe emissions of vehicles equipped with spark ignition engines

C.M. Silva, T.L. Farias & J.M. C. Mendes-Lopes
Department of Mechanical Engineering
Instituto Superior Técnico, Portugal

Abstract

A numerical code capable of predicting the dynamic and environmental performances of vehicles is presented. The program, named EcoGest, solves the dynamic laws of vehicles for specific acceleration and deceleration curves of typical driving modes. Main inputs of EcoGest are the type of driving mode, vehicle characteristics, number of passengers, time spent at idle and the route - characterized by the topography, number and localization of stop signs and maximum allowed speed. Based on those inputs EcoGest is capable of calculating along the trip the localization of the vehicle, vehicle velocity, position of the accelerator pedal, gearbox selection, and the engine rotation speed. In addition, using the throttle position and the engine speed, EcoGest is capable of estimating instantaneous fuel consumption as well as instantaneous and average NO_x, CO, CO_2 and HC exhaust emissions. These calculations are done using emissions and fuel consumption distribution maps as a function of engine speed and throttle position. These maps can be obtained either numerically, or experimentally. For numerical data, due to the lack of experimental data for a large range of engines and running conditions, a numerical model, named MotorIST, was developed which simulates the real thermodynamic cycle of a four stroke spark ignition engine were a full discretization in time is adopted. Instead of performing a driving simulation for specific acceleration and deceleration curves of typical driving modes (slow, normal and fast), EcoGest can calculate the driving parameters (such as position of the accelerator pedal and engine rotation speed needed for the calculation of fuel consumption and tailpipe emissions) from a given driving cycle (speed against time), position of speed gear box chosen by the driver along the driving time, vehicle characteristics and number of passengers inside.

1 Introduction

The emission of vehicle pollutants into the atmosphere is an important health and environmental issue. For example, hydrocarbons (HC) irritate man's mucous, some compounds have a carcinogenic effect and together with nitric oxides (NO) leads to the formation of ground level ozone which can cause lung tissue damage and respiratory illness. Also, high amounts of carbon monoxide (CO) can lead to poisoning because of it's strongest adherence to hemoglobin and can impair visual perception, manual dexterity and exercise capacity. Low concentrations of nitrogen dioxide (NO_2) are sufficient to cause lung irritation, tissue damage and irritation of mucous membranes. NO_x together with water can also lead to acid rains. Carbon dioxide has no direct effect on man at the concentrations present in engine operation but contributes to long term environmental damage caused by atmospheric changes such as global warming (greenhouse effect) - see Barrio [1] and Schäfer and Basshuysen [2]. Such a direct link between vehicle emissions and societal and environmental health shows the importance of knowing what do vehicles emit when they travel from one location to another so traffic analysts could minimize vehicle emissions in designing a roadway or timing a signal system. Besides the above, this study could also help driving schools to give a more environmental friendly education.

Although experimental studies involving on-road vehicle emissions and engine data measurement as the vehicle is driven under real world conditions have been done (see [3]), it is important to built a simulation tool (a software) that allows the same results (emissions and engine data) with the advantage of being less expensive, more flexible, powerful and user-friendly than the real world measurement. As far as authors know, EcoGest is a unique solution because it combines in a single tool driving simulation, internal combustion modeling, fuel consumption and tailpipe emissions released to the atmosphere.

2 EcoGest

EcoGest is a Visual Basic program that solves the dynamic laws of vehicles for specific acceleration and deceleration curves of typical driving modes (slow, normal and fast). Main inputs of EcoGest are vehicle characteristics, number of passengers, the route (characterized by the topography), and either the driving cycle with speed gear box selection, or the type of driving mode, time spent at idle, number and localization of stop signs and maximum allowed speed. Based on those inputs EcoGest is capable of calculating along the trip the localization of the vehicle, vehicle velocity, position of the accelerator pedal, gearbox selection, and the engine rotation speed. In addition, using the throttle position and the engine speed, EcoGest is capable of estimating instantaneous and average fuel consumption as well as instantaneous and average NO_x, CO, CO_2 and HC exhaust emissions. These calculations are done using emissions and fuel consumption distribution maps as a function of engine speed and throttle position. These maps can be obtained either numerically, or experimentally.

Figure 1 shows an input window and Figure 2 shows an example of one of the distribution maps as a function of engine speed and throttle position.

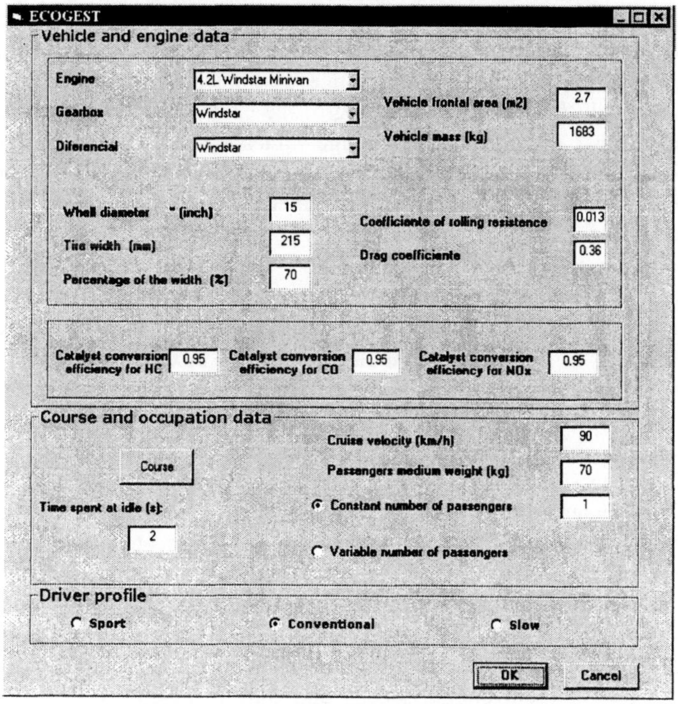

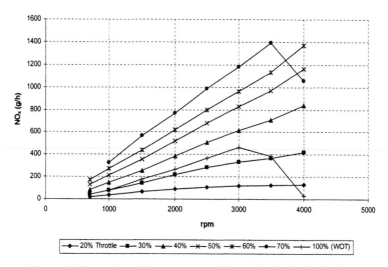

Figure 1: Imput window from EcoGest.

Figure 2: Example of the maps used for numerical calculation.

2.1 Internal combustion engine simulation: MotorIST

In order to build the fuel consumption and emissions distribution maps as a function of engine speed and throttle position, a numerical code was developed, named MotorIST, that simulates the real thermodynamic cycle of a four stroke spark ignition engine covering the range of time between the closing of the intake valves all the way to the opening of the exhaust valves. It uses a pseudo-zero dimensional approach where average values in space are considered while a full discretization in time is adopted. As input values MotorIST requires a full characterization of the geometrical parameters that characterize the engine, namely number of cylinders, bore, stroke, compression ratio, valve dimensions and geometry, valve timing (opening and closing angles) among others. In addition, it is necessary to describe the atmospheric conditions, namely ambient pressure and temperature. Finally, fuel composition (carbon and hydrogen atoms, octane number) and information about the air fuel mixture (λ) is also required. With these input variables, and considering the compression and expansions strokes as isentropic evolutions, heat transfer to the inner surface of the combustion chamber (cylinder walls, piston and cylinder head), the energy released during combustion (taking into account dissociation) and expansion (taking into account CO, H_2 and O_2 recombination due to temperature decrease), actualization of the mixture properties due to temperature and composition changes along the cycle, MotorIST allows the user to calculate, for example, the temperature, pressure, heat transfer coefficient and work evolutions along time as well as indicated and brake power, mean effective pressure, torque, engine efficiency, instantaneous fuel consumption and formation of pollutants (HC, CO and NO_x) for different engine speeds and throttle positions. The combustion modeling involves a space discretization in three zones: unburned mixture, flame (reaction zone, limited by the trailing edge and leading edge of the flame) and burned mixture in order to improve the NO_x emission simulation.

MotorIST (see Morais [4]) is being further developed within the EcoGest project. For information on internal combustion engines see Mendes-Lopes [5] and Heywood [6].

2.2 Driving simulation

Typical acceleration and deceleration curves were obtained from experimental data measured on board of a Renault Megane 2.0 IDE using Flowtronic 206-208 (a measurement system with an electronic distance sensor to be mounted onto the vehicle's wheel with a impulse cable connected to the display screen which enables the accurate measurement of distance, speed and acceleration). Some of those curves are shown in Figure 3. The sport (fast) driver has the most aggressive driving patterns. Besides the above typical curves, each driving mode is characterized by the minimal and maximum rpm at which they change the gearbox selection as shown in Table I.

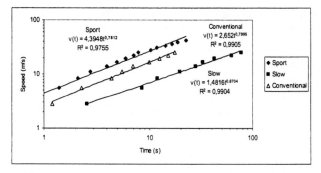

Figure 3: Experimental readings for acceleration curves.

Table I: Adopted rpm values for which the driver changes the gearbox selection for the Ford vehicles mencioned below.

	Sport	Normal	Slow
Minimal rpm	2000	1750	1500
Maximum rpm	4000 or 4500	3750	3000

The driving simulation principles, for each driving profile, are: the vehicle starts from idle (hot start is assumed), accelerates according to the driver profile (sport, conventional or slow) till it reaches the specified cruise velocity. Once reached, the driver keeps that speed. If a stop sign or any other kind of obstacle is ahead of the vehicle in such a distance that equals the necessary brake distance for that driver, decelerating process starts until iddle is reached again (at the obstacle position) and after a certain specified idling time the vehicle goes on accelerating till it reaches the cruise velocity, and so on. The actual speed is calculated knowing the prior speed and a certain acceleration/deceleration curve. The actual rpm are calculated knowing the actual speed, transmission relation and tire geometrical relations (Bosch [7]). The maximum allowed delivered power is calculate knowing rpm. The actual acceleration is calculated knowing the speed variation within the time step. The necessary power is calculated knowing inertial force (total mass multiplied by the actual acceleration), friction forces (drag and rolling resistance), gravitational force and the actual speed. The position of accelerator pedal is calculated knowing the relation between necessary and maximum power and it is directly related with throttle position. At acceleration, the vehicle's position is calculated from the polynomial rectilinear constant acceleration motion equation. At deceleration the vehicle's position is calculated knowing the distance versus speed curve (necessary brake distance curve). If a driving cycle and a speed gear box selection is given, the driving simulation principles are similar with the difference that the actual velocity is given , therefore EcoGest doesn't have to calculate it.

2.3 Tailpipe Emissions

For every rpm and throttle position of the driving simulation EcoGest uses bilinear interpolation (Press et al. [8]) to obtain instantaneous fuel consumption and emissions from distribution maps.

Both emissions obtained by bilinear interpolation from experimental or numerical distribution maps are non-treated emissions (without catalytic treatment). To calculate the vehicle's real released emissions to the atmosphere it is necessary to account for the conversion efficiency of the three-way catalytic converter (Heywood [6]).

The CO_2 emission is given by subtracting from the stoichiometric CO_2 emission the amount of CO_2 that would be formed from tailpipe HC and CO, accounting for their molecular weights.

These calculations are valid only if it is not considered the HC evaporative emissions. For the the Ford vehicles mencioned below the catalytic conversion efficiency was assumed to have a constant value of 95% corresponding to the maximum efficiency of a fresh three-way catalyst (Schäfer and Basshuysen [2]). This means that it was not considered cold start. For more information on catalytic converters see Heck and Farrauto [9].

Bilinear interpolation for a certain rpm and throttle position yields grams per second data. Numerically integrating these values with respect to traveling time yields grams per trip. Dividing the total mass emissions by the trip length yields grams per kilometer.

3 Results

With the propose of demonstrating the potentialities of the program, EcoGest was applied considering three different gasoline engines of which experimental data concerning fuel consumption and non-treated emissions were supplied by Ford Motor Company, namely: V6 2.49L, V6 4.2L and V8 4.6L. Main characteristics of the reference course selected are as follows: 10 km in length, flat, four stop signs along the course and a total time spent at idle of eight seconds (two seconds in each stop sign). The reference cruise velocity was 90 km/h with only one passenger inside the vehicle (the driver). Figure 4 shows, as an example, some results of the study made for the analysis of the impact of driving mode of the Ford Contour equipped with the V6 2.49L gasoline engine. Although 10 km is the total length of the route in those figures it is only represented part of the course in order to improve graphic readability. Similar results (not shown) were obtained for Ford Windstar Minivan equipped with V6 4.2L gasoline engine and Ford Explorer Sport Utility equipped with V8 4.6L gasoline engine. A comparison between the energetic (fuel consumption) and environmental (pollutant emissions) performances of those three vehicles was also made using the same reference situation (not shown). Main conclusions of this case study are presented in the next section.

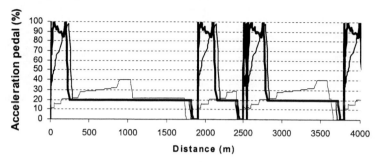

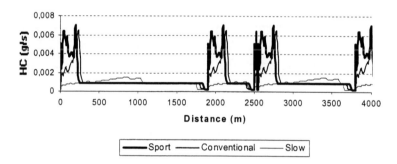

Figure 4:   Position of accelerator pedal (100% corresponding to full load) and instantaneous vehicle HC emission.

In order to validate the program concerning driving simulation and fuel consumption calculations, EcoGest was also applied to an urban bus of CARRIS (the bus company responsible for exploring the bus routes within the central area of Lisbon, Portugal). It was introduced an experimental driving cycle and the positions of the bus along traveling time, obtained with a DATRON microwave Doppler sensor M3 [10]. It was also introduced the automatic transmission (ZF 5HP_502) management and the variable weight of the bus along the traveling time due to the variable number of passengers inside it. Emission calculations were not performed due to the lack of experimental and literature data. For fuel consumption calculations, the bus' brake specific fuel consumption was known only at full load. Hence, the map shown in was built from the map for a 8 cylinder, 12 dm^3, naturally aspirated M.A.N. engine, assuming that the relation between the brake specific fuel consumption of the engine of the bus (a 6 cylinder, 11967 cm^3, turbocharged Mercedes) and of the M.A.N engine at full charge remains constant for each rpm. Results from EcoGest are 13% less than measurements from CARRIS.

Figure 6 shows vehicle speed measurements along part of the selected route of the bus and the results obtained for instantaneous and average fuel consumption.

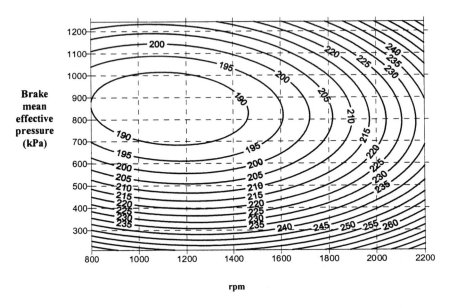

Figure 5: Estimated brake specific fuel consumption contours (g/kWh) for the engine of the urban bus.

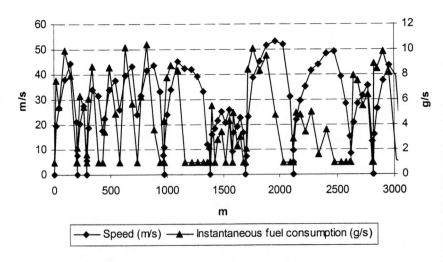

Figure 6: Speed measurements and calculated instantaneous fuel consumption of the bus. The average fuel consumption calculated for the total route was 57.7 l/100km.

4 Conclusions – future work

A numerical model named EcoGest was presented. This model simulates the driving, fuel consumption and pollutant emission for a certain type of driving mode or driving cycle and speed gear box selection, vehicle characteristics, number of passengers, time spent at idle, route (characterized by the topography, number and localization of stop signs and maximum allowed speed), conversion efficiency of the three-way catalytic converter and fuel consumption and emissions (HC, CO, NO_x) distribution maps as a function of engine speed and throttle position. These maps can be built using software named MotorIST, that was developed to simulate the real thermodynamic cycle of a four stroke spark ignition engine. A methodology for calculating the real atmosphere emissions (HC, CO, NO_x, CO_2) of gasoline internal combustion engines was presented assuming a constant conversion efficiency of the three-way catalytic converter. In order to demonstrate the potentialities of EcoGest, an application to three Ford vehicles was performed. Main conclusions of that study can be summarized as follows:

- the slow driver appears to be the most economical and environment friendly (for example it can emit less 22% of CO_2, 17% of HC, 50% of CO and 48% of NO_x than the normal driver)
- for each 20 km/h increase in the cruise velocity the vehicle can emit more 40% of CO_2, 50% of HC, 37% of CO and 86% of NO_x
- the HC emissions are the most affected with the increase in time spent at idle
- the topography of the route has a significant influence on fuel consumption and emissions
- for each additional passenger the vehicle can emit more 2% of CO_2, 3% of HC, 2% of CO and 8% of NO_x (variations in the number of passengers in the vehicle appear to be the parameter that causes less environmental impact, highlighting the importance of promoting car sharing).

In order to validate the program concerning driving simulation and fuel consumption calculations, EcoGest was applied to an urban bus of CARRIS. The results concerning fuel consumption show a difference of 13% less between CARRIS data and EcoGest results.

In summary, EcoGest is a software capable of estimate the influence of the impact of the driving mode, number of passengers, time spent at idle, cruise velocity, course inclination and type of vehicle on fuel consumption and atmosphere pollutant emissions of a vehicle equipped with gasoline internal combustion engine.

The focus of ongoing research is on the following subjects:

- study the influence of considering stationary fuel consumption and emission maps instead of transient data
- validate the model with experimental on board vehicle emission measurements using a portable exhaust gas analyzer
- extend the application of EcoGest concerning emissions to vehicles using other alternative fuels such as natural gas, methanol, diesel and biodiesel

- improve the driving simulation considering more representative acceleration and deceleration curves for the driving modes and introducing oscillations on the cruise velocity
- improve the emissions simulation considering the cold start, more accurate idle measurements and modeling the catalyst conversion efficiency with the engine exhaust flow temperature and kilometers traveled by the vehicle.

Acknowledgements

The authors would like to acknowledge the Fundação para a Ciência e a Tecnologia program POCTI/2000/mgs/35659 and 35649 for their financial contribution in this research project and Kristofor R. Norman of Ford Motor Company for his precious cooperation.

Nomenclature

WOT	wide-open throttle
λ	relative air/fuel ratio

References

[1] Barrio, Carmelo Anaya, *Livro Verde sobre o Catalisador*, Manufacturas Fonos, 1994
[2] Schäfer, F., Basshuysen, R. van, *Reduced Emissions and Fuel Consumption in Automobile Engines*, SAE, 1995.
[3] http://www4.ncsu.edu/~frey/emissions/drivingtips.html.
[4] Morais, Pedro, *Desenvolvimento e Aperfeiçoamento de Sub Modelos e Exploração de um Programa de Previsão de Desempenho de Motores de Explosão - Projecto de Termodinâmica aplicada*, DEM, IST, 1998.
[5] Mendes-Lopes, José Miguel C., *Motores de Combustão Interna- uma abordagem termodinâmica*, AEIST, 1999
[6] Heywood, John B., *Internal Combustion Engine Fundamentals*, McGraw-Hill, 1988
[7] Bosch, Automotive Handbook, 4ª Edição, Bosch, 1996
[8] Press, William H., Flannery, Brian P., Teukolsky, Saul A., Vetterling, William T., *Numerical Recipes the Art of Scientific Computing*, Cambridge University Press, 1986
[9] Heck, Ronald M., Farrauto, Robert J., *Catalytic Air Pollution Control_Commercial Technology*, John Wiley & Sons, 1995.
[10] http://www.datron.org.

Air quality alteration in a Greek town

M. Graziou
Department of Civil Engineering, Democritus University of Thrace, Greece.

Abstract

In this paper the objective is to estimate the alteration in the air pollution, during the last ten years, in a rather typical Greek town. First of all an attempt was made to document the sources of air pollution, caused by traffic and by space heating emissions. The data were applied to models, which calculate the total load of each emission: VOC, SO_2, NO_x, CO, Pb, TSP. For the computation of the actual emission, information was needed concerning the mean seasonal temperature, average speed, cylinder displacement, year of manufacturing for the conventional cars, or catalytic type used, average trip length, and the kind of the heating fuel. The maximum center and spatial averaged concentrations were estimated. Air quality is also estimated the given that all vehicles were of catalytic technology. Finally, a comparison is made between the air pollution alteration caused by traffic and that by space heating emissions.

1 Introduction

The motive for this work was the question about the range of air pollution in a typical Greek town. In urban areas, the most acute problem of air pollution is the photochemical smog. This smog is formed through atmospheric reactions, under the influence of sunlight and heat, from the primary pollutants NOx, CO and the volatile organic compounds (VOC). The dominate source, of the above primary pollutants, are the light duty gasoline powered vehicles. The NOx, CO, VOC emission factors are considerably depended on the daily mean temperature and the driving patterns. Pollutants, as the total suspended particulate (TSP), Pb and the SO_2, are also recorded.

In this paper the target is to estimate the alteration of air pollution, during the last ten years, in a rather typical Greek town. The main sources, that cause the air pollution of a small Greek town, are the traffic and the space heating emissions. A comparison between the air pollution alteration caused by these two sources is made. It is also estimated the air quality that would be if all vehicles were of catalytic technology.

2 The raw data

First of all an attempt was made to document the sources of air pollution, caused by traffic and by space heating emissions. The primary collected data concern the town of Xanthi, a typical provincial Greek town. The data are related to driving patterns, as average vehicle speed and average trip length and to information about the vehicles, as number, cylinder displacement, technology type used and year of manufacturing. Data were also collected regarding fuels and firewood quantities used for space heating. The collected data are presented in the follow tables.

Table 1: Quantities of pollution sources for the years 1991 and 2001.

Source	Unit	Quantity: Year 1991	Year 2001
Cars	number	10.000	40.000
Light duty diesel powered vehicles < 3.5 tn	number	100	200
Heavy duty diesel powered vehicles 3.5-16 tn	number	40	40
Taxi	number	117	117
Buses (urban region driving)	number	6	11
Motorcycles	number	1500	7.500
Diesel for heating	10^3 tn	18	25
Firewood	10^3 tn	5	5

Table 2: Driving Conditions for the years 1991 and 2001.

Driving Conditions	Year 1991	Year 2001
Average Speed (Km/h)	40	30
Average Trip Length (Km/y) per Car	5000	5500
Average Trip Length (Km/y) per Light duty diesel powered vehicle	10000	11000
Average Trip Length (Km/y) per Heavy duty diesel powered vehicle	8000	9000
Average Trip Length (Km/y) per Taxi	70000	30000
Average Trip Length (Km/y) per Bus (urban driving)	45000	54000
Average Trip Length (Km/y) per Motorcycle	6000	9000

Table 3: Car type distribution in relation to cylinder displacement and technology type used, for the years 1991 and 2001.

Type of car	Distribution	
	Year 1991	Year 2001
Conventional technology , cylinder displacement <1400cc	60%	29%
Conventional technology , cylinder displec. 1400cc÷2000 cc	19%	10%
Conventional technology, cylinder displacement >2000cc	1%	1%
Catalytic technology, cylinder displacement <1400cc	6%	18%
Catalytic technology, cylinder displacement >1400cc	14%	42%

Table 4: Car type distribution in relation to technology type used and year of manufacturing.

Type of car	Distribution	
	Year 1991	Year 2001
Conventional technology, year of manufacturing before 1981	10%	1%
Conventional technology, year of manufacturing 1981÷1984	30%	11%
Conventional technology, year of manufacturing 1985÷1991	40%	28%
Catalytic technology	20%	60%

3   Methods

3.1 The models

The data were applied to easily used models, which calculate the total load of each emission: VOC, SO_2, NO_x, CO, Pb, TSP. The quantities of emissions released into atmosphere depend on a number of parameters. Thus, the emission E of pollutant j can be expressed through a simple mathematical form as follows:

$$\text{Total pollutant emission loads} = \sum_{jk}^{n} E_{jk} \qquad (1)$$

$$E_{jk} = (e_j) \times (\text{Source activity k}) \qquad (2)$$

where :

E_{jk} is the emission load of the pollutant j, from the source k , and e_j is the emission factor of pollutant j, from the source k per unit activity.

The unit of activity, the mileage of the vehicle traffic in the study area and the quantity of fuel consumed for the heating, defines an acceptable way of expressing the size of a given activity. The normalized rate of the load emission factor (emission loads per unit activity) e_{jk} is almost constant,   regardless of the source activity. The emission factor e_j for the pollutant j, is expressed by the following relation:

e_j = f (Source type, source size, process or design particularities, source age and technological sophistication, source operating practices, type and quality of fuels, ambient conditions)

The above equation cannot be expressed as a continuous function form, due to the distinct nature of most parameters, as well as, due to the frequent lack of sufficient information in relation to the remaining parameters. The normalized factor e_{jk} values, of every emission load per source unit activity, are obtained from appropriate tables [1].

For the calculation e_{jk} values of NO_x, CO and VOC emissions, caused by the vehicles exhaust emissions, the following model is:

$$e_j = e^{hot} [1 + f_{cs} (m_{0.75} - 1) (0.75)^{-1}] \qquad (3)$$

where the hot-start consumption factor e^{hot} can be obtained as a function of the average speed, cylinder displacement, year of car manufacturing for the conventional cars or type of catalytic system used. The factor multiplier $m_{0.75}$ is calculated as a function of the mean temperature, average trip length, and the conventional or catalytic technology used [2]. The e^{hot} and $m_{0.75}$ factors are obtained from graphs [1]. The factor f_{cs} expresses the fraction of cold engine starts.

For the calculation the total VOC vehicle emissions, the hot soak losses, which occur when the hot engine is turned off, due to the evaporation of the fuel in the carburetor bowl and tank, and the diurnal losses, which occur while the vehicles are stationary with the engine off due to the expansion are calculated. The emission of vapor from the fuel tank, as a result of the daily diurnal ambient temperature variations are, also, calculated. The emission factors e_j for the above categories are obtained from appropriate tables [1] in relation with the average seasonal temperature, the gasoline volatility and the cylinder displacement.

Based on the above models the total rate of traffic and space heating emissions over the study area are computed through emission factors in a separate computation of emission for each basic kind of vehicle and space heating furnace for each type of fuel used. Based on a model for the dispersion of traffic and space heating emissions in urban setting [2], the computation of the long-term average concentration at city Ψ_{max} and the long-term spatial-averaged concentration over the entire urban area Ψ_{mean}, for each pollutant, is followed. For inert pollutants, the Ψ_{max} is related to the maximum population exposure and to the intensity and frequency of episodic events. The model inputs are: the effective radius of urban area R, the ratio P of pollutant emission density at the city center to the spatial-averaged, over the entire urban area, pollutant emission density (center-maximum to average), the height h from which the emission is released (effective release height), the joint frequency data from the study area, and the mixing heights L(k) as a function of the climatological mean and the nocturnal minimum mixing heights. The values of L(k) can be computed on the basis of the parametrization given in tables and graphs [1]. Ψ_{max} and Ψ_{mean} values are separately calculated, for each source type and overall. The calculation of these values, for six $\varphi(\kappa)$ values of meteorological parameters, is based on the following equations:

$$\Psi_{mean} = Q_{mean} \, \omega_{mean} \, (R, h, L) \qquad (4)$$

$$\Psi_{max} = Q_{mean}\, \omega_{max}\, (R,P,h,L) \tag{5}$$

where $\omega_{mean}\,(R,h,L) = \sum C_{mean}(k,R,0,L)\, Rh(k,h,L)\, \varphi(k)$ (6)

and $\omega_{max}\,(R,P,h,L) = \sum C_{mean}(k,R,0,L)\, Rp(k,P,L)\, Rh(k,h,L)\, \varphi(k)$ (7)

The raw meteorological data used for the $\varphi(\kappa)$ calculation are the joint frequency of six wind speed classes under the atmospheric stability class k conditions. The parameters $C_{mean}(k,R,0,L)$, $Rp(k,P,L)$ and $Rh(k,h,L)$, respectively, express the normalized spatial-average concentration for stability k and wind speed at anemometer height, the ratio of center-maximum concentration per spatial-average for stability class k and wind speed at anemometer height, and the concentration attenuation factor due to release height. The above parameters are obtained from graphs [1] as function of the model inputs R, P, h, k, L.

3.2 Assumptions and data

The formulation of the model, for the dispersion of traffic and space heating emissions in urban setting, is based on the assumption of circular study area and normal emission density profiles. For the year 1991 the effective radius of urban study area, R, is estimated equal to 1,02Km and for the year 2001 equal to 1,20 Km. The height which the emissions from traffic is released, is considered to be at ground level and for the space heating one, a typical height of buildings. Therefore, the effective release height for the traffic emissions is equal to 1m, for the emissions from buildings heated by firewood is equal to 4 m and for the space heating furnaces is equal to 13m for the year 1991 and equal to 16m for the year 2001. For the estimation of SO_2 and Pb emissions, the fuel content in S and Pb is computed based on the annual fuel specifications as they are given by the Supreme Chemical Committee of Greece. The fuel content in S and Pb and the gasoline volatility, for the years 1991 and 2001, are presented in table 5.

An homogeneous wind field is assumed. The values of the parameters $\varphi(\kappa)$, for the six categories of atmospheric stability, have been estimated as: for A(1500) the value 0.0039, for B(1000) the value 0.0226, for C(1000) the value 0.0442, for D-day (1000) the value 0.1017, for D(550)-night the value 0,0467 and for nighttime stable (100) the value 0.1409 [3].

Developing the scenario A, of all light duty gasoline powered conventional cars replaced by catalytic technology ones, it is assumed that the proportion between cars with engine less or equal to 1400 cc and those with greater engine is 50%-50%.

Table 5:The fuel content in S and Pb and their Reid Vapor Pressure (RVP).

Year	1991			2001		
Fuel Type	Fuel Content		RVP	Fuel Content		RVP
	S %	Pb gr/l	Kpa	S %	Pb gr/l	Kpa
Gasoline- Super	0,15	0,15	60-80	0,15	0,15	60-80
Gasoline-Unleaded	0,15	0,013	45-50	0,15	0,005	45-50

Table 5: The fuel content in S and Pb and their Reid Vapor Pressure (RVP). (Continuation)

Year	1991			2001		
Fuel Type	Fuel Content		RVP	Fuel Content		RVP
	S %	Pb gr/l	Kpa	S %	Pb gr/l	Kpa
Diesel-Traffic	0,30			0,35		
Diesel-Heating	0,30			0,30		

4 Results

The VOC, CO, NOx, SO2, TSP, Pb emissions caused by traffic and heating for the years 1990 , 2000 , for scenario A are presented in the table 6. The Spatial – Averaged (Ψmean), over the entire urban area, annual pollutant concentration at ground-level of VOC, CO, NOx, SO2, TSP, Pb caused by traffic and space heating for the years 1990 , 2000, for scenario A are presented in the table 7. The Central-Maximum (Ψmax) annual pollutant concentration at ground-level of VOC, CO, NOx, SO2, TSP, Pb caused by traffic and heating for the years 1990 , 2000, for scenario A are presented in the table 8. The percentage of air quality deterioration from the two main pollution sources, traffic and space heating, during the cold months, of the years 1991 , 2001 and for scenario A, are presented in the table 9.

The increase or the decrease of the Spatial –Averaged (Ψmean) and the Central-Maximum (Ψmax) annual pollutant concentration of VOC, CO, NOx, SO2, TSP, caused the traffic and space heating, during the last ten years, are presented in the table 10. The increase of Pb central maximum concentration is about 250%. The increase of cars number is 300%.

Table 6: The VOC, CO, NOx, SO2, TSP, Pb annual emissions (tn/y).

Source - Pollutant	Year	VOC	CO	NOx	SO2	TSP	Pb
Traffic		255,59	755,80	136,75	16,68	6,54	0,82
Residential Furnaces	1991	6,37	12,78	46,80	108,00	6,48	
Wood Stoves		138,00	560,00	5,60	0,80	60,00	
Residential Fireplaces		43,00	85,00	1,70	0,20	14,00	
	Total	442,96	1413,6	190,85	125,68	87,02	0,82
Traffic		1560,9	2922,6	363,67	63,91	25,96	2,59
Residential Furnaces	2001	8,9	17,7	65,00	150,00	9,00	
Wood Stoves		138,00	420,00	4,20	0,60	45,00	
Residential Fireplaces		86,00	170,00	3,40	0,40	28,00	
	Total	1793,80	3530,3	436,27	214,91	107,96	2,59
Traffic		1478,2	1831,9	59,48	62,10	24,56	1,34
Residential Furnaces	Sc. A	8,8	7,7	65,00	150,00	9,00	
Wood Stoves		138,0	420,00	4,20	0,60	45,00	
Residential Fireplaces		86,0	170,00	3,40	0,40	28,00	
	Total	1711,0	2439,6	132,08	213,10	106,56	1,34

Table 7: The VOC, CO, NOx, SO2, TSP, Pb Ψmean annual pollutant concentration   ($\mu g/m^2$).

Source - Pollutant	Year	VOC	CO	NOx	SO2	TSP	Pb
Traffic		20,02	59,20	10,71	1,31	0,51	0,065
Residential Furnaces	1991	0,25	0,50	1,82	4,20	0,25	
Wood Stoves		7,52	30,53	0,31	0,04	3,27	
Residential Fireplaces		1,67	3,31	0,07	0,13	0,55	
	Total	29,46	93,54	13,51	5,78	4,58	0,065
Traffic		98,45	184,33	22,94	4,03	1,64	0,163
Residential Furnaces	2001	0,26	0,52	1,91	4,42	0,27	
Wood Stoves		6,05	18,41	0,19	0,03	1,97	
Residential Fireplaces		2,53	5,01	0,10	0,01	0,82	
	Total	107,29	208,27	25,14	8,49	4,70	0,163
Traffic		93,34	115,54	3,75	3,92	1,55	0,084
Residential Furnaces	Sc. A	0,26	0,52	1,91	4,42	0,27	
Wood Stoves		6,05	18,41	0,19	0,02	1,97	
Residential Fireplaces		2,53	5,01	0,10	0,01	0,82	
	Total	102,08	139,48	5,95	8,37	4,61	0,084

Table 8: The VOC, CO, NOx, SO2, TSP, Pb Ψmax annual pollutant   concentration   ($\mu g/m^2$).

Source - Pollutant	Year	VOC	CO	NOx	SO2	TSP	Pb
Traffic		54,57	161,38	29,20	3,56	1,40	0,176
Residential Furnaces	1991	0,50	1,00	3,66	8,44	0,51	
Wood Stoves		8,43	34,19	0,34	0,05	3,66	
Residential Fireplaces		3,36	6,64	0,26	0,02	1,09	
	Total	66,86	203,21	33,46	12,07	6,66	0,176
Traffic		267,06	500,03	62,22	10,93	4,44	0,443
Residential Furnaces	2001	0,52	1,05	3,84	8,86	0,53	
Wood Stoves		6,78	20,62	0,21	0,03	2,21	
Residential Fireplaces		5,08	10,04	0,20	0,02	1,66	
	Total	279,44	531,74	66,47	19,84	8,84	0,443
Traffic		252,90	313,41	10,18	10,63	4,20	0,228
Residential Furnaces	Sc. A	0,52	1,05	3,84	8,86	0,53	
Wood Stoves		6,77	20,62	0,20	0,03	2,21	
Residential Fireplaces		5,08	10,04	0,200	0,02	1,66	
	Total	265,27	345,12	14,42	19,54	8,60	0,228

Table 9: The percentage   of air quality deterioration from traffic and space heating emissions, during the cold months.

Year	Pollutant	VOC	CO	NOx	SO$_2$	TSP
	Source					
1991	Heating	58%	61%	43%	81%	86%
	Traffic	42%	39%	57%	19%	14%
2001	Heating	22%	26%	43%	81%	86%
	Traffic	78%	74%	57%	19%	14%
Scenario	Heating	22%	36%	67%	83%	87%
A	Traffic	78%	64%	33%	17%	13%

Table 10: The alteration of annual Ψmean and Ψmax concentration of VOC, CO, NOx, SO2, TSP during the last ten years.

	Pollutant	VOC	CO	NOx	SO$_2$	TSP
	Source	%	%	%	%	%
Central-Maximum annual concentration Ψmax	Heating	0,8	- 24,2	2,7	4,7	- 16,5
	Traffic	389,4	209,8	113,1	207	218,2
	Total load	318	162	99	64	33
Spatial – Averaged annual concentration Ψmean	Heating	13,8	-30,3	3,4	5	-13,1
	Traffic	391,8	211,4	114	208,5	219,8
	Total load	286	131	96	53	16

It is also examined what the decrease of pollutant concentration would be, in case of conventional cars replaced by catalytic technology ones. The results are presented at the table 11. The decrease of Pb concentration is about 94%.

Table 11: The decrease of pollutant concentration in case of conventional cars replaced by catalytic technology ones

	Pollutant	VOC	CO	NOx	SO$_2$	TSP
	Source	%	%	%	%	%
Annual concentration Ψmax	Traffic	5,6	59,5	511,4	2,9	5,7
	Total load	5,3	54%	361	2	3
Annual concentration Ψmean	Traffic	5,6	59,5	511,4	2,9	5,7
	Total load	5,12	49	322	1	2

5 Conclusions

In spite of the great increase of the number of cars, the provincial towns of Greece seems not to have any problem of air pollution. The examined pollutant concentrations are lower than the U.E. and the World Health Organization air quality limit standards. The increase of the pollutant emissions, the last ten years, due to the great motorcycle and car number increase, as an effect of the urbanism (brought about by domestic immigration) and the standard of living improvement, the fuel consumption for heating increase, due to the same reasons as above, and to the speed driving decrease, mainly caused by the vehicles number increase.

In the Greek towns, the greater part of air pollution, caused by VOC, CO, NOx, Pb emissions, is due to cars traffic primarily (see table 9). The rate of VOC maximum concentration increase is similar with the car increase rate while the

CO increase is about half. The increase of the other pollutants has lesser rates (see table 10).

The conventional cars replacement by catalytic technology ones will reduce the pollutant emissions and their concentrations, especially those of CO, NOx, Pb, to percentages 54%, 361% and 94% respectively (see table 11). At the figure 1, it is represented the total annual pollutant emissions during the years 1991, 2001 and scenario A (of all light duty gasoline powered conventional cars replaced by catalytic technology ones).

The heating is, primarily, accountable for the air pollution "charge" caused by SO_2 and TSP. The percentage of the "charge" is greater than 80% (see tab. 9). The 72% of air pollution caused by SO_2 emission is due to diesel residential furnaces, so long as the "increased" CO and Total Suspended Particulate concentrations are caused by the firewood combustion used for heating. The 42% of the air pollution caused by TSP emissions is due to firewood combustion.

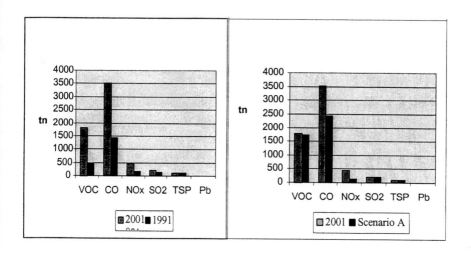

Figure 1: Total annual pollutant emissions during the years 1991, 2001 and scenario A (all cars of catalytic technology).

Acknowledgements

The author wishes to thank the manager of Xanthi Urban Transport Bureau, the directors of Commerce Department, Transport Department and Chemical Department of Xanthi Prefecture, for information on the data of this study.

References

[1] Economopoulos, A.P., *Effective Management of Air, Water & land Pollution*, Democritos University of Thrace Editions, Xanthi, Greece, 1993.

[2] Economopoulos, A.P., On the Dispersion of Traffic and Space Heating Emissions in Urban Settings, *Journal of Air & Waste Management Association*, Vol. 42 (4) pp. 448-456., 1992.

[3] Petropoulos I., and Ghikas G., A first approach to the air pollution of small Greek cities, *Proceedings of the 3rd Conference on Environmental Science and Technology*, Vol. A., pp. 482-490, 1993.

Towards a post-Kyoto sustainable transport strategy

J. A. Prades, R.Belzile, M. Labriet & J.P. Waaub
GREIGE (Environmental Management Interdisciplinary Research Group). University of Quebec in Montreal. Canada.

Abstract

Two important Documents are summarized within. Focusing on GHG emissions reduction, they elaborate two scenarios and a basic objective. Concerning the measures to be taken from now to 2010, they propose a major tightening of fuel-efficiency standards for new vehicles. For the period 2010-2025, they propose rationing transport-fuel by tradable permits, as key element of the Strategy.
Our critical comments point out the high quality of the *Documents* and the opportunity of a complementary vision concerning the impact of the new information technologies (combining locomotion and proactive logistic management) and the objective evaluation of transportation market evolution.
Our conclusion is to collect together the necessary elements of a better conceptual and practical understanding of sustainable transportation.
We thank the Quebec Ministry of Environment and the Social Sciences and Humanities Research Council of Canada for financial support.

1. Introduction

The Centre for Sustainable Transportation [01], financially supported by the Government of Canada and based in Greater Toronto area, was founded in 1996. The Centre provides leadership in achieving sustainable transportation by facilitating cooperative actions, and thereby contributing to Canadian and global sustainability. In this particular field of sustainable transportation, it is at the forefront in North America and throughout the world. Along with many important publications, its current undertakings includes the "The Longer View", a series of three nation-wide workshops on sustainable transportation in Canada. Two draft *Documents* headed respectively "Background Paper for a Post-Kyoto Transport Strategy" and " Draft Strategy for Transport in Canada for the post-Kyoto Period" had been submitted to discussion. The objective of this paper is to give a brief presentation and some critical comments of these studies, referred to simply as the *Documents* henceforth.

2. The *Documents*

The *Documents* are authorized by Richard Gilbert, an independent consultant in urban issues who specializes in transportation among other areas. The views and analyses contained in these *Documents* are those of the author and not necessarily those of Environment Canada or the Centre for Sustainable Transportation.

The *Documents* were written before the catastrophic events of September 11. The consequences of these events, especially concerning the need to reduce oil consumption, are not specifically considered here.

The overall aim of these *Documents* is to provide continued discussions on how transportation in Canada can be moved towards sustainability. More precisely, the *Documents* follow this order. 1. Setting out and justifying three scenarios for 2010 and a target for 2025. 2. Concerned relevant data. 3. Actions required to meet the three scenarios for 2010. 4. Actions required for the period 2010-2025. 5. Concluding remarks.

For simplicity, the scenarios and target are defined in terms of reductions in GHG emissions. As indicated above, the purpose of the *Documents* is to help ensure that meeting the requirements of Kyoto Protocol is regarded as a beginning of the journey towards sustainability.

As a general rule, we follow here a literal transcription of selected passages of the *Documents*. The use of quotation marks is avoided, seeming to us to be cumbersome and useless.

2.1. Scenarios and target

Three scenarios are proposed due of the high level of uncertainty considering two selected variables: the effectiveness of Canada's National Implementation Strategy on Climate Change (NIS) [02], and oil prices and oil availability [03].

Scenario A assumes that implementation of the NIS results in attainment of Canada's Kyoto commitment with respect to transportation, i.e., that total emissions oh GHGs from transport activity in Canada will have fallen to 6% below 1990 levels by 2010. This implies a reduction of about 40% from what might be regarded as the "business-as-usual" level in 2010.

Scenario B assumes partial effectiveness of the NIS, i.e. achievement of a 20% reduction from estimated "business-as-usual" levels.

Scenario C is based on the assumption of rising fuel prices. The NIS is assumed to be only partially effective (as in scenario B) but the higher fuel prices serve to reduce emissions of GHGs by the required additional 20 percentage points.

The target for 2025 for the present exercise is also set in terms of reductions in GHG emissions from transport (70% of the 1990 level).

2.2. Relevant data

The *Documents* offer relevant data on several related topics: trends in transport energy use and activity in Canada [04]; actual and projected worldwide discovery, extraction and demand for conventional oil between 1920 and 2040 [05]; trends in local pollution from transport [06]; prospects on climate change [07]. These data support the conclusion that scenario C is quite credible for the period to 2010. It could involve an 80% increase in pump prices. This could be sufficient to reduce gasoline use for personal travel by about 20% from what it might otherwise have been. The effect on freight movement may not be as strong; the effect on aviation may be stronger.

2.3. Actions required to meet the three scenarios for 2010

The tasks become essentially those of reducing fossil fuel use for transport across Canada by 40% (scenarios A and C) or by 20% (scenario B).

Several constraints on effective action by 2010 can be noted among others: land use, rail infrastructure and attitudes to transportation. Without the spur of calamity, they could require many years, perhaps decades, to change. These constraints severely limit the methods available for reaching the 2010 target for transport.

Accordingly, **the focus proposed is on** a means that has so far proved acceptable and effective under some circumstances, namely, **fuel-efficiency for new vehicles.** In order to counter potential perverse effects of the new fuel efficiency standards three ancillary measures are proposed: *increase in fuel prices, incentives and penalties to encourage fleet turnover, and investments in public transit and bicycle and pedestrian amenity.*

Only this kind of package of measures may have the prospect of being sufficiently effective during the current decade. Obviously, nothing of these measures should be taken as precluding the application of other measures (remove subsidies for oil production, tax exemption for employer-provided transit benefits, tax shifting, road pricing, better coordination of transport activity, car sharing, traffic calming, etc.).

2.4. Actions required for the period 2010-2025

Following the ideas established for the period before 2010, the key point is that reliance is placed on available technology. There appears then to be no such "technological fix" for the period beyond 2010. Much is promised –specifically in relation to fuel cells- but the potential of new technology seems too uncertain to depend on it for attaining of the target set for 2025. Accordingly this *Strategy* places reliance on measures that could work whether or not the "pollution-less" motor vehicle is developed.

Surely, sustainable transportation is not only about climate change. This is just one of several features of environmental unsustainability. The economic aspects of sustainability may be those that require the most careful attention. Continuing "business-as-usual" may in any case be more and more unbusinesslike. Therefore, three things are required in the *Strategy*. (i) that business becomes less transport dependent; (ii) that the much of the direct economic activity represented by transport is replaced elsewhere in Canada's overall economy; (iii) that in these respects Canada does not move seriously out of line with trading partners and competitors, particularly the United States. Development of these requirements is nevertheless beyond the scope of the *Documents*.

The *Documents* note also an important array of matters that should be taken into account in fashioning strategies for the period 2010-2025. Among these are increases in real transport fuel prices, increases in new vehicle prices, measures that make automobile ownership less necessary, increased use of freight by water, reducing the sprawl of urban areas, refashioning of transport activity, special attention on aviation rate of growth, etc.

As a matter of fact, the Strategy proposes a key element: **rationing transport fuel by tradable permits**. The emissions trading scheme proposed by the Netherlands government for an OECD study [08] is taken as a good example. In a well-working tradable permits scheme people would have choice. Individuals can buy or shell their allowances in permit markets.

Rationing is accepted only when there is extreme scarcity or other emergency, such as war, and then only with great difficulty. Governments can act firmly when crisis occurs. The temptation to wait until things begin to go wrong is thus understandable, but delay in the face of the inevitable can be profoundly counterproductive. This is why rationing needs before its introduction a major effort on governments' part to demonstrate the need for scarcity, and the fairness and flexibility of the tradable permit scheme. Therefore, attitude change, land use change and public transit enhancement are key complementary elements.

2.5. Concluding remarks

The principal aim of these *Documents* is to spur discussion about transport strategies for the post-Kyoto period, from now to 2010 and beyond to 2025. The challenges appear huge, beyond those that are ordinarily contemplated in thinking about transport futures. There is a disposition in our society to minimize such challenges, or not to engage in long-term planning at all. But there is a strong possibility that the tide of human good fortune is about to turn. Careful consideration of potential alternative options can help avoid severe adverse effects. Meeting the challenges will require resolute effective action of a kind encountered only in war and disaster. Achieving sustainable transportation will require tough measures as fuel rationing and new taxes on land.

3. Critical comments

3.1. Preliminary note

Our comment has a conceptual character. Its focus isn't on listing objections or remarks and on discussing the accuracy of given data and figures. The aim is to deepen the fundamental orientation of the *Documents*, to discover their genuine sense and to enrich their impact. The reason sustaining this intention is simple. We study related literature for a long time [09]. In our view, the *Documents* constitute a starting point of far-reaching effect, and address an essential topic: *to continue discussions on how can transportation be moved towards sustainability.* Our critical comments cannot therefore limit themselves to list more or less numerous shortcomings. This shall certainly be done as occasion arises. In this moment, profoundly convinced of the real value of these *Documents*, our comments come from within. Their aim is not to draw attention on debatable points of detail, but to supply complementary arguments that reinforce their solidity and their force of persuasion. The *Documents* propose an original and exemplary *Strategy*. We don't propose another one. Our concern is to enrich this *Strategy* substantively, on the basis of a theoretical integrative perspective [10].

3.2. Strong points of the *Documents*

They are numerous and significant. Following is a brief list without any pre-established order.

1. The *Documents* are elaborate, informed, well written, enlightening, moderate and constantly enriched with instructive notes and references. Their scholarly excellence is never a pure academic exercise, but a collection of sound studies oriented towards practical action in realistic and credible terms.

2. The *Documents* have the merit of focussing on a question of great actuality and in addressing a fundamental objective clearly formulated: to found a problem-solving *Strategy* that proves promising and realistic.

3. The *Documents* retain the original precaution of aiming a post-Kyoto plan of action wisely divided in middle run (2000-2010) and in long run (2010-2025).

4. The *Documents* draw particular attention on strategic factors of great significance, namely, the evolution of demographic data and of petrol production, and the climate change issue. They are also specifically sensitive to influential official texts, like "Canada's Implementation Strategy on Climate Change" [02], "Kyoto Protocol" [11], "Word Business Council for Sustainable Development" [12], OECD's Synthesis Report: Environmentally Sustainable Transport" [08].

5. The *Documents* carry an enviable societal weight appulse. They are the product of an internationally acknowledged research organization. They have been largely diffused, discussed and approved by a great number of scholars and specialists working in private and public sectors as well as in academic and associative organizations.

3.3. A complementary vision

We agree with three essential points of the *Documents*. (i) Fixing GHG's reduction scenarios for 2010 and 2025, and a target for 2025.(ii) Focusing first on a major instrument and implementing several proposed ancillary and complementary measures.(iii) Not relying inconsiderably on unproven technology (in a short and middle run perspective). On this basis, our concern is to reinforce the capacity of persuasion of the Strategy proposed by the *Documents*, in drawing particular attention on two important issues: the potential contribution of new technologies and the factual foundation of the *Strategy*, according to transportation market conditions and requirements.

3.3.1. New technologies

The *Documents* are evidently in keeping with the development of new technologies as an important element of transportation supply management [13]. An outstanding CST leader affirmed in a private mail. "We have to make a quantum jump in technology into the next phase of transportation in North America". The *Documents* agree, judiciously, under well-determined conditions.

First, new technologies could contribute a large part of what is required, but that about half of the effort will have to come from changes in transport activity. Second, we need proven, already being marketed technologies (e.g. gasoline-electric hybrid vehicle [14]) and when other ones seem too uncertain to depend on them for attainment of the target set for 2025 (e.g. fuel cells [15]), they will be welcome when full developed. We agree these premises completely. And it is in this sense that we submit some complementary reflections in order to improve the practical impact of the *Documents*.

Surely, fixing GHG reduction scenarios, key instruments and a target for 2025 is an extremely valuable objective. And we have to do every effort to attain it. But we can complete things by adding another kind of target and another key instrument.

Complementary target. 2100: the world will be equipped with thousands of kilometers of ultra high-speed train railways, in order to attain a proportionate equilibrium between road, rail, air and water transportation. 2025: several ultra high-speed trains will grow very popular in North America. 2010: first steps in this direction will be accomplished; to put into service one or more of such trains, endowed with a powerful effect of demonstration for launching an endless chain. N.B. 2100, a term fixed by the well-known IPCC, completes and enlightens fairly the 2010 and 2025 perspectives [16].

Complementary key element. We refer to changes that combine two kinds of new information technologies, *high-speed electric rail* and *proactive management*. This grouping addresses a quite essential feature on the way of sustainable transportation. Let us note some basic insights on each of them briefly.

3.3.1.1. High-speed electric rail.

Salient features High-speed electric rail constitutes a new technology proven and available. There are two grand types, HST (high-speed trains, like the French TGV [17] with peaks of 200 mph) and MLT (magnetic levitation trains, like the German Transrapid [18] with peaks of 350 mph). Both begin to call serious attention of important groups in American private and public sectors [19].

Advantages MLT more particularly presents important advantages. Very high speed. Lightness. Low noise. Inter-city and intra-city freight and people carrying capacity. Easy inter-modal connections. Entirely electronic equipment for locomotion and for responding to customers needs. Efficient use of distributed electricity. Little environmental impact if the electricity is produced from renewable resources. Low energy consumption and low operating costs. No emission of combustion gases. High security standards. Underground, surface and elevated versions. Minimal land consumption and no division of the landscape. Operational under extreme weather conditions and high protection from snow and ice. Competitive with private cars for commuting needs and with aviation short trips, the environmentally most damaging of all transportation modes [20]. At middle and long run, systematic introduction of MLT could be the best way to see congestion and pollution out of metropolitan areas all over the world.

Requirements. The best technology proves abortive without the aid of an array of complementary devices. Technological innovation is extremely expensive. It has to overcome numerous and tricky obstacles and implement indispensable requirements and conditions. In this connection, we discuss below briefly the specific need of logistic proactive management and, more generally the objective foundations of great societal innovation.

3.3.1.2. Proactive logistic management

Salient features. Technological innovation must be accompanied by a solid structure of proactive management, founded on advanced logistic and endowed with economic means in keeping with the total amount of investment in machinery. *Proactive management* [21] is the identification mark of a dynamic business. It takes into consideration the actual situation *and* the complementary elements needed to make its operations more profitable. Its specific function is to organize promotion and information in order to attract all potential customer and to retain them surely. Founded on information technologies, telecommunication, e-commerce, marketing and advertising, electronic ticketing, etc., *advanced logistics* [22], includes all operations destined to master the supply chain, from planning to delivering and after-sale service. Its function is to assure the best product, at the best place and moment, and at the best conditions for entire satisfaction of actual and potential customers [23].

Advantages. A correct combination of proactive management and new locomotion technologies opens the way of sustainable transportation and generates countless benefits. Profits for investors. Employment and revenues for wage earners. Political gains for governments. Quality of life for citizens.

Requirements. The costs of real proactive management are extremely high. All potential customers must be perfectly informed and expensive cost-benefits analysis must provide the optimal ratio between investment, promotion and development. Carmakers do it almost perfectly. Analysts put forward that 10% [24] of their turnover (billions of dollars) pay advertising costs. These costs are only a side of the coin. They are engaged because they generate profits. It must be added that as matter of fact, the implementation of new locomotion technologies isn't a simple matter of costs and benefits. Let us therefore complete our views with some thoughts on societal innovation.

3.3.2. Objective evaluation of transportation market evolution

Transportation constitutes a ubiquitous and huge world market. The evolution of transportation's supply and demand in the last 50 years of industrial civilization involves billions and billions of dollars. Transforming the transportation system in search of sustainability implies inevitably an immense structural modification of investment, in machinery and organization. If this modification has to be thought realistically, it needs of course a great mass of money, and as Max Weber brilliantly contended [25], a highly motivating *idea*. What *idea* can motivate and support so a monumental, unparalleled overturn?

The *Documents* propose the absolute necessity of such a great transformation. They suggest wisely that the *idea* that moves it, comes essentially from a combination of circumstances (intolerability of continuous air pollution, growing scarcity of oil-fuels, long term awareness and required resolute action of a kind encountered only in war and disaster). It can be added that among these circumstances, there is another one that deserves particular attention. It is indeed a kind of philosophic-historical idea that must be put in question. Let us explain it briefly.

3.3.2.1. The basic idea of the actual transportation system. The actual transportation system is not foundation-less, although its basic prevailing idea is mostly implicit. Everyone does agree indeed that huge investment combining cars, petrol and roads is the *best way* for years to come to satisfy the gigantic demand of land transportation. And everyone knows as much that this is a most powerful and rewarding business. This business is so heavy, so diversified and so solidly accumulated during long decades, that no alternative system is henceforth conceivable. Big technological and managerial changes are above our forces. Radical alternatives are therefore not available. The particular case of expanding electric high-speedy trains constitutes at best a marginal initiative. Massive introduction of these trains is absolutely unimaginable for two simple reasons: it would be exceedingly expensive and it is so poorly popular that it would never pay. Surely, many see the conventional land transportation system more and more pollutant, congestive and pricey. It is however hopeless. A radical change seems definitely impossible.

3.3.2.2. Questioning this idea. The idea is strongly established and seems invincible. In fact, it is anti-historic, simplistic, desperately backward and source of a paralyzing inertia [26]. Above all, it is very far from being objective, justified and convincing. Why?

Cars and petrol cannot be a historic exception. Before Thomas Edison it was evident that humans would ever light up with candles. Cars and trucks have proliferated like typewriters did, quite abundantly. But typewriters were replaced by personal computers in a very short time, just because the computers became affordable and a better choice. The history of technological advancement gives countless of such examples. This advancement isn't the fruit of neither positive nor negative convictions, but the consequence of important investment made with profit expectation [27]. This is why freight and people will be transported massively by high-speed electric trains, just when they will be made affordable and will constitute a better choice than cars and trucks.

Technological shift towards high-speed trains is very costly at each stage of their life-cycle (invention, application, commercialization, diffusion, saturation, senescence) [28]. Each stage requires funding, but only "learning by doing" allows costs of technology decrease exponentially and make innovation possible. Should the new system be more costly or less cost-effective than the conventional one? Who can assure it accurately? Really, the famous prevailing idea seems to lie on a very week basement and doesn't support an objective judgement.

3.3.2.3. A problem solving issue. We have on the one hand, high-speed electric trains and advanced proactive logistic management technologies that could provide important environmental and social benefits and respond to the search for alternative solutions towards transportation sustainability. We have on the other hand, a general conviction on the untouchability of our land transportation system, a seminal idea truly anti-progressive and totally unproved.

There is maybe a way to overcome this divergence surely and definitely. Three interdependent elements are required from now on, urgently. (i) A comprehensive study that (continuing and completing CST *Documents*), elaborates a *Strategy*, at short, middle and long term, on a transportation renewal, by massive and progressive implantation of high-speed electric trains combined with proactive logistic management. (ii) An unbiased assessment (environmental, social, political, economic and financial) of this *Strategy* applied to a concrete implantation plan, endowed with a powerful demonstration effect. (iii) A firm engagement in lobbying appropriate public and private experts and decision-makers, in North America quite particularly, in order to promote a substantial analysis of this *Strategy* and to fulfill its implementation if preliminary work is proving positive.

4. Conclusion

We aimed to collect together the necessary elements of a better understanding, conceptual and practical, of a *Strategy* that leads effectively toward sustainable transportation in a social and economic development perspective. We urgently need a serious effort in R&D on progressive and massive implementation of high-speed trains and proactive logistic management. We have to apply plenty of mitigation measures, but a global transformation is indispensable to serve a new transportation market expanded all over the world. We have all what is required for collaborate with experts and prominent decision-makers to fight inertia and to free ourselves from the constraint of outdated products and procedures. We can so rebuild freight and persons mobility, perfect renewable energy resources and at last meet essential requirements of contemporary society. A better understanding of this basic strategic action is a *sine qua non* condition to elaborate decision support measures involving one of the greatest challenges of our time.

References

[01] www.cstctd.org
[02] www.nccp.ca/html/media/JMM-fed-en.pdf
[03] *World Energy Outlook.* 2000. Paris. International Energy Agency.
     Campbell, CJ. & Laherrère,J.H. The End of Cheap Oil. *Scientific American*, 88, pp.78-83, 1998, available at www.energycrisis.org/de/lecture.html

[04] *Energy Efficiency Trends in Canada.*. 2000. Natural Resources Canada.

[05] See note [03]

[06] *State of the Environment Bulletin, 1, 1999,* available at
www.ec.gc./Ind/English/urb_air/Bulletin/ua_isse.cfm

[07] *Report.* U.S. National Oceanic and Atmospheric Administration, available at
www.ncdc.noaa.go/ol/climate/research/2000/ann/ann.html

[08] *Synthesis Report: Environmentally Sustainable Transport.* OECD. 2000,
available at www.oecd.org/env/ccst/est/

[09] Durkheim, E., *De la division du travail social.* Paris: P.U.F. [1893] 1960.
Prades, J.A., *Durkheim,* Paris: Presses Universitaires de France, 1997.

[10] Prades, J.A., Loulou, R & Waaub, J.-P., *Stratégies de gestion des gaz
à effet de serre. Le cas des transports,* Québec: Presses de l'Université du
Québec, 1998, see www.er.uqam.ca/nobel/greige2/ges.htm
Prades, J.A., Labriet M. & Waaub, J.-P., Structuring traffic integration,
(Chapter 3). *Urban Transport and the Environment in the 21st Century,*
ed. L.J.Sucharov & C.A. Brebbia, Southampton: WIT Press, 2001.
Prades, J.A., Labriet M. & Waaub, J.-P., GHG Management strategies and
sustainable transportation (Chapter 23). *Urban Transport and environment
in the 21st Century, ed.* L.J. Sucharov,. Southampton: WIT Pres, 2001.
Labriet, M. 2001, MARKAL/TIMES Modeling of GHG Abatement
Strategies: Canadian Case Study and World Analysis. Submitted

[11] www.unfccc.int/resource/kpstats.pdf

[12] www.wbcsd.ch/

[13] CST Monitor #5 www.cstctd.org/CSTadobefiles/STM5_English.pdf

[14] Gas-electric hybrid motor planned by GM, *Toronto Star,* Jan. 10, 2001.

[15] www.ttcorp.com/fccg/fc_what1.htm

[16] Lomborg, B., *The Skeptical Environmentalist.* Cambridge: Cambridge
University Press, 2001. IPCC www.ipcc.ch

[17] www.sncf.com/co/materiel/tgv

[18] www.transrapid.de/english/home.html

[19] Federal Railroad Administration www.fra.dot.gov/o/hsgt/index.htm.
Midwest Regional Rail Initiative htpp://sites.netscape.ne/fightthetrain/mwrri

[20] CST Monitor # 3 www.cstctd.org

[21] Porter, M., What is Strategy?, *Harvard Business Review,* 74, pp.61-78,
1996.

[22] Logistics. *Encyclopaedia Britannica* www.britannica.com

[23] www.cool-companies.org/energy/ecomm.doc

[24] Bergeron, R., *Le livre noir de l'automobile,* Montréal: Hypothèse, 1999.

[25] Weber, M., *The Protestant Ethic and the Spirit of Capitalism,* New York:
Scribner, 1930.

[26] Lecocq, F. & al., Decision Making under Uncertainty and Inertia
Constrains, *Energy Economics,* 20, pp. *539-555,* 1998.

[27] Grubler, A. & al.Modeling Technological Change: Implications for the
Global Environment, *Annual Review of Energy and Environment,* 24, pp.
545-569, 1998.

[28] Grubler, A. & al., Dynamics of Energy Technologies and Global Change,
Energy Policy, 27, pp. 247-280, 1999.

The influence of automobiles motion unevenness on harmful substances emission

N.N. Karnaukhov, L.G. Reznik & A.W. Manyashin
Tyumen State Oil and Gas University, Russia

Abstract

It is well known that vehicles are one of the main sources of environmental pollution. This negative influence is especially great in towns, which is connected with the motion unevenness of automobiles. However, the influence of motion unevenness on harmful substances emission with vehicles exhaust gases has not been sufficiently studied yet. It makes it difficult to work out scientifically based ways to reduce air pollution in towns. In this connection the theoretical and experimental investigations were carried out in Tyumen State Oil and Gas University.
The main conclusion is as follows.
- The influence of motion unevenness on harmful substances emission is different for the vehicles of different makes and models.
- This difference is highly substantial and is stipulated by different level of vehicles adaptability to this motion mode.
- Different level of adaptability to motion unevenness must be considered when evaluating vehicles ecological safety in towns.

Harmful substances emission is directly connected with fuel consumption during vehicles operation. In this connection the **goal** of the research is the evaluation of vehicles adaptability to urban motion mode by fuel consumption and directly related to it the negative influence on the atmosphere. In order to reach the set up goal it was necessary to solve some tasks, determined by the analysis of the previous researches in this field.

The unevenness coefficient K_{un} was proposed as the index of motion unevenness. It accounts of the ratio of factual medium speed v to the maximum admissible in the given conditions medium speed v_{max}:

$$K_{un} = 2\left(1 - \frac{v}{v_{max}}\right).$$ (1)

The proposed index is clear, has distinct physical sense and the possibility for practical application. Theoretically, the value of the unevenness coefficient K_{un} changes from 0 (if $v = v_{max}$) to 1 (if $v = 0.5\,v_{max}$). The latter value ($v = 0.5\,v_{max}$) is conditioned by the peculiarities of vehicle accelerating and braking process.

On the basis of analytical and experimental investigations it was determined that the dependence of fuel consumption q on the unevenness coefficient K_{un} is described by the quadratic model of adaptability:

$$q = q(v) + s \cdot K_{un}^2,$$ (2)

where $q(v)$ –   the fuel consumption as a function of even speed v, whose numerical quantity assumed equal to the value of factual medium speed, l/100 km;

s –   the parameter of sensitivity to motion unevenness by fuel consumption, l/100 km.

The quantity of $q(v)$ can be determined experimentally or by using fuel characteristics of the even motion [1]. The maximum admissible motion speed in town conditions is usually 60 km/h [2]. According to fuel characteristics of vehicles even motion the section of the curve, which corresponds to the range of speeds up to 60 km/h, is enough flat, almost horizontal. It is related to road resistance strength influencing on energy losses and connected with it fuel consumption, depending on speed changes insignificantly. Starting from the speed of 60 km/h the aerodynamic resistance influences on fuel consumption predominantly. This speed is called "transient" one. Using the term "transient speed" the authors [3] point out, that speed influence on fuel consumption should be considered only in the case when it exceeds the transient one. It is also pointed out, that for the majority of modern vehicles this speed is about 60 km/h. Thus, in urban conditions the influence of the velocity on fuel consumption is not so substantial as the influence of motion unevenness, which is proved experimentally. The exception may be the case of moving at a rather low speed on reduced gears. Therefore, at speeds below the transient one with a small error the fuel consumption may be considered independent on velocity. The value of this consumption is assumed to be equal to the control fuel consumption given in GOST – 20306-90 [1] and is given in technical characteristics of vehicles. Then the equation 2 will be transformed in the following way:

$$q = q_o + s \cdot K_{un}^2 , \qquad (3)$$

where q_o is optimum (minimum) quantity of fuel consumption at steady state speeds of motion, l/100 km (in most cases it is a control consumption).

The value of control fuel consumption is determined at a constant speed and load [1]:

- 40 and 60 km/h and total load weight (mass) are for urban buses and full-drive vehicles with total weight more than 3.5 tons.
- 60 and 80 km/h and total load weight are for trucks, freight - passengers (including full – driven), buses for special purpose, coaches and autotrains with total weight more than 3.5 tons.
- 90 and 120 km/h and a half of total load weight, but not less than 180 kg for cars (including full-drive), buses and trucks (lorries) with the total weight up to 3.5 tons.

The parameters numerical values of the last equation for cars of several makes and models were determined experimentally and their adequacy to the explored quadratic model of adaptability was proved (equations 2 and 3). The optimum value of fuel consumption for VAZ-21053 is 7.1 l/100 km (on GOST 20306-90 it is 7.1 l/100 km) and the sensitivity parameter s is equal to 15.7 l/100 km. The value of optimum fuel consumption for GAZ-31029, obtained on the results of the experiment is 8.5 l/100 km (on GOST 20306-90 the consumption equals to 8.4 l/100 km) and sensitivity parameter s equals to 52.3 l/100 km. The method to determine numerical values of equation (3) parameters by means of known technical characteristics of vehicles (control fuel consumption and consumption in urban cycle) and unevenness coefficients calculated by standard road cycles has been worked out. This method is based on motion unevenness coefficient calculation by established in GOST [1] characteristics of on road urban cycle (time, speed and road cycle sections run). At the same time fuel consumption in this cycle is the value standardized by GOST and given in technical characteristics for vehicle of any make and model produced in Russia. Besides, GOST also sets up the fuel consumption for even motion that is when $K_{un}=0$ (the control fuel consumption). The given indices enable to find the unknown parameter s in equation (3) by means of simple substitution of the values q_o, q, and K_{un} without carrying out expensive experimental investigations. Thus, the parameters numerical values of the equation (3) for fuel consumption for the vehicles of some makes and models have been determined and given in table 1. As seen from table 1 the adaptability of vehicles of different makes and models to the motion unevenness by fuel consumption is quite essentially different. There is evident considerable difference in adaptability level. For the investigated vehicles s equals from 19.2 up to 48.4 l/100km, that is it differs more than two times. It proves the necessity of differentiated accounting the adaptability for the vehicles of different makes and models.

Table 1: The equation (3) parameters

Vehicle make and model	Optimum value of fuel consumption q_0, l/100 km	Sensitivity parameter s, l/100 km
GAZ –5312	19,6	28,1
ZIL –431410	25,8	30,3
ZIL -133ГЯ	26,6	48,4
MAZ –53371	21,5	19,2
KamAZ -53212	24,4	20,6
KrAZ –250	35,0	43,6

Proceeding from the essential difference of the adaptability for the vehicles of different makes and models (table 1) 3 levels of the adaptability to the motion unevenness were set up: high, medium and low. They were found by dividing the total possible range of adaptability level values into 3 equal parts. This division into 3 levels provides the following. First of all it provides the possibility of differentiated correction fuel consumption norms depending on motion unevenness if the parameters of the equation (3) for these vehicles are unknown. In this case the level of adaptability is determined by the known adaptability level for the vehicle of analogous construction. Correction coefficients values for each adaptability level were determined beforehand. Therefore attributing the vehicle to this or that adaptability level gives the correcting coefficients values at once and enables to reduce fuel consumption. There are four ways of using the adaptability level A for reducing fuel consumption and, consequently, for decreasing harmful substances emission with exhaust gases. Four functions are used:

$$q = f_1 (q_n; R; A); \quad q_n = f_2 (q; R; A); \quad R = f_3 (q_n; q; A);$$
$$A = f_4 (q_n; q; R), \tag{4}$$

where q – fuel consumption in the given conditions;

q_n – nominal fuel consumption (basis consumption);

R – the rigor of the given operation conditions;

A – vehicle adaptation to the rigour of the given operation conditions.

For the unevenness coefficient K_{un} practical application the whole range of its values is divided into three intervals of motion mode complexity: moderate rigorous $(K_{un} =0...0.33)$, rigorous $(K_{un} =0.33...0.66)$ and very rigorous $(K_{un}=0.66...1)$. These intervals are characterized by the following values of rigour index [5]: moderate rigorous - $0...4R$, rigorous - $4R...8R$ and very rigorous - *8R...12R*. One of the most important ways of saving automobile fuel is an objective standardizing of its consumption. For this it is necessary to take into account actual operation conditions and consider the factual adaptability level to these conditions of the given vehicle. The standardization of fuel consumption begins from the determination of the base norm. It is described by the valid now in Russia Methods of fuel consumption standardization at motor transport [4]. According to this document at first the temporary base norms are determined for each vehicle make and model by special techniques. Then these norms are verified on the basis of collecting and processing factual fuel consumption statistical data and after that they obtain the constant status. To determine consumption considering unstandard operation conditions the correcting coefficient are applied [4]. According to the valid techniques these coefficients are the same ones for the automobiles of different makes and models. The correction coefficients are expressed in the form of percents of increase or decrease the base norm. For example, the normative fuel consumption for the automobiles of general purpose is determined by the formula:

$$Q = 0.01 \cdot H_s \cdot S \cdot (1 + 0.01 \cdot D),$$
(5)

where Q – normative fuel consumption, l, under given conditions;

Hs – the base fuel consumption norm for the run, l/ 100 km;

S – the run of the automobile, km;

D – correction coefficient (the total relative increase or decrease) to the base norm, %, considering the influence of the given operation conditions.

The valid now Methods [4] considers the motion mode influence on the on-road norm value by means of six correction coefficients. The norm is increased in the following cases:

- motor transport operation on the roads with a complicated plan - up to 10 %;
- operation in cities with the population over 2.5 million people – up to 20 %;
- operation in cities with the population from 0.5 up to 2.5 million people - up to 15 %;
- operation in cities with the population up to 0.5 million people - up to 10 %;
- transportation bulky, explosive-dangerous and the like of freights, requiring the reduced speeds of vehicles (up to 20 km/h) – up to 10 %.
- operation requiring often technological stops connected with loading and unloading (on the average more than one stop per one kilometer run – route buses, vehicles for mail collection, collecting money and the like) - up to 10 %;
- hourly operation of board lorries or their constant job as technological transport or as freight taxes - up to 10 %.

The norm is reduced during operation behind the boundary of urban zone - up to 15 %. The valid now correction system contains only the maximum values of the coefficients (instead of concrete value it is indicated " up to..."). The real vehicle operation mode is not considered. The main drawback is: the level of the vehicle adaptability of concrete mark and model is not taken into consideration. The important trend in practical application of the results obtained is differential correction of on-road fuel consumption norms by means of developed mathematical models application. According to the interval of motion mode complexity and in accordance with the vehicle adaptability level differentiated correction coefficients D_d to the base norm value were established. The values of these differentiated coefficients are determined by the formula:

$$D_d = \frac{q - H_s}{H_s} \cdot 100\%.\qquad(6)$$

For practical application the quantity D_d is determined by the tables of differentiated correction coefficients to the base norms of fuel consumption (table 2). The quantity D_d is determined depending on the interval of complexity R of the motion mode and depending on the level A of vehicle adaptability:

$$D_d = f(R; A).\qquad(7)$$

It is necessary to remind that formerly the level of vehicle adaptability was not considered at all:

$$D_{max} = \varphi(R).\qquad(8)$$

Through differential correction of the norms the corresponding level of vehicle adaptability and the congruent interval of motion mode complexity are found in table 2. The value D_d is on the intersection of the corresponding line and appropriate column.

Table 2: The values of differentiated correction coefficients

The level of vehicles adaptability	The correction coefficients, %, for the interval of motion mode complexity (the coefficient of unevenness)		
	Moderate rigorous ($K_{un}<0,33$)	Rigorous ($K_{un}=0,33...0,66$)	Very rigorous ($K_{un}>0,66$)
High	-13	26	59
Medium	-8	46	107
Low	1	61	119

The following vehicles with different level of adaptability to motion unevenness may serve as examples:

- with high level - VAZ-2109,
- with medium level - VAZ-1111,
- with low level - GAZ-31029.

When using all additions stipulated by the valid now official Methods accounting motion unevenness their total value is equal to $D_d = 50$ %. It corresponds to the rigorous complexity interval of the motion mode and the medium adaptability level of the vehicles: $D_d = 46$ %. One of the ways for practical application of the results obtained is the calculation of real fuel consumption, corresponding to urban movement mode. On the base of the real fuel consumption determination, using known interconnections one can determine the mass quantity of harmful substances emission into the atmosphere while vehicles operation. This approach enables to estimate the adaptability of different makes and models vehicles for operation in urban conditions both as from the point of view of fuel economy and as ecological safety. In this case it is necessary to take into account engine type, catalyst availability and other constructive and operation peculiarities. The influence of motion unevenness on harmful substances emission with exhaust gases is stipulated not only by changing fuel consumption. Changes in the processes of mixing and combustion taking place in the engines play a certain part under the conditions of uneven motion. Harmful substances emission is advisable to be estimated in the same way as with that of fuel economy. For example at the speed 90 km/h, 120 km/h and in urban mode. Setting up the norms of harmful substances emission must be started from establishing the base marginal norm. Herewith the precise definition of the concept "base" is necessary. The correction coefficients to the base norm can be applied for determination of the emission with unstandard operation conditions taken into account.

Conclusions

1. The unevenness coefficient was established as the index of motion unevenness. The unevenness coefficient is conditioned by the relationship of average actual motion speed and of maximum permissible speed in the given conditions.
2. It was determined, that fuel consumption dependence on the established index is described by mathematical quadratic model of adaptability.
3. Numerical values of this equation parameters for the automobiles of a number of makes and models were determined.
4. Three typical intervals of movement unevenness index and three typical adaptability levels of vehicles to the given factor were established.
5. The application of the new approach by calculating of fuel consumption with the vehicle adaptability level and its movement mode taken into account, enables to fulfil the differentiated correction of fuel consumption norms and directly related with it harmful substances emission.

References

[1] GOST 20306-90. *Motor Vehicle. Fuel Economie. Test Methods and Evalution*: Moscow, 1990.

[2] *The rules of road traffic*: Moscow, 2000.

[3] Hilliard D., Springer D. *Fuel economie in road vehicles powered by spark ignition engines*: Moscow, 1989.

[4] *The norms of fuel and lubrication consumption at motor transport. Official document R 3112194-0366-97*: Moscow, 1997.

[5] Reznik L.G. *The rigorous index of mashines operation conditions. Information of higher education institution. Oil & Gas*: Tyumen, pp. 112-115, 2000.

Analysis of the environmental impact of urban buses: application to a case study in Lisbon

A. M. Simões, M. C. Coelho, C. M. Silva & T. L. Farias
Department of Mechanical Engineering, Instituto Superior Técnico, Technical University of Lisbon, Portugal

Abstract

The image related with air pollution associated to urban buses is usually negative. However, quantification of the real contribution of the urban buses to the total pollutant emissions is usually not performed. Therefore, in order to quantify these emissions and compare with the emissions from the additional traffic, a study of the environmental impact of urban buses in a real inner city situation was performed. The study was focused on several routes of CARRIS, the company responsible for exploring the bus routes within the central area of Lisbon, Portugal. Based on the urban buses fleet of CARRIS, the topography of selected routes, the vehicles average speed and transported passengers, the CORINAIR methodology (that was supported by European Environment Agency's Topic Centre on Air Emissions) was used to predict fuel consumption and CO, NO_x, VOC and particles emissions from these urban buses. Experimental measurements of the bus dynamic performances and fuel consumption where performed in order to apply the CORINAIR methodology. Following this task, studies on the influence of several parameters, such as driving behavior, topography of the route and type of vehicle related with dynamic and environmental characteristics, were performed. Finally, with the purpose of predicting the influence of CARRIS fleet on the global emissions (as gram per kilometer and gram per passenger per kilometer) in comparison with the remaining road traffic as a whole, the same methodology was adopted to calculate the emissions caused by private owned vehicles (along the same routes).

1 Introduction

The present society depends of individual mobility, mainly, which promotes communication and interaction between people, cultures and countries. Mobility causes more comfort to populations, but air pollution that results from vehicles emissions (in which carbon dioxide, hydrocarbons, carbon monoxide, oxides of nitrogen, particulate matter and lead are the main pollutants) has negative impacts not only on environment, but on human health too (De Nevers [1]). This problem includes direct effects on health and global effects (greenhouse effect). In Portugal it is predictable that transportation sector contribution to CO_2 emissions global balance will rise from 24% to 31%, in the period that goes from 1990 until 2010 (Seixas *et al.* [2]).

The energy consumption by the transportation sector has increased 47% since 1985, about ten times more than the increase of the other economic sectors. CO_2 emissions from transport in the EU increased by 15% between 1990 and 1998. The European Environment Agency predicts that external costs of transport are estimated at 8 % of GDP (EEA [3]). As shown in Figures 1 and 2, the passenger transport is mainly performed by private owned vehicle and this category is responsible by the greatest amount of CO_2 emissions.

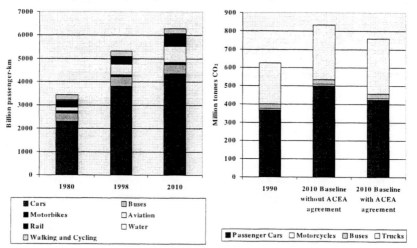

Figures 1 and 2: Distribution of passenger transport and distribution of CO_2 emissions on road transport on the EU (EEA [3])

In Portugal, the evolution of people mobility follows the same trend, that is, a greater dependence of road transport.

The urban areas expansion and the rise of citizens economical power caused a greater use of private owned vehicles, instead of public transportation, with consequent implications in the connection between transportation, energy and environment. The percentage of urban buses on Portugal fleet has decreased from 0.18%, on 1990, to 0.13%, on 1998 (Coelho [4]).

Data compiled by UITP [5], which is in the Millennium Cities Database for Sustainable Transport, show that the world average speed of buses is 11 km/h. In any of the regions related to this study the average speed is greater than 26 km/h, but a light duty vehicle has an average speed of 34 km/h.

The Carris de Ferro de Lisboa, SA is the company responsible for exploring the bus routes within the central area of Lisbon, Portugal. Carris [6] has a fleet with 835 urban buses. The public service of Carris involves a network with 105 routes that covers an 8 384 ha area of Lisbon city, where live 700 thousand citizens, and reaches the population of the Metropolitan Region of Lisbon, composed by 2,7 million of inhabitants (Carris [6]). Recently, with an increased attention to environmental questions, Carris is testing new types of fuels and enlarged its fleet with natural gas moved buses.

2 Methodology

In this work, it was studied the energetic and environmental impact of two distinct routes of Carris: route n.º 11, between Praça do Comércio and Damaia, and route n.º 44, between Cais do Sodré and Moscavide. The topography of route n.º 11 is more irregular and has a suburban zone, while route n.º 44 is mainly urban.

The main purpose in this study was a numerical analysis, in which was used Corinair methodology (EC [7]). With Corinair methodology, total emissions can be calculated by means of eqn (1):

$$E_x [g] = e_x [g/km] \times a [km] \tag{1}$$

where: E_x – each one of the contributions to total emissions; e_x – activity related emission factor; a – amount of traffic activity relevant to this type of emission.

Several parameters are needed to calculate the activity related emission factor, like vehicles average speed, load (in which the passengers transported by the bus are included) and terrain topography. To introduce these parameters in Corinair based equations, measurements of bus dynamic performances and terrain topography were performed.

Field measurements of the dynamic behavior of several types of vehicles comprising different categories were performed along each route, with the purpose of simulation of the bus behavior (specially, the stop and go situations) using a Microwave Doppler Sensor for speed and distance measurement combined with a data treatment software (DLS, from DATRON-MESSTECHNIK GmbH). The terrain topography was measured with a GPS. The measuring equipment installed in the vehicle is shown in Figure 3.

Figure 3: Test vehicle fully equipped with the measuring equipment

During this study, the following assumptions in relation to the urban buses were considered: though Corinair methodology considers the calculation of emissions and fuel consumption for the average speed range between 0 and 50 km/h (Ntziachristos and Samaras [8]), the same formulas were used in the situation of higher speed values; idle rate emissions are related to an average speed of 5 km/h, as advised by California Department of Transportation; global fuel consumption of urban buses on a certain route includes the fuel consumption related to idle situation on the stops between sections and on last stops (stopping-place at the beginning and end of the route), which have associated a certain time of delay.

On the other hand, the following presuppositions were considered in relation to passenger cars: the emissions were calculated using a weighed mean and considering an average national vehicle park; passenger cars have hot engine on the selected routes (the cold-start emissions were not considered); evaporative emissions are very small on Euro I light duty vehicles, because they are already equipped with electronic system injection (Ntziachristos and Samaras [8]); there is not inspection and maintenance program.

3 Results

3.1 Route Characterization

In Figures 4 and 5 the topography of the selected routes (corresponding to buses n.° 11 and 44, respectively) is presented followed by Figures 6 and 7 where measured buses instantaneous speed are shown. In Figures 8 and 9 the variation of buses average speed between bus stops is summarized, while in Figures 10 and 11 is presented the number of passengers transported in a typical trip of each route.

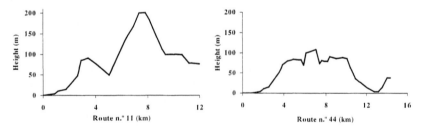

Figures 4 and 5: Topography of selected routes

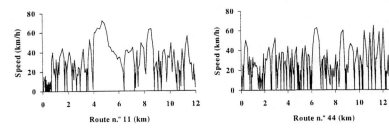

Figures 6 and 7: Instantaneous speed along selected routes

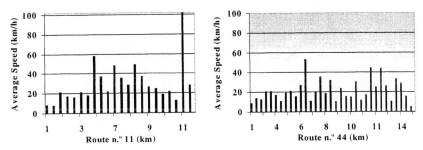

Figures 8 and 9: Average speed along selected routes

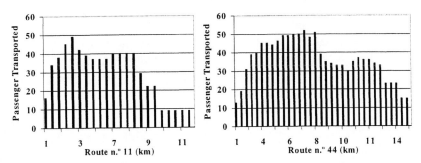

Figures 10 and 11: Passengers transported along selected routes

Main interpretation of the data presented in the above mentioned figures can be summarized as follows. Route 44 covers the central area of Lisbon where traffic is more intense. It is therefore dominated by lower average speed, more stop and go situations, higher variations of instantaneous speed, more bus stops and stop signs per kilometer and a higher number of passengers transported. All these parameters lead to expected higher fuel consumptions and pollutant emissions per kilometer.

On the contrary, route 11 covers a suburban area of Lisbon where traffic is less intense, average and instantaneous speeds are higher and the number of passengers transported is usually lower. In this route, topography is the most demanding variable.

3.2 Fuel consumption and pollutant emissions of urban buses

In Figures 12 and 13 the buses fuel consumption (on units liter/km and liter/(passenger·km) are presented, for each route, along different daily hours.

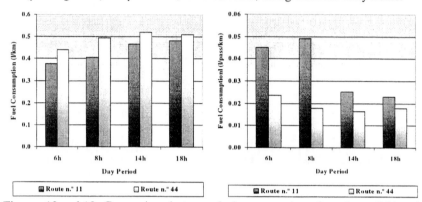

Figures 12 and 13: Comparison between fuel consumption of one bus n.° 11 and 44, on units liter/kilometer and liter/(passenger·kilometer)

As presented, the more severe traffic conditions of route 44 lead to a ca. 10% increase in the fuel consumption, when compared with route 11. However, the consumption associated with the mobility of a citizen (in liter per (passenger·kilometer)) is systematically lower in route 44.

Looking at the previous figures, it can be seen that there is not a significant variation of fuel consumption during the day (slightly increases during the afternoon). The same occurs with emissions (graphics not shown). So, the following figures are related to a specific period of the day (middle of the afternoon where traffic was more intense).

The fuel consumption that results from the application of the Corinair methodology presented in the previous figures was compared with data measured by Carris. Based on the available average daily fuel consumptions, it was possible to conclude that the variations are between 0.8 and 6.9%. These results were very encouraging, confirming the applicability of the Corinair methodology to the type of studies addressed in the present paper.

3.3 Environmental performance of urban buses versus private vehicles

A comparison of fuel consumption and pollutant emissions between a conventional urban bus, an Euro II urban bus and a typical vehicle from the national fleet, along the chosen routes, was performed. Results are shown along Figures 14 to 23.

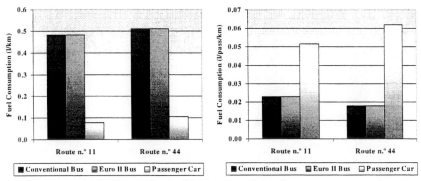

Figures 14 and 15: Comparison of fuel consumption between a conventional urban bus, an Euro II urban bus and a typical vehicle from the national fleet, on units l/km and l/(pass·km)

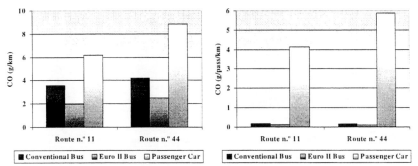

Figures 16 and 17: Comparison of CO emissions between a conventional urban bus, an Euro II urban bus and a typical vehicle from the national fleet, on units g/km and g/(pass·km)

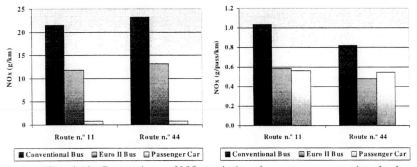

Figures 18 and 19: Comparison of NO_x emissions between a conventional urban bus, an Euro II urban bus and a typical vehicle from the national fleet, on units g/km and g/(pass·km)

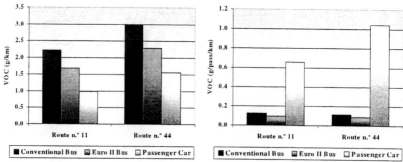

Figures 20 and 21: Comparison of VOC emissions between a conventional
urban bus, an Euro II urban bus and a typical vehicle from
the national fleet, on units g/km and g/(pass·km)

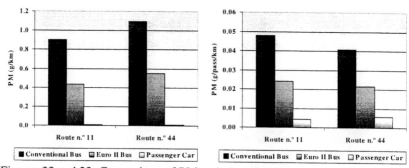

Figures 22 and 23: Comparison of PM emissions between a conventional urban
bus, an Euro II urban bus and a typical vehicle from the
national fleet, on units g/km and g/(pass·km)

Main conclusions of this study were the following:
- while the fuel consumption of a standard vehicle is typically 6 times less
  than the values patented by buses, on a passenger·kilometer basis, the
  vehicle passenger consumes 2 to 4 times more;
- CO and VOC emissions of vehicles are 2-3 times greater than the
  emissions from buses. This leads to an increase by a factor of 10 of the
  pollution of CO and VOC per vehicle passenger;
- the majority of vehicles in Portugal are equipped with gasoline engines.
  Therefore urban buses continue to be the main contributors to the
  emissions of NO_x and PM. The differences are more dramatic for PM
  where buses outscore vehicles by a factor of 10;

While the previous figures provide a useful comparison between the
performances of a bus and a private vehicle, they are not suitable to investigate
the real impact of a bus fleet on the overall environmental damage caused by
traffic as a whole. Using traffic data supplied by the traffic control center of

Lisbon, a comparison between the overall impact of the buses and the remaining traffic was performed. Main conclusions of this study are summarized in Table 1 where total emissions and fuel consumption for one hour are compared.

Emissions / Fuel	Buses		Remaining traffic	
	g/km	Percentage (%)	g/km	Percentage (%)
CO (g/km)	7790	2.8	272453	97.2
NOₓ (g/km)	35470	59.6	24047	40.4
VOC (g/km)	5869	11.1	47009	88.9
PM (g/km)	1523	86.0	248	14.0
Fuel Consumption (l/km)	1329	32.9	2708	67.1

Table 1: Comparison of emissions and fuel consumption between the buses and the remaining traffic, in one hour of the afternoon - Route n.° 44

Most citizens that live in regions dominated by constant traffic jams consider that urban buses are the main cause of pollution. Table 1 contradicts this common knowledge. In fact for the region considered (a main route in the downtown area of Lisbon) urban buses are responsible for solely 2,8 and 11% of total emissions of CO and VOCs, respectively. Buses contribute to one third of the fuel consumption – similar conclusion can be achieved for CO_2, due to the direct relationship between fuel consumption and CO_2 emissions. Because vehicles equipped with gasoline engines dominate the national fleet, buses are still the main contributors to total emissions of PM and NOx emissions (ca. 60% and 86%, respectively). However, if the Diesel market share continues to increase (as it has been happening throughout the past 10 years) private vehicles may also become the main contributors to NO_x and PM emissions.

4 Conclusions

In the present work the environmental impact of urban buses in a city was investigated. The Corinair methodology was applied to investigate emissions and fuel consumption of urban buses in two different routes in Lisbon. To apply the methodology, bus dynamic performances and terrain topography along the selected routes to introduce were experimentally characterized.

The selected routes are very different in relation with topography, average and instantaneous speed, number of stops and transported passengers. Main conclusions of the present study were as follows:

- pollutant emissions and fuel consumption per kilometer traveled do not vary considerably along the period of the day (although slightly higher during the afternoon traffic peak period). It is the traffic (i.e. the speed variations due to stop and go situations and number of stops) that dominates the fuel consumption;
- a passenger car has, in a general matter and on a passenger-kilometer basis, CO emission rates ten times higher that those for an urban bus, but

occurs the opposite in relation with NO_x (passenger car emissions are three times lower than those for the urban bus), when the number of passengers transported in each type of vehicle is taken into account. In addition, the passenger car consumes three times more fuel than the urban bus;

- finally, contradicting common knowledge, private traffic is still the main contributor to CO, VOCs and CO_2 emissions. Urban buses outscore the private vehicle in PM and NO_x emissions.

In summary, and despite the limitations of the Corinair methodology, this emission analysis is a very relevant planning tool, because it can be applied by traffic management entities to improve air quality in urban spaces.

5   Acknowledgements

The authors would like to thank Carris, for its support, and Renault Portuguesa for providing the test vehicles. This work was partially funded by Projects POCTI/35649/MGS/2000 and POCTI/35659/MGS/2000, supported by Fundação para a Ciência e Tecnologia.

6   References

[1]   De Nevers, *Air Pollution Control Engineering*, McGraw-Hill Int. Ed, 1995.
[2]   Seixas, M. J. *et al.*, *Avaliação das Emissões e Controlo dos Gases com Efeito de Estufa em Portugal*, Ministério do Ambiente, 2000.
[3]   EEA, *TERM 2001 – Indicators tracking transport and environment in the European Union*, http://themes.eea.eu.int/theme.php/activities/transport, European Environment Agency, 2001.
[4]   Coelho, M. C., Domingos, J. J. & Farias T. L., Impact of Urban Road Transport on Air Pollution. Application to a Case Study in Lisbon. Analysis of Alternative Scenarios. *Proc. of the Clean Air VI – 6th Intl Conference on Tech. and Combustion for a Clean Environment*, Porto, 9-12 July 2001.
[5]   UITP, *The Millenium Cities Database for Sustainable Transport*, http://www.uitp.com/millenium/mil.htm.
[6]   Companhia Carris de Ferro de Lisboa, http://www.carris.pt.
[7]   EC, (eds). *Meet Methodology for Calculating Transport Emissions and Energy Consumption, European Commission*, 1999.
[8]   Ntziachristos, L. & Samaras, Z., COPERT III: Computer programme to calculate emissions from road transport - Methodology and emission factors (Version 2.1), European Environment Agency, 2000.

Emissions at different conditions of traffic flow

J.Veurman[1], N.L.J. Gense[2], I.R. Wilmink[3] & H.I. Baarbé[4]
[1]*Transport Research Centre, Ministry of Transport, the Netherlands*
[2]*TNO Automotive, the Netherlands*
[3]*TNO Inro Section Traffic and Transport, the Netherlands*
[4]*Ministry of Public Housing, Spatial Planning and the Environment*

Abstract

Although it is widely assumed that congestion causes an increase in exhaust gas emissions, it has always been difficult to quantify this relationship. The project Emissions and Congestion investigated this relationship by simultaneously measuring traffic conditions and emissions. Emission factors were derived for different traffic conditions on motorways, ranging from free flow to heavy congestion.

The results clearly indicate that there are significant differences in emissions and fuel consumption for different types of traffic flow. Heavy traffic dynamics, shortcut traffic, heavy congestion and high speeds lead to significant increases of regulated emissions and fuel consumption of motorway traffic.

Efforts to reduce congestion and traffic dynamics (by traffic management measures) should be concentrated on specific routes or sections with frequent occurrence of heavy congestion and a large share of heavy duty traffic. These are the motorways in the conurbations. Tens of percents of reduction in emissions are possible. The resulting improvements on local air quality can be significant.

Lowering the speed limit to 100 km/h on all sections of Dutch motorways can significantly improve emission levels (most of Dutch motorways have a speed limit of 120 km/h).

1 Why a study of emissions at different conditions?

Last year (2000) the number of Dutch traffic jams increased with another 1000 to the number of 30.000. During peak hours traffic jams are common on major roads, especially in the Dutch conurbation of the Randstad (western part of the

Netherlands). Several traffic management measures like peaklanes (use of the hard shoulder), controlled access and dynamic route information panels, have been introduced over the last years, to reduce delays. Despite more intensive use of the existing infrastructure, pricing policy and expansion of infrastructure, congestion will be a common phenomenon in the future as well. Before we started the study there were various opinions about the effects of congestion on exhaust gas emissions and fuel consumption of road vehicles. It was unknown what the effects of congestion and traffic management measures could be on total traffic emissions and what the effects could be on the air quality along motorways. In the Netherlands, we have problems with the air quality targets established in the Framework Directive on Ambient Air Quality at different places along the Dutch motorways in the conurbation of the Randstad. The gaps in knowledge about emissions and congestion were the reason for the Dutch Ministry of Transport, Public Works and Water Management and the Ministry of Housing, Spatial Planning and the Environment to commission TNO for a study about the effects of different conditions of traffic flow on exhaust gas emissions and fuel consumption, by measuring emissions related to real world driving in less or more congested situations.

This paper presents the results of the study. The paper is structured as follows: In the next section we focus on the set up of the study (2). In the third section the emission factors and the share of each congestion category in the mileage is shown (3). In the fourth and fifth section we will go into the effects of congestion on the local (4) and the national emissions (5). Furthermore we will explore some policy suggestions (6) and desirable follow-up-research (7). Finally we summarise the main conclusions (8).

2   How did we set up the study?

The study consisted of two main elements:
- Deriving emission factors for different real world traffic conditions on motorways, ranging from free flow to heavy congestion.
- Calculation of the effects of congestion and the effects of traffic management measures for specific road sections in the conurbation of the Randstad and for the entire motorway network of the Netherlands.

2.1 Test phase

In the first stage of the project, two instrumented cars made a test drive on congested motorways in the conurbation of Western Holland, recording speed, time and traffic conditions. At the same time, tail pipe emissions were measured with on board equipment for purpose of determining the possible differences between measuring directly on the road and measuring in a laboratory. In the laboratory the emissions were measured again while projecting the recorded time/speed pattern of the test drives on a chassis dynamometer. In the laboratory measurements were made simultaneously by the lab measurement equipment and by the in-car-system, in order to be able to differentiate effects caused by the measurement equipment and those caused by driving on a chassis dynamometer.

In order to find a useful categorisation of congestion types on motorways, the data collected during the test drives were analysed. The final categorisation in 10 congestion types is mainly based on average speed and traffic volumes.

Furthermore the traffic profile of the test drive has been compared to the traffic profile derived from traffic data available from loop detectors in the road surface. Today, many Dutch motorways, especially those in the conurbations have induction loops in the road surface at regular intervals, measuring average speed and traffic volumes every minute (the Monica-system). The profiles of the test drive were compared to the data from the loops and matched quite well. It was therefore decided that the traffic data from loop detectors could be used to represent traffic conditions.

2.2 Determination of emission factors

In the second stage of the project 30 trips were made with an instrumented car (driven by 5 different drivers) in morning and afternoon peak hours, in order to collect statistical relevant speed/time patterns of travelling on Dutch highways. The trips were about 60 km long and all situated in the highly congested conurbation of the Randstad. The trips comprises all types of traffic situations form highly congested up to high speed free flow. After statistical compression of the speed/time patterns into 10 trips (one per congestion type), actual emission factors where established by measuring emissions of 20 different passenger cars driving these trips. The relative emission results per congestion type were combined with a huge amount of emission data available from the Dutch "In Use Compliance programme" resulting in emission factors for the average Dutch car. Using this set up, emission factors for CO_2, NO_x, CO, HC and PM_{10} were determined for each category of motorway traffic (and one for secondary roads). For heavy-duty traffic a different approach was used. A previously determined set of factors was adapted to the traffic categorisation used in this study.

2.3 The calculation of congestion effects

In the third stage of the project, a method was developed to calculate the total emissions on specific *road sections* or routes in the conurbation of Western Holland and on the *entire national motorway network*. Data from the Monica-system and data from a traffic counting monitoring system (Inweva) formed the basis for the calculation of the travelled kilometres by passenger cars and trucks in each congestion category.

The emissions calculated for the actual situation for road sections and for the entire motorway network were compared to the emissions that would occur in other situations: with less or more congestion, with a speed limit of 100 km/h and, if back roads were used, for parts of the trip.

More about the study set up can be found in (Gense [1]).

3 Congestion categories and emission factors

3.1 Real world driving emission factors

The first two columns of table 1 shows the description of the motorway congestion categorisation as decided on and used in this study. Ranging from heavy traffic congestion to high-speed free flow. Also included is a category for traffic on secondary roads (3). With this factor, the effect of drivers avoiding congested motorways by using back roads could also be taken into account.

	Traffic category	CO	HC	NO_x	CO_2	PM_{10}
1 a a	Stop-and-go' traffic, speed below 10 km/h	5.51	0.93	0.63	370	0.06
1 a	Stop-and-go' traffic, speed between 0 en 25 km/h	2.84	0.60	0.50	239	0.05
1 b	Congested traffic, speed between 25 and 40 km/h	1.71	0.43	0.48	178	0.04
1 c	Congested traffic, speed between 40 and 75 km/h	1.15	0.23	0.47	153	0.04
2 a	Speed 75-120 km/h, traffic volume over 1000 vehicles per lane per hour, speed limit = 100 km/h	1.13	0.14	0.49	146	0.03
2 b	Speed 75-120 km/h, traffic volume over 1000 vehicles per lane per hour, speed limit = 120 km/h	1.20	0.14	0.57	157	0.04
2 c	Speed 75-120 km/h, traffic volume below 1000 vehicles per lane per hour, speed limit = 100 km/h	0.90	0.11	0.47	146	0.03
2 d	Speed 75-120 km/h, traffic volume below 1000 vehicles per lane per hour, speed limit	1.17	0.12	0.66	173	0.04
2 e	Speed over 120 km/h, independent of traffic volume	3.42	0.16	0.98	208	0.18
3	Shortcut/back road	2.42	0.19	0.49	177	0.12

Table 1: Emission factors per congestion categorisation for passenger cars

Table 1 shows the emission factors that were found for passenger cars for the different congestion categories. In general driving in the congestion categories 1a and 1 b (= stop and go and speeds < 40 km/h), back road driving (categorie 3) and high-speed-driving (> 100/120) causes significant increases of emissions and fuel consumption. For example driving in category 1a (stop and go traffic, average speed < 25 km/h) gives almost twice the amount of CO_2 compared to the categories 2a/2c (average speed 75-100 km/h). Even driving in congestion with an average speed between 25 and 40 km/h gives an increase of about 20% CO_2.

There are different patterns for the different pollutants. But only NO_x emissions is influenced more by average speed rather than by a combination of speed and driving dynamics. Emissions from driving on a back road is rather comparable to motorway congestion (category 1b), except for PM_{10} emissions, which are quite high on backroads.

Table 2 shows the emission factors for trucks that were derived from previous research. Congestion situations and back road driving doubles the NO_x and PM_{10} emissions, whereas CO_2 increases with about one third.

Traffic category		CO	HC	NO_x	CO_2	PM_{10}
1 a a	'Stop-and-go' traffic, speed below 10 km/h	4.36	0.93	0.63	370	0.06
1 a	'Stop-and-go' traffic, speed between 0 en 25 km/h	4.32	1.50	12.65	824	0.45
1 b	Congested traffic, speed between 25 and 40 km/h	4.31	1.50	12.60	814	0.44
1 c	Congested traffic, speed between 40 and 75 km/h	4.31	1.50	12.58	809	0.43
2 a	Speed 75-120 km/h, traffic volume > 1000 vehicles per lane per/h, speed limit 100 km/h	1.45	0.46	6.53	614	0.22
2 b	Speed 75-120 km/h, traffic volume > 1000 vehicles per lane/h, speed limit 120 km/h	1.45	0.46	6.55	617	0.22
2 c	Speed 75-120 km/h, traffic volume < 1000 vehicles per lane/h, speed limit 100 km/h	1.26	0.42	6.23	568	0.20
2 d	Speed 75-120 km/h, traffic volume <1000 vehicles per lane/h, speed limit	1.27	0.42	6.27	576	0.21
2 e	Speed over 120 km/h, independent of traffic volume	1.29	0.42	6.34	589	0.21
3	Shortcut/back road	4.32	1.50	12.61	815	0.44

Table 2: Emission factors per congestion category for trucks and big vans

3.2 Emissions dominated by trucks and old cars

It must be mentioned that trucks and cars without a catalytic converter heavily put their mark on the total emission levels. It is noteworthy that truck emissions are significantly higher per vehicle kilometer than the emissions of passenger cars. Especially the CO_2, NO_x en PM_{10} emissions are dominated by trucks. NO_x emissions per kilometer are 10 to 20 times higher than for the average passenger car, depending on the congestion category.

Another remarkable point is domination of the absolute level of emission factors for passenger cars by cars without a catalytic converter. Even though their contribution to the annual Dutch mileage is only 20% and their contribution to the mileage on the motorways is only about 10%. (The emission factors from each class of technology is weighted using the share in yearly kilometers driven on the Dutch motorways.) This is caused by the fact that absolute emissions of these cars are 10 to 30 times higher than those of cars equipped with a 3-way catalyst.

3.3 Share of mileage per congestion category

After establishment of these emissionfactors total emissions were calculated for (I) specific segments of the Dutch motorways in the conurbation of the Randstad and (II) the entire Dutch motorway network. Figure 1 shows the division over congestion categories (1a-c) as found in the different analyses carried out in the study. The first column shows the congestion categories as recorded by the test vehicles, during the 30 trips in the conurbation of the Randstad. For selected *parts* of these routes, data has been collected regarding all traffic on these routes, for the periods when the vehicle was present. These division over the categories is shown in the second column. The third column shows the division when the average day (24 hours) on the entire Dutch motorway network is considered.

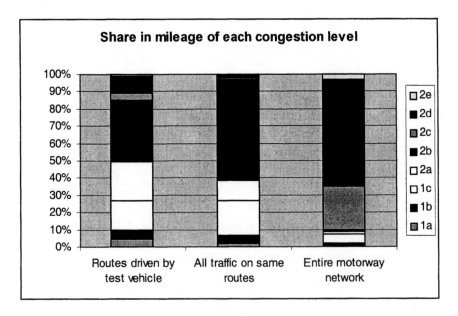

Figure 1: Share in mileage per congestion level

The share of congested traffic in the total mileage in the conurbation of the Randstad during the peakhours is much lager than when the entire motorway network and the entire day is regarded. In contrast to the situation in the Randstad during peakhours, most traffic on the entire motorway network actually drives under good conditions, given the high shares of categories 2c and 2d.

4 Improvement of ambient air quality

4.1 Effects on section level

From the analyses TNO made by considering sections (of several kilometres long) of the network of the Randstad it can be concluded that solving congestion leads to significant reduction in the local exhaust gas emissions. This holds true especially on specific routes or sections with high amounts of heavy congestion and a high share of heavy duty traffic. Like solving congestion, increasing congestion can effect the ambient air quality as well. In case of an ambient air quality bottleneck along the motorway A13 in Rotterdam it was calculated that a reduction of 20% NO_x and PM_{10} is possible by reducing traffic dynamics and speed limit enforcement. Of course we have to be conscious of the fact that the local traffic is only one of the sources that influences the ambient air quality. In addition we have to keep in mind that congestion isn't a 24 hour a day problem.

Table 3 gives a further impression of the order of emission changes caused by reducing or increasing congestion. It must be mentioned that the calculations do not take into account the effect of changes in congestion on traffic demand. The number of kilometres travelled is kept constant throughout the calculations.

Table 3: Effects of more or less congestion, on selected motorway sections

	CO	VOC	NO_x	CO_2	PM_{10}
Less congestion					
Least congested route	-7.9%	-21.3%	-10.3%	-3.4%	-10.8%
Most congested route	-21.3%	-44.1%	-20.3%	-9.6%	-21.1%
All routes	-11.5%	-29.0%	-13.6%	-5.0%	-13.9%
More congestion					
Least congested route	32.1%	67.5%	21.4%	11.6%	22.4%
Most congested route	16.1%	31.2%	10.5%	6.1%	9.6%
All routes	24.9%	53.5%	16.2%	8.7%	14.7%

4.2 Very local effects

The magnitude of the effects calculated depend on whether sections of many kilometres of the network are considered or only a small section. In this study we didn't address the very local effects of congestion. In the second stage of the study it was found that the actual tail pipe emissions of individual passenger cars and trucks increase by at least 50% (up to 800%) during heavy congestion. For local air quality this can have dramatic effects, because if traffic congestion is taking place near a densely populated area, the exposure of people to air polluting substances, will increase dramatically. The fact that in a traffic jam, dispersion of the exhaust gasses is rather poor (there is no aerodynamic turbulence behind the cars) increases the ambient concentrations of air pollution even further.

5 The limited effects of solving congestion nation-wide

The calculations of the entire motorway network resulted in much smaller effects. If we could solve all congestion on the Dutch motorways this would lead to limited reduction of emissions (see table 4). For example if we could solve all the traffic jams, without generation of extra mileages, the CO_2 emissions of the motorway network reduces with about 1,5%. This is about 0,22 Mton CO_2. In the Dutch "climate change policy implementation plan" it is presumed that the traffic sector should reduce emissions by about 3 Mton CO_2 equivalent by 2010 compared to 1990. From our study it is clear that lowering the speed by actual speed enforcement for passenger cars to 100 km/h on all sections of the motorway network can improve emission levels much more than solving all the traffic jams. For example, lowering the speed limit to 100 km/h would reduce the CO_2 emissions of the motorway network with about 7%. This is about 1 Mton CO_2 per year at current levels.

Table 4: Effects of less congestion and lowering speed limits nation-wide

	CO	VOC	NO_x	CO_2	PM_{10}
Less congestion	-4.1%	-11.3%	-4.1%	-1.5%	-4.3%
Speed limit 100 km/h	-16.6%	-2.0%	-7.1%	-6.7%	-13.4%

6 What to do with the results?

6.1 Traffic management measures

Traffic management measures should aim at keeping motorway velocities as constant as possible, or as it is called "homogenizing traffic". Traffic management measures aiming to reduce traffic dynamics of trucks – for example prohibiting of overtaking for and by trucks, and opening dedicated truck lanes - should have priority, because truck emissions are significantly higher especially in dynamic traffic situations. TNO stated that reduction of traffic dynamics is the most important ingredient for reducing the emissions of heavy duty traffic (Riemersma [2]).

Tests and implementation of traffic management measures that make traffic flows more homogeneous are indicated, since tens of percents of reduction in emissions are possible. Actually a good example is the Dutch pilot on the motorway A1. The objective of this pilot is to homogenize traffic by applying variable speed message signs, route control, providing information and "tit for tat policy" by breaking the speed limits.

Efforts to reduce traffic dynamics and congestion should be concentrated on road sections with high risks of heavy congestion and a high share of heavy duty traffic in the built-up areas. However, awareness of possible rebound effects is necessary. By reducing congestion it is possible that new traffic is generated. By making use of traffic management it is important to prevent motorway traffic from shifting towards secondary roads, because emissions on the latter are much higher.

6.2 Zoning, pricing, technology and enforcement of speed limits

In specific urban zones where the air quality is really poor, it should be taken into consideration to prohibit or restrict access of heavy duty traffic and old cars without catalytic converter. Apart from restricting access, pricing could support the air quality as well. For instance, by the kilometer-levy formula, by charging for time (higher levy during peak hours), place (higher levy for busy or sensitive environments) and/or the environmental pollution of the vehicle.

Furthermore, in the urban environment several traffic measures that lead to "stop and go" traffic situations, like speed bumps, should be considered from an air quality viewpoint as well. Actually in commission of the Flemish government, TNO looks into the emission effects of speed bumps, roundabouts and phased traffic lights.

In future other possible solutions to reduce traffic dynamics are automatic vehicle guidance or driver assistance systems like intelligent speed adaption.

Another important conclusion of this study is that lowering the speed limit to 100 km/h can improve emission levels, as most of the Dutch motorways have a speed limit of 120 km/h. A discussion about speed limits comes up time and again in the Netherlands. It is still a touchy subject. However efforts to reduce speed by way of enforcement and technical means are clearly indicated. Speeds higher than 120 km/h will have to be avoided wherever and whenever possible. Additionally, in urban areas where the air quality is poor speed limits of 100 km/h should be taken into consideration.

6.3 Using different emission factors

Furthermore it is clear that especially in the urban environment different emission factors have to be used for different congestion categories in order to calculate the ambient air quality along motorways. Until now emission factors only made a distinction between road types not between congestion categories. In congestion situations this probably leads to underestimation of the calculated ambient air quality.

7 Desirable follow-up research

In general we have to be cautious when using emission factors as absolute numbers. There are several influences on the emissions that traditionally are not considered. For example from recent studies it is obvious that driving styles, air conditioning and automatic gearboxes clearly have it's effects in fuel consumption and emissions and hence disqualify the European type approval test procedure (Eurotest) for the purpose of determining emission factors (Gense[3]).

For further improvement of emission calculations this study made clear that further attention is needed with regard to the following:

- What are the differences between measuring emissions directly on the road and measuring in a laboratory and how can they be explored. This study is not conclusive in this respect but it is clear that meteorological circumstances, and the possible more nervous throttle use during driving in the laboratory situation, can lead to differences in emissions between directly measuring on the road and measuring in a laboratory.
- Emission factors for trucks for different traffic conditions. Follow-up investigation is recommendable because the investigations of emission factors for different traffic conditions for trucks were less detailed than those for passenger cars. Besides, trucks have a great influence on the total emission levels. In the future this influence will become even more pronounced.
- Increase of knowledge of the composition of motorway traffic. For example there are differences between motorways and secondary roads in the share of number of cars without a catalytic converter. These differences have significant effects on emissions.

8 Conclusions

The study has resulted in a set of emission factors that distinguish between the levels of congestion found in actual traffic on motorways. Significant differences in emissions and fuel consumption were found for different types of traffic. High traffic dynamics, shortcut traffic, heavy congestion and high speeds lead to significant increases of regulated emissions and fuel consumption. Measures to homogenize traffic can play an important role in decreasing driving dynamics and thus lowering emissions and improving ambient air quality. Lowering and enforcing the speed limits on sections of the Dutch motorways can improve total motorway emissions levels significantly.

References

[1] Gense N.L.J., Wilmink I.R. & van de Burgwal H.C. *Emissions and Congestion - Estimation of emissions on road sections and the Dutch motorway network - Executive summary*, TNO Automotive, Delft, The Netherlands (2001)
[2] Riemersma I.J. & Hendriksen P., *Update en evaluatie van HD Testcycli*, TNO Automotive, Delft, The Netherlands (2001)
[3] Gense N.L.J., *Driving style, fuel consumption and tail pipe emissions,* TNO Automotive, Delft, The Netherlands, report number (2000)

A new simulation model of fuel consumption and pollutant emissions in urban traffic

D.C. Festa & G. Mazzulla
Dipartimento di pianificazione territoriale
Università della Calabria, Italy

Abstract

The atmospheric pollution is one of the most important impacts of vehicular traffic; air pollution levels and the over-saturated traffic conditions constitute severe problems in many cities. A large number of models, with different characteristics, has been proposed in order to simulate traffic flow and related pollutant emissions. In this paper, a fuel consumption and pollutant emission model is presented, which has three interesting features. It is based on average traffic speed, and so it can be coupled with macro traffic simulators; its range of validity (1 - 30 km/h) is well suited for urban congested traffic; it reproduces consumption and emissions in presence of accelerations, decelerations, stop and go phenomena, typical of urban traffic. The model has been developed in three steps. Many experimental journeys have been effected by a test car in a large city (Naples); space and speed have been measured by every interval of 0.5 second. Fuel consumption and pollutant emissions have been computed second by second for each journey, using an instantaneous emission model, MODEM; afterwards, total fuel consumption and pollutant emissions in each journey have been computed. Statistical relationships between consumption/emissions rates (g/km) and average speed (km/h), observed in the test runs, have been derived by the least squares method.

1 Introduction

A decision support system, used to evaluate fuel consumption and pollutant emissions in road networks, is composed of two fundamental modules: the first one is used to simulate the interactions between land use and transport system, and the characteristics of the produced traffic flows; the second one is used for calculating energy consumption and pollutant emission levels, which are functions of the relevant characteristics of the traffic flows. The first module allows the computation of the flows in the transport network, and related features, which are originated by the characteristics of the transport system and of the activity system.

A transport model, in the most general case, is used to analyse the effects on mobility, in the middle or long term, of strategical measures (eg construction of new transport facilities), or relevant modifications in the land use pattern. A transport model usually contains four main submodels. The trip generation submodel allows the computation of trips originated in each traffic zone I, in each time interval, for various purposes. The trip distribution submodel computes the probability that a trip, originated in the zone I, is directed toward the zone J. The mode choice submodel computes the probability of using a specific transport mode (e.g. car, bus, et c.), when moving from zone I to zone J. The network assignment submodel computes paths used to reach each zone J from each zone I, for every transport mode. Transport models constitute a well known tool; they operate from the urban to the regional or national scale; various models, with similar characteristics, have been developed by researchers; among all, the EMME/2 model, developed by the CRT of Montreal [1], the TRIPS model, developed in the UK by MVA Systematica [2], and the Italian MT.Model, developed by CSST and ELASYS [3], are instanced.

When the transport demand is assumed to be fixed, the transport model reduces to a simple traffic simulation model. These models are used to analyse the effects on traffic characteristics of tactical measure, as new traffic regulations, or local road network improvements. Many traffic models have been proposed in order to simulate the traffic flows on a road network; they are usually classified in three categories.

Macroscopic traffic models use a continuous flow representation (fluid approximation); user journeys on links are not explicitly traced; aggregate measures (average speed, average waiting times at intersections) are computed. These models do not capture the speed profiles of individual vehicles or groups; average travel times are estimated for each link of the road network. Macroscopic models are used to simulate large networks. The META model, proposed by Papageorgiou et al. [4], for instance, simulates speed and density on the links; the volume Q is a deduced variable.

Microscopic traffic models simulate the movements on the network of each individual vehicle, using car following, lane changing, and traffic signal response logic. Microscopic traffic simulators exhibit high levels of complexity, which constitute a severe limit to their applicability to large networks; they constitute however an efficient tool to evaluate the performances of local networks. The model Integration, proposed by Van Aerde [5, 6], assumes a basic relationship between spatial headway and speed for each link; Integration includes an algorithm, which manages vehicle interactions through the basic relationship; a rule based lane-changing model, that allows to represent the lane changing manoeuvres on multi-lane links; and a gap acceptance model, which describes vehicular interactions at on/off ramps.

Mesoscopic models are an intermediate step between macroscopic and microscopic ones. Mesoscopic models deal with platoons of vehicles, which are traced in their movement between the origin and the destination node. The model STODYN-MICE, proposed by Cascetta and Cantarella [7,8], for example, computes the running speed on links using usual speed/density relationships, and waiting times at intersections using the deterministic queuing theory.

Pollutant emissions and fuel consumption are influenced by many variables, mainly by vehicle technology, engine thermal conditions, and motion characteristics (speeds and accelerations). Emission models are used to estimate emission factors, namely pollutant emissions referred to time and distance units, or to specific driving sequences. Emission factors are related to homogeneous vehicles groups; composite emission factors reflect the actual flow composition on a specific link. Thermal conditions are specified by cold start, transient and hot-stabilized emission factors. Fuel consumption and pollutant emission models, too, have specific characteristics, depending on the model aim and the reference scale. At regional and national scale, these models are used to estimate the global energy consumption and to compute pollutant emission inventories; these parameters are used, for instance, to evaluate the effects, in the long period, of transport policies, strategical planning measures, nation-wide infrastructural plans, or more stringent regulations for vehicular emissions and so on, on the overall air quality. At urban scale, emission models are used to evaluate the effects of traffic measures, or local new transport infrastructures, on local emissions levels; the effects on local air quality may be also estimated, using pollutant dispersion model, as CALINE [9], or ITALICS.1 [10].

Emission models are usually classifies in two categories. Average models compute fuel consumption and pollutant emissions, which occur in a trip, by the average speed in the whole trip; these models are essentially used for large scale inventories purposes. The model MOBILE is used in the US since the late 1970s [11], and has been upgraded several times; the model CORINAIR has been developed for the European car park [12]; an updated version, COPERTII, has been recently released [13]. This model takes in consideration the various above mentioned factors, which affect emission rates. Instantaneous, or modal models, compute consumption and emissions, which occur in a trip, summing the values computed for each elementary time interval (usually 1 second) by the instantaneous speeds and accelerations. These models are used for local studies; they allow to compute the distribution of consumption and emissions along a road section. The model MODEM [14] calculates the emissions of four pollutants (CO, HC, NO_X, CO_2), and the fuel consumption, second by second, according to the speed curve and taking into account the acceleration, for 12 car layers (4 types of cars: gasoline cars without catalyst, complying with 15/03 or 15/04 European standard, gasoline cars with controlled catalyst, Diesel cars; and 3 classes of engine displacement: <1.4 l, 1.4 – 2.0 l, >2.0 l). Instant emission and consumption values are summed to obtain the total values in the whole driving sequence.

Emission models must be consistent with the models used to simulate traffic flows. Average emission models can be coupled with macroscopic or mesoscopic traffic simulators, which reproduce the average link speeds; modal models can be coupled with microscopic traffic simulators, which reproduce instantaneous speed and acceleration for each individual vehicle in the network. Average emission models, however, have been usually developed for regional/national inventories purposes, and they are not fit to reproduce the local congested traffic, which occurs in many urban areas; slow speed in urban traffic may be outside the range of the models (e.g. 10 – 100 km/h). These models, when used for urban traffic, usually underestimate consumption and emission rates. Instantaneous emission models, instead, are well suited to congested traffic conditions; however, they must be coupled with microscopic traffic simulators, which require an high computational effort.

Because of these reasons, much research work has been devoted to develop simpler tools in order to estimate pollutant emissions in function of macroscopic traffic variables. Pronello and Andrè [15] have implemented a modified version of MODEM, named MODEM2; this version requires the average speed and acceleration in each driving sequence, instead of the instantaneous values second by second. In this paper, a new model is presented, which has, as input values, only the average speed in the whole trip, or along an individual road section. The new model, so, can be coupled with macro and meso traffic simulators, which reproduce only aggregate traffic variables, as the average speed. However, the model has been calibrated for the average speed, which occurs in real urban driving cycles encompassing positive and negative accelerations, stop and go phenomena, and constant speed conditions too. So, the new model "statistically" reproduces the effects of instantaneous traffic variables (accelerations and speeds); the model thus overcomes the underestimation problems, which verify when average models are used in order to simulate fuel consumption and pollutant emissions in congested urban traffic.

2 Construction of driving cycles

The journey characteristics (speeds, accelerations, waiting times) used in this research work, for the construction of driving cycles, were collected by a test car; the car was a two-liter engine passenger vehicle, which can be powered by gasoline or methane (FIAT Marea Bi-Power). The car was equipped with a Global Positioning System (GPS) device and a data acquisition system. Monitored parameters include geographical coordinates (latitude and longitude), instantaneous speed, covered distance, and some engine parameters. The parameters were monitored at 500 milliseconds intervals; for each parameter, 23.829 values were recorded.

The car was used in real traffic conditions in Naples suburbs; the driver followed the main traffic stream. Test runs were performed on July 30, 1999, from 8.20 a.m. until twelve. The collected data were used for the construction of driving cycles. The test path included several urban streets, with one signalised intersection; several experiment journeys were effected; the total travel distance was about 75 km. The recorded data include two trips (about 22 km) on an urban motorway, from the car garage to the test site. Traffic flows were quite high; the test car was forced to stop and go, according to local congestion phenomena, traffic lights at the signalised intersection, and traffic rules at the unsignalised ones. Using simultaneously instant GPS and travel distance data, the car position on the test path was traced second by second. The total travel space was divided in several driving sequences; in each one, the car starts from stop conditions, runs for some time, and then again stops (fig. 1). The number of identified sequences was 99; for each one, the following parameters were computed:

- Length (metres)
- Running time (seconds)
- Stop time (seconds)
- Total travel time (running time plus stop time, seconds)
- Running speed (length/running time, metres/second)
- Travel speed (length/travel time, metres/second)
- Standard deviations of running and travel speeds (metres/second)
- Average running acceleration and average travel acceleration (m/sec^2)
- Average positive acceleration in travel and running times (m/sec^2)
- Average negative acceleration in travel and running times (m/sec^2).

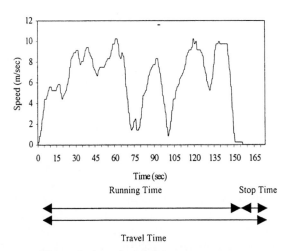

Figure 1: A typical driving sequence.

The driving sequences are classified according to the travel distance and the running/travel speeds. The average cycle length is 371.4 metres; the 90th percentile, which excludes the longer trips on the urban motorway, is 1976.9 m., the 75th percentile is 754.7 m, the 25th is 35.65 m, and the 10th percentile is 3.3 m. The average travel speed is 4.94 m/s (17.78 km/h), while the average running speed is 5.69 m/sec (20.48 km/h). The cumulate distributions of the two speeds are compared in figure 2.

The 90th percentiles are respectively 6.75 and 7.19 m/sec; the 75th percentiles 6.13 and 6.54; the 25th percentiles 0.99 and 2.01; the 10th percentiles 0.20 and 0.59; the two distributions exhibit higher differences in the lower range of speeds; it has been observed that differences among travel and running speeds are higher in short than in long trips. The average accelerations, in a driving sequence, range to 0.02 m/sec^2 in travel conditions, and 0.07 m/sec^2 in running conditions; obviously, the average value, in each driving sequence, tends to zero. The average positive acceleration ranges from 0.28 to 0.92 m/sec^2, while the average negative accelerations range to 1.56 m/sec^2.

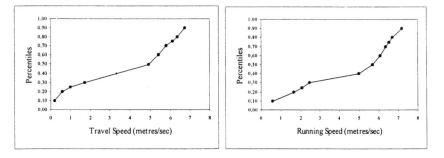

Figure 2: Cumulate distributions of travel and run speed in driving sequences.

3 Fuel consumption and pollutant emissions in the observed driving cycles

Fuel consumption and pollutant emissions, in each of the observed driving cycles, where computed by the software MODEM, using instantaneous speeds and accelerations, as measured in the test runs; obviously, speed and acceleration were zero, when the vehicle was waiting in a queue, or otherwise idling. Computations were effected for four categories of cars (ECE 15/03 vehicles, ECE15/04 vehicles, three-way catalyst vehicles, and diesel vehicles); for each category, three classes of engine displacements were considered (less than 1.4 l, 1.4 - 2.0 l, greater than 2.0 l). For each type of vehicle, the emissions of the four main pollutants, CO, HC, NOx, CO_2, and the fuel consumption, were computed for each second of each driving sequence; total values were then computed for each driving sequence. Total consumption and emissions were divided by the sequence length and duration (travel time and running time), obtaining the average consumption and emissions factors for the unit of space and time (g/km and g/sec) in each driving sequence. The values of the estimated parameters for the test car (gasoline catalyst vehicle, 2.0 litres displacement), are shown in table 1. The range of each computed value is very large; this indicates that traffic conditions affect heavily energy consumption and pollutant emissions. Differences between the same parameter in running and travel conditions are high; this indicates how the repeated stops in urban traffic constitute a serious problem non only because of the lost time value, but also because of environmental impacts.

4 Regressive models for fuel consumption and pollutant emissions

The computed data were used to produce an interpretative mathematical model which, based on statistical relations, could connect the consumption and emission rates with the average running or travel speed. A preliminary statistical analysis was performed in order to investigate the degree of correlation among the variables involved in the phenomenon:

- Pollutants emission rate in running and travel conditions (g/km)
- Fuel consumption rate in running and travel conditions (g/km)
- Length of the driving sequence (m)
- Average running and travel speed (m/sec)
- Standard deviations of running and travel speed (m/sec)
- Average positive and negative accelerations in running conditions (m/sec^2)
- Average positive and negative accelerations in travel conditions (m/sec^2)
- Total travel time (sec)
- Total running time (sec)
- Total waiting time (sec)

Table 1. Average emission and fuel consumption rates.

Parameter	Type of motion	Minimum	Medium	Maximum
CO (g/km)	Run	2.55	15.67	155.92
	Travel	0	28.58	459.18
HC (g/km)	Run	0.032	1.51	48.00
	Travel	0.037	1.63	49.11
NO$_X$ (g/km)	Run	0.27	0.96	12.12
	Travel	0.27	1.81	27.47
CO$_2$ (g/km)	Run	149.93	902.21	8,853.33
	Travel	149.96	1,962.59	34,919.58
FC (g/km)	Run	48.58	288.75	2,863.33
	Travel	48.59	630.09	11,253.90

The correlation among CO emission rates, for the test car, and the cinematic parameters, is reported in table 2. The table shows that CO emission rates are affected by each cinematic parameter, and mainly by speed, speed standard deviation, positive and negative accelerations. High correlation degrees do exist among many cinematic parameters, and collinearity problems arise, if a regressive model among CO emission rates and all cinematic parameters is estimated.

Various functional forms were so investigated, in order to produce an interpretative mathematical model, which could connect consumption and emission rates with the various cinematic parameters; the analysis showed that the two rates were mainly affected by the running or the travel speed. Two models were so calibrates, having the following equations:

- $y = a * V^n$
- $y = i + c * V + d * V^2$

where y is the pollutant emission rate or the fuel consumption rate, and V is the running or the travel speed.

Table 2. Correlation matrix of parameters (r: run, t: travel; w: wait).

	CO_r (g/km)	CO_t (g/km)	L (m)	V_r (m/sec)	V_t (m/sec)	$SD(V_r)$ (m/sec)	$SD(V_t)$ (m/sec)	a^+_r (m/sec²)	a^-_r (m/sec²)	a^+_t (m/sec²)	a^-_t (m/sec²)	T_t (sec)	T_r (sec)	T_w (sec)
CO_r	1.00													
CO_t	0.85	1.00												
L	-0.22	-0.19	1.00											
V_r	-0.55	-0.49	0.71	1.00										
V_t	-0.47	-0.43	0.74	0.95	1.00									
$SD(V_r)$	-0.57	-0.51	0.58	0.94	0.87	1.00								
$SD(V_t)$	-0.58	-0.53	0.55	0.94	0.87	0.99	1.00							
a^+_r	-0.58	-0.53	0.03	0.48	0.37	0.59	0.58	1.00						
a^-_r	0.51	0.48	-0.06	-0.50	-0.38	-0.59	-0.59	-0.73	1.00					
a^+_t	-0.57	-0.53	0.03	0.48	0.37	0.59	0.58	1.00	-0.73	1.00				
a^-_t	0.53	0.49	-0.12	-0.55	-0.46	-0.61	-0.61	-0.71	0.91	-0.71	1.00			
T_t	-0.29	-0.24	0.88	0.65	0.66	0.52	0.51	0.14	-0.14	0.14	-0.23	1.00		
T_r	-0.29	-0.26	0.89	0.67	0.71	0.54	0.53	0.13	-0.14	0.13	-0.23	0.99	1.00	
T_w	-0.05	0.09	-0.13	-0.17	-0.34	-0.12	-0.13	0.04	-0.04	0.04	0.02	0.01	-0.12	1.00

The best results were obtained by the first model, which exhibit a better statistical fit. CO emission rates, for the four categories of vehicles, are reported in table 3; similar relationships have been obtained for HC, NO_X and CO_2 emission rates. Fuel consumption rates have been reported in table 4. Figure 3 shows the regression curves between CO emission rates and running/travel speeds.

When using the model referred to running speed, fuel consumption and pollutant emissions in a driving sequence must be computed in three steps. In the first step, consumption/emissions in running conditions are computed, multiplying the driving distance (km) by the emission rates (g/km) referred to the running speed (m/sec). In the second step, consumption and emissions in waiting conditions are computed, multiplying the emission rates, referred to time (g/sec), by the time spent in waiting (sec). In the third step, the two values are added, to obtain the total consumption/emissions in the whole driving sequence. This procedure is well suited for traffic simulation models, which compute separately for each link the running and the waiting time.

When the model referred to travel speed is used, fuel consumption and pollutant emissions in a driving sequence are computed in only one step, multiplying the driving distance (km) by the emission rates (g/km) referred to travel speeds; these rates encompass consumption/emissions in running and waiting conditions.

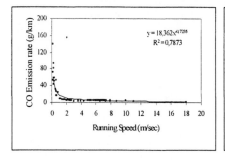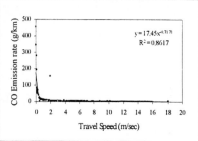

Figure 3: Regression curves between CO emission rates and run/travel speeds.

Table 3. CO emission rates (g/km).

Vehicles categories	Displacement	Running conditions		Travel conditions	
		Emission rate (g/km)	R^2	Emission rate (g/km)	R^2
ECE 15-03	< 1.4 l	$160.170*V^{-0.9279}$	0.9239	$143.110*V^{-0.8873}$	0.9304
	1.4-2.0 l	$103.03*V^{-0.8173}$	0.9017	$272.88*V^{-1.226}$	0.9301
	>2.0 l	$379.4*V^{-1.044}$	0.9523	$341.71*V^{-0.9981}$	0.9475
ECE 15-04	< 1.4 l	$103.55*V^{-0.8048}$	0.8933	$101.71*V^{-0.8192}$	0.9166
	1.4-2.0 l	$146.96*V^{-0.9049}$	0.9254	$140.68*V^{-0.9024}$	0.9360
	>2.0 l	$98.244*V^{-0.8405}$	0.9006	$102.01*V^{-0.8776}$	0.9261
Catalyst	< 1.4 l	$16.56*V^{-0.7128}$	0.7729	$16.3180*V^{-0.7237}$	0.8604
	1.4-2.0 l	$18.362*V^{-0.7235}$	0.7873	$17.45*V^{-0.7171}$	0.8617
	>2.0 l	$21.553*V^{-0.7017}$	0.7962	$20.6030*V^{-0.7014}$	0.8638
Diesel	< 1.4 l	$2.543*V^{-0.8797}$	0.8304	$2.2467*V^{-0.8308}$	0.8811
	1.4-2.0 l	$2.543*V^{-0.8797}$	0.8304	$2.2467*V^{-0.8308}$	0.8811
	>2.0 l	$4.218*V^{-0.9766}$	0.9052	$3.5940*V^{-0.9083}$	0.9132

5 Range of validity and sensitivity analysis

Fuel consumption and emission models have been estimated from driving cycles with speeds ranging from 0.1 to 65 km/h; however, near all the cycles have speeds less than 30 km/h; for this reason, the models could be reasonably used for speeds less than 30 km/h. An analysis of the model sensitivity has been effected comparing the values of pollutant emissions and fuel consumption rates, computed for some values of speed by the model referred to running speed, the model referred to travel speed, and the model CORINAIR, which is referred to average speed.

Table 4. Fuel consumption rates.

Vehicles categories	Displacement	Running conditions		Travel conditions	
		Fuel cons. rate (g/km)	R^2	Fuel cons. rate (g/km)	R^2
ECE 15-03	< 1.4 l	$296.20*V^{-0.8032}$	0.8830	$277.71*V^{-0.7941}$	0.9079
	1.4-2.0 l	$372.44*V^{-0.8269}$	0.8921	$351.48*V^{-0.8191}$	0.914
	>2.0 l	$576.34*V^{-0.8591}$	0.9014	$539.57*V^{-0.8450}$	0.9205
ECE 15-04	< 1.4 l	$274.66*V^{-0.7782}$	0.8720	$260.62*V^{-0.7761}$	0.9020
	1.4-2.0 l	$356.12*V^{-0.8126}$	0.8874	$334.83*V^{-0.8040}$	0.9104
	>2.0 l	$558.79*V^{-0.8581}$	0.8971	$535.65*V^{-0.8545}$	0.9213
Catalyst	< 1.4 l	$276.41*V^{-0.8061}$	0.8832	$262.28*V^{-0.8036}$	0.9117
	1.4-2.0 l	$539.83*V^{-1.1346}$	0.5010	$403.56*V^{-0.9977}$	0.6062
	>2.0 l	$521.97*V^{-0.8587}$	0.8982	$481.53*V^{-0.8382}$	0.9199
Diesel	< 1.4 l	$177.49*V^{-0.6747}$	0.8170	$184.29*V^{-0.7220}$	0.8798
	1.4-2.0 l	$177.49*V^{-0.6747}$	0.8170	$184.29*V^{-0.7220}$	0.8798
	>2.0 l	$411.13*V^{-0.8914}$	0.9170	$342.26*V^{-0.8211}$	0.9181

Table 5. Sensitivity analysis.

V (m/sec)	CO emission rate (g/km)			Fuel consumption rate (g/km)		
	Running conditions	Travel conditions	Corinair (average)	Running conditions	Travel conditions	Corinair (average)
0.25	50.062	47.156	2.837	2600.839	1609.101	81.258
0.50	30.319	28.686	2.763	1184.910	805.834	80.134
1.00	18.362	17.450	2.618	539.830	403.560	77.938
2.00	11.121	10.615	2.346	245.940	202.102	73.753
3.00	8.293	7.937	2.097	155.277	134.860	69.846
4.00	6.735	6.457	1.870	112.047	101.212	66.216
5.00	5.731	5.503	1.666	86.993	81.011	62.863
6.00	5.023	4.828	1.484	70.742	67.538	59.787
7.00	4.493	4.323	1.325	59.395	57.910	56.989
8.00	4.079	3.928	1.189	51.047	50.687	54.469
9.00	3.746	3.610	1.075	44.664	45.067	52.225
10.00	3.471	3.347	0.984	39.633	40.570	50.259

Values have been computed for all vehicles categories, in terms of EC regulations and engine displacements; for brevity, only CO emission rates and fuel consumption rates, computed for a three-way catalyst car, with engine displacement of 1,4 – 2.0 l, are reported in table 5. For the same speed, CO emission and fuel consumption rates, computed by the model referred to the running speed, are quite greater than values computed by the model referred to the travel speed. This is not surprising. In each driving sequence, the average running speed is greater than the average travel speed; if consumption/emission rates are computed for the same value of speed, the values in running conditions must be greater than the values in travel conditions. The difference between rates in running and travel conditions decreases when speed increases, since (statistically) the influence of time lost in waiting conditions decreases.

Emission and consumption rates, computed by the proposed models in the range 0.25 - 10 m/sec, are greater than values computed by the model CORINAIR; for higher speeds, the three models tend to predict the same rates. This is obvious, since CORINAIR has been developed for large scale inventories, and is referred to an average travel speed; the new models, instead, have been calibrated in order to reproduce emissions and consumption rates in congested urban traffic.

6 Conclusions

Pollutant emission and fuel consumption models, which have been developed to make out inventories at regional or national scale, refer to the average travel speed; they are not fit to congested traffic conditions, typical of many urban areas. Modal emission and consumption models refer to instantaneous speed and acceleration; they capture urban traffic dynamics, when are coupled to microscopic traffic simulators. These system of models are used to evaluate local traffic measures, while their use for large networks is difficult, because of the high computational effort. Simpler tools, related to macroscopic traffic variables, are so requested in order to simulate emissions and consumption in urban networks, for planning purposes. The analytical models, presented in this paper, refer only to the average speed, and so they can be coupled with usual traffic macro and meso simulators; however, their results are comparable with results produced by the more sophisticated instantaneous models.

Acknowledgements

The authors would like to thank Elasis S.C.p.A., which has provided the data base on the test driving sequences, and engineer Giuseppe Monteleone, for his cooperation in the data analysis.

References

[1] INRO Consultants, Inc. EMME/2, Release 9.2., Montreal, Quebec, Canada, 1999.
[2] MVA Systematica. TRIPS, Version seven, User's guide, 1995.
[3] C.S.S.T. S.p.A. & Elasis S.C.p.A. MT.Model Manual, Version 4.1.006, Torino, Italia, 1997.

[4] Papageorgiou M., Blosseville J.M., Hadj-Salem H. Macroscopic modelling of traffic flow on the Boulevard Périphérique in Paris, *Transportation Research B*, Vol.23B, pp.29-47, 1989.

[5] Van Aerde M. A single regime speed-flow-density relationship for congested and uncongested highways, *Presented at Transportation Research Board 74th annual meeting*, Washington, D.C., 1997.

[6] Van Aerde M. and Transportation System Research Group, INTEGRATION - Release 2, User's guide, Volume I, II, III, Queen's University, Kingston, Ontario, Canada, 1995.

[7] Cascetta E., Cantarella G.E. A day-to-day and within-day dynamic stochastic assignment model, *Transportation Research*, Vol. 25A, No. 5, 1991.

[8] Cantarella G.E., Cascetta E. Un modello di assegnazione doppiamente dinamica del traffico, *C.N.R., Progetto Finalizzato Trasporti 2, III Convegno Nazionale*, Taormina, 1997.

[9] Benson P.E. CALINE4 - A dispersion model for predicting air pollutant concentrations near roadways, Caltrans, FHWA/CA/TL-84/15, 1986.

[10] D.C. Festa. Simulation of traffic pollution in urban areas, *Transportation systems*, M. Papageorgiou, A. Pouliezos Eds., IFAC/IFIP/IFORS Symposium, Chania, Greece, 16-18 June 1997, (preprints), pp. 1150-1155, 1997.

[11] EPA, Office of Mobile Sources. Description of the MOBILE Highway Vehicle Emission Factor Model, 1999.

[12] Eggleston S., Goriβen N., Joumard R., Rijkeboer R.C., Samaras Z. and Zierock K.H. CORINAIR Working Group on Emissions Factors, Final Report Contract No. 88/6611/0067, EUR 12260 EN, 1993.

[13] EC, MEET, Methodology for calculating transport emissions and energy consumption, European Communities, EPA 1999.

[14] Joumard R., Hickman A.J., Nemerlin J., Hassel D. Model of exhaust and noise emissions and fuel consumption of traffic in urban areas - manual, INRETS, 1992.

[15] Pronello C., André M. Pollutant emissions estimation in road transport models, Report INRETS-LTE n.2007, INRETS, 2000.

Particulate matter composition in four major Italian towns

A. D'Alessandro[1], F. Lucarelli[2], P. A. Mandò[2], G. Marcazzan[3],
S. Nava[1], P. Prati[1,] G. Valli[3], R. Vecchi[3] & A. Zucchiatti[1]
[1]Dipartimento di Fisica and INFN, Genova, Italy
[2]Dipartimento di Fisica and INFN, Firenze, Italy
[3]Istituto di Fisica Generale Applicata, Milano, Italy

Abstract

The composition of particulate matter in the atmosphere of four major italian towns (Florence, Genoa, Milan and Naples) has been studied with the extensive application of IBA techniques. The aerosol has been collected simultanously in the four towns during the first weeks of year 2001, by two-stage continuous streaker samplers, which provide the separation of the particulate metter in two fractions. The concentrations in air of about 20 elements, and the total particulate mass, have been extracted in the PM2.5 and PM10 fractions with hourly resolution by PIXE, PIGE and optical analyses of about 2700 samples. IBA analyses have been performed at the 3 MeV external proton beam of the INFN accelerator facility at the University of Florence.

1 Introduction

In the last years the quantity of data produced by health authorities and other research institutes, concerning the aerosol concentration and composition in Italian urban areas, is rapidly increasing, but the differences of the used techniques often makes a comparison impossible; the aim of our investigation is to 'photograph' the aerosol characteristics in four big Italian towns, by a unique methodological approach. The four towns selected for this campaign are representative of the Italian urban environments: two cities (Genoa and Naples) lie along the sea, while the other two (Milan and Florence) are located more than 100 km far from the nearest coast. Milan has more than 3 millions inhabitants, Naples and Genoa about 1 million and Florence more than half a million. Major contributions to urban pollution are expected to come mainly from traffic, but also from industries present in the urban surroundings and domestic heating. The sampling sites had been selected in order to be representative of medium-heavy traffic urban zones; they all are close to heavy traffic roads, known to have similar annually average concentration of CO ($2.5 - 3$ mg/m^3) and are equipped to monitor meteorological variables (temperature, pressure, wind direction and speed, relative humidity, rainfall) and gaseous pollutants concentrations (CO, NO_X, SO_2, O_3). The sampling lasted four weeks starting from the 18th of January. Continuous streaker samplers [1] were used for the campaign. The combination of streaker samplers and IBA techniques is particularly useful in urban environments, since it provides elemental concentrations with hourly resolution [2]. Moreover the high sensitivity (and therefore the speed and reasonable costs) of PIXE analysis allows extended campaigns to be carried out. In this paper the methodological aspects of the campaign will be described and data related to vehicles emission will be discussed.

2 Materials and methods

Samplers, one for each town, have been installed on the roof of monitoring cabins of the municipal air quality network (Florence – *Gramsci*, Genoa – *Brignole*, Milan – *Zavattari*, Naples – *Giulio Cesare*), at about 3 m above ground. In the streaker sampler, particles are separated on different stages by a pre-impactor and an impactor. The pre-impactor removes particulate matter with aerodynamic diameter (D_{ae}) > 10 μm. The impactor deposits the aerosol coarse fraction (2.5 μm < D_{ae} < 10 μm) on a Kapton foil while the fine fraction (D_{ae} < 2.5 μm) is collected on a Nuclepore filter (with 0.4 μm pores). Since the cut off diameter of any impactor is a function of the air flow, our set up should work at 1l/min to obtain the nominal cut off of 2.5 μm. In reality the samplers ran on average at 0.85 l/min, with a moderate increase of the cut-off diameter [3]. The two collecting plates (Kapton and Nuclepore) are paired on a cartridge which rotates at constant speed ($\sim 1.8°$ per hour) for a week, and this produces a circular continuous deposition of particular matter ("streak") on both stages.

Nuclepore filters have been first analysed with an optical method [4], based on the hypothesis that for thin samples the visible light (red laser in our device, $\lambda = 633$ nm) is exponentially attenuated with thickness [5]. This method allows the determination of the total particulate thickness (μg/cm^2) on Nuclepore substrata with a sensitivity of 5 μg/cm^2, a precision of about 35% and hourly resolution. The instrument has been calibrated by measuring several PM10 and PM2.5 samples, whose thickness was known by previous weighing. The development of an analogous technique for the Kapton foils, which have very different optical properties, is still in progress.

The external beam facility in Florence is based on a Van de Graaff accelerator for light ions (protons, in this case) [6]. The projectiles energy ($E_p = 2.9$ MeV) has been chosen such that the cross section for the Na(p,p'γ)Na ($E_\gamma = 441$ keV) reaction, which is exploited for PIGE determination of Na [7], remains sufficiently constant thought the proton energy loss in the sample, being at the same time high enough to provide good sensitivity. Methodological aspects for beam energy selection, based on experimental yield, are described in ref. [8]; E_p = 2.9 MeV is also an usual energy for PIXE measurements. The beam (12 nA maximum, 10 nA average) is diffused in vacuum by an Al foil, collimated to a rectangular spot (1 x 3 mm^2) on the thin aerosol samples and finally collected on a graphite Faraday cup. The beam moves along the streak in steps corresponding to 1 hour of aerosol sampling, each step takes 5 minutes of beam time. Therefore scanning the whole streaker requires about 15 hours with, on average, 3 µC collected per step. On Nuclepore filters, on which the streak vertical size is 8 mm, the 1 x 3 mm^2 beam moves vertically along the streak to average possible inhomogeneities. On each sample (Nuclepore or Kapton) zones outside the streak have also been analysed, to evaluate the background contribution. Three detectors collect X and γ rays emitted by the sample: two Si(Li) ("small": active area of 13 mm^2 with 170 eV FWHM energy resolution, "big": 78 mm^2 with 190 eV FWHM energy resolution at 5.9 keV) at 135° from the beam, and one HPGe detector (efficiency 25% with less then 2 keV energy resolution at 1.33 MeV) at 120° from the beam. Helium gas flows in front of the "small" Si detector to reduce light X rays attenuation, while a 400 µm Mylar foil shields the Si "big". In this way, measurements on the two detectors are optimised for low and medium-high X ray energies, respectively, with a balanced counting rate. Pile-up corrections on Si detectors did not exceed 3% of the whole X spectra.

We obtain the elemental thickness by comparing peak counts per µC with a sensitivity curve [counts/µC*(µg/cm^2)] evaluated in the same geometry with a set of thin standards certified within 5% (Micromatter Inc.). During the 16 days PIXE/PIGE beam shifts, the stability of the sensitivity curve has been daily checked with NaCl and Fe standards. All the X-ray spectra have been fitted for 24 elements (Na, Mg, Al, Si, P, S, Cl, K, Ca, Ti, V, Cr, Mn, Fe, Co, Ni, Cu, Zn, As, Se, Br, Sr, Zr, Pb) using the GUPIX software package [9]. A few filters were affected by Si and Br contaminations, up to 560 ng/cm^2 for Si and 12 ng/cm^2 for Br. PIGE has been tuned to the measurement of Na concentrations, being well known that the PIXE measurement may underestimate it, because of the X ray attenuation inside the target. The measurement reliability has been tested on a multielemental standard of certified thickness and composition (BCR CMR 038). PIXE reproduces within 16% the standard composition for all elements but Na which, however, is well reproduced by PIGE. Moreover, the comparison between Na concentration deduced by PIGE and Cl measured by PIXE on sea-salt enriched aerosol (Genoa, Naples) reproduces the stecheometric ratio for NaCl. Also Al and Si concentrations in the coarse fraction are under-estimated by PIXE analysis because of the attenuation inside the particles themselves so that the estimation of a suitable correction factor is in progress. PIXE minimum detection limits (MDL), at 3σ level, range between 0.8 and 45 ng/cm^2, corresponding to 0.7 – 40 ng/m^3 for the coarse stage and between 1.7 – 100 ng/m^3 for fine one, being different the deposition area on Kapton foils and on Nuclepore filters. For Sodium MDL was 150 ng/cm^2 with PIGE analysis.

3 Results

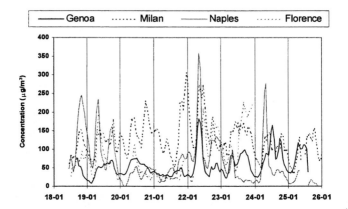

Figure 1: Total aerosol mass concentration in the fine (PM2.5) stage measured by optical method in the first week (18-25 January 2001; starting day: Thursday).

Data reduction to extract the total and elemental concentrations has been completed. The optical analysis has been performed on all the exposed Nuclepore filters obtaining the fine aerosol fraction time trends, as those showed in figure 1, concerning the first week of sampling. A similar time pattern peaked twice a day, around 8 am and 6 pm, is observed in all the four sites. With the exception of Milan, the pollution is reduced during the weekend and increases considerably on Monday morning.

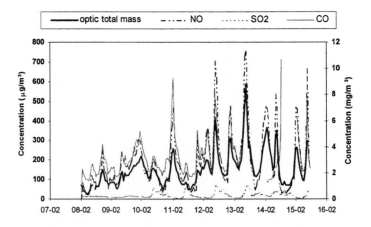

Figure 2: Comparison between optically measured total mass (fine stage) and gaseous pollutants (Milan, 8-15 February 2001; starting day: Thursday); PM2.5, NO, SO$_2$ are expressed in μg/m^3, CO in mg/m^3.

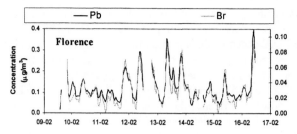

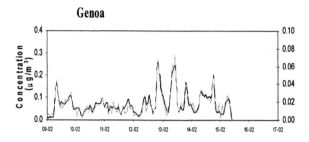

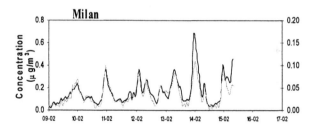

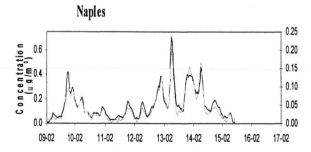

Figure 3: Br and Pb concentration (fine stage) in the four towns.

This behaviour must be mainly related to traffic as confirmed by the high correlation observed between the total fine mass, CO and NO (figure 2).

From the PIXE spectra, concentration time series have been obtained for each town and all elements, both in the fine and coarse stage [10] covering two weeks for a total of 2688 hourly samples. Hourly resolution and elemental analysis allows the identification of strong correlations due to local sources.

Traffic is known to influence the Pb and Br fine fraction time series (figure 3) which have indeed high correlation coefficient in all sites: Florence R = 0.94, Genoa R = 0.94, Milan R = 0.91, Naples R = 0.97. In Genoa, Florence and Naples the Pb/Br ratio results in the range 3.35-5.24, (Table 1) similar to those reported in literature for the traffic source profile in urban areas [11] and to the values found in our previous works [6,12,13]; in Milan the higher value (about 5) could be due to the presence of different sources of Pb [14] or to a different composition of a vehicle fleet.

Table 1: Average concentration ($\mu g/m^3$) in the two weeks for lead and bromine. Top frame: fine (PM2.) stage, middle: coarse stage; bottom: Pb to Br ratio in the fine stage.

Period	Florence	Genoa	Milan	Naples
January, 18-25	0.141	0.056	0.123	0.162
February, 8-15	0.122	0.071	0.158	0.143

	Florence	Genoa	Milan	Naples
January, 18-25	0.037	0.014	0.023	0.046
February, 8-15	0.029	0.018	0.033	0.043

	Florence	Genoa	Milan	Naples
January, 18-25	3.79	3.98	5.24	3.50
February, 8-15	4.17	4.04	4.80	3.35

The average elemental concentrations are shown in the bar diagram of figure 4. Some elements (S, K, V, Ni, Zn, Pb, Br,) are present mainly in the fine fraction, while others (Mg, Al, Si, Ca, Ti, Fe) are balanced in the two components. In all the towns Sulphur dominates the PIXE measured particulate mass in the fine stage and its time pattern is characterised by a time component varying on a few hours scale, superimposed to a generally dominant slowly varying background, typical of secondary aerosols of regional origin; a behaviour that has been already seen in previous campaigns [15]. This element is in fact present in the fine particulate mainly as sulphate particles, which can be emitted directly from fossil fuel combustion process, but are mainly produced by oxidation (in the atmosphere) of SO_2, which is also emitted from fossil fuel combustion process. Sodium and Cl enrichments appear, as expected, in the two marine cities, in the coarse stage. Florence receives a remarkably high contribution of Fe and Ca in both stages, while the high fine Zn concentration is a distinctive sign in the Milan particulate.

Bromine and Pb concentration in Genoa are about one half of those measured in the other sites: these could be related to the traffic restriction adopted in this town (not -catalyzed vehicles can not circulate between 7.30 and 11 a.m. during working days) but also to the peculiar meteorological conditions (northern and strong winds "clean" quite frequently the atmosphere in Genoa during winter). This trend is confirmed also by the optical measurement of the PM2.5. During the whole sampling period the average PM2.5 concentration in Genoa was 60 $\mu g/m^3$ against 80, 120 and 70 $\mu g/m^3$ measured in Florence, Milan and Naples respectively. It should however be remembered that the uncertainties on these concentrations are quite high.

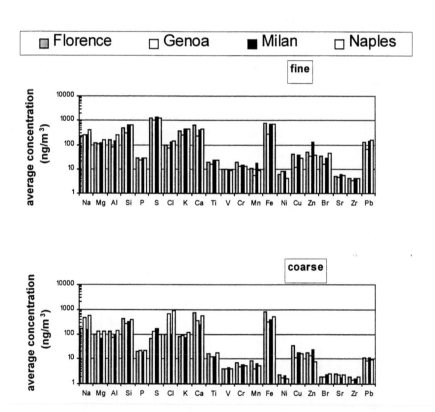

Figure 4: Average aerosol composition in the fine and coarse stage.

4 Conclusions

The first results obtained by the analysis of time series give indication of urban pollution processes that are quite understood from previous work. The particulate fingerprint in each town shows differences that have to be described in terms of contributing sources and their apportionment. In the four sampling sites traffic is clearly the dominant source of particulate matter also if significant differences have been detected and discussed for the four towns. Some episodes common to the time series in different towns suggest a sharper investigation of both particulate and meteorological data to understand processes on a larger scale. A statistical study, including PCA and APCA, is therefore in progress.

A new sampling campaign has been organised in the same sites and with the same techniques in July 2001. PIXE analyses on the esposed filters are still in progress but we expect to obtain interesting comparisons with the winter period. In Genoa, for this second campaign, we installed also a TEOM (Tapered Element Ocillating Monitor) sampler [16] equipped with a PM10 inlet. The sampling period included the days of the "G8" summit in Genoa: around the sampling site and in the whole centre of the town we had 4 days (July 19th-22th) without any substantial vehicle circulation. In figure 5 the TEOM measurements are reported and the PM10 reduction is evident in the period of the summit.

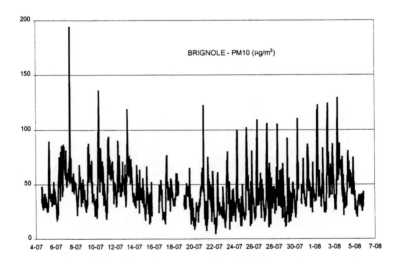

Figure 5: PM10 concentration measured in Genoa-Brignole between July 4th and August 6th 2001 by the real-time TEOM monitor.

Acknowledgements

We thank the local authorities of Florence, Genoa, Milan and Naples for the permission to use structures and data, and for their valuable assistance.

References

[1] PIXE International Corp., P.O. Box 7744, Tallahassee, FL 32316, USA

[2] P. Prati , A. Zucchiatti , F. Lucarelli , P.A. Mandò, Atm. Env. **34** (2000), 3149

[3] P. Formenti , P. Prati , A. Zucchiatti , F. Lucarelli, P.A. Mandò, Nucl. Instr. and Meth. **B113** (1996), 359.

[4] E. Filippi, P. Prati, A. Zucchiatti, F. Lucarelli, P. A. Mandò, V. Ariola, P. Corvisiero, Nucl. Instr. And Meth. **B150** (1999), 370.

[5] J. D.Lindberg, R. E.Douglass, D. M.Garvey, Appl. Opt. Vol. **38** No. **12** (1999), 2369.

[6] P. Del Carmine, F. Lucarelli, P. A. Mandò, G. Moscheni, A. Pecchioli, J. D. MacArthur, Nucl. Instr. and Meth. **B45** (1990), 341.

[7] C. Boni, A. Caridi, E. Cereda, G. Marcazzan, Nucl. Instr. and Meth. **B47** (1990), 133.

[8] F. Calastrini, P. Del Carmine, F. Lucarelli, P. A. Mandò, P. Prati , A. Zucchiatti, Nucl. Instr. and Meth. **B136** (1998), 975

[9] J.A.Maxwell, W.J.Teesdale, J.L.Campbell, Nucl. Instr. and Meth. **B95** (1995), 407.

[10] V. Ariola, L. Campajola, A. D'Alessandro, P. Del Carmine, F. Gagliardi, F. Lucarelli, P. A. Mandò, G. Marcazzan, R. Moro, S. Nava, P. Prati, G. Valli, R. Vecchi, A. Zucchiatti, Studio del particolato atmosferico nelle frazioni PM2.5 e PM10 nelle città di Firenze, Genova, Milano e Napoli, internal report, Univ. of Genoa, June 2001

[11] G. D. Thurston, J. D Spengler, Atmosph. Envir. **19** n. 1 (1985), 9.

[12] P. Del Carmine, F.Lucarelli, P. A. Mandò, M. Valerio, P. Prati, A. Zucchiatti, Nucl. Instr. and Meth. **B150** (1999), 450.

[13] F.Lucarelli, P. A. Mandò, S. Nava, P. Prati, A. Zucchiatti, Nucl. Instr. and Meth. **B161** (2000), 819.

[14] G. M. Braga Marcazzan, Nucl. Instr. and Meth. **B109** (1996), 429.

[15] S. F. Bongiovanni, P. Prati, A. Zucchiatti, F. Lucarelli, P. A. Mandò, V. Ariola, C. Bertone, Nucl. Instr. and Meth. **B161** (2000), 786.

[16] Rupprecht & Patashnick Co., Inc. 25 Corporate Circle, Albany, NY 12203, USA

Measurements of roadside air pollution and traffic simulations

Y. Tsubota[1] & H. Kawashima[2]
[1]*Keio Senior High School, Japan.*
[2]*Keio University, Japan.*

Abstract

Air pollution levels at the roadside were measured and traffic flows were analyzed in order to determine the dynamic features of air pollutants. Moreover, a traffic simulator was used to simulate observed traffic flows and to evaluate proposed strategies. It was found that temperature-inversion above the road surface due to vehicle exhaust emissions might suppress the vertical dispersion of air pollutants in the early morning. It was also found that concentrations of air pollutants at the roadside near traffic lights had periodicity corresponding to the traffic signal cycle. But the phase of nitrogen dioxide concentration was different from that of suspended particulate matter. It was found that total traffic volume depended mainly on the number of small car, but level of air pollution along the roadside seemed to depend on mainly on the number of heavy-goods vehicles. A vehicle-actuated signal-control system that enables reduction of the air pollution level at the roadside is proposed.

1 Introduction

Urban air pollution due to road traffic is a serious problem [4]. Traffic congestion in urban area due to the increasing number of vehicles is the main cause of urban air pollution. Attempts have been made to reduce traffic congestion by building more roads, but new road construction has resulted in a larger volume of traffic. Thus, new road construction can have an undesirable effect on the environment. Is there an effective means for reducing urban air pollution caused by road traffic?

Many countries have been adapted so-called Intelligent Transport Systems (ITS). The ITS are designed to improve the infrastructure of road networks, which could make safer and smoother traffic flow possible [1]. A strategy for using the ITS is vehicle-actuated signal-control, which requires real-time traffic information and real-time traffic signal control capability. However, possible environmental impacts of this microscopic strategy would not be detected by currently used networks for macroscopic monitoring of air pollution.

The objectives of this study were to reveal the dynamic features of air pollutants at the roadside and to develop a reliable method for evaluating tool for ITS-related strategies. For these purposes, we have been carrying out measurements of roadside air pollution, counting numbers of vehicles, and analyzing traffic signal patterns since 1997 in order to determine the microscopic behaviors of air pollutants in relation to traffic patterns. We have also used a traffic simulator to simulate observed traffic flows and to evaluate proposed strategies.

2 Measurements of the roadside air pollution

Measurements of air pollution at roadsides near traffic lights were carried out during winter, when concentrations of pollutants often exceed environmental standards. The weather in Kawasaki in winter is generally fair. Nocturnal radiation cooling induces temperature inversion near the ground, which suppresses the dispersion of air pollutants. Thus, in fair weather conditions, such as nitrogen oxides (NO_x) and suspended particulate matters (SPM) accumulate near the ground. Details of the measurements are shown in Table 1.

Table1. Dates and sites of measurements, items measured, and instruments used.

Date	Location	Traffic Obs.	Met. Obs.	NOx	CO2	SPM
01/26/97	Marukobashi, Kawasaki	x	x	x		
03/06/98	Hiyoshi, Yokohama	x	x	x	x	
12/01/99	Ikegami-Shincho, Kawasaki	x		x		
12/15/99	Ikegami-Shincho, Kawasaki	x	x	x	x	
10/26/00	Ikegami-Shincho, Kawasaki	x				
12/22/00	Ikegami-Shincho, Kawasaki	x	x	x	x	x
12/21/01	Ikegami-Shincho, Kawasaki	x	x	x	x	x

Weather Observation	: Vaisala MAWS
NOx Measurement	: Horiba AP NA-360
CO2 sensor	: Vaisala GMD20
SPM measurement	: Shibata L20 and LD-3, ME pDR1200

Video cameras were used to record traffic counts and traffic signal patterns. Vehicles were classified into three types: small automobiles, heavy-goods vehicle, and motorcycles. Traffic counts were aggregated by vehicle type and vehicle movement at the intersection (i.e., turning left or turning right or proceeding in a straight line). Traffic signal patterns (each duration of red, yellow and green signal rights) were analyzed in order to simulate real conditions.

As can be seen in Figure 1, the vertical temperature structure showed a maximum temperature at about 120 cm above the road surface when the weather was fair and calm.   This temperature structure was different from the usual temperature inversion due to nocturnal radiation cooling that disappeared from the ground surface after sunrise.   The temperature maximum at 120 cm above the road surface must be due to the exhaust gas emitted by vehicles.   A temperature inversion above the road surface was observed after sunrise until 9:30 a.m.   This temperature structure could affect the dispersion of air pollutants over the road.

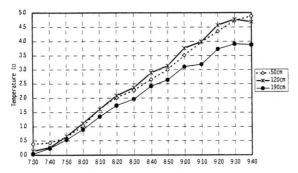

Figure 1.   Changes in temperature and temperature (January 26, 1997 in Kawasaki).

Variations in NO_x concentration showed a similar periodicity to that of traffic signal cycle, as shown Figure 2. NO_x increased just after the traffic light turned red and then decreased after the light turned green.   Local maximum and minimum NO_x levels were observed just before the traffic light changed from red and green, respectively, suggesting that appropriate signal control could reduce the NO_x concentration at the roadside.

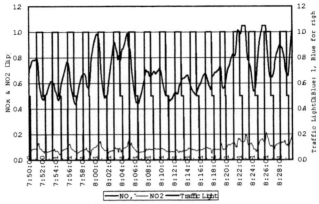

Figure 2. Measurement of NOx at the roadside near traffic lights (December 22, 2000 in Kawasaki).

Bulky and expensive equipment is needed for NO_x measurements. However, relatively small devices are needed to monitor the microscopic variation of NO_x concentration at the roadside. A carbon dioxide (CO_2) sensor is smaller and cheaper than an NO_x sensor. CO_2 emissions from engines are correlated with NO_x emissions. Both CO_2 and NO_x sensors were used, and the results were compared. As can be seen in Figure 3, variation in the concentration of CO_2 was similar to that in the concentration of NO_x. The CO_2 concentration can be used as an index of NO_x concentration. However, the periodicity of fluctuation in CO_2 was longer than that of NO_2. That might be due to the response time of the CO_2 sensor.

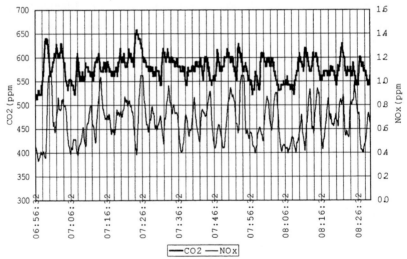

Figure 3. Comparison of CO2 and NOx variations (December 15, 1999 in Kawasaki).

The concentrations of SPM were only measured on December 22, 2000 and July 12, 2001. The periodic change in SPM concentrations was similar to that of NO_2 concentrations as shown in Figure 4, but it was out of phase. The local maximum of SPM concentration was often observed when the traffic light was red and did not coincide with the NO_x maximum. Thus, the SPM concentration might be controlled not only by the exhaust emission from vehicles but also by other factors. Other factors might be friction between the tires and the road, the vehicle's movement, and wind. Based on the measurements, traffic simulation enabled NO_x emissions from vehicles to be calculated, but variation in SPM concentration at the roadside could not be simulated. Also, the simultaneous reduction of NO_x and SPM concentrations by means of traffic signal control would be difficult.

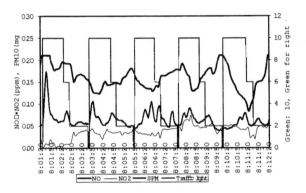

Figure 4. Measurements of SPM, NO_2 and Traffic signal pattern (July 12, 2001).

3 Computer simulations of roadside air pollution using a traffic simulation

The traffic simulator VISSIM, developed and sold by PTV in Germany, was used to simulate observed traffic flows and to evaluate the proposed signal control system. The VISSIM is a microscopic traffic simulator that enables simulation of each vehicle's movement and calculation of exhaust emission based on the vehicle's speed [3]. The VISSIM can compute any emissions from vehicles if the emission coefficients based on the vehicle's speed are provided. We used the VISSIM to analyze NO_x and SPM concentrations with respect to signal control system. The emission tables for NO_x and SPM were taken from research report by the Tokyo Metropolitan government [4]. After confirming the reliability of the simulation model, the effectiveness of several different signal control methods in reducing environmental impacts was investigated.

Since computer simulation of traffic flow is a stochastic process, ten simulations were carried out using ten different random seeds for each case. Then ten results for each case were averaged in order to compare with different case. A screen image of the VISSIM traffic simulation is shown in Figure 5.

Figure 5. A screen image of VISSIM simulation of traffic at an intersection in Kawasaki.

The simulated traffic flow was compared with observed traffic flow, as shown in Figure 6. The correlation coefficient between them was 0.974. We therefore concluded that our traffic model could reproduce observed traffic flow and could be used to evaluate proposed traffic signal control systems.

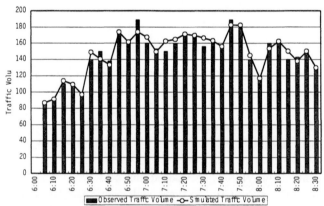

Figure 6. Simulated and observed traffic flow patterns on December 22, 2000.

4 Results and Discussion

The periodic fluctuations in NO_x and SPM concentrations observed at the roadside were reproduced by the VISSIM, as shown in Figure 7.

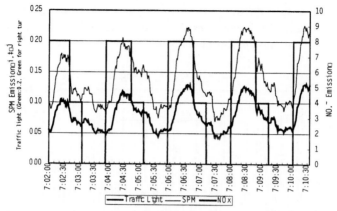

Figure 7. Simulated NO$_x$ and SPM concentrations and Traffic signal pattern.

After the reliability of the model had been confirmed, several traffic signal-control methods were applied to the observed traffic flow. The Results showed that there was an appropriate signal cycle that would minimize the NO$_x$ concentration under the observed traffic condition as shown in Figure 8. However, the best signal cycle depends on the traffic volume, whereas real signal control system uses a fixed traffic signal cycle. The fixed signal cycle observed was different from the signal cycle that had shown the minimum concentration in simulations. Therefore, we introduced vehicle-actuated signal-control to the simulations in order to minimize the environmental impact. The signal cycle was determined by the traffic volume, which was detected by a traffic counter set for each traffic lane. The results showed that the introduction of vehicle-actuated signal-control reduces NO$_x$ concentration by 5% (Figure 8).

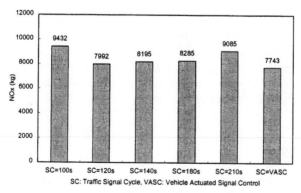

Figure 8. Reduction of the NOx concentration along the roadside.

The simulated SPM variations based on vehicle's speed were similar to the variations in NO$_x$ (Figure 7). These results disagreed with observational data, which showed a phase difference between NO$_x$ and SPM. We therefore tried to compute NO$_x$ and SPM emissions based on acceleration, deceleration and velocity [2]. The results are shown in Figure 9.

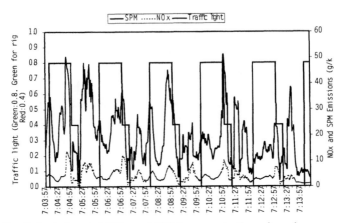

Figure 9. Calculations of NO$_x$ and SPM concentrations based on acceleration, deceleration and speed of each vehicle.

5 Conclusions

We found followings through our measurements and traffic simulations:

(1) The temperature inversion above the road surface due to vehicle exhaust emissions might suppress the vertical dispersion of air pollutants in the winter morning.

(2) The concentrations of air pollutants at the roadside near traffic lights have periodicity corresponding to that of traffic signal cycle.

(3) The CO$_2$ concentration can be used as an index of NO$_2$ concentration.

(4) Utilization of the vehicle-actuated signal-control system enables reduction of the air pollution level at the roadside.

(5) A microscopic traffic-simulator is a useful tool for evaluating ITS features.

However, a simple microscopic traffic simulator is not sufficient for estimating SPM concentration. Improvements in the traffic simulator and/or inclusion of a microscopic atmospheric model are needed for accurate estimation of SPM conditions.

Acknowledgments

Sincere thanks are extended to Mrs. Masahiro Kohda, Naohito Matsumoto, Takuya Hara, and Kazunori Watanabe for helping with data collection and simulations and to Mr. Frederick C. Lee for his help in editing the final manuscript. This research was commissioned by the National Institute for Land and Infrastructure Management.

References

[1] ITS America(1996)., *A comparison of Intelligent Transportation System Progress around the World through 1996*, ITS America: USA, 1996.

[2] Joumard, R., A. J. Hickman, J. Nemerlin and D. Hassel, *Modeling of emissions and consumption in urban areas - final report*, INRETS: France, 54p, 1992.

[3] PTV System (1998), *USER'S MANUAL VISSIM, PTV System*, PTV: Germany.

[4] Tokyo Metropolitan Government, *Environmental White Paper for Tokyo 2000 (in Japanese)*, Tokyo Metropolitan Government: Japan, 2000.

Source apportionment model for PAHs in a complex urban area

G. Vitali[1] & G. Fava[2]
[1]Dept. of Agro-Env. Science and Tech., Univ. Bologna, Italy
[2]Dept. of Materials and Env. Eng. and Physics, Univ. Ancona, Italy

Abstract

The present analysis was carried out to test a method for extracting information from outputs of incomplete experimental frameworks. The method is based on the definition of an imputation vector based on the Box Model assumptions, and is applied to the identification of sources of polycyclic aromatic hydrocarbons (PAHs). Even if the data set showed that the sampling site was set in a non favourable point with respect to the winds scenario, the method provided important information, allowing to identify the angular location of major sources. The present analysis can be suitably carried out for selecting a suitable interpretative dispersion model, as much as an optimal location for new sampling stations.

1 Introduction

Identifying the source of pollutants like Polycyclic Aromatic Hydrocarbons (PAH's) can only be achieved by means of a large amount of high quality observations and complex and expensive measuring campaigns [1,3,4]. On the other hand most of Italian towns are already monitoring atmospheric PAH's concentrations as required by the existing rules on atmospheric pollution control. Therefore the possibility of analyzing data collected at one of these measuring sites, has been considered to realize if such a data set could be useful in understanding local pollutant dynamics and particularly source apportionment.

The case of the town of Ascoli (Italy), already studied in the past [2], is emblematic: after the ruling law requirements, the local authorities equipped one sampling station with air samplers for PAH's and particulate analysis, plus standard meteorological observations. The related experimental framework assumes implicitly that source emissions are uniform over the area and does not consider the possibility of analyzing output data with more detailed models.

Even if the following method seems hardly comparable to the complex and fully recorded experimental frameworks settled ad hoc in many studies of source apportionment [6,7], it faces a problem common to environmental data analysis: when a variable known over a region of the space or over a time scale greater than that of other variables, supplementary hypotheses have to be supplied by the researcher. In the present analysis there are two kind of variables, PAH's concentration which are daily average, and meteorological information, which are hourly; both are sampled in a single site located exactly in the middle of a complex landscape (Figure 1).

Figure 1 - Ascoli map. The course of Tronto river is visible from WSW to SE, black dots point to SGL plant chimneys. Lines separates main pollution originating sectors; the vertex corresponds to the sampling site.

The aim of this study is to evaluate the possibility of identifying PAH's originating direction and possibly the sources contributing to the records, starting from the sole data sampled according to current laws.

2 Problem analysis

The area - Ascoli (figure 1) is a town of 54.000 inhabitants located in central Italy, 30 km from the sea (at NNE), surrounded by mountains (up to 400 m from valley bottom) and at the junction of three rivers, the main (Tronto) drawing both the course of the valley and the direction of recurrent breezes (in figure 2 both sea breeze from NNE and land breeze from SSW are well visible).

Figure 2 - Hourly wind directions at PAHs sampling date (105 days).

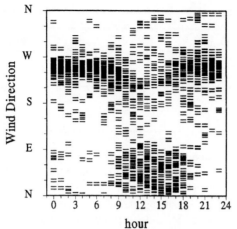

The sources – The known pollution sources for the area considered are: AS) traffic, with well known complexity due to variability of type and age of vehicles, time dependence (featured at seasonal, weekly or daily) and location of transportation flows; SGL) a carbon electrode production plant, SGL Carbon, located at less than 1 km from downtown as well as from sampling site. SGL has a main role in welfare of the area, so the sustainability of constant fossil coal processing with a healthy lifestyle forced the industry to adopt advanced abatements devices at the base of its 4 chimneys: three of these were active in the analysed period with physical heights ranging from 50 to 100 meters.

The sampling site - A sampling station has been located in a green area N-E from the historic centre (the vertex in figure 1), conveniently more for a management than for micro-meteorological logic: the choice of the sampling site is not specifically indicated by the Italian laws and regulations. The station has been equipped with a standard set of meteorological sensors (see table 1) with hourly recording of the output. PAHs, because of low concentrations, are analysed (in laboratory) on air samples collected continuously from 0 to 24, at intervals of five-to-seven days. The period of observation chosen for this analysis was 1992-1995, during which many missing data, especially during the summer season, restricted the number of samples to 105.

The 19 PAHs analysed together with particulate are listed in table 2: the list includes the 3 PAH considered by Italian laws, namely BenzoAnhtracene, BenzoFluoranthene and BenzoPyrene. Table 2 also reports some statistics, from which it is evident that only five PAH values have been significantly greater than analysis bias (of 2 ng/mc).

Table 1 – Meteorological data recorded hourly at measurement station

Channel	Meas. Units
- Global Solar Radiation	W/mq
- Air Temperature	°C
- Relative Air Humidity	%
- Precipitation	Mm
- Wind Velocity	m/s
- Wind Direction	°N cw

Moreover, a first statistical analysis has shown a significant linear relation between concentration values of all the PAHs, allowing to focus the analysis on one of them: the Pyrene (PYR) was chosen, and the coefficients (a and b) indicated in table 2 are the linear regression parameters between PYR and other PAHs concentrations. Particulate did not show any relation with any PAHs, so it has been studied separately.

Table 2 – Chemicals observed in the period 1/1/1994 - 31/12/1995
[values in ng / mc , particulate in mg/mc, ns = not significant].

Code	Chemical	Mean	StDev	a	b	R^2
DBTF	DibenzoThiophene	1.6	1.6	1.2	0.044	0.10
FT	Phenanhtrene	14.9	10.7	19.	0.36	0.14
ANT	Anthracene	0.3	0.5	0.19	0.010	0.08
2-MF	2-MethilPhenanthrene	1.2	0.9	0.66	0.043	0.31
FL	Fluoranhtene	23.2	21.2	3.4	1.8	0.94
PYR	Pyrene	12.0	11.6	-	-	-
BF	Benzo(b)Fluorene	1.6	1.6	0.96	0.057	0.13
BNTF	BenzoNaphtoThiophene	2.2	2.1	1.0	0.096	0.55
BB	Benzo(c)Phenanthrene	2.1	1.5	0.81	0.085	0.68
BA	Benzo(a)Anthracene	2.1	2.4	0.05	0.15	0.65
TFC	Triphenilene+Chrisene	11.4	15.4	5.3	0.41	0.48
BFT	Benzo(b+j+k)Fluoranthene	10.0	7.8	6.4	0.31	0.27
BEP	Benzo(e)Pyrene	4.3	3.1	2.5	0.12	0.29
BAP	Benzo(a)Pyrene	1.0	1.1	0.15	0.060	0.53
PER	Perylene	0.5	1.1	n.s.	n.s.	-
IP	Indano(1,2,3-cd) Pyrene	2.2	1.6	1.1	0.060	0.45
DBA	Dibenzo(a+h)Anthracene	0.1	0.3	-0.03	0.014	0.29
BP	Benzo(g+h+i)Perylene	1.7	1.2	0.79	0.058	0.55
COR	Coronene	0.4	0.6	n.s.	n.s.	-
POL	Particulate	41.6	105.7	n.s.	n.s.	-

3 The model

The main goal of the following analysis is to evaluate the contribution to PAHs concentration of all possible sources identified by their angular location with respect to sampling station. Even if each daily concentration is the average of instantaneous values over the receptor from 0 h to 24 h, it is possible to treat such an average as a discrete one with hourly steps, being that both the characteristic time scale of planetary boundary layer (PBL) [7], and sampling time interval of meteorological variables are hourly.

Now, as a first guess it is possible to state that the meteorological variable which mostly affects the pollutant records is wind direction, because of the selective effect over the sources: the receptor can only perceive upwind sources. It follows that each daily chemical concentration in the atmosphere is the average of source contribution weighted by wind direction.

In fact, together with wind direction, other variables play fundamental role, such as wind velocity and turbulence (as well as, at an higher approximation level, complex terrain dynamics together with radiation, air temperature and other pollutants, which affect chemical transformation) which mainly affect chemical dilution and complete the well known 'chromatographic' paradigm improved in the Box Model [8]: given a box with height H (constant) where a wind of velocity V is blowing from a direction parallel to the side of length L, in absence of chemical reactions, the average concentration C [ML^{-3}], at a downwind section is given by:

$$C = E L [H V]^{-1} \tag{1}$$

where E is a uniform emission from the ground of the box [$M L^{-2} T^{-1}$].
Assuming that wind direction is changing hourly, downwind daily average concentration has to account for different box scenarios made of hourly emission intensity E_h, box depth L_h, height of the PBL H_h and wind speed V_h, as follows:

$$C = \sum_{h=1, 24} L_h E_h [H_h V_h]^{-1} \tag{2}$$

The PBL height H has been estimated on the basis of relations with atmospheric stability. Following Stull's indications [7], under unstable conditions (stability index S < 4) H is assumed to decay linearly with S: H is hypothesised constant (Hmin) for S ≥ 4 (Pasquill's D and E class) and becomes five times greater (5 Hmin) at the highest instability. (S = 1, Pasquill A Class).

The method developed here consists in using the Box Model in an indirect manner, being emissions E unknown, obtaining an expression for a weighted average of meteorological values, in particular wind direction, yielding average value to be assigned to each chemical daily value.

The resulting expression for daily Wind Direction Dg is:

$$Dg = \frac{\left[\sum_{h=1,24} \left((Hh^* \, Vh)^{-1} \, Dh\text{-}x\right)^2 + \sum_{h=1,24} \left((Hh^* \, Vh)^{-1} \, Dh\text{-}y\right)^2\right]^{1/2}}{\left[\sum_{h=1,24} (Hh^* \, Vh)\right]} \qquad (3)$$

where the reference value of Hmin disappeared leaving the place to the ratio H*= H/Hmin, while Dh-x and Dh-y are wind direction components.

In the following analysis the results of the expression (3), indicated as **HA** (from **H**-dependent Average), has been compared to the ones based on a conventional average (**CA** ; obtaining neglecting weights) and to those from an an intermediate procedure (**RA** from **R**eference **A**verage) obtained from **HA** by neglecting the estimated effect of PBL (H*=1).

The results of such transformations are visible in Figure 3 where each concentration value is displayed in correspondence of three angles, one for each variant of the method. The figure also shows three peaks of concentration, two of them corresponding to known sources, AS (230°) and SGL (300°), the last being more evident from HA averaging method, even if with an increased spread. A distinct third peak (around 45°) could be ascribed to a formerly unconsidered effect of a quite far downstream industrial area and/or to particular atmospheric conditions: it will be referred to as ZI.

Figure 3   − Pyrene and Particulate concentrations against Wind
Directions calculated following CA, HA, RA methods.

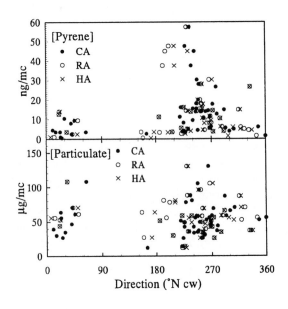

Now the second step of the method is introduced: the results of figure 3 have been used to obtain a more definite angular location of the three sources, difficult to be pursued from figure 1 only.

Table 3 - Estimate of angular domains related to detected sources: each domain is described by an average main direction θ_o and half-angle σ_θ.

Name	Source	θ_o (°N cw)	σ_θ (°N cw)
AS	Ascoli town	230	60
SGL	SGL – Carbon	300	15
ZI	Virtual source	45	50

The angular domains obtained are finally used as parameters of a set of distribution functions used to evaluate the ownership of concentration records to each source. The expression used (4) has the shape drawn in figure 4.

$$P = 1 - e^{-[(\theta - \theta o)/\sigma_\theta]^6} \tag{4}$$

Figure 4 – Ownership functions used to group together wind directions used to calculate the Imputation Vector.

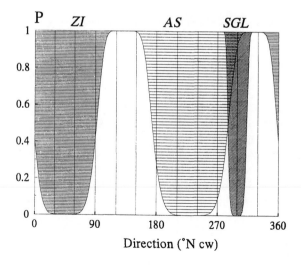

Now the set of ownership functions allows the correlation of each concentration record, which comes with a CA-averaged upcoming direction, with a set of values: the **imputation vector P,** which can be **defined** as that **collection of probabilities that a record can be ascribed to a certain source.**

The computed imputation vectors, conveniently drawn in the triangular diagram of figure 5, immediately shows a marked domain of breeze masking the effective contribution of sources: P values are all flattened around Ascoli direction.

Figure 5 Imputation Vector attributed to the individuated sources (AS,SGL,ZI).

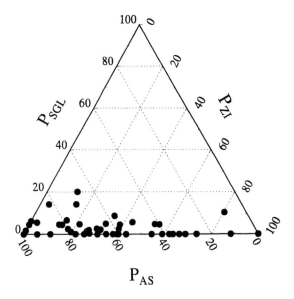

Things become more interesting when P values are reported as a function of concentration (figure 6), where it is possible to observe that, apart from SGL-related values (breeze dominance makes the plant poorly visible to the sampler), AS and ZI P-values show significant linear trends (figure 6).

However, while imputation to Ascoli increases for high Pirene concentration, the reverse occurs for ZI imputation, a behaviour which can be explained only considering more advanced transportation models.

Figure 6 – Imputation Vectors in relation to the Particulate and Pyrene air concentrations values measured. Also reported the statistical parameters of the significant linear regressions. (at right)

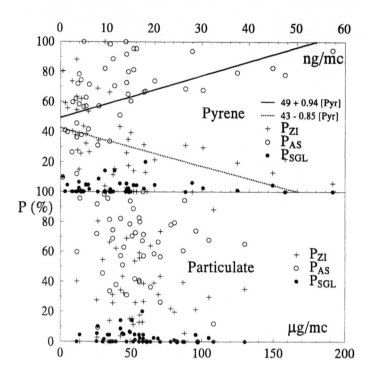

Conclusions

The proposed analytical method proved to be a valid preliminary investigation tool, showing how valid hypotheses may help in extracting hidden knowledge from observations recorded from reduced and incomplete experimental frames. However the difficulties encountered and the limits of validity of results certainly enforces the recommendation to build experiments as adherent as possible to some interpretative model or, in other words, that the experimental framework be decided after the development of some even simple behavioural hypothesis.

In the particular case, the breeze regime has masked considerably the contribution of SGL to the pollution of the area related to PAHs, making the present analysis useful to select suitable interpretative dispersion model accounting for micro-circulation, as much as for possible re-location of sampling site(s). Finally, the possibility of taking into account unstable conditions and chemical transformations, together with more accurate traffic and house heating parameterisation, is certainly hoped for.

References

[1] **Broddin.G, Cautreel W., Van Cauwenberghe K., (1980)** On the aliphatic and polycyclic aromatic hydrocarbon level in urban and background aerosols. Atm.Env 14,895-910

[2] **Corradetti et al.** Indagine sull'inquinamento atmosferico da PAHS nella zona sud-est della città di Ascoli Piceno Ascoli 1993

[3] **Cretney J.R., et al (1985)** Analysis of PAHs in air particulate matter from a lightly industrialised urban area. Envir.Sci.Technol. 19, 397-404

[4] **Daisey J.M., (1982)** Receptor Source apportionment models for two PAHs special Conference on Receptor models applied to contemporary pollution problems. APCA Ed. pp 384-357 Denvers Mass.

[5] **Fava G. et al (1992)** Ripartizione solido/gas, diffusione e trasporto di sostanze organiche semivolatili emesse da fonti stazionarie. Atti del congresso" Omaggio scientifico a Renato Turriziani Roma 23-24 Aprile 1.417-426

[6] **Gordon G. et al (1984)** Considerations for design of source apportionment studies Atm.Env. 18,1567-75

[7] **Stull R.B. (1988)** An Introduction to Boundary Layer Meteorology. Kluwer Ac.Pub. 400pp.

[8] **Zannetti P. (1990)** Air Pollution Modelling: theories, computational methods and available software. Van Nostrand Reinhold NW 440 pp.

The external costs of air pollution by motorcycles

L. Int Panis, L. De Nocker & R. Torfs
Vito, Flemish Institute for Technological Research, Belgium

Abstract

The main goal of this paper is to evaluate the consequences for air quality of modal shifts between passenger cars (incl. car-pooling), motorcycles and city buses. This evaluation is based on the calculation of environmental external costs. The analysis will be complemented with a literature review of congestion and accident related externalities of different modes to allow a meaningful comparison. The assessment of environmental impacts through air pollution is based on the ExternE methodology, which was developed within a European wide project, co-funded by the European Commission. It is based on a detailed 'impact-pathway analysis', which aims to quantify impacts on human health, crops, materials and ecosystems in 4 consecutive steps: specification of emissions, dispersion simulation, impact assessment with dose-response functions and monetary valuation.

Motorcycles are the third category of road vehicles for passenger transport for which we have calculated externalities with this methodology. This paper is the first in which our results for motorcycles are presented and discussed. Motorcycles with different cylinder capacities between 50 and 750cc are compared. Based on the results of previous studies on passenger cars and buses, we can now compare three major vehicles for passenger transport while taking differences in capacity into account. Calculations with a simplified world model provide us with a means to distinguish the different impacts that are dominant in cities, rural areas and on highways. We assess which pollutants are dominant in the assessment of external costs and which measures could be taken for the abatement of motorcycle emissions. This could result in recommendations for the drafting of Euro2 emissions standards for motorcycles by the European Commission.

1 Introduction

1.1 Scope of the research projects

The results presented in this paper were obtained from an ongoing series of research projects at Vito. These projects, funded by national and European authorities, aim to estimate the external costs of all major transport modes. Results for passenger cars and buses have been published before [1, 3] and results for Heavy Duty Vehicles (HDV, lorries) will be published shortly [4]. This paper is the first to discuss the results for motorcycles.

In contrast to some other, mainly southern European countries, Belgium's fleet of powered two-wheelers is rather small. Most motorcycles in Belgium (98% of the fleet) are equipped with a four-stroke petrol-fuelled engine. Despite the spectacular increase of the fleet in recent years (+60% between 1990 and 1997), the fleet's mileage remains almost constant. The average mileage per vehicle is less than half that of passenger cars. This reflects the fact that motorcycles are mainly used for recreational purposes and not for commuting. It is estimated that only about 1% of all passenger.kilometres in road transport can be attributed two powered two-wheelers.

1.2 Objectives of this paper

The first objective of this paper is to present our first estimates of external costs of different types of motorcycles. In this paper we will only address vehicles with 4-stroke engines larger than 50cc. Two-stroke motorcycles with an engine capacity over 50 cc are negligible and are not included in our analysis. Two-stroke engines and mopeds (<50cc) generate emissions with a very different composition and will therefore be dealt with in a forthcoming publication.

Our second and most important objective is to compare the environmental performance of motorcycles with cars and buses. We assess which emissions are dominant in the external costs and which measures could be taken for the abatement of air pollution by motorcycles. This could result in recommendations for the drafting of Euro2 emissions standards for motorcycles by the European Commission. Finally we address the question whether motorcycles are an alternative to cars and buses from an environmental perspective.

2 Methodology

2.1 The Impact Pathway Methodology

Our estimates of environmental externalities are based the ExternE-methodology. This methodology was developed over the course of a number of projects in the European Joule research program and is implemented in a common accounting framework. It uses an impact-pathway approach to trace a pollutant from its emission through its dispersion until it causes an impact. The magnitude of an impact is calculated from the concentration increase of a pollutant with exposure-response functions. The impact is then converted to a monetary value (damage) so that different impacts can be compared and summarised into a single figure. Generally there are 4 types of impacts that are considered: human health, crop loss, damage to materials and ecosystems. This 'impact pathway' methodology is illustrated in Figure 1.

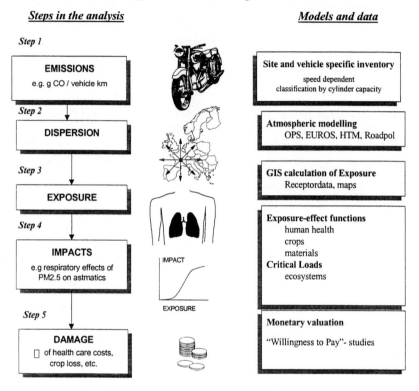

Figure 1. The impact pathway methodology.

A more detailed description of the general methodology was given by De Nocker et al. [1]. For a detailed description of the methodology, including exposure-response functions and monetary valuation of different health end-points, the reader is referred to the new ExternE report that is due to be published later this year [2].

Although a discussion of methodological details is clearly beyond the scope of this paper, it should be stressed here that the accounting framework has undergone profound improvements. New findings in the epidemiological literature have prompted the ExternE team to make alterations to the exposure-response functions for human health. In addition a new approaches to the marginal impacts of ozone and global warming impacts were adopted. These improvements have reduced some of the uncertainty and enhanced the credibility of the results. Comparability with earlier results is not an issue because we are not aware of any other externality estimates for motorcycles.

2.2 The implementation of the Impact Pathway Methodology

2.2.1 Calculation of emission factors

In the ExternE methodology emission factors are calculated with the speed dependent functions from MEET [5]. MEET distinguishes controlled and uncontrolled motorcycles, but only differentiates the uncontrolled vehicles in three classes according to cylinder capacity (<250cc, 250-750cc, >750cc).

The speeds that were used for the calculations in this paper are given in Table 1.

Table 1: Average speeds (km/h) for different vehicle types and road types under normal traffic conditions

Vehicle type	Average speed (km/h)		
	urban dense / normal	rural dense / normal	highway dense / normal
Passenger car	*15 / 22*	*25 / 51*	*25 / 110*
Public bus	*11 / 15*	*25 /45*	*25 / 80*
Motorcycle	*15 / 25*	*25 / 51*	*25 / 110*
Moped	*15 / 25*	*25 /31*	*25 / -*

It is assumed that speeds are similar for passenger cars and motorcycles in rural driving conditions and on highways, but it cannot be ignored that motorcycles have a slightly higher average speed in urban traffic.

2.2.2 Assessing spatial variation

Earlier results have shown that environmental externalities from transport are very site specific. To calculate public health impacts we must accurately take the population density into account, especially when applying the methodology to urban environments. To achieve this goal, the ExternE has developed embedded GIS-tools for the accounting framework Ecosense which allows to precisely calculate exposure for any given trajectory.

To answer policy related questions; generalised results are more useful than fully detailed modelling results. Therefore we have included data from multiple Ecosense runs to derive a simplified world model ExTC (External Transportation Costs) (Vito). This model allows the fast calculation of total and marginal external costs for typical trajectories. It is designed to combine high speed with reasonable accuracy by elimination of the need for repeated atmospherical modelling. ExTC was used to calculate externalities for three typical situations: rural (or country average), urban (Brussels) and highway.

3 Results

3.1 Environmental damage costs of uncontrolled motorcycles and cars

Traditionally motorcycles are considered to be cleaner vehicles than cars. Very often the lower fuel consumption is cited as one of their major environmental advantages. In Figure 2 we have illustrated the environmental damage costs of uncontrolled motorcycles in different driving conditions. It is clear that motorcycles do perform better from an environmental perspective when compared with uncontrolled passenger cars. The main impacts however are not caused by CO_2 or global warming (which is directly linked to fuel consumption). The adverse health effects of nitrates, particles (PM2.5) and ozone are much more important

Nitrates are formed from NOx emissions by chemical reactions in the atmosphere. Their effect is mainly regional (Europe-wide), and therefore little difference is found between the three locations shown in Figure 2. Particles on the other hand have a local effect and are found to dominate in urban locations, where population densities are highest.

Uncontrolled motorcycles have lower emissions of NOx and PM2.5 than uncontrolled (pre-catalyst) cars. This explains why the impacts are generally 20-50% lower. There is an interesting parallel between the emissions and the size of the engine. Heavy motorcycles (that were designed for higher speeds) have lower emissions in highway driving. Smaller engines (<250cc) which are often used to power scooters have lower emissions at low speeds (e.g. in urban traffic)

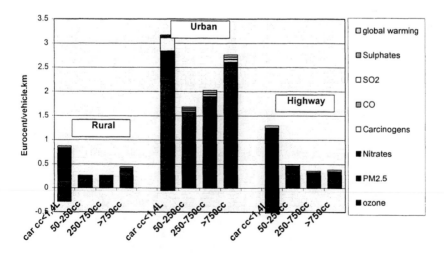

Figure 2 : Environmental external costs of uncontrolled motorcycles compared to small petrol cars in different locations

Emissions of VOC's from motorcycles are relatively high. This leads to the formation of ozone that can causes significant impacts. But for some vehicles negative values (benefits) are found because of the (local) depressing effect of high NOx emissions on O_3 formation in some countries.

3.2 Controlled motorcycles

Figure 3 shows the results for "controlled" motorcycles, compared to common passenger cars. It is clear at first glance that motorcycles have lost their environmental advantage over cars. Only in large cities they have slightly lower externalities than cars.

Although tighter emission standards for motorcycles have been set in 1999, they have not achieved a similar effect on external costs as in passenger cars [1]. Most significant reductions where those of VOC's and particles. However compliance with the emission standards did not necessitate the introduction of three-way catalytic converters as in passenger cars. As a result emissions of NOx from motorcycles have not decreased.

Taking into account the January 1st 2000 introduction of Euro 3 emission standards for cars, the low penetration of controlled motorcycles and the number of passengers per vehicle (see 3.3); we conclude that motorcycles are now environmentally outperformed by cars.

The reduction of NOx from tail-pipe emissions has proven to be the single most important technological achievement in lowering external costs in passenger cars. Despite the success of catalysts in cars, motorcycles with catalysts are rare and implementing them involves technological problems unlike those in passenger cars 10 years ago. It is therefore unlikely that EC directives will impose emissions standards that force the introduction of catalysts in the near future.

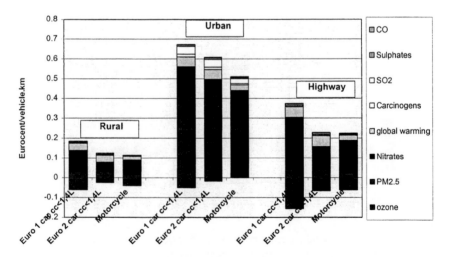

Figure 3 : Environmental external costs of controlled motorcycles compared a small petrol car in different locations

Last year, only two major manufacturers could offer a motorcycle with a catalyst and one of them withdrew its model because of disappointing sales. Given the relative importance of nitrate impacts in rural and highway driving, it is expected that motorcycles could regain their favourable environmental image with the mandatory introduction of three-way catalytic converters. At that point, the lower fuel consumption of motorcycles may again make a difference.

3.3 Environmental performance in urban peak traffic

There seems to be only one exception to the comparison of present-day vehicles made above. In urban peak traffic, when speeds are low, NOx emissions are also much lower. Combined with the large population at risk, we find that local health effects of primary particles dominate externalities (see Figure 2 & Figure 3). The reduction of particulate emissions in controlled motorcycles has been adequate to ensure that impacts per vehicle.kilometre are lower than for passenger cars (Figure 5).

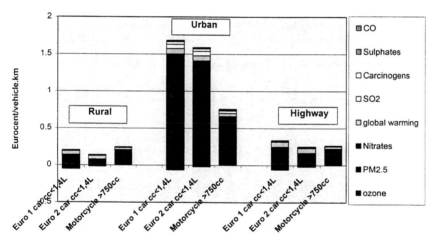

Figure 4 : Air pollution impacts from urban peak traffic

This apparent advantage of motorcycles quickly evaporates when occupancy rates are taken into account. Obviously passenger cars and public buses can carry many more passengers than a motorcycle. Although the average occupancy of cars and buses is low (1.3 and 15 passengers respectively), these could be increased significantly (e.g. in peak traffic). Policy makers may therefore consider that promoting car-pooling and public transport with buses are just as effective for reducing externalities as a modal shift to motorcycles.

3.4 Other external costs

It would be misleading to compare motorcycles with other transport modes in terms of impacts by tail-pipe emissions only. In urban peak traffic, air pollution is but one of several causes of external costs. Other possible externalities include Life Cycle Impacts (LCI) as well as impacts from noise, accidents and congestion. Despite the severe lack of useable data from literature, we have attempted to create a graph with preliminary estimates for some of these impacts. Life Cycle impacts and external costs of noise were included in Figure 5 to provide a comparison with externalities through air pollution. It shows that air pollution impacts from tailpipe emissions are usually the most important environmental costs.

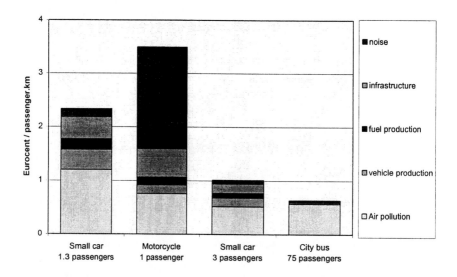

Figure 5: Summation of different types of externalities for different means of urban passenger transport (peak traffic, Eurocent/passenger.km)

External costs resulting from the production of motorcycles and their fuel are lower than for cars because of their low weight and low fuel consumption (based on ExternE data from IER, Bickel pers. comm.). An increase of the average occupancy rate of cars (car-pooling) however can achieve a similar reduction in the costs per passenger.km. For busses, air pollution costs are much larger than other externalities

We have found no applicable literature on the external costs of noise from motorcycles. European emission standards are now at the same level as for heavy lorries (80 dB). Therefore it can be expected that noise externalities will be at least 10 times higher than for cars. This means that noise may be the major impact from motorcycles in urban traffic (based on data from Mayeres & Van Dender, pers. com.).

Two other types of (non-environmental) external costs are derived from the interaction of motorcycles with other vehicles in real life traffic situations: external accident costs and external congestion costs. The external accident cost (the risk that someone else gets injured) for motorcycles appears to be much higher than for other vehicles. Recent studies shown that this cost may amounts to 0.17 Euro/km, dwarfing the externalities shown in Figure 5 (based on data from Mayeres, pers. com.). The main uncertainty however lies with external cost of congestion. None of the recent studies of externalities have addressed the specific impacts of motorcycles. For cars, these costs are by far the most important category (up to 30 times as high as all other costs combined in urban peak traffic). Unfortunately, there is no obvious relationship between the external congestion costs of cars and motorcycles.

3.5 Opportunities for motorcycles in Belgium

In contrast to data for passenger cars (see [3] for a summary), no official figures are available on yearly activity of motorcycles and mopeds in Belgium. Mileages from motorcycles as reported in MEET for Belgium (3000 km) are very different from those for Austria (7800 km) and France (6500 or 9000 km). According to European statistics, the average mileage of Belgian motorcycles has decreased by 30% since 1990. Their estimate (6200 km/y) is very close to Vito's assessments of motorcycle mileage (6390 km/y; De Vlieger, pers. com.) which are therefore believed to yield the best estimates of motorcycle mileage.

The number of new motorcycles sold in Belgium has risen sharply over the last few years. Although this growth mainly occurred in the heavier segment of the fleet, it can be expected that small scooters (some of them with 2-stroke engines) will appear in urban traffic as congestion problems worsen. On the other hand, the introduction of a separate driver's license for motorcycles and passenger cars may inhibit some drivers to make this modal shift.

4 Conclusions

-   Since the introduction of the three way catalyst for petrol cars, motorcycles have higher air pollution impacts than (small) petrol cars, because the strengthening of emission standards for motorcycles went less far. Only in cities, the higher NOx impacts from motorcycles are compensated by higher particle impacts from petrol cars.
-   However, based on emission standards, noise impacts from motorcycles could be the dominant impact in urban areas and result in higher total environmental externalities from motorcycles.
-   Motorcycles need to improve their environmental performance (air pollution and noise) to be seen as a clean alternative for petrol cars.
-   Other external costs of motorcycles such as accidents and congestion have hardly been studied and are poorly understood.

5 Acknowledgements

This paper is based on work co-financed by the Belgian Federal Office for Scientific, Technical and Cultural Affairs (OSTC) in the 'Sustainable Mobility' program and by the JOULE III program of the European Commission.

References

[1] De Nocker, L., Int Panis , L. & Torfs, R. External costs of passenger transport in Belgian cities, *Proceedings of the 5th International conference on Urban Transport and the environment for the 21th* century, ed. L.J. Sucharov, WIT press, pp. 501-510 , 1999.
(see website: http://papers.ssrn.com/paper.taf?ABSTRACT_ID=206549)
[2] European Commission, DGXII, Science, Research and Development, JOULE, *External costs of Transport. Final Report.*, 2000, In prep.
[3] Int Panis, L., De Nocker, L, De Vlieger, I. & Torfs, R. Trends and uncertainty in air pollution impacts and external costs of Belgian passenger car traffic, *Proceedings of the 9th International scientific Symposium on Transport and Air pollution*, INRETS., 2000.(in press)
[4] Int Panis , L., De Nocker, L. & Torfs, R. External costs of heavy duty vehicles for goods transport and buses, *Proceedings of the 6th International conference on Urban Transport and the environment for the 21th* century, WIT press , 2000. (in press)
[5] European Commission. MEET - Methodology for calculating transport emissions and energy consumption, Office for Official Publications of the European Communities, Luxembourg, 1999.

Influencing factors on air pollution in Ahwaz

S. A. Tabatabaie
Faculty of Engineering
Chamran University of Ahwaz, Iran

Abstract

The city of Ahwaz is one of the biggest cities in Iran, capital of Khozistan province, situated on both sides of Karoon river, with a population of one million the climate of this city, during most seasons, particularly summer, is very hot and humid reaching 50-55 degrees centigrade. According to environmental studies, the climate is very polluted, so much so that Ahwaz is among the high-risk cities.

A number of factors affect the pollution. In this study an attempt has been made to identify and to some extent, determine the range of some of these factors.

In fact, unusual development and growth of the city, undesired placement of heavy industries, such as iron and steel plants, airport, and exploration of Oil wells in a nearby city, in addition to heavy traffic and number of small polluting factories operating inside the city, have made the city like an island of heat and pollution. Fuel is the other important factor, which is to be considered.

It seems, studies on transportation phenomena suffer from lack of continuity and enough mutual understanding.

In this study some practical and scientific solutions, are suggested, in order to reduce the pollution in this city.

1 Introduction

Effects on human health and an increase in mortality levels caused by air pollution have been described extensively in international literature.

In fact, pollutant levels are very often influenced from local variables (composition and maintenance level of vehicles running in the town, driver behavior, particular weather conditions of the town) and difficult to be estimated or modeled by analytical formulas.

2 Problem dimensions

Combustion of transportation fuels releases several contaminants in to the atmosphere, including carbon monoxide, hydrocarbons, oxides of nitrogen, and lead and other particulate matter. Hydrocarbons, of which more then 200 have been detected in exhaust emissions, are the result of the in complete combustion of fuel.

Particulate are minute solid or liquid particles that are suspended in the atmosphere; They are aerosols, smoke, and dust particles. Photochemical smog is the result of complex chemical reactions of oxides of nitrogen and hydrocarbons in the presence of sunlight. [1]

3 Background of the air pollution by traffic

Atmospheric pollution is a major problem facing all nations of the world. Rapid urban and industrial growth has resulted in vast quantities of potentially harmful waste produces being released in to the atmosphere. [2]

In fact, pollutant levels are very often influenced from local variables (composition and maintenance level of vehicles running in the town, driver behavior, particular weather condition of the town) difficult to be estimated or modeled by analytical formulas. [3]

It is evident that cross roads represent critical one for car traffic, in fact there are a lot of concomitant situations that contribute in significant raising of polluting emissions, that is: condition of engine deceleration rate when car is arriving near cross roads, condition of engine bottom gear for stops originated by queues or "red" phase of traffic lights, condition of engine pick - up rate during start again phases. [4]

4 Ahwaz city

Khuzistan province (64,664) km^2 is located in the southwest part of Iran. This province contains 13 township's, 24 cites and 30 towns and 113 villages.

Ahwaz City is fifth largest city in the Iran in terms of population, populations growth of Ahwaz city and khuzistan province is very high. [5]

Year	Ahwaz	Kh – Province
1956	120000	1278000
1966	200375	1707000
1976	334399	2187118
1986	619966	2681978
2000	1000000	3242519

Ahwaz city (220 km^2 in area), owing to its characteristics was designated as the center of agricultural and industrial poles. The establishment of heavy industry, power plants, oil and gas industries and agri-industrial company of sugar can have brought back its former importance.

The maximum temperature in summer (Apr-Oct),reaches 52 degree of centigrade Industrial activities dominated the economy of the region until now. A usual practice was the installation of industrial plants close to residential areas, so neighborhood complaints were very frequent and, in several cases, there were situations of health risks.

Still there is much work to do, especially in relation to transportation related sources. Another important point is that in the city of Ahwaz there is a strong heat island effect, an increase of air temperature in the most dense urban area of about 12 degrees centigrade in relation to neighboring rural areas. The heat is land is strongly related to areas where pollution levels are higher.

Ahwaz size and layout have also created environmental problems such as traffic congestion air and noise pollution. Many government departments are located in the center of the city.

Wind direction and velocity is considered as decisive factors on pollution spreading.

5 Transportation systems and study trips

The investigation of origin-destination studies shows that nearly 28% of the total urban movement (trips) were carried by bus.

Transportation system. Bus system is regarded as the main system of the city transportation.

According to the origin-destination results, the total daily trips made are equaled to 1,800,000 trips. Table (1) show the rate of trip generation and trip attraction of different traffic areas.

Table 1: No of trips

Type of system	P.Car	Taxi	M.Bus	Bus	Motor-bic	bicycle	Walk and others	Total
No of trips	265646	324323	111380	531454	69248	56945	573385	1,800,000
Percen tags	13.75	16.78	5.76	27.5	3.58	2.95	29.64	100%

6 Air pollution in Ahwaz city

Still there is much work to do especially in relation to transportation related and others sources. Air quality management in Ahwaz started-based upon air quality standards and in emission standards for stationary sources, present day standards are shown in table (2)

Table 2: Iranian national air quality standards $(\mu g / m^3)$

Pollutant	Primary standard	Secondary standard
Carbon monoxide	20,000 (1- hour average) 10,000 (8- hours)	same as primary
Nitrogen dioxide	100 (annual mean)	100 (annual mean)
Sulfur dioxide	365 (24 hours average) 80 (annual mean)	260 (24 hours average) 40 (annual mean)
Hydro carbon	160 (3 hours max) (6-9 A.M)	Same as primary
Suspended particles	75 (annual mean 260 (24 hours max)	60 (annual mean) 150 (24 hours max)
Photochemical Dioxide	160 (1 hours max)	Same as primary

Table (3) show the inventory of emissions from mobile and industries sources in Ahwaz in 2000.

Table 3: Emissions in Ahwaz City kg/day

Source Type	CO	HC	NOX	SOX	Particles
P.Car	464877	1993	17931	8367	1593
Taxi	23625	102	912	4253	87
M.Bus	260	605	972	792	476
Bus	333	565	908	739	444
Motor. Bic	60550	259	2335	10899	225
Total	551945	3524	23058	100360	3616

Table 4: Emissions in Ahwaz City due to industries kg/year

	CO	HC	NOX	SOX	Particles
Process of production	121.8×106	—	—	—	10309124
Combustion of fuel	330451	2281987	2956854	4695633	275906

Parameter includes CO, HC, NOX, SOX and particles can be compared to the national standards of air quality in order de define control strategies.

Other factors that influence the air pollution of Ahwaz city are as follows:

1- Existence of much oil wells in the vicinity of the city.

2- Existence of two black carbon factories in addition to the pipe factory of the Iranian national oil company inside the city.

3-High temperatures in warm seasons

4-consumption of fuels such as gas oil and oil at major workshops inside the city.

5- In correct utilization of landuse that leads to increase of travel concentrations at particular regions of the city.

6- Passage of khorramshahr and Bandere - emam trains through the city

7- Location of steel industries in the vicinity of the city.

8- Severe lack of grasses and trees inside the city.

9- Oldness and wear of the main transportation vehicles in the city.

10- Low speed of the traffic flow in the city.

7 Recommendations

1- Changing land utilization, by a long-term plan.
2- Imposing a controlled traffic area, a few hours of each day over C.B.D
3- In avgurtion of light rail transit system
4- Regular technical examination of cars.
5- Reinforcement of public transportation systems.
6- Increasing traffic flow speed by imposing provisions.
7- Father studies on bicycle and pedestrian transportation.
8- Teaching driving provisions along with appropriate law imposing mechanisms.
9-
10- Increasing green areas up to the standard level.
11- Omittion of lead from gasoline.
12- Using gas-consuming engines.

8 Conclusions

The evaluation of air quality in Ahwaz area is very important and related to human and economic activities, as well as To meteorological conditions.

Data above-mentioned show that air pollution control programs were not effective.

Unfortunately there are not surveys about disease due to air pollution in Ahwaz. Still there is much work to do far this problem.

The variation of the traffic management structure, the increase of the general transportation vehicles and the study and execution of light rail transit.

References

[1] Papacostas, C.A, (university of Hawaii at Manoa), Fundamentals of transportation engineering, Prentice Hall of India private limited: New Delhi - 110001, pp 346, 1990

[2] Elson, D., Atmospheric pollution, Basil Blakwell, oxford, 1989

[3] S.Amoroso and M.Migliove, Neural networks to estimate pollutant levels in canyon roads, seventh international conference on urban transportation and the

environment for the 21st century, urban transport Vll, Wessex Institute of Technology, UK. pp.381 - 389,2000

[4] F.patana, G.Siracusa and A. Gagliano, Air pollution drops by technique of urbon traffic integrated control system in Catania City (Italy). Seventh inter national conference on urban transportation and the environment for the 21st century, urban transport Vll, Wessex Institute of technology, UK. Pp.389 - 397,2000

[5] Population and housing censuses selected year s plan and budgct organization,Iran. 1998

Section 8:
Environmental noise

The air and noise pollution in several Andalusian metropolitan areas

J. de Oña López, F. Delgado Ramos, F. Osorio Robles
Department of Civil Engineering, University of Granada, Spain

Abstract

As the century has been advancing, the Andalusian cities have been changing from a model of compact city, characteristic of the Mediterranean cities, toward a model of diffuse city that is more characteristic of the Anglo-Saxon pattern. A diffuse city is characterised by the population and employment decentralisation and it drives to the expansion of the urban peripheries, giving origin to the metropolitan areas. In the compact cities the majority of the displacements could be carried out on foot or in public transportation, while in the new metropolitan areas, where the conventional public transportation services don't adapt to the new necessities, a massive use of the private vehicle takes place, causing a high energy consumption, and an important atmospheric and acoustic contamination. In the case of the Metropolitan Area of Granada (AMG) these problems are increased by the importance that the old centre has in the operation of the city. In the present communication the environmental problems that the AMG faces are analysed, as well as the projects that are being carried out to give solution to those problems. Data are also given from other Andalusian metropolitan areas of similar dimensions to that of Granada. These data allow a comparative study of the problems of each one of them to be carried out.

1 Introduction

The work presented in this article approaches an analysis of the environmental levels of atmospheric and acoustic contamination caused by the road traffic in ten Andalusian cities. These cities have been chosen following a certain number of criteria that are explained later. It is also analysed their causes and their evolution in the time.

Granada is the noisiest capital in Andalusia because of the traffic that maintains congested the urban centre almost all the time. But it is the high number of circulating motorcycles, one of the highest in Spain, the element that more decisively contributes to become Granada in the second city with more decibels of all the municipalities with more than 50000 inhabitants in Andalusia [1]. The Concepción's Line only overcomes it. Indeed, in Granada there are near 43000 motorcycles, which represents almost the 30% of all the vehicles registered in the capital [2].

Although Granada is, during the day and during the night, the noisiest city between the eight Andalusian capitals, the difference with the others is minimum. The eight capitals of the Andalusian community move in a band that oscillates during the day between 66 and 69 decibels and between 58 and 62 decibels at night [1].

The level of environmental noise is produced mainly by escapes of motor vehicles in the roads of slow circulation. As significant fact, it is enough to point out that the average speed of the Granada's urban buses is 13 km/h [3]. And the acoustic emissions in downtown overcome to almost all hours the 70 dB that is the maximum allowed by the municipal ordinance [1].

2 Metropolitan areas' description

The metropolitan areas selected in Andalusia have been the eight county capitals together with the urban population centres of Jerez and Algeciras, these are metropolitan areas whose population overcomes 100.000 inhabitants. There are other Andalusian cities that overcome this population but they have been excluded from the study for not having data so representative.

In the following table the ten finally elected cities are shown with their corresponding population and their vehicles' park in 1998 [2]. It is included: *"all the vehicles, with motor, excepts special vehicles that theoretically circulate"*.

Table 1: Population and vehicles' park at the studied cities.

City	Population	Vehicles
Algeciras	101.972	40.636
Almería	168.025	64.723
Cádiz	143.129	41.560
Córdoba	309.961	108.718
Granada	241.471	104.397
Huelva	139.991	53.465
Jaén	107.184	38.582
Jerez	181.602	68.320
Málaga	528.079	208.067
Sevilla	701.927	274.394

Source: INE [2].

3 Atmospheric contamination

3.1 Andalusian Contamination Vigilance and Control Net

The Andalusian Atmospheric Contamination Vigilance and Control Net is integrated by a series of fixed and mobile stations that evaluate in a continuous way the quality of the air in the main urban and industrial population centres of this Community [4].

In figure 1 it is shown the Andalusia map with the location of these stations.

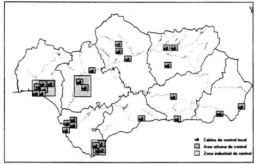

Source: Junta de Andalucía [4].

Figure 1: Location in Andalusia of the stations object of the study

Figure 2: Location of the stations in the municipality of Granada

The atmospheric pollutants evaluated in the stations are the followings ones: suspended particles (SPM) ($\mu g/m^3$), dioxide of sulphur (SO_2) ($\mu g/m^3$), dioxide of nitrogen (NO_2) ($\mu g/m^3$), monoxide of carbon (CO) ($\mu g/m^3$), ozone (O_3) ($\mu g/m^3$). The measured meteorological parameters are: air temperature, wind speed, wind direction, air relative humidity, solar radiation, rain and atmospheric pressure.

All these systems operate continuously and uninterruptedly (24 hours a day, 7 days a week). They offer an integrated concentration value every 30 minutes. The information is transmitted to the control centre.

3.2 Atmospheric contamination in Andalusia [5]

a) Particles: The activities that emit the biggest quantity of particles are: those from extractive type, in particular the metallic minerals processing (35,4%), the lime and plaster production (30,2%), the extraction and transformation of quarries' products (15,6%), the clay and ceramic factories (9,1%), the coal mining (2,8%) and the cement production (2,7%), following in importance the road traffic sources (1,5%). In Andalusia it also exists great quantity of particles in suspension of natural origin, coming in great measure from the north of África.

During 1998, the Andalusian Atmospheric Contamination Vigilance and Control Net has not detected any particles levels above the limits settled down by the legislation.

b) Dioxide of sulphur: The emissions of dioxide of sulphur are originated mainly by the industry, and especially by the energy and chemistry industry. The road traffic sources, on the other hand, contribute 10,8% of the total emissions of dioxide of sulphur in the region.

In 1998, the values of dioxide of sulphur have overcome the values guides settled down in the legislation at the industrial environments of Huelva and Algeciras, causing nuisances in the citizens and the action of the corresponding administrations.

c) Monoxide of carbon: The urban and road transports are responsible of the almost entirety of the emissions of CO in our region. They produce the 96,8% of the total in the region. The industry contributes the rest. Between them, the chemistry highlight with 1,5% of the emissions of this gas, the energetic sector with 0,7%, or the alimentary one with 0,5%.

The overcomes that have taken place in 1998 have been in Granada and in Seville, in stations located in commercial environments, and in the days previous to the festivity of Christmas. The reasons were the big traffic jams with the rising associate monoxide.

d) Nitrogen oxides: The road traffic sources are responsible of the 74,4% of the total emissions of nitrogen oxides in the region. After these ones, the energy industry appears (14,2%), the cement production (5,8%), and the chemical industry (3,6%)

The established limits has not been overcome during 1998 for these oxides.

e) Ozone: This pollutant (typically urban) represents nowadays one of the main problems of contamination in our cities.

The ozone levels have been overcome fundamentally during summer time, in urban environments with abundant traffic and in the petrochemical complex surroundings. During 1998, in Almería, Cádiz, Córdoba, Huelva and Sevilla overcomes of the value 180 g/m^3 in one hour have taken place.

Table 2: Air quality classification in the ten metropolitan areas

City	Station	Particles	SO$_2$	NO$_2$	Ozone	CO
Almería	Mediterráneo	43	7	39	-	-
	Pza.Concordia	43	5	38	52	1
Cádiz	Avd.Marconi	38	13	23	79	1
	Cádiz	49	14	27	82	1
Algeciras	Algeciras	48	28	47	-	1
Jerez	Jerez	58	28	50	52	2
Córdoba	Gran Vía Parque	65	7	38	47	2
	Puerta Colodro	63	11	53	32	2
Granada	Avd.Cádiz	50	24	90	-	3
	Con.Ronda(AG)	47	17	60	-	1
	Constitución(PF)	37	19	70	39	2
Jaen	Avd.Madrid	57	9	44	51	1
	Hospital Ciudad Jaen	35	9	37	51	1
Málaga	C/Hilera	43	13	44	44	3
	Paseo de Martiricos	46	9	42	59	1
Huelva	Barriada La Orden	33	13	28	71	-
	El estadio	21	16	33	-	2
	Los rosales	62	23	41	-	2
	Manuel Lois	36	12	17	70	-
	Marismas del Titán	68	13	22	-	2
Sevilla	Enramadilla	52	16	64	-	2
	Los Príncipes	47	10	41	-	1
	Macarena	38	7	43	-	1
	Ranilla	56	13	55	33	2
	Reina Mercedes	36	3	36	-	1
	Torneo	33	13	50	31	1

Source: Own elaboration

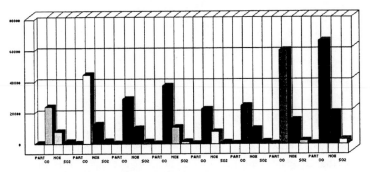

Almería   Cádiz   Córdoba   Granada   Huelva   Jaén   Málaga   Sevilla
Source: Junta de Andalucía [4]. Units: Tm/year.

Figure 3: Pollutants caused by road traffic.

The previous graph corresponds to the data of pollutants dues to road traffic sources, expressed in Tm/year. It is necessary to highlight the significant value of emissions in Granada, keeping in mind that the contributed data are absolute.

3.3 Atmospheric contamination in Granada

The monthly average values of the different pollutants obtained in the Granada Avenida de la Constitución station are presented in the next table [6].

Table 3: Atmospheric contamination in Granada (Avda. Constitución Station)

	Jan	Feb	Mar	Apr	May	Jun	Jul	Aug	Sep	Oct	Nov	Dec
CO	1,9	2	1,4	1,1	1,5	1,3	1,3	1,3	1,5	2,3	2	3
NO_2	73,2	80,5	79,7	63,3	60,9	62,8	66,9	56	62,1	79,7	66,4	87
Ozone	26,8	33,8	42,7	48,4	48	49,4	58,3	57,1	37	23,9	19,8	18
Particles	62,9	53,6	56,2	23,4	24,5	28,5	31,3	34,2	31,7	29,5	29,3	43,4
SO_2	25,1	21,4	26	14,5	11	11,4	12,6	13,8	12,9	17,2	20,6	37,6

Note: Monthly average values in 1998.
Source: Own elaboration.

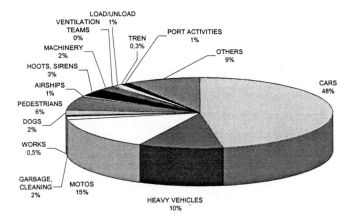

Source: Junta de Andalucía [1]

Figure 4: Origin of the urban acoustic contamination in Granada

4 Acoustic contamination

The noise levels have grown during the last decades and only in Spain it is calculated that at least 9 million people support average levels of 65 decibels, being the second country in the world, behind Japan, with a higher index of exposed population at high levels of acoustic contamination.

As it can be observed in figure 4, the high measured noise levels have as main origin the road traffic with a contribution of almost 80% to the problem of acoustic contamination.

The European legislation marks 65 db during the day and 55 db during the night as an acceptable limit, since the auditory capacity gets damaged between 75 and 125 db and it passes at a painful level when 125 db is overcome. The pain threshold comes to 140 db.

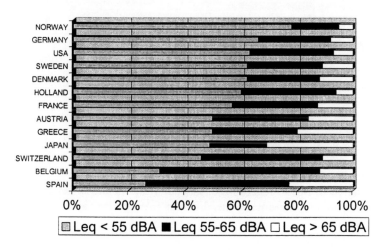

Source: Junta de Andalucía [1]

Figure 5: Population exposed to the noise in different OECD countries.

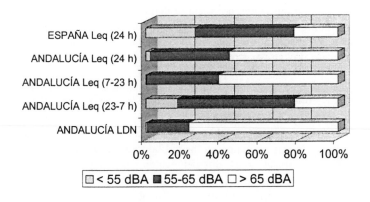

Source: Junta de Andalucía [1]

Figure 6: Population exposed to the noise in Spain and Andalusia

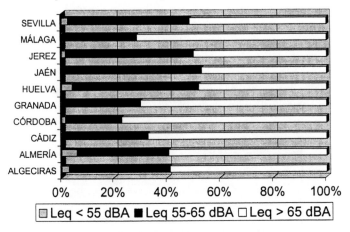

Source: Junta de Andalucía [1]

Figure 7: Population exposed to the noise in the different cities of the study

Previously there are a series of graphs that illustrate the situation of the contamination in Spain, regarding other countries; Andalusia regarding Spain; and a comparative one among the different metropolitan areas object of the present study.

5 Solutions to these problems

In the last years the City Council of Granada has been developing, in collaboration with others administrations, diverse projects in order to give a solution to these problems.

Some of these projects are: a project of demand management called "De 3 en 3", for promoting the car sharing; the "Plan Director de Bicicletas", to foment the use of this transportation mode in the city; and "El Día sin coches", during which the main downtown streets are reserved for the pedestrians, prohibiting the car use.

The population understanding of the contamination and noise problem caused by the road traffic becomes notorious when we can observe the increase of the public transportation use in the last years.

However, this increase has taken place basically inside the municipality of Granada. While in this municipality the public transportation represents 27,66% of the motorised displacements, this percentage lows in 10 points (17,48%) for the outlying displacements with origin or destination in Granada, and other 10 points (until 5,67%) for the displacements among outlying municipalities.

In the following graph it is appreciated how Granada is one of the few Andalusian cities that has achieved in the considered period to reduce their acoustic contamination, although it continues being the one that presents the biggest levels.

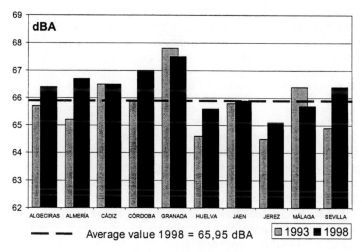

Source: Junta de Andalucía [1]

Figure 8: Evolution of the acoustic contamination from 1993 to 1998.

Table 4: Savings in Km. and travellers caused by the increment in the use of public transport, during the period 1992/1998

	Travellers	**Travellers increase regarding 92/93**	**Travellers saved in private vehicle**	**Km saved in private vehicle**
1992/93	23.269.301			
1993/94	23.415.711	148.441	123.675	618.375
1994/95	24.060.073	790.772	658.976	3.294.883
1995/96	24.244.671	975.370	812.808	4.064.042
1996/97	25.613.145	2.343.844	1.953.203	9.766.017
1997/98	27.059.452	3.790.151	3.158.459	15.792.296
Total		8.048.547	6.707.121	33.535.613

Source: Own elaboration.

To foment the use of the public transportation among the residents in the peripheral municipalities of the Metropolitan Area of Granada, in next dates, it is going to enter into operation a Demand Responsive Transport Service, using shared taxis as vehicles.

It has been carried out a study to evaluate the operation of this system applying a new methodology that has been designed keeping in mind the characteristics of this kind of services [7]. This methodology allows to quantify improvements of mobility and accessibility, modal changes, economic benefits for the users and environmental benefits for the society.

The results of the application of this methodology in Granada show that, although users from the car are captured, environmental improvements don't take place due basically to the bus users that start using the shared taxis. This causes that the environmental improvements taken place by the reduction on car usage are counteracted by the increasing taxi usage.

6 Conclusions

The atmospheric and noise problems that face all the Andalusian metropolitan areas dues to the road traffic have been patent, and especially in Granada. This is causing a widespread worsening of the residents' quality of life.

The involved administrations and the population are aware of these problems and they are carrying out actions to give solutions to the same ones. The atmospheric contamination and noise levels are descending in the last years. However, these levels go on staying above the average in Spain.

It is necessary and urgent that more measures are adopted to reduce the road traffic in all the Andalusian metropolitan areas. The use of public transportation should be incentivated, the use of private vehicles should be restricted and it is very important to involve the population in all these actions [8].

References

[1] Junta de Andalucía, *Análisis de los niveles de ruido ambiental y su evolución durante el periodo 1992-1998 en las ciudades de más de 50000 habitantes de la Comunidad Autónoma de Andalucía, Expediente 20/97/C/00*, 1998.

[2] INE, *Censos de población y estadísticas de transportes,* 1998.

[3] Junta de Andalucía, *Estudio de Transportes de la Aglomeración Urbana de Granada*, 1998.

[4] Junta de Andalucía, *SINAMBA*, 1998.

[5] Junta de Andalucía, *Informe 1998: Medio Ambiente en Andalucía*, 1998.

[6] Junta de Andalucía, *Red de vigilancia y control de la contaminación atmosférica en Granada. Informes mensuales Enero-Diciembre 1998*, 1998.

[7] Oña, J. *Metodología para la evaluación de un sistema de transporte optimizado a la demanda. Aplicación en el Área Metropolitana de Granada*, Tesis Doctoral, 2001.

[8] Taylor, D. & Tight, M., *Public attitudes and consultation in traffic calming schemes*, Transport Policy, Vol. 4, pp. 171-182, 1997

A study of highway noise pollution in Tehran

M. Vaziri
Department of Civil Engineering
Sharif University of Technology, Iran

Abstract

Urban noise pollution has been a steadily growing problem for developing countries. Urban growth is accompanied by increased highway traffic which is a major contributor to noise pollution. Control laws and management rarely accompany the noise pollution growth. The Greater Tehran Metropolitan Area, GTMA, inhabitants along major highways are being continuously exposed to severe traffic noise health hazards. The objective of this research was to evaluate and model noise pollution due to highway traffic in the GTMA. The study database consisted of relevant information about the noise level, traffic, roadway and meteorological characteristics. The collected noise level information at the roadway sound level meter receptor site included equivalent noise level. The traffic information included traffic flows, traffic speed and composition. The roadway information included number of lanes, median type, roadway functional and location types. The meteorological information included air temperature. The univariate statistical analysis of the database shed some lights on the GTMA noise pollution. The noise level measured at reception points along the GTMA highways was found often in breach of noise standards. The noise level was found significantly correlated with distance from the roadway, traffic conditions, roadway conditions and local weather characteristics. The stepwise multiple regression analysis was used to develop highway noise level descriptive models. These models proved to be simple tools for noise level prediction and management. Although the study findings are for the GTMA and problem specific, the same methodology can be applied in any urban transportation noise pollution study.

1 Introduction

Traffic noise is generated by the engine and exhaust systems of vehicles, by aerodynamic friction, and by the interaction between the vehicle and roadway. The key sources of vehicle noise are the engine, inlet, exhaust, fan, transmission, road surface, tires, brakes, body and load. Traffic noise at a specific point adjacent to roadway at any instant is the total of all the noises generated by roadway vehicles at various distances from that point. Standard procedures for measuring the noise from individual vehicles under specified conditions by sound level meter have been established in developed countries. The sound level meter is used for evaluation of sound pressure on linear or weighted scales. Its microphone picks up the air pressure waves and its meter reads the sound pressure level, directly calibrated into decibels, or using filtering curves, into weighted scale decibels. Roadway traffic noise can be directly measured by sound level meter or can be predicted by noise information of individual vehicles [1].

The equivalent sound level, L_{eq} is the most common roadway traffic noise exposure index, also recommended by the International Organization for Standardization, ISO [2]. The L_{eq} is computed according to the following equation:

$$L_{eq} = 10 \log \left(\Sigma\, f_i\, \sqrt{10^{\,(L_i/10)}} \right)^2. \tag{1}$$

Where L_i is the sound level in A-weighted decibel, dB(A), and f_i is the fraction of time that L_i is in progress. Empirical traffic noise models have long been developed, such as the following model which is more than half a century old [3], [4], [5]:

$$L_{50} = 68 + 8.5 \log V - 20 \log D. \tag{2}$$

Where L_{50} is mean noise level 50 percentile, exceeded 50 percent of time, measured in dB(A), V is traffic volume in vehicle per hour and D is distance from a traffic line to the observer in feet.

Individuals residing and/or working along traffic arteries are most severely affected by the negative health and welfare impacts of noise pollution. Indeed, traffic noise gives rise to psychological and physiological problems of adjacent roadway inhabitants. It also reduces adjacent roadway property and land values. Most countries have standards and regulations for both interior as well as exterior vehicle noise levels. Most countries have also established community noise standards and regulations. Noise barriers reduce road traffic noise levels and their effects to adjacent properties. Their effectiveness depends on the characteristics of barriers, the topography of the site, changes in the level of the roadway and the distance of the receptors from the noise sources [6].

As the GTMA auto travel continues to grow, noise pollution assails its inhabitants and the due cost to public health and environment escalates dramatically. The GTMA population has grown from about 0.7 million in year

1941 to more than 9 millions in year 1999. Its current population, surface area and energy consumption are 15%, 0.16% and 20% of the nation, respectively. The average population density is about 10000 persons per square kilometer with higher values in the GTMA central parts. The average trip rate is 1.5 trips per day per capita with more than 30% by personal automobile. The highway fleet consisted of more than 1.5 million vehicles with an average age of 17 years. More than 80% of total roadway vehicle fleet is consisted of automobiles when more than 80% are built in Iran [7].

The Iranian Environmental Protection Agency, IEPA, undertook the first GTMA noise level survey in 1977, and found its levels in the range of 55 to 88 dB(A). The Iranian Ministry of Housing, IMH, undertook the second GTMA noise level survey in 1983, confirming the first study results and identifying higher noise levels along urban highways. The GTMA Municipality is currently conducting the third noise level survey with results to become available in near future. The IEPA has established vehicle and community noise standards; nevertheless, they have not been effectively enforced. The objective of the research reported herein was to shed some light on the status of traffic noise pollution in the GTMA using the IMH 1983 database and limited field survey.

2 Data collection and analysis

The study relevant GTMA traffic noise level information consisted of two parts namely files A and B. The first part, file A, consisted of information extracted from the IMH 1983 databases. The file A consisted of relevant information for 288 roadway sites in the western part of GTMA. The noise level measurement had been carried out by a B&K 2203 sound level meter located at the pavement edge. The traffic noise level L_{eq} had been recorded for durations of 5, 15 and 30 minutes, respectively. The second part, file B, consisted of the field survey information gathered by a B&K 2203 sound level meter in June 1999. The limited resources confined the field survey data collection to 4 roadway sites. The selected sites were typical roadways with minimum environmental interference and were located in the western part of GTMA. The noise level measurements were taken at distances of 0, 10, 20 and 30 meters from pavement edge, respectively. The traffic noise level L_{eq} was recorded for 5 minutes duration. The study database files A and B consisted of 288 and 120 records, respectively.

The database univariate analysis shed some lights on the status of GTMA traffic noise pollution. The minimum, mean, maximum, range and standard deviation of the variables for 408 records are summarized in Table 1. The table has 16 and 8 variables from files A and B, respectively. For the nominal variables CBA, TAA, TBA, TCA, TDA and MDA, the minimum and maximum are listed as 0 and 1, respectively. The table shows similarity of files A and B regarding the means and standard deviations. The mean value of variables LAA, LBA, LCA and LQB were 74.86 dB(A) , 75.15 dB(A), 75.05 dB(A) and 76.74 dB(A) respectively. According to the Organization for Economic Cooperation and Development, OECD, noise levels above 55 dB(A) are undesirable. Urban

Table 1. Results of univariate statistical analysis.

vari able	description	file	min.	mean	max.	st. de.	dimen -sion
VHA	vehicle flow rate	A	17	2161	11988	2130	veh/hr
CRA	car flow rate	A	17	1753	10608	1059	veh/hr
CBA	central business district	A	0	0.052	1	0.226	n/a
TAA	expressway	A	0	0.115	1	0.321	n/a
TBA	arterial	A	0	0.283	1	0.452	n/a
TCA	collector	A	0	0.243	1	0.438	n/a
TDA	local street	A	0	0.358	1	0.475	n/a
LNA	number of traffic lanes	A	2	4.351	10	1.405	lane
LAA	5 minute L_{eq}	A	54.6	74.86	84.4	6.45	dB(A)
LBA	15 minute L_{eq}	A	55.7	75.15	85.5	6.29	dB(A)
LCA	30 minute L_{eq}	A	54.9	75.05	85.1	6.41	dB(A)
MOA	motorcycle flow rate	A	0	318	3481	459	veh/hr
SPA	speed	A	10	47.6	110	18.95	km/hr
TPA	temperature	A	2	19.9	34	6.77	celsius
MDA	median	A	0	0.27	1	0.44	n/a
TKA	truck flow rate	A	0	88	672	119	veh/hr
MOB	motorcycle flow rate	B	0	51	241	59	veh/hr
TKB	truck flow rate	B	0	367	1798	185	veh/hr
DSB	distance to pavement	B	0	15	30	11.25	meter
CRB	car flow rate	B	660	1545	3180	369	veh/hr
VHB	vehicle flow rate	B	960	1962	3542	456	veh/hr
LQB	5 minute L_{eq}	B	70.4	76.74	85.6	4.24	dB(A)
SPB	speed	B	65	78.96	85	5.75	km/hr
TPB	temperature	B	15	21	28	3.22	celsius

areas with noise levels above 70 dB(A) are not permitted for housing development in France. Table 1 shows that the GTMA roadway traffic is a major noise pollution generator contributing significantly to the overall levels of its environmental pollution. Although the observed traffic noise levels were in breach of noise standards, mitigation measures and noise barriers have not been utilized effectively. Table 1 confirms the severity of traffic noise pollution in the GTMA when relevant noise management schemes such as noise barrier, traffic and land use control have considerable potentials for preventing inhabitants' exposure to excessive traffic noise.

To develop an understanding of the interrelationships among the files A and B variables, pairwise correlation analyses were performed. The size of 16 by 16 and 8 by 8 correlation matrices prevented their display herein. The matrices revealed a number of interesting patterns and were found useful in modeling phase of the study. Many pairs of variables were found significantly correlated. On the average, each of the variables was correlated, at a level of significance 0.05, with 38 percent of the others in its file. The results of correlation analyses conformed to expectations. Traffic flows and speed variables of VHA, CRA, MOA,, TKA and SPA demonstrated positive associations with equivalent noise level variables of LAA, LBA and LCA. Traffic flows and speed variables of VHB, CRB, MOB, TKB and SPB demonstrated positive associations with equivalent noise level variable LQB. Distance variable DSB demonstrated negative association with equivalent noise level variable LQB.

3 Regression modeling

Stepwise regression analysis was carried out to develop noise equivalent level prediction models. For file A, variables LAA, LBA and LCA, and for file B, variable LQB were used as dependent variables. For file A, variables VHA, CRA, CBA, TAA, TBA, TCA, TDA, LNA, MOA, TKA, SPA, MDA and TPA were candidate independent variables. For file B, MOB, TKB, DSB, CRB, VHB, SPB and TPB were candidate independent variables. Many models were developed and evaluated.

Based on coefficient of determination and independent variables' description, the following five models were selected from file A:

$$LAA = 67.34 + 0.0016 \text{ VHA} + 0.08 \text{ SPA}. \tag{3}$$

$$LAA = 70.19 - 4.56 \text{ TDA} + 1.16 \text{ LNA} + 3.07 \text{ CBA} + 0.0008 \text{ VHA}. \tag{4}$$

$$LAA = 69.59 - 4.12 \text{ TDA} + 1.21 \text{ LNA} + 0.0025 \text{ MOA} + 0.0074 \text{ TKA}. \tag{5}$$

$$LBA = 69.29 - 4.16 \text{ TDA} + 0.75 \text{ LNA} + 0.04 \text{ SPA} + 0.0007 \text{VHA}. \tag{6}$$

$$LCA = 68.64 - 3.77 \text{ TDA} + 0.73 \text{ LNA} + 0.05 \text{ SPA} + 0.0007 \text{VHA}. \tag{7}$$

Where variables are defined in Table 1. Eqn (3) shows the effect of traffic flow rate and traffic speed on 5 minute L_{eq} with a coefficient of determination of 0.40. Eqn (4) shows the effect of existence of local street, number of traffic lanes, existence of central business district and traffic flow rate on 5 minute L_{eq} with a coefficient of determination of 0.43. Eqn (5) shows the effect of existence of local street, number of traffic lanes, motorcycle flow rate and truck flow rate on 5 minute L_{eq} with a coefficient of determination of 0.46. Eqn (6) shows the effect of existence of local street, number of traffic lanes, traffic speed and traffic flow rate on 10 minute L_{eq} with a coefficient of determination of 0.51. Eqn (7) shows, the effect of existence of local street, number of traffic lanes, traffic speed and traffic flow rate on 15 minute L_{eq} with a coefficient of determination of 0.52.

Based on coefficient of determination and independent variables' description, the following two models were selected from file B:

LAB = 67.11 − 0.35 DSB + 0.14 SPB + 0.022 TKB + 0.008 CRB.　　　(8)

LAB = 67.78 − 0.34 DSB + 0.12 SPB + 0.011 VHB.　　　(9)

Where variables are defined in Table 1. Eqn (8) shows the effect of distance from pavement edge, traffic speed, truck flow rate and car flow rate on 5 minute L_{eq} with a coefficient of determination of 0.88. Eqn (9) shows the effect of distance from pavement, traffic speed and traffic flow rate on 5 minute L_{eq} with a coefficient of determination of 0.89. Eqns (3) to (9) can be used in equivalent noise level prediction. Based on the study field survey reliability, variable description and coefficient of determination, eqn (9) is suggested as the best-developed model.

4 Conclusions

Roadway traffic noise pollution for the GTMA was studied. Relevant information was extracted from the IMH 1983 noise level survey databases and was also collected from a field survey. The study database consisted of 408 records with relevant information about the noise level, traffic, roadway and meteorological characteristics. The univariate statistical analysis of the database 24 variables shed some lights on the GTMA noise pollution. The equivalent noise level at reception points along the GTMA roadways was found often in breach of noise standards. The minimum, mean, maximum, range and standard deviation of the variables revealed a number of interesting patterns and were found useful in multivariate statistical analysis and modeling phases of the study. The equivalent noise level was found significantly correlated with traffic flow rates, traffic composition, traffic speed, roadway type, roadway location and distance from roadway pavement. This study is the first effort to develop prediction models for equivalent traffic noise level for the GTMA. Although the study findings are based on a rather limited database and are location specific, the same methodology can be applied in future traffic noise pollution studies.

Acknowledgements

The Research Office of Sharif University of Technology provided partial funding for this study. The author wishes to thank Mr. B. Hashemloo for extensive data extraction process.

References

[1] Watkins, L.H. Environmental impact of roads and traffic (Chapter 2). *Vehicle and Traffic Noise*, Applied Science Publishers, London, pp. 10-49, 1981.
[2] Sincero, A.P. and Sincero, G.A. Environmental engineering, a design approach (Chapter 14). *Noise Pollution and Controls*, Prentice-Hall International Inc., London, pp. 686-752, 1996.

[3] Papacostas, C.S. Fundamentals of transportation engineering (Chapter 10). *Air Quality, Noise, and Energy Impacts*, Prentice-Hall International Inc., London, pp. 343-374, 1990.

[4] Parida M. and Jain S.S. Urban noise modeling and abatement measures. *Proc. of the 2nd Asia Pacific Conference & Exhibition on Transportation and The Environment, Volume 2*, People's Communications Publishing House, Beijing, pp. 869-877, 2000.

[5] Yuan, W., Cao, W., and Zhang, Y. Test research on sound intensity of traffic noise of city roads. *Proc. of the 2nd Asia Pacific Conference & Exhibition on Transportation and the Environment, Volume 2*, People's Communications Publishing House, Beijing, pp. 883-888, 2000.

[6] Haling, D. and Cohen, H. Residential noise damage costs caused by motor vehicles. *Transportation Research Record*, No. 1559, pp. 84-93, 1996.

[7] Haj-Nasrlahi, K. and Tabatabai, A. Development of urban rail transport for Tehran, *Traffic Engineering Issues*, Vol. 7, pp. 36-42, 2000.

A microlevel method for road traffic noise prediction

J. Heltimo[1], J. Niittymäki[1] & E. Björk[2]
[1]Transportation Engineering,
Helsinki University of Technology, Finland.
[2]Department of Environmental Sciences,
University of Kuopio, Finland.

Abstract

Traffic noise is a major environmental concern and a source of an ever-increasing level of discomfort particularly in urban areas with traffic congestion. In a microscopic noise model for urban areas both the noise sources and the noise propagation have to be modeled. The main objective of our study was the integration of a very detailed traffic microsimulation model (HUTSIM) with an accurate and commonly used model of noise dispersion (Nordic Traffic Noise Computing Model). This integration enables more accurate estimations of traffic noise in changing situations in urban areas. The use of computer simulation rather than case studies or physical models should provide a greater degree of reliability and flexibility to the results achieved.

This study is a part of the DIANA-project (Development of Integrated Air Pollution Modeling Systems for Urban Planning), where the aim is to create a model that would be accurate in modeling urban air quality and its changes depending on the traffic situation. The noise study is made at HUT in cooperation with the Laboratory of Transportation Engineering and the Department of Environmental Sciences at University of Kuopio.

The microsimulation model used in this study is HUTSIM, which is developed at Helsinki University of Technology. The results are analyzed by using graphs produced by HUTSIM-analyzer. The approach of developed noise distribution model is macroscopic and the main input parameters are speed limit, traffic flow and the distribution of vehicles.

The results were calculated in the application phase. Dividing each approach and departure direction at the intersection area in smaller, ten metres, elements carries out the observation of traffic at the intersections. Each of these elements is then studied separately by using the Nordic Traffic Noise Computing Model. The main benefit of the developed method is that more accurate information is obtained of the traffic situation.

Introduction

One of the main concerns about the growth of traffic is the state of the environment, which is deteriorating especially in cities. The ever-growing traffic is a highly topical problem in both industrialized and developing countries; declining air quality decreases the quality of life in cities, and exposes people to different kinds of respiratory diseases. The knowledge of the cause and behavior of emissions helps to evaluate different control strategies in preventing and minimizing environmental strain in cities, where the main cause of pollution is traffic. In modeling emissions it is therefore important to understand the impact of vehicle movements and delays in generating accurate urban emission dispersion models. Furthermore, the opportunity of being able to correctly model emissions and the dispersion of air pollution is a means to a greater understanding of the characteristics of urban environment.

Traffic noise, in addition to other emissions, is an important environmental health problem affecting the health and well being of the people exposed. Growing pressure on road space underlies increasing public concern about the environmental impact of road traffic, particularly in terms of air quality, but also noise and visual intrusion. The amount of people being exposed to road traffic noise is increasing in addition to the growth of traffic. Especially in urban areas the noise environment is totally different than that on highways in general because of changing traffic situations. In urban areas the fluency of traffic units is the key to the noiseless and emission free environment.

The aim of the DIANA-project was to create a comprehensive modeling system that could be used in evaluating traffic volumes, emissions, atmospheric dispersion, and noise in cities. This paper deals with the integration of a very detailed traffic microsimulation model (HUTSIM) with commonly used model of noise dispersion (Nordic Traffic Noise Computing Model). This integration enables more accurate estimations of traffic noise in changing situations in urban areas, like intersections.

DIANA-study

This study was done as a part of the DIANA (Development of integrated air pollution modeling systems for urban planning) project. The different sub-models of the program are shown in Figure 1. The bolded arrows show the areas this paper concentrates on.

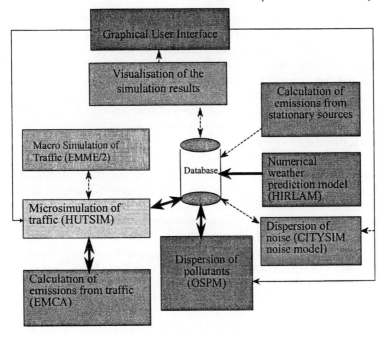

Figure 1: The sub models of DIANA

The organization behind the study was the Finnish Meteorological Institute (FMI). FMI accounted also for the expertise of air quality modeling and management while Helsinki University of Technology (HUT) was in charge of traffic simulation and planning. University of Kuopio was responsible for the noise modeling.

Traffic simulation

Road traffic simulation was introduced in the early days of computer-aided calculation of traffic demand and flows in a network system. Computer simulation has become a widely used tool in transportation engineering with a variety of applications from scientific research to planning, training and demonstration. Traffic systems are an excellent application environment for simulation-based research and planning techniques. Traffic systems are also an application area where the use of analytical tools, though very important, is limited to the level of subsystem and sub-problem. The reasons to use simulation in the field of traffic are the same as in all simulation; the problems in analytical solving of the question at hand, the need to test, evaluate and demonstrate a proposed course of action before implementation, to do research (to learn), and to train people.

Traditional traffic simulation has been macroscopic. However, the use of macroscopic simulation requires such generalizations in the traffic environment that, it can sometimes be an inflexible and inappropriate way of modeling traffic. In macroscopic simulation, for example, vehicles are treated as traffic flows, and individual vehicles are not separated from it. In microscopic simulation of traffic, on the other hand, each vehicle has its own characteristics. This brings in the real dynamics of the traffic phenomenon, and thus increases the sensitivity of the simulation. The planner and researcher can also follow the traffic phenomenon as it develops as a function of time. Visual presentation and animation of real-time (or faster) action gives the viewer a comprehensive view that helps him or her in interpreting statistical printouts depicting the traffic situation and performance.

Model integration

Integration of traffic simulation models to traditional analytic prediction models is a potential way to create new efficient tools to evaluate the harmful effects of traffic more and more accurately. The aim of this study was to find out how a traffic micro simulation model could be used with a traditional noise prediction model. Basically this meant that the micro simulation model HUTSIM [4] was used as a tool in producing the variables the analytic model needed. The analytic model used was The Nordic Road Traffic Noise Prediction Model.

The prediction models are commonly used for traffic noise evaluation. In the models both the noise emission and the noise propagation are modeled. The noise emission of road traffic is modeled mostly for example in The Nordic Road Traffic Noise Prediction Model [1] on a macrolevel as a noise emission of a line source. The model does not take into account that there may be a local increase of noise emission at road intersections courtesy of the influence of driving pattern. The modeling of noise source and propagation on a macrolevel is not very suitable for computer modeling of noise near road intersections and in cities, where the traffic flow and noise emission are not locally steady. In this paper a basis for prediction of traffic noise emission and propagation on a microlevel is described.

The macrolevel road traffic noise prediction models are based on line sources. In the microlevel method each lane is divided into point sources. In this work a ten metres part of a lane forms a point source. The noise emission of each point source is predicted and the evaluation of noise propagation is made using point source models.

The traffic noise emission in macrolevel models is predicted as a noise level for example at 10 m from the centerline of the road, caused by the traffic flow. In the microlevel method the traffic noise emission is predicted as the noise emission level of each point source. The noise emission level is defined as the equivalent A-weighted sound power level during the time interval considered. The noise emission level of each vehicle at each point is predicted by using empiric data. The vehicle noise emission level is normalized to one second. The vehicles are divided in different categories. The relationship between noise emission and speed and acceleration must be determined empirically in each vehicle category. The noise emission level of each point is the sum of the noise emission levels of all vehicles at this point during the time interval considered.

In this state of the art the dependence of the noise emission of light (<3.5 ton) and heavy (>3.5 ton) vehicles on speed is documented. In this first application model of the microlevel method the noise emission levels of light and heavy vehicles were derived from the empiric nomograms and formulas of The Nordic

Road Traffic Noise Prediction Model. The effect of acceleration on noise emission is not documented before. In this study that relationship was predicted supposing that it is alike the effect of the road gradient in the Nordic model. We hypothesized that the effect of acceleration is linear and that 0.4 m/s^2 corresponds to the road gradient 100 per thousand i.e. + 2 dB(A) for light vehicles and + 8 dB(A) for heavy vehicles. It was also found that vehicle type approval tests supported this assumption. The possible effect of deceleration on noise emission was eliminated.

Modern automatic traffic counting systems can classify cars into about 10 classes instead of two classes of the Nordic model. For developing the model it is necessary to measure noise emission of different kind of vehicles in different weather and traffic conditions. The statistical distribution of noise emission of different vehicle types must be measured. Using this database the noise emission at any traffic composition can then be more reliably predicted.

In current acoustic theory there are five main sound propagation attributes that are considered to be the most important for the design of a noise prediction model: attenuation due to geometrical divergence, attenuation due to air absorption, attenuation due to screening, attenuation due to the ground effect, and effects of reflections. The acoustic theory is quite advanced and standardized with the factors, which affect the propagation of sound from a point source outdoors [2]. The computer modeling enables the accurate modeling of the basic acoustic forms on which today's acoustic theory is based. That is why the microlevel method is suitable for evaluation of the road traffic noise propagation.

The noise emission of vehicles has a directional pattern. This may be significant for prediction of noise immission in the vicinity of road intersections. The microlevel method makes it possible to utilize also the directivity data of vehicle noise emission. In the microlevel modeling of noise propagation the noise levels in any receiving point are computed integrating the sound levels caused at that point from noise emissions of all the point sources.

The next presented new method of calculating and evaluating the traffic noise emissions enables the observation of a noise emission from single vehicle at each point of the lane. Microscopic variables of each vehicle, which are speed, acceleration and deceleration, can be interpreted from the results of simulation and then used as a part of the analytic calculation. In other words the evaluation of noise emission has jumped from macro level to microlevel, which makes new applications possible.

Case study

In this study there were two different intersections under research: a T-intersection and a three-leg-roundabout (Figure 2). In both intersections two legs were chosen to represent the main direction.

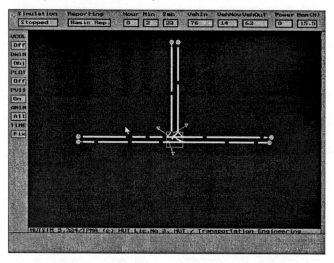

Figure 2: The simulation model of T-intersection.

The intersection models were constructed very simple, which in some cases turned out to be a little problem. However, the models corresponded well enough to the reality and enabled the production of needed microscopic variables for vehicles simulated.

Because the chosen intersection types were very different on their function it was possible to assume there to be some difference between the noise emissions. Roundabouts contains only accelerating and decelerating traffic while T-intersections also have vehicles with steady speed. However, it can be said that the noise emission of an intersection is dependent on fluency of the traffic in the intersection area. So the more there are stopped vehicles and delays the more there is accelerating and decelerating traffic, which increases the noise emission.

The idea was to find out the noise emissions of the chosen intersections in different traffic situations. Simulations were made for both intersections in six different traffic situations, where the number of vehicles per hour and speed limit varied. The speed limits when approaching intersection area were 50 km/h and 70 km/h and three different traffic situations were then modeled:

- Low demand traffic: main direction 300 veh/hour, minor 60 veh/hour.
- Day traffic: main direction 600 veh/hour, minor 120 veh/hour.
- Rush hour traffic: main direction 800 veh/hour, minor 160 veh/hour.

In simulations the road before the intersection (intersection area) was divided into smaller parts of ten metres and noise emissions were then calculated separately to each part. The total emission of the intersection in question could then be calculated by summarizing the effects of smaller parts. The critical examination intersection was extended up to 50 meter so that each leg had five point sources, which all contained two smaller elements (Figure 3). Each smaller element contains three different flows, which means different driving situations: steady speed, acceleration and deceleration.

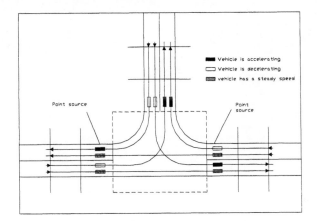

Figure 3: Dividing intersection in smaller parts and the formation of point sources.

So, each point source contains noise emissions from different flows with different behaviors. Average speed, acceleration, and the amount of heavy and light vehicles was calculated for each flow inside the element. Acceleration was calculated from the speed differences between sequential elements. With this information the effect of each point source was calculated with the new microlevel method where The Nordic Model was modified so that it notices the microscopic variables. In practice the whole calculation process was programmed in Microsoft to make whole process easier and also suitable for future research.

The duration of each simulation was 30 minutes. Both intersections had six simulations where the number of vehicles and speed limit varied. The simulated traffic flows that went trough the intersection were manipulated in several ways to correspond to the real traffic situation. First of all, the lanes (pipes) around the intersection were given a speed limit (50 or 70). Speed limits at the intersection were given based on field studies. In this way vehicles observe the geometry of the intersection and some acceleration and deceleration can be found. The vehicle objects simulated in to model also included speed distribution so that 70 % of all vehicles aimed at the speed limit and 15 % either 10 km/h lower or higher speed. The portion of heavy vehicles was 12 %.

The results of the simulations were expressed by using HUTSIM-Analyzer. Analyzer enables the presentation of results in graphic form. From the graphics it was possible to see the trajectory of each vehicle at intersection as function of time, distance or speed (Figure 4).

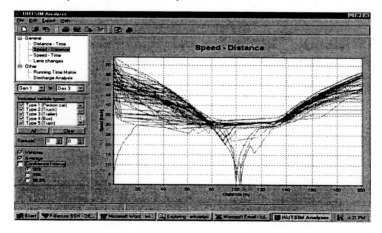

Figure 4: A distance-speed-graph from HUTSIM Analyzer.

Results of case studies

The table that was used in the calculations gave directly the equivalent A-weighed sound power level at the distance of 100 meter ($L_{aeq,100m}$) from the intersection. So, the noise level that each intersection creates in various cases was observed from that distance.

The noise emission from the intersections was first calculated with the Traditional Nordic model. In this case the simulation process was not needed, because the only input parameters were speed limit, the amount of simulated vehicles and the vehicle type distribution. Because of the macroscopic character of the model both intersections gave the same results for noise level (Figure 5).

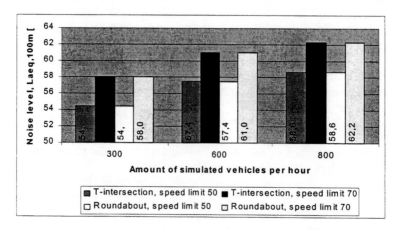

Figure 5:   Calculated noise emission from intersections in different traffic situations with the traditional method.

Next the noise emission from intersections was calculated with the new microscopic method. The microscopic input variables that model needed were collected from the graphs of HUTSIM Analyzer. This meant that the speed values were more realistic than in the traditional method where they were the same as the speed limit. Also the effect of acceleration on noise emission was now noticed separately for heavy and light vehicles in a way described earlier in this paper.

In cases where speed limit was 50 km/h the noise emission from both intersections was a little bit higher than what the traditional method gave. In cases of higher speed limit the microlevel method gave 2-3 dB(A) higher noise levels than the traditional method (Figures 5 and 6). Acoustically this means a doubling of sound power, which can be considered as a significant result.

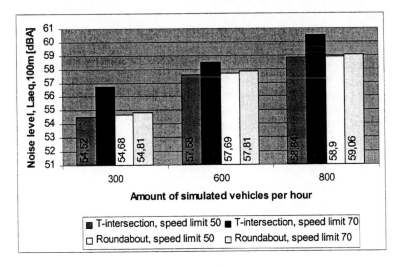

Figure 6: Calculated noise emission from intersections in different traffic situations with the microlevel method.

Conclusions

The main objective of this study was the integration of a very detailed traffic microsimulation model (HUTSIM) with an accurate and commonly used model of noise dispersion (Nordic Traffic Noise Computing Model). According to the results, this integration enables more accurate analysis of traffic noise in changing situations at urban areas, like intersections. The use of computer simulation rather than case studies or physical models should provide a greater degree of reliability and flexibility to the results achieved.

The Traditional Nordic model gives too high noise levels in inconstant traffic situations, because in real life the speed in intersection area is lower than the speed limit on the same road. Because of that the noise emission due to vehicle speed, is lower. On the other hand acceleration was supposed to greatly increase the noise emission, but obviously its effect is not as big as the effect of speed or the factor set to reflect the effect of acceleration was too small. In addition to the comparison results between the traditional and the microlevel method something can be said about the influence of intersection type on noise emission. This is actually one of the main results of this study. Because the traditional method does not make any difference between intersections the conclusions are based on the results from the developed microlevel method.

With lower speed limit, which means lower average speeds, the difference between noise emissions from T-intersection and roundabout was very small. This is interesting, because the operating principle of these two intersections is very different: all vehicles in a roundabout are either accelerating or decelerating at intersection area while a T-intersection also contains vehicles, which are having a steady speed. The reason why there is no difference between intersections with this speed might derive from our inaccurate assumption about the effect of acceleration on noise level.

In case of higher speed limit T-intersection turned out to be much noisier than roundabout. Mainly this is a result of two factors. First, the average speeds in a roundabout intersection area are lower because there are no vehicles with steady speed like at T-intersections. Speed is, however one of the main reasons affecting noise levels. Secondly, the fluency of the traffic in a roundabout was much better than at T-intersection. The amount of stopped vehicles at roundabout was almost zero in all cases while in T-intersection vehicles had to wait for suitable time gap much longer.

References

[1] Bendtsen, H., *The Nordic prediction method for road traffic noise, The Science of The Total Environment*, pp. 331-338, 1999.
[2] ISO 9613-2, *Attenuation of sound during propagation outdoors, Part 2. A general method of calculation.*
[3] Heinrich, S., *Effects of noise limits for powered vehicles on their emission in real operation,* Proceedings of the 1995 noise and vibration conference, 1995.
[4] Kosonen, I., HUTSIM - *Urban Traffic Simulation and Control Model: Principles and Applications*, 248 p., 1999

Noise pollution due to air and road traffic at Corfu's international airport (Greece)

E. Matsoukis[1] & D.G. Tsouka[2]
[1]*Transport and Traffic Engineering Study Unit, University of Patras, Greece.*
[2]*Civil Aviation Authority, Hellinikon, Greece*

Abstract

Corfu International Airport is located in the vicinity of the highly populated city of Corfu and next to the main national road of the island, which connects its northern with the southern part. Important environmental impacts, namely noise, have been observed at the surrounding area of this airport due to the airport operation and the road traffic; this especially applies for the summer periods, where both seasonal air traffic peaks and road traffic peaks are being recorded.
Regarding air transport, in year 2000 approximately 1,9 million passengers (out of which 90% referred to international flights) were served. In year 2020 this number is expected to exceed the 3,0 million passengers. Major interventions and construction works are under way in this airport and in the surrounding areas, on the basis of its Master Plan design, which was recently completed [1].
In the context of this paper, the air and road traffic noise pollution impacts on the surrounding area of the Corfu airport and on the urban complex of Corfu city up to the design-year 2020 are estimated and assessed. The assessment as far as air noise pollution is concerned is based on noise recordings [2] and relative noise calculations, as produced by the Integrated Noise Model (INM) [1,3,4], a well-known and internationally widely used model.
Special measures regarding operational procedures, road schemes and compatible land uses are proposed. The scope is to achieve a well – integrated and environmentally acceptable solution for the system: airport, airport road access, and urban areas, considered as a total.

1   Introduction

Corfu island is a traditional resort with nice weather and lots of natural beauties and beaches, that every year attract many tourists from several countries. The island presents important hotel and entertainement infrastructure, that assures a pleasant staying to the visitors. According to recent statistics, approximately 370 hotels with 36.000 beds are distributed over several sites of the island. First class hotels share a 30% of total number of beds on the island. Regarding load factors of hotels and beds, these factors reach 90%-100% values in July and August, 80% in June and in September, and 40%-60% in May and in October. Major hotel expansions are planned or under construction to further improve the hotel accommodation.

The main transport modes for the international tourism arrivals are sea- and air-modes, where the air mode shares a 80% of the total volume. This means that Corfu Airport is the main international entrance to the island. The international traffic is characterized by a clearly increasing trend.

Corfu International Airport is located at the vicinity of the densely populated city of Corfu and next to the main international road of the island. The latter connects the northern with the southern part of the island, and coincides with the periphery of the airport at a length of 1 km.

Important noise impacts have been observed at the surrounding area of this airport due to airport operation and road traffic. This especially applies for the (extended) summer period May to October, where both seasonal air and road traffic peaks have been recorded [1,7].

2   Environmental impacts

In the context of an Environmental Impact Assessment [2], an extensive environmental study was carried out at many locations in the surrounding area of Corfu Airport. This study included noise measurements during flight operations (landing, take-off, etc), as well as background noise measurements recorded in the absence of flight operations.

Also, road noise measurements were carried out in the absence of flight operations, for a comparative environmental analysis of the noise produced by airport operation and road traffic.

The above mentioned noise was recorded in time series of SPL (Sound Pressure Level), and in noise levels L_n in A-weighted figures (dB(A)), for samples of 5 minutes duration.

The airport noise was calculated in NEF levels (Noise Exposure Forecast), and this in accordance to the Greek law 1178/1981. For comparison reasons, both the noise measurements and the general assessment of the acoustic environment have been recorded in dB(A) levels.

Based on the noise recording program of the above study, more than 130 acoustic measurements were carried out at 79 various geographical locations in the airport surrounding terrain. More specifically, the following areas had been examined:

➢ Corfu airport (apron, runway ends 35 and 17), airport road access, main national road, road to Agia Eleni, Katakali, Mamali, Akti Savoura, road to Kanoni, hotel area in Kanoni.

The examination of the noise measurements (Table 1) showed that the acoustical environmental noise in the urban area around the airport is considerably high during flight operations, as compared to the background noise. In some cases, levels L(A) $_{max}$ of more than 90 dB(A) were recorded. Especially in the areas of Kanoni and Akti Savoura (which connects suburban areas of Corfu city), the disturbance was high during the use of R/W 35 for landings and R/W 17 for take-off operations.

It was also found that the noise levels due to road traffic are high in the investigated area, so that the acoustical annoyance produced by flight operations is shown as reduced. It is mentioned, that there had been estimated a yearly mean daily traffic volume of about 7.000 cars on the main national road Corfu-Lefkimi and of 3.000 cars on the airport access road.

Table 1: Available noise measurements in the area around/ in Corfu airport, in context to the airport Environmental Impact Assessment study, 1993 [2].

Region	Max noise levels during flight operations	Time duration of the air noise impact	Road traffic noise, L_{max}	Background noise
Katakali (in the western part of Chalkiopoulou lake)	56-77 dB(A)	20'' and 1'30'' by the usage of R/W35	81 dB(A)	
Mamali region (in the northwestern part of the main runway)	62-100 dB(A)	>1'50'' by the usage of R/W 35	83-89 dB(A)	50-54 dB(A)
Road to Corfu city next to R/W17.	71-98 dB(A)	36''-1,10'	81-88 dB(A)	61-63 dB(A)
Corfu city (in the northern part of R/W 17)	75-90 dB(A)	26''-34''		
Across the Corfu-Kanoni road (eastern of R/W)	68-87 dB(A)			42-54 dB(A)
Kanoni (in the eastern part of R/W 35)	86-105 dB(A)	>1'	81 dB(A)	
Akti Savoura. Pontikonisi (in the southern part of R/W)	70-108 dB(A)		71-87 dB(A)	50 dB(A)
Corfu airport (internal area)	78-106 dB(A)			
Airport road access			80-105 dB(A)	64-71 dB(A)

By application of the INM model, the LAmax noise level distribution in the surrounding area of Corfu airport, as produced by aircraft types of B757 (Figure

1), and B737-400 and B767 was recorded, during take-off operation from R/W 17. A significant correlation was found between the calculated LA_{max} noise levels and the relative measurements –the latter had been made at specific locations during corresponding flight operations.

Figure 1 shows that the LA_{max} 80 curve remains almost within the airport boundaries; there is only a restricted extension outside of these boundaries at the northern and southern parts of the airport.

3   Noise pollution in years 2000 and 2020

By further applying the Integrated Noise Model, the noise curves LA_{max} 70, 80 and 90 around Corfu Airport and within the city's urban complex were made available, for years 2000 and 2020 (Figure 2). This index has been chosen for a better examination/ correlation of the impacts produced by air and road traffic noise.

It should be noted that the number of aircraft movements in year 2000 was approximately 15.000; in year 2020 this is expected to double. The annual air traffic in 2000 was 1.9 million passengers, in 2020 these are expected to be more than 3,0 million passengers. Finally, in year 2000 we had 123 aircraft movements in the typical peak day; in year 2020 there are expected about 176 movements [1].

According to the results, it is observed that the areas included in the LA_{max} 90 noise curve are within the boundaries of the airport terrain for the year 2000. In year 2020, the situation remains the same. However, the noise curve LA_{max} 80 will be extended towards the eastern direction (Corfu city), as well as towards the southern direction (the later one falls within the sea area). Therefore, a slight airport noise increase is expected in Corfu city and measure must be taken to reduce these expected to be affected noise sensitive areas.

Finally, the LA_{max} 70 curve between years 2000 and 2020 is extended towards the northern and southern directions. The relevant areas fall within the sea. Furthermore, this curve is also slightly extended towards the eastern and western directions.

4   Conclusions

The Corfu airport is located next to a highly populated residential area, which is highly affected by road traffic and airport operations noise impacts [2]. The noise assessment was carried out in LA_{max} levels, because this index allows the quantitative comparison of the impacts produced by these different transport modes in urban areas [3,4].

According to various researches and investigators [3,4], the LA_{max} 90 level should be the limit, which cannot be exceeded outdoors in any residential area; the LA_{max} 80 level and less, are generally compatible for residential areas. For LA_{max} values among these levels, building improvements are proposed.

In the context of this paper, the correlation of the LA_{max} levels calculated by application of the INM model, to the airport actual noise levels measured at specific locations in the surrounding area [5], for relative flight operations, was shown to be significant. According to these measurements and the relative noise calculations, the noise distribution in the surrounding area was found.

Furthermore, for a decisive noise control at the affected surrounding area, it is proposed to undertake an effective noise abatement strategy. This will incorporate the following measures:

➢ Definition of flight paths, runway ends use distribution, flight operations and procedures of reduced noise impacts on noise sensitive areas, for the high air traffic season.

➢ Restrictions to the extension of any further urban and residential activities and house constructions in the zone included in the noise curve LA_{max} 80.

➢ Definition of specific activities and land uses to be developed in the area included in the LA_{max} 80 curve, which will be compatible to the seasonal character of the airport operations.

➢ Construction of noise barriers in proper sites.

References

[1] University of Patras, Transport and Traffic Eng., "Master Plan of Corfu Airport", Ministry of Transport - Hellenic Civil Aviation Authority - General Air Transportation Dept, 1998-2000.

[2] Ministry of Transport - Hellenic Civil Aviation Authority - General Air Transportation Dept, "Environmental Impact Assessment Study at Corfu Airport", 1993.

[3] D.G.Tsouka, "Contribution to the Airport Noise Prediction by the Application of Computational Models", PhD Thesis, Aristotelion University of Tessaloniki, Civil Engineering Dpt, 1996.

[4] D.G.Tsouka, "Noise Prediction at the International Airport of Thessaloniki MACEDONIA by the Application of Original and Revised INM Models", INTER-NOISE 97, Budapest, Hungary, 1997.

[5] ICAO, "Manual on Air Traffic Forecasting", Doc 8991-AT/722/2, 1985.

[6] ICAO, "Airport Planning Manual, Master Planning", Doc 9184-AN/902/1, 1987.

[7] Evangelos Matsoukis, D.G.Tsouka, "Noise Capacity at Airports of High Seasonality", International Conference "Environmental Capacity at Airports", Manchester Metropolitan University, April 2001, United Kingdom.

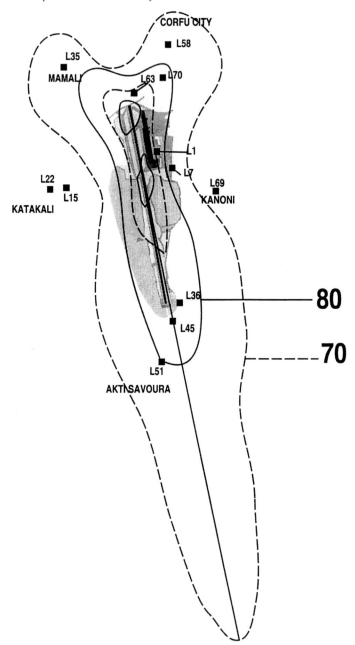

Figure 1: LAmax noise curves at Corfu airport produced by a B757 take-off
operation.

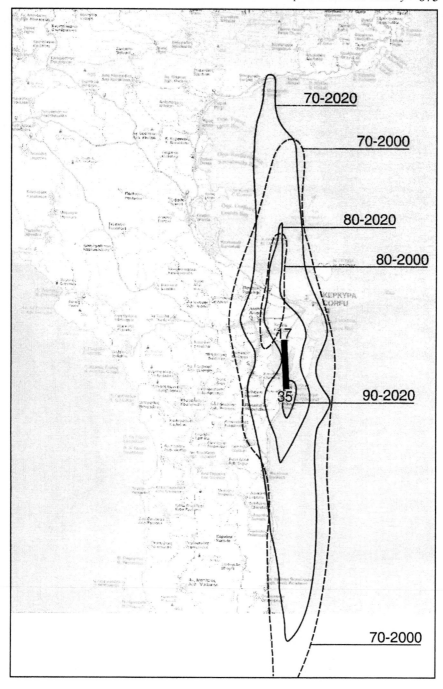

Figure 2: LAmax noise curves for 2000 and 2020 for Corfu airport.

Section 9:
Economic and social impact

An index for impact assessment of a motorway – Case study of Egnatia motorway

M. Pitsiava-Latinopoulou[1], S. Basbas[2] & E. Zacharaki[1]
[1]*Aristotle University of Thessaloniki, School of Technology*
Faculty of Civil Engineering, Laboratory of Transportation Engineering
[2]*Aristotle University of Thessaloniki, School of Technology*
Faculty of Rural & Surveying Engineering

Abstract

The construction and operation of an important transport axis of the scale of Egnatia Motorway, with the improved accessibility that provides, undoubtedly has direct and indirect impact to the spatial development of Northern Greece and more generally of the Greek territory. Aim of this paper is to present a system of indices, that have been developed in the framework of the Observatory for the Spatial Impacts of Egnatia Motorway, the use of which is an important tool for assessing the impacts from the operation of Egnatia, with the presumption of a diachronic monitoring and an effort to identify the relations between them.

Broadly, the research on which this paper is based, develops a system of indices, which concerns three topics: transport sector, socio-economic sector and environmental sector, assessing the impact on issues like the access to markets of goods and services, the location of the settlings' network and the environmental protection. For the topic of transport sector twenty-two (22) indices have been developed out of the total forty-five (45), which characterized as "Road Network Operation Indices". These indices categorized as Basic, Framework and Special Indices and a number of them (nine out of the total twenty), have been considered in depth during a pilot implementation, which took place in the framework of this research.

Therefore, the present paper will focus on the basic transportation indices and their characteristics, the main parameters that influence them and the proposed methodology for their estimation. In addition, some preliminary results of the pilot implementation are given.

1 Introduction

Transport system and the related infrastructure in general cannot be considered in isolation. As movement is a means to an end and not an end in itself, improvements in transport infrastructure results in better accessibility and more mobility. This means that there is an opportunity for land use allocation that leads to changes in land use distribution and land values, and growing demand for movement. The new pattern of land uses and the improved accessibility due to the new infrastructure have an impact on the following three entities, socioeconomic characteristics of the affected population, road operation characteristics and environmental conditions of the adjacent area, which in turn have an impact on the land use system. The above interrelationships are shown in Figure 1.

Observatories give a qualitative or quantitative description of these interrelationships, having as framework a system of indices. Through them it is possible to monitor the effects of the infrastructure and to produce a useful tool for impact assessment of new transport schemes. The objective of this paper is to present the system of indices, which describes the impact from the construction and operation of Egnatia Motorway on the entity of Road Operation.

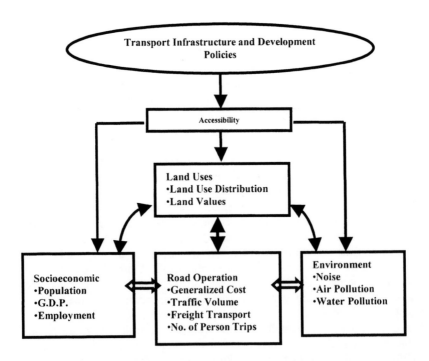

Figure 1: Interrelationships between transport investments and development policies with land uses, socioeconomic, transport and environmental parameters.

2 System of Indices

In the context of the utilization of Egnatia Motorway Observatory, a set of twenty-two indicators have been developed (Table 1), in order to describe the impacts on Road Operation (RO). These indicators correspond to different levels of significance and priority. There are three classification levels: Basic, Framework and Special Indices.

The first category -Basic Indices (B)- includes indices that refer to critical impacts and the observatory should monitor them continuously and maintain a high degree of readiness and updating. So the Basic Indices will form the backbone in the regular reports of the Observatory.

The Framework Indices (F) on the other hand refer to more general phenomena that interact with those monitored by the Basic ones. These allow the understanding and explanation of the observed trends and the observatory develops expertise for the proper use of these indicators.

The Special Indices (S), finally, concern specific categories of impacts and phenomena and their estimation whenever will be considered there is a special demand or need. For this level it is possible to elaborate specific methods or even special research work.

Table 1: Road Operation Indices and Classification Levels.

No.	Level	Index
1	Basic	Traffic Volumes (A.A.D.T.)
2	Basic	Traffic Composition
3	Basic	Number of Person Trips
4	Basic	Average Vehicle Occupancy
5	Basic	Travel Time
6	Basic	Travel Speed – Spot Speed
7	Basic	Time Distance between Cities and Terminals
8	Basic	Generalized Cost of Transport
9	Basic	Freight transport
10	Basic	Road Safety
11	Framework	Road capacity
12	Framework	Level of service (A,B,C,D,E,F)
13	Framework	Generated traffic
14	Framework	Movements in the frontier areas
15	Framework	Combined transport
16	Framework	Automobilists service areas
17	Framework	Changes of residential areas in the axis zone
18	Framework	Changes of industrial development in the axis zone
19	Framework	Changes in the land values in the axis zone
20	Special	Trip generation rates
21	Special	Changes in the choice of the place to live and place of employment (commuting)
22	Special	Shifts to modal split

2.1 Basic indices

The basic indices include the basic parameters, which describe the traffic (traffic volume and travel speed) and their derivatives (number of person trips, travel time), the freight transport, the generalized cost of transport and road safety. The interrelationships between the basic indices and their origin from primary sources are described in Figure 2.

The traffic volume expressed either as hourly volume or as annual average daily traffic (A.A.D.T.) and its analytical derivatives (traffic composition, average vehicle occupancy e.t.c.), is the output of the vehicle surveys by the roadside, after the application of appropriate coefficients, in order to take into account the influence of the various vehicle types. Traffic volume is a determining factor in creating a clear picture about the traffic conditions per road link and also in helping to restrict and tackle problems in the perceived level of road safety and to form a maintenance program of the road infrastructure.

The number of person trips is an index, which is obtained by passenger surveys and gives the demand for certain origins and destinations for passenger movements.

The indices of travel time in links, travel speed, spot speed, and time distance between cities and terminals are all based on the data of travel time and length of the links. They describe the easiness of movements between the links of the newly constructed motorway and at the same time they help to regulate speed limits based on real data in order to maintain acceptable safety levels. Here it is important to highlight two points. First, as travel time is considered the running time between two points including as well all the delays due to congestion, stops at toll stations etc, and second, as spot speed is used the 85th percentile of all the instantaneous speeds of vehicles at the observation site.

Both the traffic volume and the travel speed are determinants of the prevailing level of road safety. It seems important to mention here that in the concept of an Observatory, this index involves the diachronic collection and analysis of data for accidents in order to investigate the level of safety "before" and "after" the construction of a motorway and to define the "black spots" in the control area.

The index of freight transport identifies the effects of road provision on such kind of transport and also the trends in transit movements at national level. They also assist the tracking of dangerous goods and the scheduling of the road maintenance program and thus, various kinds of regulatory actions can be taken, like the average allowed weight of heavy goods vehicles, or even a schedule for the running of these vehicles, etc, based on real data.

Having as information travel times and the demand for movement between various sets of origins and destinations arises the parameter and thus the index of generalized cost. As generalized cost, in the framework of the Observatory, is defined the space distance between the activities, thus the opportunity to participate in certain activities of an area using the road system, in economic means. It includes the operating cost (fuel and maintenance), the value of time and the toll payment. This index forms a centrum index for assessing the impact from Egnatia's operation, which is strongly related with the concept of accessibility. Also it forms an important parameter for the choice of location in an area and decisive parameter for the promotion of the development plans.

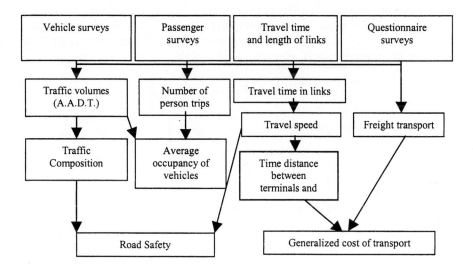

Figure 2: Sources and interrelationships with Basic Indices.

2.2 Framework indices

The framework indices, as it has been already mentioned, depend on the basic indices. In more detail, traffic volume, travel speed, generalized cost and freight transport stabilize the context of the framework indices through a set of three subcategories. The first of them gives the quality of the traffic patterns, the second includes the consequences of the accessibility changes and the third one describes the effects of the changes on freight transport. This pattern is presented descriptively in Figure 3.

The synergy between traffic volumes and travel speed gives a quantitative and qualitative description of the prevailing traffic conditions in the road links, through the road capacity and the level of service respectively. The systematic estimation of these two indices gives the limits for glide traffic and identifies needs for new or alternative routes in the road network.

The second subcategory tries to comprise and describe the direct impacts from the changes in accessibility, which is expressed by the generalized cost. These impacts are the generated traffic which is due to the new motorway as a result of the improved accessibility for some destinations and the changes in the allocation of residential and industrial land uses -even changes on land values- as result of the different levels of accessibility after the construction and operation of the new motorway.

The third subcategory of the framework indices, which is related to freight transport, gives the prospective increasing trends and the complementarities between different modes of transport. A motorway of the range of Egnatia shoulders the long distance freight transport and thus the possibility for the combination of two or more modes for a certain origin and destination rises and the pressure for related infrastructure increases. Therefore this subcategory includes the movements in the frontier areas, the combined transport and the automobilists service areas.

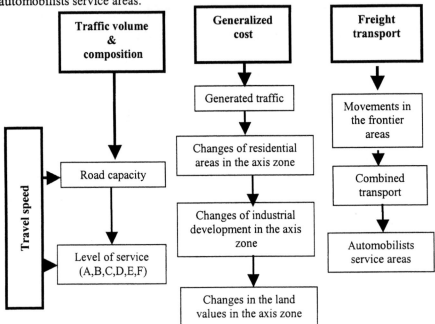

Figure 3: Basic Indices and interrelationships with Framework Indices.

2.3 Special indices

The last level of indices, which is mainly described by using models and characterized as special indices, concerns the trip generation rates, the changes in the choice of the place to live and the place to work (commuting) and the shifts to modal split. All of them are based on the concept of accessibility and thus on the generalized cost, when at the same time there exist interactions between each other. Aim of this set of indices is to visualize these interactions and interrelationships and to give the framework for such forecasts.

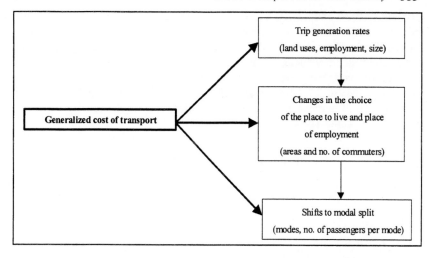

Figure 4: Basic Indices and interrelationships with Special Indices

2.4 Basic sources

As discussed previously the system of indices is based on a number of primary data and thus, sources that involves vehicle and passenger counting, measurements of travel time, completion of questionnaires. Trying to codify these various sources the potential categories are:
- Observers for field work
- New technologies and mechanical means for the data collection
- Questionnaire based surveys at the road side, Organizations, Chambers, etc
- Official records of Organizations, Chambers, Companies, etc
- Forecasting models

3 Pilot Application Indices

The pilot application includes initially an analytical description of all the above mentioned road operation indices in a common form and at a second stage a detailed estimation of nine indices selected to represent the basic and the framework levels of the system of indicators. This pilot took place along a road section of Egnatia Motorway of about 10 kilometers, within the administrative border of the Kavala prefecture and more specifically between the interchanges of Saint Andreas and Saint Sillas. In the next paragraphs a synoptic description of the proposed methodology for the calculation of the nine indices as well as the preliminary results of this application is given. Analytical information on the methodology, the data sources and the problems associated with the evaluation of the indicators is included in the Final Report of this research program.

For the traffic volumes (A.A.D.T.), the traffic composition and the number of person trips a roadside survey by a number of observers was accomplished on March 2001. The selected data of number of vehicles per category (cars and taxis, light good vehicles-LGV, heavy goods vehicle-HGV and buses) and number of passengers were analyzed and the average values of them were derived. Afterwards, the average vehicle occupancy was estimated from the combination of number of persons and vehicles. The results for these indices are presented in Table 2.

Table 2: Results for four basic indices.

	Cars and Taxis	LGV	HGV	Bus
Traffic volumes (A.A.D.T.in pcu/day)	5364			
Traffic composition (% in pcu and %in vehicles)	54 / 68	5 / 6	39 / 25	2 / 1
Number of person trips (persons/day)	4164	325	1079	1360
Average vehicle occupancy (persons/vehicle)	1,6	1,4	1,2	34

At the same time period a second survey concerning the travel time was accomplished using an experimental vehicle. From the analysis of data obtained during this survey and taking into consideration the length of the links, the average travel time and travel speed between junctions were derived (Table 3).

Table 3: Results for two basic indices.

Index	Link 1	Link 2
Travel time (min)	3,95	3,91
Travel speed (km/hr)	79	107

For the estimation of generalized cost, the following parameters were taken into consideration: the value of travel time, the operating cost (fuel and maintenance) including toll payment, with distinction for three vehicle types: car, bus, HGV. It should be pointed out here that for the value of time, the trip purpose has been taken into consideration (work and non-work trips) for the car trips only. The results from this process are presented in Table 4.

Table 4:Results for the Generalized Cost Index.

Mean	Generalized Cost (EURO/Km)	
	Link 1	Link 2
Cars (work)	1,29	1,50
Cars (non-work)	0,86	1,08
HGV	3,88	4,68
Bus	4,00	4,84

Finally combining the traffic data from the roadside surveys, the topographic characteristics of the study area and the geometric elements of the road layout, the road capacity as well as the level of Service (A,B,C,D,E,F), according the Highway Capacity Manual Methodology were estimated (Table 5).

Table 5: Results for two framework indices.

	Road Capacity (pcu/hr)	Level of Service
Link 1	2327	A
Link 2	2026	A

4 Conclusions

The basic conclusions of the present research can be summarized in the following three points:

- Observatories and the corresponding system of indices produce a framework for assessment of the direct and indirect impacts from the construction and operation of a new motorway.

- The values of Road Network Operation Indices should not considered in isolation from the values of other categories indices, i.e. socioeconomic and environmental indices. It is important to identify and describe the interfaces between them and to search for a framework able to relate them in a diachronic base.

- The results of the pilot application have not the potential to produce accurate estimates for the indices under consideration, due to the partially construction and operation of the Motorway, but they form a very useful "example" of how a system of indices can be defined and work.

References

[1]   Aristotle University of Thessaloniki – Hellinic Institute of Transport, *Feasibility study for the implementation of an Observatory for the spatial impacts of Egnatia Motorway*, Egnatia Odos S.A., Thessaloniki 1999.

[2]   Aristotle University of Thessaloniki – Hellinic Institute of Transport, *Observatory for the spatial impacts of Egnatia Motorway: A ilot application of a system of indices*, Final Deliverable, Egnatia Odos S.A., Thessaloniki 2001.

[3]   Barnett V., *Sample Survey: Principles & Methods*, Edward Arnold, UK, 1991.

[4]   Eratosthenis Ltd., *Model Development and Forecasting*, EGNATIA S.A., July 1997.

[5]   Frantzeskakis, I., Giannopoulos G., *Transport Planning and Traffic Engineering, Volume 1*, 3rd Edition, Paratiritis 1986.

[6]   Frantzeskakis, I., Pitsiava-Latinopoulou, M., Tsamboulas, D., *Traffic Management*, 1st Edition, Papasotiriou 1996.

[7]   Giannopoulos, G., *Transport Planning and Traffic Engineering*, Volume 2, 2nd Edition, Paratiritis, 1986.

[8]   O'Flaherty, C.A., *Transport Planning and Traffic Engineering*, Edward Arnold, Uk, 1997.

[9]   Ortuzar-Willumsen, *Modelling Transport*, Second Edition, Wiley, 1999.

[10]   Pitsiava-Latinopoulou, M., *Land use and transport interactions at urban areas*, PhD Dissertation, Department of Civil Engineers, Aristotle University of Thessaloniki, Thessaloniki, 1984.

[11]   SACTRA (The Standing Advisory Committee on Trunk Road Assessment) *Trunk Roads and the Generation of Traffic*, DETR, HMSO, 1994.

[12]   SACTRA (The Standing Advisory Committee on Trunk Road Assessment) *Transport and the Economy*, DETR, HMSO, 1999.

Container railcar versus container lorry transport - a comparative study

F. R. Haferkorn
Fachhochschule Dortmund / University of Applied Sciences

Abstract

The system advantages of rail transport: minimal rolling resistance, trains of any length with excellent wind shadowing, small motive performance required and energy consumed, high velocity, safety and reliability (just in time) and automated operation may all be derived from the strong connection of steel wheels to steel rails. They make railway transport economically and environmentally acceptable.

We have used our simulation tool AERORAIL and the Dortmund formulae to calculate air resistance of vehicles and trains. This tool was tested with data from simulations, measuring series in wind tunnel and literature and until now proved to be correct. Nevertheless vehicles and systems based on formula calculations have to be tested as scale prototypes and in pilot projects in real reality.

The recently developed container railcar CargoSprinter was compared to container transport on lorries using the interport line between Rotterdam and Kaliningrad as a background. Our economic calculations depend on a system of technical cost indicators: Number of trains/lorries required as a model for staff costs, motive performance installed for depreciation, and motive performance applied for operational costs. Limitations were an overall transport impulse of 1 million tkm/h and a heavy lateral storm adding continuously 80 km/h to the rolling velocity.

Railway trains, especially the streamlined version, showed much more efficiency than lorries. Of course we omitted infrastructure costs for both competitors, trains and lorries. In Germany rail customers are exempt from such costs only during pilot projects.

We think that generally infrastructure costs ought to be raised by the governments and the rail network must be opened for everybody with a suitable train fleet. By this way private and neighbouring railway companies will be able to compete and co-operate on the European rail network, supplying an effective and environmentally reasonable network for users.

Introduction

Providing sustainable mobility and reducing energy consumption and air pollution in traffic is an important challenge for our society.

Many different solutions to achieve both aims have been discussed. The solutions vary from new technologies e.g. exhaust catalysators in automobiles to political measures e.g. environmental taxes and traffic prohibitions in smog situations.

The task, 1 million tkm/h between Rotterdam and Kaliningrad

The line between Rotterdam and Kaliningrad with stops in Bremen, Harburg, Schwerin, Szczecin and Gdynia was chosen because of several reasons:
- The line is plain and not far from the North Sea and Baltic Sea, so we could take as the worst case for all competitors a heavy lateral storm adding another 80 km/h to the rolling speed and prefering vehicles with a good near-streamlined surface.
- Because containers of 40 feet length and 30 t payload had to be shipped, Rotterdam as Europe's biggest container port and Kaliningrad as the last harbour with rail connection in normal gauge seemed to be the best choice.
- Four European countries, the Netherlands, Germany, Poland and Russia, had to co-operate on shipping containers on this line.

An assumption was made about source and destination traffic and the relations between the seven stations, so that the charge between Rotterdam and Schwerin was almost the same and decreased towards Gdynia and Kaliningrad. The data in Figure 1 are calculated for a total of 1 million tkm/h.

Different time tables all producing about 1 million tkm/h

To get a basis for further calculations three different time tables were constructed as shown in Figure 2. Originally, they were supposed to allow velocities of 80, 160 and 240 km/h and payloads of 600, 1200 and 1620 t for 32 convoys of 20 lorries, 8 CargoSprinter and 4 AeroSprinter trains. This part of our study will have to be repeated to be adjusted to the assumptions made and results achieved in the meanwhile.

Nevertheless these timetables seem to be useful examples to demonstrate the strong relationship between velocity, payload and number of vehicles required. We decided to continue the study with the formula

$$n = 1e6 \text{ tkm/h} / V / mN,$$ where n is the number of trains, V is

velocity and mN is payload.

from\to	Ro	Br	Hb	Sw	Sz	Gd	Ka	Total	charge	km
Ro		57	71	57	52	62	52	351		
Br	57		24	10	5	15	5	116	**351**	417
Hb	71	24		24	20	29	20	188	**353**	115
Sw	57	10	24		5	15	5	116	**351**	123
Sz	52	5	20	5		10	1	93	**285**	253
Gd	62	15	29	15	10		10	141	**214**	353
Ka	52	5	20	5	1	10		93	**93**	226
Total	351	116	188	116	93	141	93	1098		
charge		**351**	**353**	**351**	**285**	**214**	**93**		[Containers/24 h]	
km		417	115	123	253	353	226			

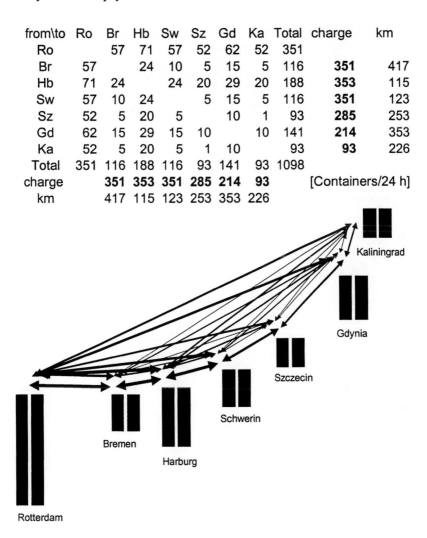

Figure 1: The task, 1 million tkm/h between Rotterdam and Kaliningrad

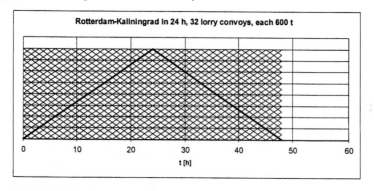

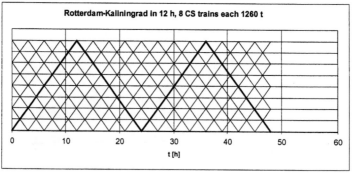

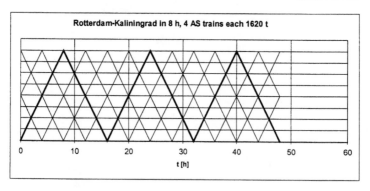

Figure 2: Different Time Tables all producing about 1 million tkm/h

Lorry, freight trains,   CargoSprinter, AeroSprinter

Figure 3 shows the five competitors: Lorry, the two different freight trains FT and FTE, CargoSprinter and AeroSprinter.

To be as fair as possible to the main competitor lorry, all competitors were loaded with 40 ft sea containers. Two 20 ft containers would be too heavy and two C782 containers would be too long for one lorry, whereas one 20 ft or one

C782 would be too light.

The CargoSprinter is a recently developed container diesel railcar which is able to carry all types of containers at a maximum velocity of 120 km/h. As compared to ordinary freight trains, it is well powered with more than 8 MW per train. So it fits well into the schedules of passenger trains.

To have a container train that suits even the schedules of express passenger trains we imagined a streamlined AeroSprinter with 25 m long understructures on 6 axles, all of the same design, all driven by two Diesel motors and allowing for 2 containers 40 ft, 4 containers 20 ft and 3 containers C782.

The freight trains have been redesigned on the basis of CargoSprinter to test the effects of weak performance, reduced payload and wide gaps respectively of empty containers to fill the gaps.

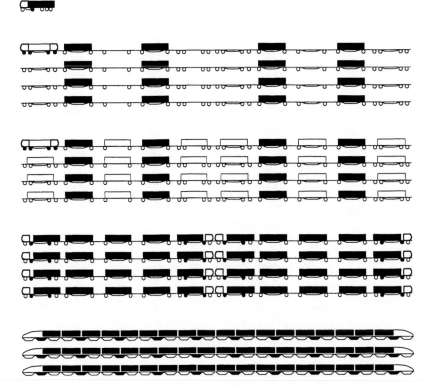

Figure 3: The Competitors Lorry, Freight Trains, CargoSprinter, AeroSprinter

The profile area of them all is about 10 m^2, the length of a lorry is 18 m whereas all trains are about 750 m long. While lorry, Cargo- and AeroSprinter are fully loaded with 1, 40 and 54 containers respectively, the freight trains are loaded with 16 containers only, FT has wide gaps whereas FTE closed the gaps with empty containers. Payload is calculated to 30 t per container, and the gaps according to 12 m per container. The gross mass of lorry is assumed to 40 t, the freight trains' to 1280 and 1300 t, and the Cargo- and AeroSprinters' to 2000 t.

Motive performances P vary strongly: 0.265 MW for lorry, 2.65 MW for the freight trains, 8.5 MW for CargoSprinter, 15.9 MW for AeroSprinter. Air and rolling resistances, maximum velocity according to performance and resistances and the cost indicator iC will be discussed in the following chapters.

Air and rolling resistances assumed for the competitors

Figure 4 shows the Rolling Resistances of radial tyres for lorry as taken out of literature [3] and of steel wheels on steel rails [1]. Besides limited payload rolling resistance is a lorry's worst handicap which will be shown in this study. Compared to a lorry the rolling resistance of trains is about one tenth and might be neglected.

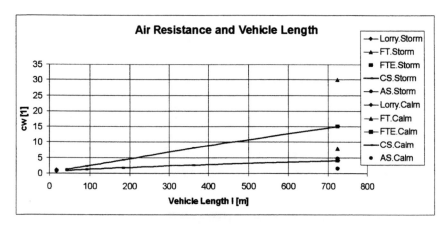

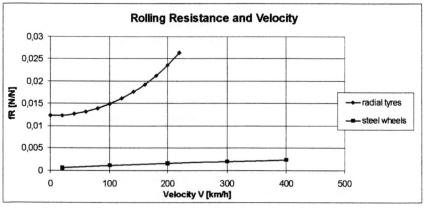

Figure 4: Air and Rolling Resistances assumed for the Competitors

Figure 4 also shows the air resistance cw for CargoSprinters of different length and both for calm air and lateral storm as calculated with our prototyping kit AeroRail [2]. The values for a well shaped lorry are taken from literature [3], and the ones for freight trains and AeroSprinter are estimations.

Performance, number of vehicles and velocity

As an input to the calculation of the Cost Indicator iC which is described in the following chapter and for a proper time table we have to find out the maximum velocity.

As the line Rotterdam to Kaliningrad is traced horizontally without any hills, the only resistances to speed and performance are rolling and air resistances. The rolling resistance force FR is calculated according to the formula

$$FR=fR*m*g,$$ where fR is the dimensionless rolling resistance of Figure 4, m is the vehicle gross mass in [kg] and g is the gravitation constant

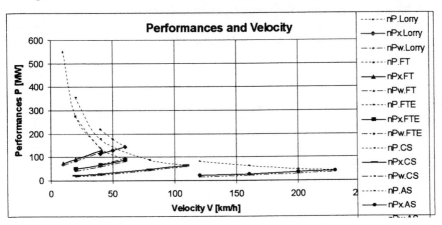

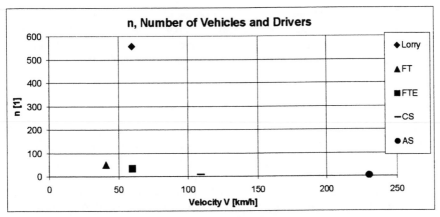

Figure 5: The technical values Performance, Number of Vehicles and Velocity

9.81 m/s^2.

The air resistance force Fw is calculated acccrding to the formula

Fw=cw*A*ρ/2*v^2 with the dimensionless air resistance cw of Figure 4, the profile area A of vehicles (about 10 m^2), the air density ρ (about 1.3) and the air velocity v in m/s. As we assume a heavy lateral storm, the driving velocity has to be increased by 80 km/h.

Both forces, FR and Fw, are added to withstand acceleration. They may be multiplied by velocity v [m/s] so blind performance Px=PR+Pw works against performance P until at maximum velocity V, Px and P become equal as shown in Figure 5.

With this velocity and payload the number of vehicles is calculated as required for 1 million t km/h: n=1e6/V/mN. The results are plotted in Figure 5, too.

The result, payload, velocity and cost indicator iC

To be able to compare the competitors we prepared the same task for all competitors, to transport an impulse of 1 million tkm/h in 40 ft sea containers each with a payload of 30 t in a lateral storm adding 80 km/h to the velocity of vehicles. To achieve the task the competitors required a number n of vehicles or trains and a total performance n*P. At maximum velocity V the required performance n*Px equals the installed performance n*P.

For personnel costs, operational costs and depreciation for one competitor we assumed n, n*Px and n*P. We assumed that for lorries 40 % of the transportation costs were for personnel, 40 % for operation and 20 % for depreciation. With n, n*Px and n*P required for lorry transport we calculated three factors to multiply the technical values of all competitors so that lorry transport got 100 %, freight train FT 58 %, freight train FTE 40 %, CargoSprinter 28 % and AeroSprinter 18 %. These percentages we called the Cost Indicator iC.

In Figure 6 Cost Indicators of the competitors are plotted against payload and against velocity for detailed discussion. It seems that transportation costs are not only a function of payload and velocity. Comparing the freight trains FT and FTE there may be an influence of surface shape as well. And comparing lorry to the trains the rolling resistance of rubber tyres on asphalt seems to be a handicap.

Conclusions

The question arises why in real life lorries have an advantage to trains. One part of the answer is that CargoSprinter and AeroSprinter with excellent results in our model are not yet part of the business, CargoSprinter is still in the test phase and AeroSprinter only exists in this paper. Shipping empty containers to improve train surface and cost indicator as does FTE is not yet usual practise on railways. So freight train FT with an iC of 58 % is the only really existing competitor to the lorry. The difference to 100 % may be declared by the amount of infrastruc-

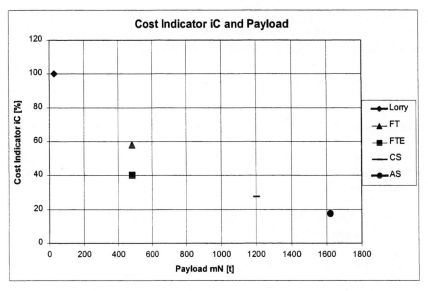

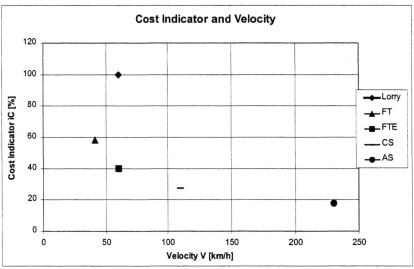

Figure 6: The Result, Cost Indicator iC as a Function of Payload and Velocity

tural costs that always have been spent by the railways and always have been paid by governments for lorries, ships and aeroplanes.

But let us be optimistic: the competitors lorry and railways might start to co-operate in alliances and to learn from each other. Railways e.g. might learn how to speed up trains and rising payload by filling the gaps not only with empty containers but rather with additional cargo canvassed by a very flexible pricing and information system. And railways should speed up operation using the fast and flexible railcar trains CargoSprinter and AeroSprinter.

References

[1] Breimeier, R. Transrapid und Eisenbahn, Wettbewerb zweier Spurführungssysteme oder gegenseitige Ergänzung? *ZEV+DET Glas. Ann.* Nr. 124 (2000) 9. September

[2] Haferkorn, F.R. Vehicle surface geometry optimisation Computers in Railways VII, WIT Press 2000

[3] Hucho, W.-H. (Hrsg.): Aerodynamik des Automobils Eine Brücke von der Strömungsmechanik zur Fahrzeugtechnik 3. Auflage, Springer 1999

[4] Peters, J.L.: Computational design and aerodynamic optimization of locomotive nose shapes Computers in Railways VII, WIT Press 2000

Analysis and forecast of air transport demand in Sardinia's airports as a function of tourism variables

R. Devoto, C. Farci & F. Lilliu
Sezione di Trasporti, Dipartimento di Ingegneria del Territorio, Facoltà di Ingegneria, Università degli Studi di Cagliari, Italia

Abstract

The potential of an econometrics approach for forecasting air transport demand is examined. The aim is to identify and select the most significant variables for multivariable linear regression models. Each independent variable has been evaluated by means of ARIMA models after rendering the historical series stationary. The variables for the different cases examined have been chosen using Student's t-test and the correlation matrix to determine their level of significance and of correlation. The resulting models have been tested on three airports in Sardinia (Cagliari, Olbia and Alghero) in order to identify the most suitable and characteristic variables for representing air transport demand.
Time series for annual passenger movements have been constructed for each airport expressed in absolute terms and index number.

1 Introduction

The transport system is a complex system composed of three main subsystems:
- Planning and programming
- Structures and infrastructures
- Production and management

The objectives of the present study, concerned with transport planning, were to identify those factors generating air transport demand and to build a model for forecasting travel demand.

The purpose of the analysis was to highlight some fundamental characteristics of air transport, the past trend and evolution of air traffic, the future prospects and the effect that particular socio-economic variables and variables typical of transport systems have had in generating air travel demand.

For forecasting purposes a knowledge of the system's characteristics and the influencing variables are essential for determining the functional relationship between demand trends and the behaviour of the main demand parameters.

The most widely used forecasting techniques in the transport sector are *demand projections* and *econometric models.*

The model constructed here has allowed to develop passenger flow projections in each airport over the next 5-10 years using socio-economic variables and historical traffic data.

Furthermore, as new data are acquired it will be possible to update forecasts and the model itself, insomuch as rather than the classic deterministic methods, highly inflexible and constrained to the reference time interval, we adopted a probabilistic approach. Probabilistic methods are able to take account of the intrinsic randomness of air travel demand generating a flexible function that can be adapted to the observed data and continually updated over time.

In this way, a forecasting tool of general validity has been developed which, by introducing specific variables, is applicable to airports other than those examined here.

The choice of functional form of the econometric model constructed for demand forecasting, was dictated by estimation accuracy and ease of application.

2 Choice of analytical method

Forecasting passenger travel demand by means of econometric models requires the construction of functions for estimating both the independent variables of significance and the demand itself. A review of the pertinent literature showed that in the majority of applications a deterministic approach is adopted to tackle this problem, approximating the trend of the variables by means of a regression curve chosen from among those that best interpolate the observed data. Introducing the values thus obtained into the equation chosen for the dependent variable, one obtains an inflexible model, that is unable to account for the real dynamics of air travel demand and bases estimates of future demand on historical data alone.

This implies that the model will not remain valid over time, inasmuch as the smallest variation in the hypothetical trend will invalidate the projections.

Here an attempt has been made to use primarily the Box-Jenkins probabilistic techniques for addressing the problem, thereby relaxing the constraints imposed on the projections by the inflexibility of the regression. In this way a flexible model is achieved that better interprets the trend in the time series examined and can, if necessary, be updated with the latest data.

An econometric forecasting model has been constructed with a multivariable linear regression function. The choice of linear form stems from the fact that it is fairly simple to express mathematically and sufficiently reliable.

Comparison with other more complex mathematical forms showed that the linear form requires a smaller number of parameters to be estimated, thus reducing error margins.

Furthermore, as the function is multivariabile, it takes into account the different variables influencing determination of air demand. In this regard, note that the independent variables to be introduced into the model have been chosen after significance testing on the major factors influencing growth in air travel demand. The analytical work comprised the following steps::

- *Choice of independent variables*. The independent variables were selected on the basis of Student's t-test for the statistical significance of the parameters and analysis of multi-collinearity, examining the correlation matrix .

- *Model construction for the independent variables chosen*. We chose the most suitable models for representing the variables. Both regression models and the so-called Box-Jenkins *ARIMA* models were considered. The models were calibrated with historical data on a 10 year basis.

- *Calibration of the econometric model*. This entailed estimating the parameters of the multivariable linear regression using the values of the independent variables calculated with the above models for the period 1980-1994. Two models with different variables were then chosen ,the final choice falling on the model that was more appropriate for demand forecasting.

- *Testing the econometric model*. The goodness of fit of the models was tested by comparing the calculated data with the data recorded for the previous five year period.

- *Air travel demand forecasting*. Demand forecasts were developed for the next five years with respect to the last available data.

3 Air travel demand forecasting

Annual scheduled airline passenger movements (arrivals + departures) were analysed for the three major Sardinian airports:

- *Cagliari – Elmas*
- *Olbia – Costa Smeralda*
- *Alghero - Fertilia*

The historical annual passenger traffic flows for scheduled services were constructed for these three airports. Passenger movements were expressed both in absolute terms (pax/year) and in terms of percentage increase with respect to the reference year (1975), using the index number (IN).

Air travel demand has been forecasted by means of econometric models expressed as a function of significant socio-economic variables including variables typical of tourist accommodation in Sardinia, namely:

- *Resident population (P)*
- *Number of tourist beds (B)*
- *Per capita beds (B_{pc})*
- *Tourist arrivals (A)*

The choice of independent variables to be introduced into the forecasting models relied on the statistical *Student's t test* and the correlation matrix: The first test determines the degree of significance of the variable considered for determining demand: The second indicates the degree of correlation between pairs of variables.

Table 1:   Passenger movements and index number of the resident population and tourist arrivals variables in Sardinia over the period 1975-1995.

year	Resident population		Tourist arrivals	
	B	IN (%)	A	IN (%)
1975	1,550,498	100	652,526	100
1976	1,562,149	100.75	704,200	107.92
1977	1,572,549	101.42	762,800	116.90
1978	1,581,274	101.98	764,662	117.18
1979	1,588,960	102.48	783,970	120.14
1980	1,594,175	102.82	855,347	131.08
1981	1,594,627	102.85	932,294	142.87
1982	1,605,410	103.54	1,014,658	155.50
1983	1,617,265	104.31	988,129	151.43
1984	1,628,690	105.04	974,567	149.35
1985	1,638,172	105.65	1,013,933	155.39
1986	1,643,789	106.02	1,182,943	181.29
1987	1,651,218	106.50	1,261,888	193.39
1988	1,655,859	106.80	1,335,699	204.70
1989	1,657,562	106.91	1,336,219	204.78
1990	1,664,373	107.34	1,313,261	201.26
1991	1,646,771	106.21	1,376,475	210.95
1992	1,651,902	106.54	1,351,421	207.11
1993	1,657,375	106.89	1,261,821	193.37
1994	1,659,466	107.03	1,336,385	204.80
1995	1,660,701	107.11	1,400,483	214.62

Examination of the correlation matrix revealed the possibile presence of collinearity. A more in depth investigation of this phenomenon, by means of stationarity analysis, allowed to eliminate those pairs of variables that were effectively correlated.

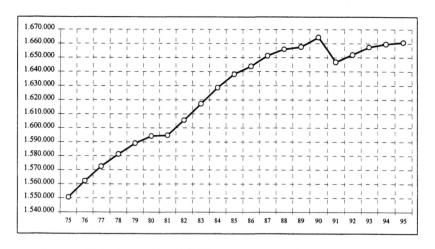

Figure 1:   Trend of the resident population variable.

The figures and tables show the data and graphs for the socio-economic variables considered.

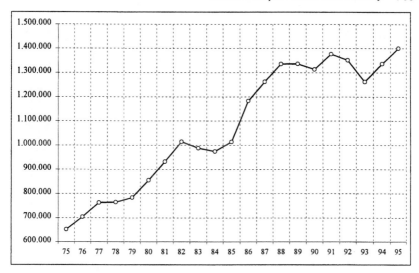

Figure 2: Trend of the tourist arrivals variable.

Table 2: Time series and index numbers of the number of tourist beds and per capita tourist beds in Sardinia for the period 1975-1995.

year	Number of tourist beds		Per capita beds	
	B	IN	B_{pc}	IN
1975	33,540	100	0.0216	100
1976	34,688	103.42	0.0222	102.65
1977	36,672	109.34	0.0233	107.80
1978	39,503	117.78	0.0250	115.49
1979	56,004	166.98	0.0352	162.93
1980	57,859	172.51	0.0363	167.78
1981	80,037	238.63	0.0502	232.03
1982	75,324	224.58	0.0469	216.90
1983	82,328	245.46	0.0509	235.33
1984	87,854	261.94	0.0539	249.36
1985	101,780	303.46	0.0621	287.21
1986	106,489	317.50	0.0648	299.48
1987	110,781	330.30	0.0671	310.14
1988	119,507	356.31	0.0722	333.64
1989	118,146	352.25	0.0713	329.50
1990	108,455	323.36	0.0652	301.23
1991	111,849	333.48	0.0679	313.98
1992	118,082	352.06	0.0715	330.45
1993	120,576	359.50	0.0728	336.31
1994	122,392	364.91	0.0738	340.95
1995	127,247	379.39	0.0766	354.21

The ability of each equation obtained to fit the real data was evaluated considering different indexes, including the *coefficient of determination R^2*, which indicates the reliability of the results in terms of matching the real phenomenon.

The regression analysis was performed calibrating the models on the data for the period 1975-1996. The models were verified using the data for the years 1997-2000.

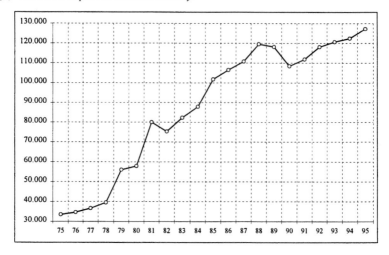

Figure 3: Trend of the number of tourist beds variable.

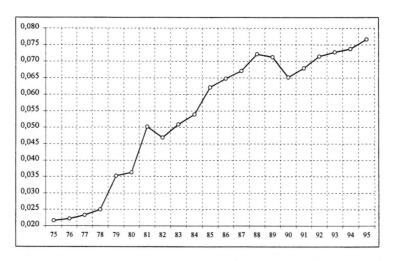

Figure 4: Trend of per capita beds variable.

3.1 Cagliari - Elmas Airport

Based on the results of the significance test conducted on the historical passenger movements data for **Cagliari – Elmas** airport, the socio-economic variables number of tourist beds (B) and resident population (P) were chosen.

The functional relationship of the forecasting model obtained is:

$$IN_{CAGLIARI} = 0.38\ B + 0.54\ P \qquad (1)$$

The *coefficient of determination* is:

$$R^2 = 99.25 \qquad (2)$$

Table 3: Scheduled airline passenger movements and forecasts for Cagliari-Elmas airport.

year	Passengers/year	Δ_{year} (pax/year)	Δ_{year} (%)	IN (%)	Δ_{1975} (pax)
CAGLIARI – ELMAS AIRPORT					
1975	720,859	-	-	100	-
1976	744,562	23,703	3.29	103.29	23,703
1977	800,906	56,344	7.57	111.10	80,047
1978	744,759	-56,147	-7.01	103.32	23,900
1979	736,049	-8,710	-1.17	102.11	15,190
1980	735,375	-674	-0.09	102.01	14,516
1981	783,199	47,824	6.50	108.65	62,340
1982	858,040	74,841	9.56	119.03	137,181
1983	868,618	10,578	1.23	120.50	147,759
1984	855,985	-12,633	-1.45	118.75	135,126
1985	930,644	74,659	8.72	129.10	209,785
1986	975,579	44,935	4.83	135.34	254,720
1987	1,078,254	102,675	10.52	149.58	357,395
1988	1,185,924	107,670	9.99	164.52	465,065
1989	1,294,039	108,115	9.12	179.51	573,180
1990	1,330,059	36,020	2.78	184.51	609,200
1991	1,283,338	-46,721	-3.51	178.03	562,479
1992	1,343,235	59,897	4.67	186.34	622,376
1993	1,310,410	-32,825	-2.44	181.78	589,551
1994	1,313,152	2,742	0.21	182.16	592,293
1995	1,288,862	-24,290	-1.85	178.80	568,003
1996	1,460,630	171,768	13.33	202.62	739,771
1997	1,680,566	219,936	15.06	233.13	959,707
1998	1,750,882	70,316	4.18	242.89	1,030,023
1999	1,824,385	73,503	4.20	253.08	1,103,526
2000	2,063,514	239,129	13.11	286.26	1,342,655
Growth from 1975 to 2000 = 1,342,655 pax = 186.26%					
Mean annual growth = 53,506 pax/year = 4.45%					

	DEMAND FORECASTS TO THE YEAR 2010		
year	Passengers/year	Δ_{year} (%)	IN (%)
2001	2,115,310	2.51	293.44
2002	2,167,106	2.45	300.63
2003	2,218,902	2.39	307.81
2004	2,270,698	2.33	315.00
2005	2,322,494	2.28	322.18
2006	2,374,290	2.23	329.37
2007	2,426,086	2.18	336.55
2008	2,477,892	2.14	343.74
2009	2,529,688	2.09	350.93
2010	2,581,484	2.05	358.11
Growth annual mean = 36,922 pax/year = 2.26%			
Growth with respect to 2000 = 517,970 pax = 25.10%			
Growth with respect to 1975 = 1,860,625 pax = 258.11%			

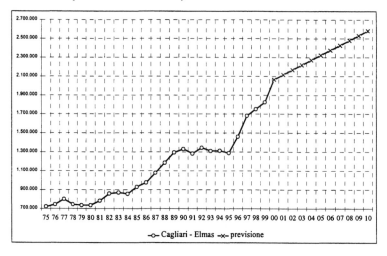

Figura 5: Scheduled airline passenger movements at Cagliari – Elmas airport
from 1975 to 2000 and forecasts up to 2010.

3.2 Olbia – Costa Smeralda Airport

With regard to air travel demand estimates for the **Olbia – Costa Smeralda**
airport, the socio-economic variables *tourist arrivals (A)* and *resident population
(P)* proved to be significant.

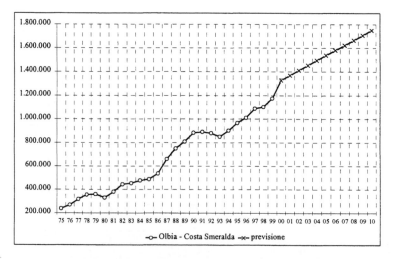

Figure 6: Scheduled airline passenger movements and forecasts for Olbia –
Costa Smeralda airport from 1975 to 2000 and demand forecasts to
the year 2010.

The following results were obtained:

$$IN_{OLBIA} = 2.69\,A - 1.88\,P \qquad (4)$$

$$R^2 = 99.23 \qquad (5)$$

Table 4: Scheduled airline passenger movements and forecasts for Olbia – Costa Smeralda airport.

year	Passengers/year	Δ_{year} (pax/year)	Δ_{year} (%)	IN (%)	Δ_{1975} (pax)
OLBIA – COSTA SMERALDA AIRPORT					
1975	238,169	-	-	100	-
1976	269,707	31,538	13.24	113.24	31,538
1977	317,373	47,666	17.67	133.26	79,204
1978	355,757	38,384	12.09	149.37	117,588
1979	360,482	4,725	1.33	151.36	122,313
1980	329,947	-30,535	-8.47	138.53	91,778
1981	380,744	50,797	15.40	159.86	142,575
1982	443,765	63,021	16.55	186.32	205,596
1983	454,060	10,295	2.32	190.65	215,891
1984	477,107	23,047	5.08	200.32	238,938
1985	487,124	10,017	2.10	204.53	248,955
1986	535,977	48,853	10.03	225.04	297,808
1987	660,132	124,155	23.16	277.17	421,963
1988	749,999	89,867	13.61	314.90	511,830
1989	808,545	58,546	7.81	339.48	570,376
1990	883,988	75,443	9.33	371.16	645,819
1991	891,120	7,132	0.81	374.15	652,951
1992	880,272	-10,848	-1.22	369.60	642,103
1993	850,250	-30,022	-3.41	356.99	612,081
1994	902,291	52,041	6.12	378.84	664,122
1995	965,714	63,423	7.03	405.47	727,545
1996	1,011,110	45,396	4.70	424.53	772,941
1997	1,087,116	76,006	7.52	456.45	848,947
1998	1,102,311	15,195	1.40	462.83	864,142
1999	1,174,479	72,168	6.55	493.13	936,310
2000	1,327,275	152,796	13.01	557.28	1,089,106
Growth from 1975 to 2000 = 1,089,106 pax = 457.28%					
Annual mean growth = 43,564 pax/year = 7.35%					
DEMAND FORECASTS TO THE YEAR 2010					
year	Passengers/year	Δ_{year} (%)		IN (%)	
2001	1,369,364	3.17		574.95	
2002	1,411,465	3.07		592.63	
2003	1,453,554	2.98		610.30	
2004	1,495,655	2.90		627.98	
2005	1,537,744	2.81		645.65	
2006	1,579,845	2.74		663.33	
2007	1,621,934	2.66		681.00	
2008	1,664,035	2.60		698.68	
2009	1,706,124	2.53		716.35	
2010	1,748,225	2.47		734.03	
Growth annual mean = pax/year = 2.79%					
Growth with respect to 2000 = 420,950 pax = 31.72%					
Growth with respect to 1975 = 1,510,056 pax = 634.03%					

3.3 Aeroporto Alghero - Fertilia

Air transport demand at **Alghero – Fertilia** airport was found to depend significantly on the *per capita beds (B_{pc})* and *resident population (P)* variables

Table 5: Scheduled airline passenger movements and forecasts for Alghero – Fertilia airport.

year	Passengers/year	Δ_{year} (pax/year)	Δ_{year} (%)	IN (%)	Δ_{1975} (pax)
		ALGHERO – FERTILIA AIRPORT			
1975	274,069	-	-	100	-
1976	226,666	-47,403	-17.30	82.70	-47,403
1977	241,011	14,345	6.33	87.94	-33,058
1978	287,311	46,300	19.21	104.83	13,242
1979	267,133	-20,178	-7.02	97.47	-6,936
1980	253,611	-13,522	-5.06	92.54	-20,458
1981	289,283	35,672	14.07	105.55	15,214
1982	309,775	20,492	7.08	113.03	35,706
1983	307,149	-2,626	-0.85	112.07	33,080
1984	301,631	-5,518	-1.80	110.06	27,562
1985	306,748	5,117	1.70	111.92	32,679
1986	348,641	41,893	13.66	127.21	74,572
1987	393,488	44,847	12.86	143.57	119,419
1988	418,117	24,629	6.26	152.56	144,048
1989	466,448	48,331	11.56	170.19	192,379
1990	509,691	43,243	9.27	185.97	235,622
1991	506,384	-3,307	-0.65	184.77	232,315
1992	520,177	13,793	2.72	189.80	246,108
1993	502,618	-17,559	-3.38	183.39	228,549
1994	484,419	-18,199	-3.62	176.75	210,350
1995	472,974	-11,445	-2.36	172.57	198,905
1996	495,464	22,490	4.76	180.78	221,395
1997	550,337	54,873	11.08	200.80	276,268
1998	562,488	12,151	2.21	205.24	288,419
1999	588,169	25,681	4.57	214.61	314,100
2000	668,023	79,854	13.58	243.74	393,954
	Growth from 1975 to 2000 = 393,954 pax = 143.74%				
	Mean annual growth = 15,758 pax/year = 3.95%				

	DEMAND FORECASTS TO THE YEAR 2010				
year	Passengers/year	Δ_{year} (%)		NI (%)	
2001	686,415	2.75		250.45	
2002	704,809	2.68		257.16	
2003	723,200	2.61		263.88	
2004	741,591	2.54		270.59	
2005	759,982	2.48		277.30	
2006	778,379	2.42		284.01	
2007	796,770	2.36		290.72	
2008	815,161	2.31		297.43	
2009	833,552	2.26		304.14	
2010	851,948	2.21		310.85	
	Growth annual mean = 15,008 pax/year = 2.46%				
	Growth with respect to 2000 = 183,925pax = 27.53%				
	Growth with respect to 1975 = 577,879 pax = 210.85%				

The following results were obtained:

$$IN_{ALGHERO} = 0.35\,B_{pc} + 0.44\,P \qquad (6)$$

$$R^2 = 98.69 \qquad (7)$$

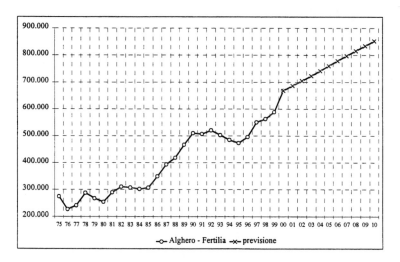

Figure 7: Scheduled airline passenger movements for Alghero - Fertilia airport from 1975 to 2000 and demand forecasts to the year 2010.

References

[1] C.S.S.T., *Modelli Econometrici per la domanda di trasporto. Viaggiatori a lunga distanza*, Centro Studi sui Sistemi di Trasporto Roma, Quaderno N.11, 1976.

[2] ICAO, *The Economic Situation of Air Transport, Review and Outlook, 1978 to the year 2000*, Circular 222-AT/90, International Civil Aviation Organization, Montreal, Canada, 1989.

[3] Lupi, M., *Modelli per la Macroanalisi della Domanda di Trasporto Aereo*, Trasporti e Trazione 2/96.

[4] Marbach, G., Mazziotta, C., Rizzi, A., *Le previsioni – Fondamenti logici e basi statistiche*, ETASLIBRI, 1991.

[5] Piccolo, D., Vitale, C., *Metodi statistici per l'analisi economica*, Il Mulino, Bologna, 1984.

[6] Reitani, G., Costa, A., *Analisi e Previsione della Domanda di Trasporto Aereo nella Comunità Europea: un modello econometrico multivariabile*, Università degli Studi di Pavia, Quaderni del Dipartimento di Ingegneria del Territorio, 47, PI-ME, Pavia.

[7] Vajani, L., Analisi Statistica delle Serie Temporali, Vol.1,2, CLEUP, 1980.

GIS in road environmental planning and management

E. Sfakianaki & M. O'Reilly
School of Engineering, Kingston University, UK.

Abstract

The urban growth of the last few decades has resulted in increasing demands for infrastructure in urban sites. Access to and quality of road transport systems is often considered an index of industrial and social development. The construction of new roads may ease congestion and reduce travel time, but it is also a host of environmental impacts. It is increasingly recognised that it is necessary to develop and upgrade transport systems so that the physical, social and environmental impacts are minimised. The development of Environmental Impact Assessment (EIA) tools and methodologies is critical to ensuring that all potentially adverse impacts are identified and assessed, and are given consideration in the decision-making process. One tool that has considerable potential for supporting road EIA and ultimately planning is the Geographical Information System (GIS). The same tool is also employed to account for uncertainties in the EIA process. More specifically GIS is used to investigate how different traffic volumes will influence noise levels using a case study.

1 Introduction

Roads often bring significant economic and social benefits, but they can also have substantial negative impacts on communities and the natural environment. As the public becomes more aware of the adverse repercussions and legislation on a national and international level becomes tighter, there is a growing demand for the techniques and skills needed to incorporate environmental considerations into road planning and management. It is perceived that Environmental Impact Assessment (EIA) is an excellent preventive planning tool, provided that it is implemented early in the project development process.

EIA aims to assess the potential impacts of a proposed project on the environment in advance with potential to improve decision-making [4]. One tool that has considerable potential for supporting road EIA is the Geographical Information System (GIS). GISs are computer systems used for storing, retrieving, analysing and displaying spatial data. Considering the spatial nature of many environmental impacts, GIS provide a useful platform for the EIA process as they can account for the fact that many impacts are functionally related to the distance of a location from a project.

They can be employed to provide information concerning the sensitivity of the existing environment; identify direct impacts such as the passage of a proposed road through a site of archaeological importance; incorporate sophisticated models to enable the prediction of indirect impacts such as the spread of air pollution; perform spatial analysis and modelling; and contribute to the reduction of risks and uncertainties involved in the process. The way that GIS can contribute to different EIA stages is illustrated in the following section.

2 The EIA Process and the GIS contribution

Road planning involves several different stages starting with the need for the development stage, feasibility, engineering design, construction and operation and maintenance. On the other hand, the most important stages of the EIA process are:

- Before the preparation of the Environmental Statement (ES), (initial stages)
- During the preparation of the ES;
- Mitigation of impacts and public participation; and
- After the preparation of the ES (post development).

The Environmental Statement (ES) is the legal documentation, which includes all the information pertinent to the proposed project, together with the actual assessment of impacts. It is important therefore to synchronise environmental studies with the project development process to minimise environmental impacts. Ideally therefore an EIA should be considered and provided for from the outset in the budget of all road projects. The potential contribution of GIS to the different EIA stages is investigated in the following.

2.1 Initial stages

At the preliminary stages of the EIA process, GISs can assist in positioning the proposed road into a geographical context, describe the project's surrounding environment and topography (Figure 1). During screening, GIS, due to its mapping and data gathering capabilities, can precisely identify the geographic context and ensure that the project requires an EIA (e.g. identify whether a proposed project requires an EIA due to its proximity to a sensitive land-use, such as an ancient woodland). Since projects, which need an EIA, are often defined by reference to their proximity to certain features or other spatial consideration, this will enable projects that do not require a full EIA to be screened out. GISs could also speed up the scoping process by the creation of databases of local information. The databases will be constantly up-dated by consultees on different areas such as ecology, archaeology, noise, and air quality. Subsequently, the risk of neglecting a number of pertinent environmental factors that might be impacted by the proposed development is minimised.

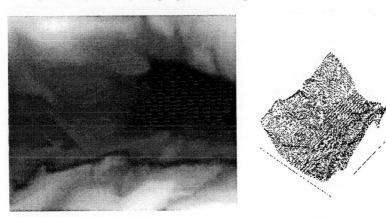

Figure 1:   Digital Elevation Map (DEM) for the area also illustrated in Figure 3, and 3-Dimensional orthographic perspective DEM of the study area

2.2 Preparation of the ES

During the preparation of the ES, typical GISs operations such as overlay analysis can beneficially contribute to the identification of impacts. For example, if the air pollution map is overlaid with the residential land-use map, possible adverse impacts can be investigated. Typical operations such as overlaying are much more powerful, accurate and flexible in a GIS and there are no restrictions on the number of layers used. New maps are automatically produced and different computations can easily and quickly be made, increasing both the quality of presentation and accuracy of data. Combinations of GISs modelling tools with existing process models enable the rapid and objective prediction of impacts. Using a GIS, alternatives including the 'do-nothing' option can be compared. Sensitivity analysis can be carried out rapidly and different assumptions can be checked on whether and how they could alter decision-making.

2.3 Mitigation and public participation

GIS as a tool for modelling and spatial illustration of impacts could further be used to indicate locations that should be preferred or avoided. In cases where the only effective mitigation measure is to abandon the project altogether, GISs could be used to rapidly evaluate other alternatives. Furthermore, interactive analysis of GISs along with the necessary tools such as on-screen digitising allows for the computerised design of potential mitigation measures. Conversely, if CAD packages are employed, then results imported to a GIS will enable the revision of different designs. In terms of public participation, GISs, due to their visual display capabilities can assist in the better illustration of a proposed development to the public. If combined with multi-media and visual technologies, their visualisation and presentation capabilities could further be enhanced. In this respect, misinformation about the proposed development can be prevented.

2.4 Post ES

For the post-development stages, GIS can serve as a database for processing and storing monitoring data. It enables the comparison of the actual outcomes with the outcomes that had been predicted and illustrates the changing values of impacts with time contributing to environmental management and sustainability (Figure 2).

Year	1997	2005	2010	2015
Predicted Noise Levels	X1	X2	X3	X4
Actual Noise Levels	Y1	Y2	Y3	Y4
Compare	i.e. If X-Y <0 then go back to models, more mitigation, check thresholds			

Figure 2: Noise Impact Map for a proposed route for a residential area – GIS Database for monitoring and auditing predictions with actual impacts

3 Accounting for uncertainty

The straightforward use of GIS in EIA is not novel and represents an obvious application of developing technology to EIA. The authors are currently engaged on research into an aspect of the application of GIS, which has hitherto received scant attention, namely the GIS's ability to account for uncertainties.

There are many aspects of uncertainty associated with the EIA process. The following classification may be used:

- Uncertainty about what the environment is. For example:
    - the impact of a project on species A cannot be assessed with accuracy unless there is accurate information about the population, status and distribution of A in the environment under consideration
    - the impact of a project on the hydrogeological regime in an environment unless an accurate assessment of the current regime is available
- Models used to compute physical impacts have limitations. For example:
    - empirically derived models are not applicable to all conditions
    - theoretically constructed models depend on assumptions which may not be valid in the given conditions
    - interactions between impacts may not be fully modelled; for example, the physical location of a project may cause fauna to move its location. The impact of pollutants on that fauna needs to take into account the revised location rather than the original location.
- Models to compute ecological impacts are very sensitive to the actual conditions in place at any time and one cannot place high confidence on the results of simulations. For example:
    - noise transmission depends upon ground cover (which may vary over time) and atmospheric directions (which obviously change over short time scales)
    - subsurface transmission of pollutants depends on groundwater conditions, which will vary over time

Uncertainties consequently will affect the accuracy of predictions and ultimately the decisions taken. GIS offers a platform from which issues of probability and confidence in predictions can be addressed. Ranges may be attached to predictions reflecting the degree of confidence in the solution and different weighting combinations can be incorporated to identify areas that show greater sensitivity or potential for development. GISs can be used to generate sensitivity data and hence prioritise data collection; if, for instance, the relationship between parameter A and parameter B is such that whatever the changes in A there is little change in B, then no further information may be needed. However, where the effect is much more variable, there may be a need for further information.

Furthermore, the physical and socio-economic environments evolve over time and space. As such the standard approach to EIA based on data collected at a specific time and place, can often be out-of-date before the planning or development are completed. Such changes in time and space can be modelled in the GIS environment to allow spatial and time predictions of environmental interactions. Thus, plans could be made for how to handle present and future needs promoting therefore the ultimate goal of sustainability. Clearly the best check on the accuracy of predictions is to check on the outcomes of the implementation of a project after the decision which concerns the stages of monitoring and auditing. Conversely, the monitoring of outcomes of similar projects may provide useful information for the project in hand. Eliminating uncertainties in the EIA process is almost impossible but GIS can certainly assist in reducing them.

4 Using GIS as an analysis/sensitivity tool

The use of mathematical models for impact prediction is relatively commonplace. One of the major difficulties when assessing environmental impacts is the accuracy of input parameters. GIS provides an effective basis for an integrated sensitivity input parameter analysis tool. In the following, it will be examined how one of the most important factors in any road EIA, the traffic volume, can affect different noise predictions. Although the specific factor can influence a number of other parameters (such as air quality), the present paper will investigate only noise levels.

Application is illustrated using the A69 Sunderland to Carlisle trunk road Haltwhistle Bypass, UK as a case study [2]. The principal function of the bypass was to relieve traffic using the A69 through Haltwhistle. The road has now been constructed and was opened to the public in 1997. Several alternatives were considered before the final decision was made. The GIS selected as, the development platform, was 'IDRISI' [1].

Figure 3 illustrates some of the land-uses. The existing route (A69), the actually constructed bypass (Green) and one of the alternatives considered are superimposed. An area of 3.25 km × 2.71 km was considered following the area studied in the Environmental Statement. Each block (pixel) corresponds to a 20 m x 20 m area of land.

The assessment of **Road Noise** is based upon the Manual for the Calculation of Road Traffic Noise [3]. The analysis was simplified to consider a single segment only with the basic noise level being derived solely from the estimated traffic flow. The attenuation of noise is a function of distance from the road. No account is taken of screening. One further simplification that should be considered is that the road under consideration is assumed to be the only source of road noise in the area. Minor roads and side-roads are neglected.

A simplified **Road Noise Impact Model** was therefore developed which was subsequently implemented into the GIS IDRISI (for a more analytical description of the model development see [5]). The application of the model produced impact maps illustrating how the different alternatives including the do-nothing scenario would affect different areas. The focus of the present study is the residential area.

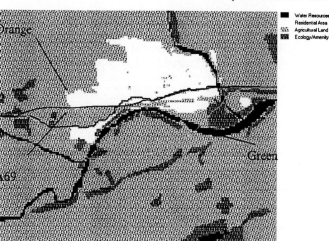

Figure 3: Land-use map for Haltwhistle

Figure 4 compares the three routes in terms of the percentage of the residential area falling within specified noise ranges. The Green route, which represents a bypass for Haltwhistle, is likely to result in reduced noise levels when compared with the A69 and the orange route. That is because the Green route is positioned to the south of the residential area, whereas the other two routes go through the residential area. These predictions are in broad agreement with the findings of the published Environmental Statement. It should be noted however that the model used was rather simplified and many effects which were given full consideration in the ES were not accounted for here. However, it is entirely feasible to implement every stage of the road noise calculation procedure [3].

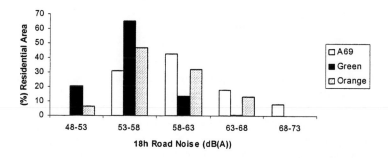

Figure 4: Comparison between road noise impacts for the A69 and the two alternative routes

The comparisons in Figure 4 were based on the predictions of traffic flows presented in the ES. The Road Noise Impact Model was further used to investigate how different traffic flows could make a route less or more favourable. Sensitivity analysis was undertaken to investigate how the noise levels would fluctuate in accordance with different traffic values. In this case, the traffic flow initially predicted was altered in the range of ±75% in 25% intervals. Some of the results are illustrated in Fig. 5-6.

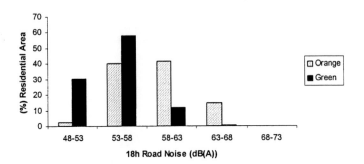

Figure 5: Comparison between road noise impacts for the two alternatives assuming an increase of 25% in traffic flows.

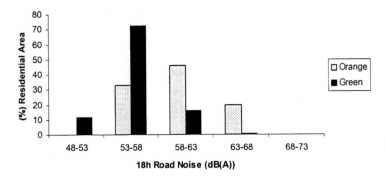

Figure 6: Comparison between road noise impacts for the two alternatives assuming an increase of 50% in traffic flows.

It could be said that the increased noise levels were expected. However what makes GIS a particularly useful tool at this stage is the speed and accuracy with which it enables such calculations for many different combinations. It can also increase the level of presentation since it can illustrate in a clear manner differences in predictions.

In Figure 7 the residential are of Haltwhistle has been extracted, and the predicted noise levels for the green route have been subtracted from the orange route noise levels assuming there is a 50% increase in the traffic flows originally predicted. As anticipated, most of the area would experience a substantial reduction in road noise levels (typically 0 – 6 dB(A)) with the green route, which is positioned further to the south than the orange route.

In the immediate vicinity of the orange route reductions are even more substantial (6 – 18 dB(A)).

Figure 7: Difference between road noise levels for the residential area of Haltwhistle for the green and orange routes if traffic flows increase 50% from the original predictions

The development of a more rigorous and automated sensitivity GIS tool which will employ a set of deterministic and simulation methods, depending on the parameter examined, to investigate different input parameter combinations and how they can affect decisions seems to have a lot of potential. Such a tool would certainly be advantageous at the preliminary stages of planning where different scenarios are examined and could suggest areas that show potential or should be avoided.

5 Conclusions

Urban growth has resulted in considerable development in the area of urban transport. This development in turn has resulted in significant degradation of the environment. Environmental Impact Assessment is now a well-known process that focuses on the effects of projects on the environment and naturally, planning and management move to more strategic approaches to satisfy the goals of sustainable development. One tool that has considerable potential for supporting road planning and management through the EIA process is the GIS since it recognises the spatial variability of impacts. Despite the well-acknowledged capabilities of GIS for EIA, it seems that it is better known as a tool for map and report preparation, rather than data modelling and analysis.

The research presented in this paper has demonstrated that GISs can serve as a platform for data modelling and analysis but also as a tool for uncertainty calculations. In particular GIS was employed to investigate how different traffic volumes will influence noise levels. A Road Noise Impact Model was produced. The model is relatively simplistic and the intention is for the model to be refined at a later stage. The model was applied to a real case study and the results produced are in broad agreement with the published Environmental Statement. The model was also used to investigate the sensitivity of the outcomes when traffic flows were changed. Noise levels for the alternatives examined were quickly calculated and clearly presented.

Suggestions were made on how the GIS sensitivity tool can be further enhanced to provide clearer insight on the impact of different alternatives and how uncertainty with respect to input parameters can be further investigated. Future work will consider the investigation of other input parameters and their incorporation in a single GIS sensitivity tool.

References

[1] Clark Labs, *The IDRISI32 Applications Programming Interface User's Guide Version 1.0*, 2000.

[2] DoT, *A69 Sunderland to Carlisle Trunk Road Haltwhistle Environmental Statement*, London UK, 1993.

[3] DoT/Welsh Office, *Calculation of Road Traffic Noise*, HMSO, 1988.

[4] Glasson, J., Therivel, R. & Chadwick, A., *Introduction to Environmental Impact Assessment*, (2nd edn), UCL Press, 1999.

[5] Sfakianaki, E. & Stovin V. R., A spatial framework for environmental impact assessment and route optimisation. *Proceedings of the Institute of Civil Engineers Transport*, in press.

Effectiveness and macroeconomic impact analysis of policy instruments for sustainable transport in Korea: A CGE modeling approach

S. Lee[1] and J. Lim[2]
[1] Institute for Transport Policy Studies, Japan
[2] Korea Energy Economics Institute, Korea

Abstract

In evaluating policy measures' applicability, information on policy measures' effectiveness and its possible macroeconomic consequences would be essential for policy makers especially in cases where severe macroeconomic consequences are anticipated. In the transport sector various policy measures are being considered for satisfying specific environmental quality objectives and these policy instruments usually have macroeconomic implications in their implementation.

In this paper we first analyze the policy measures' effectiveness and we develop a computable general equilibrium model where the macroeconomic impacts of environmental and economic policy variables can be analyzed in the Korean context. We analyze the impacts of widely considered policy instruments for sustainable development in the transport sector. These include fuel pricing, public transport promotion and modal shift in freight transport. Changes in macroeconomic indicators such as GDP, trade account balances and government expenditures are estimated according to the change in the policy variables. The findings from this study can be consulted in prioritizing or analyzing feasibility of environmental policies in the transport sector.

1. Introduction

After the ratification of Kyoto Protocol in 1997, Annex B countries have to take on binding responsibility for their greenhouse gas (GHG) reductions. At the same time, increasing pressure is placed on developing countries requesting sharing the burden of GHG reduction from these unregulated countries. In light of this, Korea has been trying to find the way to share the burden and to develop consensus among governmental agencies, industrial sectors, academics and general public about how Korea should respond to the issue. As its economic development so heavily dependent on energy consumption, South Korea needs an effective domestic policy (portfolio) to control the growth GHG while avoiding unbearable adverse impacts on its economy. Therefore, the comprehension of the features of each policy instrument and the synergetic reconciliation with objectives other than GHG abatement is important.

The policy instruments that can be implemented in transport sector are diverse and comprehensive, ranging from economic incentives to control or guiding approaches. Given a number of issues surrounding various types of policy instruments, choice of appropriate domestic policy is very important. In addition to the usual command and control measures, various policy measures have been introduced or have been contemplated for implementation in order to reduce GHG emissions in the transport sector. These include fuel pricing, public transport promotion and modal shift in freight transport. However, these policies based on economic incentives and infrastructure provision might have severe economic consequences when implemented.

The objective of this study is to analyze and compare the impacts of widely considered policy instruments for sustainable development in the Korean transport sector. For analysis, a dynamic computable general equilibrium (CGE) model – called Korean Trade and Environment Model (KORTEM) - with extensively disaggregated energy sectors and nested structures for economic agent behaviors has been employed.

We first analyze the effectiveness of representative policy measures on reducing GHG emissions. This represents the bottom-up part of the analysis, which considers the reduction potential of a policy measure and the results from this analysis can also be used as an input to the macroeconomic impact analysis. Based on the findings from the bottom-up analysis, macroeconomic impact analysis is conducted for the policy measures. Information on the macroeconomic implications of the policy measures will be very beneficial for the policy makers to choose proper sets of policy measures for achieving the objectives while minimizing the adverse impact on the economy.

2. Modeling approach

KOTEM is a detailed dynamic model of the Korean economy designed specifically to analyze the economic impacts of national and international climate change policy on the Korean economy. Korea is a relatively small open economy that relies heavily on fossil fuel imports and on energy/emission intensive industries for export earnings. This implies that climate change response policies at both the national and international levels will have significant impacts on the Korean economy and trade. These include impacts on the competitiveness of energy intensive export industries, on non-traded energy related services such as transport and on fossil fuel imports. KORTEM also allows assessment of the impacts of domestic emission abatement on Korean economy and industries.

As a general equilibrium model, KORTEM include all the major structural details of, and interrelationships between, the different sectors of the Korean economy. Given the pervasive use of energy in the economy, policies affecting energy use have widespread ramifications that can be accounted for only in a general equilibrium setting. KORTEM is a dynamic model that is essential for climate change analysis to allow the impacts of emission abatement to be tracked over time and the impacts of alternative timetables for implementing emission abatement policies to be examined. KORTEM incorporates stock flow dynamics in investment and in labor force and population growth.

In KORTEM, there are 103 industries and commodities including 19 energies and 10 margins with 4 transport margins (i.e. road, rail, air and sea transportation). There are three types of primary factors – labor, capital and land. Labor is divided into eight different types in terms of occupations. With the detailed representation of the labor market, KORTEM has the capacity for detailed analysis of policy changes on various labor types and income distribution. Each commodity is supplied from two different sources – domestic and imported – with imperfect substitution (i.e. Armington elasticity).

Realistic specification of key energy using sector is essential for modeling climate change policies. KORTEM adopted the approach of nested production functions at this stage. KORTEM allows for inter-fuel and energy-capital substitution over a range of different technologies. For example, the adoption of more energy efficient but more costly equipment is modeled as energy-capital substitution. The extent of substitution is constrained to preclude unrealistic substitution possibilities.

The detailed treatment of margins is incorporated in KORTEM. The services of various trade (for example, wholesale trade, retail trade and insurance) and transport industries are often required for the transfer of goods and services between producers and purchasers (These industries account for about 20 percent of Korean GDP). KORTEM takes explicit account of margins in the supply chain. Apart from allowing simulation of the effects on the margin industries of structural change elsewhere in the economy, KORTEM allows substitution between different modes of transport. This allows the assignment of freight transport tasks between road, rail, sea and air in response to changes in relative freight costs. KORTEM, therefore, is able to capture any changes in the freight task arising from actions to reduce greenhouse gas emissions.

KORTEM also includes specific treatment of the government sector. The government sector purchases goods and services and collects taxation revenue from a number of sources. The explicit treatment of the government sector allows KORTEM to examine the fiscal dimensions of climate change policy. A key fiscal consideration for government is the revenue collected, or not collected, from market based instruments used to mitigate GHG emissions. For example, KORTEM has the capacity to assess the fiscal implications of carbon taxation versus domestic tradable emission permits. Furthermore, KORTEM allows detailed analysis of revenue recycling, such as the replacement of inefficient taxation by carbon taxation, that can confer benefits to the Korean economy - the so-called "double dividend".

A fundamental requirement for greenhouse policy analysis is the ability to account for all greenhouse gas emissions. In many current general equilibrium models, carbon dioxide (CO_2) from fossil fuel combustion is the only gas and source covered. KORTEM, however, incorporates a system of emission accounts that cover three major GHG gases – carbon dioxide, methane and nitrous oxide - from various sources – energy, industrial processes, agriculture and waste.

3. The reference case

A key determinant of the economic impact of the policy employed in transport sector for GHG emissions reduction is the deviation of projected GHG emissions level under a 'no policy' scenario – referred to here as the reference case – from its targeted emission level. The reference case projections determine the extent of emissions abatement required to meet the given target. The reference case does not include the impacts of policies that are currently being implemented or negotiated in response to concerns of climate change. Here, reference case GHG emissions, energy consumption and macro economy to year 2020 are presented. The reference case projections are based on current assumption about GDP and population growth and energy technology and, as such, should not be considered a prediction of the future.

Table 1. Macro-economy and energy consumption, reference case

Economic and environmental indicators	1995	2000	2010	2020	Growth rate *		
					1996-2000	2001-2010	2011-2020
Real GDP (1000 billion won)	377.4	442.4	729.6	1,067.6	3.23	5.13	3.88
Population (million)	45.0	47.2	50.8	52.4	0.96	0.74	0.30
GHG emissions (million TC)	120.0	138.1	215.1	313.5	2.85	4.53	3.84
Final energy consumption (million TOE)	120.9	149.6	253.1	380.9	4.35	5.40	4.17
Energy intensity (mil. TOE/1000 billion won)	0.320	0.338	0.347	0.357	1.08	0.26	0.28
Emission intensity (TC/million won)	0.318	0.312	0.295	0.294	-0.37	-0.57	-0.04

* Annual average growth rate

Korean economy has achieved the rapid recovery from the Asian financial crisis. The real GDP has grown by 3.23% a year over the period 1996-2000. The real GDP is projected to rise approximately by 5.1% and 3.9% a year over the period 2001-2010 and 2011-2020 respectively. Population growth rate is projected to be 0.74% and 0.30% respectively for the same period. The growth rate of final energy consumption is projected to be higher than that of real GDP. This is projected to raise energy intensity of production defined as the ratio of aggregate energy consumption to aggregate output (real GDP). On the other hand, as the GHG emissions are projected to increase by 4.53% and 3.84% a year over the period 2001-2010 and 2011-2020 respectively, the emission intensity of production defined as the ratio of aggregate emissions to aggregate output is projected to fall.

Table 2. Growth rate of energy consumption and GHG emissions in transport sector, reference case

	Energy consumption		GHG emission	
	2001-2010	2011-2020	2001-2010	2011-2020
Rail	5.71	6.63	4.38	5.09
Road	3.33	3.15	3.52	2.55
Sea	3.92	2.90	3.79	3.79
Air	4.25	3.35	5.87	6.08
Total	3.56	3.19	3.58	2.72

* Annual average growth rate

Energy consumption of transport sector in total is projected to increase by 3.56% and 3.19% a year over the period of 2001-2010 and 2011-2020 respectively. The growth rate of energy consumption of rail is projected to be higher than that of other transport sectors. In terms of GHG emissions, emissions from rail and air are projected to lead in increasing emissions in transportation sector, highlighting the importance of the future abatement efforts of rail and air in reducing emission growth in transportation sector.

4. Policy scenarios and their effectiveness analysis

To compare the economic and environmental impacts of policy instruments for sustainable development in the Korean transport sector, this paper analyzes three different policy scenarios that are widely considered in Korea. They include fuel pricing, public transport promotion and modal shift in freight transport.

4.1 Public transport policy

Our first policy scenario is about maintaining current transport share of public transport up to year 2020. Current trend indicates that the share of public transport, especially the share of bus transport will be decreasing significantly in the future. Table 4 compares the base scenario with the public transport promotion policy. Table 5 estimates the potential savings from the increased public transport patronage in the Korean context. The estimated emission unit of private passenger car is 40.8 g-C/person km. The emission units of bus and subway are estimated to be 37.0% and 7.4% of passenger car's respectively due to the high occupancy rate.   As shown in Table 5, it is estimated that 3.72% of the total transport emission can be reduced by the public transport promotion policy in 2020.

Table 3. Public transport policy scenarios

Scenario	Assumptions
BAU Scenario	Current trends scenario: Declining public transport modal share
Public transport scenario	Bus: Maintaining current modal share (9.96%) up to 2020. Subway: Maintaining current modal share (9.49%) up to year 2020.

Table 4. Passenger transport demand forecast by public transport policy scenario

Unit: million person km

		2000	2005	2010	2015	2020
BAU Scenario	Passenger car	168,126	217,043	280,194	361,718	466,963
	Bus	27,695	25,917	24,253	22,695	21,238
	Subway	28,365	34,445	38,899	51,541	61,170
	Total	224,186	277,405	343,345	435,954	549,371
Maintaining public transport modal share	Passenger car	168,126	207,477	258,367	330,241	418,397
	Bus	27,695	35,254	42,842	53,297	66,032
	Subway	28,365	34,673	42,136	52,417	64,942
	Total	224,186	277,405	343,345	435,954	549,371

Table 5. Estimation of CO_2 emission under public transport policy

Unit: thousand TC

		2000	2005	2010	2015	2020
BAU Scenario	Passenger car	6,853	8,847	11,421	14,745	19,035
	Bus	417	390	365	342	320
	Subway	85	103	117	155	184
	Sub-total	7,355	9,341	11,903	15,241	19,538
	Total Emission[1]	18,681	22,176	26,565	31,044	34,748
Maintaining public transport modal share	Passenger car	6,853	8,457	10,532	13,461	17,055
	Bus	417	531	645	803	994
	Subway	85	104	126	157	195
	Sub-total	7,355	9,092	11,303	14,421	18,244
	Estimated reduction compared with the total[2]	-	249 (1.12%)	600 (2.26%)	820 (2.64%)	1,294 (3.72%)

1) Total emission in the transport sector
2) The estimated reduction is in comparison with the total transport emission.

4.2 Modal shift in freight transport

The freight transport sector accounts for 30.9% of the total transport CO_2 emission and it is also regarded the most inefficient sector of Korea's transport. The road transport, especially less efficient private freight vehicles plays the dominant role in Korea's freight transport sector. Various efforts are now being made to reduce this dependency on road sector and to increase the more energy efficient railway's share by increasing the capacity of the more environmentally friendly freight mode.

The emission units by each freight transport modes are calculated from the current emission and activities data. The results are shown in Table 6. Table 7 represents the target freight modal share set by the ambitious government plan to provide more environmentally friendly infrastructure.

Table 6. CO_2 emission units by freight transport modes (1999)

	Private freight vehicle	Commercial freight vehicle	Rail	Water	Air
Freight ton km (million ton-km)	33,376	9,227	10,072	33,699	151
Share (%)	38.6	14.6	11.6	38.9	0.2
CO_2 emission (thousand TC)	5,251.3	1,167.7	-	-	-
CO_2 emission unit (g-C/ton km)	157.3	126.6	7.1	10.0	402.0

Table 7. Proposed freight modal share change

Unit: %

	1997	2010	2020
Road	56.6	48.2	41.2
Rail	14.2	15.5	20.3
Water	35.8	36.0	38.1
Air	0.1	0.3	0.4

Table 8. Freight modal shift policy scenarios

BAU Scenario	Current trend and no infrastructure investment
Modal shift scenario	Government infrastructure investment and modal shift plan

Table 9. Freight modal demand forecasting by scenario

Unit: million ton km

		2000	2005	2010	2015	2020
BAU Scenario	Road Private	34,379	40,006	46,841	55,201	65,491
	Road Commercial	9,504	11,060	12,950	15,261	18,106
	Rail	10,375	12,073	14,136	16,659	19,764
	Water	34,712	40,394	47,295	55,736	66,125
	Air	156	182	213	251	298
	Total	89,126	103,715	121,435	143,108	169,784
Infrastructure & modal shift policy scenario	Road Private	34,379	38,448	40,972	41,468	41,971
	Road Commercial	9,504	10,417	17,560	22,494	27,980
	Rail	10,375	14,592	18,822	25,477	34,483
	Water	34,712	40,007	43,717	53,178	64,688
	Air	156	252	364	491	662
	Total	89,126	103,715	121,435	143,108	169,784

As shown in Table 10, it is estimated that 6.64% of CO_2 emission can be reduced by the long-term modal shift policy measures. This increased efficiency comes from the modal shift to more energy efficient modes such as rail and also from a shift to more efficient commercial vehicles within the road sector.

Table 10. CO_2 emission forecasting and reduction potential under the
infrastructure and modal shift policy

Unit: thousand TC

		2000	2005	2010	2015	2020
BAU Scenario	Road Private	5,409	6,294	7,370	8,685	10,304
	Road Commercial	1,203	1,400	1,639	1,931	2,291
	Rail	74	86	101	119	141
	Water	347	404	473	557	661
	Air	63	73	86	101	120
	Sub total	7,096	8,257	9,668	11,394	13,518
	Total	18,681	22,056	26,565	30,855	33,869
Infrastructure & modal shift policy Scenario	Road Private	5,409	6,049	6,446	6,525	6,604
	Road Commercial	1,203	1,318	2,222	2,847	3,541
	Rail	74	104	134	182	246
	Water	347	400	437	532	647
	Air	63	101	146	197	266
	Sub total	7,096	7,973	9,387	10,282	11,304
	Reduction potential	-	284 (1.29%)	282 (1.06%)	1,111 (3.60%)	2,214 (6.54%)

4.3 Fuel price policy

We first need to specify the policy scenario of fuel price increase. In our scenario fuel price is assumed to increase at a rate of 5% per annum in addition to the base scenario for eight consecutive years from the year 2001. In the base scenario, an annual 1.9% increase is adopted from the price change forecasting as a part of the base scenario. This represents an additional 48% increase in fuel price at the end of the policy period.

Table 11. Scenario for fuel price policy

Scenario	Assumptions
BAU	Annual increase rate of 1.9%
Fuel price increase	Additional 5% fuel price increase from 2001 for 8 years

There are two ways that the fuel price change can affect the carbon dioxide emission in the transport sector. The assumed fuel price change has some impact on the future vehicle ownership since our long-term vehicle ownership forecasting equation has fuel price as a component of the cost variable. And then the increased fuel price affects the vehicle travel according to the price elasticity.

Table 12 shows the estimated impact of fuel price increase on the vehicle ownership. It is estimated that the assumed fuel price hike will reduce the vehicle numbers by almost 1.4 million in the long run. This represents about 7.8% reduction of passenger cars compared with the BAU scenario.

The estimated reduction in the CO_2 emission is shown in the Table 13 below. It is estimated that about 4.8% of the total emission reduction can be expected under the fuel price policy. The estimated reduction in this case is measured against the total emission in the transport sector that was calculated by the emission units.

Table 12. Forecasting of vehicle ownership under the fuel price policy scenario

Unit: vehicles

		2000	2005	2010	2015	2020
BAU Scenario	Passenger car (Gasoline)	7,624,013	10,319,880	13,470,977	15,710,622	17,535,395
	Bus (Gasoline)	44,993	52,837	58,379	67,320	73,877
	Truck (Gasoline)	62,473	73,364	81,059	93,474	102,578
	Subtotal	7,731,4797	10,446,081	13,610,415	15,871,416	17,711,850
Fuel price policy scenario	Passenger car (Gasoline)	7,624,013	9,943,312	12,317,773	14,567,116	16,542,085
	Bus (Gasoline)	44,993	50,012	52,443	61,323	68,467
	Truck (Gasoline)	62,473	69,442	72,817	85,147	95,067
	Subtotal	7,731,479	9,888,036	12,226,579	14,457,605	16,414,932
	Estimated reduction of vehicle numbers	-	558,045	1,383,836	1,413,811	1,296,918

Table 13. Estimated reduction of CO_2 under the fuel price policy

Unit: thousand TC

		2000	2005	2010	2015	2020
BAU Scenario	Passenger car (Gasoline)	7,024	9,436	12,317	14,364	16,033
	Bus (Gasoline)	50	58	64	74	81
	Truck (Gasoline)	77	89	99	114	125
	Subtotal	7,151	9,583	12,480	14,552	16,239
	Total Emission	18,681	22,176	26,565	31,044	34,748
Fuel price policy scenario	Passenger car (Gasoline)	7,024	8,809	10,726	12,684	14,404
	Bus (Gasoline)	50	54	56	65	73
	Truck (Gasoline)	77	83	86	100	112
	Subtotal	7,151	8,946	10,868	12,849	14,589
	Estimated reduction of CO_2 emission*	-	637 (2.87%)	1,612 (6.07%)	1,703 (5.49%)	1,650 (4.75%)

* The estimated reduction is in comparison with the total emission in the transport sector

5 The impacts on macro economy, energy consumption and GHG emissions

An assessment of the impacts of various policy scenarios to mitigate GHG emissions in transport sector is provided in this section. The economic and environmental impacts are measured by comparing results from counter factual runs of the model and the reference case.

Table 14. Changes in economic and environmental indicators relative to the reference case

Economic and environmental indicators	Scenario 1 (Public transport promotion)		Scenario 2 (Modal shift in freight transport)		Scenario 3 (Fuel pricing)	
	2010	2020	2010	2020	2010	2020
Real GNP	0.31	0.45	-0.80	1.13	-0.51	-0.45
Household consumption	0.44	0.60	-1.11	1.70	-1.08	-0.91
Investment	0.32	0.49	-0.33	1.09	-0.09	-0.10
Government Consumption	0.44	0.60	-1.11	1.70	-1.08	-0.91
Export	-0.38	-0.49	1.04	-2.06	0.85	0.47
Import	-0.33	-0.02	0.75	-0.22	-0.08	-0.25
GHG emissions	-0.42	-0.74	-0.67	-1.95	-2.16	-2.63
Energy consumption	-0.80	-1.26	-0.97	-3.42	-2.54	-2.99
Energy intensity	-1.12	-1.70	-0.18	-4.50	-2.04	-2.55
Emission intensity	-0.77	-1.24	0.13	-3.18	-1.74	-2.29

Table 14 presents the impacts of three different policy scenarios on macro economy, aggregate energy consumption and aggregate GHG emissions in Korea. Scenario 1 (public transport promotion) is projected to increase real GDP by 0.31% and 0.45% relative to the reference case in 2010 and 2020 respectively, while GHG emissions is projected to be reduced by 0.42% and 0.74% in same year. The increase of real GDP relative to the reference case is led by the increase of household consumption, government consumption and investment. However, the deterioration of trade account partly offsets the increase of real GDP. The reduction of GHG emissions is mainly led by the decrease of emissions from driving private car. As GHG emissions fall and real GDP increases, the emission intensity is projected to decrease by 0.77% and 1.24% relative to the reference case in 2010 and 2020 respectively. Since the energy consumption is projected to decrease, the energy intensity is also projected to fall by 1.12% and 1.70% in same year.

On the other hand, scenario 2 is projected to decrease real GDP by 0.80% in 2010 and increase by 1.13% in 2020, while it is projected to reduce GHG emissions by 0.67% and 1.95% in 2010 and 2020 respectively. The significant reduction of road in freight transport after 2010 under scenario 2 is projected to lead the reduction of GHG emissions after 2010. Until 2010, the emission intensity is projected to increase by 0.13% led by small reduction of GHG emission relative the real GDP. However, the increase of real GDP is projected to contribute to the decrease of emission intensity in 2020 relative to the reference case. The increase of real GDP in 2020 is due to an increase of household consumption, investment and government consumption, while the trade account is deteriorated. As a result, scenario 2 is projected to shrink the economic activity during the short and middle terms with the reduction of GHG emissions. However, it is projected to expand the economy in the long run with the increased contribution of environment friendly road and sea transportation in total freight transportation.

Under scenario 3, fuel pricing, real GDP is projected to decrease by 0.51%

and 0.45% in 2010 and 2020 respectively, while GHG emission is reduced with the higher rate (2.16% and 2.63%) than real GDP. Therefore, the emission intensity is also projected to fall. This result shows that the scenario 3 is effective for the abatement of GHG emissions, however it accompanies the curling up of economic activity. The reduction of real GDP is mainly due to the reduction of household and government consumption, while the trade account is projected to improve.

6. Summary and policy implications

After the climate change negotiation reaches an agreement in near future, the next main issue to be addressed is the way of involvement of developing countries in emission abatement commitments. Despite having no emission abatement commitments under the Kyoto Protocol, Korea is projected to face the increasing pressure from international society to contribute to the global efforts for greenhouse gas emission reduction. As Korea participates to the global efforts, it is believed that it will create the structural changes of Korean economy. This new situation will bring Korea to an unfamiliar economic and social environment.   In this study we first analyze the policy measures' effectiveness and we develop a computable general equilibrium model where the macroeconomic impacts of environmental and economic policy variables can be analyzed in the Korean context. By utilizing a dynamic computable general equilibrium (CGE) model, this paper analyzed what kind of scheme for policy instruments in transport sector to reduce GHG emissions are desirable for Korea in complying with the international efforts to mitigate climate change, by focusing on three different policy scenarios.

This study shows that the policy focusing on the increase of fuel price (scenario 3) is projected to be effective in reducing GHG emissions. However, this kind of policy approach accompanies the shrinkage of economic activity simultaneously. On the other hand, even if the effectiveness in reducing GHG emission is lower than the case of fuel pricing, policies such as public transport promotion and modal shift in freight transport are found to be more feasible policy options in designing domestic policies in transport sector.

References

[1] Korea Energy Economics Institute, July 2000, *Energy Statistics Monthly*.
[2] IPCC, 1996. *Revised 1996 Guidelines for National Greenhouse Gas Inventories: Reference Manual*, (IPCC: Intergovernmental Panel on Climate Change).
[3] Japanese Ministry of Transport, 1999, *The Survey on Transport Energy*, Japanese Ministry of Transport.
[4] The Korea Transport Institute, 1999, *National Logistics Visions and Policies for the 21st Century*. (The Korea Transport Institute).
[5] Lee, Sungwon, Meeyoung Shin et al. 1999. *Comprehensive Policy Measures*

for Environment Friendly Transport, (The Korea Transport Institute).

[6] Lee, Sungwon, Jaekyu Lim, Myungmee Lee et al., 2001, *Macroeconomic Impacts Analysis of Environmental Regulations in the Transport Sector*, (The Korea Transport Institute and Korea Energy Economics Institute)

[7] Ministry of Construction and Transport, 1999. *National Strategy for Transport Arteries* (Ministry of Construction and Transport, Korea).

[8] Ministry of Environment, 1998, *Environment Statistics Yearly*.

[9] National Statistics Office of Korea, 2000, *Korea Statistics Annual*.

Locating P&R facilities based on travel behaviour: a Dutch case study

R.E.C.M. van der Heijden[1,2] & E.J.E. Molin[2]
[1] *Nijmegen School of Management, Nijmegen University, the Netherlands*
[2] *Department of Transport Policy & Logistics, Delft University, the Netherlands*

Abstract

Finding the right location for P&R facilities in urban agglomerations is important for the success of these facilities. Plans for P&R facilities are sometimes dominated by political considerations, resulting in location choices with limited success of the facility. Our knowledge of decision making by potential users should be improved to counterbalance these considerations.

This paper addresses a quick scan study regarding the location choice of a large-scale P&R facility in the agglomeration of The Hague, the Netherlands. The study has been performed in co-operation with the regional authorities to find indications for the best location from the perspective of commuters. A choice based stated preference approach was applied to identify preferences of employees of offices in The Hague, living at a certain distance from The Hague. A focus was laid on travelling in one specific corridor. Based on the analysis of the collected data, the conclusion was drawn that the politically preferred location does not fit well to the preferences of commuters. It will lead to a considerable risk of non-use of the planned P&R facility.

1 Introduction

Many urban agglomerations suffer from a heavy pressure by motorised traffic. The pressure on the urban system induces inbound and outbound traffic congestion, noise disturbances, much use of scarce space for parking, traffic accidents, deterioration of living quality, and so on. One of the strategies to tackle these problems is to improve public transport facilities. Traditionally, public transport has been considered as a transport means to accommodate door-to-door travel behaviour. Hence, travellers are strictly segmented into 'car users' and 'non car user'. This last category can further be divided into public transport users and bicyclists.

In recent years however, professionals in traffic management increasingly stress the need for accommodating chain travel behaviour. 'Chain travelling' implies the use of different transport modes during one door-to-door trip. For example, the use of a bus or car to go to the train station, then use the train to the city of destination and a rented bike or a taxi to the final destination. Typical for chain travelling is the combined use of private and public transport means. Consequently, the 'old' approach of segmenting travel markets is increasingly inadequate and should be replaced by a chain focus, including attention for integrating transport services, information provision, infrastructure facilities and adjacent parking and traffic management policies. A chain approach could overcome the typical disadvantage of public transport being strong with respect to point-to-point mass transport but weak in linking the place of origin or destination to the bundled transport services.

To accommodate chain travelling, P&R facilities play a significant role (e.g. Turnbull [1]). There exists a lot of variation in the features of these facilities. This variation ranges from small-scale bike and car parking facilities at peripheral bus or train stops, to large-scale parking facilities at higher order train stations with various commercial facilities. To attract people to use these facilities and switch from private to public transport demands for a careful planning, including choices regarding the target group, the capacity and location of the facility, the system of informing travellers, the price and the addition of extra commercial services. Choices in this respect that have not been carefully matched with travel behaviour, easily result in investments in facilities and services that will not efficiently and effectively be used. Non viable facilities will in the end result in deterioration of the facility and further loss of share in the travel market.

In the Netherlands we have faced the investment in various large-scale P&R facilities since mid nineties, that were dominated by political wishes (creating a distinguishing profile of the city), spatial considerations (where is sufficient space available?) and the idea to combine them with large football facilities. Insufficient study was made on chain travel behaviour of target groups. This has caused a situation of (very) disappointing use of the facilities in the early years. Also the city of The Hague recently announced the idea to invest in such a large-scale facility close to the city, to be combined with a new football arena. However, regional authorities argue that this plan is insufficiently based on the analysis of travel behaviour of target groups. These doubts triggered a small-scale explorative (quick scan) study performed by a Masters student of the Delft University (Van Iperen [2]). The focus of this study was to explore the preferences of commuters with respect to the use of a P&R facility to switch from car to some public transport service. The aim of this paper is to describe the research approach and the main findings.

The paper is structured as follows. In section 2, the study area will be briefly introduced. Section 3 then describes the methodology applied and the data collection. In section 4 the model is described while in section 5 the main results are presented. Finally, in section 6 some conclusions will be drawn.

2 Study area

As mentioned, the study area (Figure 1) is the region of The Hague ('s-Gravenhage), the Netherlands, called 'Haaglanden'. The region consists of various smaller and larger urban nodes, including the city of The Hague. Different motorways facilitate long distance access to the area. One of them is motorway A12, linking the Utrecht region with The Hague. For the part of this motorway between the city of Zoetermeer and the centre of The Hague (about 15 km), the congestion probability will increase up to a level of 25% within a few years according to recent traffic studies for this area. The congestion probability for the other motorways, linking The Hague with respectively Schiphol Airport and Amsterdam (A4) and Rotterdam (A13) is comparable to these figures.

Adjacent to the A12 high-level railway facilities exists, including 2 train stations in new-town Zoetermeer (110.000 inhabitants). The discussion on the P&R facility focuses on a location close to motorway A12 either close to the edge of The Hague (in fact the node of A12 with A4) or more to the east near to Zoetermeer. Apart from the railway line Utrecht –The Hague, Zoetermeer is linked with The Hague by a second rail line.

Notwithstanding the good rail connections to The Hague, more than halve of the commuters from Zoetermeer to The Hague travel by car. It was decided therefore to focus the study on the preferences of these commuters. In the next section, the analytical approach will be described.

Figure 1: map of the study area

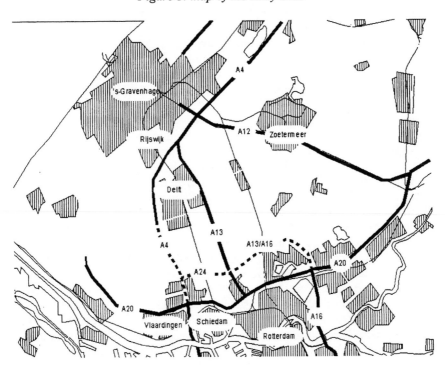

3 Methodology and data collection

The analysis of overt travel behaviour of commuters would not give a sufficient and reliable insight in their possible change in behaviour due to the construction of a large-scale P&R facility. The number and variety of facilities is simply too low to accommodate such an analysis. Therefore, a different approach was chosen. Good results have been reached with the stated preference methodology. It is referred to Molin [3] for an extended overview. Stated preference research is based on the assumption that overt choice behaviour is based on preferences of individuals with regard to their choice alternatives. These preferences are the result of the personal perception and evaluation of the attributes of these alternatives. Choice behaviour in thus based on making an individual trade-off between evaluations of attributes. Different operational measurement methods have been elaborated on this concept. In our study, a choice based stated preference measurement technique was applied.

The application of this technique involves a sequence of steps. First, the choice alternatives for a commuter have to be specified. In our study it is evidently necessary to have a choice option "car". Next, an alternative is a P&R facility near to The Hague at the highway node ("P&R node"). Finally, an alternative is a P&R facility near to Zoetermeer. In fact, for commuters living in Zoetermeer this third alternative would imply the option for using existing (or improved) public transport services ("public transport").

The second step is the specification of the attributes to characterise the choice alternatives. These attributes are selected by studying reported success and failure factors of operational P&R facilities. Although a variety of attributes seem to play at least some role, only the most important attributes were included in the study to limit measurement complexity (see Table 1).

In the third step the attribute levels had to be specified. This was done using information on actual or planned travel times and actual or planned costs. The attribute levels have been summarised in Table 1. As indicated in this table, 6 attributes vary in level: 2 specific for the "car" alternative, 2 specific for the alternative "P&R node" and 2 for both of them. The alternative "public transport" has fixed attribute values and therefore does not vary between the choice sets. Hence, it is considered to be a base alternative.

In the fourth step different attribute levels are combined to generate theoretical choice options (so called 'profiles'). Data collection involves the presentation to a commuter a choice set including some profile for the "car" alternative, some profile for the alternative "P&R node" and the profile for the alternative "public transport". The first two alternatives vary per choice set; the third one is fixed. The commuter then chooses one alternative per choice set out of these three alternatives. The problem is that due to the variety in attribute levels, too many choice profiles can be generated to handle in such an evaluation task. Therefore, a selective set of profiles is generated, based on statistical considerations (so called fractional factorial design). It is assumed that the part-worth utility of an attribute level is independent from the presence of other attribute levels. Hence the interaction effects are assumed to be zero. In total 8 choice sets resulted. Based on the choice of commuters of one alternative per set (the attached overall utility), the part-worth utilities of each attribute level can be statistically assessed.

Table 1: attributes included in the stated preference study

Attributes	Attribute levels	
Alternative "car"		
Travel time node to inner city	a.	10 minutes
	b.	20 minutes
Parking costs at office	a.	free
	b.	Dfl. 10,- per day
Alternative "P&R node"		
Average waiting time public transport	a.	2 minutes
	b.	5 minutes
Costs of P&R service	a.	free use
	b.	Dfl. 8,- per day including transfer
Alternatives "P&R node" and "car"		
Travel time to highway node	a.	20 minutes
	b.	40 minutes
Road pricing	a.	not introduced
	b.	Dfl. 5,- per day
Alternative "public transport"		
Travel time home to railway station	10 minutes	
Travel time public transport	10 minutes	
Travel time end stop to destination	10 minutes	
Costs public transport	Dfl. 6,- per day	

In the fifth step a questionnaire was designed including the choice tasks and some additional questions. After some preliminary tests, in the sixth step data were collected among commuters. Due to limited time available, it was decided to ask Haaglanden authorities, located in the inner city of The Hague and employing about 135 people, for their co-operation. The co-operation involved attending employees living in Zoetermeer on the questionnaire that was made accessible on the Intranet. Within 2 weeks 36 respondents filled in the questionnaires. They appeared not to live all in Zoetermeer. However, all respondents indicated to be able to fill in the questionnaire due to their good awareness of the situation. It appeared that 56% of the respondents was male and 44% female. A test on the age distribution of the respondents indicated a relatively high percentage of younger respondents (up to 45 years).

4 The model

Based on the choices of the respondents, the well-known multinomial logit model can be assessed that can be used to forecast the probability that a certain alternative i (i= 1,...,n) will be chosen, given its' attribute levels. The model is:

$$P_i = \exp (V_i) / \Sigma_i \exp (V_i) \qquad (1)$$

with

P_i: the probability that alternative i will be chosen
V_i: the utility attached to alternative i

In this model V_i is assumed to equal the sum of some basic level (intercept) plus the part-worth utilities for the attribute levels, according to equation (2):

$$V_i = C + V_{i1} + V_{i2} + \ldots\ldots + V_{im} \qquad (2)$$

with

V_{ij}:   part-worth utility of attribute j (j=1,...,m) of alternative i
C: intercept

The part-worth utility attached to attribute j of alternative i is calculated as the product of the relative weight of the attribute and the attribute level:

$$V_{ij} = \beta_j X_{ij} \qquad (3)$$

with

β_j: weight parameter for attribute j
X_{ij}:   level of attribute j for alternative i

The assessment of the parameters β requires the attribute levels X to be coded to standardise the parameter values. After assessment the parameter values are tested whether they significantly differ from 0. The standard significance level of 5% is adopted. The predictive value of the model is expressed in terms of Rho^2:

$$Rho^2 = 1 - (LL(\beta) / LL(0)) \qquad (4)$$

with

$LL(\beta)$:   the loglikelihood of the assessed model
$LL(0)$:   the loglikelihood of the 'zero model'

Starting point for this indicator is the assumption that none of the attributes influences choice behaviour ('zero model'). In case the assessed model does not differ significantly from the 'zero model' the Rho^2 will be close to 0.

5 Findings

The findings are based on the choices made by 36 respondents. The assessed aggregate model is specified in terms of parameter values for each of the included attributes. The part-worth utilities for the attributes for the alternative "public transport" are by definition set equal to 0 (by the coding scheme used as input for parameter assessment). This expresses that we consider the use of public transport as a base option and are interested in the degree to which the two other alternatives generate higher or lower appreciation by the respondents. The first analysis indicated that not all attributes are significant: the intercept for the car alternative, the travel time from the P&R node to the office and the average waiting time at the P&R node were found not being significantly differed from 0.

In a second analysis therefore, it was decided to eliminate the least significant attribute: the travel time from the P&R node to the office. Due to that, the part-worth utilities slightly changed. They have been summarised in Table 2.

Table 2: overview of part-worth utilities adapted model

alternative	Intercept/Attribute	Part-worth utility	significance
"car"	intercept	1,36	0.01
	Travel time to highway node	-0.06	0.00
	Road pricing	-0.16	0.01
	Parking costs at office	-0.16	0.00
"P&R node"	intercept	1.52	0.05
	Travel time to highway node	-0.06	0.00
	Road pricing	-0.16	0.01
	Average waiting time public transport	-0.31	0.06
	Costs of P&R service	-0.34	0.00

The interpretation of the part-worth utilities in Table 2 is the following. The intercepts of the two alternatives "car" and "P&R node" indicate the basic utility attached to these alternatives as compared to the alternative "public transport". The positive values indicate a higher preference (on average) for both options as compared to using public transport from Zoetermeer to The Hague. However, how robust this preference is, depends upon the values of the travel time and cost attributes. Evidently, these attributes receive negative part-worth utilities. In particular the costs to be paid for the P&R option (parking plus connecting train service) and the average waiting time at the P&R node weight relatively heavy. The Rho^2 of the adapted model was calculated as 0.80, which indicates that the model appears to be quite satisfactory explaining observed choice behaviour.

The model might be further simplified by combining different attributes for time and/or attributes for costs. Basically, it was found that the explanatory value of the model does not significantly changes. The interpretation of this simplified model is that the various costs and time components distinguished in the model are not differently weighted. To choose, the respondents simply added the costs and time component. Various respondents confirmed this. The simplified model therefore might give the best representation of the respondents' choice process.

A final (internal validity) test of the model was to use it to predict the choices by the 36 respondents with respect to a special (9th) choice set. This so called "hold out" set was not included in the data for the parameter estimation. The set is described in Table 3. The observed data involved the (intended) choices by the respondents regarding this special set. The model predicted that 1 person prefers alternative "car" (probability of choice: 4%), 1 person prefers alternative "P&R node" (probability of choice: 3%) and 34 respondents prefer alternative "public transport" (probability of choice: 93%). These predictions appeared to perfectly match the (intended) choices of the respondents.

Table 3: hold out profile

Attributes	Attribute levels
Alternative "car"	
Travel time to highway node	40 minutes
Travel time node to inner city	not significant; not included
Road pricing	Dfl. 5,- per day
Parking costs at office	Dfl. 10,- per day
Alternative " P&R node"	
Travel time to highway node	40 minutes
Road pricing	Dfl. 5,- per day
Average waiting time public transport	5 minutes
Costs of P&R facility	Dfl. 8,- per day including transfer
Alternative "public transport"	
Travel time home to railway station	10 minutes
Travel time public transport	10 minutes
Travel time end stop to destination	10 minutes
Costs public transport	Dfl. 6,- per day

The constructed model was in addition used for evaluating the effects of possible scenarios for commuters from Zoetermeer inbound The Hague. These scenarios differ in terms of the values of the attributes. This type of analyses can be considered as a kind of sensitivity analyses of market shares of the various alternatives given certain conditions. We included 5 scenarios in the analyses (see Table 4). Moreover, in this table the predicted impacts on alternative choice are presented in terms of the distribution of choices.

Scenario A represents a situation that optimises the conditions for car users. This implies no extra costs and only limited congestion. According to the model half of the commuters will use the car, while only few will choose for switching at the P&R node. The share for public transport from Zoetermeer is 47%, which is only slightly higher than the actual share within the response group (about 45%). Scenario B describes a situation that maximises the conditions for using the P&R node near to The Hague. The choice for only car use drops to 14% as compared to scenario A while the combination of parking and additional public transport at the P&R facility generates 22%. Scenario C maximises the use of public transport from Zoetermeer (in fact a P&R at Zoetermeer), by assuming congestion between home and the office and assuming significant parking costs at the office. The share of public transport increases up to a level of 95%.

The two remaining scenarios are based on adding the P&R node to the present conditions. Scenario D assumes the least favourable attribute levels for this facility while in scenario E the most favourable attribute levels in scenario E are included. As is shown in Table 4, the market share with regard to the response group for the P&R facility near to the city of The Hague varies from 2% to 8%. It should be noted that in both cases the model gives an under-prediction of car use and an over-prediction of public transport use, as compared to the observed modal split. This is at least partly due to the biases in the response group regarding mode choices (relatively many public transport users).

Table 4: predicted impacts of different scenarios

	Car	P&R node	Public transport
Scenario A: No car use restrictions	49%	4%	47%
No road pricing			
Free parking at office			
Congestion from P&R node to office			
Costs P&R node plus shuttle: Dfl. 8,-			
Average waiting time train: 5 minutes			
Scenario B: Stimulate The Hague P&R use	14%	22%	64%
No road pricing			
Costs parking at office: Dfl. 10,-			
Congestion from P&R node to office			
Free use P&R service			
Average waiting time train: 2 minutes			
Scenario C: Maximise P&R Zoetermeer	3%	2%	95%
Road pricing: Dfl. 5,-			
Costs parking at office: Dfl. 10,-			
Congestion from home to office			
Costs P&R node plus train: Dfl. 8,-			
Average waiting time train: 5 minutes			
Scenario D: Add-1 P&R to actual situation	27%	2%	71%
No road pricing			
Free parking at office			
Congestion from home to office			
Costs P&R node plus train: Dfl. 8,-			
Average waiting time train: 5 minutes			
Scenario E: Add-2 P&R to actual situation	25%	8%	67%
No road pricing			
Free parking at office			
Congestion from home to office			
Free use P&R service			
Average waiting time train: 2 minutes			

6 Conclusions and discussion

In this paper an explorative study was described to asses the possible impacts of locating a full P&R facility close to the city of The Hague on mode choice behaviour of commuters. The study was based on a small data set collected among the employees. Consequently, the results can only be regarded as indicative. The conclusion is that for commuters living in the corridor Zoetermeer – The Hague, the attractiveness of such a P&R facility is limited.

This is due to the fact that commuters first have to travel a substantial part of their home-office trip by car in a heavily congested situation. Even with no costs of P&R service use and a high frequency of additional shuttle service, the market share does not exceed 8%. In contrast, public transport from Zoetermeer to The Hague is a much more attractive option and will even receive a very strong impulse in case some mode of road pricing is introduced. This makes it far more logical to extend P&R facilities near to Zoetermeer.

Evidently, the practical value of this study for decision making is limited due to various aspects. First, the study only looked at commuters in one of the three main corridors inbound The Hague. Commuters from the north or the south might also use a P&R facility at the A12/A4 node. Secondly, as mentioned, the number of respondents was very limited. Moreover, respondents are employees of one company. This strongly limits generalisation. Not described in the study (due to space limitations) is that in a second step we collected and analysed some additional preference data among respondents working in 2 other companies. These additional analyses legitimate the same conclusions as described above.

Important is that this study illustrates that with relatively limited efforts and within a short period of time (the whole study as described took a few months), one is able to get a better feeling of the nature of decision making of potential users of P&R facilities. The stated preference approach appears to be a strong analytical tool in this context. It improved our knowledge on a key success factor important to counterbalance innocent political arguments. Evidently, the development of a more balanced (more attributes) and validated model is required. Such a model is under construction. The authors will publish on the progress in that modelling effort in the near future.

References

[1] Turnbull, K (1995): *Effective use of Park-and-Ride facilities*, National Academy Press, Washington
[2] Van Iperen, E.: *Transferia binnen het stadsgewest Haaglanden* (Transfer points within the Haaglanden region) (in Dutch), Master thesis Delft University of Technology, April 2001
[3] Molin, E.J.E. (1999): *Conjoint Modeling Approaches for Residential Group Preferences*, Dissertation, Series Bouwstenen 53, Eindhoven University of Technology

Section 10:
Safety

Modelling fatal pedestrian accidents in Montreal's metropolitan area 1995-1997

J.P. Thouez[1], A. Rannou[2], H. Bélanger-Bonneau[2],
J. Bergeron[3], R. Bourbeau[4] & J. Nadeau[1]
1. *Department of Geography, University of Montreal*
2. *Direction de la Santé Publique – DSP Montreal-Centre*
3. *Department of Psychology, University of Montreal*
4. *Department of Demography, University of Montreal*

Abstract

In order to help prevent pedestrian accidents, it is necessary to identify the environment and circumstances of the accidents and the characteristics of the persons involved. To study these issues a three component model has been elaborated, the first component included characteristic of the environment at the locus of the accident, the second component characteristics related to the driver involved in the accident and the type of vehicle and the third component characteristics relating to the fatally-injured pedestrian. Using a logistic regression as a method of analysis we decompose the variation in fatal pedestrian automobile accidents between the city of Montreal and the periphery of the region of Montreal. Results of the study showed that age of the pedestrian killed in traffic collisions is an important explanatory variable for the two territories. The elderly are more likely to be involved in fatal pedestrian crashes than are the other age groups. Some variables related to the characteristics of the driver and those of the striking vehicle were included in the final model but there are some differences between the two territories for example, high posted speed limits is associated with fatal pedestrian crashed within the city of Montreal but was not statistically significant at the periphery. Variables related to the characteristics of the environment at the site of the accident were roadway alignment and lighting conditions. Roadway alignment (grade-curve and flat-straight categories) is an important exploratory variable for the periphery and lighting conditions – roadway lighted at night for the city of Montreal. In conclusion, from the demographic and environmental point of view, it is important to make a distinction between geographical areas for exploring the mechanisms by which certain population groups may experience hi gher rather than lower rates of pedestrian fatal injuries

1 Introduction

Injuries of pedestrians in automobile-related accidents is still a major public health and safety problem in urban areas. Over the past five years on the Island of Montreal 247 pedestrians have died and 1603 have been severely injured in accidents involving motor vehicles.

A number of authors have studied the problem of accidents involving pedestrians from the demographic and epidemiological point of view. Joly et al showed that in an urban setting the accident rate among children in poorer neighborhoods is from five to eight times higher than that in the rest of the urban area. Singh et Yu found that accidents as pedestrians involving children are the single greatest cause of death in the states of Massachusetts, New York and Rhode Island. In a report by Cohen more than half of all pedestrian deaths by automobiles in the United States occur on neighbourhood streets. As a group, senior citizens (persons aged 65 and over) are almost twice as likely to be killed by an automobile as members of the general public. Studying Virginia urban areas, Worthington showed that elderly pedestrians encounter greater difficulty than younger persons in the negotiation of potentially complex situations, such as crossing the street in a densely populated urban area. They are also more likely to die as a result of the impact. In France, Fontaine and have performed a factorial analysis of the main characteristics of pedestrians and they have identified four groups of pedestrian fatalities: children involved in day time accidents in urban areas whilst playing or running; elderly pedestrians who were crossing a road in an urban area; intoxicated pedestrians in night-time accidents in the country while walking on the highway; pedestrians involved in secondary accidents and accidents associated with changes in the mode of transport.

In order to help prevent pedestrian accidents, it is necessary to answer questions about the circumstances of pedestrian accidents and the characteristics of the persons involved. This paper describes the results of logistic regression analyses of fatal pedestrian crashes on the Island of Montreal between 1995 and 1997. The rationale and design of the research is described further. The investigation is part of an on-going, interdisciplinary research program designed to determine the differences of exposure of pedestrians to automobile accidents in the provinces of Quebec and Ontario and to propose suitable action to prevent such accidents.

2 Analysis

Road accident statistics are, understandably, the subject of considerable interest on the part of media, policy makers and the general public. Instances in which accident counts are, for some reason, unusually high receive particular attention. They are interpreted as a change in the underlying accident risk and tend to generate some form of public action or out cry. But accident counts are influenced by numerous factors other than the risk level. First, they are subject to random variation. Second, they are strongly influenced by exposure levels. Third, they are affected by environmental conditions. Fourth, they depend on the accident reporting routines by the police.

The model which guided the analysis in this paper had three components: characteristics concerning the environment at the locus of the accident (e.g. accident location, environmental conditions, environmental land use, light, road surface conditions, time of the accident, speed limit zone); characteristics related to the driver involved in the accident and the type of vehicle (e.g. sex and age of the driver, vehicle type, vehicle manoeuvres, traffic signals, visibility); characteristics relating to the fatally-injured pedestrian (e.g. sex and age of the fatally injured-pedestrian, pedestrian action, number of persons injured in the accident) (Fig. 1). The type of measurement is nominal. The environmental variable conditions, for example, is divided into five categories. This conceptual framework suggests that a fatal pedestrian accident is influenced by three sets of characteristics: those of the pedestrian, those of the driver of the striking vehicle and the roadway environment at the moment of the accident. The relationship between the independent and dependent variables was unidirectional. Logistic regression was chosen as the method of analysis for three reasons :

(1) the outcome of interest is dichotomous. For example, these data does not reflect the behaviour related to alcohol either of the driver and the pedestrian.
(2) the factors are categorical variables
(3) the nature of the relationships between the independent and dependent variables are described by a logistic function

3 Methods

Data for this study came from all traffic accidents involving pedestrians in the region of Montreal between January 1, 1995, and December 31, 1997. The accident data were provided by the provincial public automobile insurance agency (SAAQ). In addition, the population data were provided by the provincial statistical office (BSQ). Since the age effect must be taken into account, we used the direct method of standardisation. A system of weights (wi) was described as the percentage of population by sex and age group in Canada from the 1996 census.

The standardised pedestrian mortality rate is given by :

$$T_{sj} = \Sigma_i w_i \frac{d_{ij}}{n_{ij}}$$

T_{sj}: Standardised mortality rate by age in the territory j
i: age group
wi: weight for the age group

dij: number of fatalities by age in the territory j
nij: person-years in the territory j and age group i

The ratio of standardised mortality rates (RTS) is given by the ratio between the adjusted mortality rate in territory j (TSj_1) and the adjusted mortality rate of the province of Quebec (TSj_2). This ratio (RTS) made it easier to compare the adjusted death rates between the city and the region of Montreal. This was accomplished by using the formula :

$$RTSj_1 = \frac{TSj_1}{TSj_2}$$

For a territory j_1 to test the null hypothesis ($H_o : RTSj_1 = 1$) one may calculate the z value :

$$z = \frac{\ln TSj_1 - \ln TSj_2}{\sqrt{\text{variance } (\ln RTSj_1)}}$$

using an a priori normal distribution (0, 1).

The variance of the reperien logarithm, important measure to evaluate z, is defined by :

$$\text{Variance } (\ln RTSj_1) = \frac{\text{Variance } TSj_1}{\text{Variance } TSj_1{}^2} + \frac{\text{Variance } TSj_2}{\text{Variance } TSj_2{}^2}$$

Therefore the measure of the variance is : $TSJ = \Sigma_i w_1{}^2 \dfrac{dij}{nij^2}$

In order to test the result, Morson's classification was used.

The analysis of the model described above is calculated using SPSS. For the outcome a hierarchical model was constructed by entering each block of variables shown in the analytical model (see fig. 1) in an additive fashion (ie first the "environment" block, then the pedestrian "block", then the "driver" block), keeping only those variables which contributed to the model and removing those which did not, before adding the next block of variables. Models were run using a stepwise backward elimination algorithm within each block. Variables were judged to contribute to the model if: (a) the significance level for the Wald inclusion test statistic was 0.10 or lower; or, (b) the significance level was greater than 0.10 but a contribution to the model was indicated via a partial correlation greater than zero and/or an improvement in the percentage of respondents correctly classified. Once all exploratory variables were identified (table 1), their first-order interaction terms were entered using a forward-stepwise solution.

The aim of this research is to assess how much variation in the fatal pedestrian accident counts is typically attributable to the above variables within each block.

4 Results

Men represent 54% of pedestrians killed and half of those involved in accidents with injuries are within the region of Montreal. An over-risk of being killed in accidents is highest for elderly persons 65 years and above in the City of Montreal and in the periphery of the region (see table 2). The vulnerability of elderly people is well known: among those over the age of 65 the lethal rates (ratio adjusted fatalities rates divided by adjusted severely injured rates) are the highest compared to the other age groups (see table 2).

Table 3 presents the ratio of standardised mortality and morbidity rates among severely injured and not severally injured. A comparison with the adjusted mortality and morbidity rates for the province of Quebec gives a significant over-risk of being killed or injured in the city of Montreal. In the periphery of the region not severely injured victims are the only statistically significant group (see table 3).

The significant explanatory variables in the models (presenting in Fig 1) were few and included some characteristics of the fatally injured pedestrians, of the driver and those of the striking vehicle and from the environment at the site of the accident. The logistic regression model for the city of Montreal had a p^2 of 0.25 where p^2 measures goodness of fit (see table 4). It is defined as one minus the ratio of the maximum like hood values of the fitted and constant-only-terms models. p^2 ranges from zero to one; values ranging from 0.2 to 0.4 represent a very good fit of the model. The periphery of the region had a p^2 of 0.28 (see table 4). The models have a relatively low specificity (i.e. the percentages of persons not fataly injured and who were correctly predicted) at 50 % but higher sensitivity (i.e. the percentage of pedestrians killed who were correctly predicted) at 97.7% for the City of Montreal and 97.6 % for the periphery of the region. The models correctly classified 97.6 % and 97.4 % of fatally injured pedestrians for the city of Montreal.

The Relative Odds (R.O.) and Confidence Intervals (C.I.) associated with each variable are also indicated in the table 4 Relative odds (e^β) is the factor by which the odds of having the outcome variable changes when the independent variable changes from one category to another. If β is positive the relative odds are >1, which means that the odds are increased. If β is negative, the relative odds are <1 meaning that the odds are decreased. Using the age of the pedestrian as an example (see table 4) the relative odds were 3.51 for the 45-54 age group, 7.39 for those 65-74 and 12.86 for those 75 years and over in the City of Montreal.

These age groups are more likely to be at risk of being killed than the other age groups. In the periphery of the City of Montreal one age group the group 75 years and over is more likely to be killed. The confidence interval shows that the relative odds for these groups of age is statistically significant.

Based on the significant single effects in the model, fatally injured pedestrians in the City of Montreal are more likely at risk if the striking vehicle is a bus, a truck or an emergency vehicle as opposed to an automobile, if the posted speed limit at the site of the fatal crash is high, if the crash occurred at night on a lighted roadway, if the number of persons injured at the crash site is two or more.

5 Discussion

Approaches to reducing pedestrian-motor vehicle collisions in urban areas included engineering changes following driver and pedestrian education and methods to alert drivers and pedestrians to one another's presence. To explore the feasibility of a program directed toward preventive measures to prevent fatal injuries or to assist countermeasure planning it is useful to know the pattern and character of the pedestrian crash problem in urban areas, the characteristics of the driver and the pedestrian involved in these collisions and the roadway and environmental factors at the site of the accident. Various studies have been conducted to obtain this information.

Most research conducted in North America indicates that the young and the elderly are more involved in fatal pedestrian crashes than are the other age groups [Cohen et al, 1997]. However, recent research suggests that pedestrian fatalities have declined more than other motor vehicle fatalities with the greatest decline being among children. Explanations for the vulnerability of older persons in fatal pedestrian crashes have been offered by several investigators. In crashes where pedestrians are struck by the front of a vehicle, the elderly appear more likely to sustain severe and critical injury on the MAIS (Maximum Abreviated Injury Scale). The major factors most frequently cited in the literature that contribute to fatal pedestrian crashes are risk-taking behaviour or negligence by the elderly. The elderly are more likely than others to emp loy a strategy for crossing the street that places them more at risk. For example, they may delay before crossing the street, spend more time at the curb, take longer time to cross the road and make more head movements before and during crossing. In addition, age related perceptual and cognitive deficits may play a substantial role in many of the crashes involving older pedestrians. Contrary to this stereotypical portrayal of older pedestrians several studies show that this group is more cautious under the most potentially hazardous crossing conditions when roadways are covered with snow or ice and when traffic is slow or moderate [Harrell, 1991; Jorgensen, 1988].

Most research points out that the driver is not at fault in the majority of fatal pedestrian crashes. The most common factors are speeding, driving recklessly hit and run situations. However, recent studies indicate that drivers and pedestrians are nearly equally likely to have made at least one critical error leading to crash occurrence. This is in sharp contrast to earlier studies that indicated pedestrians were far more likely to have made critical errors and is consistent with the change in crash type distribution toward fewer midblock dart - crashes and more turning vehicle crashes. In addition, passenger cars and light trucks are the most common types of vehicles that strike pedestrians. However, the heavier the striking vehicle, the more likely it is that the pedestrian will be killed.

The type of roadway, intersection-related factors, speed limits and weather and lighting conditions play a part in the frequency and severity of fatal pedestrian crashes. In general, crash sites are straight, level roadways. The posted speed limit at the site of the fatal crash is generally high. In the United States approximately half of fatal pedestrian crashes occur at intersections controlled by traffic signals. In Canada, Simpson and Warren have found that the majority of pedestrians were killed in clear weather and Bernard et al (2000) show that fatal pedestrian accidents are more frequent in summer than in winter. In addition, in the majority of fatal pedestrian crashes driver visibility was not obscured by roadway or environmental factors.

6 Summary and conclusions

There are two points of particular interest which follow from the results of this research. One concerns the variables which did or did not emerge as significant in the models. The other concerns the potential application of the findings.

Several remarks arise in relation to the first point. Age of the pedestrian was the important explanatory variable for the two territories. The number of persons injured at the crash site was significant in the City of Montreal only. The other pedestrian characteristics such as gender and pedestrian action did not contribute to the model at stage one. Pedestrian action (e.g. crossing the street against a red light, running, walking along roadway) could be a precipitant factor leading to the crash. This is not inconsistent with the literature which indicates pedestrian risk-taking behaviour or negligence may play a substantial role.

Second two variables related to the characteristics of the driver and those of the striking vehicle were included in the final model. In addition to passenger cars, bus (in the two territories) and light trucks (for the City of Montreal) are the most common types of vehicles that strike pedestrians. Also, fatal pedestrian crashes became more likely with an increase in the speed limit. In other words, in urban areas, speed kills. The relationship between fatal pedestrian crashes among the elderly and this precipitant factor is highly correlated. The variable driver visibility was not included in the model at stage one.

Third, variables related to the characteristics of the environment at the site of the accident were roadway alignment and lighting conditions. Roadway alignment is an important explanatory variable in the periphery of the region of Montreal but not statistically significant for the City of Montreal. The final model identified roadway lighted at night as a contributing factor in urban pedestrian crashes. Variables related to the weather conditions were not included at stage one.

Accident counts are influenced by numerous factors particularly, they depend on the accident reporting routines currently in effect and or the changes occurring in those routines over time. The limits of the data on police reports are not clearly specified in this study and they may prevented comparisons with other studies . In addition, given the number and diversity of variables in the models, there is no support for a simple cause and effect relationship. However, our results show that it is necessary to develop an education adapted to the pedestrian group, and particularly the age group, to be addressed, insofar as the problems are different in each category. It is also important to create an adequate environment to lower vehicle speeds in urban areas -such as the development of traffic calming measures- in order to facilitate the movements of the populations which are at risk for accidents.

Acknowledgments

This research was supported by a grant from the Quebec insurance agency SAAQ, the Quebec Ministry of Transport MTQ and the "Fonds pour la formation des chercheurs et l'aide à la recherché" FCSR

References

[1] Cohen BA, Wiles R, Campbell C, Chen D, Corless J. 1997. Mean Streets Washington. *Environmental Working Group and Surface Transportation Policy Project*, 80 p.

[2] Joly MF, Foggin PM, Pless BI. 1991. Geographical and Socioecological Variations of Traffic Accidents among Children. *Soc Sci Med* 33(7) pp. 765-769.

[3] Singh GK, Yu SM. 1993. US Childhood Mortality 1950 through 1993: Trends and Socioeconomic Differentials, *Am J Public Health* 86, pp. 505-512.

[4] Worthington ME. 1991. Factors Associated with Fatal Pedestrian Crashes in Virginia's Urban Area 1985-1987. Virginia Transportation Research Council, rapport 91-R30.

[5] Fontaine H et Gourlet Y. 1997. Fatal Pedestrian Accidents in France: a Typological Analysis. *Accident Analysis and Prevention* 29(3) pp. 303-312.

[6] Fridstrom L, Ifver J, Ingebrigtsen S, Kulmala R, Krogsgard Thomsen L 1995. Measuring the Contribution of Randomness, Exposure, Weather and Daylight to the Variation in Road Accident Counts. *Accid Anal & Prev* 27(1) pp. 1-20.

[7] Rannou A, Thouez JP, Joly MF, Bourbeau R, Bussière Y. 1996. Accidents de la route, flux, espace social et piétons âgés. Le cas de la Communauté de Montréal. *Recherche Transports Sécurité* 50, pp. 63-73.

[8] Wrighley N. 1985. *Categorical Data Analysis for Geographers and Environment Scientists*, New York: Longman.

[9] Norusis MJ. 1990. *SPSS Advanced Statistics Student Guide*, Chicago: SPSS Inc.

[10] Sarkar S, Nedewen AJ, Polo A. 1993. Renewed Commitment to Traffic Calming Measures for Pedestrian Safety. *Transportation Research Record* 1578, pp. 11-18.

[11] Jensen SU. 1999. Pedestrian Safety in Denmark. *Transportation Research Record* 1674, pp. 61-69.

[12] Virkler MR. 1998. Signal Coordination Benefits for Pedestrians. *Transportation Research Record*, 1636, pp. 76-82.

[13] Persaud BN, Retting RA, Garder PE, Lord D. 2000. *Crash Reductions Following Installation of Roundabouts in the United States*. Arlington VA. Insurance Institute for Highway Safety, Research report, 15 p.

[14] Blomberg RD, Cleven AM, Edwards JM. 1993. *Development of Safety Information Materials and Media Plans for Elderly Pedestrians*. Final report to the National Highway Traffic Safety Administration, Washington DC, report no OA 91-2.

[15] Koening DJ. 1994. The Impact of a Media Campaign in the Reduction of Risk-taking Behaviour on the Part of Drivers. *Accident Analysis and Prevention* 26, pp. 623-625.

[16] Lord D (1995) *L'utilisation des conflits routiers dans le cadre des analyses de sécurité routière*. École Polytechnique, Université de Montréal, Centre de Recherche sur les transports.

[17] Doyle DP and Tidwell JE. 1995. Driver and Pedestrian Comprehension of Pedestrian Law and Traffic, Control Devices. *Transportation Research Record* 1502, 119-128.

[18] Preusser DF, Wells JK, Williams AF, Weinstein HB. 2000. *Pedestrian Crashes in Washington DC and Baltimore*. Arlington VA. Insurance Institute for Highway Safety, Research report, 14 p.

[19] Sjögren H, Bjornstig U, Erikson A, Sonntag-Öström E, Öström M. 1993. Elderly in the Traffic Environment: Analysis of Fatal Crashes in Northern Sweden. *Accid Anal & Prev* 25(2) pp. 177-188.

[20] Harrell WA. 1990. Perception of Risk and Curb Standing at Street Corners by Older Pedestrians. *Perceptual & Motor Skills* 70(3-2) pp. 1363-1365.

[21] Jorgensen NO. 1988. Risky Behaviour at Traffic Signals: A Traffic Engineer's View. *Ergonomics* 31(4) pp. 657-661.

[22] Simpson HM, Warren RA. 1979. Characteristics of Fatally-injured Impaired Pedestrians. *Canadian Society of Forensic Science Journal* 12(1) pp. 31-40.

Table 1. Explanatory variables in final logistic models

City of Montreal

Variable	Type	Coding (reference category is underlined)
Pedestrian variables		
Age	Categorical	14 vs 15-24, 25-34, 35-44, 45-54, 55-64, 65-74, 75 and more
Number of victims	Categorical	1 vs 2, 3 and more
Pedestrian action	Categorical	Crossing with the signal vs crossing on a marked right of way, crossing along the edge of the road/sidewalk, leaving or entering vehicle, other types of movements, crossing against the signal, crossing outside of the diseperated, crossing on a diagonal (Jaywalking)
Driver and striking-vehicle characteristics		
Age of the driver	Categorical	Less than 16, vs 16-24, 25-34, 35-44, 45-54, 55-64, 65-74, 75 and more
Vehicle type	Categorical	Automobile vs bus, truck, motor cycle, taxi, emergency vehicles, others
Visibility	Categorical	Not obscured vs obscured by weather conditions. Observed by the environment (tree, building) obscured by headlight glare.
Driver and striking-vehicle characteristics		
Vehicle manœuvres	Categorical	Going straight vs making right turn, left turn, stopping or parking, passing, other
Environmental crash sites		
Posted speed limit	Categorical	Less than 50 km/hr vs 50 km/hr 50 km/hr and more
Lighting conditions	Categorical	Daylight vs mid darkness (day), roadway lighted (at night), roadway not lighted (at night)

Table 1(suite). Explanatory variables in final logistic models

Periphery of the region

Variable	Type	Coding (reference Category is underlined)
Pedestrian variables		
Age	Categorical	14 vs 15-24, 25-34, 35-44, 45-54, 55-64, 65-74, 75 and more
Driver and striking vehicle		
Characteristics vehicle type	Categorical	Automobile vs bus, trick, motto, taxi, emergency vehicles, others 1 vs 2, 3 and more
Vehicle manoeuvres	Categorical	Going straight vs making Right turn Left turn Stopping or parking Passing Other
Environmental crash sites		
Posted speed limit	Categorical	Less than 50 km/hr vs 50 km/hr 50 km/hr and more
Roadway alignment	Categorical	Flat/straight vs Flat/curve Grade/straight Grade/curve

Table 2. Frequency observed and standardised rates of morbidity and mortality
City of Montreal and the periphery of the region, 1995-1997

City of Montreal

	Male						Female					
	Fatal injury			Severely injury			Fatal injury			Severely injury		
	N	To	ta	N	to	ta	N	to	ta	N	to	ta
≤4	1	1.13	0.07	17	9.62	0.64	1	1.35	0.09	5	6.75	0.43
5-14	2	1.74	0.24	86	29.93	4.06	3	2.16	0.28	31	22.37	2.93
15-19	3	1.86	0.13	44	27.25	1.85	1	1.09	0.07	27	29.52	1.93
20-24	6	2.51	0.17	40	16.71	1.13	3	1.88	0.12	22	13.79	0.91
25-54	22	1.52	0.69	190	13.09	5.97	9	1.33	0.60	83	12.28	5.53
55-64	8	2.83	0.24	40	14.14	1.21	4	2.08	0.18	11	5.71	0.49
65-74	16	6.18	0.44	51	19.71	1.39	5	3.29	0.25	27	17.76	1.34
≥75	17	8.90	0.45	36	18.84	0.35	11	9.77	0.61	17	15.09	0.94
TOTAL	79	2.59	2.42	506	16.53	17.20	37	2.32	2.20	223	13.97	14.50

Table 2 (suite). Frequency observed and standardised rates of morbidity and mortality
City of Montreal and the periphery of the region, 1995-1997

Periphery of the region

	Male						Female					
	Fatal injury			Severely injury			Fatal injury			Severely injury		
	N	To	ta	N	to	ta	N	to	ta	N	to	ta
≤4	-	-	-	9	12.30	0.84	1	0.70	0.05	4	6.32	0.40
5-14	4	2.94	0.41	18	13.25	1.85	4	1.50	0.20	16	12.26	1.61
15-19	2	2.81	0.20	14	19.69	1.39	2	1.42	0.10	9	11.19	0.73
20-24	1	1.42	0.10	9	12.79	0.89	1	0.70	0.05	7	6.87	0.45
25-54	6	1.25	0.58	37	7.71	3.57	8	0.79	0.36	22	4.36	1.96
55-64	3	2.72	0.23	7	6.34	0.54	6	2.55	0.22	15	11.77	1.01
65-74	1	1.17	0.08	4	4.69	0.31	2	1.01	0.07	7	7.66	0.58
≥75	2	4.12	0.16	13	26.81	1.02	9	6.25	0.31	15	22.93	1.43
TOTAL	19	1.77	1.75	111	10.33	10.42	33	1.45	1.36	95	8.16	8.18

Table 3. Ratio of standardised mortality and morbidity ratio (RTS)

	Fatal	Severely injured	Not severely injured
Region/Quebec	1.24	1.59[xx]	2.05[xx]
City/Quebec	1.47[x]	1.99[xx]	2.60[xx]
Periphery/Quebec	0.90	1.08	1.32[xx]

[x] p = 0.05

[xx] p = 0.01

Table 4. Results of the logistic regression using forward-stepwise selection

Variable	Periphery of the region of Montreal Number of fatal and non fatal crashes involving pedestrians (985) number of fatally injured pedestrians (52) R.O. (C.1)	City of Montreal Number of fatal and non fatal crashes involving pedestrians (2561) number of fatally injured pedestrians (116) R.O. (C.1)
Roadway alignment		
1. flat-straight		
2. flat-curve	7.38ˣ (1.32-41.18)	7.05ˣˣˣ (2.29-21.71)
3. grade-straight	3.61 (0.92-14.21)	5.52ˣˣˣ (2.91-10.47)
4. grade-curve	70.62ˣˣ (3.47-1443.6)	1.16 (0.11-12.78)
		0.70 (0.09-5.32)
		27.32ˣ (1.61-46.80)
		1.90 (0.23-16.11)
Vehicle type		
1. automobile		
2. bus	7.09ˣˣ (1.85-27.20)	
3. truck	3.90 (1.40-10.90)	
4. moto	0.00	
5. taxi	0.00	
6. emergency vehicle	0.00	
7. others	22.28ˣ (1.98-251.09)	

Table 4 (suite). Results of the logistic regression using forward-stepwise selection

Vehicle manœuvres		
1. going straight		0.16 (0.04-0.71)
2. making right turn		0.05 (0.01-0.24)
3. making left turn		0.00
4. stopping or parking		0.75 (0.05-10.40)
5. passing		0.15 (0.04-0.52)
6. others		
Posted speed limits		
<50 km/hr		
50 km/hr	2.36 (0.60-9.32)	3.26 ( )
>50 km/hr	43.58$^{×××}$ (5.68-334.5)	11.92 ( )
Lighting conditions		
1. daylight		
2. mid-darkness (day)		1.63 (0.43-6.25)
3. roadway lighted (at night)	3.20$^{×××}$ (1.75-5.83)	
4. roadway not lighted (at night)	0.00	
Number of persons injured at the crash site		
1. one victim		
2. two victims		3.89$^{××}$ (1.68-9.04)
3. three and more		10.50$^{×××}$ (2.68-41.18)

Table 4 (suite). Results of the logistic regression using forward-stepwise selection

Age of the pedestrian

<14	0.00			0.52	(0.13-2.05)
15-24	0.22	(0.02-2.92)		0.79	(0.20-3.16)
25-34	0.61	(0.09-4.08)		1.30	(0.39-4.38)
35-44	1.40	(0.24-8.05)		3.51^{x}	(1.15-10.71)
45-54	4.35	(0.99-19.15)		2.52	(0.69-9.13)
55-64	1.46	(0.24-8.90)		7.39^{xxx}	(2.57-21.31)
65-74	7.92^{xxx}	(2.23-28.12)		12.86^{xxx}	(4.40-37.54)
>75					

p2 : 0.28
Sensitivity : 97.6 %
Specificity : 50.0 %

p2 : 0.25
Sensitivity : 97.7 %
Specificity : 50.0 %

% correctly classified : 97.46 %   % correctly classified : 97.62 %
^{x} p < 0.05, ^{xx} p < 0.01, ^{xxx} p < 0.001

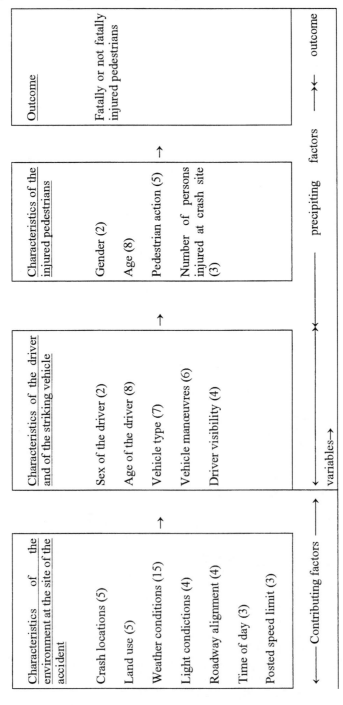

Figure 1. Analytical model for fatal pedestrian accidents

The practice of road safety audits

H.C. Chin
Department of Civil Engineering, National University of Singapore, Singapore.

Abstract

In recent years, road safety audits have been introduced in a number of countries as a proactive means of improving road safety and rectifying potential safety deficiencies on the road. In contrast to the usual accident investigation procedure that is undertaken after crashes are observed, road safety audits seek to identify safety problems prior to crash occurrence and even before the road project is completed. This paper presents a brief history of the development in the practice of safety audits and outlines the common procedure undertaken in such audits. The benefits and liability concerns associated with such audits are also discussed. The paper also describes a methodology of risk assessment not found in the most manuals on road safety audits.

1 Introduction

For many years, safety researchers and practitioners have made concerted efforts to reduce crash occurrences on the roads. While there seems to be general improvements in safety standards in our vehicles and on the roads [1], the increase in motorization continues to inflict an unacceptable fatality and injury toll on road users worldwide.

Traditional safety programs tend to be reactive, i.e., safety improvement schemes are designed based on and following observed crashes. Such an approach is unlikely to result in substantial decrease in crash reduction occurrences and road casualties. In recent years, there have been calls by various authorities to achieve quantum reduction in fatality rates [2]. This has led many agencies to explore more proactive strategies to deal with the root causes of safety deficiencies in the road system.

In the 1970s and 1980s, there were various attempts in North America and Europe to examine traffic conflicts, which were considered to precede crash occurrences. Though more proactive than many accident investigation programs, traffic conflict studies [3] still require road projects to be completed before actions can be taken.

It seems sensible that a more proactive road safety enhancement strategy is one that examines the crash risks or potential of road projects even before such projects are completed. This principle underlies the practice of road safety audits.

AustRoads [4] defines a road safety audit as a Aformal examination of an existing or future road or traffic project, or any project which interacts with road users, in which an independent, qualified examiner reports on the project's accident potential and safety performance@. Such audits were first introduced in the 1980s in the United Kingdom based on the safety audit concepts originally developed for railroad networks during the Victorian Period. It was done as part of a Quality Assurance Scheme in a number of County Councils to facilitate a systematic check of highway projects prepared by the County Councils [5]. This practice was formalised in the United Kingdom in 1990 with the publication of The Institution of Highways and Transportation on Guidelines for the Safety Audit of Highways [6]. The guidelines were subsequently revised [7] when the Department of Transport in United Kingdom made it mandatory for all major national trunk roads and motorways to be audited.

At the same time, a similar safety audit process was initiated in New Zealand when the newly formed Transit New Zealand was given the responsibility to conduct post-construction safety reviews of road projects [8]. Initially, pilot reviews were conducted for state highway projects, but by 1993 a set of policies and procedures [9] was already developed and implemented for all types of roads.

In Australia, road safety audits were first introduced in the State of New South Wales in 1990 [10]. The practice was quickly followed by other states and in 1994, the Australian Road Authority, AustRoads [4] has published its own guidelines on auditing roads in Australia.

In the last decade, road safety audits have been adopted in similar fashion in other countries in Europe [11-12], North America [13-14], Africa [15] and Asia [16-17].

2 Objectives and benefits of road safety audits

Road safety audits were introduced as an attempt to implement quality assurance in organisations involved in planning, design, construction and operation of road projects. Hence they are some form of quality control checks undertaken at specific points in time so as to ensure quality is maintained throughout the life

cycle of a road project. Specifically, road safety audits are aimed at achieving the following objectives:
1. To identify potential safety problems faced by all road users and others who may be affected by the road project;
2. To ensure adequate measures are considered to eliminate or minimise the potential safety problems.

Most road designs tend to favour the drivers rather than non-drivers. For example, the criteria for establishing curvatures in horizontal and vertical road profiles are solely based on the performance of drivers in maintaining adequate sight distances and speeds. Consequently, other road users may be inadvertently forgotten in the design process. A failure to provide adequate and appropriate facilities for vulnerable road users can often lead to unsafe conditions for these road users who may resort to taking unsafe actions. By considering all road users, particularly the vulnerable ones in the examination, road safety audits seek to cover whatever lapses in safety considerations in the design process.

There are identifiable benefits in conducting road safety audits. Evidently, the necessity of safety audits makes those who are responsible for road development and maintenance become more aware of the safety requirements in their projects and will indirectly help to promote a better road safety culture among road providers and operators. Potentially, safety audits should reduce the likelihood of crash occurrences as well as severity of crashes on the roads. Such reductions can mean significant economic benefits to the road users and operators as well as to society as a whole. When hazards are identified early and measures to eliminate them are taken promptly, there will be a reduced possibility of having to undertake expensive remedial works on the completed road system subsequently. Furthermore, by noting design deficiencies that are highlighted in a safety audit, designers can work to incorporate safety features into their future designs, bringing about improved designs and facilitating a more efficient way of updating design standards and procedures. The extensive documentation required in safety audits can also lead to better appreciation of the principles of road safety engineering among highway engineers and operators.

While there appears to be potential benefits in road safety audits, there are few quantitative assessments to confirm these benefits, despite the numerous safety audits that have been undertaken to date. It has been argued [18] that since road safety audits are unlikely to cost more than accident blackspot programs which have been shown to result in significant economic benefits, the benefit to cost ratio of safety audits should be high. Based on some early work done in New Zealand [9], the potential benefit to cost ratio of 20:1 seems to be attainable.

3 Types of road safety audits

As a formal process of assessing the crash potential and safety performance of a road project, the safety audit requires an independent and qualified team to be the assessor. Such an examination is not considered to be a design check as it deals only with safety issues. However, as a complete safety check, the concerns of all road users, including motorcyclists, pedestrians and cyclists, must be taken into account.

Road safety audits can be undertaken throughout the entire life cycle of a road project from conception to operation. Various types of road safety audits have been defined in road safety audit manuals and these are conducted at the different stages of the life cycle in the road development, as follows:

1. *Feasibility stage.* In this case the review looks at the route options, layout options and treatment options. The audit allows an assessment of the relative safety performance of scheme options and identifies the specific safety needs of the various potential users based on the adjacent land use. It may also highlight the need to reprogram other nearby road or traffic projects to safely accommodate changes in traffic.

2. *Preliminary Design Stage.* At this stage, the issues such as intersection or interchange layout and the alignment details are addressed along with considerations on the design standard to be chosen.

3. *Detailed design stage.* Once the design details are available, the geometric design, traffic signing scheme, line marking plans and landscaping plans are examined in relation to the operational safety of the road.

4. *Post-Construction Stage.* A critical safety audit is undertaken just before the road is opened to the public; hence the audit done at this stage is also regarded as one at the Pre-Opening Stage. Site inspections are made under various conditions (e.g. day and night setting) and the safety impact is examined for all road users who will likely use the road. This audit ensures that hazards identified earlier have been rectified and are in place before traffic is allowed on the road. Other deficiencies not apparent on the drawings are easily identified at this stage.

5. *Existing Roads.* A safety audit can also be conducted on roads that are in operation. Safety aspects of the road network may have changed significantly since the road was first built. For example, the development of adjacent land and new roadside features such as new signage or commuter facilities may have a safety implication on the operation of the road.

6. *Temporary Road Works.* In a major road-upgrading program, there can be many elements in the road scheme that may be hazardous to the road users. A safety audit during this stage can significantly improve operational safety and ensure that the usually tight road construction schedule does not compromise on safety.

Audits may not be conducted at every stage of the road project. Indeed, there are differences in what are required in the various safety audit guidelines. The AustRoads guide [4] recommends only the first five categories. In New Zealand, the audit of existing roads is applicable only at a network level and while the audit of temporary road works may not appear in the audit guide [9], its practice has been encouraged [19]. The British manual [7] has only the first four categories because it considers the traditional accident investigation programs to be equivalent to audits of existing roads. Nonetheless, there is a subtle difference – as a proactive approach, an audit of existing roads need not be called only when crashes have occurred. This may explain why many County Councils in UK have carried out audits on existing roads [20]. In Singapore, audits are not carried out at the feasibility stage because there is usually little time gap between the feasibility stage and the preliminary design stage.

4 The audit process

There are specific steps in the audit process that are spelt out in the various guides. AustRoads [4] details 7 steps from the point of selecting an audit team to taking follow-up actions after the audit. These steps are discussed below.

Selection of the audit team
The first logical step in the audit process is selecting the audit team. This may seem straightforward, but concerns raised at this step are those centred on the qualifications and composition of the audit team.

The need for a qualified team stems from the requirement that the road safety audit has to be a formal exercise. Consequently, members in the audit team are to have both the relevant educational qualifications and experience, typically, in traffic engineering, road safety engineering or accident investigation and prevention. In some instances an understanding of the local issues is seen to be an advantage although it may be argued that someone with a different cultural background may provide a more objective assessment on safety. For the audit to be carried out without bias, it is also necessary that the audit team should have no direct involvement in the design or execution of the road project. This independence is necessary to ensure that the project will be evaluated with "a fresh pair of eyes". Furthermore, it is considered desirable for auditors to consider only safety issues and not be biased by design considerations known to the design team.

The composition of the audit team is also an important consideration though there appears to be no consensus on its requirements. Ideally, the team should comprise several individuals with diverse backgrounds and experience, who will complement each other in evaluating the safety performance. Based on audit exercises undertaken in training classes, it has been found that in general, audits are better conducted and more safety issues are raised by teams whose members are drawn from professionals with different training and experience in road design, construction, maintenance, traffic operation or traffic management. However, in practice, it may be difficult and costly to muster a large and varied team. Consequently, some authorities have allowed one-member audit teams to audit their smaller road projects.

Provision of Background information

Before the audit team takes on the job, the road designer or project manager will need to prepare the necessary background materials and supporting documents for the audit team.

The information to be gathered depends on the type of audit to be undertaken. The background to the road project may include information related to the intended function of the road section to be audited as well as information on the adjacent streets and intersections. The existing or projected vehicular flows and pedestrian flows and the kinds of vulnerable road users expected are also made known. Where applicable, the accident history of the site may also be needed.

In all cases, drawings of the road project such as the traffic plans, layout plans, horizontal and vertical profiles as well as typical road sections are essential. The audit team also needs other documents such as design specifications and constraints as well as reports of previous audits, at this stage. In audits of temporary road works, operational safety procedures for workers as well as emergency plans are also reviewed.

Commencement meeting

The formal meeting between the project team and the audit team marks the commencement of the audit proper. In this meeting, the project team briefs the audit team on the road project to be audited.

The idea of having one=s work to be audited is often uncomfortable and the commencement meeting can generate some tense moments of hostility. It is known that road designers have found it difficult to accept that their design skills are questioned by those who have little or no experience in road design [21]. Setting the right atmosphere in the commencement meeting and treating designers with respect for their professional work can gain invaluable support from the designers, which can lead to higher quality in the reviews [22]. Emphasizing the complementary roles in promoting safety can also bring about greater mutual benefits in professional developments.

Safety Analysis

The purpose in a safety analysis is to identify the crash potential of the road project. To do this, the audit team needs to examine the drawings as well as carry out site inspections under various conditions. All audits, irrespective of the stage of the road project, should include a site visit so that ground conditions can be properly understood [23].

Whether on the drawing or at the site, the auditors have to undertake a systematic appraisal of the risk potential. Few road safety audit guidelines provide a rigorous methodology on how this is to be done. One of the more structured approaches is that adopted by Singapore Land Transport Authority (LTA), which followed the concept based on military risk assessment [24].

Applied to road safety audits, risk assessment is the decision making process that seeks to evaluate and control the likelihood of occurrence and the severity of a crash. The process involves identifying the potential hazards, evaluating the extent of the risks involved and establishing further controls and precautions needed to mitigate the risks.

The steps in the risk assessment methodology are as follows:

1. *Risk identification:* Specific hazards are identified and described. A road hazard is defined as any unsafe condition on the roadway that can generate an incident that will inflict potential injury or harm to any road user. Risk is a measure of the potential for such a dangerous incident being realised. Hence, the concept of risk is a combination of two elements: the likelihood of a crash and the severity of the crash. In reporting the hazard it is important to indicate both the location and nature of the hazard, i.e., how the unsafe condition may result in an undesirable unsafe outcome. The description should include not only the type of vehicles and road users that will be involved but also the manner the crash will likely occur. Since different road users are involved, there may be several hazards at a single location.

2. *Impact assessment:* For each of the hazard identified, its severity is next determined according to some ordinal scale. The level of crash severity is influenced by the nature of the crash and the vulnerability of the road users involved. Table 1 shows the four categories of severity adopted by LTA [25] together with the corresponding definitions and examples. Since severity may be reduced by possible evasive actions of the road users and the kind of safety protective devices used, the choice of the severity level can be subjective and dependent on the judgement of auditors.

Table 1: Crash Severity

Category	Definition	Examples
High	Multiple fatalities and/or serious injuries	Head-on crash High-speed crash
Medium	Single fatality or severe injury with possible other minor injuries	Pedestrian or cyclist struck by car Side-swipe crash
Low	Minor injuries or property damage only	Low speed crash Cyclist fall
Negligible	Property damage only	Car reverses into post Car crashes into guard rail

3. *Probability estimation:* Following impact assessment, the expected frequency of occurrence in the hazardous event is determined by estimating the likelihood of occurrence. This estimate also requires good professional judgement from the auditor. Four categories of accident frequency are proposed in the LTA guidelines [25], ranging from frequent to improbable. These are defined and illustrated in Table 2.

4. *Risk Rating:* The category of risk for each hazard is evaluated by mapping the impact and probability values against the risk matrix as shown in Table 3. The risk rating establishes whether the risk of any potential hazard is acceptable or not.

Table 2: Crash Frequency

Category	Definition
Frequent	More than 10 times a year
Occasional	From 1 and 10 times a year
Remote	Once in 10 years to once a year
Improbable	Less than once every 10 years

Table 3: Risk Rating

Risk Category		Accident Severity Category			
		Negligible	Low	Medium	High
Accident Frequency Category	Frequent	B	A	A	A
	Occasional	C	B	A	A
	Remote	D	C	B	A
	Improbable	D	D	C	B

A: Intolerable – Risk shall be reduced by whatever means possible
B: Undesirable – Risk shall be accepted only if cost of risk reduction is disproportional to gain
C: Tolerable – Risk shall be accepted if cost of improvement is high
D: Acceptable – Risk is minimal

5. *Risk management*: Once the risk rating is known, the appropriate courses of action needed to manage or mitigate the risk can next be worked out. Where the risk rating is exceptionally high, it is imperative that such risks should be reduced by whatever means possible. On the other hand, the risk level may be so low that nothing needs to be done to reduce it further. In most cases, risk ratings fall into the region where the risk needs to be managed. In such cases, the decision to mitigate the risk is based on a comparison between the expected benefit in a risk reduction measure and the likely cost incurred. In general, risks should be reduced as much as practically possible and economically feasible.

To assist the review team in the tasks of risk assessment, checklists or prompts are often used. A set of the customised checklists is usually included in the most guidelines on road safety audits. These typically show the sort of issues and problems that can potentially arise at the relevant stages of the road project. The main advantage of using such checklists is that this formalised checking procedure can help ensure that potential problems will not be overlooked. Checklists may also be helpful for the designers to review their work before it is subjected to a formal audit by the audit team.

Safety report
As a formal process, the safety audit will require a report to be produced. The report details the findings related to road safety deficiencies identified and makes

the necessary recommendations for mitigating these identified hazards. The report usually contains a background description of the road project with a map or location plan. As plans and designs are modified constantly, it is important to know which sets of drawings have been audited. Thus, the report will usually include a list of the plans, drawings and documents and their versions that have been examined.

The main part of the report is devoted to hazard description. For each hazard identified in the audit, the location of the hazard and how it may develop is presented together with the nature of the potential crash and the result of the risk assessment. The risk rating and the recommended remedial measures to eliminate the risk are also included. To facilitate ease of reference, these are usually organised and presented in a tabular form. This is supplemented by a set of appropriate photographs showing the hazards and the surrounding road conditions. The list of the hazards and their ratings, together with the recommendations are summarised in a form at the end of the report. This summarised list is intended for the project team to document their response to the audit findings.

Completion meeting
Following the submission of the safety audit report, it is usual for the audit team to orally present the findings to the project team. This is done at the final meeting. With the help of visual aids and photographs to describe the hazards and road conditions, this presentation of audit findings can sometimes be more effective than the written report in bringing across the safety concerns observed by the audit team. While the project team needs to examine all the recommendations in order to make an appropriate response, it is not normal for the project team to respond to any of the recommendations during the meeting itself.

Response report
The indirect consequence of having a formal safety audit is that there needs to be a response from the project designer or builder to the recommendations raised in the audit report. In responding to each of the safety deficiencies identified, the designer or project manager may choose to accept or reject the existence of such a potential hazard. Where there is concurrence on the existence of the hazard, the project team may choose to agree or disagree on the risk rating. Finally, the project team may decide to adopt the recommended remedial actions or suggest an alternative or even to reject the recommendation and take no action. Whenever the design team or project team differ from the assessment of the audit team, it is normal to document the reasons for the differing opinions.

The safety audit submission and the response report are usually presented to the next level of management overseeing the project. In smaller projects, the reports may end up with the immediate superiors of the designers or builders but in larger projects, it is not uncommon for a high-level safety review committee to examine the safety and response reports.

5 Liability concerns

One of the main stumbling blocks to having more extensive use of road safety audits is the concern over professional liability. The manner in which liability implications are viewed may depend on the cultural setting of the country and practice of governance. In Australia, anyone alleging professional negligence must prove that the party charged with the duty of care has failed to act with reasonable diligence. Thus in calling for road safety audits, the authorities or road providers can show themselves to have acted with due diligence and hence become less subjected to litigation. In New Zealand, where the national insurance program does not permit lawsuit for personal injury, the liability issue in road safety audit does not arise.

Safety auditors have always expressed concerns over liabilities should there be mishaps arising from safety deficiencies that have not been identified in the audit. Some have argued that the role of auditors is different from that of accident investigators. In a safety audit, the intention is to identify safety problems so that safety deficiencies can be fully considered [18]. On the other hand, accident investigation seeks to apportion blame or award compensation. Hence, following this argument, the liability of reviewers should not be an issue.

There are still serious debates over the legal implications arising from the conduct of road safety audits, particularly in the United States where government decisions are subject to intense legal scrutiny. One concern is whether a team, agency or authority would become liable to those crashes that occur following the rejection of a safety audit recommendation. Such fears may indeed discourage agencies from carrying out safety audits. However, as safety audits deal with potential hazards while accident analysis deal with manifested hazards, then assuming that potential hazards cannot be treated as evidence for lack of safety, it has been argued [18] that agencies are no more liable in conducting safety audits than in executing programs to identify hazardous locations.

6   Conclusion

For the road safety process to be successful there should be commitment to the audit process at all levels, from the management of an organisation to the various working levels of staff and contractors. Often the audit process is perceived to be a challenge to the competence and professional judgement of the designer or road builder. This can inhibit the sharing of vital information. On the other hand, the audit process may also be treated as an approval of the design. In this case, designers and contractors have known to adopt a more careless attitude, knowing that their failings will be picked up. For the process to work well, all the stakeholders must view the audit process as an important avenue to promote road safety and to prevent the occurrence of crashes. It seems that much work is still required to encourage the various parties to agree on this common goal.

In the last decade, there has been significant progress in the development of safety audit practices around the world. Yet there remain numerous challenges ahead. As in many safety initiatives, there are as many sceptics as advocates. There are those who remain unconvinced that there is enough evidence of real safety benefits. It has also not been proven that the objective of creating a safer road environment and inculcating a safety culture among road professionals through safety audits has been achieved. Furthermore, there needs to be more research work to improve the assessment methodology. The manner of assessing risk as described in this paper, though more rigorous than what is reported in existing road safety audit manuals, is still far from perfect.

References

1. Lamm, R., Psarianos, B. and Mailaender, T., Highway Design and Traffic Safety Engineering Handbook, McGraw Hill Co., New York, 1998.
2. Gerondeau, C., Report of the High-Level Expert Group for European Policy for Road Safety, OECD, Paris, France, 1991.
3. Chin, H.C., and Quek, S.T., Measurement of Traffic Conflicts. Safety Science, 1997, Vol. 26, No. 3, 169-185.
4. AUSTROADS, Road Safety Audit. AustRoads, Melbourne, 1994.
5. Bulpitt, M., Safety Audit - An overview, Proc, Institution of Civil Engineers, Paper 10616, May 1996.
6. The Institution of Highways and Transportation (IHT), Guidelines for the Safety Audit of Highways. London, 1990.
7. The Institution of Highways and Transportation (IHT), Guidelines for Road Safety Audit. London, 1996.
8. Appleton, I. And Jordan, P., Progress with the Introduction of Road Safety Audit in Australia and New Zealand, 18th ARRB Transport Research, Vol 1, 1994, p. 101-106.
9. Transit New Zealand, Safety Audit Policy and Procedures. Transit New Zealand, 1993.
10. Ogden, K. W. and Jordan P. W., Road Safety Audit: An Overview. Proc. Pacific Rim Trans Tech Conference, Seattle, 1993.
11. Cardoso, J. and Bairrao, L., Application of road safety audits in Portugal, Safety Standards for Road Design and Redesign, Laborataorio Nacional de Engenharia Civil, 1998.
12. Kooi, R. M. van der (ed), Road Safety Audit, Tools, Procedures, and Experiences: a Literature Review and Recommendations. Leidschendam, SWOV, 1999.
13. Professional Engineers Ontario (PEO), Report of the Highway 407 Safety Review Committee. North York, Ontario, 1997.
14. Lipinski, M. E. and Wilson, E.M., Road safety audits - a summary of current

practice. Proc., Conference on Traffic Congestion and Traffic Safety in the 21st Century, American Soc. Civil Engineers, New York, 1997, 111-117.

15. Department of Transport, Road Safety Audits - Guidelines for South African Road Authorities. Contract Report CR 97/025. CSIR TRANSPORTEK, 1997, Pretoria.

16. Lagunzad, L.V. and Garsuta, R.T., Introducing road safety audits in the Philippines. International Symposium on Traffic Safety, Singapore, 1998.

17. Stolz, D.R. and Wong, W.K., Building Safety into the Road Design Process, CitiTrans Conference >99, Singapore, 1999.

18. Federal Highway Administration, FHWA Study Tour for Road Safety Audits, US DOT, Oct 1997.

19. Transfund New Zealand, Draft Procedures for the Safety Audit of Traffic Control at Roadwork Sites, 1998.

20. Hampshire County Council, Safety Audit Handbook.

21. Sabey, B.E., Safety Audit Procedures and Practice. Traffex '93, Birmingham, UK.

22. Ogden, K.W., Safer Roads: A guide to Road Safety Engineering, Monash University, 1996.

23. Belcher, M and Proctor, S., The Use of Safety Audits in Great Britain. Traffic Engineering & Control, Vol. 34, No. 2, 1993, pp. 61-65.

24. Defense Systems Management College, Risk Management: Concepts and Guidance, Fort Belvoir, Virginia, 1989.

25. Safety Department, Project Safety Review for Road Projects - Procedure Manual, Land Transport Authority, July 2001.

Comparative analysis of pedestrian-vehicle crashes

A.S. Al-Ghamdi
Department of Civil Engineering, King Saud University, Saudi Arabia

Abstract

In 1999 there were 450 fatalities due to road crashes in Riyadh, the capital of Saudi Arabia, of which 130 were pedestrians. Hence, every fifth person killed on the roads is a pedestrian. The aim of this study is to investigate pedestrian-vehicle crashes in this fast-growing city with the following objective in mind: to analyze pedestrian collisions with regard to their causes, characteristics, and most common patterns. Data from 638 pedestrian-vehicle crashes reported by police were used. The analysis showed that the pedestrian fatality rate per 10^5 population is 2.8 (2.1 in the USA). The analysis revealed that 77.1 percent of pedestrians were probably struck while crossing a roadway either not in a crosswalk or where no crosswalk existed. The paper also includes some international comparisons, in particular with the USA and UK.

1 Introduction

Motor vehicle crashes result in approximately 6,000 pedestrian injuries and 1,000 pedestrian deaths in the Kingdom of Saudi Arabia each year (Official Statistics 1999). More than one-fourth of the severe crashes in this developing country are pedestrian related. During 1999, there were 450 fatalities due to road crashes in Riyadh, the capital of Saudi Arabia; of these, pedestrians accounted for 130 (29 percent). Hence, every fourth person killed on the roads is a pedestrian. In this city Koushki (*1988*) studied walking characteristics and found that the average walking distance was about 859 m, which when compared with corresponding distances in other Asian cities was fairly low (Tanaboriboon and Jing 1999). In fact, since the oil boom in the early 1970s, the motorization rate in Saudi Arabia has increased dramatically (about 50-fold). The typical mode of travel in this country is the private car (MOC 1997). However, the problem of pedestrian crashes is still increasing (Official Statistics 1999).

Pedestrian-vehicle collisions are a serious concern because of the severe nature of injuries to those who are struck by vehicles. Past research has established that pedestrians suffer very serious injuries compared with vehicle occupants. The traditional view of pedestrian traffic safety tends to place the burden of responsibility on the behavior of pedestrians and emphasizes education as the means to prevent accidents (Harruff et al. 1998). This view has been investigated by data from developed countries showing that educational efforts are less effective than efforts aimed at modifying the physical and social environment of the transportation system (Roberts and Coggan 1994). In order to help prevent pedestrian accidents, it is necessary to answer questions about the circumstances of pedestrian accidents and the characteristics of the persons involved (Fonaine and Gourlet, 1997). This study attempts to determine the extent of pedestrian responsibility in crashes between motor vehicles and pedestrians in Riyadh. The objectives therefore are twofold: to analyze pedestrian collisions with regard to their causes, characteristics, and most common patterns.

2 Data

To achieve the study objectives, 638 pedestrian-vehicle crashes in Riyadh (over the period 1997-1999) were analyzed. Using data collected from traffic police and hospital records, some of the characteristics of these crashes were examined. A brief summary of the investigative crash records was made, and a database was constructed containing the circumstances of the crash in which the pedestrian was involved. It appeared during this stage that not all necessary data could be found in crash records. The problem with crash data in terms of completeness, clarity, and accessibility is still a major issue in this country, as previous researchers have indicated (*Al-Amr et al. 1998;Al-Ghamdi 1998*). Data collection and record keeping are not computerized but are still done manually. Therefore, the study data, which had been entered manually, were obtained from archived files in the Riyadh Traffic Police Department. A systematic sampling technique was followed in which every third record was used.

3 Analysis and results

The counts in number of victims (in each crash one victim (i.e., injury or fatality) is involved), and proportion of occurrence of the study variables related to pedestrians involved in pedestrian-vehicle crashes are summarized in Table 1. For those variables shown in this table, the frequencies were sufficiently large to perform confidence-interval analyses assuming a normal distribution. It should be emphasized that the primary purpose of this initial table was to provide an overall view of the data and to suggest variable levels or factors for further analysis.

Table 1: Pedestrian data and 95 percent confidence intervals.

Variable	Frequency	Proportion of Sample (%)	95 percent CI
Age			
0-15	272	42.63	(0.38 – 0.47)
16-30	104	16.30	(0.14 – 0.19)
31-50	160	25.08	(0.22 – 0.29)
50+	92	14.42	(0.12 – 0.17)
Unknown	10	1.57	(0.01 – 0.03)
Sex			
Male	517	80.88	(0.78 – 0.84)
Female	121	18.97	(0.16 – 0.22)
Education			
Literate	269	42.17	(0.39 – 0.46)
Illiterate	201	31.50	0.28 – 0.35)
Unknown	168	26.33	(0.23 – 0.30)
Nationality			
Saudi	295	46.24	(0.42 – 0.50)
Non-Saudi	338	52.98	(0.49 – 0.57)
Unknown	5	0.78	(0.003 – 0.019)
Social Status			
Married	204	32.0	(0.28-0.36)
Single	330	51.72	(0.48-0.56)
Unknown	104	16.30	(0.14-0.19)
Cause			
Play on roads	36	5.64	(0.04 – 0.08)
Not paying attention	55	8.62	(0.07 – 0.11)
Crossing not at crosswalk	225	35.27	(0.32–0.39)
The above two causes	209	32.76	(0.29-0.37)
Pedestrian not at fault	98	15.36	(0.13–0.18)
Other	15	2.35	(0.01-0.04)

3.1 Age, sex, and nationality

The age of pedestrian victims ranges from about 2 to 67 years, with an average of 28.02 years (st.dev.=11.1). From Table 1, it can be seen that the largest proportion of victims was aged 15 years and under (42.63 percent). The fatality data among those victims (75 deaths out of 272 victims) also revealed that that the fatality rate (fatalities per victim) is highest for this group (27.57 percent), indicating that there is a need for close attention to the analysis for this age group.

Figure 1 shows the distribution of age-specific fatality rates based on the population of Riyadh (*National Census 1998*). The overall fatality rate per 10^5 population is 2.8. The rates were lowest in the age range 20 to 29 years; compared with this group, the childhood (1 to 9 years) and young adult (10 to 19 years) groups had slightly higher rates and the old-age groups (60 to more than 80 years) had the highest rates (Figure 1).

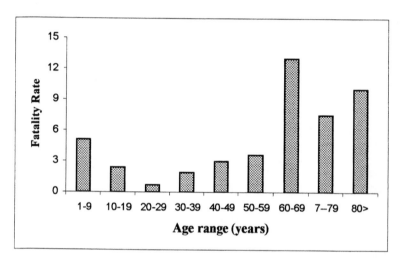

Figure 1: Distribution of age-specific fatality rates (deaths per 10^5 population).

Although women involved in pedestrian crashes accounted for only 18.97 percent of the sample (versus 80.88 percent for men) and their sex is underrepresented in the city (risk index (i.e., the ratio of percent crash involvement in group to percent population in group) of 0.43 versus 1.5 for men), their fatality rate (deaths per 10^5 population) is much higher than that for men, 28.93 percent versus 19.15 percent. Further analysis based on sex will be given later.

It appears from the data in Table 1 that more non-Saudis were involved in pedestrian-vehicle crashes on the basis of the study sample (52.98 percent). To read the picture more accurately, a risk index based on the proportion of non-Saudis in the population of this city was obtained. Accordingly, the risk index for non-Saudis is 1.6 (versus 0.68 for Saudis), indicating that the involvement of this group in pedestrian-vehicle crashes is disproportionate to their representation in the population (they are overrepresented). In other words, non-

Saudis are at much greater risk than Saudis to be involved in such crashes. It should be noted that this result is considered general because of the lack of data on unit exposure (e.g., walking distance traveled). Other characteristics are listed in Table 1.

3.2 Time of crashes

For day of crash, it appears from the study data that Saturday (the first day of the week in Saudi Arabia) has the highest proportion of pedestrian-vehicle crashes (16.93 percent) and Friday has the least (12.07 percent). The weekend days in this country (Thursday and Friday) reported the lowest proportion of crashes among all days. This result is consistent with the general trend in traffic accidents for the country. Official statistics show that Saturday has the highest number of crashes (Official Statistics 1999).

From the study data, it is clear that pedestrian-related crashes were more likely during the night (52.82 percent). Although 56 percent of all traffic crashes occurred in this city during the day (Official Statistics 1999), pedestrian crashes occurred more during the night, which can be attributed to visibility problems, particularly when it is known that more than one-third of such crashes in the study sample (35.31 percent) occurred during weak light conditions.

3.3 Driver characteristics

Looking at the data for drivers in this study, illegal-age drivers (under 18 years) were responsible for about 8 percent (significant at the 5 percent level) of pedestrian-related crashes. Under-age driving is a serious problem in this developing country (Official Statistics 1999). The group with the greatest involvement in these crashes is aged 21 to 30 (39.18 percent. It is clear that the three youngest groups (30 years and under) account for more than half of the driving population (61.49 percent). By nationality, although non-Saudis form about one-third of the population in Riyadh, their involvement proportion (29.31 percent) is less, indicating that this involvement is disproportionate to their representation in the population (the risk index is less than 1, i.e., 0.94).

3.4 Location of crashes

Most pedestrian-vehicle crashes (59.88 percent) in this sample occurred on divided roadways where posted speed limits were fairly high (from 70 km/h to 120 km/h). It should be noted that divided roads in Riyadh are typically busy with business activities (i.e., very congested). This result (i.e., median roadways have higher crashes) does not seem consistent with U.S. or European Studies. However, the study data show that more than two thirds (68.6%) of the women involved in pedestrian crashes (based on the study sample) were struck on median roadways and we know that women wear black clothing (cultural cloth), which might lead to visibility problems and hence higher crashes on this type of roadway. In short, one can say that women with their cultural clothing may over-represent the problem of such crashes on median roadways in Riyadh.

Unlike results from international research, fewer crashes (less than 5 percent) occurred at intersections, which may be partly because pedestrians like to cross anywhere, even where no crossing is marked, and partly because of the absence of crosswalks at locations where they should be available (Al-Faraj 1998).

Residential streets account for 15.2 percent of victims (97 victims), the second-highest proportion. In Riyadh, no school bus system is available for public schools. Each neighborhood has at least one public school. Breaking down the 97 victims by age, it is apparent that more than half (55.67 percent) of the victims were 15 years old or younger, indicating the great risk for children of this age to be involved in a crash on this type of road. Another study showed that a typical mode for a school trip in residential neighborhoods is walking and that children use residential roads as play areas (Al-Faraj 1998).

In Riyadh the definition of a crosswalk does not depend upon markings on the pavement, and from the data it was sometimes difficult to determine whether the pedestrian was in a marked crosswalk or not in any defined crosswalk at the time of the crash. Unfortunately, even medical examiner reports did not always make a distinction between pedestrians struck within marked crosswalks and those struck in unmarked areas.

Table 2 shows that most pedestrians (77.12 percent) were probably struck while crossing a roadway either not in a crosswalk or where no crosswalk existed (more than 80% of pedestrian causalities in UK occurred while pedestrians were crossing the carriageway(Hunt et. Al 200)). Of those, 48.12 percent were crossing the roadway where no crosswalk existed within 500 m, indicating that there is an availability problem (i.e., a crosswalk is not available where it might be used). On the other hand, 29 percent were crossing where a crosswalk was available within 100 m, indicating either that pedestrians are not aware enough of the danger of crossing at an unmarked place or that the crosswalk is not conveniently placed.

Table 2 also reveals that discipline in crossing roads is not generally observed in Riyadh. This result is consistent with a field survey conducted by Al-Faraj (*1998*), who studied the attitudes of pedestrians in Riyadh toward crossing facilities. He found that pedestrians were not enthusiastic about using crossing facilities (either at signalized intersections or at underpass or overpass facilities). Similar attitudes have been observed in other developing countries (Tanaboriboon and Jing 1999).

Table 2: Location of crossing activity.

Crossing Activity	Frequency	Proportion of Sample (%)
Crossing roadway at crosswalk	36	5.64
Crossing roadway not at crosswalk[a]	185	29
Crossing roadway where no crosswalk exists[b]	307	48.12
No crosswalk defined	110	17.24

[a]When marked crosswalk is available within 100 m.
[b]When no marked crosswalk is available within 300 m.

Compared with those crossing the roadway, pedestrians less commonly (less than 2 percent) were struck as they were walking along or just standing in the roadway or on its shoulder. This finding might be due to the typical curb design in this city, which is higher from the pavement by at least 20 cm and thus may make it less likely for a vehicle to run onto the shoulder. Of all the cases studied, 13 pedestrians (2.04 percent of the sample) were struck as they were working on or otherwise attending to their own stalled vehicles or providing assistance to another motorist.

3.5 Vehicles involved

The study data shows the types of vehicles involved in the crashes studied. Light vehicles, including passenger cars and light trucks, were responsible for 66.9 percent and 22.1 of the cases, respectively. Heavy vehicles (trucks and buses) and vans together accounted for 10.4 percent of all cases.

3.6 Causes

More than half of pedestrian crashes (76.65 percent) were caused by not paying attention and by crossing the roadway without being in a crosswalk, as listed in Table 1. Overall, the proportion of crashes in which drivers were at fault accounted for more than half (47.65 percent) of all crashes. This result may indicate that drivers do not yield the right-of-way properly to pedestrians, who share this right-of-way with drivers. From the pedestrians' point of view, 45.61 percent were reported to be at fault (26% in UK due to pedestrian non-compliance (Hunt et. Al 2000)), indicating that many pedestrians do not pay attention and cross the roadway improperly, as shown from the large proportion mentioned earlier (57.68 percent). It seems from the two proportions (47.65 percent and 45.61 percent, of which the difference is insignificant, p-value = 0.40) that drivers and pedestrians share the burden of responsibility. Although there is a problem with availability and accessibility of marked crosswalks, as discussed earlier.

4 Conclusions

The study provided insight into pedestrian-vehicle crashes in Riyadh. A total of 638 pedestrian-related crashes were analytically investigated.

The study illustrated that young and old age groups are at a higher risk of being involved in pedestrian-vehicle crashes. Divided roadways with fairly high posted speeds and residential streets are the most likely locations for this type of crash.

With respect to causes of crashes, pedestrians and drivers bear the responsibility equally for being involved in pedestrian-vehicle crashes. Not paying attention and crossing a roadway either not in a crosswalk or where no crosswalk exists are the most common causes among pedestrians. Many drivers often do not respect the right-of-way of pedestrians.

The results from this study provide a better understanding of some of the risks and problems related to the age of pedestrians involved in these crashes. This knowledge could help in targeting certain age groups in the population with better designed educational and awareness programs to improve pedestrian traffic safety.

References

[1] Agresti, A. *Categorical Data Analysis*. John Wiley & Sons, New York, 1990.

[2] Al-Amr, S. et al. *Camel-Vehicle Crashes in Saudi Arabia*. Funded Project. King Abulaziz City of Science and Technology, Riyadh, 1998.

[3] Al-Faraj, H. *Pedestrian Accidents in Riyadh: A Field Survey*. Master's degree thesis. Naif Academy for Arabs Security Sciences, Riyadh, 1998.

[4] Al-Ghamdi, A. S. Injury Severity and Duration of Hospital Stay for Urban Road Accidents in Riyadh. In *Transportation Research Record 1635*, TRB, National Research Council, Washington, D.C., 1998, pp. 125-132.

[5] Al-Ghamdi, A. S. *Road Accidents in Saudi Arabia: A Comparative and Analytical* Study. Proc. Of The 2nd International Conference on Urban Transport and the Environment for the 21st Century, Barcelona, Spain, 1996, pp. 231-253.

[6] Al-Ghamdi A. S. Pedestrian-Vehicle Crashes and Analytical Techniques for Stratified Contingency Tables. Accepted for publication at *J. Accident Analysis And Prevention*, 2001.

[7] Al-Ghamdi A. S. Pedestrian-Vehicle: Saudi Arabia Case Study. ITE Annual Meeting , Chicago, August 2001.

[8] Fontaine, H. and Gourlet, Y. (1997). Fatal Pedestrian Accidents in France: A Typological Analysis. *Accident Analysis and Prevention*, Vol. 29, No. 3, 1997, pp. 303-312.

[9] Harruff, R.C., et al. Analysis of Circumstances and Injuries in 217 Pedestrian Traffic Fatalities. *Accident Analysis and Prevention*, Vol. 30, No. 1, 1998, pp. 11-20.

[10] Hunt J., et al. Evaluating alternative operating strategies at Pelican crossings. *Traffic Engineering Control*, Vol. 41, No. 10, 200, pp. 402-409.

[11] Koushki, P.A. Walking Characteristics in Central Riyadh, Saudi Arabia. *Journal of Transportation Engineering*, ASCE, Vol. 114, No. 6, 1988, pp. 735-744.

[12] MOC. *Public Transit in Riyadh*. Unpublished Report, Ministry of Communications (MOC), Riyadh, 1997.

[13] National Census. *Statistical Report*. Agency of Public Census, Ministry of Planning, Riyadh, 1998.

[14] *Official Statistics: Annual Traffic Statistics*. Ministry of Interior, Riyadh, 1999.

[15] Roberts, I., and C. Coggan. Blaming Children for Child Pedestrian Injuries. *Society, Science, and Medicine*, Vol. 38, 1994, pp. 749-753.

[16] Santner, T.J., and E. D. Diane. *The Statistical Analysis of Discrete Data*. Springer-Verlag, New York, 1989.

[17] Tanaboriboon, Y., and Q. Jing. Chinese Pedestrians and Their Walking Characteristics: Case Study in Beijing. In *Transportation Research Record 1441*, TRB, National Research Council, Washington, D.C., 1999, pp. 16-26.

Cluster analysis for road accidents investigation

M.N. Postorino & G.M.L. Sarnè
Faculty of Engineering -
" Mediterranea" Reggio Calabria University, Italy

Abstract

Road accidents and particularly urban accidents are one of the most important negative impacts produced by travel, involving both users and non users of the transport system. The number of fatal injuries has increased in the last decades and their social cost has become more and more relevant requiring an in-depth study in order to resolve the problem. This paper proposes an analysis of accidents based on cluster techniques. Cluster techniques need a suitable database in order to group sets of "similar" objects and to identify the most relevant elements that represent the group. The identification of the relevant aspects common to different types of accidents is the first step for a conscious intervention in the transportation system, because the knowledge of the principal causes of accidents can help the analysts of the transportation systems both in the construction of mathematical relationships among accident and causes and can support the choice of suitable actions for reducing the number of accidents (mainly the fatal accidents).

1 Introduction

Road safety is an important aspect of urban and extra urban transportation systems, particularly due to the high social costs it involves. While different actions have been started for resolving the problem of the atmospheric pollution caused by the vehicles moving on the transportation networks as well as different efforts have been made to limit the environmental pollution at the end-of-life of the vehicles, in the safety field the situation is still very serious. The resources devoted to the road safety each year are largely smaller than the real needs; users spend more than 60 billion of ECU for accident refunds by means of the insurance companies, while the amount devoted to the prevention of accidents is very lower. The situation is different from Country to Country, both for the differences in the regulations in force and for the different sensibility of users to the safety problem. To limit and reduce the number of accidents on the urban and extra urban roads, a first step is the increase of funds for improving the transportation system; in fact, if well designed, the improvement of the road network is one of the more efficient solutions for reducing the number and the severity of accidents in the time.

The social cost due to the accidents both in terms of medical and economical assistance weighs on the community and is really high. In 1990 the U.S.A. registered a total cost due to the accidents near to 137.5 billions of dollar per year. Similar analyses carried out in Europe valued the direct cost due to road accidents equal to 45 billions of ECU, with about 45000 fatal accidents registered on the European roads [12].

Different studies carried out in this field linked the risk of accidents, the percentage or the number of accidents, the number of fatal accidents (dependent variables) to different factors or explanatory variables (independent variables) such as: age, and/or sex of the driver, expert or inexpert drivers, speed, length of the network, use of the safety belts, meteorological conditions and so on [2], [3], [4], [5], [7].

Other kinds of studies concern the aggregate description of the accidents occurred in a region [1], [4], [10], [13], by using indicators for identifying the trend of some relevant variables (total number of accidents, number of fatal accidents, and so on, in a given location and in a given time period) and the black points.

However, this kind of analyses allows relating the event "accident" with one or more relevant variables or describing the trend in the space and in the time period considered, but it does not allow understanding which are the causes that produced the accident. In other words, these analyses cannot establish the degree of similarity among even apparently different events. On the other hand, the knowledge of the main causes producing the event "accident" is very important in order to decide if actions of information and user education are more relevant than actions on the road network or more generally on the network system [8], [6].

In this paper we propose the use of the cluster technique for grouping similar accidents, in order to identify some representative types for each group and then the representative accident of the category, following the approach proposed by Pas [11] for the classification of daily travel activity patterns. The analysis of the identified standard accidents allows better understanding the reasons that causes the beginning of the accident.

2 Main characteristics of urban accidents

As a general agreement, one considers that an "accident" has occurred when at least one vehicle moving along a road gets involved and moves away from the roadway; alternatively, it is considered that an accident has occurred when a vehicle collides with another vehicle, a person or an obstacle. If one or more people involved in an accident die by thirty days, the accident is classified as "fatal".

Analysis of accidents can be performed by different points of view, because there are a very large number of factors that interact among them to produce the "accident event": human factors, technological factors and environmental factors. Studies already carried out attribute 10-11% of accidents to the non-observance of the safety distance, 15% to driver inattention, 2-3% to meteorological conditions and 52% to undefined causes.

Then, undefined factors are one of the most important causes of accidents, but the large class of factors collected in this set is not useful for analysis. On the other hand, the knowledge of the principal causes of accidents (not due to human factors) is a crucial aspect for the analysts of the transportation systems if some intervention have to be made for reducing the number of accidents (and mainly the fatal accidents).

The knowledge of the factors that contribute to cause an accident is a fundamental aspect because that knowledge allows conceiving methods for improving the road safety.

Road accidents can be considered the consequence of the interactions among the users of the urban or extra urban transportation system and the environment in which they move. An accident is then the result of a sequence of actions and events, due to the interaction among the users and among the user and the system; the strong complexity of this interaction makes difficult to establish which factor could be the main cause of the accident and how little variations on the initial conditions could transform a slight accident in a fatal one.

Furthermore, a large set of factors could be considered for describing the accident, making more complex the classification. In order to reduce the number of possible causes, causal factors and contributory factors can be identified, with the following meaning:

the causal factors are the deficiencies in the system and the manoeuvres that immediately precede the beginning of an accident, where the "deficiencies" of the system represent a condition of inefficiency that increases the risk of accident;

the contributory factors represent the causes of some specific deficiencies and manoeuvres; then, each causal factor is linked to one or more contributory factors.

Studies on causal and contributory factors have been carried out in UK within a project of accident analysis developed by the Transport Research Laboratory [3], [4], [5]. The analysis carried out allowed linking the most usual pairs of causal and contributory factors in order to understand the dynamic of accidents.

Finally, an important aspect in the investigation of accidents is the standardisation of the data for verifying similarities among events occurred in different places. At European level, there is a project, called CARE [14], whose aim is the construction of a unified accident data base, at different level of information, for all the Countries of the European Community. Statistics and indicators at European level about the accidents are one of the outputs provided by the system.

3 Cluster analysis for grouping similar events

In order to group similar events in few homogeneous sets, an equal number of factors has to be defined for each event, specifically the accident. Let N be the total number of factors considered for each accident; an example of such factors is given in table 1. Naturally, the kind of factors considered in the table 1 can change to match the specific objective of the analyst in describing the accident. All the considered factors are qualitative and then a subsequent coding needs in order to make them quantitatively comparable.

Table 1 - An example of some main factors describing the accident

human factors	age, sex, type of job, psychological conditions, physical conditions,
technological factors	type of vehicle, weight, age of the vehicle, number of kilometres already travelled
environmental factors	Meteorological conditions (sun, rain, fog, snow), pavement conditions, light conditions, locations, type of location (one way road, intersection, urban road, extra urban road, and so on);

The procedure presented for the classification of the accidents is briefly depicted in figure 1 and in the following the different steps are described more carefully.

Step 1
Step 1 produces the description of the accidents by means of the relevant factors previously identified; the result is a synthetic $N{\times}M$ matrix, where N is the number of factors and M the number of accidents to be examined. This matrix is the input of the step 2.

Step 2
This step produces an analytical comparison among pairs of accidents, defined by their factors, in order to verify similarities or differences; the result of this step is a similarity (or distance) matrix, whose elements are a measure of the degree of similarity among pairs of accidents. The construction of the similarity matrix has been performed by using the following similarity index [11]:

$$s_{ij} = \frac{\sum\limits_{k=1}^{N} W_k S_k (x_{ik}, x_{jk})}{\sum\limits_{k=1}^{N} W_k} \tag{1}$$

where:
   s_{ij} is the similarity index between the accident i and the accident j;
   x_{ik} is the observed value of the factor k for the accident i;

W_k the weight (if considered) of the factor k;
S_k a score function of the factor k
N the number of factors used for describing the accident i.

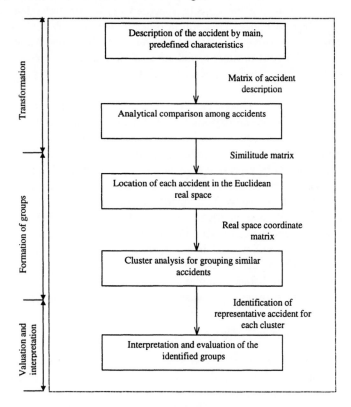

Figure 1 – Representation of the proposed clustering procedure

Because of the factors x_{ik} are defined with a code and they can have only few, predefined values, the score function used is simply:

$$S_k(x_{ik}, x_{jk}) = \begin{cases} 1 \text{ if } x_{jk} = x_{ik} \\ 0 \text{ otherwise} \end{cases}$$

The result of the step 2 is a similarity matrix S, symmetric with element on the principal diagonal equal to 1 (each event i is perfectly similar to itself); the generic element of this matrix describes the degree of similarity between the accident i and the accident j, on the basis of the weighted average of the similarities among pairs of factors. The matrix S is the starting point for the identification of similar objects.

Step 3

Step 3 produces the location of the accidents in the Euclidean real space N-dimension, being N the number of factors.

The relationship among the objects, specified by the similarity matrix, can be represented in a real space [11] and in order to achieve this goal the similarity matrix has to be positive semidefinite. Gower [15], [16] showed that a matrix of indices of similarity is positive semidefinite if all data of the set of observations are considered. Particularly, each object has to be valued and compared to all the others.

Because of each object (specifically the accident) is defined by the same number of factors and there are no reasons for eliminating an object from the process of valuation and comparison, it can be argued that the all data in the observed set are considered and then the similarity matrix is positive semidefinite. In this way, the matrix can be represented in the real Euclidean space: each accident can be represented by a point and the distances among the different point reproduce the relationship expressed by the similarity matrix.

The result of this step is then a matrix of spatial coordinates that allows identifying each accident as a point in the N-dimension space.

The clustering algorithm used in the literature can directly use the similarity matrix for identifying similar object, but if we want to identify the centroid for each group and the distance among each element of the group and the centroid the step 3 cannot be omitted because this kind of information cannot be directly deduced by the similarity matrix.

Step 4

In this step similar accidents are grouped together, on the basis of their location in the Euclidean real space and then it provides a clustering of similar accidents on the basis of the similarity relationships defined at the previous step two.

Each clustering process involves loss of information; in fact the object are grouped on the basis of their similarity but because of the similarity cannot be identified with a perfect equality, the clustering reduces the specific characteristics of each object, specially if the cluster is identified by only one representative element. On the other hand, if we increase the number of cluster for maintaining the peculiarity of the objects, this number will tend to coincide with the number of objects.

The loss of information produced by the clustering process, particularly when each cluster is represented by only one centroid, can be defined in terms of sum of the squares of the errors. More specifically, if N is the dimension of the considered space, referred to the number of factors, G the number of groups and N_g the number of observations in the group g, the following expression holds:

$$WSS_G = \sum_{g=1}^{G} \sum_{i=1}^{N_g} \sum_{n=1}^{N} (X_{gin} - \underline{X}_{gn})^2 \tag{2}$$

where:

WSS_G is the sum of the squares of the errors for the G groups;

X_{gn} is the location along the dimension n of the observation i of the group g;

$\underline{X}_{gn}$ is the average location along the dimension n of the observations of the group g.

Among the different techniques of cluster analysis, the hierarchical agglomerative can be used. Particularly, the algorithm proposed by Ward [17] is one of the most known for resolving the problem. It minimizes the sum of the squares of the errors provided by eqn (2) at each step of the clustering procedure. Furthermore, the algorithm of Ward implicitly assumes that the relationships among the objects, specified by the similarity matrix, can be represented in a real space. At the end of the clustering process, a set of groups is obtained, each one of them includes accidents similar among them.

Step 5

The last step analyzes the results obtained at the previous step and identifies the accident representative of each cluster. Because of the aim of the clustering is the identification of homogeneous groups and then the discussion about the characteristics of the objects in the cluster, the final step is the identification of relevant elements that can represent the group. A barycentre (centroid) can be defined in each cluster, as representative of the group; however, the centroid not necessarily has to coincide with an element of the cluster. Furthermore, for each element of the cluster the distance from the centroid can be calculated. Particularly, beginning from the centroid a specific distance can be defined that identifies a boundary: all the elements whose distance from the centroid is less then the boundary distance can represent the group.

The following relationship can be defined [11]:

$$d_{ig} \leq d_g + a\sigma_g \tag{3}$$

where:

d_{ig} is the distance among the centroid and the ith element of the cluster g;

d_g is the distance among the centroid and the element nearer to the centroid of the cluster g;

σ_g the standard deviation of the distance among the elements and the centroid of the cluster g;

a an experimental parameter.

This relationship allows considering more than one representative element of the cluster, based on the not-homogeneity degree of the cluster measured by σ_g that estimates the dispersion into the group.

In fact, eqn (3) allows depicting an ideal circle whose centre is on the centroid and whose diameter is equal to the expression at the second hand of the eqn (3). All the elements that are into the circle can represent the cluster.

If σ_g is very large (i.e., the cluster is formed by elements not homogeneous among them) the diameter of the circle increases and the circle is larger. If σ_g is very low (i.e., the cluster is formed by elements homogeneous among them) the diameter decreases and the circle is smaller, collapsing into the centroid.

In this way, even the elements farther from the centroid can be represented, and the information they contain is preserved.

4 An example

In this section a test example is presented by using a set of accidents data collected in the medium size city of Reggio Calabria, in the south of Italy. The use of only a test example is due to the impossibility of having all the data in a short time, because a large part of this data are reported in a widely descriptive format while the procedure described needs encoded data.

In this stage, 7 significant groups are identified (table 2). Groups with less than three elements are not considered because they are too specific and they cannot identify a standard event; furthermore, the number of accidents in each group is decreasing from the top to the bottom in table 2, by implicitly defining more frequent and less frequent standard event.

Table 2 – Test example: the identified standard accidents

cluster	Description of the standard event representative of the cluster
1	Accident occurred at the intersection, with faint light, no fog, no rain, in normal pavement conditions; driver less than 35, inattentive; age of the car less than five.
2	Accidents occurred along a two-way road, with faint light, rainy weather, normal pavement conditions; driver less than 35, high speed driving; age of the car less than five.
3	Accident occurred along a two-way road, good light conditions, no fog, no rain, bad pavement conditions; driver less than 35, inability to control the car; age of the car more than five and less than ten.
4	Accident occurred along a two-way road, good light conditions, rainy weather, normal pavement conditions; driver less than 35, inability to control the car; age of the car more than five and less than ten.
5	Accident occurred at the intersection, with good light conditions, no fog, no rain, in normal pavement conditions; driver more than 35 and less than 50, inattentive; age of the car more than five and less than ten.
6	Accident occurred along a one-way road, good light conditions, no fog, no rain, bad pavement conditions; driver less than 35, high speed; age of the car more less than five.
7	Accidents occurred along a two-way road, with faint light, no fog, no rain, normal pavement conditions; driver less than 35, high speed driving; age of the car less than five

As showed in table 2, the accidents identified as representative are characterized by different combination of the considered factors; particularly, in this first stage only a subset of the factor previously indicate in table 1 are here considered. A complete standardisation of the accidents in the medium size sample city considered cannot be extracted because of the analyses are still in progress. However, even if still incomplete, the analyses carried out with the procedure described shows that accidents can be standardised although the apparently large number of cases. When the most relevant standard events are identified, they can be analyzed in order to verify which factors are determinant for the beginning of the accident. In other words, the identification of the standard events is the starting point for linking the accident with the relevant factors and for verifying quantitatively the weight they have in explaining the origin of the accident.

5 Conclusions

In this paper a procedure for the evaluation of the accidents has been described, in order to obtain a clustering of similar accidents on the basis of their characteristics. The procedure is formed by different interrelated steps that allow identifying homogeneous groups of accidents.

The clustering of accidents in homogeneous groups allows separating the elements that are not similar, but, at the same time, the individual characteristics of each event is maintained in the group.

Further developments can be expected by defining a different score function (that in this work is a simply binary one) and above all by constructing an analytical function that links the main identified factors for each representative event to the generic accident, in order to verify the impact produced by modifying one or more of the values of the factors. This last aspect is already object of the search in progress.

References

[1]   AA. VV. DUMAS: Developing Urban Management and Safety – Work package 4: Accident Investigation, *Progetto DUMAS*, 1998

[2]   Aron M., Biecheler M.-B., Hakkert S., Peytavin J.F. Headways, rear-end collisions and traffic: the case of French motorways, 7th *International Conference on Traffic Safety on Two Continents*, 1997

[3]   Broughton J., Markey, K.A. In-car equipment to help drivers avoid accidents, *TRL Project Report 198: Transport Research Laboratory*, Crowthorne, 1996

[4]   Broughton, J. A study of causation factors in car accidents, *Road Safety in Europe Conference*, Birmingham, 9-11 September, 1996

[5]   Broughton, J. A new system for recording contributory factors in road accidents, 7th *International Conference on Traffic Safety on Two Continents*, 1997

[6]   Brouwer M Road safety information system: Key information supporting traffic safety policy in the Netherlands, *7th International Conference on Traffic Safety on Two Continents*, 1997

[7]   Ernvall T. Risks exposures and accident data, *7th International Conference on Traffic Safety on Two Continents*, 1997

[8]   Fluery D., Jourdan Y., Cadieu J.-P. Conception d'un plan de securité pour la ville de Rennes, *Rapport INRETS n. 199*, 1995

[9]   ISTAT. Statistica degli incidenti stradali, *Informazioni n. 21*, Roma, 1998

[10] Koornstra M.J. The quantifying of road safety developments. *Proceedings of the Conference Road Safety in Europe*, Birmingham,U.K., 1996

[11] Pas E.I. A flexible and integrated methodology for analytical classification of daily travel-activity behaviour. *Transportation Science*, vol. 17 No 4, 1983

[12] Preston G. Introduction to the road safety problem. Plenary session, *7th International Conference on Traffic Safety on Two* Continents, 1997

[13] Rodrigues E., Picado-Santos L. A study on road accident in urban environment, *7th International Conference on Traffic Safety on Two Continents*, 1997

[14] Yannis G., Golias J., Kanellaidis G. Road accident database with disaggregate data in the two continents, *7th International Conference on Traffic Safety on Two Continents*. 1997

[15] Gower J. C. A note on Burnaby's character-weighted similarity coefficient, *Journ. International Assoc. Math. Geol.*, 2, 1970

[16] Gower J. C. A general coefficient of similarity and some of its properties, *Biometrics*, 27, 1971

[17] Ward J.H. Hierarchical grouping to optimise an objective function, *Journ. Am. Statist. Assoc.*, 58, 1963

An experiment of fire risks in tunnels: an application of the numerical analysis

A. de Lieto Vollaro, S. Grignaffini & A. Vallati
Technical Physics Department,
Rome University "La Sapienza", Italy.

Abstract

The purpose of this work is to assess through numerical analysis the thermofluidynamic conditions in underground railway and road tunnels following a fire, so as to implement a mathematical model that could be used in the future to identify a security indicator associated with every tunnel. The phenomenon of the thermal field has been assessed through a numerical analysis by way of the software Fluent 5.3. The mathematical model utilized has been applied in comparing the results available in literature relative to noted experiments taken in a tunnel, in relation to a fire of small dimensions, reaching a maximum power of 2.5MW for reasons tied to the feasibility of the carrying out of measurement in the field. Our mathematical model though, once validated, will be able to simulate fires of greater dimensions in which the thermal field and the temperatures reach the limit values of the stability of the structures. The comparisons were made between some points positioned at different distances from the hearth and at different heights from the road. An attempt was made to reproduce the natural ventilation conditions present within the tunnel and special attention was given to the discretitation grid to which an independent solution was obtained from what was chosen. The results reached were in accordance with the amount experimented with, allowing to assume the possibility to utilize this mathematical model for other underground and road tunnels, assessing in particular, the eventual labor necessary to carry out complete security.

1 Introduction

The current growth of subsoil use that is materializing in the development of subterranean networks in railway and road tunnels that have become longer and more dangerous, implies a consequent increase of risk factors, requesting more than ever renewed attention and interest to security problems. In particular, the recent events that took place in the Mont Blanc and Gottardo tunnel, as well as the Kaprun cable car incident in Austria, have dramatically increased the interest of the public, that is, brought to their attention, the importance of the consequences derived from a fire in a tunnel which may not have been adequately treated for many years. The risk associated to any event is definable once the probability that the event will take place and the consequent damage of the event itself is known, measured from time to time according to the variable most suited to characterize it. The probability that an accident will occur is defined through the observation of similar incidental surveys that verify likewise in transport systems set against a time span of 30 years. The harm we find ourselves dealing with is a harm to human beings involved, who would lose their lives in a hypothetical situation. This is, from time to time, dependent upon how the observed system, confined environment, fire, material, emergency equipment, human factor, reacts when stimulated by an emergency situation like that in this study. It is understood therefore, that to estimate this type of damage, requires being up to date with a series of information necessary to specifically define the thermofluidynamics that will be established in the environment under examination, as well as an analysis of a crowds exit from the tunnels. Such information can be determined from time to time, or through diverse empirical formulas that is available through literature or, as in the case suggested, resorting aid through the numerical analysis by means of CFD.

2 About a fire

Without getting into the details of the chemical processes that govern this phenomenon, one could say that a fire is provoked by an uncontrolled combustion reaction of materials accompanied by products developed in various quantities generally distinguished: heat, gas, smoke. So that such reactions can take place, the presence of three different agents, that is combustible is necessary, the comburent and heat, that together form a so-called triangle of fire. Therefore, to foresee the consequences of a phenomenon like a tunnel fire, means to foresee combustible products, in terms of smoke, heat and toxic substances, as well as the transmission of these internally within the environment in which they develop. It is understood then that the parameters which intervene to define a fire setting is dependent not only by the comburet but the environmental characteristics of the tunnel. In each event of fire, three relative stages develop while the temperature in the environment advances: a developing phase, an expansion phase and an extinction phase.

The developing stage presents a situation of great instability of processes, depending on instant, energetic balances that are established; a distribution of various, increasing temperatures is present and progressing at points around the premises, as the fire remains localized.

The expansion stage of the fire starts with the development of a general combustion (flash over). To follow, a stabilizing of the combustion velocity at the rate of 15 kg/min and medium temperature elevation, associated to considerable development of heat and production of considerable quantities of smoke and inflammable gas due to distillation.

The extinction stage begins after the point in which the temperature has reached maximum, (700°C÷2500°C) in accordance with the total igniting of combustible materials that evolve more or less rapidly in relation to the quantity of heat produced by the combustion of residue and those of the walls of the premises. The fire extinguishes when the temperature of the premises results around 300°C [1].

From what is anticipated above, it is understood how the knowledge of materials involved in the combustion consents to extract, further to appropriate process of analysis, the spectrum of emissions of toxic products, as well as the thermal power emitted within the time.

3 Security tunnel

In the last few years, security aims have been concluded to a rise of efforts and from resources in the field of a research turned over to new technology, materials and equipment to determine service in tunnels.

The whole technical installation system, which is necessary to furnish a tunnel with, has to stand up to the various situations of risk, transforming the tunnel into an active system able to react in real time to a certain number of stimuli, and to supply the users in different situations, the indications concerning the behaviour more appropriate to follow.

The aspects relating to the tunnel project, like civil engineering, combined with technical systems, constitute the necessary package needed to reach a determined level of security.

Nevertheless, in addition to these two requisites, it is necessary to keep in mind the operative conditions of emergency management, so emergency plans should be created, on the basis of possible intervention. There are numerous studies conducted around the world on the security of tunnels in relation to fire hazards, that seem to show the great importance possessed by the ventilation parameter that controls these events in such particular environments [6], [12]. Such factors, which in any type of fire plays a very important role in both the spreading of them and of combustible products, seems to be determining for subterranean locations, both to carry out prevention measures and to deal with possible emergencies. It follows that, ventilation equipment in a tunnel is necessary and should develop a course able to impose within tunnels areas of greater movement to those of just smoke; only this way will it be possible to fulfil a subdivision of the environments, planning protected areas for escape and aid to those involved. However, attention should be given not to supply the environment with excessive ventilation. The elevated turbulence introduced in this case would cause, in fact, a disturbance from the layer of smoke that deposits below the tunnel ceiling with consequent invasion of itself within the internal environment [4]. Forced ventilation imply furthermore an excessive supply of flames with consequent increase in the thermal capacity and products of combustion.

4 Numerical model and calibration

The purpose of this work is to study the behaviour of fire in a tunnel through the use of numeric analysis.

In order to verify the validity of the simplified hypothesis taken to represent this phenomenon, it is believed opportune to tackle the case study of a fire in real scale, from which experimental measures were noted.

In particular, the case of this study regards a fire test conducted in 1999 at the Central Studies and Experience of the National Fire-fighters Corps.

The road tunnel no longer in use, "Colli Berici" utilised for the fire test is positioned long axis road Milano-Vicenza of highway A4, between the tollbooth exits of Vicenza East and Vicenza West.

To allow the campaign of measurements the materials used for the creation of the hearth were; water, gas, and petrol, in such quantities that the temperature reached were notibly inferior to the temperatures which are critical to the stability of the structure of the gallery.

The focal point of this fire realization was positioned in proximity to the longitudinal centre lane of the tunnel. A large number of thermometric probes were installed because of the importance of the temperature evaluations following the fire test, concerning the time temperature graph generation characterized by the fire, and the determination of the thermal stress agents on the structure (see Figure 1).

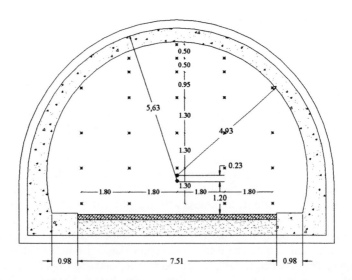

Figure 1: Transversal section of the tunnel whit the measurement points.

Five stations were determined from the long axis measure of the tunnel where the temperature survey of the area was carried out (see Figure 2).

Each measure section of the tunnel includes diverse thermometric probes distributed transversally. The number and the position of the probe, at each level, existed to dictate information at different altitudes in respect to the street level, increasing the number there, where it was thought likely to point out significant variations in the area temperature.

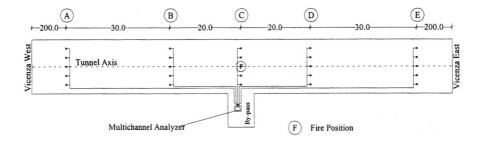

Figure 2: Longitudinal section of the tunnel whit the measurement section.

The fire was modelled like a pure thermal and chemical source, therefore disregarding the problem of the chemical reaction that develops. And so the comparison between the numerical results and experimental, will only be conclusive verifying the correspondence between the temperature values.
In regards to the temperature, being aware of the maximum thermal power developed, and knowing the profile with which it was made to vary with time, it is possible to completely reproduce the phenomenon according to the methodology hypothesized.
To fulfill the numeric simulation, it was needed to create a model that adequately represented both the geometry of the environment and the physics of the fire phenomenon studied. Particular attention was given to the conditions of the surroundings. The portals of the tunnel, modelled according to the conditions of the surroundings "velocity inlet" were completed to reproduce the conditions of natural ventilation present the day of the test, therefore the estimate of the velocity was arranged in longitudinal direction equal to 0.4 m/s. The square formed surface represented the focal point of the fire and was positioned exactly at the centre of the tunnel. It was formed like a thermal source which was realized in the experimental test. The percentage of heat left from the source is not constant, but variable in time according to a reference graph followed during the course of the test [4].
A structured mesh was carried out for this model, achieving a solution independent from the mesh.

Subsequently, the relative sequences were reported of the isothermal visualization respectively in the five sections observed (see Figure 3), in the longitudinal section of the centre lane (see Figure 4) and a transversal section (see Figure 5).

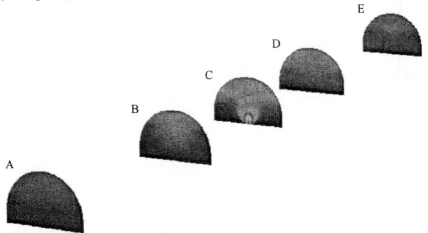

Figure 3: Isothermal Visualization of the five measurement sections.

Figure 4: Isotherm Progress of the longitudinal section of the tunnel.

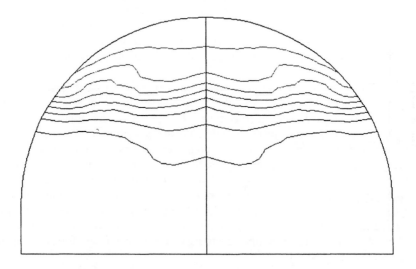

Figure 5: Isotherm Progress of the transversal section of the tunnel.

In Figures 6 and 7 the relative graphs comparing the two sections are reported, the products resulting from the numeric analysis and from the experimental data.

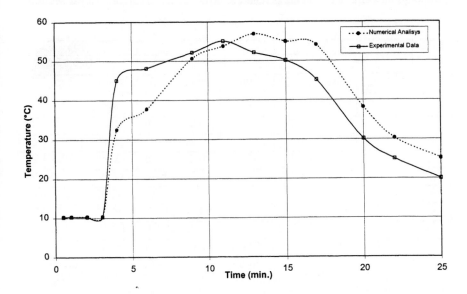

Figure 6: Comparison between experimental data and values obtained from the numerical simulation for section A to the quota H=5.85m.

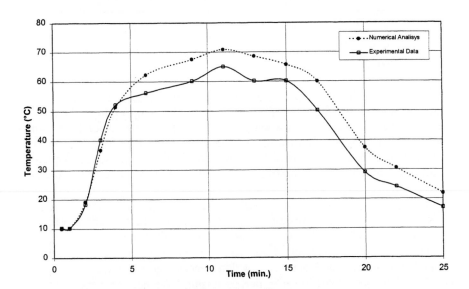

Figure 7: Comparison between experimental data and values obtained from the numerical simulation for section B to the quota H=5.20m.

In Table 1 the detailed list is proposed in three different traversal sections of the estimates extracted from the numerical simulation, those deduced by the campaign measurement and the percentage errors checked (ε).

Time (min.)	A H= 5.85m			B H= 5.20m			D H= 5.85m		
	Num. Analysis °C	Exp. Data °C	|ε| %	Num. Analysis °C	Exp. Data °C	|ε| %	Num. Analysis °C	Exp. Data °C	|ε| %
0.5	10.3	10.22	0.78	10.03	10.21	1.76	10.08	10.2	1.17
1	10.32	10.23	0.87	10.09	10.22	1.27	20.15	20.1	0.24
2	10.33	10.24	0.87	19.1	18.25	4.65	31.6	32.3	2.16
3	10.35	10.26	0.87	36.8	40.21	8.48	46.08	42.15	9.32
4	32.5	45.03	27.82	51.4	52.13	1.40	52.03	48.11	8.14
6	37.8	48.1	21.41	62.3	56.14	10.97	54.11	45.21	19.68
9	50.6	52.15	2.972	67.5	60.12	12.27	57.12	50.12	13.96
11	53.8	55.06	2.288	70.86	65.03	8.96	62.2	55.13	12.82
13	56.9	52.13	9.150	68.55	60.13	14.00	66.14	60.03	10.17
15	55	50.09	9.802	65.67	60.12	9.23	60.08	50.2	19.68
17	54.1	45.12	19.90	60.01	50.11	19.75	46.11	35.6	29.52
20	38.2	30.11	26.8	37.5	29.11	28.82	29.66	22.7	30.66
22	30.3	25.01	21.15	30.55	24.13	26.60	24.2	20.35	18.91
25	25.2	20.02	25.87	21.9	17.1	28.07	19.5	16.44	18.61

Table 1: Numerical estimates, experimental and error percentages (ε) for three different sections of measurement (A, B and D) and for three different height inquiries.

Notice a slight difference from the data verified in the highest part of the tunnel, and one most substantial convergence between the temperature data in the inferior layers. Nevertheless the maximum gap between the experimental and numerical estimates verified reaches 30% in some points measured. The results obtained through the model set up have retained more than satisfactory, a quality account of the model hypothesized, especially keeping in mind the following considerations:

• The increasing rate of the fire focal point is noted purely from a theoretical point of view, having been practically impossible during the test for the National Fire-fighters Corps to follow the increasing curve recalled above.

• The ventilation conditions of the tunnel are not uniform, being caused by natural air movement and moreover noted in a very rough manner.

• The temperature data noted in our possession have been surveyed with an acquisition time of 10 seconds; this interval in certain instances of time seems to excessively reveal itself from the moment in which notable gradients of temperature verify in time, and is therefore difficult to stabilize the real temperature measured.

5 Conclusions

Seeing that the mathematical model implemented gave satisfactory results, it is possible to utilize it to study other typologies of tunnels and verify in this case the relative parameters of the security of railway and road tunnels. It is possible to extend the use of this method for fires of large dimensions. Up until now, such problems of great topical interest, had been strictly associated to the problems of carrying out real fire simulations which obviously cannot always be executed. With the advent of numerical simulation, such problems are easily overcome, maybe making tunnels more secure. One can conclude that the methodology introduced at the right moment, opportunely assisted by a numerical analysis, offers that essential tool, and not only to classify simply the security of the infrastructure of subterranean transport in relation to fire cases. In fact, above all, the aim is to construct an instrument with which to foresee, measuring on an arbitrary scale, the effects added by eventual interventions realized in management by the achievement of major security standards, as well as constructing a reference based on which to plan diverse strategic possibilities of intervention, in relation to the possible settings.

Again we can add that the fundamental role played by the typology, altimetry and dimensions of the environment, in the spreading of the products of the combustion, allows to assume that the employment of CFD is quite desirable in the planning phase of the infrastructure.

References

[1]   Barosso F., "Impianti Antincendio". Manuale della climatizzazione". Tecniche Nuove, 1989.
[2]   Blume G., "SMOKE AND HEAT PRODUCTION IN TUNNEL FIRES- SMOKE AND HOT GAS HAZARDS", Insitut fur Baustoffe, Massivebau und Brandshutz der Technischen Universitat Braunnschweigh, 1994
[3]   Center d'etudes des tunnels, "SMOKE CONTROL IN ROAD TUNNELS IN CASE OF FIRE".
[4]   Doc. Vigili del Fuoco. Prova a fuoco in galleria stradale. 1999.
[5]   Drysdale D., "AN INTRODUCTION TO FIRE DYNAMICS", 1990, A Wiley interscience publication.
[6]   Haak A., "INTRODUCTION TO THE EUREKA-EU 499 FIRETUN PROJECT" Studiengesellschaft fur unterirdische verskehrstantagen- STUVA- Cologne.
[7]   International Tunnelling Association "TUNNEL AND UNDERGROUND SPACE TECHNOLOGY" vol.13, Working group n°4, 1998.
[8]   Patankar S. V., "NUMERICAL HEAT TRANSFER AND FLUID FLOW". Washington hemisphere publishing corporation, 1980.
[9]   Patankar S. V., "RECENT DEVELOPMENTS IN COMPUTATIONAL HEAT TRANSFER". Journal of heat transfer. Vol 110, 1988.

[10] Peacock R.D. e E.Broun, 1999, "FIRE SAFETY OF PASSENGERS TRAINS, PHASE 1: MATERIAL EVALUATION (CONE CALORIMETER)", National Institute of Standards and Technology, NIST IR 6132, U.S. Department of Commerce, Gaithersburg.

[11] Peacock R.D., R.W.Bukowskj, W.W.Jones, P.A. Reneke, V. Babrauskas e J.E. Broun,1994, "FIRE SAFETY OF PASSENGERS TRAINS: A REVIEW OF CURRENT APPROACHES AND OF NEW CONCEPTS", National Institute of Standards and Technology, NIST IR 6132, U.S. Department of Commerce, Gaithersburg.

[12] PIARC Commitee on Road Tunnels: Statfan Bengtsan,"OBJECTIVES OF FIRE AND SMOKE CONTROL" Fire and smoke control in road tunnels- second draft, 1996

[13] Society of Fire Protection Engineers (SFPE), 1990,"THE SFPE HANDBOOK OF FIRE PROTECTION ENGINEERING" SFPE, Boston, Massachussets

[14] Studiengesellschaft Stahlanwendung (STUSTA), 1995, Report, "FIRES IN TRANSPORT TUNNELS, REPORT ON FULL SCALE TESTS", Eureka Project EU499: Firetun

Section 11:
Vehicle technology

Study on power transmitting efficiency of CVT using a dry hybrid V-belt.

J. Yamaguchi[1], K. Okubo[1], T. Fujii[1], R. Kido[2] & M Takahasi[2]
[1]Department of Mechanical Engineering and Systems,
Doshisha University, Kyoto Japan
[2]BANDO Chemical Industry, Japan

Abstract

This paper presents the net power transmitting efficiency of CVT using a newly developed dry hybrid V-belt. The efficiency was measured by using a devised testing machine, which eliminates other power losses due to peripherals such as shaft flanges. Torques on both pulleys were measured with high accuracy by using strain gauges which were glued on the cantilever shafts.

The CVT efficiency is divided into three regions with respect to applied torque. At a low range of applied torque: region I, the efficiency of CVT increases sharply with respect to the applied torque, because the bending loss is almost constant for applied torque but the torque increases the total transmitting power. At region II (a middle range of applied torque), the efficiency is also constant with respect to transmitting torque since the relative energy loss due to belt bending decreases while the energy loss due to elastic slip increases with increasing the transmitting torque. They are equivalent with each other at this region. The efficiency sharply decreases at region III due to the remarkably increasing of the slip. The transmitting efficiency increases with the low contraction force. The CVT shows the high transmitting efficiency at the speed ratio 1.0.

The transmitting efficiency decreases when the CVT system has the misalignment, because the sharing deformation of the belt strand influences the transmitting efficiency as well as the bending deformation. The appropriate initial setting misalignment exists to reduce the influence of the misalignment.

It is found that the relationship between the traction coefficient and the transmitting efficiency is independent on the contraction force, speed ratio and the misalignment. The traction coefficient could be a non-dimensional applied torque for characterizing the efficiency of the dry hybrid V-belt type CVT.

1. Introduction

The Continuously Variable Transmissions (CVT) using dry hybrid V-belts have higher power transmitting efficiency than metal pushed V-belt type CVT due to high frictional coefficient between a V-belt and pulleys. Because lubrication oil and devices for lubrication are not necessary to operate "the dry CVT".

On studying the dry CVT efficiency, we have three topics in our research. At first: some papers reported that this dry CVT has over 95% efficiency [1], but in their study, the efficiency of them were totally measured in a unit. There were several power losses such as bearing, torque-meter loss and others in such a system. Therefore we measured the efficiency excluding such losses with high accuracy. Secondly: it can be also said that deference of the speed ratio causes to change the transmitting efficiency. The applicable indicator for the transmitting efficiency should be proposed independent on the speed ratio for easy evaluation of the CVT system. At last: current type CVT has a structural misalignment [2] to change the speed ratio in wide range by moving the one side of the pulley flange. It is important to investigate the influence of the misalignment on the transmitting efficiency of the dry CVT. However, few reports have been published describing the efficiency of the dry hybrid V-belt CVT considering the above three topics.

This paper describes the characteristics of the transmitting efficiency, and proposes the applicable indicator to show the variation of the efficiency of dry hybrid V-belt CVT with high accuracy. The mechanism that explains the change of the transmitting efficiency is also discussed when the CVT has the misalignment.

2 Experimental apparatus

2-1 Structure of dry hybrid V-belt

Figure 1 shows the schematically illustration of a CVT belt used in this study. The structure of the belt is hybrid, made of blocks and tension members. A couple of tension members are inserted into grooves between two multiple arms of 204 pieces of lateral H-shaped blocks. Blocks consist of aluminum alloy covered with a heat resisting resin. Rubber tension members are reinforced by aramid fiber. Blocks sustain the pulley thrust with high stiffness and produce the frictional force for applicable power transmission. Tension members should be flexible for which the belt fits with pitch radii in spite of high tensile strength to the elevated tension. The belt has 26 degree wedge angle, 25mm pitch width and 612mm belt length.

2.2 CVT test machine and test conditions.

Figure 2 shows a schematic view of the CVT running test machine and torque measuring system in this study. This test machine consists of the dry hybrid V-belt, driver and driven pulleys. The groove widths of the pulleys were fixed to constant. The machine has AC motor that provides constant input revolution speed, and weights for applied torque and contraction force. The contraction force Fs was measured by a load cell and revolution speed at each shaft N_{in} and N_{out} are measured by proximity sensors. Eight sheets of strain gages were glued on cantilever shafts attached slip-rings to measure net torque on the pulleys with high accuracy as shown in figure 2(b). The measured torques Tr_{in} and Tr_{out} does not included other torque occurring at bearings or torque-meters by this system. In this study, speed ratio i, contraction force Fs, applied torque Tr_{out}, misalignment distance C were changed.

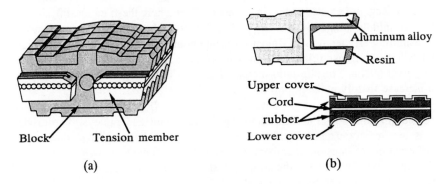

(a)   (b)

Figure 1: (a) Dry hybrid V-belt assembly and (b) consists of a block and tension member.

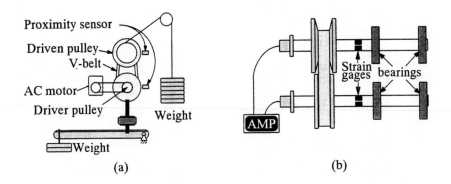

(a)   (b)

Figure 2: (a)Experimental apparatus and (b) newly measuring method.

3. Results and discussion

3.1 Three region of the transmitting efficiency

The transmitting efficiency η was calculated by equation (1), and the slip ratio was calculated by equation (2), where N_{out0} is the revolution speed of driven pulley at no applied torque. Figure 3 shows the transmitting efficiency η and the slip ratio s with respect to the applied torque Tr_{out}.

$$\eta = \frac{Tr_{out} N_{out}}{Tr_{in} N_{in}} \times 100 \tag{1}$$

$$s = \frac{N_{out} - N_{out0}}{N_{out0}} \times 100 \tag{2}$$

The variation of η with respect to the Tr_{out} can be divided into three regions. Region I existed at the Tr_{out} under 30Nm where the η increasing sharply. In the middle range of the Tr_{out} (Tr_{out}=30~60), there was region II where transmitting efficiency was almost constant about maximum efficiency. Region-III where the transmitting efficiency decreasing suddenly was observed at the Tr_{out} over 60Nm. The slip ratio increased linearly in the region I and II, and then it increase sharply in the region III.

The variations of η with respect to the Tr_{out} can be explained by considering the power losses occurring between belt and pulleys. The driving loss are mainly caused by following two. One is bending loss due to the deformation of tension members to bend on the pulley, which is given by equation (3)[4]. The other is the slipping loss due to elastic deformation of the belt to transmit the power given by equation (4).

$$\Delta P_b = \frac{EI\pi}{30R} N \tag{3}$$

$$\Delta P_s = \frac{v}{2EAR^2} Tr^2 \tag{4}$$

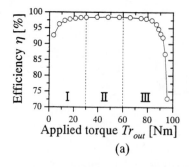
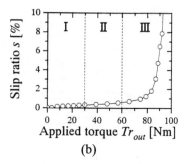

(a)　　　　　　　　　　(b)

Figure 3: Variations of (a) transmitting efficiency and (b) slip ratio with respect to applied torque. Speed ratio 1.0, contraction force 2.0kN.

Where, E is Young's modulus, I is the moment of inertia of area, A is the cross section of the tension member along the belt and v is the belt velocity. In this study, the ΔP_b can be considered almost constant for any conditions if speed ratio is constant. But ΔP_s depends on the applied torque. Figure 4 shows calculation results by the equations (3) and (4) describing the relationship between the Tr_{out} and the η. The calculated result well agree with the experimental result in the regions I and II.

In a low range of the applied torque: the region I, the efficiency of the CVT increases sharply with respect to the applied torque, because the bending loss is almost constant for the applied torque but the torque increases the total transmitting power. In region II , the efficiency is also constant with respect to the transmitting torque since the relative energy loss due to belt bending decreases while the energy loss due to elastic slip increases with increasing the transmitting torque. They are equivalent with each other at this region. The efficiency sharply decreases in the region III due to the remarkably increasing of the slip.

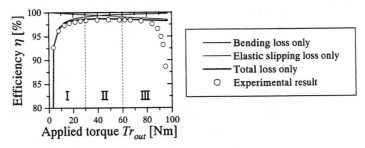

Figure 4: Comparison between calculation results and experimental result. speed ratio 1.0, contraction force 2.0kN.

3.2 Influence of the running condition on the transmitting efficiency

3.2.1 contraction force

Figure 5(a) shows the transmitting efficiency η and the slip ratio s with respect to the applied torque Tr_{out} when the contraction force Fs changed. Figure 5(b) shows the transmitting efficiency at Tr_{out}=20N for any conditions of the Fs. The η decreased with increasing Fs because frictional force increased due to the belt penetration to the pulley radius direction.

The traction coefficient λ is calculated by equation (5), and it has been generally used to evaluate the transmitting ability regardless belt types. Where T_t is the tight side tension, T_s is the slack side tension and θ is the angle of strand.

$$\lambda = \frac{T_t - T_s}{T_t + T_s} = \frac{Tr_{out}}{R_{DN}} \frac{\cos\alpha}{Fs} \tag{5}$$

The slip ratio was generally expressed for the function of the traction coefficient as the applicable indicator of the transmitting capacity. Gerbert analyzed pulley thrusts considering the belt motion in pulleys of a rubber V-belt type CVT and expressed the contraction force and the pulley thrust as the function of the traction coefficient [3]. Figure 6 shows the transmitting efficiency η and the slip ratio s evaluated by using the traction coefficient λ. The λ can divide the η into three as well as the Tr_{out}. Furthermore there is the region I in $\lambda=0\sim0.3$, the region II in $\lambda=0.3\sim0.6$ and the region III in $\lambda=0.6\sim$ at any Fs. It can be seen that the variations of the η and the s almost independent on the Fs in the regions I and II. If the Fs increases, the transmitting power increases at the same traction coefficient λ, because the λ is the non-dimensional applied torque. However, the bending loss is constant at any traction coefficient. Therefore the transmitting efficiency η increases when the contraction force Fs increases at any λ in the regions I and II

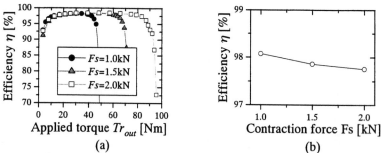

Figure 5: (a) Variations of transmitting efficiency with respect to aplied torque.
(b) Transmitting efficiencies at applied torque 20Nm.

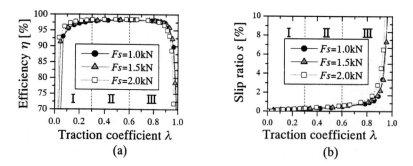

Figure 6: Variations of (a) transmitting efficiency and (b) slip ratio with respect to traction coefficient. Speed ratio 1.0.

3.2.2 speed ratio

Figure 7 shows the η and the s with respect to the λ when the speed ratio i changed. It can be seen that the variations of the η and the s with respect to the λ almost independent the i as well as the contraction force Fs changed. The transmitting efficiency at $i=1.0$ has the highest of the three other ratios in all regions. Figure 8 shows the calculated bending losses with respect to the λ when the speed ratio i changes. This means that the η shows maximum at $i=1$.

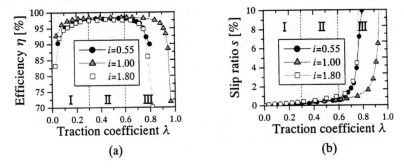

(a)   (b)

Figure 7: Effect of speed ratio on (a) transmitting efficiency and (b) slip ratio. Contraction force 2.0kN.

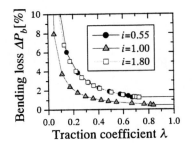

Figure 8: Difference of bending loss. Contraction force 2.0kN.

3.3 Influence of the misalignment

Figure 9 shows the η and the s with respect to the λ when the misalignment distance C changed. The misalignment is the offset of each pulley to axial direction due to changing the speed ratio. The variations of the transmitting efficiency with respect to the traction coefficient were divided into three regions even if the misalignment distance C was changed.

As shown in this figure when the C increased, the η decreased in the regions I and II; however, less difference was observed in the region III. It can be supposed that the slip ratio is not affected by the misalignment. The misalignment of the CVT should make the shearing deformation at strands as shown in figure 10. Shearing deformation causes constant quantitative loss as the bending loss, much affects of the C on the η was observed in the region I. Figure

11 shows the influence of the misalignment on the η when the speed ratio changes. The η at $i=1$ shows the highest because that has the longest strand i.e. the shearing deformation is the smallest at $i=1$.

Figure 12 shows the absolute value of the sharing deformation with respect to the speed ratio when the initial setting misalignment C_{inii} changed. C_{inii} is the misalignment distance at the speed ratio $i=1$. The relationship between the speed ratio and the misalignment was calculated by equation (6) [3].

$$C = \left[(R_{DN} - R_{DN0}) - (R_{DR0} - R_{DR})\right]\tan\frac{\alpha}{2} \tag{6}$$

Where, R_0 is the pitch radius at the misalignment distance $C = 0$ and α is the wedge angle of the V-belt. Maximum of the sharing deformation shows the smallest at $C_{ini}=0.384$. I.e. there is the applicable initial misalignment to reduce the influence of the misalignment on the transmitting efficiency.

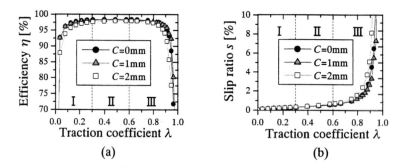

Figure 9: Effect of misalignment distance on (a) transmitting efficiency and (b) slip ratio. Contraction force 2.0kN, speed ratio 1.0.

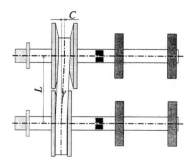

Figure 10: Sharing deformation of belt strand due to misalignment distance.

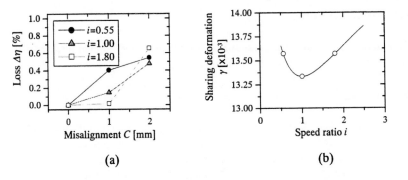

(a)

(b)

Figure 11: (a) Effect of misalignment distance on transmitting efficiency.
(b) variation of sharing deformation with respect to speed ratio.

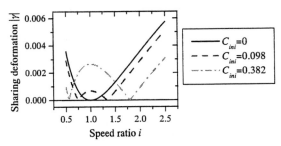

Figure 12: Effect of initial setting misalignment distance on absolute value of sharing deformation.

4. Conclusions

1. Variations of the transmitting efficiency can be divided into three regions, and it changes increasing, constant and decreasing in each region. The bending loss influences the transmitting efficiency in the region I, and bending loss and slipping loss influence the efficiency in the region II. the slipping loss influences in the region III.
2. Regardless of the contraction forces, the speed ratios and the misalignments, the traction coefficient can characterize the variations of the transmitting efficiency. In the region II, at the $\lambda=0.3\sim0.6$, the transmitting efficiency shows high and constant.
3. The transmitting efficiency decreases when the CVT has the misalignment especially in the region I. The influence of the misalignment on the transmitting efficiency is the least at speed ratio i=1 where sharing deformation is the smallest.
4. There is the applicable initial setting misalignment distance to reduce the influence of the misalignment on the transmitting efficiency.

Acknowledgement

The author would like to express special thanks to BANDO chemical Industries, Ltd. for their fruitful support to continue this work.

References

[1] Takahashi M., Design and Development of a Dry Hybrid Belt (BANDO AVANCE) for CVT Vehicles, *proc. of the International Congress on Continuously Variable Power Transmission CVT'99*: The Netherlands, 1999.
[2] A J Robertson and K B Tawi, "Misalignment equation for the Van Doorne metal pushing V-belt continuously variable transmission", *Proc. Instn. Mech. Engrs. Vol. 211 Part D*, pp121-128, 1977
[3] G. B. Gerbert, "Traction belt mechanics", Kompendiet-Goteborg: Sweden, 1999.

Uncertainty in the implementation of automated vehicle guidance

V. Marchau & W. Walker
Faculty of Technology, Policy and Management,
Delft University of Technology, The Netherlands.

Abstract

Much has been written about the technologies of Automated Vehicle Guidance (AVG) -- electronic systems that support the driver in controlling his vehicle in a better way. Within these articles there is usually a focus on specific AVG technologies and/or a specific aspects of AVG implementation. Broader pictures of AVG implementation, in which the various AVG applications, their possible consequences for transportation system performance, and societal conditions for implementation are treated in an integrated way, are seldom presented. As such, the current value of these studies is highly limited with regard to public policy making. In this paper we take a systems view of AVG implementation. We examine how the different pieces might fit together given general transport goals, and how to proceed with implementation so that it can reach its potential. Major problems in this context involve the uncertainty associated with AVG implementation. A generic typology of uncertainties, their causes, and a possible way to deal with them is presented. This typology is based on the view that policymaking basically concerns making choices regarding a system (e.g. the transport system) in order to obtain desired system outcomes. We apply this typology to the field of policymaking with respect to AVG implementation, showing that large uncertainties exist about the outcomes of AVG policy decisions and about the valuation of the outcomes by stakeholders involved in or affected by AVG policy decisions. In order to deal with these uncertainties, a flexible or adaptive policy is proposed which allow adaptations in time as knowledge about AVG accumulates and critical events for AVG implementation take place.

1 Introduction

Modern societies are increasingly confronted with the growing externalities of road traffic, i.e. congestion, reductions in safety levels, consumption of scarce space, use of energy, and increased emissions. To a large extent, these problems can be attributed to improper or suboptimal vehicle driving behaviour. It has been estimated that some 90% of all traffic accidents can be attributed to human failure [1]. Congestion is, among other factors, the result of drivers' trip-making decisions and minute-by-minute driving behaviour [2]. In order to improve this driving behaviour, various technological systems are developed and (gradually) implemented that support drivers in controlling their vehicles in a better way. These systems are known as Automated Vehicle Guidance (AVG) systems, which automate, to a certain degree, the driver's acceleration, braking, and steering tasks.

The range of possible AVG applications researched and developed these days is wide. They range from systems that support the driver in one specific driving task (e.g. distance keeping, lane keeping, speed control) to highly advanced systems in which the driver's steering, acceleration, and braking tasks are totally taken over (e.g. the autopilot). The technological feasibility of AVG is not the main issue anymore. This has been demonstrated within several experiments and pilots. In these (and other) studies, AVG proved to have potential for improving road traffic efficiency and safety significantly. For instance, it has been estimated that the use of systems that support the driver in keeping a proper distance to the nearest vehicle ahead (adaptive cruise control) could increase road capacity up to 25% [3]. The large-scale implementation of collision avoidance systems, which support the driver in case of imminent crash danger with oncoming vehicles or obstacles, could reduce road fatalities up to about 45% [4] [5]. The first AVG applications have already entered the market [6]. Well-known examples involve adaptive cruise control and collision warning systems. Consequently, the focus in this field is now gradually shifting from technology development towards the possibility of AVG implementation on a large scale [7].

Transport policymakers in various countries are becoming increasingly interested in the large-scale implementation of AVG. However, policy development regarding AVG is hindered by large uncertainties related to AVG technology development, the contribution of this development to general transport policy goals, and societal conditions for AVG implementation [8]. Until now, the development of AVG systems has been strongly technology driven and the performance and impacts of most AVG prototypes has been assessed only in experiments under strictly controlled conditions, implying limited real-world validity [9]. AVG technology development and its impacts are strongly related to the societal conditions that have to be fulfilled for implementation. For instance, in the field of legal regulations, it might be necessary to change rules in the context of liability and third-party insurance in case of AVG systems that take drivers out of the driving loop [10]. Another issue involves societal acceptance. It is often argued that drivers will reject AVG, since it reduces their freedom and their responsibilities for making their own decisions [11].

A major problem in the context of public policymaking, therefore, involves the uncertainty associated with AVG technology implementation. Current policymaking is often characterised by a 'sit and wait' attitude in reaction to this uncertainty, allowing developments to be largely determined by market forces. This could hinder AVG development in an early stage or lead to the implementation of AVG applications that serve producers and individual consumers' interests only, not more general transport policy goals. Hence, there is a need for an AVG policy course that recognises the existence of uncertainties without neglecting the possibilities and responsibilities of public authorities with respect to general transport policy goals. In this paper a first set-up for such a course is given by focussing on strategies for identifying and handling relevant uncertainties within the context of AVG policymaking. In Section 2, a framework for structuring uncertainty is presented. In Section 3, relevant uncertainties within the context of AVG policymaking are identified according to this framework. A strategy for handling these uncertainties is discussed in Section 4. We draw some conclusions in Section 5.

2 A framework for structuring uncertainty

In general, uncertainty can be defined as *missing knowledge; i.e.,* the absence of information. With respect to policy and decisionmaking, uncertainty refers to the gap between available knowledge and the knowledge needed in order to develop and implement good policies [12]. Evidently, this uncertainty in policymaking clearly involves subjectivity, since it is related to the satisfaction with existing knowledge, which is coloured by the underlying values and perspectives of policymakers. Many classifications or typologies of uncertainties have been made, differing in point of view and objective. The aim of this paper is not to discuss these different typologies, their advantages and shortcomings, but to focus on a typology that considers two dimensions [12]:

- the elements about which uncertainty exists
- the reasons for or causes of these uncertainties.

Such a typology has recently been developed by Walker [13]. This typology is based on the view that policymaking concerns making choices regarding a system (e.g. the transport system) in order to change the system outcomes in a desired way. The typology is summarised in Figure 1. It distinguishes between uncertainty about *outcomes* of policy decisions and uncertainty about the *valuation of the outcomes* of policy decisions.

Outcomes of policy decisions refer to the characteristics of the system (the transport system) that are considered relevant criteria for the evaluation of policy measures. For transport policies, these criteria involve, among others, the level of emissions by motor vehicles, the number of road casualties, the level of freight transport and the level of congestion probability on the road network (e.g. [14]). Uncertainty about outcomes can result from uncertainty about *external inputs* and/or uncertainty about *system responses* to these external inputs. Uncertainty about external inputs refers to inputs that are not controllable by the decisionmaker but may influence the system significantly, i.e. exogenous influences. Well-known exogenous influences on the transport system involve demographic, economic, spatial, social, and technological developments in society. Uncertainty about these developments is usually handled by means of scenarios: descriptions of plausible alternative future developments in the environment of the system of interest. Scenarios themselves are based on two types of uncertainties: (1) those that result from uncertainty about the variables to be included in the scenario (i.e. *the relevant external inputs*), and (2) the possible *values of these relevant inputs.*

Even if there were certainty about the external inputs to the system (that is, we knew how the system-external world would develop), there might still be uncertainty about how the system would respond to those external inputs. The system response might be uncertain because of *model uncertainty* and/or *parametric uncertainty.* Model uncertainty refers to the selection of the relevant system components and the identification of the relationships among these components (e.g., the functional form of the relationships). Even if we were sure about the components and their relationships, there may still be uncertainty regarding the values of the parameters describing the relationships. In modelling terms, this is often called *parameter* uncertainty.

The second category of uncertainty refers to the *valuation of outcomes*: i.e., the (relative) importance given to the outcomes by crucial stakeholders. It involves uncertainty about how stakeholders value the results of the changes in the system, such as improved traffic efficiency, fewer fatalities, reduced emissions, etc. One can distinguish uncertainty about *current values* and *future values* of parties involved in or affected by outcomes. The uncertainty about current values is related to different perceptions, preferences and choices the system's stakeholders currently have regarding outcomes. Even if the outcomes are known and there is no uncertainty about the current valuation of outcomes, values may change over time in unpredictable ways, leading to different valuations of future outcomes than those made in the present. For instance the occurrence of a

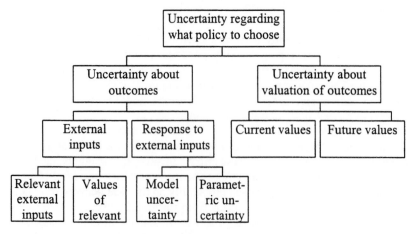

Figure 1: A typology of uncertainty

specific event (crash of a ship or airplane, explosion in a tunnel), unexpected cost increases, or new technologies can lead to changes in values. These changes in values can affect policy decisions in substantial ways.

3 Uncertainty related to AVG implementation

Given the generic typology on uncertainty, we are now able to identify and structure the different types uncertainties related to AVG implementation, based on the current knowledge and experiences reported in the literature. The results of this exercise are presented in Table 1.

Uncertainty about the influence of *external inputs*, including AVG development, has been almost completely ignored up until now. Of course, there are several studies in which possible future developments of AVG have been hypothesised (see [8] for an overview). In these studies, a gradual change of the present car system, based on assuming an incremental absorption, a slowly intensifying use, and increasing driving assistance of AVG technologies is argued. Although of interest, these trajectories are unlikely to occur, since they are based on simplistic conceptualisations of transport technology development, in which technological progress determines the implementation process. In particular, the studies neglect the co-evolution of technology and society [15]. Therefore, a broader view on future AVG development together with other, non-technological, relevant developments is needed.

Only few studies have been found in which scenario approaches have been used for studying the development of AVG systems in relation to the overall context of the transport system (e.g. Van Arem & Smits [16]; Heyma [17]; Helmreich & Leiss [18]). Others have argued the importance of exogenous events for the development of AVG, like urban sprawl, dispersion of work centres, working flexibility, etc (e.g. Hanson & Tsao [19]; Hayward et al. [20]). These studies are of interest, since they are typically the basis for constructing scenarios. Both the relevant inputs and their values differ significantly among the studies, resulting in widely differing scenarios. As such, it is difficult to identify a single set of robust scenarios. Furthermore, the way in which these scenarios might affect the transport system differs widely among the studies. Most assume static relationships, while it is likely that the relationships might change over time [21]. As such, the scenario exercises found in the literature are unlikely to be very useful.

Review of research undertaken regarding *the response to external inputs* including AVG implementation reveals that current knowledge is restricted to evaluating the intended impacts of specific AVG systems. More safety, more driver comfort, and better performance are claimed. The question is how strong the basis of these claims is. The literature reports potentially significant positive impacts of intelligent speed adaptation (e.g. De Visser et al. [22]; Carsten et al. [23]). Adaptive cruise control could contribute significantly to less head/tail crashes, but (dependent upon the specific operating characteristics of the system) could also reduce road capacity use (e.g. Minderhoud [3]). Moreover, both

The *valuation of outcomes* of AVG implementation by crucial stakeholders will determine future actions and decisions. If these valuations between stakeholders differ substantially, implementation might be obstructed. Therefore, it is important to analyse the willingness and possibility of relevant parties to act. The identification of the uncertainty about the valuation of outcomes of AVG implementation points out that most research involves studying the (current) preferences and choices of vehicle drivers regarding AVG systems. It appears that empirical findings for consumer preferences regarding AVG systems often show different, unexplained results. Some of these differences might have methodological causes. Several approaches have been used to assess user preferences regarding AVG including questionnaires, interviews, focus group meetings, etc., sometimes in combination with driving simulator experiments or road experiments. Furthermore, background-related characteristics might explain preference differences among individuals, for example in their risk behaviours, driving styles, traffic accident histories, vehicle operating costs, etc. [25, 27]. Hence, the relationships among different driver support features and the preferences of consumers to buy and use these systems is still subject of further empirical research [28].

Efforts to explore the values of stakeholders regarding the outcomes of AVG implementation have started only recently. As such, there is only limited information available in the literature. For instance, Lathrop & Chen [29] studied the attitudes of private users and non-users, fleet-operators, vehicle- and electronics industries, insurance companies and public authorities concerning Automated Highway Systems (AHS). The results reveal not only that significant differences exist among stakeholders, but also among members representing a single stakeholder, indicating the need for a more diverse representation.

A recent European study on stakeholder needs regarding AVG applications in general indicated that different stakeholders have rather similar opinions concerning the severity of current traffic problems (safety, efficiency, costs, etc.) [30]. However, stakeholders differ in their opinion about how the severity of traffic problems will develop in the future. This results in different needs among the stakeholders regarding future AVG implementation. Hence, the future valuation of AVG outcomes, in this study, showed conflicting results. As such, implementation might be obstructed for the near future.

Some general reasons why future valuation of outcomes may change in unpredictable ways, leading to other valuations than those made in the present, has already been argued in Section 2. An AVG-specific reason in this context involves the valuation of legal issues concerning the implementation of AVG. For example, for manufacturers and road authorities the threat to be held liable for certain types of future accidents may discourage them to support AVG implementation. As such, the uncertainty of how the risks of the new technology will and should be allocated may slow down or even obstruct the introduction of certain AVG applications. Another issue is that that current legal frameworks may contain barriers for the introduction of AVG. New technologies may conflict with existing laws on vehicle standards. Furthermore, legislative interventions may be needed to gain or guarantee the necessary support of the different stakeholders involved (including public authorities) to facilitate the intelligent speed adaptation and adaptive cruise control might generate unexpected driver behaviour (less alertness, over-expectation, compensation for freedom limitations), which could eliminate positive safety impacts (e.g. Endsley & Kiris [24]; Hoedemaker [25]). Furthermore, experts indicate that the impacts of these systems on environmental performance are hardly known [8]. Finally, the implementation of AVG is intended to shorten travel times due to higher average vehicle speeds. However, the 'law of constant travel time budget' suggests that high speeds will not necessary lead to time savings on travelling, as these savings will immediately be used to make new or longer trips [26]. In conclusion, so far, figures on traffic performance improvements are hardly more than indications that depend strongly on the systems' specific operating characteristics, driving behaviour, and actual traffic conditions (e.g. flow density, speed, the mix between manual and instrumented vehicles).

Table 1: Uncertainty about Outcomes of AVG implementation

Type of Uncertainty	Specific Element of Uncertainty	Reason for Uncertainty
External Inputs	- relevance of external inputs for AVG implementation - future AVG technology development in terms of AVG key-technology and future AVG functional specification - future infrastructure-technology development	- lack of knowledge about external factors influencing transportation performance - long-term nature of implementation of AVG - inherent ill-predictability of (levels of) most of these factors in the long term
Responses to external inputs	- developments in basic needs in driving and travel behaviour - impacts of AVG on traffic safety, emissions, fuel consumption, and efficiency - interference between AVG intended outcomes and other general transport policy goals	- poorly known key relationships determining transport system performance from AVG implementation - focus on evaluation of single AVG application on intended outcome(s) - lack of research with an integrated approach and focus on causal relation
Valuation of outcomes	- Stakeholder configuration - core values to be respected in using new AVG technology - Shifting values and standards in judging policy impacts - developments in attitudes for driving, travelling and activities	- Passive role and ignorance of policymakers - Occurrence of specific events that work as "catalysts" - Long-term nature of implementation of ITS

deployment of AVG. Examples could be the ability for public authorities to guarantee some safety level through type approval standards or other measures and legal arrangements concerning privacy and liability.

4 Handling AVG uncertainties

The current handling of the AVG uncertainties reflect an "individualised goal" model. Under this model, stakeholders (producers, users and governance bodies) pursue their own goal-oriented activities, with little or no regard for commonly held goals. Individuals act on the basis of their own expectations about technological capabilities, future conditions, and consumer preferences. Uncertainties tend to be neglected. Systems are currently entering the market that serve only producers' interests and individual consumers' interests, not more general transport policy goals. It has even been suggested that there may be little or no contribution of AVG to general transport policy goals for the next two decades, or that the contribution might even be negative [8]. Hence, there is a need for an AVG policy course that recognises the existence of uncertainties without neglecting the possibilities and responsibilities of public authorities with respect to the general transport policy goals.

Such a policy course might be derived from the "common goal" model, which is the opposite of the "individualised goal" model. Under this model, significant change in the surface transportation system occurs primarily as the result of an enlightened policy analytic effort that envisions a new set of capabilities and system goals, and then works systematically to achieve those goals, applying traditional top-down policy analysis. Under the "common goal" model, a synoptic systems view allows decisionmakers to envision radically different concepts of system operation and system paradigms. Proponents of this model of system development view a common goal as essential for enabling the surface transportation system to take full advantage of advances in information and communications technologies. Without a common goal, they believe system change tends to be incremental, overly constrained by "what is", and incapable of moving towards radically different configurations that "might be" from a technical standpoint, but that are too different or too incompatible with current system configurations.

Of course, there are multiple manifestations of the common goal model. In what follows, we adopt the version called "adaptive policy analysis," which has been developed by Walker et al. [31]. Under this model, significant change in the surface transportation system occurs primarily as the result of an enlightened policy analytic effort that envisions a new set of capabilities and system goals, and then works systematically to achieve those goals, adapting tactics and strategy as conditions change. The key activities of "adaptive policy analysis" are the determination of a set of common goals, monitoring progress towards those goals, and the adaptation of policies as exogenous and endogenous conditions change over time. Within this framework, individual actors carry out their activities. But policymakers, through monitoring and mid-course corrections, try to keep the system headed toward the common goals. In particular, the following major steps are proposed for creating and implementing an adaptive policy [31].

The first activities constitute the *stage-setting* step in the policymaking process. This step involves the specification of objectives, constraints, and available policy options. For illustrative purposes, consider the field of traffic safety. Suppose the goal involves improving road traffic safety. Outcomes of interest for policymakers might be reductions in accident fatalities, injuries and material damage, as well as minimising the secondary consequences of accidents (secondary accidents, congestion, etc). The constraints could be those imposed by costs, vehicle-throughput, travel time, comfort, convenience, etc. Next to more traditional, preventive measures, like driver-educational campaigns and legislation, policy options could include measures that directly intervene in vehicle driving tasks using AVG technology. In particular the application of intelligent speed adaptation has shown large potential in improving traffic safety. These systems take into account the local speed restrictions and warn the driver in case of speeding or even automatically adjust the maximum driving speed to the posted maximum speed. Intelligent speed adaptation requires some information source on local speed regulations. This source could be vehicle-based; using advanced digital maps mediated by GPS, or communicates with beacons along the road [32]. The estimated safety effects of the use of full-automatic speed control devices involve up to a 40% reduction of injury accidents [33], and up to a 59% reduction of fatal accidents [23].

In the next step, a *basic policy* is assembled. It involves (a) the specification of a promising policy and (b) the identification of the conditions needed for the basic policy to succeed. A promising basic policy might be to implement speed adaptation for 'unsafe' drivers (e.g. younger drivers) on 'unsafe roads' (e.g. urban roads) under 'unsafe' traffic conditions (e.g. fog, darkness, snow). Accident statistics might be of use in specifying unsafe 'speeding markets' in this context. There are several necessary conditions for the success of this basic policy. An essential condition is the availability of reliable and accurate technologies for speed control. Another important condition involves a basic level of willingness among drivers to use the systems as they were intended to be used.

In the third step of the adaptive policymaking process, the remainder of the policy is specified. This involves (a) the identification of vulnerabilities or adverse consequences of the basic policy and (b) the translation of necessary conditions for success into signposts that should be monitored in order to be sure that the underlying analyses remain valid, that implementation is proceeding well, and that any needed policy interventions are taken in a timely and effective manner. A fairly certain vulnerability of the new policy might be that the speed control technology is not sufficiently reliable or accurate in case of incidental speed limits (work-zones, accidents, etc). An action to mitigate the negative effects of this situation on the success of the policy would be to build in some redundancy, by providing temporary vehicle-roadway communication around incidents. Another fairly certain vulnerability involves low drivers' acceptance for speed adaptation, especially with regard to fully automated speed control. A more uncertain vulnerability involves the adverse driving behaviour that speed adaptation devices might induce. Experimental results indicate that, with speed adaptation devices implemented, drivers exhibit riskier gap-acceptance, loss of vigilance, increased frustration, and increased impatience [34]. Therefore the driving behaviour of drivers with speed adaptation should be monitored closely. "Triggers" should be defined that would implement corrective policy actions when certain pre-defined levels of risky driving behaviour develop. A major (highly uncertain) vulnerability of AVG systems, but one with large consequences, is a serious technological failure. Accidents with AVG systems due to malfunctioning technology have been reported [35]. For instance, recently, in the Netherlands, a bus equipped with an electronic gas pedal automatically accelerated due to electromagnetic interference. Suppose, for instance, that in an urban area, rural or motorway speed limits are being automatically transmitted to speed adaptation devices and drivers are relying on the system to regulate their vehicle speed. A malfunctioning system might result in severe accidents with large societal impacts. The adaptive policy must include hedging actions to reduce or spread the risk of the possible adverse effects.

Once the above policy is agreed upon, the final step involves *implementation*.

In this step, the events unfold, signpost information related to the triggers is collected, and policy actions are started, altered, stopped, or extended. The adaptive policymaking process is suspended until a trigger event is reached. As long as the original objectives and constraints remain in place, the responses to a trigger event have a defensive or corrective character – that is, they are adjustments to the basic policy that preserve its benefits or meet outside challenges. For instance, in case the predefined levels of risky driving behaviour are reached, corrective actions might be undertaken. These could include the exclusion of 'unsafe' drivers from those road-types on which unsafe driving behaviour has appeared. Also, in addition to speed limiting devices, the vehicles of the unsafe drivers could be equipped with black-boxes in which real-time vehicle driving data are stored.

Under some circumstances, neither defensive nor corrective actions might be sufficient. In our malfunctioning technology case, if the result was a large accident, the entire policy might have to be reassessed and substantially changed or even abandoned. If so, however, the next policy deliberations would benefit from the previous experiences. The knowledge gathered in the initial adaptive policymaking process on outcomes, objectives, measures, preferences of stakeholders, etc., would be available and would accelerate the new policymaking process.

5 Conclusions

In this paper, the complexity of the implementation of AVG technology from the perspective of public policy decisionmaking has been studied. On the one hand, several studies and pilot projects have shown that AVG technologies have great potential to contribute to general transport policy goals. On the other hand, public policy and decisionmaking is confronted with the existence of large uncertainties related to the future of AVG development and implementation. A generic typology of uncertainties and their possible causes was presented. This typology is based on the view that policymaking basically concerns making choices regarding a system (e.g. the transport system) in order to obtain desired system outcomes. We applied this typology to the field of policymaking with respect to AVG development and implementation. This showed that large uncertainties exist about the outcomes of AVG policy decisions and about the valuation of the outcomes by stakeholders involved in or affected by AVG policy decisions. The challenge for enlightened policymaking is to develop innovative approaches to handle these uncertainties.

We proposed an approach involving a flexible or adaptive policy, which allows adaptations in time as knowledge about AVG proceeds and critical events for AVG implementation take place. In particular, policymakers are encouraged to first develop a normative view and then guide the experimentation and adaptation process and stimulate knowledge creation, knowledge availability, and knowledge integration.

References

[1] Smiley A. & K.A. Brookhuis, Alcohol, drugs and traffic safety. *Road users and traffic safety*, eds. J.A. Rothengatter & R.A. de Bruin. Van Gorcum, Assen, p. 83-105, 1987.

[2] Lindsey R. & E. Verhoef, Congestion Modelling. *Handbook of Transport Modelling*, eds D.A. Hensher & K.J. Button, Elsevier Science Ltd, Oxford, pp. 353-373, 2000.

[3] Minderhoud M. M., *Supported Driving: Impacts on Motorway Traffic Flow*. TRAIL Thesis Series T99/4, The Netherlands TRAIL Research School, Delft University Press, Delft, 1999.

[4] Hiramatsu K., K. Satoh & F. Matsukawa, Estimation of the number of fatal accidents reduced by advanced safety vehicle (ASV) technologies. *Proceedings of the 4th World congress on Intelligent Transport Systems*, ITS Congress Association, Brussels, 1997.

[5] Sala G., N. Clarke, P. Carrea & L. Mussone, Expected Impacts of Anti-Collision Assist Applications. *Proceedings of the 4th World Congress on Intelligent Transport Systems*, ITS Congress Association, Brussels, 1997.

[6] Bishop, *A Survey of Intelligent Vehicle Applications Worldwide: Overview*. Richard Bishop Consulting, Granite, USA, 2000.

[7] Heijden R.E.C.M. van der & M. Wiethoff (eds). *Automation of Car Driving: Exploring societal impacts and conditions*. TRAIL Studies in Transportation Science No. S99/4, Delft University Press, Delft, 1999.

[8] Marchau V.A.W.J., *Technology Assessment of Automated Vehicle Guidance: Prospects for automated driving implementation*. TRAIL PhD Thesis Series T2000/1, Delft University Press, Delft, 2000.

[9] Marchau V.A.W.J. & R.E.C.M. van der Heijden , Policy aspects of driver support systems implementation: results of an international Delphi study. *Transport Policy*, vol. 5, no. 4, Elsevier Science Ltd, pp. 249-258, 1998.

[10] Wees K.A.P.C. van, Driver support systems and product liability. *Proceedings of the 4th TRAIL Year Congress: Competition, innovation and creativity*, Part 2, TRAIL Research School, Delft, 15 p., 1998.

[11] Dingus T.A., S.K. Jahns, A.D. Horowitz & R. Knipling, Human factors

design issues for crash avoidance systems. *Human factors in Intelligent Transportation Systems*, eds. W. Barfield & T.A. Dingus, Lawrence Erlbaum Associates, Mahwah New Jersey, pp. 55-93, 1998.

[12] Geenhuizen M. en Thissen, Uncertainty and Intelligent Transportation Systems: implications for Policy. *International Journal of Technology, Policy and Management*, Volume 1, Number 3, 2001. (forthcoming)

[13] Walker W.E., An Uncertainty Topology for Model-Based Policy Analysis, 2002.(forthcoming)

[14] Loop H. van der & M. Mulder, To measure - to know: results of a transport policy monitoring system in The Netherlands. Paper presented at the 9th World Conference on Transport Research, Seoul, 2001.

[15] Geels F.W. & W.A. Smit, Failed technology futures: pitfalls and lessons from a historical survey. *Futures*, 32, pp. 867-885, 2000.

[16] Arem B. van & C.A. Smits, *An exploration of the development of automated vehicle guidance systems*. TNO-report; INRO/VVG 1997-13, TNO Infrastructure, Transport and Regional Development, Delft, 1997.

[17] Heyma A., *Impact assessment of new transport concepts*. European research project RECONNECT, Deliverable 4. TNO-report 00/NV/160, TNO Inro Department Traffic and Transport, Delft, 2000.

[18] Helmreich W. & U. Leiss, *Forecasting and Assessment of New technologies and Transport Systems and their Impacts on the Environment*. European research project Fantasie, European Commission, Brussels, 2000.

[19] Hanson M. & H.S.J. Tsao, Leveraging Exogenous Events for AHS Deployment. *Proceedings of the Third Annual World Congress on Intelligent Transportation Systems*, ITS America, Washington D.C., 1996.

[20] Hayward M., M. Traversi & E. Barreto, Deployment issues affecting intelligent driver support systems for the control of road vehicles. *Proceedings of the 4th World Congress on ITS*, ITS Congress Association, Brussels, 1997.

[21] Button K. & S. Taylor, Linking Telecommunications and Transportation - The Macro Simplicity and the Micro Complexity. *International Journal of Technology, Policy and Management*, Volume 1, Number 3, 2001. (forthcoming)

[22] Visser W. de, V.A.W.J. Marchau & R.E.C.M. van der Heijden, The cost-effectiveness of future driver support systems. *Proc. of the 32nd International Symposium on Automotive Technology & Automation*, ed. D. Roller, Automotive Automation Ltd, Croydon, pp. 421-428, 1999.

[23] Carsten O., M. Fowkes & F. Tate, Implementing intelligent speed adaptation in the UK: Recommendations of the EVSC project. *Proceedings of the 7th World Congress on Intelligent Transport Systems*, 6-9 November, Turin, Italy, 2000.

[24] Endsley M.R. & O.E. Kiris, The out-of-the-loop performance problem and the level of control in automation. In: *Human Factors*, 37 (2), Human Factors Society, Santa Monica, pp. 381-394, 1995.

[25] Hoedemaeker M. *Driving with Intelligent Vehicles. Driving behaviour with Adaptive Cruise Control and the acceptance by individual drivers*. TRAIL Thesis Series T99/6, The Netherlands TRAIL Research School, Delft

University Press, Delft, 1999.

[26] Hupkes G. The law of constant travel time and trip rates. *Futures*, 14, pp. 34-86, 1982.

[27] Marchau V.A.W.J. & E.J.E. Molin, Users stated preferences regarding vehicle driving automation. *International Journal of Technology, Policy and Management*, Volume 1, Number 3, 2001. (forthcoming)

[28] Shladover S.E., Intellectual challenges to the deployability of AVCSS. *Proc. of the 78th Meeting of the Transportation Research Board*, Transportation Research Board, Washington DC, 13 pp, 1999.

[29] Lathrop J. & K. Chen, *National Automated Highway System Consortium: modelling stakeholder preferences project*. PATH research report, UCB-ITS-PRR-97-26, Institute of Transportation Studies, University of California, Berkeley CA, 1997.

[30] Heijer T., H.L. Oei, M. Wiethoff, S. Boverie, M. Penttinen, A. Schirokoff, R. Kulmala, J. Heinrich, A.C. Ernst, N. Sneek, H. Heeren, A. Stevens, E. Bekiaris, S. Damiani, *Problem identification, User Needs and Inventory of ADAS*. European research project ADVISORS, Deliverable D1/2.1, European Commission, Brussels, 2000

[31] Walker W.E., S.A. Rahman & J. Cave, Adaptive policies, policy analysis, and policymaking. *European Journal of Operational Research*, Vol. 128, Issue 2, pp. 282-289, 2001.

[32] Brookhuis K. & D. de Waard, Limiting speed, towards an intelligent speed adapter (ISA). *Transportation Research Part F: Traffic Psychology and Behaviour*, Volume 2, Issue 2, , pp. 81-90, 1999.

[33] Varhelyi A. & T. Makinen, The effects of in-car speed limiters: field studies. *Transportation research. Part C, Emerging technologies*, Vol. 9C, no. 3, pp. 191-211, 2001.

[34] Comte S.L., New systems: new behaviour? *Transportation Research Part F: Traffic Psychology and Behaviour*, Volume 3, Issue 2, pp. 95-111, 2000.

[35] Heijden R.E.C.M. van der & K.A.P.C. van Wees, Introducing Advanced Driver Assistance Systems: Some legal issues. *European Journal of Transport, Infrastructure and Logistics.*, Vol 1., No 4, 2001. (forthcoming)

Urban freight movement: a quantity attraction model

F. Russo & A. Comi
Department of Computer Science, Mathematics, Electronics and Transportation,
"Mediterranea" University of Reggio Calabria, Italy

Abstract

The freight that is transported each day in an urban centre may be grouped into various categories. From the analysis of vehicle flow for freight transport in an urban context, the transport of foodstuffs and household products accounts for between 70% and 82% [1]; moreover, such goods are purchased by end consumers in their zone of residence.

A general classification for freight demand models is given by Garrido and Regan [2]. Urban freight models can be classified into several classes: gravitational [3,4,5,6,7,8,9]; input-output models [10]; spatial equilibrium of the prices [11].

A multi-step model, that considers different decision-makers, presented [12]: quantity attraction and distribution models, an acquisition model, models for the choice of service and vehicle type, and path choice model.

Models for the aggregate estimation of quantities of goods bought and sold for o/d pairs constitute the first block of models required for simulating urban freight traffic [13]. To obtain preliminary results some surveys were conducted in a medium-size city. In this paper, in relation to the first step, the following attraction model will be specified and calibrated for perishables and household products, in terms of quantity, and for durable goods in terms of goods trips.

1 Introduction

Today, in urban areas the delivery of goods chiefly occurs by road, because few businesses have private areas equipped for loading and unloading operations.

Operators, customers and sectoral experts express the need to increase the productivity of goods transport, but they almost always encounter considerable barriers.

In the last few years many firms have taken on board the concept of just-in-time (JIT), which allows numerous advantages: better productivity and efficiency, better quality, small used spaces, elimination of each superfluous activity that does not add value to the good in the process of transformation, and better motivation and staff involvement; this has led to the use of smaller, more frequent consignments, and smaller quantities in stock. This new distribution policy has caused more traffic of goods vehicles in metropolitan areas with consequent increases in congestion, accidents and pollution.

Thus urban goods transport needs solutions that reconcile two conflicting objectives, between which a potential trade-off exists. On the one hand there is the need to guarantee an efficient distribution system and be able to respond to customer demands, characterized by a high level of service, and on the other, the wish to set limits to goods traffic to minimize the environmental impact. It has been estimated that urban freight transport in Europe accounts for about 34 per cent of the total freight traffic expressed in kilometer tonnes, that is 50 per cent of only road transport. Besides, of the total of vehicles moving inside the city, 20 per cent is freight vehicles, which effect 32 per cent of total trips in the urban area.

To underline the extent of the phenomenon in question, we report the results of two recent studies [14] conducted in France and Switzerland (Table 1).

Table 1: Freight transport in urban areas.

	Population	Quantity transported (tonnes/day)	Quantity transported (ton)/Population	km/day travelled
Basle	168,735	44,000	0.26	327,000
Geneva	172809	30,000	0.17	
Berne	123,254	34,000	0.28	257,000
Lucerne	57,193	21,000	0.37	117,000
Zurich	336,821	100,000	0.30	828,000
Bordeaux	215,363			138,000

From surveys conducted for Iveco, analysing a fleet of 118,700 vehicles in 9 European countries, it was estimated that 48% of vehicles circulate within town and city centres and 32% in the suburbs [14]. In Italy, the destination of over 70% of transported freight is within the region of origin. More than 50% is transported within a range of 50 km and 25% within urban areas.

In industrialised countries, the number of studies and surveys in the field of urban goods movement has increased in the recent years, Routhier et alii [15] make an international comparison of the methods and results in this sector, considering several countries of Europe, America and Asia.

Despite the number of trips undertaken by freight vehicles in urban areas, the modelling of this fundamental mobility segment has not been developed to the same extent as passenger transport modelling. In Italy, some studies have tackled various aspects of long-haul freight mobility [16, 17, 18, 19, 20, 21, 22, 23].

The systems of models [21, 22] developed to simulate freight demand at a national scale derive from the integration of two classes:

- macro-economic models, which simulate the level (quantity) and spatial distribution of goods traded between various zones and ultimately produce Origin-Destination matrixes; within the scope of macro-economic models, two groups of models have been proposed, which have given rise to various specifications of what is to be simulated: spatial equilibrium models of prices and intersectoral models;
- models that simulate modal split and route choice on representative transport service networks.

Similarly, models at an urban scale may be analysed, breaking them down into parts: the first concerns calculation of the demand by freight type, and by o/d consumption pair and by d-w restocking pair, while the second concerns determination of the mode, service and vehicle used as well as the route chosen for restocking sales outlets.

This paper analyses the set of movements in relation to urban freight transport. In the first part a general multi-step model to simulate urban freight transport is recalled [12, 13]. In the second part the specification, calibration and validation of attraction models are reported.

2 General multi-step modelling for urban freight movement

2.1 The main references on urban movement

Freight demand models are one of the key components of transport plants at the strategic, tactical and operative level. Local authorities need to predict future transport requirements both for passengers and freight so as to plan the development of infrastructures and related human resources. The private sector requires models to predict transport service demand in order to evaluate future needs. This applies both to transport service managers, producers of consumer goods and firms using transport services, as well as manufacturers of commercial vehicles.

A major difficulty in analysing freight mobility is the identification of decision-makers involved in the process. In the case of freight, there is no sole decision-maker who chooses trip characteristics, but rather a complex set of decision-makers responsible for production, distribution and marketing who, in turn, operate in different fields as producers, who have an economic function and deal with the production of goods, or as consumers, who are freight consumers and become producers of semi-finished goods, destined for the markets and hence towards end-consumers [24].

A general framework for a freight demand model is given by Garrido and Regan [2]. The models for analysing the demand for urban freight transport could be classified into several classes: gravitational models, similar to those used for urban passenger travel analysis [3, 4, 5, 6, 7, 8, 9]; input-output models by Harris and Liu [10]; spatial equilibrium of prices [11]. Recently, in France (April 2000), a study was carried out in the cities of Bordeaux, Dijon and Marseilles that led to the formulation of a model for the evaluation of the instant use of the network by the vehicles in circulation and parking in each zone [1, 25]. In the United Kingdom the Government has attached great importance to the problem of freight distribution in urban areas [26, 27, 28, 29], being one of the principal factors of the development and pollution of the urban areas. The paper of Browne et alii [30] treats, the research conducted in the United Kingdom, the techniques adopted and the principal results of the study.

2.2 The multi-step model used

The used freight transport multi-step models are relative to a medium-size city and consider a disaggregated approach for each level of decision. In figure 1 a schematic representation of data and models is pictured.

- Quantity attraction and distribution models. From the general population data (residents, number of employed, stores, etc.) the quantity for each category of freight is calculated that reaches each traffic zone o in one day arriving from each zone d; in this case it is assumed that the decision-maker is the end consumer;
- Acquisition model (or large scale distribution). From the data on the location of logistic bases, general stores, etc. it is possible to calculate for a general retailer in zone d the d-w probability of purchasing, in the generic zone w, the goods that are on sale in his/her store;
- Models for the choice of service and vehicle type. The type of vehicle used for each goods class, with the quantity that it transports and the type of service effected by it [31] (one-to-one, one-to-many, many-to-many, many-to-one) is obtained by means of a logistic model;
- Path choice model. For each type of service the probability of each path is evaluated.

3 The quantity attraction model

3.1 Data and models involved

For estimating the quantity of goods attracted from each zone the decision-maker is assumed to be the family. On the basis of the number of present families in each zone it is possible to estimate the number of trips effected from/to the same zone, classifying the attracted goods in homogeneous categories. From the data relative to the families and the trips effected for shopping and from the goods classification the quantities acquired may be estimated.

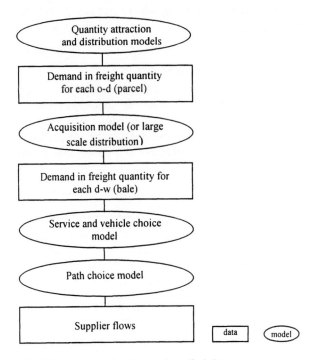

Figure 1: Model system to simulate urban freight movement.

The freight that is transported each day in an urban centre may be grouped into various categories. The first phase of the study consists in the identification of homogeneous categories in which to aggregate the daily purchasing trips. A macro segmentation of trip types is given by: durable good purchases and non-durable good purchases [21].

The non-durable goods are formed by general foodstuffs and household product categories. In the following a model to estimate the quantities for each category in a disaggregated way, is proposed for purchases of durable goods. The procedure is not so straightforward. In fact, this class includes several categories and the models have to be specified to evaluate the number of purchases for each category. For durable goods, in this paper we propose a model to estimate the number of trips produced for each category and compare the virtual number thereby obtained with the aggregate values found in the literature [21].

The model structure is reported in figure 2. The part in bold refers to the models found in the literature, while the part in standard type refers to models analysed in this paper, the outlined part referring to the model requiring further analysis.

From the literature [21] it emerges that for durable (Purchases Durable Goods, PDG) and non-durable goods (Purchases Non-durable Goods, PNG) the number of trips, N_{trip}, with N_{fam} number of families , is:

$$N_{trip} = \beta\, N_{fam} \qquad\qquad [trips/day]$$

and $\beta_{PDG} = 0.25$ e $\beta_{PNG} = 0.11$.

Section 3.2 reports specification and calibration of the attraction model in quantities for categories of non-durable goods; in section 3.3 we focus on the durable goods class, proposing disaggregation into freight categories, specifying and calibrating models to evaluate the number of purchases for each category. Models to estimate the quantities of non-durable goods are in course of development.

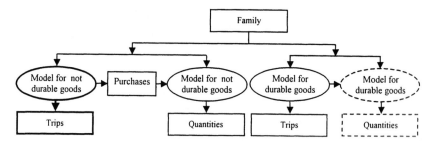

Figure 2: Structure of modelizzation.

3.2 Specification and calibration of the attraction model for non-durable goods

From the analysis of vehicle flows for freight transport in an urban context, the transport of foodstuffs and household products accounts for between 70% and 82% [1]. Moreover, such goods are purchased by end consumers in their zone of residence. The attraction model will be specified and calibrated for perishables and household products.

Models for the aggregate estimation of quantities of goods bought and sold for o/d pairs constitute the first block of models required for simulating urban freight traffic [13]. From the population data (residents) the quantity of freight is calculated per category that reaches each traffic zone every day for consumption. Data of the commercial structure of the zones (employees, m^2 of retail space) allow us to calculate in which zone the goods are purchased; in this case it is assumed that the decision-maker is the end-user.

The proposed model is the index by category type; it supplies the quantity of freight that is attracted every day by each zone into which a city is subdivided. To obtain some preliminary results, two different surveys were conducted, one for families (50 interviews) and one for retailers (32 interviews) in the southern

Italian city of Reggio Calabria (about 170,000 inhabitants). A homogeneous district was chosen for which it is possible to hypothesize that all the resident families (attraction) purchase in the zone and the retailers (distribution) sell only to families of the zone. Accordingly, two models were calibrated independently and the results obtained were compared. From road surveys [13] the main categories have been confirmed as the following:

- General foodstuffs
  - Fruit and vegetables,
  - Meat and fish,
  - Other food products,
- Household products.

The retailers were asked about the siting of the business itself, the number of employees and number of customers served daily, as well as the quantity of goods sold, aggregated by product class. The second survey gave information on family composition, the consumption of goods subject to daily turnover and the consumption of goods with weekly turnover.

The model expresses the average quantity Q(s), in kg/day, for the generic goods of category s that is required (origin and destination), as a linear function of explicative variables N_{res}, average number of residents in the zone:

$$Q(s) = \beta_s \, N_{res} \qquad [kg/day]$$

Table 2 reports the estimated values of parameters for each category. The homogeneity of the results for fruit and vegetables and household products categories emerges, while for the other categories, given the deviation encountered, further investigations are required.

Table 2. Calibration results: attraction model.

Survey		Families	Retailers
Fruit and vegetables	β_s	0.5	0.4
	t	16.2	9.0
	ρ^2	0.3	0.8
Meat and fish	β_s	0.2	0.5
	t	8.0	6.1
	ρ^2	0.2	0.5
Other foodstuffs	β_s	0.7	0.4
	t	13.8	10.7
	ρ^2	0.2	0.7
House products	β_s	0.2	0.3
	t	15.5	11.1
	ρ^2	0.6	0.9

3.3 Emission model specification and calibration

As reported in the literature, there are aggregated models to estimate urban trips for purchase. Below a disaggregated generation model will be specified and calibrated for the non-durable goods category. The models used are once again descriptive of the index type per category. Hence for each category the average number of trips is directly estimated.

The number of daily purchases generated by each zone o for the freight j, $Npur_j$, is obtained as a linear function of the average number of families, N_{fam}, living in each zone, by the following relation:

$$Npur_j = \beta_j \, N_{fam} \qquad \text{[trips/day]}$$

In table 3 the calibrated indexes of trips β_j are reported. The information necessary for the calibration phases of the models was obtained from the families, as described in section 3.2. The classification used derives from the ATECO 91 (Economic Activity Code) classification.

Comparing the obtained results with the aggregate parameter, 0.11 recalled in section 3.1, it emerges that for each trip many purchases are made. But the obtained results are important: as they associate to each category a size of purchase a first valuation of the attracted quantities for zone can be obtained.

Table 3: Calibration results: emission model.

Clothing	β_j 0.03	Herbal chemist's	β_j 0.03	Toys	β_j 0.01	Gold jeweller's	β_j 0.008
	t 5.8		t 2.3		t 4.9		t 2.8
	ρ^2 0.5		ρ^2 0.7		ρ^2 0.6		ρ^2 0.3
Footwear	β_j 0.01	Health care	β_j 0.07	Books	β_j 0.03	Optician, Photos	β_j 0.007
	t 3.75		t 5.15		t 5.6		t 6.3
	ρ^2 0.6		ρ^2 0.8		ρ^2 0.5		ρ^2 0.3
Stationery	β_j 0.04	Hardware	β_j 0.03	Electrical material	β_j 0.02	Sports goods	β_j 0.02
	t 9.45		t 6.07		t 5.1		t 3.3
	ρ^2 0.8		ρ^2 0.4		ρ^2 0.4		ρ^2 0.3
Household appliances	β_j 0.01	Flowers	β_j 0.005	Music	β_j 0.04	Tobacco	β_j 0.46
	t 6.51		t 1.6		t 4.8		t 6.6
	ρ^2 0.4		ρ^2 0.3		ρ^2 0.5		ρ^2 0.5

References

[1] Gerardin B., Patier D., Routheir J. L., Segalou E., Diagnostic du Transport de Marchandises dans une agglomération. Programme National Marchandises en Ville. 2000, www.transports-marchandises-en-ville.org. Accessed September 2000.

[2] Regan A. C., Garrido R. A., Modeling Freight Demand and Shipper Behavior: State of the Art, Future Directions. *Preprint of IATBR*, Sydney, 2000.

[3] Hutchinson B. G. Estimating urban goods movement demands. *Transportation Research Record*, 496, pp. 1-15, 1974.

[4] Odgen K. W., *Urban Goods Movement*, Ashgate, Hants, England, 1992.

[5] List G. F. and Turnquist M. A., Estimating truck travel patterns in urban areas. *Transportation Research Record*, 1430, pp. 1-9, 1994.

[6] Taylor S. Y., A Basis for Understanding Urban Freight and Commercial Vehicle Travel. *ARRB Transport Research Report*, ARR300, February, 1997.

[7] Fridstrom L., A stated preference analysis of wholesalers' freight choice. Institute of Transport Economics, Norwegian Centre for Transport Research, Working paper of June, 1998.

[8] He S. and Crainic T. G., Freight transportation in congested urban areas: iusses and methodologies. *8th World Conference on Transport Research*, 12-17 July, 1998, Antwerp, Belgium.

[9] Gorys J. and Hausmanis I., A strategic overview of goods movement in the Great Toronto Area. *Transportation Quarterly* 53 (2), pp. 101-114, 1999.

[10] Harris R. I. and Liu A., Input-output modelling of the urban and regional economy: the importance of external trade. Regional Studies, 32 (9), pp. 851-862, 1998.

[11] Oppenheim N., A combinated, equilibrium model of urban personal travel and goods movements. *Transportation Science* vol. 27, n° 2, pp. 161-171, May 1993.

[12] Russo F., *Un sistema di modelli per l'analisi degli spostamenti merci a scala urbana*, Quaderno del Dipartimento Informatica Matematica Elettronica e Trasporti, University of Reggio Calabria, 2001.

[13] Russo F., Cartisano A. G., Comi A., Modelli per l'analisi degli anelli finali della distribuzione delle merci. *Modelli e metodi dell'Ingegneria del traffico* a cura di G. E. Cantarella e F. Russo, Franco Angeli, 2001.

[14] BFS, 1996. www.bestufs.net. Accessed February, 2001.

[15] Routhier J., Ambrosini C., Patier-Marque D., Objectives, methods and results of surveys carried out in the field of urban freight transport : a international comparison. *Proceeding of 9th World Conference on Transport Research,* Seoul, 2001.

[16] Cascetta E., Nuzzolo A., Biggiero L., Russo F., Passenger and freight demand models for the Italian transportation system. *Proceeding of 7th World Conference on Transport Research,* Sydney, 1996.

[17] Russo F., Un sistema di modelli per il calcolo di tempi e costi delle spedizioni di merci su strada e su ferrovia. *Modelli e metodi dell'Ingegneria del traffico* a cura di G. E. Cantarella e D. C. Festa, Franco Angeli, pp. 185-216, 1997.

[18] Nuzzolo A. and Russo F., Modal split at international level: a system of models for Italy-based freight. *Proceeding of 25th PTRC, Europe Transport Forum*, London, 1997.

[19] Russo F. and Conigliaro G., Integrated macro economic and transport models for freight demand. *Preprint of 8th IFAC*, Chania 1997, Greece.

[20] Nuzzolo A. and Russo F., A logistic approach for freight modal choice models. *Proceeding of 26th PTRC, Europe Transport Forum*, London, 1998.

[21] Cascetta E., Teoria e metodi dell'ingegneria dei sistemi di trasporto. UTET, Torino, 1998.

[22] Cascetta E. and Iannò D., Calibrazione aggregata di un sistema di modelli di domanda merci a scala nazionale. *Metodi e Tecnologie dell'Ingegneria dei Trasporti* a cura di G. E. Cantarella e F. Russo, Franco Angeli, pp. 156-178, 2000.

[23] Russo F., Trasporto intermodale delle merci. *Introduzione alla Tecnica dei Trasporti e del Traffico con Elementi di Economia dei Trasporti*, a cura di G. E. Cantarella, UTET, Turin, 2001.

[24] Harker, P.T., *Predicting intercity freight flows*. VNU Science Press, Utrecht, The Netherlands, 1986.

[25] CERTU. Plans de Deplacements urbains. Guide Methodologique. Ministere de l'Equipement, des Transports et du Logement, 1998.

[26] DETR, *A new Deal for Transport: Better for everyone*. The Government's White Paper on the Future of Transport, Cmnd. 3950, The Stationery Office, London, 1998.

[27] DETR, *Sustainable Distribution: A Strategy*. DETR, London, 1999.

[28] DETR, *Transport Statistics Great Britain*. The Stationery Office, London, 2000.

[29] DETR, *Guidance on Full Local Transport Plans*. DETR, London, 2000.

[30] Browne M., Allen J., Anderson S., Jones P., Urban freight transport and logistics systems: moving towards sustainability. *Proceeding of 9th World Conference on Transport Research*, Seoul, 2001.

[31] Daganzo C., *Logistics Systems Analysis*. Spring-Verlag, 1991.

Index of authors

Hybrid Vehicle Propulsion

C.M. JEFFERSON, Hybrid Transport Technology Ltd., Bristol, UK and R.H. BARNARD, University of Hertfordshire, UK

Bringing together information from a wide range of sources such as recent conferences and publications, this unique book provides a thorough introduction and guide to hybrid vehicle propulsion. The authors cover many issues ranging from the reasons for the development of such vehicles, to control strategy and systems. Other topics examined are hybrid propulsion configurations, energy storage options such as batteries and flywheels, the choice of appropriate prime mover, and performance and limiting factors, while case studies of existing cars, trams, buses and rail vehicles are also included. The mathematical content is small and kept to a low level.

- Features numerous tables, graphs, line illustrations and black-and-white photographs.
- Clearly references all sources used in order to aid further investigation.
- Written for engineering and technical staff working in the road and rail vehicle industries, final year undergraduates of mechanical and automotive engineering, postgraduates, transport planning personnel and technically literate readers with an interest in this subject.

Series: Advances in Transport, Vol 10

ISBN: 1-85312-887-2
2002 apx 250pp
apx £82.00/US$127.00/€133.00

Modelling Urban Vehicle Emissions

M. KHARE, Indian Institute of Technology, India and P. SHARMA, Indraprastha University, India

Vehicular air pollution poses the main threat to urban air quality and is therefore one of the major components of urban air quality studies. Air quality models can play an effective role in the efficient management of such pollution.
This unique book presents various air quality modelling techniques, previously scattered throughout the literature, together with their applications. Comprehensive and well-organised, it also provides a step-by-step guide to using these models, followed by case studies to illustrate the points discussed. A methodology for formulating a local air quality management programme, including a discussion of the significance of different air quality models, is also featured.
Partial Contents: Urban Air Quality Management and Modelling; Air Pollution Due to Vehicular Exhaust Emissions - A Review; Development of Vehicular Exhaust Models; Application of Vehicular Exhaust Models.

Series: Advances in Transport, Vol 9

ISBN: 1-85312-897-X
2002 232pp
£79.00/US$123.00/€129.00

WITPress
Ashurst Lodge, Ashurst, Southampton, SO40 7AA, UK.
Tel: 44 (0) 238 029 3223
Fax: 44 (0) 238 029 2853
E-Mail: witpress@witpress.com

Air Pollution X

Editors: **C.A. BREBBIA**, *Wessex Institute of Technology, UK and* **J.F. MARTIN-DUQUE**, *Universidad Complutense, Spain*

Bringing together recent results and state-of-the-art contributions from researchers around the world, this book contains papers first presented at the Tenth International Conference on the Modelling, Monitoring and Management of Air Pollution. Emphasis is placed on the development of experimental and computational techniques, which can be used as tools to aid solution and understanding of practical air pollution problems.

Scientists working in industry, research organisations, government and academia, on the monitoring, simulation and management of air pollution problems will find this book invaluable.

Contents: Air Pollution Modelling; Air Quality Management; Urban Air Pollution; Urban and Suburban Transport Emissions; Monitoring and Laboratory Studies; Global Studies; Comparison of Modelling with Experiments; Indoor Pollution; Pollution Engineering; Fluid Mechanics for Enviromental Problems; Chemistry of Air Pollution; Aerosols and Particles; Health Problems; Chemical Transformation Modelling; Emission Inventories; Indoor Pollution.

Series: Advances in Air Pollution, Vol 11

ISBN: 1-85312-916-X
2002   apx 650pp
apx £214.00/US$332.00/€348.00

Air Quality Management

Editors: **J.W.S. LONGHURST**, *University of the West of England, UK,* **D.M. ELSOM**, *Oxford Brookes University, UK and* **H. POWER**, *Wessex Institute of Technology, UK*

This book evaluates and reviews the development and application of the air quality management process from a European, North American and Australian perspective. The contemporary approaches and experiences described provide a critical assessment of practice as well as important pointers for the future.

Contents: Application of the Air Quality Framework Directive to Portugal - A Strategic Evaluation;   Air Quality Management in the United Kingdom - Development of the National Air Quality Strategy;   Air Quality Management Experience in Budapest; Operation of the Air Pollution Warning System in Cracow During Pollution Episodes; Air Quality Management in Prague;   Air Pollution Management in Australia - The Example of Newcastle, NSW; Air Quality Management in the Bulkley Valley of Central British Columbia, Canada; Model-Based Decision Support for Integrated Urban Air Quality Management;   Statistical Models for Air Quality Evaluation and Emissions Reduction Assessment.

Series: Advances in Air Pollution, Vol 7

ISBN: 1-85312-528-8
2000   312pp
£98.00/US$149.00/€156.00

All prices correct at time of going to press but subject to change.
WIT Press books are available through your bookseller or direct from the publisher.

WIT*PRESS*

Structural Integrity and Passenger Safety

Editor: **C.A. BREBBIA**, *Wessex Institute of Technology, UK*

The safety of railways is now high on the list of operators' concerns. Speeds have risen considerably with new generations of high-speed trains and, consequently, a relatively small fault can result in devastating consequences. Featuring the work of internationally acknowledged experts from Japan, Sweden, Germany, France, Poland and the Czech Republic, this title provides broad coverage of this important topic and is an essential addition to the literature.

Contents: Integrity Assessment of the Shinkansen Vehicle Axle using Probabilistic Fracture Mechanics; Stainless Steel Carbodies for High Structural Integrity and Safety; Safety of High-Speed Maglev Trains of the "Transrapid" Type; Development and Practical Use of a Capacity Model for Railway Networks; Track and Rolling Stock Quality Assurance Related Tools; Passenger and Equipment Safety in Railway Transport; Train Real-Time Position Monitoring Trials at Czech Railways; Boundary Element Analysis of the Cycle of Stress Intensity Factors for Cracks in Wheels.

Series: Advances in Transport, Vol 3

ISBN: **1-85312-784-1**
2000   192pp
£65.00/US$108.00/€113.00

Innovations in Freight Transport

Editors: **E. TANIGUCHI**, *Kyoto University, Japan and* **R.G. THOMPSON**, *University of Melbourne, Australia*

Intelligent Transport Systems (ITS), such as advanced information systems, automatic vehicle identification systems, and global positioning systems, have recently been developed and deployed achieving improvements in cost reduction, better service to customers, and traffic congestion. Illustrating recent progress in the subject, this title also highlights innovative concepts for the management of logistics systems.

Contents: Introduction; Intelligent Transport Systems I; Intelligent Transport Systems II; Vehicle Routing and Scheduling Problems; Logistics Terminals; Intermodal Freight Transport; Transport Demand Management; New Freight Transport Systems; Economic Perspectives; Supply Chain Management; E-Commerce; Future Perspectives.

Series: Advances in Transport, Vol 11

ISBN: **1-85312-894-5**
2002   apx 264pp
apx £89.00/US$138.00/€145.00